DAVIES

PRINCIPLES
OF
TAX LAW

FOURTH EDITION

by

Professor David W. Williams, LL.M., Ph.D., A.T.I.I.,
SOLICITOR
Visiting Professor of Tax Law,
Queen Mary & Westfield College, University of London and
The Technical University, Vienna

Professor Geoffrey Morse, LL.B., BARRISTER
Professor of Law, University of Nottingham

LONDON
SWEET & MAXWELL
2000

First Edition (1980) Introduction to Revenue Law
by F.R. Davies
Second Edition (1985) Introduction to Revenue Law
by F.R. Davies, David Williams and Geoffrey Morse
Third Edition (1996) Davies: Principles of Tax Law
by Geoffrey Morse, David Williams and David Salter
Fourth Edition (2000) Davies: Principles of Tax Law
by Geoffrey Morse and David Williams

Published in 2000 by Sweet & Maxwell Limited of
100 Avenue Road, London, NW3 3PF
Typeset by YHT Ltd., London W13 8NT
Printed in England by MPG Books, Bodmin

No natural forests were destroyed to
make this product; only farmed timber was used and replanted.
A CIP catalogue record for this book is available
from the British Library.

ISBN 0 421 722 703

PREFACE TO THE FOURTH EDITION

It soon becomes apparent to anyone who has to deal with it that tax law in the United Kingdom is both far too complex and far too long. Moreover that volume and complexity increases year on year with each successive Finance Act. The statutory material alone, on which the subject is entirely based, fills several inches on bookshelves, even in a consolidated form, and when analysis and commentary are added a substantial library is needed. In time electronic means of accessing all this information may render bookshelves irrelevant—but that will not solve the basic problems of either length or complexity. It is the view of the editors, however, that it is still possible to distil from this labyrinth some basic principles upon which the principal taxes operate and moreover that there are principles of tax law in addition to those of taxation. It is the aim of this, as in previous editions, to present those legal principles in as readable a form as possible for those coming face to face with tax law principally for the first time or only from time to time.

There is also some light at the end of the tunnel in the form of the Inland Revenue's Tax Law Rewrite project which aims to rewrite the UK's primary direct tax legislation so that it becomes clearer and easier to use, but without changing its general effect. Several documents have already been published by the teams involved in this project, so far covering parts of income tax. The intention of the project is to provide a fundamental restructuring of the legislation into a more logical and helpful order and in this edition we have gratefully adopted the classification of income as used by the project in relation to income tax. Legislation will follow in the form of 'rewrite' Bills and one on capital allowances is expected soon.

There are also some structural changes to this edition. The abolition of advance corporation tax has substantially simplified the basic structure of corporation tax so that we have removed it as a separate section, incorporating it into the income tax section as a single chapter. For reasons of space we have omitted the section on stamp duty. On the other hand there is the growing importance of VAT, both in terms of revenue raised and litigation. The consequent development of several fundamental legal principles underlying the tax arising, not least, from its EC framework, has meant that that section has been restructured and expanded. VAT cannot be regarded any longer as simply a mass of detailed rules imposed on a simple framework.

There have, of course been many changes to tax law, both by Parliament and the courts, since the previous edition and we have incorporated those which relate to the structures and basic charges of the various taxes covered in this book. Of these it is capital gains tax which has undergone the most radical change, with the abolition of the relief for the effects of inflation and the introduction of one based on length of ownership and the nature of the asset.

The most difficult aspect of writing any book on tax law is how to keep it up to date during its lifetime. A book of this size cannot be published in a loose-leaf format. To this end therefore the publishers and the editors have agreed to open a dedicated page on the publisher's web site for *Davies*, accessible to all readers (www.sweetandmaxwell.co.uk/academic). It is the intention to publish each September, at least, an update on that page linked to the current text so that readers will be able to use the book with that additional information to hand. In addition the web page will contain various hyper-links to relevant web sites on tax so that further information may be obtained on specific areas. This is a relatively new venture in student textbook publishing and we would welcome comments from readers as to its effectiveness.

The editors would like to thank the publishers for their help and co-operation, Claire Jennings for her help in setting out some of the tables, and our wives, Christine and Elisabeth for all their encouragement and support, not least in arranging joint meetings between us. We would also like to thank David Salter for his work on the previous edition of this book and regret that other commitments prevented him from taking any part in the preparation of this edition.

This edition is written on the law as known to the editors on July 31, 2000.

Geoffrey Morse
David Williams

CONTENTS

Preface   v
Table of Cases   viii
Table of Statutes   xxiii
Table of Statutory Instruments   xxxiii

PART ONE INTRODUCTORY

Chapter 1   Understanding Tax   3
Chapter 2   Handling Tax Laws   20

PART TWO TAXATION OF INCOME

Chapter 3   Assessment of Income Tax   55
Chapter 4   Income and Capital   64
Chapter 5   Trading Income   68
Chapter 6   Employment Income   96
Chapter 7   Property Income   128
Chapter 8   Capital Allowances   138
Chapter 9   Trading Losses   147
Chapter 10   Savings and Investment Income   152
Chapter 11   The Taxation of Trusts and Estates   164
Chapter 12   The Taxation of Individuals   174
Chapter 13   The Taxation of Companies   187

PART THREE TAXATION OF CAPITAL GAINS

Chapter 14   Capital Gains Tax   203
Chapter 15   Gains and Losses   234
Chapter 16   Exemptions and Reliefs   254

PART FOUR INHERITANCE TAX

Chapter 17   The Evolution of Inheritance Tax   271
Chapter 18   Chargeable Transfers   274
Chapter 19   Exemptions and Reliefs   291
Chapter 20   Computation   309

CONTENTS

Chapter 21   Settled Property   323
Chapter 22   Liability and Incidence   347
Chapter 23   Administration and Collection   353

PART FIVE VALUE ADDED TAX

Chapter 24   The Charge to Value Added Tax   361
Chapter 25   Computation and Payments   382

PART SIX INTERNATIONAL TAX

Chapter 26   Income Tax   401
Chapter 27   Value Added Tax   418

Index   425

TABLE OF CASES

ABERDEEN CONSTRUCTION GROUP LTD v. IRC [1978] A.C. 885; [1978] 2 W.L.R. 648; [1978] 1 All E.R. 962, HL 15–03
Administrators of the Estate of Caton v. Couch [1997] 970, CA
    15–03
Alexander v. IRC [1991] S.T.C. 112, CA 20–11
Alloway v. Phillips [1980] 1 W.L.R. 888; [1980] 3 All E.R. 138, CA 5–19
Anglo-Pension Oil Co. Ltd v. Dale [1932] 1 K.B. 124 5–12
Apple and Pear Development Corporation v. Customs and Excise Commissioners [1988] 2 All E.R. 922, S.T.C. 221, ECJ 24–04, 24–10
Argos Distributors Ltd v. CEC [1996] S.T.C. 1359, ECJ 25–07
Att.-Gen. v. Seccombe [1991] 2 K.B. 688 18–07

B.S.C. FOOTWEAR LTD v. RIDGWAY [1972] A.C. 544; [1971] 2 W.L.R. 1313, HL 5–10
Baird v. Williams [1999] S.T.C. 635 6–18
Baker v. Archer-Shee [1927] A.C. 844 11–01
Ball v. Johnson [1971] T.R. 147 6–05
— v. National & Grindlay's Bank [1973] Ch. 127; [1972] 3 W.L.R. 17; [1971] 3 All E.R. 485 13–09
Barclays Bank Trust Co. Ltd v. IRC [1998] S.T.C. (SCD) 125 ... 19–16
Baron Inglewood v. IRC. See Inglewood (Lord) v. IRC
Batey v. Wakefield [1982] 1 All E.R. 61, CA
Barrett v. Powell [1998] S.T.C. 283 .... 16–11 16–05
Beecham Group Ltd v. Fair (H.M. Inspector of Taxes) (1984) 57 T.C. 733 6–21
Belgium v. Ghent Coal Terminal NV [1998] S.T.C. 260, ECJ ... 25–12
Benham's Will Trusts, Re (1995) 22–01
Bennett v. IRC [1995] S.T.C. 54 19–04
Bentley v. Pike (1981) 53 T.C. 590 15–01
Bentleys, Stokes & Lowless v. Beeson [1952] 2 All E.R. 82, CA .. 5–13
Bird v. IRC [1989] A.C. 300, HL 2–08
Blackpool Marton Rotary Club v. Martin (Inspector of Taxes) 62 T.C. 686, CA 13–01
Bond (Inspector of Taxes) v. Pickford [1983] S.T.C. 517, CA 14–27
Booth v. Ellard [1980] 1 W.L.R. 1443; [1980] 3 All E.R. 569, CA 14–22
Booth (E.V.) Holdings Ltd v. Buckwell (1980) 53 T.C. 425 15–03

Boots Co. plc v. CEC [1990] S.T.C. 387, ECJ 25–07
Bothupswana National Corp. Ltd v. CEC [1993] S.T.C. 702,
    CA 24–11
Bowden v. Russell & Russell [1965] 1 W.L.R. 711; [1965] 2 All
    E.R. 258 5–13
British Airways plc v. CEC [1990] S.T.C. 643, CA 24–11
British Insulated and Helsby Cables Ltd v. Atherton [1926] A.C.
    205, HL 5–12
British Salmson Aero Engines Ltd v. IRC [1938] 2 K.B. 482, CA
                                                                                                        5–12
British Transport Commission v. Gourley [1956] A.C. 185;
    [1956] 2 W.L.R. 41; [1955] 3 All E.R. 796, HL 6–19
Brown v. Bullock [1961] 1 W.L.R. 1095, CA 6–18
— v. National Provident Institution [1921] 2 A.C. 222, HL 2–05
Buccleuch v. IRC [1967] 1 A.C. 506; [1967] 2 W.L.R. 207;
    [1967] 1 All E.R. 129, HL 20–16
Bullivant Holdings Ltd v. Ellam [1998] S.T.C. 905 14–08
Butler v. Evans [1980] S.T.C. 613 14–06

CAIRNS v. MACDIARMID (INSPECTOR OF TAXES) [1983] S.T.C.
    178, CA 10–02
Calvert v. Wainwright [1947] K.B. 526; [1947] 1 All E.R. 282 ... 6–05
Campbell v. IRC [1970] A.C. 77; [1968] 3 W.L.R. 1025, HL 10–04
Campbell Connelly & Co. Ltd v. Barnett (Inspector of Taxes)
    [1993] S.T.C. 50, CA 16–08
Capcount Trading v. Evans (Inspector of Taxes) [1993] 2 All
    E.R. 125, CA 15–01
Card Protection Plan Ltd v. CEC [1999] S.T.C. 270, ECJ 24–11
Carr (Inspector of Taxes) v. Sayer [1992] S.T.C. 396 8–09
CEC v. Blackpool Pleasure Beach Co. [1974] S.T.C 138 25–02
— v. BT plc [1999] S.T.C. 758, HL 24–11, 25–07
— v. Bugeja [2000] S.T.C. 1 25–07
— v. Church Schools Foundation Ltd [2000] S.T.C. 651 24–10
— v. Colour Offset Ltd [1995] S.T.C. 85 25–02
— v. Diners Club Ltd [1989] S.T.C. 407, CA 24–11
— v. FDR Limited, (2000) STC 672, CA 24–13
— v. Ferrero UK Ltd [1997] S.T.C. 883, CA 25–02
— v. Harpcombe Ltd [1996] S.T.C. 726, QBD
— v. Littlewoods Organisation plc [2000] S.T.C. 588 ... 24–10, 25–07
— v. Oliver [1980] 1 All E.R. 353 24–08
— v. Plantiflor Ltd [2000] S.T.C. 137, CA 24–11, 25–07
— v. Professional Footballers Association [1993] 1 W.L.R. 153;
    [1993] S.T.C. 86, HL 24–11
— v. Redrow Group plc [1999] S.T.C. 161, HL 25–12
— v. Robert Gordon's College unreported, HL, 1995 2–13
— v. Royal Exchange Theatre Trust [1979] S.T.C. 728 24–13
— v. Safeway Stores plc [1997] S.T.C. 163 25–02
— v. Telemed Ltd [1992] S.T.C. 90 24–11
— v. United Biscuits (UK) Ltd [1992] S.T.C. 325 24–11

— v. Wellington Hospital [1997] S.T.C. 445, CA 24–11
— v. Westmorland Motorway Services Ltd [1998] S.T.C. 431,
   CA 25–07
Chaloner (Inspector of Taxes) v. Pellipar Investments Ltd [1996]
   S.T.C. 234 14–10
Chinn v. Collins [1981] A.C. 533; [1981] 2 W.L.R. 14; [1981] 1
   All E.R. 189, HL 11–05
Clark (Inspector of Taxes) v. Oceanic Contractors Inc. [1983]
   A.C. 130 12–03
Clarke v. BT Pensions [1998] S.T.C. 1075 2–16
Clarke v. Mayo [1994] S.T.C. 570 16–11
Clore, dec'd (No. 3), Re [1985] 1 W.L.R. 1290; [1985] 2 All
   E.R. 819 .... 22–01, 23–01
Colquhoun v. Brooks (1889) 14 App. Cas. 493 .... 5–01, 26–12
Commissioner of Taxation v. Squatting Investment Co. Ltd
   [1954] A.C. 182, PC 5–09
Congreve v. IRC [1948] 1 All E.R. 948, HL 26–22
Conservative and Unionist Central Office v. Burrell [1982] 1
   W.L.R. 522; [1982] 2 All E.R. 1 .... 2–08, 13–01
Co-operative Wholesale Society Ltd v. CEC [1999] S.T.C.
   1096 24–11
Cooke (Inspector of Taxes) v. Blacklaws (1984) 58 T.C. 255 6–03
Copol Clothing Ltd v. Hindmarch (Inspector of Taxes) [1984] 1
   W.L.R. 411, CA 8–09
Corbett v. IRC [1938] 1 K.B. 567 11–01
Countess Fitzwilliam v. IRC [1993] 1 W.L.R. 1189; [1993] 3 All
   E.R. 184, HL 2–14, 21–10
Craven (Inspector of Taxes) v. White [1988] 3 W.L.R. 423;
   [1988] 3 All E.R. 495, HL 2–14
Crowe v. Appleby [1975] 1 W.L.R. 1539; [1975] 3 All E.R. 529
                                               14–22

DAPHNE v. SHAW (1926) 43 T.L.R. 45 8–03
Davenport (Inspector of Taxes) v. Chilver [1983] Ch. 293;
   [1983] 3 W.L.R. 481 14–10
Davis v. Powell [1977] 1 W.L.R. 258; [1977] 1 All E.R. 471 14–10
De Beers Consolidated Mines v. Howe [1906] A.C. 455 26–03
Drummond (Inspector of Taxes) v. Austin-Brown (1983) 58
   T.C. 67 14–10
Duple Motor Bodies v. Ostime. See Ostime v. Duple Motor
   Bodies
Dyer v. Dorset County Council [1989] Q.B. 346 16–05

EC COMMISSION v. UK [1998] S.T.C. 456, ECJ 25–02
Edwards v. Bairstow and Harrison [1956] A.C. 14; [1955] 3
   W.L.R. 410; [1955] 3 All E.R. 48, HL ... 1–12, 3–05, 5–02, 6–02
— v. Clinch [1981] Ch. 1; [1981] 3 W.L.R. 707; [1981] 3 All
   E.R. 543; [1982] A.C. 845, HL 6–02

Eilbeck v. Rawling [1982] A.C. 300; [1981] 2 W.L.R. 449;
    [1981] 1 All E.R. 865, HL 15–03
Elida Gibbs Ltd v. CEC [1996] S.T.C. 1387, ECJ 25–07
Ellesmere v. IRC [1918] 2 K.B. 795 20–11
EMI Group Electronics v. Coldicott [1999] S.T.C. 803 6–04
Emmerson v. Computer Time International [1977] 1 W.L.R.
    734; [1977] 2 All E.R. 545, CA 15–01
Empire Stores Ltd v. CEC [1994] S.T.C. 623, ECJ 25–07
Ensign Tankers (Leasing) Limited v. Stokes (Inspector of Taxes)
    [1992] 1 A.C. 655; [1992] 2 W.L.R. 469; [1992] 2 All E.R.
    275, HL 2–13, 2–14, 2–16, 5–03
Erichsen v. Last (1881) 8 Q.B.D. 414 5–03
Ewart v. Taylor (Inspector of Taxes) [1983] S.T.C. 721 14–28

FALL v. HITCHEN [1973] 1 W.L.R. 286; [1973] 1 All E.R. 368 .. 6–02
Falmer Jeans Ltd v. Rodin (Inspector of Taxes) [1990] S.T.C.
    270 13–16
Fetherstonhaugh v. IRC [1985] Ch. 1; [1984] 3 W.L.R. 212,
    CA 19–16
Fielder (Inspector of Taxes) v. Vedlynn Ltd [1992] S.T.C. 553 .. 15–02
Finanzamt Bergisch Goldbach v. Skripalle [1997] S.T.C. 1035,
    ECJ 24–02
Finanzamt München III v. Mosche [1997] S.T.C. 195, ECJ 24–02
Fischer v. Finanzamt Donaueschingen [1998] Q.B. 883 24–02
Fitzpatrick v. IRC (No. 2) [1994] 1 W.L.R. 306; [1994] 1 All
    E.R. 673, HL 6–18
Frankland v. IRC [1997] S.T.C. 450, CA 19–20, 21–18
Furniss v. Dawson [1984] A.C. 474; [1984] 2 W.L.R. 226;
    [1984] 1 All E.R. 530, HL 2–14, 2–16, 7–09

G v. G. (1975) 6 Fam. Law 8 19–19
Gallagher v. Jones (Inspector of Taxes) [1994] Ch. 107; [1994]
    2 W.L.R. 160, CA 5–06
Garner v. Pounds Shipowners and Shipbreakers Ltd [2000]
    S.T.C. 19, HL 15–02, 15–03
Glantre Engineering v. Goodhand (Inspector of Taxes) [1983] 1
    All E.R. 542, DC 3–06
Global Plant v. Secretary of State for Social Security [1972] 1
    Q.B. 139; [1971] 3 W.L.R. 269 6–02
Goodbrand v. Loffland Bros North Sea Inc. [1998] S.T.C. 930,
    CA 15–02
Goodwin v. Curtis [1998] S.T.C. 475, CA 16–05
Gordon v. IRC [1991] S.T.C. 174 16–09
Government of India v. Taylor. See India (Government of) v.
    Taylor
Graham v. Greene [1925] 2 K.B. 37 5–05
Gray v. IRC [1994] S.T.C. 360, CA 20–16
Great Western Railway Co. v. Bater [1922] A.C. 1, HL 6–02
Gregg v. CEC [1999] S.T.C. 934, ECJ 24–02

Grey v. Tiley (1932) 16 T.C. 414 5–19
Griffin (Inspector of Taxes) v. Craig-Harvey [1993] S.T.C. 54 ... 16–05

HALL (INSPECTOR OF TAXES) v. LORIMER [1994] 1 W.L.R. 209;
  [1994] 1 All E.R. 250, CA 6–03
Hamblett v. Godfrey (Inspector of Taxes) [1987] 1 W.L.R. 357;
  [1987] 1 All E.R. 916, CA 6–04
Harthan v. Mason [1980] S.T.C. 94 14–22
Hatton v. IRC [1992] S.T.C. 140 18–04
Hayes' Will Trusts, Re [1971] 1 W.L.R. 758; [1971] 2 All E.R.
  341 2–15
Hillyer v. Leeke [1976] S.T.C. 490 .... 5–14, 6–18
Hinton v. Maden & Ireland Ltd [1959] 1 W.L.R. 875; [1959] 3
  All E.R. 356, HL 5–11
Hitch v. Stone [1999] S.T.C. 431 2–14
Hoare Trustees v. Gardner [1979] Ch. 110; [1978] 2 W.L.R.
  832, 839; [1978] 1 All E.R. 791 14–27
Hochstrasser v. Mayes [1960] A.C. 376; [1960] 2 W.L.R. 63;
  [1959] 3 All E.R. 817, HL 6–04
Hoechst Finance Ltd v. Gumbrell (Inspector of Taxes) [1983]
  S.T.C. 150, CA 13–10
Honour (Inspector of Taxes) v. Norris [1992] E.G.C.S. 35 16–05
Horton v. Young [1972] Ch. 157; [1971] 5 W.L.R. 348; [1971]
  3 All E.R. 412, CA 5–14

ICAEW v. CEC [1999] S.T.C. 398, HL 24–13
Ian Flockton Developments Ltd v. CEC [1987] S.T.C. 394 25–12
India (Government of) v. Taylor [1955] A.C. 491; [1955] 2
  W.L.R. 303; [1955] 1 All E.R. 292, HL 2–06
Inglewood (Lord) v. IRC [1993] 1 W.L.R. 866, CA 21–22
Ingram v. IRC [1999] S.T.C. 37, HL 18–07
IRC v. Barclay, Curle & Co. Ltd [1969] 1 W.L.R. 675; [1969] 1
  All E.R. 732, HL 8–03
— v. Brander & Cruickshank [1971] 1 W.L.R. 212; [1971] 1 All
  E.R. 36, HL 6–02, 6–19, 24–14
— v. Church Commissioners for England [1977] A.C. 329, HL . 4–02,
                                                                           10–04
— v. Cock, Russell & Co. Ltd [1949] 2 All E.R. 889 5–10
— v. Crawley [1987] S.T.C. 147 10–05
— v. Duke of Westminster [1936] A.C. 1, HL 2–14, 10–04
— v. Green [1982] S.T.C. 485 16–05
— v. Land Securities Investment Trust Ltd [1969] 1 W.L.R. 604;
  [1969] 2 All E.R. 430, HL 10–04
— v. Livingston (1927) 11 T.C. 538 5–04
— v. Lloyds Private Banking Ltd [1998] S.T.C. 559 21–03
— v. Lord Rennell [1964] A.C. 173; [1963] 2 W.L.R. 745;
  [1963] 1 All E.R. 803, HL 19–05
— v. Macpherson [1988] 2 W.L.R. 1261; [1988] 2 All E.R. 753,
  HL 18–04, 21–09, 21–18

— v. Maxse [1919] 1 K.B. 647 5–05
— v. National Book League [1957] Ch. 488; [1957] 3 W.L.R.
  222; [1957] 2 All E.R. 644, CA 10–04
— v. National Federation of Self-Employed and Small Businesses
  [1982] A.C. 617; [1981] 2 W.L.R. 722; [1981] 2 All E.R.
  93, HL 3–10
— v. Plummer [1980] A.C. 896; [1979] 3 W.L.R. 689; [1979] 3
  All E.R. 775, HL 11–05
— v. Ramsay (1935) 20 T.C. 79 18–01
— v. Richard's Executors [1971] 1 W.L.R. 571, HL 15–03
— v. Scottish and Newcastle Breweries [1982] 1 W.L.R. 322;
  [1982] 2 All E.R. 230, HL 8–03
— v. Slater (Helen) Charitable Trust [1982] Ch. 49; [1981] 3
  W.L.R. 377; [1981] 3 All E.R. 98, CA 16–13
— v. Spencer-Nairn [1991] S.T.C. 60 18–05
— v. Stannard [1984] 1 W.L.R. 1039; [1984] 2 All E.R. 105 22–01
— v. Wattie [1998] S.T.C. 1160 4–02
— v. Willoughby [1997] 1 W.L.R. 1071; [1997] S.T.C. 995,
  HL 1–12, 2–13, 2–14, 26–22
— v. Wolfson [1949] 1 All E.R. 865, HL 11–06

JARMIN (INSPECTOR OF TAXES) v. RAWLINGS [1994] S.T.C.
  1005 16–11
Jenkins (Inspector of Taxes) v. Brown [1989] 1 W.L.R. 1163 14–22
John Pimblett and Sons Ltd v. CEC [1988] S.T.C. 358, CA 25–02
Johnston v. Britannia Airways *The Times*, July 20, 1994 5–06
Jonas v. Bamford [1973] S.T.C. 519 3–05
Jones v. Leeming [1930] A.C. 415 5–19
Jones (Samuel) & Co. (Devondale) Ltd v. IRC (1951) 32 T.C.
  513 5–15
Julius Fillibeck Söhne GmbH & Co. KG v. Finanzamt Neustadt
  [1998] S.T.C. 513, ECJ 24–10

KEEPING NEWCASTLE WARM v. CEC [2000] S.T.C. 454 25–07
Kelsall Parsons & Co. v. IRC (1938) 21 T.C. 608 5–08
Kidson v. MacDonald [1974] Ch. 339; [1974] 2 W.L.R. 566;
  [1974] 1 All E.R. 849 .... 2–06, 14–22
Kirby (Inspector of Taxes) v. Thorn EMI plc [1988] 1 W.L.R.
  445; [1988] 2 All E.R. 947, CA 14–06, 14–10
Kirkham v. Williams (Inspector of Taxes) [1991] 1 W.L.R. 863,
  CA 5–04
Kuwait Petroleum GB Ltd v. CEC [1999] S.T.C. 488, ECJ 24–11,
                                                                      25–07

LAKE v. LAKE [1989] S.T.C. 865 19–20
Landboden Agrardienste GmbH & Co. KG v. Finanzamt Calau
  [1998] S.T.C. 171, ECJ 24–10
Law Shipping Co. Ltd v. IRC (1924) 12 T.C. 621 5–15
Leader v. Counsel [1942] 1 K.B. 364 5–19

Lennartz v. Finanzamt München III [1995] S.T.C. 514, ECJ 25–12
Letts v. IRC [1957] 1 W.L.R. 201; [1956] 3 All E.R. 588 18–07
Levene v. IRC [1928] A.C. 217 26–04
Lewis (Inspector of Taxes) v. Lady Rook [1992] 1 W.L.R. 662,
    CA 16–05
Lewis v. Walters (Inspector of Taxes) [1992] S.T.C. 97 15–05
London and Thames Haven Oil Wharves Ltd v. Attwooll [1967]
    Ch. 772; [1967] 2 W.L.R. 743; [1967] 2 All E.R. 124, CA . 5–07
London County Council v. Attorney-General [1901] A.C. 26,
    HL 1–07, 4–01
Lord Fisher v. CEC [1981] S.T.C. 238 24–13
Lowe v. Ashmore [1971] Ch. 545; [1970] 3 W.L.R. 998; [1971]
    1 All E.R. 1057 7–04
Lucas v. Cattell (1972) 48 T.C. 353 5–13
Lurcott v. Wakely & Wheeler [1911] 1 K.B. 905 5–12
Lyon (Inspector of Taxes) v. Pettigrew (1985) 58 T.C. 452 14–12

McClure (Inspector of Taxes) v. Petre [1988] 1 W.L.R.
    1386 7–04
Macfarlane v. IRC [1929] S.C. 453 11–03
McGowan v. Brown and Cousins [1977] 1 W.L.R. 1403; [1977]
    3 All E.R. 844 5–09
McGregor v. Adcock [1977] 1 W.L.R. 864; [1977] 3 All E.R.
    65 16–11
McKnight v. Sheppard [1999] S.T.C. 669, HL 5–13
MacNiven v. Westmoreland Investments [1997] S.T.C. 1103 2–14
Macpherson v. IRC. See IRC v. Macpherson
Makins v. Elson [1977] 1 W.L.R. 221; [1977] 1 All E.R. 572 ... 16–05
Malik v. CEC [1998] S.T.C. 537 25–02
Mallalieu v. Drummond [1983] 2 A.C. 861; [1983] 3 W.L.R.
    409; [1983] 2 All E.R. 1095, HL 5–11, 6–18
Mairs (Inspector of Taxes) v. Haughey [1994] 1 A.C. 303;
    [1993] 3 W.L.R. 393; [1993] 3 All E.R. 801, HL (N.I.) 6–04
Markey (Inspector of Taxes) v. Saunders [1987] 1 W.L.R. 864 . 16–05
Marks and Spencer plc v. CEC [2000] S.T.C. 16, CA; [1999]
    S.T.C. 205 .... 24–02, 25–02
Marren v. Ingles [1980] 1 W.L.R. 983; [1980] 3 All E.R. 95,
    HL 14–10
Marriott v. Lane [1996] S.T.C. 704 16–11
Marsden v. IRC [1965] 1 W.L.R. 734; [1965] 2 All E.R. 364 6–18
Marson v. Marriage [1980] S.T.C. 177 14–12
Marson (Inspector of Taxes) v. Morton [1986] 1 W.L.R. 1343 .. 5–02,
                                                                                                7–09
Martin v. Lowry [1927] A.C. 312 5–04
Mason v. Innes [1967] Ch. 1079; [1967] 3 W.L.R. 816; [1967]
    2 All E.R. 926, CA 5–10
Melville v. IRC [2000] S.T.C. 628 .... 16–01, 18–02
Midland Bank plc v. CEC [2000] S.T.C. 501, ECJ 25–05, 25–12
Miller v. IRC [1987] S.T.C. 108 21–03

Minden Trust (Cayman) Ltd v. IRC [1985] S.T.C. 758, CA 21–01
Mirror Group Newspapers Ltd v. Customs and Excise Commissioners [2000] S.T.C. 156 24–08
Mitchell and Edon v. Ross [1960] Ch. 498; [1960] 2 W.L.R. 766; [1960] 2 All E.R. 218, CA 6–02
Moodie v. IRC [1993] 1 W.L.R. 266; [1993] 2 All E.R. 49, HL 2–16
Moore v. Griffiths [1972] 1 W.L.R. 1024; [1972] 3 All E.R. 399 6–05
— v. Thompson (Inspector of Taxes) [1986] S.T.C. 170 16–05
Moore & Osborne v. IRC [1985] Ch. 32 21–03
Moorhouse v. Dooland [1955] Ch. 284; [1955] 2 W.L.R. 96; [1955] 1 All E.R. 93, CA 6–05
Munby v. Furlong [1977] Ch. 359; [1977] 3 W.L.R. 270; [1977] 2 All E.R. 953, CA 8–03
Munro v. Commissioner of Stamp Duties [1934] A.C. 61, PC ... 18–07
Murray v. Goodhews [1978] 1 W.L.R. 499; [1978] 2 All E.R. 40, CA 5–09

Nadin v. IRC [1997] S.T.C. (SCD) 107 19–04
National and Provincial Building Society v. UK [1997] S.T.C. 1466 2–06
Newsom v. Robertson [1953] Ch. 7; [1952] 2 All E.R. 728, CA 5–11
Nicholls v. IRC [1975] 1 W.L.R. 534; [1975] 2 All E.R. 120, CA 18–07
Nicoll v. Austin (1935) 19 T.C. 531 6–14
Norbury Development Ltd v. CEC [1999] S.T.C. 511, ECJ 24–02
North Anderson Cars Ltd v. CEC [1999] S.T.C. 902, CS 25–07
North of England Zoological Society v. CEC [1999] S.T.C. 1027 25–03

Oakes v. Commissioner of Stamp Duties of New South Wales [1954] A.C. 57; [1953] 3 W.L.R. 1127; [1953] 2 All E.R. 1563, PC 18–07
O'Brien v. Benson's Hosiery Ltd [1980] A.C. 562, HL .. 14–06, 14–10
Odeon Associated Cinemas Ltd v. Jones [1973] Ch. 288; [1972] 2 W.L.R. 331; [1972] 1 All E.R. 681, CA 5–15, 15–02
Odhams Leisure Group Ltd v. CEC [1992] S.T.C. 332 25–02
O'Grady v. Bullcroft Main Collieries Ltd (1932) 17 T.C. 93 5–15
O'Kelly v. Trusthouse Forte [1984] Q.B. 90; [1983] 3 W.L.R. 605; [1983] 3 All E.R. 456, CA 6–02
Oram v. Johnson [1980] 1 W.L.R. 558; [1980] 2 All E.R. 1 15–03
Ostime v. Duple Motor Bodies [1961] 1 W.L.R. 739; [1961] 2 All E.R. 167, HL 5–10
Owen v. Elliott (Inspector of Taxes) [1990] Ch. 786; [1990] 3 W.L.R. 133, CA 16–05
— v. Pook [1970] A.C. 244, HL 6–08, 6–18

Page (Inspector of Taxes) v. Lowther [1983] S.T.C. 799, CA 7–09

Palmer v. Maloney [1999] S.T.C. 890 .... 1–14, 16–11
Park, dec'd (No. 2), Re [1972] Ch. 385; [1972] 2 W.L.R. 276;
    [1972] 1 All E.R. 394, CA 19–05
Parker Hale Ltd v. CEC [2000] S.T.C. 388 24–08
Parsons, Re [1943] Ch. 12 18–03
Partridge v. Mallandine (1886) 18 Q.B.D. 276 5–05
Pearson v. IRC [1981] A.C. 753; [1980] 2 W.L.R. 872; [1980] 2
    All E.R. 479, HL 21–03
Pepper v. Hart [1993] A.C. 593; [1992] 3 W.L.R. 1032; [1993]
    1 All E.R. 42, HL 2–09, 2–13, 6–08, 16–11
Pexton v. Bell [1976] 1 W.L.R. 885; [1976] 2 All E.R. 914, CA 14–26
Pickford v. Quirke (1927) 13 T.C. 251 5–04
Pilgrims Languages Courses Ltd v. CEC [1999] S.T.C. 876, CA 24–11
Pilkington v. Randall (1966) 42 T.C. 662, CA 7–09
Plumbly v. Spencer [199] S.T.C. 677, CA 16–11
Polsar Investments Netherlands BV v. Inspecteur der Invoerrech-
    ten en Accijnzen te Arnhem (C-60/90) [1991] E.C.R. I-3111 24–13
Prest v. Bettinson (1982) 82 T.C. 437 16–13

R. v. IRC, EX P. NATIONAL FEDERATION OF SELF-EMPLOYED
    AND SMALL BUSINESSES. *SEE* IRC V. NATIONAL FEDERATION
    OF SELF-EMPLOYED AND SMALL BUSINESSES 3–10
— v. Barton, unreported, October 29, 1999 3–09
— v. Customs and Excise Commissioners, ex p. Building Societ-
    ies Ombudsman Co. Ltd [1999] S.T.C. 974 24–02
— v. Dimsey [1999] S.T.C. 846 3–09
— v. W [1998] S.T.C. 550 3–09
Ramsay v. IRC [1982] A.C. 300; [1981] 2 W.L.R. 449; [1981] 1
    All E.R. 865, HL 2–13, 2–14, 18–04
Randall v. Plumb [1975] S.T.C. 191 15–02
Ransom v. Higgs [1974] 1 W.L.R. 1594; [1974] 3 All E.R. 949,
    HL 5–03, 5–11
Ratcliffe, Re [1999] S.T.C. 262 22–01
Ready Mixed Concrete (South East) v. Minister of Pensions and
    National Insurance [1968] 2 Q.B. 497; [1968] 2 W.L.R.
    775 6–02
Regent Oil Co. Ltd v. Strick [1966] A.C. 295; [1965] 3 W.L.R.
    696; [1965] 3 All E.R. 174, HL 5–12
Rendell v. Went [1964] 1 W.L.R. 650; [1964] 2 All E.R. 464,
    HL 6–07
Ricketts v. Colquhoun [1926] A.C. 1 6–17
Robert Gordons College v. CEC [1993] V.A.T.T.R. 159 2–14
Robinson v. Scott Bader Co. Ltd [1981] 1 W.L.R. 1135; [1981]
    2 All E.R. 1116, CA 13–04
Rolfe v. Nagel [1982] S.T.C. 53, CA 5–09
Roome v. Edwards [1982] A.C. 279; [1981] 2 W.L.R. 268;
    [1981] 1 All E.R. 736, HL 14–27
Rosgill Group Ltd v. CEC [1997] S.T.C. 811, CA 24–10, 25–07
Roskams v. Bennett (1950) 32 T.C. 129 6–18

Russell v. IRC [1988] 1 W.L.R. 834; [1988] 2 All E.R. 405 19–16,
                                                19–20
Rutledge v. IRC (1929) 14 T.C. 490 5–04

SALT v. CHAMBERLAIN [1979] S.T.C. 750 5–04
Sansom v. Peay [1976] 1 W.L.R. 1073; [1976] 3 All E.R. 353;
    [1976] B.T.R. 259 16–05
Sargent v. Barnes [1978] 1 W.L.R. 823; [1978] 2 All E.R. 737 .. 5–14,
                                                   6–18
Schuldenfrei v. Hilton (1999) 3–02
Schlumberger v. CEC [1987] S.T.C. 228 3–02
Scorer (Inspector of Taxes) v. Olin Energy Systems Ltd [1985]
    A.C. 645; [1985] 2 W.L.R. 668; [1985] 2 All E.R. 375, HL

                                                     3–02
Scott v. Ricketts [1967] 1 W.L.R. 828; [1967] 2 All E.R. 1009,
    CA 5–16, 14–06
Sea Containers Services Ltd v. CEC [2000] S.T.C. 82 24–11
Secretan v. Hart [1969] 1 W.L.R. 1599; [1969] 3 All E.R. 1196 14–01
Seymour v. Reed [1927] A.C. 554, HL 6–05
Shah v. Barnet London Borough Council. See Akbarali v. Brent
    London Borough Council 26–02, 26–04
Sharkey v. Wernher [1956] A.C. 58; [1955] 3 W.L.R. 671; [1955] 3
    All E.R. 493, HL 5–08, 14–13
Shilton v. Wilmshurst (Inspector of Taxes) [1991] 1 A.C. 684;
    [1991] 2 W.L.R. 530, HL 6–04
Shove v. Downs Surgical plc [1984] 1 All E.R. 7 6–19
Simpson v. Reynolds (John) & Co. (Insurances) Ltd [1975] 1
    W.L.R. 617; [1975] 2 All E.R. 88, CA 5–09
— v. Tate [1925] 2 K.B. 214 6–17
Skerrits of Nottingham Ltd v. Secretary of State for the Environ-
    ment, *The Times*, March 8, 2000 16–05
Smith (Inspector of Taxes) v. Abbott. See Fitzpatrick v. IRC
    (No. 2)
— v. Schofield (Inspector of Taxes) [1993] 1 W.L.R. 398, HL ... 15–10
Smiths Potato Estates Ltd v. Bolland [1948] A.C. 508; [1958] 2
    All E.R. 367, HL 5–14
Snushall v. CEC [1982] S.T.C. 537, CA 25–02
Société Financière d'Investissements SPRL v. Belgium [2000]
    S.T.C. 164, ECJ 24–02
Spectros International plc v. Madden [1997] S.T.C. 114 15–02
Staatssecretaris van Financien v. SAFE BV [1991] S.T.C. 627,
    ECJ 24–08
Stamp Duties Commissioner of New South Wales v. Permanent
    Trustee Co. of New South Wales [1956] A.C. 512; [1956] 3
    W.L.R. 152; [1956] 2 All E.R. 512, PC 18–07
Stanley v. IRC [1944] K.B. 255 11–03
Stanton v. Drayton Commercial Investment Co. Ltd [1983] A.C.
    501; [1982] 3 W.L.R. 214; [1982] 2 All E.R. 942, HL 15–03
Starke v. IRC [1995] S.T.C. 689, CA 19–17

Steibelt v. Paling [1999] S.T.C. 594 16–08
Stenhouse's Trustees v. Lord Advocate [1984] S.T.C. 195 21–03
Stephenson v. Barclays Bank Trust Co. Ltd [1975] 1 W.L.R.
   882; [1975] 1 All E.R. 625 14–22
Stevenson (Inspector of Taxes) v. Wishart [1987] 1 W.L.R.
   1204; [1987] 2 All E.R. 428, CA 11–03
Strong & Co. Ltd v. Woodfield [1906] A.C. 448 5–13
Swales v. IRC [1984] 3 All E.R. 58 .... 21–03, 21–04, 21–22
Swires (Inspector of Taxes) v. Renton [1991] S.T.C. 490 14–27

Taylor v. Good [1974] 1 W.L.R. 556; [1974] 1 All E.R. 1137,
   CA 5–04
— v. Provan [1975] A.C. 194; [1974] 2 W.L.R. 394; [1974] 1
   All E.R. 1201, HL 6–08, 6–18
Taylor Clarke International Ltd v. Lewis [1998] S.T.C. 1259,
   CA 14–17
Tennant v. Smith [1892] A.C. 150 .... 6–13, 6–24
Todd (Inspector of Taxes) v. Mudd [1987] S.T.C. 141 16–08
Tolsma v. Inspecteur der Omzetbelasting Leenwarden [1994]
   S.T.C. 509, ECJ 24–10
Tomlinson v. Glyn's Executor Co. [1970] Ch. 112; [1969] 3
   W.L.R. 310; [1970] 1 All E.R. 381 14–22
Trustees of Nell Gwyn House Maintenance Fund v. CEC [1999]
   S.T.C. 79, HL 24–11, 25–07
Tucker v. Granada Motorway Services Ltd [1979] 1 W.L.R.
   683; [1979] 2 All E.R. 801, HL 5–12
Turner v. Follett [1973] S.T.C. 148, CA 14–08

Van Boeckel v. CEC [1981] 2 All E.R. 505 3–02
Van den Berghs Ltd v. Clark, unreported, 1935 .... 4–01, 5–08
Varty v. Lynes [1976] 1 W.L.R. 1091; [1976] 3 All E.R. 447 16–05
Vesty v. IRC [1962] Ch. 861; [1962] 2 W.L.R. 221; [1961] 3 All
   E.R. 978 10–04
— v. — [1980] A.C. 1148; [1979] 3 W.L.R. 915; [1979] 3 All
   E.R. 976, HL 26–22
Virgin Atlantic Airways Ltd v. CEC [1995] S.T.C. 341 24–11
Vodafone Cellular Ltd v. Shaw [1995] S.T.C. 353 13–06

Wakeling v. Pearce [1995] S.T.C. (SCD) 107 16–05
Walding v. IRC [1996] S.T.C. 13 19–16
Walton v. IRC The Times, December 11, 1995 20–11
Wase v. Bourne [1996] S.T.C. 18 16–11
Watkins (Inspector of Taxes) v. Ashford Sparkes and Harward
   [1985] 1 W.L.R. 994; [1985] 2 All E.R. 916 5–13
Watton (Inspector of Taxes) v. Tippett The Times, December
   21, 1995 .... 14–09, 16–08
Weight v. Salmon (1935) 19 T.C. 174, HL 6–14
West v. Phillips (1958) 38 T.C. 203 5–04
Whitechapel Art Gallery v. CEC [1986] S.T.C. 156 24–13

Whitehouse v. Ellam [1995] S.T.C. 503 14–08
Wilkins v. Rogerson [1961] Ch. 133; [1961] 2 W.L.R. 102;
    [1961] 1 All E.R. 358, CA 6–08, 6–14, 6–15
Williams v. Bullivant [1983] S.T.C. 107 14–11
— v. Evans [1992] S.T.C. 498 16–08
Williams (Inspector of Taxes) v. Merrylees [1987] 1 W.L.R.
    1511 16–05
Wimpey International v. Warland [1989] S.T.C. 273, CA 8–03
Woolwich Building Society v. IRC [1993] A.C. 70; [1992] 3
    W.L.R. 366; [1992] 3 All E.R. 737, HL 2–05
Wright v. Boyce [1958] 1 W.L.R. 832; [1958] 2 All E.R. 703,
    CA 6–05

YARMOUTH v. FRANCE (1887) 19 Q.B.D. 647 8–03
Yoga for Health Foundation v. CEC [1984] S.T.C. 630 24–02
Young, Re (1875) 28 Ch. D. 705 26–03
Young and Young v. Phillips (Inspector of Taxes) (1984) 58
    T.C. 232 14–06
Young and Woods Ltd v. West [1980] I.R.L.R. 201, CA 6–03
Yuill v. Fletcher (Inspector of Taxes) (1984) 58 T.C. 145, CA 7–09
— v. Wilson [1980] 1 W.L.R. 910; [1980] 3 All E.R. 7, HL 7–09

ZIM PROPERTIES LTD v. PROCTER (INSPECTOR OF TAXES) [1985]
    S.T.C 90 .... 14–06, 14–08, 14–10

TABLE OF STATUTES

1706 Act of Union (c. 7) . 2–06
1803 Income Tax Act (43
Geo. 3, c. 122) 2–03,
2–07, 2–16, 4–01
Scheds. A–E 2–07
1842 Income Tax Act (5 &
6 Vict., c. 35) 2–03
1853 Income Tax Act (16
& 17 Vict., c. 34) ... 2–03
1880 Employers' Liability
Act (43 & 44 Vict., c.
42) 8–03
1890 Inland Revenue
Regulation Act (53 &
54 Vict., c. 21) 1–10
Partnership Act (53
& 54 Vict., c. 39) . 12–07
1894 Finance Act (57 & 58
Vict., c. 30) 2–03
1918 Income Tax Act (8 &
9 Geo. 5, c. 40) 2–03
1925 Trustee Act (15 & 16
Geo. 5, c. 19)
s. 31 ..... 11–02, 11–07,
21–03, 21–04,
21–22
(i)(ii) 21–03
s. 32 21–22
Law of Property Act (15
& 16 Geo. 5, c. 20)
s. 184 18–08
Administration of
Estates Act (15 & 16
Geo. 5, c. 23)
s. 34 22–01
s. 47A 19–20
Sched. 1
Pt. II ... 22–01

1934 Law Reform
(Miscellaneous
Provisions) Act (24 &
25 Geo. 5, c. 41) 10–02
1936 Finance Act (26 Geo.
5 & 1 Edw. 8, c. 34) ....
2–03, 2–13
1940 Finance Act (c. 29)
Sched D, Case 6 .. 7–01
1945 Income Tax Act (8 &
9 Geo. 6, c. 32) 8–01
1948 Agricultural
Holdings Act (11 &
12 Geo. 6., c. 63) . 14–10
1952 Income Tax Act (15
& 16 Geo. 6 & 1
Eliz. 2, c. 10) 2–03, 2–13
1963 Finance Act (c. 25) . 7–01
1965 Finance Act (c. 25) . 2–03
1967 Leasehold Reform
Act (c. 88) 15–05
1968 Capital Allowances
Act (c. 3) 2–03
1969 Finance Act (c. 32) . 7–01
1970 Taxes Management
Act (c. 9) 1–10, 2–03,
13–01
s. 8 3–02
s. 9A(1) 3–04
s. 12B(1)(a) 3–04
s. 29(3) 3–01
s. 31 1–12
s. 34 3–08
s. 36 3–08
s. 40 3–08
s. 50(6) 3–05
s. 54 3–02
s. 56 .... 1–12, 2–16

1970	Taxes Management Act
	s. 56A 1–12
	B 3–05
	Income and Corporation Taxes Act (c. 10) 2–01, 2–13
	European Communities Act (c. 68) 26–07
1974	Finance Act (c. 30) . 2–04
1975	Finance Act (c. 7) 18–09, 19–01, 19–17
	ss. 39–42 18–09
	s. 39 18–09
	s. 40 18–09
	s. 41 ...... 18–09, 18–12
	s. 42 18–09
	Social Security Act (c. 14) 2–04
	Inheritance (Provision for Family and Dependants) Act (c. 63) 19–21
1976	Finance Act (c. 40)
	s. 115 18–12
1978	Finance Act (c. 42) . 6–16
1979	Customs and Excise Management Act (c. 2) 1–11
1980	Housing Act (c. 51) 16–05
1982	Supply of Goods and Services Act (c. 29) 24–08
1983	Oil Taxation Act (c. 56) 2–06
1984	Finance Act (c. 43) 8–01, 8–02
	Capital Transfer Tax Act (c. 51) 17–01
	Inheritance Tax Act (c. 51) 17–01, 18–06, 18–09, 19–01, 20–16, 26–07, 26–09
	Pt. III 21–01
	s. 1 .... 2–07, 18–01
	s. 2(1) 18–01

1984	Inheritance Tax Act— contd
	s. 3 20–01
	s. 3(1) 18–01
	(2) 18–01
	(3) ... 18–01, 21–18
	(4) 21–08
	s. 3A 18–06
	s. 4 .... 18–03, 19–11, 19–19, 20–16, 21–08
	(1) 18–08
	(2) 18–08
	s. 5 .... 19–10, 20–07, 20–08, 21–04, 21–06
	(1) ... 18–01, 20–16
	(2) 18–03
	(5) 20–09
	s. 7 20–01
	(4) 20–02
	s. 10 ..... 19–19, 19–22, 21–18, 21–23
	(1) 18–01
	s. 11 19–19
	(1) 19–19
	(6) 19–19
	s. 12 19–22
	s. 13 19–23
	s. 14 19–24
	s. 15 ...... 18–01, 19–25
	s. 16 19–26
	s. 17 19–20
	s. 18 19–01
	ss. 19–22 21–08
	s. 19 19–02
	s. 20 19–03
	s. 21 19–04
	s. 22 19–05
	s. 23 19–06
	s. 24 19–07
	s. 24A 19–08
	s. 25 19–09
	s. 27 19–14
	s. 29A 19–20
	ss. 30–35A 19–14
	ss. 36–42 22–06
	s. 41 22–01
	s. 43 ...... 20–14, 21–01

1984	Inheritance Tax Act—*contd*	
	s. 47	21–04
	s. 48	21–04
	(1)(a)	21–23
	s. 49	21–06
	(1)	21–04
	s. 50	21–03
	(6) . 20–14, 21–04	
	s. 51	21–08
	s. 52	21–08, 21–13
	(1)	21–08
	(2)	21–10
	(3) . 21–09, 21–18	
	(4)	21–10
	s. 53(2) . 21–10, 21–23	
	(3)	21–10
	(4)	21–10
	s. 54	21–10
	s. 54A	21–13
	s. 54B	21–13
	s. 55	21–23
	s. 56(2)	19–01
	ss. 58–85	21–14
	s. 58(1) . 21–14, 21–21	
	s. 59	21–14
	s. 60	21–15
	s. 61	21–15
	s. 64	21–15
	s. 65(1)	21–18
	(2)	21–19
	s. 66	21–17
	(2)	21–17
	(6)	21–17
	s. 67	21–17
	s. 68	21–20
	s. 69	21–20
	s. 70	21–22
	s. 71	21–22
	s. 76	21–18
	s. 80	21–15
	s. 90	21–10
	s. 91	21–04
	s. 92	18–03
	s. 93	19–20
	ss. 94–98	18–09, 21–12
	s. 94	18–10
	s. 96	18–10

1984	Inheritance Tax Act—*contd*	
	s. 98	18–10
	s. 99	21–12
	s. 101	21–12
	s. 102	18–04, 18–05
	ss. 103–114	19–16
	s. 106	21–17
	ss. 115–124C	19–17
	s. 115(2)	19–17
	(3)	19–17
	ss. 125–130	19–18
	s. 131	20–02
	s. 141	19–13, 21–11
	ss. 142–145	19–20
	s. 142	18–01, 19–20
	(1)	19–20
	s. 143	19–20
	s. 144	19–20
	s. 145	19–20
	s. 146	19–21
	s. 150	19–15
	s. 152	19–10
	s. 154	19–11
	s. 155	19–12
	s. 160	20–11
	s. 161	20–13
	(1)	20–13
	s. 162(5)	20–07
	s. 163	20–12
	s. 164	20–07
	s. 165	20–07
	s. 167	20–15
	s. 170	20–14
	ss. 171–177	18–03
	s. 171	20–16
	(2)	18–08
	s. 172	18–03, 20–16
	s. 173	20–16
	s. 176	20–13
	ss. 178–189	20–16
	ss. 190–198	20–16
	ss. 199–214	22–01
	s. 202	18–09
	ss. 215–261	23–01
	s. 215	23–01
	s. 216	23–01
	s. 218	23–02
	s. 219	23–03

1984 Inheritance Tax Act—
      contd
      s. 219A 23–03
          B 23–03
      s. 220 23–03
          A 23–03
      ss. 221–225 23–04
      ss. 226–236 23–05
      s. 237 23–06
      s. 238 23–06
      s. 245 23–01
          A 23–02
      s. 256 23–01
      s. 262 .... 18–09, 18–11
      s. 263 .... 18–09, 18–13
      s. 264 20–05
      s. 265 20–03
      s. 266(1) 20–04
          (2) 20–04
      s. 268 ...... 2–15, 18–04
          (2) 18–04
          (3) 18–04
      s. 272 18–04
      Chap. II 21–13
      Chap. III 21–13
      Sched. 1 20–01
      Sched. 3 19–09, 19–14
1985 Companies Act (c. 6) ....
                    13–05, 13–19
      Housing Associations
      Act (c. 69) 19–08
1986 Finance Act (c. 41)
      s. 102 ... 18–07, 18–08,
                           332
          A 18–08
          (2) 18–08
          (3) 18–08
          (4)(b) 18–08
          (5) 18–08
          B 18–08
          C(6) 18–08
      s. 103 .... 20–09, 20–10
          (5) 20–09
      s. 104 20–09
      Sched. 20 18–07
              para. 6 ....
                           18–07
1986 Insolvency Act (c. 45)
      s. 341 19–15

1988 Income and
      Corporation Taxes
      Act (c. 1) 2–05, 2–07,
              2–13, 2–17, 4–01
      Pt. XV 11–05
      s. 1 .... 2–05, 2–07
          A 10–08
      ss. 6–13A 13–01
      s. 6 .... 2–05, 2–07,
                    4–01, 13–01
      s. 7(1) 10–03
      s. 9 13–04
          (1) 13–01
      s. 15 (Sched. A) .. 2–07,
              4–01, 6–17, 7–01,
              7–02, 7–03, 7–04,
              7–05, 7–06, 7–07,
              7–08, 9–01,
              11–02, 12–04,
              12–08, 13–06,
                           26–11
      s. 17 (Sched. C) . 10–01
      s. 18 (Sched. D) . 2–07,
              2–08, 4–01, 5–01,
              5–14, 5–19, 8–03,
              6–18, 6–19,
              10–04, 12–08,
              24–04, 24–14,
              26–11, 26–12
          (1) 5–01
          (a)(ii) 26–12
          (2) 26–13
          (3) ... 5–01, 10–07
          Case 1 2–05,
              4–01, 4–02, 5–01,
              5–05, 5–10, 5–11,
              5–19, 6–01, 6–18,
              7–01, 7–05,
              10–08, 12–02,
              12–04, 12–08,
              13–01, 13–06,
              13–07, 24–13,
              26–12, 26–14
      s. 18 Case 2 2–07,
              4–01, 5–01, 5–05,
              5–11, 5–19, 6–01,
              6–02, 6–18,
              10–09, 13–01,
                           24–13

1988 Income and Corporation
Taxes Act—*contd*
    Case 3 2–07,
        4–01, 5–19,
        10–01, 10–04,
        10–05, 10–08,
        10–09, 11–03,
        12–02, 13–07,
        13–20, 26–12,
        26–14
    Case 4 2–07,
        4–01, 5–19,
        10–01, 26–14
    Case 5 2–07,
        4–01, 5–19, 10–01,
        26–12, 26–14,
        26–20
    Case 6 2–07,
        4–01, 5–17, 5–19,
        7–02, 7–06, 7–09,
        9–01, 10–02,
        10–09, 11–06,
        11–07, 11–08,
        13–15, 14–06,
        26–23, 26–15,
        26–22
    s. 19 (Sched. E) .. 2–07,
        2–13, 3–06, 4–01,
        4–02, 5–01, 5–11,
        5–14, 5–19, 6–01,
        6–02, 6–04, 6–18,
        6–19, 6–20, 6–21,
        6–22, 6–23, 6–24,
        12–05, 12–22,
        13–01, 24–14,
        26–03, 26–14,
        26–16, 26–19
      (1) 6–01
    Case 1 6–01,
        6–04,
        26–17, 26–19
    Case 2 6–01,
        26–18
    s. 19 Case 3 6–01,
        26–19
    s. 20 (Sched. F) .. 2–07,
        4–01, 10–01, 10–10,
        13–19, 26–20
    s. 21A 7–05

1988 Income and Corporation
Taxes Act—*contd*
    s. 32 ....
    ss. 34–39 7–07
    s. 34 7–07
      (1) 7–07
      (2) 7–07
      (4) 7–07
      (5) 7–07
    s. 35 .... 7–07, 13–01
    s. 36 7–07
    s. 38 7–07
    ss. 43A–43G 7–08
    s. 53 5–04
    s. 54 5–04
    s. 63 13–01
    s. 64 10–05
    s. 69 5–19
    s. 74   5–11, 5–14, 7–06
      (a)–(q) 5–09
      (a) 5–11,
        5–14, 5–15
      (b) 5–11
      (d) 5–11, 5–15
      (e) 5–11
      (f) 5–11
      (g) 5–11, 5–15
      (k) 5–11
    s. 75 13–10
    s. 76 13–10
    s. 84 5–09
    ss. 103–110 5–17
    s. 103 5–17
      (2) 5–17
    s. 104 5–17
    s. 107 5–19
    s. 110(3) 5–17
    s. 111 12–06
    s. 119 10–02
    s. 120 10–02
    s. 125(1) 10–03
    s. 131(1) .. 4–01, 6–03,
        6–05, 6–17
    s. 134 5–01
    s. 141 6–15
    s. 143 6–15
    s. 145 6–17
      (4) ... 6–09, 6–17
    s. 148 .... 6–05, 6–19,

1988 Income and Corporation
Taxes Act—*contd*
 ss. 153–168 6–06
 s. 153 6–08
 s. 154 6–08
 s. 155A 6–12
 s. 155AA 6–13
 s. 156 6–08
 s. 157 .... 6–10, 6–25
 s. 158 6–10
 s. 159 6–10
 s. 159AA 6–10
 s. 159AB 6–10
 s. 160 .... 6–11, 6–12
 s. 161(1) 6–11
 s. 162 6–12
 s. 163 6–09
 s. 166 6–08
 s. 168A 6–10
 s. 168F 6–10
 s. 188 6–19
 s. 190 4–01
 s. 198 5–11
  (1) 6–18
 s. 201 6–18
 s. 202B 6–22
 ss. 203F–203L 6–22
  G 6–15
  I 6–15
 ss. 209–218 4–01
 s. 209(2)(a) 4–01
 s. 212 13–20
 s. 218 13–20
 ss. 213–218 13–21
 ss. 257–278 12–16
 s. 257(5) 12–17
  AA 12–19
 s. 275C 12–16
 s. 313 6–17
 s. 314 5–01
 s. 329 10–02
 s. 334 26–03
 s. 335 26–03
 s. 336 26–03
 ss. 337–344 13–01
 s. 338 13–07
  (4) 13–09
 s. 340 13–09
 s. 343 13–16

1988 Income and Corporation
Taxes Act—*contd*
 s. 344 13–16
 s. 347A 10–03, 10–04,
   11–05, 11–10
  (1)
  (7)
 s. 347B
 s. 348 ..... 4–01, 10–02,
  10–05, 10–08, 10–12
  (2) 10–07
 s. 349 .... 4–01, 9–03,
  10–02, 10–05, 10–08
  (1)(b) 10–09
  (2) . 4–01, 10–08
 s. 350 9–03
 s. 353 .... 6–10, 9–03
  (3) 12–11
 s. 380 .... 9–02, 9–03
 s. 381 9–05
 s. 384 ...... 9–02, 13–14
 s. 385 9–03
  (4) 9–03
 s. 386 9–03
 s. 387 9–03
 s. 388 9–04
 s. 390 9–03
 ss. 392A–413 13–01
 s. 393 13–12
  (9) 13–07, 13–13
 s. 393A 13–12
 s. 397 ...... 9–02, 13–14
 s. 402 13–18
 s. 403(1) 13–18
  (7) 13–09
 s. 414–422 13–22
 s. 477A 10–08
 s. 480A 10–08
 s. 503 7–06
 s. 504 7–06
 ss. 559–565 5–01
 s. 577 .... 5–11, 5–14
 s. 580(3) 6–19
 s. 592 .... 5–14, 6–20
 s. 592(4)–(6) 5–11
 s. 594 6–19
 s. 595 5–14
 s. 596 6–20
 s. 617 .... 6–01, 6–21

1988 Income and Corporation
Taxes Act—*contd*
ss. 619–629 5–18
ss. 630–655 5–18
ss. 639–646 6–19
s. 639 5–18
s. 641 5–19
s. 642 5–19
s. 643(2) 5–19
s. 656 10–07
s. 660A . 11–05, 11–06
11–07, 11–08,
11–09
(1) 11–06,
11–07, 11–09
(2) 11–06
(3) 11–06
(4) 11–06
(5) 11–06
(6) 11–06
(8) 11–06,
11–09
(9) 11–09
(10) 11–06
s. 660B   11–05, 11–06,
11–08
(1) 11–07
(2) 11–07
(3) 11–07
s. 660D(1) 11–06,
11–07
s. 660G(1) 11–05
s. 677 .... 11–05, 11–08
(2) 11–08
(4) 11–08
(9) 11–08
(10) 11–08
s. 678 .... 11–05, 11–08
s. 686 .... 11–02, 11–08
(2)(b) 11–08
(6) 11–04
s. 687 11–02
s. 739 26–22
ss. 747–756 26–22
ss. 757 *et seq.* ... 26–23
s. 765 26–22
s. 768 13–17
s. 768A 13–17
s. 770 5–10

1988 Income and Corporation
Taxes Act—*contd*
s. 776 .... 2–13, 7–09,
7–10
(1) 7–09
s. 779 7–07
s. 780 7–07
s. 787 12–11
s. 788 26–07
s. 790 26–09
s. 811 26–09
s. 817(1) 5–11
ss. 831–842A 13–01
s. 832 .... 2–08, 5–03
s. 833 12–07
(4)(c) 5–19
s. 835 12–01
s. 837 6–17
A 5–07
Sched. 6 6–10
Sched. 6A 6–10
Sched. 8AA 26–12
Sched. 12A 6–18
Sched. 13 12–19
Sched. 28AA 5–10
Finance Act (c. 39) . 7–01
s. 66 26–03
s. 78 6–16
s. 80 6–16
1989 Finance Act (c. 26)
ss. 67–74 6–16
s. 67 6–16
s. 76 5–14
Sched. 5 6–16
1990 Capital Allowances
Act (c. 1) 2–03
2–17, 2–18, 8–01
s. 18 8–09
(7) 8–09
s. 24 8–03
s. 27 .... 8–01, 8–07
ss. 34–36 8–08
s. 37 8–08
s. 61 8–03
s. 61(4) 8–03
s. 67A 8–03
s. 79 8–03
s. 140 9–03
Sched. AA1 8–03

1991　Finance Act (c. 31)
　　　　s. 72 9–02
　　　　s. 117 13–01
　　　　Sched. 18 13–01
1992　Social Security
　　　　(Contributions
　　　　and Benefits) Act
　　　　(c. 4) 2–04
　　　　Pt. I 6–23
　　　　s. 2(1) 6–24
　　　　s. 3(1) 6–24
　　　　s. 6 6–24
　　　　s. 10 6–25
1992　Social Security
　　　　Administration
　　　　(Northern
　　　　Ireland) Act (c.
　　　　8) 6–22
　　　　Taxation of
　　　　Chargeable
　　　　Gains Act (c.
　　　　12) 2–07, 14–01,
　　　　　15–05, 26–07, 26–09
　　　　s. 1(1) 14–03
　　　　s. 2 26–21
　　　　　(1) 14–06
　　　　　(2) ... 14–04, 15–12
　　　　　A 15–07
　　　　　(2) 15–12
　　　　　A(5) 15–07
　　　　　A(6) 15–12
　　　　　A(9) 15–08
　　　　s. 3 .... 14–02, 15–01
　　　　　(5)(a) 15–12
　　　　　(b) 15–12
　　　　　(7) 14–02
　　　　s. 4 14–02
　　　　s. 8 .... 13–01, 13–06
　　　　s. 10(1) 14–06
　　　　　(4) 14–06
　　　　s. 10A 14–06
　　　　s. 12(1) 14–06
　　　　ss. 15–20 15–01
　　　　s. 15(2) 14–04
　　　　s. 16(1) . 15–01, 15–12
　　　　　(2) 15–12
　　　　s. 17 ..... 14–08, 14–12,
　　　　　15–02, 16–01,
　　　　　16–09, 16–12

1992　Taxation of Chargeable
　　　　Gains Act—contd
　　　　s. 18(2) 14–08
　　　　　(3) 15–12
　　　　　(5) 14–06
　　　　s. 21(1) 14–06
　　　　　(b) 14–08
　　　　　(2) . 14–09, 14–10
　　　　s. 22 14–10
　　　　　(1) . 14–10, 14–12
　　　　　(2) 14–10
　　　　s. 23 14–11
　　　　s. 24 237
　　　　　(1) 14–11
　　　　　(2) 14–11
　　　　s. 28 14–12
　　　　s. 35 15–09
　　　　　(2) 15–09
　　　　　(5) 15–09
　　　　ss. 37–52 15–01
　　　　s. 37(1) 14–09
　　　　s. 38(1) 15–03
　　　　　(4) 15–03
　　　　s. 39 15–01
　　　　s. 40 15–03
　　　　s. 42 15–04
　　　　s. 44(1) 15–05
　　　　s. 45 16–07
　　　　s. 48 14–12
　　　　ss. 53–57 15–08
　　　　s. 53(1A) 15–08
　　　　s. 54 15–08
　　　　　(1A) 15–08
　　　　s. 55(2) 15–09
　　　　s. 59 14–05
　　　　s. 60 14–22
　　　　s. 60(1) 14–25
　　　　　(2) 14–22
　　　　s. 62(1) 14–21
　　　　　(2)
　　　　　(4) 14–21
　　　　　(6)–(9) 14–21
　　　　s. 64(2) 14–21
　　　　　(3) 14–21
　　　　s. 68 14–22
　　　　s. 69 14–27
　　　　　(4) 14–29
　　　　s. 70 14–23

1992 Taxation of Chargeable
       Gains Act—*contd*
       s. 71 ...... 14–26, 14–27
          (1) . 14–24, 14–25
               14–26, 14–27
          (2) 14–24
       s. 72 14–26
          (1) . 14–24, 14–26
       s. 73 14–26
          (1)(a) 14–25,
               14–26
             (b) 14–25
       s. 76(1) 14–28
          (2) 14–28
          A 14–28
       ss. 104–114 15–11
       s. 105 15–11
       s. 106A 15–11
             (5) 15–11
       s. 107 15–11
       s. 110A 15–11
       s. 115 16–03
       s. 117 16–03
       s. 122 14–14
       ss. 126–140 14–14
       s. 137 14–14
       ss. 152–159 16–08
       s. 155 16–08
       s. 159 16–08
       s. 161(1) 14–13
             (2) 14–13
       s. 161(3) 14–13
       s. 162 .... 14–16, 16–09
       s. 163 16–11
       s. 164 16–11
       s. 165 16–12
       s. 210 16–04
       ss. 222–226 16–05
       s. 222 16–05
             (6) 16–05
       s. 223(4) 16–05
       s. 224 16–05
             (3) 16–05
       s. 225 16–05
       s. 248A 16–10
             B 16–10
       s. 251 14–17
             (4) 14–17
       s. 253 14–17

1992 Taxation of Chargeable
       Gains Act—*contd*
       s. 256(1) 16–13
          (2) 16–13
       s. 257 16–13
       s. 260 16–01
       s. 262 16–06
       s. 271 6–19
          (1)(h) 5–19
       s. 275 .... 14–07, 26–21
       s. 286 14–08
          (2) 14–08
          (8) 14–08
       s. 288(3) 14–02
       Sched. 1
             para. 2 14–02
             A 15–07
       Sched. 2 15–10,
               15–11
       Sched. 4A 14–28
       Sched. 6 16–11
       Sched. 8 15–05
             para. 5(1) 14–09
       Sched. 9 16–03
       Finance Act (No. 2)
          (c. 48)
          s. 59 7–06
          Sched. 10 7–06
1992 Tribunals and
       Inquiries Act (c.
       53)
          s. 11 24–04
1994 Finance Act (c. 9) ... 3–04
               6–22
          s. 117 8–03
          s. 249 26–03
       Value Added Tax Act
          (c. 23) 24–03
          s. 1 .... 2–07, 24–06
          s. 3(1)
          s. 4(1) 24–06
             (2) ... 24–06, 24–12
          s. 5(2) ... 24–06, 24–08
          s. 19 25–07
          s. 26 25–12
          s. 36 25–13
          s. 43A 24–13
          s. 83 .... 1–12, 24–04
          s. 94 24–13

1994 Value Added Tax Act—
      contd
      s. 94(4) 24–14
      s. 96 24–09
      Sched. 4 24–09
          para. 1 24–09
          para. 3 24–09
      Sched. 8 25–02
      Sched. 9 24–12, 25–03
1995 Finance Act (c. 4) ....
                    7–01, 11–09
      s. 154 19–17
      s. 160 2–03
1996 Finance Act (c. 4) .. 2–09,
          10–02, 12–07,
          13–01, 24–13
      Pt. IV Chap. II . 13–01,
                        13–07
      s. 82 13–07
      s. 83 13–07
1998 Finance Act (c. 36) 6–22,
          26–12, 26–22
      s. 38 7–02

1998 Finance Act—contd
      s. 42 5–07
      Sched. 5 7–01
      Sched. 7 4–01
1998 Human Rights Act (c.
          42) 1–12, 2–06
1998 Scotland Act (c. 46) 2–06
1999 Finance Act 2–19, 24–13
1998 Social Security
          Contributions
          (Transfer of
          Functions) Act . 6–23
2000 Finance Act . 7–08, 8–01,
          10–12, 13–01, 26–22
      ss. 38–45 10–12
      s. 40 13–09
      s. 41 10–06
      s. 141 3–09
      Sched. 8 6–15
      Sched. 12 6–03
      Sched. 14 6–16
      Sched. 22, para.
          41 2–15

TABLE OF STATUTORY INSTRUMENTS

1979 Social Security
(Contributions)
Regulations (S.I.
1979 No. 591) ... 2–09,
6–23, 6–24,
reg. 19 6–24
(1)(d) 6–24
1981 Capital Transfer Tax
(Delivery of
Accounts)
Regulations (S.I.
1981 No. 880) .. 23–01
Capital Transfer Tax
(Delivery of
Accounts) (Scotland)
Regulations (S.I.
1981 No. 881) .. 23–01

1987 Inheritance Tax
(Double Charges
Relief) Regulations
(S.I. 1987 No. 1130) ....
20–10
1995 VAT Regulations
(S.I. 1995 No.
2518) 2–05, 25–12
1998 Inheritance Tax
(Delivery of
Accounts)
Regulations 1998
(S.I. 1991 No.
1431) 23–01

Part One

Introductory

PART ONE

Introduction

UNDERSTANDING TAX

The question "What is a tax?" is surprisingly difficult to answer. **1–01**
It is tempting to rely on the well-known reply of the child who
was asked to define an elephant. "An elephant is large and grey,
and lives in a herd of elephants." Some payments are not clearly
one of the herd. This is so, for example, of the profits made on
postage stamps or the fees paid to government for the right to
operate independent television channels. Clarity is not helped
because some politicians find it convenient to say that things are
not tax when they certainly seem to look like taxes. An example
is national insurance contributions.

Defining taxes

So, as the elephant definition does not seem to work, we must
try to define a tax. A tax has three characteristics. It is *a compulsory levy imposed by an organ of government for public
purposes*. The legal essence of this definition lies in the compul-
sion. Law requires that the payment be made. The political
essence lies in the public purposes for which the payments are
made. Even the definition reflects the disagreements that often
take place about tax.

Another way to define taxes is by way of a list of levies that are,
beyond doubt, taxes. Listing all the payments that might be
regarded "currently" as taxes in force in the United Kingdom
would be contentious and perhaps tedious. Here is a list of the
principal taxes, in order of importance to government: income
tax, value added tax, national insurance contributions, corporation tax, the business rate, excise duties, council tax, capital gains
tax, stamp duty, inheritance tax, petroleum revenue tax, vehicle
excise duty, and insurance premium tax. We have left out customs duty? Yes and no: customs duties are European taxes, and
there is now no British law imposing them. British customs
officials are collecting them for the European Union. We should
perhaps also include hidden taxes like the national lottery levy,
sugar levy, fossil fuel levy, climate change levy, and ports levy—
but then it does get tedious.

1–02   *Why do we tax?*

Before we look in detail at the present United Kingdom tax system, it is valuable to spend a little time thinking about tax policy. Why do we tax the way we do? What are the political, economic, social and administrative pressures that have contributed to the shape of our tax system?

The primary purpose of taxation is to raise revenue for government expenditure. The government can raise revenue by borrowing, by "printing" money, and by selling things, but in practice it is unavoidable that taxation should raise most of the government's fiscal requirements. The government spends part of the money on services which private enterprise cannot provide, such as defence and law and order. It also pays for services that it is thought are better provided on a universal basis, such as social security benefits, and education. Attitudes to taxation depend to some extent on the views of taxpayers as to the merits of these items of government expenditure. Do you, for example, think it the job of government to provide a health service, or consumer protection laws, or pensions? If raising money to pay for these things was the only reason for taxes, however, we could have a much simpler system. If we raised the rate of income tax by 2 per cent, we could abolish inheritance tax and capital gains tax and still make money. Or we could raise the rate of value added tax and abolish most of income tax. Would that be fair? Would it be efficient?

Another purpose behind taxation is the redistribution of wealth and income. Certain aspects of this idea are generally agreed. It is generally—but not universally—agreed that income tax should be "progressive", and that some government revenue should be spent on welfare services. This was a major reason why the poll tax was so unpopular. People thought it unfair that everyone should pay *the same* tax, whether they were rich or poor, just because they lived in the same town. An unpopular tax is a failure—it loses politicians votes, and it proves too expensive to collect. Of course, for any tax the questions of rate and amount are of immense importance. *How* progressive should income tax be? *How much* should be spent on social services? Once upon a time it was considered right that income tax had a top rate of 98 per cent. Does anyone think that right now? Few do, but "once upon a time" was only 25 years ago. Fashions change in tax as in all else.

Another purpose behind imposing taxes is control of the economy. Changes in taxation can and do affect the economy, but control is also exercised by adjusting the money supply and

4

credit. A good example of using tax to control behaviour is the use of customs duties. There used to be a very high customs duty on imported leather. The aim was to protect the Scottish leather industry. This tax was successful because it collected no money! This also shows that taxes are not used only to raise money. That is an important point. One main way in which taxes are used to influence people is by what is *not* taxed. For instance, we put value added tax on most things that people buy, but we do not tax medicines.

Taxes may also be used as a kind of social control. We see this idea concerning the taxing of alcohol and tobacco. More recently, politicians have decided that cars are less of a good thing, so they have been increasing the cost of taxes on them.

We can also use taxes to make sure people pay the full price for something. This is the idea of a pollution tax. When I buy goods, I pay the price the seller asks. That makes the seller a profit and meets the costs. What if the seller has polluted the local area while making the goods? Perhaps the seller has made something that I am going to dump untidily when I have finished with it (like car tyres or plastic bags)? Taxes can be used to impose the cost of destroying the tyre and collecting up the bags. This is a matter of debate at present. It is not widely used as a form of tax in Britain. There is an informal levy imposed by sellers on the price of every tyre to pay for its destruction. In 1996 a landfill tax was introduced. Others may follow.

Principles of Taxation 1–03

Choices of taxes, and the reasons for taxes, is a fascinating topic of academic analysis and discussion. It leads on to an easy question that it is almost impossible to answer: what is the best form of tax? That debate was started in this country by a former customs official, Adam Smith in *The Wealth of Nations* (first published in 1776). Smith set out four "canons" that, in his view, lead to better taxes. In modified form, they still influence official thinking today. The four axioms are:

- people should contribute taxes in proportion to their incomes and wealth;
- taxes should be certain, not arbitrary;
- taxes should be levied in the most convenient way;
- the costs of imposing and collecting taxes should be kept minimal.

To this we must add a modern canon: taxes should be both convenient and competitive internationally. We are a trading nation, and we trade in a global economy.

Taxation, then, can be used for several purposes other than collection money. For more detailed discussion, see Kay and King, *The British Tax System.*[1] There is another side to the question of "better" taxes. If a tax operates in a certain way that they can sidestep (such as stamp duty taxing documents, but not oral transactions), people will change the way they do things to pay less tax. That is human nature. A tax that does not alter behaviour is said to be *neutral.* The aim of those designing taxes is to create neutral taxes, unless policy requires a tax to be non-neutral. In practice, taxes often have unintended side-effects. The United Kingdom suffers, some allege, from this problem of non-neutral taxes.

1–04   *Is taxation fair?*

Let us look at the tax system from the point of view of justice. The current thinking on this matter concentrates on *equity*, which in this context means fairness. *Horizontal equity* is the idea that people in equal circumstances should pay an equal amount of tax. *Vertical equity* means that people in different circumstances should pay an appropriately different amount of tax.

Horizontal equity commands strong support. It was the reason that Adam Smith advocated an income tax, and it is a major reason for that form of tax today. Those with similar levels of income should pay similar levels of tax. Why should that be so? There are several ways of justifying the levels of tax paid by individuals. One economic view is the ability-to-pay argument. On that basis, those with equal ability to pay should pay equally. Another economic view is the benefit argument. Those who pay tax should do so according to the benefits they gain. Leaving aside personal circumstances (for example, that A needs more help than B because A is older/younger/less fit than B), again those with similar means should be paying similar taxes. The same result is achieved by taking the lawyer's view of fairness that "we are all equal before the law", or the democratic view that we are all members of the same society, and are equal within it.

Vertical equity is much more controversial. It is generally agreed that the richer should pay more tax than the poorer. That was why so many people did not like the poll tax, and found it "unfair". Incidentally, they effectively threw out the benefit argu-

---

[1]   Oxford University Press.

ment in so doing, and dismissed the "equal before the law" view as insufficient. But how much more should the richer be paying? Even with a proportional tax the richer do pay more than the poorer. If there were an income tax at a flat rate of 30 per cent, someone with an income of £100,000 would pay £30,000 in tax. This is more than the £300 that someone with an income of £1,000 would pay. Should the person with £100,000 pay more tax than the person with £1,000 not merely absolutely but also proportionally? This is where a progressive tax comes in. Instead of paying at 30 per cent, those on £100,000 income should pay rather more (at least, on part of their income), and those with £1,000 rather less. Again the details become as important as the principle. Precisely what percentage? And on precisely what part of the income? Why?

An important aspect of the justice—or otherwise—of the tax system is the *tax base*. The base of a tax means the thing, transaction, or amount on which the tax is raised. All taxes have bases—whether the base is you (in the case of a poll tax), your income, your wealth, the number of shoes you buy, or whatever. This means the precise boundary of what is taxed as distinct from what is not taxed. Let us take an example. Hal has £100,000 in hand. He uses it to buy a house in which he then lives, paying no rent. Cher also has £100,000 in hand. She spends it on buying company shares. She lives in a rented house. Hal pays no tax on the use he has made of his £100,000 (the occupation of his house). Cher does pay tax on the use she has made of her £100,000 (the dividends). Is this fair?

As Adam Smith pointed out, another aspect of justice is certainty. The tax system should be clear, so that a taxpayer can see in advance how much tax must be paid. Secondly, enforcement should be consistent and universal. There is nothing more destructive of taxpayer morality than the suspicion that others are not paying. If you pay only half your income tax because of a trick, why should I pay more than that? Equally, if you get some form of special allowance, why should I not get one too? But if neither of us understands the law, we do not know if we are paying enough. So, certainty also requires rules that can be understood. This thought leads to another of the paradoxes of tax. The simpler the rules are, the less fair they are (because they ignore justified differences). But the fairer they are, the more complex they are. The more complex they are, the harder they are to understand and put into effect. Therefore they are less certain and, arguably, therefore less fair. If both simplicity and complexity lead to unfairness, is there a happy medium?

1–05   *Is taxation efficient?*

The fourth Smithian canon is cost-effectiveness. The effectiveness of a tax system is partly a matter of success in enforcement, and partly a matter of the total cost of running it and complying with it. Some think that enforcement, in the case of income tax, is not showing a very high success rate. There has grown up what we call the black economy, meaning moonlighting and other forms of tax evasion. Moonlighting is the practice of earning and paying tax on a source of income properly, but then undertaking a second job without declaring the tax. Then there are the ghosts—those who do not appear on any tax department records, and therefore pay no tax. Or do they? In practice, they may pay no direct income tax, but they would be hard put also to avoid all VAT.

Currently, the cost of collecting the Inland Revenue taxes is about 2 per cent of the total net yield, and the cost of collecting the Customs and Excise duties varies from tax to tax. But, of course, this deals only with the direct government costs. There are also hidden *compliance costs*, that is, the costs incurred by taxpayers in paying taxes. Two notable examples of these compliance costs are the costs of an employer for staff hours acting as an unpaid collector of income tax for the Revenue under the PAYE system, and the costs of a trader in complying with the VAT system. Both may also incur substantial costs for professional assistance and advice concerning tax affairs.

There is also an even more deeply hidden cost, a kind of social cost, which the community as a whole pays as part of the price of taxation. What we have in mind is the expenditure (one might almost say waste) of brain-power. Some of the best brains in the country are exclusively devoted to tax matters; some on the Revenue side, some against the Revenue. This brain-power could be better employed in increasing the wealth, health or happiness of the community. In the past, this brain-drain was closely linked to the immensity of the rates of tax. If someone is asked to pay 98 per cent income tax, or even 75 per cent tax, there is a high premium on good advice to avoid it. If income tax had a maximum rate of, say, 10 per cent, much less time and effort would be devoted to escaping the tax. But what would the state stop doing in return?

As for the effects of taxation, we are afraid that this is a topic where asking questions is easier than answering them. Does a high rate of income tax encourage people to work harder or does it discourage them? Most people would say that it discourages them, that it is a disincentive. But it is quite possible to argue that, on the contrary, it spurs people on to earn more, so that even when the tax is paid they will have enough left to live on. Does a high rate of tax on business raise prices? Does a high rate of tax on individuals raise wages and salaries? No one seems to know the answers. A high *average* rate of tax is probably an incentive to work, whereas high *marginal* rates are disincentives.

Of course, the ideal position for the taxpayer confronted with this dilemma is to ensure that whatever others pay, I pay no more tax than I must. In considering this, it is very important to emphasise the distinction between *tax avoidance* and *tax evasion*. Tax avoidance is so arranging my affairs within the rules that I pay the smallest tax bill that is possible. This is perfectly lawful. Tax evasion is when you escape tax by unlawful means. This usually involves some form of dishonesty, ranging from omitting to state some item of income in a tax return to forging a document to create untrue "facts". It is not easy to see (and keep to) the distinction between evasion and avoidance—if needed, evasion involves some crime where avoidance involves no crime. Two factors blur this distinction in practice. First, some quite honourable people think that a tax crime is not "really" a crime at all. What is "really" wrong with omitting to mention in a tax return some jobbing gardening or book-reviewing done at weekends? We tend to think that what we do ourselves is not really criminal at all. What others do is always bigger and badder. The second factor is that crime versus no crime is not the last word on the subject. Elaborate schemes of tax avoidance that have no other purpose may not be criminal, but they are distasteful to many taxpayers and to some judges. Some schemes come near the line—so much so that a word has been coined for them, avoision.

Some taxes are more easily avoided than others. For example, income tax is more easily avoided than VAT. It is partly for this reason that governments have made a big switch from income tax to VAT. We did not have VAT as a tax in 1970. Just 30 years later it is our second biggest tax. Indeed, replacement of income tax by an expenditure tax is advocated in some quarters. The merits of this are said to be that it would be less easily avoided or evaded, it would encourage saving, and it would be cheaper to administer. (Remember that the cost of collecting Customs and Excise duties is less than the cost of collecting Inland Revenue taxes). On the other hand it contradicts the progressive principle. An expenditure tax hits the poor harder than it would hit the rich.

International aspects   1–06

We added a new principle to those of Adam Smith. It is that our rules have to work in the international arena. There are two aspects to this. First, we are now part of the European Union, and must comply with its rules. Secondly, there is strong tax competition between states. Tax systems are as much part of the global marketplace as any other aspect of a country. Both are extremely important in any overall view of current British tax policy. There is another dilemma here: we must both join them and beat them.

Say it softly, but Britain's entry into the E.U. limited the powers of the British Parliament and Government in respect of taxation. Certain Articles of the E.C. Treaty prohibit rules of tax that would discriminate against persons in other Member States. Another Article provides for Member States to work towards tax harmonisation, at least on indirect taxes—those on goods. This movement has progressed farthest in the field of VAT. It is partly why VAT is now so important as a British tax, but it is not the only reason. For most of British—and before it, English—history, the extraordinary revenues of the Crown (as taxes were called) came from customs duties on imports, and from excises. Excises have now been replaced by VAT—a European tax. Customs have now been replaced by the Community customs regime. So much so is this that to call the relevant collection department "Her Majesty's Customs and Excise"—as we do—is a bit of a misnomer. It would be more accurate to call it "Her Majesty's VAT and Duties"—but it is nothing like as romantic. It would be even less romantic, and even more accurate, to call it "Her Majesty's part of the European VAT and Duties". But that might invoke the response given to Alice by the Queen of Hearts.

Our direct taxes have not been affected by the rising tide of E.U. law. Well, even that is not true, as we shall see. We might avoid the E.U. tide. We cannot avoid the currents caused by global tax competition. Ours is a world of offshore jurisdictions, tax havens (or tax heavens as French students consistently mistranslate "paradis fiscaux"), customs unions, free trade zones, enterprise zones, special regimes, jurisdictions, tax holidays, free depreciation regimes ... in short, a highly competitive marketplace. We shall return at the end of the book to some international issues that our tax system has to solve. But we must now begin at the beginning.

1–07   **Introducing the Taxes**

We want to finish this introduction, and start our detailed analysis of tax, by introducing the taxes dealt with in this book and then by referring generally to the kinds of taxes that exist, and the issues that each tax must tackle. We want to try to state in a very few words what it is that each tax is taxing.

First, **income tax**. Why? Because it is in government terms the largest revenue raiser, and therefore the most important tax. And because, with corporation tax, it is the most complex tax, and the hardest to understand. And because it involves significant efforts by lawyers and accountants to ensure that their clients comply with the law, and avoid its excesses. What does it tax? In a famous aphorism in *London County Council v. Attorney-General*, HL, Lord Macnaghten said: "Income tax, if I may be pardoned for saying so, is a tax on income." This is largely, but not absolutely, true. There are some items of income that are not taxed; for example, student grants. So income tax is not a tax on all income. On the other hand, there are some charges to income tax that are imposed on receipts that are not income tax receipts, but rather capital receipts. This is so, for example, of taxing premiums received on leasing land. Anyway, what is income? Such questions are why we wrote a good part of this book!

Secondly, **VAT** (which is what the Act imposing value added tax calls it, so we shall too). Why? Because it recently became the second most important tax in fiscal terms. Secondly, it has become the most litigated of the taxes, and is gaining in complexity and practical importance each year.

Thirdly, social security contributions (or **NI contributions** as everyone and everything except the law itself terms them), which are the third source of government finance, and, for most people, a second income tax. The law is less complex and comprehensive than income tax law, so requires less extended treatment.

Fourthly, **corporation tax**. This is simply income tax and capital gains tax imposed on companies. Well, not simply—parts are fiendishly complicated, although we avoid the worst of it!

Fifthly **capital gains tax (CGT)**. Its fiscal significance is trivial compared with the taxes so far listed. Nevertheless, its complexity—and therefore its nuisance value to lawyers—far outweighs its importance in filling a gap in the income tax. What it taxes is the gain represented by the difference between the price at which an item was acquired and the price at which it is sold. Since 1982 this taxes the *real* gain (taking account of inflation), not the *cash* gain.

Sixthly, **inheritance tax (IHT)** or, as it used to be called before they thought it fun to change its name, capital transfer tax. It is a tax on capital transfers, and has never been a tax on inheritances, but what does that matter? It is a tax on transfers of property by certain gifts, by transfers into trust, and by operation of law on someone's death from that person's estate. Although whether or not it is accurately named does not matter, accurate advice on where it may affect capital transfers is important. Again we must examine it in detail.

1–08   *Collecting taxes*

All these taxes, and all other taxes in Britain, can be grouped under three broad heads of taxation in terms of the way they are imposed and collected: withholding taxes, taxation related to particular transactions or their effects (called transactions taxes for short), and taxes based on profits or wealth of any kind (called assessed taxes, but normally now self-assessed). British taxes are of all these kinds, frequently muddled up together.

A withholding tax is a tax imposed on the payer of a sum so that the recipient receives less than would otherwise be received. For example, someone paying patent royalties to another person will be required to deduct from that sum an amount equal to the basic rate of income tax. If this is done, the recipient is treated as having paid tax on those royalties. The tax authorities are always on the lookout for ways of increasing the payment of taxes at source in this way. Most income tax and NI contributions are now collected in this way through the PAYE system. Under most forms of withholding tax, the payer is liable to pay the tax to the tax authorities even though they did not deduct it from the payment and even though it was the *recipient* who is really paying the tax.

Transactions taxes are those based on particular transactions or their results. VAT is usually imposed on any supply of goods or services made by a business. Stamp duty is imposed whenever a document is used (as it must be) to transfer land. Inheritance tax and capital gains tax can be regarded as being, in one sense, transactions taxes.

Assessed taxes are the most usual kinds of taxes in Britain although most are now self-assessed by taxpayers. Income tax raises most of its money from the income of the employed, the self-employed and those with investment income. So does the National Insurance Fund through NI contributions. Then there are the special assessed taxes like petroleum revenue tax.

1–09   *Anatomy of a tax*

Whichever form of tax we adopt, and whatever the fiscal or other reasons for its adoption, the lawyer's task is to identify when it is payable and when not. Tax law, or revenue law as many also call it, is there to define when taxes shall be charged. In respect of each tax this definition will contain the same elements:

- the tax base;
- the incidence (including the rate) of the tax; and
- the taxpayer, or person liable to pay.

The rate is often the most important point politically or commercially, but rarely detains the lawyer long. The other issues need further thought.

The tax base, as we have seen already, is the asset, transaction, profit or other thing which is liable to the tax. This may be anything from a television to the net profits of a year's trading. Each tax will have a limited tax base, the limits being of two kinds: the general limits on that kind of tax, and specific exceptions. Clearly, the wider the tax base of a tax, the more revenue it will collect. The more exceptions that are allowed, the smaller the return from the tax. Over the years, all our main taxes have become subject to important exceptions. This is partly because granting an exception is very easy politically, and votes are not easily won for removing it later. Nonetheless, in the last few years more attention has been turned to both the limits on the tax bases of our taxes and the width of exceptions. It has become commonplace to regard exceptions as tax expenditures, that is, subsidies created by the tax not collected. The cost of these tax expenditures has often been worked out. As a result, some longstanding exceptions and reliefs from tax have been removed, such as the life assurance relief that lasted from 1842 to 1984. This trend is continuing.

The second issue is the identity of the taxpayer. Economists talk of this as the incidence of the tax, distinguishing between the *formal incidence* of the tax (who is required by law to pay it) and the *effective incidence* (who ends up paying). Lawyers are concerned only with formal incidence. In most cases under modern laws different people can be made to pay in respect of some taxes, especially when withholding taxes are used to collect the tax. For example, if someone makes a gift of shares to someone else on which inheritance tax ought to be paid, the authorities can try to collect the tax from the donor, the recipient and most subsequent owners of the shares.

Tax Authorities   1–10

Two main government departments administer our taxes: the Inland Revenue and Customs and Excise. Customs and Excise is responsible for VAT, but all the other taxes described in this book are administered by the Inland Revenue.

The **Revenue** is more formally known as the Commissioners of Inland Revenue. The commissioners are appointed under the Inland Revenue Regulation Act 1890 for the collection and management of inland revenue. The powers of the commissioners to deal with income tax, corporation tax and capital gains tax are set out in the Taxes Management Act 1970. Formally, the care and management of these are in the hands of the commissioners acting together as the Board. The Board is based at Somerset House on the Strand in London.

The Revenue is run through the head office in London, supported by specialist offices (for example for NI contributions, petroleum revenue tax, and valuation questions) with a national network of district offices under a regional structure. Inspectors (known formally as Her Majesty's Inspectors of Taxes) are appointed for each district. Your local inspector will therefore be the inspector for the district responsible for collecting your taxes. For the self-employed this will be a local office (for example, Oxford). For employees, it is the office that deals with the employer (for example Wrexham 1, the office dealing with employers in part of London). The inspectors have the formal power to require information and make assessments. They are supported by specialist staff in the regional and national offices.

The processes of assessment and collection have recently gone through a complete change. The traditional approach was "us and them", where all assessments and demands were made by inspectors or collectors, with the taxpayer supplying information or following procedures in a passive role. Over the last few years the whole of the revenue operation was computerised and placed on a self-assessment basis. This has involved simplifying and codifying laws and practices. It also involves transferring the duty to decide tax liability to the taxpayer. These processes of codification, mechanisation and self-assessment are also adopted for NI contributions.

Customs is the colloquial term used for Her Majesty's Commissioners of Customs and Excise. Tradition, and law, provides that they are appointed under the Great Seal of the United Kingdom. The pomp and circumstance perhaps reflects the long history behind those officials, presiding jointly over the oldest government department of all. In practical terms, the powers of Customs now arise directly under E.U. law. In practice, customs officers have the widest powers of any government officials. This is because one part of their job is tackling smuggling, contraband, arms trading and, above all, illegal drugs sales. That part of their functions is separate from the VAT organisation. This is based at Southend, and is run through a national network of local VAT offices. The local office is responsible for all aspects of the operation of the tax locally, although it is supported by both national computer facilities and national staff. Most of the task of determining and collecting VAT is placed on those registered for VAT. The main job of VAT staff is therefore checking that the tax is being collected properly.

Why do we have two tax departments? Increasingly, countries are combining their tax departments into one, for example the Danish Customs and Tax Department. The more that tax administration becomes the province of the computer and self-assessment, the less sense it makes to have separate tax departments that may compete and may conflict. Nor does it make much sense to have different powers, or even different registration numbers, for different taxes. Once upon a time, the reason for different administration was a deliberate inbuilt inefficiency in the tax service, and the sharply different nature of customs work to tax work. Then there were several different sets of tax officials. Evidence that the historical justifications have weakened came when NI contributions were transferred from the Department of Social Security to the Revenue in 1999.

Controlling the tax authorities   1–11

It is important to note that each of the tax authorities is constrained to act only within the legislative powers at its disposal. As we explore in the next chapter, the United Kingdom has no constitution. It therefore has no constitutional limits on executive action. History is replete with examples of tax authorities being used to extract taxes for dubious official use. In most advanced states, there are therefore constitutional checks on such action. Lacking such limits in the United Kingdom, it has been left to judges to prevent the use of arbitrary power. They have been alert to ensure that a tax authority has clear legal authority both to collect a tax, and to carry out the procedures necessary to do this. Taxpayers have also been alert to ensure that any apparent stepping beyond the limits is challenged. The result is a developed administrative law of taxation. If you look at any book on constitutional and administrative law, you will see a significant number of tax cases cited. It is precisely because it is only through such cases that the balance has been struck between the Executive and the taxpayer.

At the same time, the fair enforcement of a tax such as income tax depends heavily on taxpayers honestly providing information about what they are earning. Authorities need strong powers to obtain information and collect taxes from those who do not comply readily or who are dishonest. A balance has to be struck between giving powers to the tax authorities on the one side, and on respecting rights of taxpayers on the other. In particular, individual taxpayers do not expect their privacy to be invaded by tax officers, nor do businesses wish to sacrifice commercial confidentiality. Both will want to be inconvenienced to the minimum extent by the process of collecting and paying taxes.

The balance is struck in three ways. First, the powers of the tax authorities are limited by law, and often subject to internal safeguards. These are found in the Taxes Management Act, the Customs and Excise Management Act, and the Acts providing for individual taxes. Secondly, a dispute about either the law or the facts (and often also the procedure) can be referred to independent tribunals and courts. Thirdly, independent reviewers can check the fairness and efficacy of administrative issues.

1–12   *Tax appeals*

Tax appeals against assessments to the Inland Revenue taxes go to appeal tribunals or to the courts. The appeal tribunals are, confusingly, called the General Commissioners and the Special Commissioners. General Commissioners (or, formally, Commissioners for the General Purposes of the Income Tax) are roughly the tax equivalent of a local magistrates' court. The Commissioners are often not experts in the law or tax, but are local people with financial ability and experience. They meet in divisions, each division having a clerk. Procedure is informal and to some extent varies from division to division. The Specials (Commissioners for the Special Purposes of the Income Tax) are based in London, although they also sit elsewhere. They are tax experts drawn both from the professions and from former Revenue officials, and often sit singly. Their proceedings are more formal.

There is a right of appeal against any assessment or amendment of self-assessment to income tax, corporation tax or CGT given by section 31 of the Taxes Management Act. Taxpayers can choose whether to appeal to the local General Commissioners or to the Specials. The Commissioners have the right to transfer cases between them. The Commissioners, when they hear a case, have the right to look anew at any matter of law or fact referred to them, and they can dismiss or alter any assessment in any way they consider to be justified.

Appeal from the Commissioners to the courts is only allowed on a question of law: sections 56 and 56A of the Taxes Management Act. This restricts the rights of the courts to interfere in the administration of taxes. It effectively prevents judges from deciding a tax case as such. The distinction between law and fact is, however, not an easy one. We explore it in the "Escape to Victory" decision in the next chapter, but you should also read *Edwards v. Bairstow* (1952) (see paragraph 3–05). Appeals from the Commissioners are made to the Chancery Division.

Reports of the decisions of Commissioners were long kept secret, as were the hearings. The taxpayer could technically release them, but hardly ever did. A change in the law now allows decisions to be released for publication. Selected decisions are published commercially as *Simons Tax Cases Special Commissioners' Decisions*.

VAT appeals go to the VAT and Duties Tribunal (VADT), mainly because of section 83 of the Value Added Tax Act. This contains a long, but not comprehensive, list of matters that can be appealed. The VADT headquarters is now at the same offices (in Bedford Square) as the Specials, and the President of the VADT is the same person as the Presiding Special Commissioner. There are also a number of individuals who are both VADT chairmen and Special Commissioners or Deputy Special Commissioners. However, there are also still considerable differences between the VADT and the Specials, but there is pressure to form a unified tax tribunal.

Appeals from the VADT are treated as appeals on administrative law and therefore go as part of the Administrative Court of the Queen's Bench Division. Consequently, they are heard by different judges to the income tax appeals. This sometimes leads to interesting contrasts of approach in the High Court between the two taxes on similar questions.

Appeals go from both divisions to the Court of Appeal and— often in tax cases—to the House of Lords. Cases may leapfrog direct to the Court of Appeal, as did *Willoughby* (1995) (see paragraph 2–09). If a point of European law is involved, cases can go direct to the European Court of Justice under Article 234 (the old 177) of the E.C. Treaty at any level. The VADT has referred several important issues direct to the ECJ without waiting for the British courts to be involved. The Commissioners and VADT also operate in Scotland and Northern Ireland, but appeals on questions of law go to the Scottish and Northern Irish courts. We discuss how this appeal system works in the next chapter.

The Lord Chancellor's department published a consultation paper, *Tax Appeals*, in 2000. This suggested major reforms to the way tax appeals are handled, including the effective addition of the General commissioners. While both the introduction of self-assessment and the Human Rights Act 1998 indicate scope for reform, changing a system that dates back four centuries may prove controversial. But the general review of all tribunals by the Leggatt Committee in 2001 will probably add impetus for change.

1–13 *Tax reviews*

There are two more informal ways in which taxpayers can get cases reviewed. The first is to refer matters to the Revenue Adjudicator (who is also the Customs Adjudicator, and the Adjudicator for contributions questions). The office of adjudicator is informal, but provides a way in which a dissatisfied customer (as taxpayers are called in marketspeak) can get a file reopened and looked at afresh.

The Parliamentary Ombudsman provides a semi-formal method of reviewing complaints of taxpayers. The Parliamentary Ombudsman is an officer of parliament who has the specific job of investigating allegations that injustice has been caused to complainants by means of maladministration by a government department. Complaints to the Ombudsman are routed through the complainant's M.P. Complaints can result in financial redress. This may be appropriate where no formal appeal is possible, or where the Revenue or Customs have applied a rule in a way that may strictly be correct, but has worked unfairly (for example, they have enforced the rule unevenly).

1–14 *The tax professions*

Our final introductory topic is that of the professional status of those who advise on tax matters. The Revenue has its own high grade training operation, and Customs also does much training, but this training is aimed at the personnel of the tax departments.

Taxpayers' advisers may belong to several professions or to none. Unlike the legal profession, but following the general approach taken to accountants in the country, the tax profession is an open profession not a closed profession. This means that a tax practitioner does not need a specific qualification to deal with tax affairs. Qualifications are only needed to represent a taxpayer before an appeal tribunal, and there the qualifications of both lawyers and accountants are recognised.

More generally, the complexity of tax makes a professional training advisable to any tax practitioner. There are, however, three separate routes to such status. The only specialist body covering the full range of taxation is the Chartered Institute of Taxation, whose members style themselves chartered tax practitioners. Many tax practitioners are also lawyers (perhaps associated with the Revenue Bar or specialist solicitors), or accountants (where they may be associated with the Tax Faculty established by the Institute of Chartered Accountants of England and Wales). More recently, an Institute of Indirect Tax Practitioners has been established. A fourth source of private tax practitioners is former staff of the tax departments. However, as the profession is an open one, so that no qualification is needed to claim expertise in tax, there is also a range of less formally qualified advisers, and also limited companies, operating in the field. As this book shows, it is increasingly difficult to justify expertise in the field without a formal qualification. In Germany, for example, where tax is largely a closed profession, it has been stated that no individual can properly claim to be an expert in the whole field of taxation. It could be argued that tax is noticeably more complicated in the United Kingdom than Germany.

It may be for this reason that we are now starting to see reported cases about the (alleged) negligence of tax professionals: see *Palmer v. Maloney* (1999), where the Court of Appeal could not agree.

Tax laws may be compared more with an iceberg than an elephant. They are certainly vast and often grey to the outsider. But they are also capable of sinking *The Titanic*! In practice, you will find that there is a lot more to the subject when you examine it closely than is seen by those who merely view it from a distance. Let us learn how to handle the ice.

HANDLING TAX LAWS

2–01   Tax is often regarded as being about numbers. Tax law is about words. It is an odd thing that many lawyers seem worried about tax, because they are worried about the numbers, while many others are worried about tax, because they are worried about the words! What needs to be understood by many lawyers is that you can be a completely sound tax lawyer yet leave the numbers for others to work out. That is the approach taken in this book. Any examples will be simple ones! At the same time, it is of the highest importance that a tax lawyer is fully competent at interpreting and applying the laws that impose taxes. This is because, quite simply, every tax case is a case about statutory interpretation and application.

The purpose of this chapter is to make an initial survey of the raw material of a tax lawyer's work—the statutes and other materials to be used in finding out what the relevant tax law for a particular matter is, what that law means, and how it is to be applied. To do this we must first reflect on the history of tax law. Despite Mr Ford's views on such things, it is not bunk. We must also examine the territorial extent of the tax laws. Having set the scene, we look at the forms of tax legislation, and the current high levels of criticism about those forms. Another point of importance is finding out about the current law. Tax law changes with extreme rapidity, and to be out of date is easy but useless. How are tax questions researched? That we must explore. We then look at how the laws are handled—the methods of interpretation and application, including some thoughts on the use of techniques to avoid the application of tax laws. Some of what we say is relevant to the study of any statute law. That does not make it any less important. On the contrary, the techniques involved are central to a lawyer's skills, and repetition of them is always justified.

2–02   **History**

It is no coincidence that some of the oldest documents in existence are tax returns. We hold tax laws from over four millennia ago in the British Museum archives. Wherever there is social organisation, there is also tax, unless there is almost total slavery or serfdom. Even in the shorter history of England (and the much shorter history of Great Britain) taxation played a central role. It lay behind several rebellions (including, of course, that of the American colonies) and the failure of governments, both ancient and modern. We will not stray into those areas now, fascinating as they are, just for their own sake. Happily, others have chronicled the subject with care. Pre-eminent among recent historians is Basil Sabine, whose *History of Income Tax* and well-written contributions to the *British Tax Review* are of considerable help. Stephen Dowell's *History of Taxation*, written at the beginning of last century, spans the previous 600 years, but is sadly found in too few libraries.

Is not the history of tax yet more clutter in the study of a complex subject? We think not. We need to examine the backgrounds of our taxes. This is because some of them are old and understandable only in the context of their origins. Others of our taxes may be new but there are lessons to be learnt from previous experiments that are of continuing relevance.

The oldest regular taxes are the **stamp duties**. These were introduced in 1694 by William of Orange. They were a direct import from his home territories. The proceeds were exported, in the shape of the English Navy, to fight the French. The taxes have changed little since, although technology is now overtaking them.

Income Tax 2–03

The next tax to be introduced was the **income tax**. Its proceeds were also exported to fight the French although, arguably, the tax was the invention of a Frenchman, Colbert. It was adopted in 1799 as a temporary tax to finance the war against Napoleon. At the time, it replaced, and to some extent copied, what were known as the assessed taxes and land tax that had been used for over a century before. The need for new revenue was desperate. The usual practice until then had to be to tax things. In large part this was done by customs duties, the takings from which were reduced sharply by the war at sea. In Britain itself, the usual practice was to put excise taxes on things—windows, servants, tea, wigs—but these were not enough. Pitt introduced a "contribution on property, profits and income". It was based on a voluntary declaration that the sum of money paid was "not less than ten per centum" of the contributor's income. Not surprisingly, it did not raise much. In 1802, after a lull in the fighting, the tax was repealed. In 1803, it was reintroduced by Addington in a more efficient form. So efficient, indeed, was it that the tax still

21

has much of the form given it by the 1803 Act—and a surprising amount of the original wording. Addington's Act lasted to 1815, when peace finally arrived and the tax expired automatically. For 27 years, land taxes and trade taxes were again used, but they proved too weak a tax base for the emerging industrial economy. In 1842 the income tax, still much in its 1803 form, was reintroduced as a temporary measure. The need for revenues might again have had something to do with ships, as that year we seized Hong Kong. Income tax has been with us ever since, although it is still in form a temporary measure.

During its long history the details of the income tax have been chopped and changed by governments. For example, in 1910 we needed some more ships, so a higher rate of tax (in the guise of supertax) was proposed. That is one reason why the present tax is so difficult to understand. It is not the work of any one committee or team of drafters, but a patchwork of the efforts of innumerable minds with differing and often unstated aims. Every so often, someone has a go at sorting it out, but they have rarely succeeded in changing much.

It was always thus. Back in 1752, Lord Chesterfield and other "backbench" reformers wanted to change the calendar to get rid of the extra 11 days that had crept into the measurement of the year under the Julian calendar. In those days the official year started on March 25 (Lady Day). Lord Chesterfield and colleagues got their way and, despite rioting, the middle of September (mid-year) was removed in 1752. The end of the year was left as March 24, 1753—except for the Treasury. Then, as now, to lose 11 days from a financial year was just too expensive. So the tax year continued to April 5, 1753. For income tax, it still does, 250 years later. With the daily revenue from the tax exceeding £2 billion, it is unlikely to change.

There have been some spirited attempts to knock the income tax into shape. A Royal Commission on Income Tax had a go in 1920 (Cmd. 615). A few changes followed. More ambitious was a Codification Committee in 1936 (Cmd. 5131). This conducted the monumental task of sieving through our then tax laws to find the principles and the problems. It is a fascinating study which still repays the reading, but it was never implemented. There was another Royal Commission in the early 1950s, reporting in 1953 (Cmd. 8671), 1954 (Cmd. 9105) and 1955 (Cmd. 9474). It led to several changes but no substantial restructuring. There was an unofficial attempt by a committee on the structure and reform of direct taxation (and published by the Institute for Fiscal Studies under that name), chaired by Sir James Meade, a Nobel Laureate in economics. It advocated scrapping income tax to replace it by an expenditure tax. It didn't happen. But the work had some effect, in particular invigorating economic thought about our taxes and spawning work such as the brilliant summary by Kay and King, *The British Tax System* (paragraph 1–03). If anything beyond black letter law interests you, read it.

None of these initiatives did anything to improve the shape of the income tax. Finally (so far), a more serious attempt was started in 1995 when years of grumbling boiled up into a most unusual statutory requirement that something be done (see section 160 of the Finance Act 1995, passed against the wishes of the government). We discuss below what is being done. But even this looks as though it will be a reform within the thinking imposed in 1803, and there is much caution in changing key terminology despite—or because of—the passage of two centuries. There is just a faint chance that now we don't need so many ships, the income tax (which was in essence always a war tax) may be allowed to fade away. Otherwise we are entering the new millennium with a law framed by those whose thinking pre-dated the French Empire. The inertia of a system that raises so much revenue is too great.

Only one improvement has been achieved over the years. This is the regular consolidation of the income tax. The 1842 Act did a bit of tidying, and some more was done in 1853. That was kept going until 1918 when, under the strains of yet another war, the laws were consolidated. The 1918 text was strengthened on several occasions (notably 1936 and during the next war). It lasted until 1952 when a new consolidation changed the structure of the tax and attempted to give it a more modern appearance. It was given another structure and another consolidation in 1970, and yet another structure and yet another consolidation in 1988. But until the Tax Law Rewrite Project which started in 1995, it had never been simplified, just allowed to grow. For example, by 1999 the 1988 Act had grown from 845 sections to over 1350, and 17 Schedules had been added to the original 31—with hundreds of pages of additional law in the Finance Acts passed since 1988. Hidden at the heart of it is still the old flagship of the Napoleonic fleet, the 1803 Act, never codified and never reformed. It still cruises on, as old as the *Victory*, but never dry-docked and with a hull encrusted with the sharp barnacles of decades of judicial precedent and corroded by decades of administrative compromise. We must treat it, as the Navy treats the *Victory*, with the respect due to it. But we must not be surprised if it does not always feel as comfortable as a modern vessel.

Alongside the main Act are other supporting Acts. The 1970 consolidation split the 1952 Income Tax Act into three: an

Income and Corporation Taxes Act (1970), a Taxes Management Act (1970) and a Capital Allowances Act (1968). The current Acts are now the 1988 Income and Corporation Taxes Act, the 1970 Taxes Management Act, and a 1990 Capital Allowances Act.

2–04   Later taxes

Compared with the old taxes, the other taxes in this volume are comparatively modern. **Corporation tax** was introduced in the Finance Act 1965, as a modernisation of a profits tax on companies introduced in the last world war. It was, despite its name, devised as a parasite on the income tax and integrated into the 1970 consolidation Act. It was reformed heavily in 1972, again in the 1980s, and yet again in the 1990s. Only in the last few years do we see it emerging as a separate tax, with separate rules for calculating income, rather that something best described as "the same, but different".

Capital gains tax (CGT) also appeared in 1965. In reality, it was and is a device for plugging obvious gaps in the tax base of income tax. In some other countries it is part of the income tax. Maybe it should be here too.

National Insurance contributions, in their present form, came into being in 1973. The law was consolidated into a Social Security Act in 1975, and into a Social Security Contributions and Benefits Act 1992. The idea of special contributions towards funding social insurance dates back to 1911, when the idea was adopted from Germany. It was modified in 1948, and again in 1973. Since 1973, contributions on both employees and the self-employed have been a second form of income tax, but only since 1999 have the two taxes both been collected by the Revenue.

Value added tax (VAT) also appeared in 1973, but for a very different reason. VAT is a peace tax. Several of our taxes were introduced in order to help us beat our European neighbours. This one was introduced so we could join them. The adoption of VAT was a precondition of our entry into the European Community—now the European Union. It is the only permissible form of general indirect tax, or sales tax, in the Member States of the E.U. This is because it proved to be the only major tax that could offer a neutral way of taxing production and consumption, and also handle international transactions neutrally. It was first introduced in the E.C. in 1967. Its main framework was established in 1977, and now applies not only in all E.U. states, but throughout Europe.

Inheritance tax (IHT) has a shorter but odder (and in one way longer) history. It was introduced in 1974 and 1975 as a tax called capital transfer tax, to replace estate duty (dating from 1894) and to succeed to a tradition of taxing estates on death which predates even William of Orange. It had its name changed in 1984 to the present title, although it was not changed into an inheritance tax. It has been reformed since then, but now looks in some ways rather more like the 1894 Act than the 1974 Act! It has been threatened with abolition, but then so have most of the other taxes in this list. If it is abolished, it will only be the third time in our history that an estate duty has been abolished. Each time it has reappeared in a new guise, and with the same problems.

Old ideas and new forms   2–05

History therefore offers us a range of taxes, some 20 years old and some over 200 years old. It confronts us with a range of approaches and a range of reasons for the form of tax used. More important to us as lawyers, it confronts us with a wide variety of language. Some is the product of the word-processor, while some is only a little younger than the later plays of Shakespeare. It also confronts us with old ideas in new shapes—but we must remember that they are old ideas if we are to treat them correctly.

One old idea is that taxes are annual. Parliament still has to re-enact the income tax legislation every year. If it does not, then there would be no income tax next year. Read section 1 of the Income and Corporation Taxes Act 1988. You will see that it does not operate unless in any year there is a Finance Act imposing the income tax. Then read section 6. You will see that no such provision is necessary for corporation tax. Nor is it a necessary approach for income tax, save for our history. Read the preamble to any Finance Act. You will see that taxes are still granted annually to the Crown, not imposed by it. It is, we are supposed to believe, a voluntary offering. This fiction has the consequence that the income tax this year is different to the income tax last year. Further, a judge cannot assume that there will be an income tax next year. So any case about income tax can only look at what happens this year. If, for example, tax is imposed on a form of income, that form of income must exist this year to be taxed. It is not enough that it existed last year, or might exist next year.

The judicial reaction to the annual nature of income tax is called the source doctrine: see *Brown v. National Provident Institution* (1912), HL. The doctrine means that if, say, a trader retires in one year, and receives income in the next, that income can be taxed in neither year. It was not received in the first year.

There was no trade in the second year. It will not surprise you to learn that there are statutory provisions designed to prevent tax avoidance this way, but the doctrine still remains.

Another old approach that also haunts us still is the schedular nature of taxation. Old taxes like the income tax, customs duties, excise taxes and the stamp duties were drawn up as lists: so much to pay on this, and so much to pay on that. They are what is called schedular taxes. Modern taxes like VAT are comprehensive taxes. With a schedular tax, the tax authorities can only collect tax if they can show that what they are trying to tax appears in the list of things to be taxed. There was an extra reason for this in England. Our older taxes emerged at a time when the Stuart kings had developed a habit of raising taxes without asking for parliamentary help. (Like their successors, they needed to raise money for ships.) This was not too popular and led to a change of government and the Bill of Rights. This said that taxes could only be imposed by assent of parliament. For a tax to be imposed, therefore, it has to be shown that parliament has agreed to it. Without clear authority, a tax cannot be raised. This old idea still receives warm support from the judges. Lord Goff said in *Woolwich Building Society v. IRC* (1992):

> "the retention by the state of taxes unlawfully exacted is particularly obnoxious, because it is one of the most fundamental principles of our law ... that taxes should not be levied without the authority of Parliament."

2–06 ## Geography

Our diversions into the past have forced us to talk about England and Britain as well as the United Kingdom. This is because taxes only apply to the territory whose government authorises them. This reflects international practice. One state will not enforce the tax laws of another state without express agreement. Our courts apply this rule: *Government of India v. Taylor* (1955). They also operate on the basis that United Kingdom tax laws apply only in the United Kingdom: *Clark v. Oceanic Contractors* (1983).

For tax purposes, the United Kingdom consists of its four constituent countries together, since 1973, with the territorial sea and continental shelf. This includes, of course, the North Sea oilfields. They have their own tax, the petroleum revenue tax. This is imposed by the Oil Taxation Act 1983. But it is too specialist for a principles book like this.

Even defining the extent of the United Kingdom causes problems in modern tax practice. First, the United Kingdom is legally a union formed of states with a single tax system, but three different legal systems: those of Scotland and Northern Ireland cannot be ignored in the detail of our taxes. In addition, the Scots and Northern Irish have their own appeal systems, generating separate precedents. They are subject only to the unifying influence of the House of Lords—and the European Court of Justice.

For centuries, British governments have followed two key tax policies. First, all internal tax-collecting powers are centralised at national level. Second, our tax policies should support our national position as traders. But the wheels keep turning! We had just finished the final centralisation of all our taxes (by "capping" the powers of local councils to increase local tax rates), when we decided to re-create the Scottish Parliament and the Northern Ireland Assembly, and set up the Welsh Assembly. Much of *The Act of Union* with Scotland 1701 is about tax and trade, and it sets up a customs union. But it leaves unstated the shift of taxing powers to London. Indeed, the main Scottish concern appears to be that the English should stop using taxes to block the import of Scotch beef — how things change! The Scotland Act 1998 gives little back. The Scottish Parliament can change the rate of income tax by up to 3p, and can decide its own limits on local taxes. But while it can alter the rates, it cannot alter the laws. Neither Northern Ireland nor Wales have any powers over their own national tax rates.

The problem of Scottish law is a real one. Its contract laws, property laws, divorce laws, trust laws, and laws of succession are different to those of England. Yet the tax laws are supposed to be enforced throughout the kingdom in an even-handed way. Sometimes this results in separate Scottish terms, or separate Scottish sections. Often the problem is ignored, and the judges are left to do the best they can. This may mean generalising not just the Scottish law, but the English law too: for example *Kidson v. MacDonald* (1974).

Another aspect to the shifts of taxing powers is the unavoidable fact that the United Kingdom is part of the E.U. As a direct result, some of "our" taxes are European taxes, not British taxes at all. The United Kingdom is now part of a single customs union with the other members of the E.U. and the rather wider European Economic Area, together with Turkey and small states and territories such as Monaco and the Channel Isles. This is a vast single market with a single customs law. There is also a single form of VAT throughout the E.U. together with a legal prohibition against any Member State adopting a second VAT. As you will see in the discussion on VAT, most of the key VAT laws are European laws, and much of the case law is that of the European Court of Justice. For both reasons, a tax expert also has to be a European law expert! Repeatedly, we find that it is the European rule, not the British rule, which is to be followed.

The effect of European law on direct taxes is more sensitive politically and is still subject to national vetoes.

The Human Rights Act 1998 adds another European dimension to our taxes. That Act introduces the principles of the European Convention of Human Rights internally into all aspects of our laws. It also imposes the duty on judges to ensure that human rights are protected, if necessary, by ruling that Acts of Parliament breach them. It remains to be seen how taxpayers seek protection in the courts against the tax authorities. For example, does the protection of privacy mean that all tax cases should be anonymous? To date, the leading tax case at the European Court of Human Rights is *National and Provincial Building Society v. UK* (1997).

2–07   **"A Tax Shall Be Charged"**

The key sections in any tax law are the charging sections. These are the sections that actually impose the tax. Take them out, and the rest is mere verbiage. They are often signalled by the draftsman stating unambiguously that "a tax shall be charged ... ". Look for this language in section 1 of the Value Added Tax Act 1994, of the Inheritance Tax Act 1984 or of the Income and Corporation Taxes Act 1988.

These are not the only charging sections in the Acts. Others are often found lurking in the more obscure parts of the Acts, particularly in the 1988 Taxes Act and its many amendments. The multiplicity of charging provisions is particularly important in the income tax and corporation tax. Look again at section 1. It refers us to "the Schedules". What are they? They are a throwback to the 1803 Act. Nowadays, Schedules are added at the ends of Acts and given arabic numerals to identify them. Not so two centuries ago. Then, Schedules appeared in the body of the text, after the sections incorporating them, and were given capital letters for identity. The 1803 Act contained several, though some merely contained procedural provisions. Schedules A to E, however, set out the basis of charge on different kinds of income. That form has been carried on without a break since then, even down to the inclusion of the Schedules in the body of the Act—despite a whole retinue of new-style Schedules at the end. And the Schedules are still divided into cases, just as they were then.

Further, tax practitioners all talk of "Schedule E" rather than "the tax on earnings", or Case I instead of "taxation of trades". The shorthand is extremely useful.

Income tax used to be divided into five Schedules. These grew to six, then shrank to five in 1990, and to four in 1996: A, D, E and F. Of these, Schedules D and E are divided into cases. However, there are now only two Schedules that apply to companies: A and D. Let us explain:

Schedule A (in section 15) charges tax on the *annual profits from a business carried on* with land in the United Kingdom. It replaced a former charge to tax on the value of ownership of land in 1963. It was rewritten (again) in 1998.

Schedule B (repealed in 1988) charged tax on the occupation of commercial woodlands. It was not, in fact, an income tax but a property tax. In its last years it was a mere shadow of a former provision that had lasted in similar form from long before 1803.

Schedule C (repealed in 1996) charged tax on *profits arising from public revenue dividends*. So did Case III of Schedule D. Eventually, someone got round to rationalising this, and this Schedule was no more. A pity, perhaps, as it managed almost two centuries with hardly any litigation.

Schedule D (section 18) charges tax on a range of forms of property and profits.

Case I taxes the *annual profits or gains* from trades (including any employments and vocations of companies): (section 6).

Case II taxes the *annual profits or gains* from professions and vocations of individuals. As noted, these receipts are caught under Case I for companies.

Case III taxes investment income or, as it puts it, *interest, annuities and other annual payments* plus discounts, and a variety of anti-avoidance charges. Since 1996, Case III has a different form for companies to that for individuals.

Case IV is a charge on overseas income from securities. It has now been absorbed into Case III for corporation tax purposes.

Case V originally paralleled Case IV in charging overseas income from *possessions*. Now it stands alone for companies as the basis of charge for overseas income (although in practice the charging provisions are usually those in our double taxation agreements—see paragraph 26–07).

Case VI covers *any annual profits or gains not falling under any other Case of Schedule D, and not charged by virtue of Schedule A or E.* This sounds wider than the judges have let it be—and it is

29

narrower for companies than individuals. It is a sweeper clause, rather than a major extra tax charge.

In the past, the Schedule has had Cases VII and VIII as well. You may still come across Case VIII in the cases. It was what is now Schedule A.

Schedule E (section 19) is fiscally the most important but legally the most obscure. It is a tax on all *offices or employments on emoluments therefrom*. If you have never heard of the gloriously ancient word "emoluments" before, you have now. It comes, of course, straight from 1803. This Schedule has three Cases, but their function is to deal with international aspects of employment rather than different kinds of income, so we will return to them in chapter 26.

Schedule E, as we have noted, does not apply to companies.

Schedule F (section 20), is the newcomer, dating back only to the introduction of corporation tax. It is a tax on *all dividends and other distributions of companies* that are resident in the United Kingdom. It applies only to income tax, as United Kingdom companies do not pay tax on dividends received from other United Kingdom companies. (If you look carefully, you will see that Schedule F applies only to income tax, while the other Schedules apply to "tax".)

The remarks about corporation tax reflect that it is, from many points of view, a different tax to income tax. It also has a separate charging section, section 6.

Now read the list of Schedules again. Better still, read the sections in which these are contained. How many of them charge tax on *income*? Only two—Cases IV and V of Schedule D. What is more, you won't find a charge on income in either section 1 or section 6 either. The disparate phraseology of the income tax both causes and conceals problems, as we shall see later. Just to complicate things, most talk about profits and gains. So does the Taxation of Chargeable Gains Act 1992.

2–08   **The Relationship Between Taxes and Charging Provisions**

Faced with this battery of separate provisions, important questions arise. Can any form of income be charged under two cases, two Schedules, or even two taxes at the same time?

As regards income tax and corporation tax, only one can apply to any one taxpayer on any item of income. Corporation tax applies to companies (defined as bodies corporate by section 832), and income tax to anyone or anything that is not a body corporate. Income tax therefore covers trusts and partnerships. For a fascinating case that decided that the Conservative Party under Mrs Thatcher was not a body corporate (because it consisted of Mrs Thatcher!) see *Conservative Central Office v. Burrell* (1982). History does not record whether the tax inspector in that case was duly promoted.

There is also a clear ranking between income tax and capital gains tax (or the corporate equivalents). In every case, it must first be asked if income tax applies. Only if we conclude that it does not do we ask whether there is a charge to capital gains tax. A charge cannot arise to the two taxes at once. Case law establishes that the Revenue may raise alternative assessments under both taxes, but can only collect tax under one of them: *Bird v. IRC* (1989).

This rule of mutual exclusivity also applies to the income tax Schedules. Whatever may be the theoretical possibilities, a form of income can be charged under one Schedule only. If the legislation does not make clear which Schedule that should be, it will be for the judges to decide. The reason for this is that income tax is regarded as a single tax, not a series of taxes. It follows that only one set of provisions of that tax can apply to any taxable income at any one time. However, the judges do not apply that reasoning to overlap between rules within a single Schedule. If income falls within two cases of the same Schedule (usually Schedule D) it is for the Revenue to decide which applies, and there may be alternative assessments.

These rules are necessary because it is not clear from the words of the legislation alone that there is no overlap between the taxes, Schedules or cases. Any other rule would, in principle, be unfair. Note that the rule does not apply to other kinds of taxes. The relationship between VAT and income tax, for example, does not exist. It is therefore irrelevant in law that something is or is not subject to income tax for VAT purposes. In other words, the mutual exclusion rule only applies to similar taxes.

More generally, both the eighteenth-century idea that income can be taxed by a series of separate "schedules" with separate rules and the nineteenth-century idea that "income and capital" are fundamentally different, are unlikely to survive far into the twenty-first century. There are several reasons for this. One is that the inherent flexibility of British law means that it is relatively easy to convert an income payment into a capital payment (or the reverse), or otherwise to convert one kind of income into another. A second is that the old distinctions may make no commercial accounting sense. A third is that any significant losses of tax by reason of changes in the form of a transaction are likely to be countered by anti-avoidance legislation deeming the income or capital to be something that it is not.

One way forward is the intention of the Tax Law Rewrite to remove the old schedules and Cases and rewrite the existing law in a more coherent form. The proposals of the Rewrite Project (at the time of writing) are noted throughout this book. The emphasis is on broad "types" of income, such as trading income. Another way forward is the creation of self-contained "regimes" with their own charging provisions. For example, the loan relationships provisions for companies largely ignore both the distinction between income and capital and the distinction between trading income and investment income. Other examples are the self-contained provisions dealing with pension-related payments and with payments to beneficiaries from estates. Once the Schedules and Cases are abolished, these can be seen more clearly to be free-standing, separate taxing provisions.

2–09   **Tax Legislation**

As we have seen, one of the few clear principles that can be said to be constitutional in the United Kingdom is the Bill of Rights of 1688/89 providing that taxes cannot be imposed save by consent of parliament. There is no common law of tax, nor any prerogative or other inherent rights to tax. Nor can taxes be imposed by treaty without parliamentary authority to recognise and collect them.

For this reason, we must locate the express authority of parliament to impose a tax on every occasion on which we wish to collect tax. If there is no authority, there is no liability to tax. Applying that approach to our tax laws may once have been a simple operation. Now it is enormously complicated. This is because there have been new tax provisions passed by parliament at least once a year for at least 130 years without any break. Since 1894 there has been at least one omnibus **Finance Act** each year. These have rarely shortened the extant law, even when taxes have been abolished.

The primary legislation imposing our main taxes is therefore of formidable dimensions. As indicated above, some sort of order has been imposed on parts of this vast array of provisions by a series of **Consolidation Acts**. But the laws have never been codified. This creates genuine problems of interpretation, as we note below. At the same time, it means that there is likely to be some provision covering most forms of income or transaction, and determining whether or not it comes within the tax. We cannot, however, assume this. Leaving aside, for the moment, the problems of interpreting tax laws, the rule remains that unless there is a provision that covers the income or transaction in point, no tax can be collected. At the heart of this process lies the simple fact that the purpose of a tax law is to impose tax on certain things, and not on other things. There may be a range of reasons why parliament has decided to do that. But, following the traditions of British legislation, the reasons why are normally left unstated. The question is always: "is this activity or thing within the scope of a taxing provision?"

Traditionally, parliament has added extra levels of complexity to the process of imposing taxes by insisting that all major rules of tax are imposed by primary legislation. **Delegated legislation** is therefore limited. This means that any significant detail must be set out in a section of an Act, not in delegated legislation. This rule was in particular applied to the income tax. There were good democratic reasons for this. Every word of every section of a Finance Act is open for political and technical debate and may be the subject of a separate vote. This is restricted in the case of Schedules to the decision whether a Schedule "stand part". It is even more restricted in the case of statutory instruments to a vote whether the instrument be (or not be) made. Despite, or perhaps because of, these limitations, much greater use is made of Schedules and statutory instruments in the more modern taxes. Much of VAT is, for example, to be found in the new VAT Regulations 1995, while many important aspects of National Insurance contribution law is found in the much amended Social Security (Contributions) Regulations 1979.

Nonetheless, it is a pretence to claim that there is an open technical debate on every tax provision. Time does not allow it. A few selected provisions are subject to a high profile political debate on the floor of the House of Commons. Other selected provisions are subject to more technical debate in the Finance Bill committee. Other provisions pass without comment. All provisions pass without comment in the House of Lords, because they are (since the Parliament Acts were passed) effectively debarred from interfering in tax laws. The fact that this results in what some regard as our most important laws being subject to the least thorough scrutiny by parliament is of course justified by an appeal to history and democracy. Perhaps that is another of the principles of our constitution. If so, perhaps, now that the Queen also pays taxes, we should change it.

Some of our tax laws receive even less parliamentary scrutiny. These are the rules imposed by the **European Union Treaties**,

Regulations and Directives. Most important is the Community Customs Code (Regulation 2913/92). By virtue of the European Community Treaty (Article 249) it is directly effective in all Member States without further enactment. No pretence was made to enact it in the United Kingdom. VAT is also based on extensive E.U. law, although most of this is in the form of directives. Many of the provisions of these directives apply directly in the same way as provisions in regulations. This is so, even though a Finance Act provision says otherwise. Why? Because E.U. laws prevail over United Kingdom laws. Is that part of our constitution?

Of course, as all readers know, we don't have a **constitution**. In tax matters that is most important. Constitutions almost always contain rules limiting aspects of the right to impose taxes. We have no such rules. Even the simple rule in the Bill of Rights is no longer right unless we amend it to include tax laws imposed by the authority of the E.U. More generally, we can observe only that, constitutionally, parliament may choose to tax anything it wishes in any way it wishes, and under any name it wishes. Once it has so wished, we must pay. Or must we?

Before leaving the topic of tax legislation, we must notice another curiosity. This is the collection of **extra-statutory concessions** (ESCs) issued alongside all our main tax laws. ESCs are truly curious. They are not law, yet they prevail over the law in practice. The courts cannot enforce them or interpret them, because they have never been enacted, but yet they, arguably, can ensure that others enforce them. They exist in a sort of constitutional never-never land, supposedly authorised by ministers (who have no legal power to do it), and tolerated by a parliament that has no time to enact them (except when it does have time, as in the Finance Act 1996). In short, parliament, by an extrastatutory procedure, allows us to ignore its enactments. Against that, it is said that the system works. It is also argued that a lawyer who ignores any ESCs would be negligent to the client. If so, it is a curious law system indeed that holds a lawyer negligent for failing not to observe the law!

Even then, our list is not complete. The United Kingdom has ratified over 100 **double taxation agreements**. These are given formal effect as Orders in Council, each of which is then given precedence over internal law by general enabling provisions in the primary legislation for dealings between taxpayers and the United Kingdom and the treaty partner. We note these in the final part of the book.

Finding the Law   2–10

The first rule in trying to find the current law imposing a tax is not to do so from the Acts of Parliament themselves. Even where there is a recent consolidation, this would be an excessively time-consuming occupation. It is also pointless, because there are splendid commercial consolidations of the law published annually by several publishers. One or other of these consolidations is indispensable for a proper study of tax law. They are also available on CD-Rom for those who think computers should replace books and, more recently, also on the Internet.

These commercial consolidations are particularly useful because they give the history of sections in the consolidation measures, and cross-reference texts to other relevant provisions. They also set out the S.I.s, the E.U. law, and the ESCs.

Using Tax Laws   2–11

There are traditionally two approaches to deciding how a tax law works. One is to try and determine its meaning. The other is to try and determine what the tax authorities think it means. These are often different things, and require different techniques. For a professional adviser, which is the appropriate technique depends on the client. One approach is to seek to establish with the maximum certainty whether the tax authorities will demand that a tax be levied on a transaction. The other approach is to form an independent view about whether tax applies, and be prepared to argue the point before the courts if necessary. But even the most law-abiding taxpayer is unlikely to do this to increase a personal tax bill. The first of these approaches is the process of *tax compliance*, that is, of ensuring that the law is obeyed at minimum cost and risk. The other is the process of *tax planning*, under which a taxpayer seeks to explore the law to mitigate a tax burden, or possibly to remove it altogether, within the terms of the law.

Self-assessment has caused these two traditional approaches to coalesce. The aim of self-assessment is to transfer to the taxpayer any decision about the extent to which something should be taxed. Decisions about the relevance of any tax provision to a set of facts, or of interpretation and application of the law to those facts, is for the taxpayer. Of course, tax officials check on the accuracy of the taxpayer's judgment. Self-assessment has also made it more important for the tax authorities to clarify their own views on what taxpayers should be doing. We will look at how they make their views known first, and then how tax laws are interpreted.

2–12   The Official View

In addition to the laws themselves, the tax authorities must in a range of ways ensure that the laws actually work in practical terms. Both the Revenue and Customs have spent considerable time in recent years trying to do this. In part, they have been spurred on by the process of automation of our taxes. Computers demanding "yes or no" answers will not accept "perhaps", nor will they accept inconsistencies. In part, the shift to self-assessment has also forced a removal of issues previously left vague, such as transfer pricing.

The Inland Revenue produce guidance and information to assist taxpayers, or their own staff, in several forms. Together these add up to a substantial body of published statements. However, in every case it must be remembered that these express only the Revenue's view of the law. Save as noted below, the guidance is always general, and does not relate to individual taxpayers. The cumulated texts of these forms of guidance are published in the commercial compilations of Revenue material and are now on the Internet.

Extra-statutory concessions. These were mentioned above together with the statutes from which they purport to derogate. In fact, ESCs as they are usually called, are a motley list of matters, some reflecting interpretations of the law, others examples of faulty procedures, and others aiming at dealing with gaps in the law. They are known by a code such as ESC A85 (removal expenses), because there are so many of them. Even the Tax Law Rewrite Project is having trouble trying to remove some of them.

Statements of practice. SPs, as they are known, were first issued in a methodical way in 1978. They seek to apply the law (or ESCs), and can be quite lengthy. For example SP 5/95 on the taxation of insurance and personal pension scheme commission is 24 paragraphs long. Prior to 1978, these statements were often made through Parliament. SPs are published as Inland Revenue press releases.

Press releases. A steady stream of press releases are issued by the Revenue, covering all changes to a Finance Bill, SPs, announcements of other publications and background information. They are also all on the Internet.

The most important set of press releases are the huge bundle issued on the day of the Budget announcement. These often include details left out of the Chancellor's speech.

Parliamentary proceedings. Ministerial statements and planted parliamentary questions have long been used for making minor announcements about taxes. Since 1978, this practice is less common, although answers to other PQs may still reveal interesting points. Parliament rarely debates the tax affairs of an individual (and when it does, ministers rarely do more than give general answers). The Finance Bill debates have gained a new importance since the decisions in *Pepper v. Hart* (1992), discussed under "Interpreting the Law" below. The adjudications of the Parliamentary Ombudsman on tax cases (published as House of Commons Papers), although also anonymous, give interesting insights to the otherwise mysterious workings of the tax authorities when things appear to have gone wrong.

The main parliamentary proceeding of relevance is the Budget speech and debate each year. Along with this the Treasury publishes a "red book": the Budget Statement and Financial Forecast for the year. It is important background reading to the budget process. It is also available on the Internet.

Tax Bulletin. First published in 1991, this regular publication states Revenue interpretations on difficult points, and some decisions on contentious issues.

Guidance leaflets. These have been published for many years, but they have gained considerably in appearance and readability since the Revenue started taking the Plain English Campaign seriously, and they now regularly win praise for clarity. Guidance is issued with most standard forms (for example the coding notices sent to most individuals, and the annual returns). There are also a series of leaflets and booklets made generally available on a wide variety of issues. For example IR 20 deals with questions of residence, and is important enough to be referred to in context as the "Revenue code". These are also available in full text on the Internet.

Instruction manuals. Open government appeared to take a step forward when the Revenue agreed to publish all its volumes of instruction manuals to staff. They are now available on the Internet.

Indirect guidance. The Inland Revenue also has the commendable habit of reaching agreement with taxpayer representatives and professional associations about the operation of the taxes in its charge. Agreements may be by way of a fairly formal statement of agreement with appropriate groups, or by way of a letter sent to a group in response to representations. These sometimes receive restricted publication, but bodies such as the Tax Faculty of the Institute of Chartered Accountants, the Chartered Institute of Taxation and the Law Society's Revenue Law Committee regularly publish their own views, and exchanges with the Revenue, on points of law.

A similar list of sources could be prepared for the guidance given on NI contributions and by Customs and Excise to deal with value added tax

2–13	**Interpreting the Law**

This should be the easy bit. It is not. Consider the following provisions:

> "*Interest* means both annual and yearly interest and interest other than annual or yearly interest."
>
> "*Interest* includes dividends and any other return (however described) except a return consisting of an amount by which the amount payable on a security's redemption exceeds its issuing price."
>
> "*Interest and dividends* do not include any interest or dividend which is a distribution"
>
> "*Distribution* ... means ... any dividend payable by a company ... "
>
> "*Trade* includes any trade, manufacture, adventure or concern in the nature of trade"
>
> "*Trade* includes vocation and also includes an office or employment"
>
> "*Profits* means income and chargeable gains"
>
> "*Profits* or *gains* shall not include references to chargeable gains"
>
> "*Income* includes any amount on which a charge to tax is authorised to be made under any of the provisions of this Act"

Rule number one of interpreting legislation should be to note the meanings given to the language by parliament. In tax law, as the above illustrations (all drawn from the Tax Acts) show, this has to be modified by two reflections. The first is that the definitions may themselves add no extra meaning. The second is that words change their meaning from one part to another of the tax legislation. Or, as T.S. Eliot observed, "words strain, crack and sometimes break, under the burden." The job of the lawyer is to ensure that any words that do suffer in this way are patched back up again.

Words can have two kinds of meaning: a technical meaning given by the judges as a matter of law, or "the ordinary English meaning". Which kind of meaning is given to a word is itself a decision of law, but decisions about the language of the tax laws are not consistent on this point. The *Ensign Tankers* case discussed below (see "Escape to Victory?") illustrates this in the way it seeks to apply the simple word "trade". It also illustrates another dilemma of interpretation. If a word has an ordinary meaning, then it is for the tax authorities and the appeal tribunals to determine its meaning. It cannot be appealed to the higher courts, because it gives rise to no question of law. If, however, the word has a technical meaning, then that is a question of law and can be appealed to the courts. The *Ensign Tankers* case also illustrates this problem. How do we decide the meaning of a word?

Decisions on the meanings of words and the phrases in which they appear are guided by the rules of statutory interpretation. For a long time, judicial thinking was that tax laws should be interpreted strictly. Judges justified this by references to analogies with the criminal law and by reference to the Bill of Rights. The result could be an excessively literal reading of the words of a tax provision in isolation from its context. More recently, judges have been seeking to establish the view that interpreting tax statutes is no different from interpreting other legislation, save that the words have to be clear before tax can be imposed. The judgment of Lord Wilberforce in the *Ramsay* case (1981) is formative:

> "A subject is only to be taxed on clear words, not on 'intendment' or on the 'equity' of an Act. Any taxing Act of Parliament is to be construed in accordance with this principle. What are 'clear words' is to be ascertained on normal principles; these do not confine the courts to literal interpretation. There may, indeed should be, considered the context and scheme of the relevant Act as a whole, and its purpose may, indeed should be, regarded ... "

Unfortunately, this statement cannot be left without further comment. First, we must remind you that the Acts being interpreted are frequently consolidation measures. An attempt to look at the purpose of a consolidation measure means looking at the purpose of the provisions lying behind it. In a real sense, what the drafters have stitched together for presentational purposes has to be unstitched to establish what is meant. For an example of the complexities that result from such unstitching, see the Court of Appeal decision in *IRC v. Willoughby* (1995).

Part of the reason for the complexity in unstitching is the decision of the House of Lords in the tax case of *Pepper v. Hart* (1992). This decided that in cases of ambiguous language, it was proper to look to the record of the House of Commons for any ministerial statements about the intention of parliament behind a specific provision. In the *Willoughby* case, the logic of this was to look through not only the 1988 Act, but also the 1970 Act and the 1952 Act back to original enactment of the provision in question in 1936. While this might help deal with ambiguities, the resulting need effectively to ignore the consolidation measure for interpretation purposes is not conducive to an easy operation of the law. It means that a "proper" consolidation should identify where each part of the consolidated provision comes from. None of the consolidations currently available do this. This is also a problem for the Tax Law Rewrite Project.

A second reason for complexity is the constant adjustment in the precise terms of sections to deal with both the need to counter avoidance, and the need to avoid injustice in special cases. Some sections have therefore seen considerable amendment during their working lives, including reshaping during the consolidation process. Take the definition of "trade". In 1803, this was defined as including any trade, manufacture, art or mystery. The word was used in a phrase identical to that now in section 19 of the Taxes Act, but its statutory definition has changed. The words are the same as in 1803, but not the extended meaning. Had the relevant minister made its main meaning clear then, should we return to it now? Here again, we have the problem of some words and phrases being "ordinary" while others are "technical".

Because of the need to prevent avoidance, tax law is also at times aimed very widely. The sections in the *Willoughby* case are good examples. Another is section 776, which starts: "This section is enacted to prevent the avoidance of tax by persons concerned with land or the development of land." Does a statement like that make it easier to interpret a phrase such as "any arrangement ... effected as respects ... land which enables a gain to be realised by any indirect method ... by any person who is ... concerned in the arrangement"?

A further reason for complexity in interpretation is the influence of E.U. law. Some parts of our law are now subject to reference to the European Court of Justice (ECJ). It is their interpretation, and therefore their techniques of interpretation, that must prevail in these areas. This may lead to inconsistencies, where the courts find that the approach taken by the ECJ is different to that which they would take in a purely national context. Given that VAT is a mixture of European and United

Kingdom provisions, the result may be untidy. See, for an example, the House of Lords decision in *CEC v. Robert Gordon's College* (1995).

Applying the Law   2–14

A reference to the ECJ emphasises another aspect of handling tax cases. The ECJ takes the view that it can interpret E.U. law, but it cannot apply the law to the facts. In the United Kingdom, these two stages in a case are often conflated. Take, for example, the child's definition of an elephant as something large and grey and living in a herd of elephants. The definition is that it is large, grey, and sociable. Whether the group of creatures is a herd of elephants is an application of the law to the facts. Application of law to facts in tax matters can be an issue of considerable complexity. If you wish to see how difficult, take a piece of paper and draw a diagram on it of the transactions described by the House of Lords in *Ramsay v. IRC* (1981). Then try the same thing with the *Ensign Tankers* case discussed below.

Until the *Ramsay* case, judges would accept any series of transactions, however complicated, as something to be taken at face value. The underlying approach was one said to have been approved by the House of Lords in *IRC v. Duke of Westminster* (1936). It was that the *form* of a transaction should be followed, not its *substance*. That doctrine has been modified by a series of cases including the *Ramsay* and *Ensign Tankers* cases but of which the most important is another House of Lords case, *Furniss v. Dawson* (1984).

In *Furniss*, Lord Brightman, on behalf of the House, and following the lines already set out in *Ramsay*, propounded the rule that the court did not have to look at the form in isolation in certain series of transactions, or complex transactions. A broader view of the whole operation could be taken where the series was preordained, and where one or more steps in the series existed for no other purpose than tax avoidance. This broad view allowed the courts in both *Ramsay* and *Furniss* to look at what happened without getting caught up in the interstices of complex constructions which, in substance, had replaced much more straightforward transactions. A later House of Lords case, *Craven v. White* (1988) emphasised that the new approach only applied where the conditions were strictly met. A further decision of the House in *Countess Fitzwilliam v. IRC* (1993), stressed that the courts could look through a series of artificial transactions to the real transaction underneath if the conditions were met. However, this had to be done to the transactions as a whole, and the

Revenue could not pick and chose parts of the series to look through, while taking other parts at face value. However, in *Moodie v. IRC* (1993), the House reaffirmed the underlying principle, and applied it notwithstanding an inconsistent decision of the House of an earlier date dealing with the transactions under question.

In its modified form, the *Ramsay* and *Furness* approach is now part of the standard analysis applied by the Revenue in confronting suspected avoidance. See, for example, *McNiven v. Westmoreland Investments* (1997) and compare it with *Hitch v. Stone* (1999).

The fact that so many decisions of the House have concerned this issue in the last 20 years shows its importance. The precise extent of the operation of the new approach is still a little unclear, but it does allow judges to look through artificial schemes to the reality underneath. It also represents an attitude to the facts, rather than to the law, which has a wider implication of the kind shown in the *Ensign Tankers* case. It is that courts are encouraging the tax authorities to take a broad view of the facts, rather than a narrow view, and one which takes fully into account the need to be realistic about tax avoidance. This may be further encouraged by the views of the courts in criminal prosecutions for tax evasion, noted below.

Where does that leave tax planning? The *Robert Gordon* case suggests that it is alive and well for VAT purposes both in a straightforward way, and in less obvious ways. The *Willoughby* case provides a most interesting test of the extent of the legitimacy of tax avoidance where parliament has itself encouraged avoidance. *Ensign Tankers* suggests, however, that complicated manoeuvres which have little external effect save for alleged tax saving and which form a composite whole will save little direct tax. However, as *Ensign Tankers* shows only too well, the judicial process carries with it a level of uncertainty. It can also be time-consuming, and introduce inefficiency and inconsistency in an area where both add to the cost of an already costly process.

2–15   **General Anti-avoidance Provisions**

In many countries there are general statutory provisions dealing with avoidance either under general law or specifically for tax law. The French approach is the doctrine of *abus de droit*; in the Netherlands there is a principle of *fraus legis*. Put at its broadest, they require that any interpretation and application of the tax laws must be consistent with the purposes of those laws. In the United States, the judiciary have introduced rules of substance over form, while in other common law states such as Canada, Australia and Ireland, there are general anti-avoidance provisions in tax legislation.

The United Kingdom has a broad anti-avoidance provision for inheritance tax in section 268 of the Inheritance Tax Act (associated operations), but none for the main direct taxes. As noted above, the British approach has been the "hole and plug" approach. If a particular form of avoidance of tax is found to be unacceptable, then it is stopped by a specific legislative provision. This will often take effect from the date of its announcement but will rarely operate retrospectively. Much direct tax law was first enacted in this way.

When it was decided to rewrite direct tax law, consideration was also given to the introduction of a general anti-avoidance rule such as those adopted by Ireland or Australia. The Revenue published a useful discussion paper on this, *A General Anti-Avoidance Provision* (1998). This commented on a possible form of wording. The paper reached no particular conclusion , and the subsequent debate similarly stopped without any serious attempt being made to legislate a GAAR.

Instead, the Revenue continues to rely on individual clauses, combined with a steady broadening of general provisions. Avoidance techniques often depend on precise wording and original ways of arranging transactions. Given the flexibility of English trust laws, company and agency laws, forms of transaction are possible which could not be undertaken in less flexible law systems. That flexibility is one of the great strengths of English commercial and financial laws. There is clearly a reluctance to see tax laws cutting down that flexibility. But the price is a freedom to avoid direct taxes that is not possible in many legal systems. Against that, there is probably less evasion. In the recent past, the British solution has been to deal with both by shifting the tax burden from avoidable taxes (such as income tax on investment income) to less avoidable taxes (such as specific excise taxes or NI contributions).

There are some signs of a change of approach by Government. For example, the tonnage tax introduced in 2000 is subject to a GAAR: "It is a condition of remaining within tonnage tax that a company is not a party to any transaction or arrangement that is an abuse of the tonnage tax regime": Finance Act 2000, Sched. 22, para. 41.

2–16   Escape to Victory?

The tale of how a tax appeal is handled is best told by a case study. The case chosen here is formally known as *Ensign Tankers (Leasing) Ltd v. Stokes (Inspector of Taxes)*. The reports of the case are at [1989] S.T.C. 705 (case stated by the Special Commissioners, and decision of Millet J.), [1991] S.T.C. 136, CA and [1992] S.T.C. 226, HL. It came to be a most important decision on the boundary between acceptable and unacceptable tax avoidance. A little less usually for a tax case, the plot involves Michael Caine, Sylvester Stallone and Bobby Moore! How did they come to be involved with a tanker leasing company?

The story starts with an Inland Revenue Statement of Practice, SP 9/79. This announced the Revenue's view that the Revenue would accept claims for capital allowance for expenditure on plant in respect of the cost of master prints of films. In effect, this was a decision in favour of potential investors in the film industry, allowing them to write off against their profits (or claim losses) on the capital cost of producing the master print of any film for distribution. Ownership of the master print carries with it the rights to exploit and distribute the film.

A number of professional tax advisers were attracted by this statement of practice towards devising tax efficient ways of securing investment in the film industry. At the same time, the taxpayer company, previously a profitable leasing business, was finding it harder to make profits, and was looking to the film industry as a possible source of new business. As a result of complicated negotiations, the taxpayer company became a limited partner of a partnership known as the Victory Partnership with the intention of making a film called *Escape to Victory*. This was filmed in Hungary in 1980. (For the curious, it was about a football match that led to prisoners of war escaping.) Commercially, it proved a failure.

A little after filming started, a meeting took place in London of the limited partners of the Victory partnership at which 17 documents were completed. These included the partnership agreement and a series of loan and financial agreements. Through them, in broad terms, the partnership put up capital of $3.25 million, of which Ensign put up $2.38 million. A further $9.75 million was lent to the partnership by the film production company, funded by an American bank. This was a non-recourse loan, that is, the film production company could not demand repayment of the loan from the partnership, only from the proceeds of the film. The partnership bought the partly completed film from the production company, and agreed to pay the production company a fixed amount to finish the film. Under other provisions, the partnership were to have 25 per cent of the proceeds from the film, while the production company were to receive 75 per cent towards repayment of the loan to the partnership. In other words, the partnership put up about $3 million of the $13 million that the film was budgeted to cost, but came to own the film outright subject to charges on the proceeds from the film. In tax terms, therefore, the partnership could claim an allowance for the cost of its master print of *Escape to Victory*, although it would in due course be subject to tax on the whole proceeds of the film.

The secret of the scheme lay partly in its cash-flow advantages, and partly in the fact that the taxpayer could not lose from its investment after taking account of tax. This was because it received the benefits of its share of the tax allowances for making the film in 1980 as offsets to the considerable profits being made by the group of companies of which it was a member. It would be taxed only later if profits were made. If they were not made, it still received an allowance against tax for a sum equal to about four times its actual investment. This was because the corporation tax rate was then 52 per cent, so the company received a right to claim a loss worth more in tax terms than its original investment. (The full details of how this happened are in the 1986 report of the case.) The film, unfortunately, did make a loss, so the company claimed the tax allowances (a setoff against profits of about £5 million) in its 1980 tax returns. The inspector refused them. Why?

To claim the tax relief, the company had to show that the partnership was a person "carrying on a trade". In the inspector's view, the partnership was not doing that. It was engaging in tax avoidance, not trading. This view was accepted by the Special Commissioners in a lengthy decision made after 18 days of hearings in 1986. They rejected evidence of one of the key witnesses that the scheme was a commercial scheme and held, as a matter of law, that the partnership was not trading. They were asked to consider also whether the case fell within the principles of the decision in *Furniss v. Dawson*, and found on the facts that it did, but that this was not necessary to their decision.

The case went on appeal to the Chancery Division where it was heard by Millett J. for six days in 1989. He upheld the taxpayer's appeal on the ground that the Commissioners had reached a decision that no person acting judicially and properly instructed as to the law could have made. In particular, in his view the partnerships were trading. However, he could not make that finding of fact with authority, so the case had to go back to the Commissioners for a rehearing. This is a good illustration of a

45

judge not being able to change a decision on the facts, but only to see if the Commissioners took a decision that was correct in law. It reflects the limits on the judicial role in section 56 of the Taxes Management Act 1970. It means that the result of a successful appeal is that the process of appeal must start again.

The Revenue (usually referred to, as in this case, as the Crown) appealed to the Court of Appeal. The case was heard by the Vice-Chancellor and two Lords Justice of Appeal over four days at the end of 1991. Put shortly, they allowed the appeal by the Crown, but also found that the Commissioners had made an error of law (identified by Millett J.) in their decision, so referred it back for rehearing. In the view of the Court of Appeal, Millett J. was wrong in saying that the only possible interpretation of the facts was different to the interpretation adopted by the Commissioners. So, in the view of the Court of Appeal, both lower levels of appeal had been wrong, and it was remitted to start again.

A little over a year later, the case was heard for a further six days before the House of Lords on an appeal and cross-appeal by both parties. The judgment of the House was given by Lord Templeman, a judge who earned during his judicial career a formidable reputation as a judge determined to see tax law applied with common sense and in the common interest. The other four members of the House agreed with his decision.

To Lord Templeman, the case was concerned about a tax avoidance scheme. His opinion on this issue should be read as a concise review of judicial thinking on tax avoidance (see pages 235 to 244 of the report). In forthright terms, Lord Templeman dismisses the operation of the scheme used by the taxpayer in this case as "play acting". Under his guidance, the House reached the decision that all three lower levels of appeal had been wrong. The case was therefore remitted to the Commissioners again, but this time with a direction to allow a claim for a loss equal to the actual amount put into the partnership (and lost) by the taxpayers—the sum of $2.38 million dollars, not the inflated sum the taxpayer had claimed, or the refusal of any claim by the inspector and Commissioners.

Thirty-four days of hearings therefore produced four different answers from the four levels of appeal, although three levels were merely, in the words of Lord Templeman, overseeing the task of the Commissioners to "find the facts and apply the law, subject to correction by the courts if they misapply the law." The answer, 12 years after the original taxable activity, was based to some extent on judicial decisions made after the deal was first incurred but equally was expressed as an interpretation of a simple word: *trade*. Who was right? Read the decisions for yourself and decide with which of the four levels of appeal you most agree. In one way, each of the four decisions could be said to be a permissible use of the accepted techniques of interpretation and application of the law (although, of course, the precedent system means that three are wrong, and only the last one is actually technically correct).

With which of the four decisions do you most readily sympathise? Why? That will tell you much about your own views on the taxing process. Whichever decision you do support, the story, which might be better entitled as *Escape To Where You Came From*, is also a comment on the weaknesses, as well as strengths, of a multi-layered system of tax appeals. What *does* the word "trade" mean? For a powerful recent discussion by a single judge see *Clarke v. B.T. Pensions* (1998), disagreeing with the specials. Perhaps the 1803 Act was right in including mysteries in its definition.

The Tax Law Rewrite Project   2–17

It has always been fashionable to criticise tax legislation. In reality, much of this criticism is aimed at the rates of tax or the policies behind the laws. But the income tax law itself has long been subject to criticism for its length, complexity, lack of structure, archaic language, patchiness and convoluted style. That criticism reached a crescendo with Finance Bill 1993. Plans were mooted to simplify and codify the law. In the 1995 Budget the new Chancellor announced a long-term project to rewrite the whole of the primary legislation imposing direct taxes. It was at first called "tax law simplification" but that title itself proved to be over-simplistic!

The project became the Tax Law Rewrite. It consists of a separate unit of the Inland Revenue, including parliamentary drafters, working with two independent committees. The project is overseen by a steering committee. This is chaired by Lord Howe, the former Chancellor, and includes M.Ps, judges and senior practitioners. It is supported by a consultative committee, consisting of representatives of professional bodies (such as the Plain English Campaign and the Consumers Association), and individuals.

The project has several teams working to rewrite units of the legislation. The process involves a thorough analysis of existing law (including case law, concessions and practices not reflected in the primary legislation), followed by the reordering and rewriting of the relevant provisions. In some areas the reordering is as important to the rewrite as the redrafting. It allows the accretions of history to be rationalised and obsolete provisions to be dropped. When a team has completed its analysis and drafting, it consults the two committees and, with their approval, releases an Exposure Draft (ED). This consists of draft clauses plus a commentary. (ED 1 was on trading income of individuals and was published in July 1997.) The professions, interested parties and public are all invited to comment on the ED, which is available free both in printed form and on the Internet.

The team then reworks the ED and the commentary with the aim of preparing a bill for Parliament. The first bill is to be the Capital Allowance Bill. It is a rewrite of the Capital Allowance Act 1990 (see chapter 8). The many statutory amendments since 1990, some of the case law and practices, and some parts of the Income and Corporation Taxes Act 1988. The bill was released with a commentary as a working draft in late 1999. By the time it gets to Parliament, most of it will have been discussed twice by the expert committees and it will have been open to public consultation. This is a far cry from the rush and secrecy of the usual Finance Bills.

2–18   **General rewrite problems**

The Tax Law Rewrite Project had to surmount a series of problems in reaching even its first bill. One is the need to change the structure and format of long Acts of Parliament, and to some extent of all bills Acts. One direct result of the Tax Law Rewrite is the Parliamentary presentation of all Acts is to be in a clearer style from 2000. Another is agreement to a special procedure to ensure Rewrite bills do not get rewritten all over again while being enacted. The drafters have also had to deal with widely but inconsistently used techniques such as deeming, the use of Schedules rather than sections, naming and numbering of parts, chapters and sections, and internal "signposting". The project has had to take views on the use of duplication of language, the need to state principles emerging from case law rather than the rules from which those principles were derived, and the consistent use of language and definition throughout a long Act.

If progress of the rewrite has been slow, it is because the project has been dealing with the problems of the enactment process and the conventions of the British drafting style as well as with the complexities of the tax law itself. The results, now slowly emerging, will be of value to the legislative process as a whole. A minor example is the abandoning of marginal notes to sections in favour of headings for each section.

The work is already of value to any tax student. This is because of the painstaking analyses produced with each exposure draft, and because of the exacting work undertaken to ensure that a logical structure emerges where possible. For example, many provisions are to be listed in the order of practical importance. And the whole exercise is freely available on the Revenues web pages.

The shape of the new law

One of the early victims of the project was the idea of the "Income Tax Schedules". Instead, there is a series of rules about different kinds of income. Another difference of approach is the separation of income tax from corporation tax. Hallowed wording, such as "emoluments" are given less prominence, and terms devoid of meaning outside narrow contexts (such as "the relevant portion") are avoided where possible.

The final shape of the new income tax provisions is not yet clear. There will continue to be a separate Capital Allowances Act. There will probably be separate Acts on income tax, capital gains tax and corporation tax. Current thinking at the time of writing favoured a series of bills rather than a repeat of previous blockbusters.

The current plan for the Income Tax for Individuals is that it will have the following structure:

- core provisions;
- main obligations and rights;
- trading income;
- employment income;
- property income;
- savings and investment income;
- pension income;
- social security income;
- foreign income;
- miscellaneous income;
- exempt income;
- losses and reliefs;
- other rules (including tax avoidance and special types of individual).

E-tax

2–19

When Ron Davies wrote this book in 1979, the idea that taxation would be conducted by electronic means was still in the realms of science fiction. It was some years before one of us saw in

Manchester what may have been the first tax software programme in Britain. It had been programmed by the son of a
partner of a major accounting firm based there. If that was the
first e-tax programme, it would be appropriate, because the
world's first computer was programmed in Manchester 30 years
before. Half a century later, e-tax is here to stay. Taxpayers can
download information from the Internet, work out tax liabilities
on free software provided by the Revenue or Customs, and email
returns to their tax office. And, of course, they can instruct online
bankers to pay the tax electronically. The Revenue can check
returns by computer and respond electronically. The necessary
authority for e-tax was given in the Finance Act 1999.

You can now gain a wealth of information about tax from the
Internet. That includes, as you will see, information about this
book. But we should begin with official Web pages. Each year the
Treasury publishes full details of that year's Budget on the day it
is delivered. This includes the Chancellor's speech, the Red Book
(in which the official figures are published) and the Budget Press
Releases from the Treasury, the Revenue, Customs and other
departments. Often research papers are published too. You will
find them listed at www.hm-treasury.gov.uk/siteindex.html. For
an influential alternative policy view, visit the Institute for Fiscal
Studies website at www.ifs.org.uk.

The Revenue maintains an excellent website with an efficient
search engine. It is clear, comprehensive and user-friendly. You
can download all the relevant Revenue booklets and practice
statements, and also all the materials produced by the Tax Law
Rewrite Project. For serious students, www.inlandrevenue.gov.uk
is a must. And do not neglect another effective site run by HM
Customs and Excise at www.hmce.gov.uk, again with a search
engine.

Nearly all the recent primary source material you will need is
also fully online. Acts of Parliament and statutory instruments
are at www.hmso.gov.uk. Those and other official documents are
listed on and linked from www.official-documents.co.uk/
menu.htm. There is a good collection of tax treaties at
www.danzigerfdi.com/dtas/taxtreaty.htm, and supporting material on the OECD website at www.oecd.org.

Increasingly, the case law can also be found online. Since
1997, House of Lords judgements are all put online at the
Parliament website. The Court of Appeal's judgements may be
found on www.courtservice.gov.uk or www.smithbernal.com,
the website of the official reporters. The Combined Tax Tribunals also have webpages run by the Court Service. The index is
at www.courtservice.gov.uk/tribunals/comtax/index.htm. The

entire jurisprudence of the ECJ is online, with a strong search facility, at curia.eu.int/jurisp/cgi-bin. And the Scottish courts are not outdone. Their website at www.scotscourts.gov.uk is also worth visiting.

Taken together, the official sites provide a comprehensive access to British primary sources produced since 1997. If you are interested in straying to other countries, there are many similar national sites. There is an extremely useful list of them at the excellent website maintained by the Chartered Institute of Taxation at www.tax.org.uk. You will also find other national links from the web pages of the International Fiscal Association at www.ifa.nl.

The Chartered Institute of Taxation website also has a most useful list of links to professional sites maintained by leading firms of accountants and lawyers, including the leading barristers' tax chambers. There is a wealth of technical detail on these pages, though much is beyond the entry-level to the subject.

Nor are the academic websites to be neglected. There is a long list of academic websites listed on the Sweet and Maxwell website at www.smlawpub.co.uk/links/acad_display. This is based on British sites, and there are others, particularly in the USA , also worth chasing for international and policy material.

Which brings us to our own web page. Sweet and Maxwell have the comprehensive website and coverage now to be expected of major law publishers. Its homepage is at www.sweetandmaxwell.co.uk. Either through that, or direct, you should visit our page on the Sweet & Maxwell academic website at www.sweetandmaxwell.co.uk/academic//. You will find an expanded copy of this page online there with hypertext links to all the pages expressly mentioned. You will also find that we will add updating pages to bring the text up-to-date to take account of Finance Acts and bills, Budgets, and other major developments taking place after publication. Visit us there!

And, if you want to give us suggestions to add to the page, contact the academic team at Sweet & Maxwell who will forward them to us.

PART TWO

Taxation of Income

ASSESSMENT OF INCOME TAX

In this chapter we trace the steps in an income tax case. In 3–01
practice the most litigated rules of income tax are those dealing
with trades and professions. So let us look at the position of a
trader. Traditionally, assessment by the Revenue rather than self-
assessment by the taxpayer has been fundamental to the initiation
and development of an income tax case. However, the Finance
Act 1994 started a fundamental reform of personal tax administration when it outlined the structure of a system of
self-assessment for income tax and capital gains tax which
applies for the tax year 1996–97 and subsequent years. It is
essentially a system which gives taxpayers who used to complete
a tax return (often traders and professionals) the opportunity to
compute their own tax liability. Not surprisingly, a change of this
magnitude has had considerable "knock-on" effects, perhaps the
most significant of which is the change to a current year basis of
assessment for all sources of income. The Revenue is now in a
position to issue the taxpayer with a statement which shows all
income from whatever source in a year. Many other facilitative
measures have been taken, not the least of which on a practical
level has been the design, after public consultation, of a user-
friendly tax return form.

An outline of the major features of self-assessment is given later
in this chapter. Initially, however, regard must be given to its
forerunner (assessment by the Revenue), which we have loosely
called the traditional approach. This approach dominated
income tax for nearly two centuries.

The Steps in an Income Tax Case   3–02

1. *The Traditional Approach*

Any person could be required by an inspector (under section 8
of the TMA 1970) to make a return disclosing "such information
as may be required" for the purpose of assessing income tax. In
practice a trader submitted a return which simply said "see
accounts". And he (or his accountant) sent with the return a
profit and loss account, a balance sheet and a "computation".

This latter was simply an adjustment bringing the commercial accounts into line with income tax requirements, the most common adjustment being that depreciation had to be added back for income tax purposes.

The next step was for the inspector to make an assessment on the trader. The inspector's powers to make an assessment gave the inspector a number of linked possibilities. If satisfied that the trader's return afforded correct and complete information, "he shall make an assessment accordingly". If dissatisfied with a return, or no return has been made, the inspector made an assessment "to the best of his judgment" (section 29(3) of the TMA 1970).

The estimated assessment, which is still in use, is based on the inspector acting "to the best of his judgment". This should rule out wild guesses as to the trader's potential liability to tax, but there is hardly any income tax case law about the limits, if any, of the inspector's power. By contrast a similar power to assess for value added tax has been the subject of many tribunal decisions and the decision in *Van Boeckel v. CEC* (1981) shows there are clearly some limits (see also *Schlumberger v. CEC* (1987)).

If the trader does not appeal against the assessment and does pay the amount charged by the assessment, that is the end of the matter. If he does not pay up, the Revenue can sue him. Or, instead of suing, the collector can distrain on the lands or goods of the debtor. Such a distress can be levied without the Revenue having first to obtain a judgment against the debtor; all they need is a finalised assessment, and a warrant issued by a justice of the peace.

If the trader does appeal against the assessment, the inspector may enter into an agreement with the trader that the assessment should be upheld or varied, or discharged or cancelled. Such an agreement has the same effect as a determination of the appeal by the Commissioners. This is covered by section 54 of the TMA 1970, which also gives the taxpayer a generous 30-day "cooling-off period" to resile from the agreement. This is provided that the taxpayer has agreed: *Schuldenfreit v. Hilton* (1999). On the other hand, it prevents a taxpayer from withdrawing an appeal until the inspector has had 30 days to consider preventing the withdrawal, and has chosen not to prevent it. It is thus possible for an inspector to force an appeal by a high estimated assessment, and then to prevent the taxpayer withdrawing the appeal. Where a point has been subject to an appeal, and, following disclosure of all material facts by the trader, the appeal was settled by a section 54 agreement, the Revenue cannot go back on that agreement by using section 29(3) (see *Scorer v. Olin Energy Systems Ltd* (1985), HL).

2. Self-assessment   3–03

The introduction of the system of self-assessment gives the taxpayer the opportunity to compute his own tax bill. If the taxpayer opts to calculate the tax due, the tax return must be delivered by January 31 (the filing date) following the year of assessment and include an assessment of the taxpayer's liability to income tax (and capital gains tax) for that year.

When a taxpayer does not wish to calculate the tax due this will be done for him, provided the taxpayer delivers the return by September 30 following the year of assessment. If the return is filed after the earlier date of September 30, but without a completed "self-assessment" of the tax due, then in law the return is incomplete. In practice a Revenue officer will calculate the tax due, but the Revenue has indicated that it cannot guarantee to notify the taxpayer of the tax due in time for the January 31 payment date. If the tax due is paid late then interest and surcharge will be payable in the normal way.

Where a business is carried on in partnership a partnership return is required. This return requires details of the profits made by the partnership and of the shares of profit allocated to each partner. But no assessment will be made on the partnership and therefore there will be no joint liability for the tax due on partnership profits. Instead each partner is required to include his share of the partnership profit in his own return (and self-assessment) and will be liable for the tax due on that share.

When a taxpayer fails to file a return (and self-assessment) by the January 31 filing date a Revenue officer may make a determination of the tax due 'to the best of his information and belief'. This determination is then treated as the taxpayer's self-assessment for the relevant year until such time as the taxpayer actually files his return (and self-assessment). Superficially this resembles the traditional practice of raising estimated assessments (see above, p. 53). But the determination is automatically replaced by the taxpayer's own self-assessment once filed.

Correction of Errors and the Power to make Enquiries   3–04

The Revenue may correct obvious errors in a taxpayer's self-assessment within nine months of the delivery of the return. Otherwise, the Revenue may only conduct an investigation into a return if a notice in writing is given to the taxpayer indicating the intention "to make enquiries into the return". The notice must be served usually within 12 months of the filing date (section 9A(1) of the TMA 1970, inserted by the Finance Act 1994). If such enquiries are undertaken, a taxpayer may be required by notice in writing to produce documents and accounts which might reasonably be required for the purpose of determining the accuracy of the return. A self-assessment may be amended in the light of information unearthed during an enquiry, although there is a right of appeal to the Commissioners against the amendment. On completion of an enquiry, no other enquiry into that return may be made, unless the Revenue "discovers" later an error in the return because of information not previously available or due to fraudulent or negligent conduct by the taxpayer. In such circumstances, the Revenue may raise an "old-style" discovery assessment against which the taxpayer may appeal to the Commissioners.

A taxpayer may amend a return within 12 months of the filing date, although this right is not exercisable during a Revenue enquiry.

Section 12B(1)(a) of the TMA 1970 requires a taxpayer to keep all records which enable him to deliver a correct and complete return in a given tax year. For a trader, this includes details of all receipts and expenses of the trade and any supporting documentary evidence, *e.g.* accounts and books. Moreover, he must preserve those records for five years from the filing date (a "nontrader" must preserve records for one year from the filing date). Failure to keep or preserve records in this way will lead to the imposition of a penalty not exceeding £3,000.

3-05   *3. Appeals*

If there is no agreement between the trader and the inspector the appeal goes to the General (or Special) Commissioners. We have already seen that the "Generals" are the laymen and the "Specials" are the professionals.

At the hearing of the appeal the onus is on the taxpayer. Section 50(6) of the TMA 1970 says: "If, on an appeal, it appears to the majority of the Commissioners present at the hearing, by examination of the appellant on oath or affirmation, or by other "evidence", that the appellant is overcharged by any assessment, the assessment shall be reduced accordingly, but otherwise every such assessment shall stand good. This is an enormously important point. It provides the Revenue with a very strong lever indeed with which to extract from the taxpayer all necessary information. The assessment is right unless it is shown by the taxpayer to be wrong. This is particularly important where the Revenue raise an assessment based on "best of judgment" or a "discovery". It may be that the Revenue can no more prove it right than the taxpayer can prove it wrong. It was emphasised in *Jonas v. Bamford* (1973) that that did not matter. So, in practice, a taxpayer who is shown to have means well in excess of that declared for tax will have to prove he gained them from betting or Great Aunt Maud. Mere assertion is not enough.

The practice and procedure followed by Commissioners is governed by regulations made by the Lord Chancellor under section 56B of the TMA 1970. At the hearing before the Commissioners, normally the inspector appears for the Revenue and the trader may represent himself or be represented by a barrister, solicitor or accountant. For many years, hearings before the Commissioners were secret in the sense that they were not open to the public (nor to journalists) and in the sense that they were not reported. However, as a result of the regulations made in furtherance of section 56B, hearings before the Specials have, since 1994, usually been held in public, whilst the publication of reports of Specials' decisions is also sanctioned.

The Specials have been empowered since September 1994 to award costs where either party to a hearing has acted wholly unreasonably. The Generals have no power to award costs. Changes to these rules are being considered as part of the review of tax appeals noted in paragraph 1–12.

An appeal lies from the Commissioners to the court, but only on a point of law, not on fact (see below for the importance of this).

Any party to proceedings before the Generals may, within 30 days of the Generals' decision, declare, in writing, dissatisfaction with that decision and require the Generals to "state and sign a case for the opinion of the High Court". The "Case Stated" is a document prepared by the Generals setting out their findings of fact, the contentions of the parties, and the Commissioners' conclusions of law. It is drafted in agreement with both the Revenue and the taxpayer. By this procedure of Case Stated an appeal is taken to the court. The Appeal is heard by a judge of the Chancery Division of the High Court. Thereafter, appeal lies from the Chancery judge to the Court of Appeal, and thence to the House of Lords in just the same way as in other branches of law.

Either party to proceedings before the Specials may, on receipt of the written decision of the Specials, appeal, if dissatisfied, against that decision. In most cases, the appeal is heard initially (as with appeals from the Generals) by a judge of the Chancery Division, although, exceptionally, an appeal may go direct to the Court of Appeal.

3–06
Law and Fact

It is very important to keep in mind the point made earlier that an appeal lies from the Commissioners to the court only on a point of law. The leading authority on this matter is *Edwards v. Bairstow and Harrison* (1956), HL. The question at issue was whether certain transactions carried out by the respondents in relation to the buying and selling of textile machinery constituted an adventure in the nature of trade, in which case the profits were taxable, or whether they did not, in which case the profits were not taxable (though they would now be taxable as capital gains). The General Commissioners decided that there was no adventure in the nature of trade. The High Court and the Court of Appeal held that it was purely a question of fact and that the court could not interfere. But the House of Lords took a more robust stand. True, trade or no trade is a question of fact, but if the only reasonable conclusion to which the Commissioners could come on a consideration of all the facts contradicts the conclusion to which they did come, then their finding can be reversed by an appellate court. Naturally, this decision of the House of Lords greatly widened the scope for appealing from the Commissioners to the courts. But it still quite often happens that the court holds that it has no power to interfere with a decision of Commissioners because they are the sole judges of fact (see, for example, *Glantre v. Goodhand* (1983) (Schedule E)). It should be borne in mind that when this occurs the case is not much of an authority for the future. Where, on the other hand, the court does reverse a decision of Commissioners the judgment is of greater authority.

3–07
Penalties and Criminal Proceedings

So far the litigation that we have been considering has been purely civil litigation; the taxpayer and the Revenue have been arguing as to which of them is right on the facts or on the law. But there can be criminal proceedings by the Revenue and also quasi-criminal proceedings for penalties. Proceedings for penalties usually arise out of "back duty cases", that is, instances where the Revenue are investigating the possibility that a person has not paid all the tax in the past that should have been paid.

3–08
PENALTIES

The Revenue may take penalty proceedings against a person in a number of different circumstances. The main instances are where a person has failed to make a return at all or where a person has made an incorrect return. The latter is much the more important in practice. A penalty is incurred if there is negligence or fraud—not otherwise. The maximum penalty is 100 per cent of the tax underpaid, *i.e.* the difference between the amount of tax payable and the lesser amount of tax which would have been payable if reliance had been placed on the incorrect return or accounts submitted. This penalty is additional to the tax itself. A person who knowingly assists in the preparation or delivery of an incorrect return or accounts may incur a penalty of up to £3,000. Automatic penalties are used to encourage compliance with self-assessment. Anyone failing to get a self-assessment tax return in by January 31 following the tax year is subject to an automatic £100 penalty, with a further £100 if default continues for six months. There is a further penalty at a daily maximum rate of £60 for continuing defaulters. An instalment of tax must also be paid on that date. If it is late, an automatic 5 per cent surcharge applies after 28 days. There is a further 5 per cent surcharge after six months, together with a liability to pay interest.

The Board has a discretionary power to mitigate any penalty. At first sight it might seem that a penalty could be exacted from the taxpayer without making any assessment. But on reflection it is obvious that an assessment is needed in order to establish how much tax has been lost, and therefore how much the penalty should be. Normally, this kind of assessment will be based on the "best of judgment" power.

How far back can the Revenue go in making an assessment? The basic rule (in section 34 of the TMA 1970) is that an assessment may be made at any time not later than five years after January 31 following the end of the tax year to which the assessment relates. This is called the "ordinary time limit". However, in cases of fraud or wilful default, there is a time limit of 20 years for assessments for tax lost because of fraudulent or negligent conduct (see section 36 of the TMA 1970). This period runs from the end of the year of assessment (or accounting period) to which the fraudulent or negligent conduct relates.

Assessments on the personal representatives of a deceased taxpayer are restricted. First, the time allowed for making an assessment shall in no case extend beyond the end of the third year following the year of assessment in which the death occurred. Secondly, when the deceased had been guilty of fraudulent or negligent conduct the Revenue can only go back as far as the year of assessment which ended not earlier than six years before the death (see section 40 of the TMA).

3–09   CRIMINAL PROCEEDINGS
The Revenue tradition over many years has been to accept cash
settlements in most cases of evasion, rather than to prosecute.
Consequently, criminal prosecutions for tax offences were rare.
Most evaders had the sense to pay-up and avoid the publicity.
More recently, this approach has given way to a more aggressive
stance. In *R v. W* (1998) the Court of Appeal agreed that the
Crown Prosecution Service could pursue a prosecution against an
evader although the Revenue had declined to do so because a
settlement had been reached. In *R v. Barton* (1999) the Revenue
and Customs mounted a successful joint prosecution using elaborate information technology resources to marshall evidence
totalling 60,000 pages. Most significantly, *in R v. Dimsey* (1999)
the Court of Appeal upheld convictions for the common law
offence of "cheating the public revenue" against taxpayers and
advisers engaged in what some considered as avoidance not
evasion. Parliament strengthened this approach by enacting a
general criminal offence of fraudulent evasion of income tax in
section 141 of the Finance Act 2000. It is left to the criminal
courts to define "evasion".

3–10   Reviewing the Reviewers

One question of principle worth noting here is the extent to
which the Revenue and their decisions can be appealed or
reviewed. Some consideration has been given to the appellate
system earlier in this chapter. An application by a taxpayer for
judicial review may be appropriate in order to control improper
conduct on the part of Revenue in dealing with the taxpayer's
affairs (or, exceptionally, with other taxpayer's affairs, see *R. v.
IRC, ex p. National Federation of Self-Employed and Small
Businesses* (1982), HL), or by the Commissioners in the course of
hearing an appeal. Where an application for judicial review is
made, the court is exercising a supervisory as opposed to an
appellate jurisdiction. It does not determine facts nor does it
become involved with the merits of the case. Its concern is to see
if, on the facts presented to it, there has been a misuse of power
which results in an injustice. For example, a court may be called
upon to determine whether a decision taken by the Revenue was
such that no authority acting reasonably and directing itself
correctly as to the law could have reached it. A court, however,
will only invoke its power of review when there is no alternative
procedure available which is just as convenient and effective.
Thus, if a matter is properly resolvable on appeal then this is the
course which should be taken. See, for example *R v. North*

London General Commissioners (1999). For some instances where there is no remedy apart from judicial review, see Lord Woolf, "Tax and Judicial Review" [1993] B.T.R. 219.

Allegations of maladministration may be pursued outside the courts. Thus, the Parliamentary Ombudsman may be called upon to investigate a taxpayer's grievance. Similarly, a matter may be referred to the Revenue Adjudicator who was appointed in 1993 by (although independent of) the Revenue in furtherance of the Taxpayer's Charter and whose remit is to consider complaints about the way in which the Revenue has dealt with a taxpayer's affairs.

CHAPTER 4

INCOME AND CAPITAL

4–01   A WORD ON WORDS

Income tax, Lord Macnaghten stated wittily, but inaccurately, in 1901 (*L.C.C. v. A.G.*) is a tax on income. Capital gains tax, we are told by the Taxation of Chargeable Gains Act 1992, is a tax on capital gains. As long ago as 1935 Lord Macmillan helpfully advised us (in *Van den Berghs Ltd v. Clark*) that:

> "The Income Tax Acts nowhere define income any more than they define capital . . . What constitutes income they discreetly refrain from saying . . . Consequently it is to the decided cases one must go in search of light."

But wait a minute. In Chapter 2 we set out the wording of all the main charging sections of the Income Tax Acts. What is more, we asked you to reread the list. You will have found that the word "income" was rarely used. Instead, the 1988 Act spoke of "property, profits and gains" just as did the 1803 Act. In 1803 the tax was not called income tax at all. It was a "contribution" on "property, profits and gains". It still is.

Before we set off on our detailed exploration of income tax, we must take careful note of problems within the key words and phrases of the charging sections, and one fundamental problem behind them.

The problems within the words lie in the meanings of "income", "profits", "gains" and "annual". All these words are hopelessly ambiguous when taken out of their contexts, and their use must be carefully controlled. Take the word "profits". This is used in Schedule A, Schedule D, Cases I, II, III and VI and section 6, the corporation tax charging section. Yet it means several different things. As used in the phrase "annual profits or gains" in Schedule D, Cases I and II it means *net profit*, that is, revenue income less revenue expenditure. In Schedule D, Case VI it can mean *either* gross revenue income *or* net revenue income. Finally, to confuse us, "profits" in section 6 means both revenue and capital profits, that is, income and capital gains. We find the word again in section 131(1) in the definition of the key word of the charge to Schedule E, emoluments. Emoluments include "all . . . profits whatsoever".

The same problems exist for "gains", a word which serves both as one of the key words of the charge to capital gains tax, whilst at the same time featuring in a totally different sense in the Income Tax Acts. But things were made a lot better by Schedule 7 to the 1998 Finance Act. This removed 190 "unnecessary references to gains" from the 1988 Act!

"Annual" is also a chameleon word. It usually means "yearly" to the layman, as in the phrase "annual interest". Confusingly, the Taxes Act uses "annual interest" and "yearly interest" in relation to the same section, presumably meaning the same thing: see the marginal note to section 349 and section 349(2). What that same thing is has caused judges a lot of problems. Broadly, it has been held to be interest on a loan which may continue for more than a year, even if it does not do so in fact. "Annual payments" (as in sections 348 and 349 and Schedule D, Cases III and VI) are recurrent payments, that is, payments which continue beyond a year. By contrast the word takes a totally different meaning in the phrase "annual profits or gains". No recurrence is needed here. It means merely profits or gains *of a revenue or income nature*.

So we are back to the word "income". If "annual" is chameleon, we can only say "income" is kaleidoscopic. One must invoke the warning of Humpty Dumpty to Alice: "When *I* use a word it means just what I choose it to mean,—neither more nor less." At times it is used to mean *net* income, at other times *gross* income; elsewhere it means everything coming in, in a jurisdictional sense (as in Cases IV and V of Schedule D), that is, income remitted to the United Kingdom. In a general sense "income" in the phrase "income tax" means neither more nor less than those things which are caught by the charging sections of the Income Tax Acts.

These definitions can best be tested by reference to yet another meaning of income, that given by economists following Simons in 1938. He defined income as being the sum of the gain (or loss) in wealth over a set period, together with total expenditure incurred during that year. For example, if Shirley is worth £10,000 at the beginning of the year, and £20,000 at the end of the year, and has spent £25,000 during the year, then Shirley's income for the year is £35,000.

The charges to income tax can be both wider and narrower than this definition. It is, though, a very useful definition against which to judge the true scope of various charging provisions and, in particular, the limits on the charge on trading and similar income.

The closest that the charging sections come to the wide, Simons' definition is in Schedule E and Schedule F. Schedule F charges "dividends and other distributions". That phrase has complicated definition in sections 209 to 218 of the Taxes Act 1988. All dividends are included, including a capital dividend: s. 209(2)(a). It does not matter whether the receipt is revenue or capital for company law purposes: both are caught for tax.

The same is true for Schedule E, where "emoluments" are charged. This is a much wider word than "wages and salaries". Anything which arises "from" employment is, it seems, an emolument, whether or not it is income or capital in the sense used for Schedule D. Both Schedule E and Schedule F aim to catch everything that "comes in" to the taxpayer from the relevant sources. By contrast, Cases I, II and III of Schedule D catch "annual profits and gains", meaning net revenue income, as compared with capital receipts. But what is a capital receipt and what is capital?

4–02   **Income and Capital**

Some cases make a distinction between fixed capital and circulating capital. There is some value in this distinction, but it must be borne in mind that an item which would be fixed capital in one person's hands may be circulating capital in another person's hands. To take an example, an office building owned by X, a manufacturer, is fixed capital. If X sells the building at a profit, the profit is of a capital nature and is not chargeable to income tax. A building owned by Y, who makes a living by buying and selling office buildings, is circulating capital. If Y sells a building, the receipt is trading income and is an item in calculating taxable profit. In practice, the distinction may be difficult to draw. See, for example, *IRC v. Wattie* (1998).

The distinction between capital receipts and income receipts has its parallel in a distinction between two kinds of expenditure. But because "income expenditure" would be rather an absurd expression, it is usual in this context to speak of capital expenditure and revenue expenditure ("revenue" with a small "r", of course). If X (above) buys a new office building, that is capital expenditure, and is not deductible in calculating X's income. If Y (above) buys a building that is revenue expenditure and is deductible.

At first sight one might think that a payment must either be capital in the hands of the payer and in the hands of the recipient, or it must be revenue in the hands of the payer and in the hands of the recipient. But this is not necessarily so. Suppose X (above) buys a building from Y (above): X's payment is a capital payment, but Y's receipt is an income receipt. (For another instance of the principle see the House of Lords case of *IRC v. Church Commissioners for England* (1977).) And the converse may also occur: if Y buys a building from X, Y's payment is revenue expenditure, but X's receipt is a capital receipt. This is a general point worth remembering. The nature of the payment does not determine the nature of the receipt, or vice versa.

At one time, if a receipt were held not to be an income receipt but a capital receipt, it was not chargeable to any tax at all. Nowadays a capital receipt may be, though not chargeable to income tax, chargeable to capital gains tax. The taxes remain distinct notwithstanding the fact that since 1988 capital gains have been taxed at the taxpayer's marginal rate of income tax.

As well as the distinction between income and capital, there is also a distinction between income (that is, taxable income) and casual receipts. Tips received by a taxi-driver are taxable; pocket-money received from an aunt or uncle are not. How does this difference arise? The explanation must lie in the source doctrine. The nephew has no source. The aunt or uncle is not a source, because a source must be a state of affairs which falls within one or other of the Schedules and Cases. The taxi-driver's tips have a source which falls either within Schedule E or within Schedule D, Case I, depending on whether the driver is an employee (of a taxi company) or self-employed.

Most casual receipts (such as pocket-money) are gifts. Here again (as with capital receipts) at one time gifts were not taxable at all, but now they may be chargeable, if large enough, to inheritance tax, and (if they are not in the form of money) to capital gains tax as well.

CHAPTER 5

TRADING INCOME

INTRODUCTORY

We now leave the more generalised aspects of income tax, and begin a study of each particular kind of income. It is convenient to begin with income from a trade or profession or trading income, as the Tax Law Rewrite Project calls it.

The basic section is section 18(1) of the Taxes Act. Section 18 sets out the broad provisions of Schedule D as a whole. So far as concerns trades and professions it provides that: "Tax under this Schedule shall be charged in respect of—(a) the annual profits or gains arising or accruing—. . . to any person residing in the United Kingdom from any trade, profession or vocation, whether carried on in the United Kingdom or elsewhere . . . " Section 18(3) sets out the various Cases of Schedule D and says that "The Cases are—Case I—tax in respect of any trade carried on in the United Kingdom or elsewhere; Case II—tax in respect of any profession or vocation not contained in any other Schedule . . . "

It has been held by the House of Lords in *Colquhoun v. Brooks* (1889) that, despite the words "or elsewhere", Case I does not apply to a trade carried on *wholly* outside the United Kingdom.

As we have seen, "profits" and "gains" (in this context) mean the same thing. It is legislative tautology. And the word "annual" carries very little weight. It only means that profits, to be taxable, must be of an income nature; it does not mean that they must be recurrent.

What we must define are the words "trade" in Case I and "profession or vocation" in Case II. Each of these definitions, and Cases, presents in practice a major problem requiring considerable thought in drawing the lines around activities caught within the words. Apart from these problems, the principles of the two cases are broadly the same, although we will note a few differences. We will therefore follow the Tax Law Rewrite in assuming trading income includes professional income unless stated otherwise.

The Case I problem is this: Is a given sum a trading profit or a capital gain? In the good old days a capital gain was entirely free of tax; since 1965 it has been subject to capital gains tax. Capital gains tax is distinct from income tax (this is unaffected by the unification of the rates of capital gains tax and income tax). Each tax has its own regime for the computation of gains/losses, and the characterisation of a particular gain/loss can have important repercussions for a taxpayer.

The Case II problem is this: Is a given person's exercise of a profession (or vocation) carried on within an office or employment, in which case he is to be taxed under Schedule E or is it carried on outside any office or employment, in which case he is to be taxed under Schedule D? Remember that section 18(3) in reference to Case II says "tax in respect of any profession or vocation not contained in any other Schedule". The issue is between Schedule D and Schedule E. It is nowadays accepted that the distinction falls to be made on the same principles as in the law of tort, and also employment law. In tort the distinction is important in connection with vicarious liability, and it is generally described as the distinction between a servant (or employee) and an independent contractor.

Employed or Self-employed   5–02

In employment law the same distinction has led to considerable case law, especially on the questions of unfair dismissal and redundancy payments. In tax law it is described as the distinction between employees (Schedule E) and the self-employed (Schedule D). In all contexts it is the distinction between a contract of service and a contract for services. For example, a solicitor in private practice,[1] either as sole principal or as a partner, is self-employed and falls under Schedule D. A solicitor engaged in local government or in, say, Unilever Limited, is employed and falls under Schedule E. So does an employed solicitor in private practice; that is, a person qualified as a solicitor who works otherwise than as a partner in a firm of solicitors. And, of course, the same person can be employed and self-employed at the same time.

Is there any importance in this distinction? Yes, there is. The tax rules are different as between Schedule D and Schedule E. In particular, a Schedule E earner is subject to PAYE and the rules governing expenses are less generous.

Although the advantages are not all one way, most people would rather be taxed under Schedule D than under Schedule E.

---

[1] A solicitor is said to be "in private practice" in the same circumstances in which an accountant would be said to be "in public practice". Curious.

It is not surprising to find that Parliament has intervened to determine whether liability to tax should be under Schedule D or E. One such instance concerns what is called "The Lump". The Lump means those in the construction industry who, though performing the functions of employed persons, claim the status of self-employed persons by means of "labour only" sub-contracting. Several attempts at dealing with this situation have been made, and currently the position is governed by sections 559–565 of the Taxes Act. Except where a sub-contractor holds an "exemption certificate," the contractor must deduct from each payment that it makes to the sub-contractor a sum equal to the basic rate of tax, after allowing for the sub-contractor's expenditure on materials. So a sub-contractor, though nominally remaining under Schedule D, is to suffer deductions as though under Schedule E. That is the theory of the thing: in practice it does not always work very well.

Attention has also been directed towards "workers supplied by agencies." Section 134 of the Taxes Act provides that these workers shall be taxed under Schedule E. Examples of workers caught by this provision are secretaries, typists and nurses.

A third group of workers have been dealt with differently. These are "divers" and "diving supervisors". Section 314 of the Taxes Act provides that "the Income Tax Acts shall have effect as if the performance by [a diver or a diving supervisor of his duties] constituted the carrying on by him of a trade within Case I of Schedule D; and accordingly Schedule E shall not apply ... " This is the reverse of the treatment meted out to "The Lump" and to agency workers; it is a case of treating employed persons as self-employed. One gathers that the reason for this generous treatment is the political or economic reason that if it were not done these divers and diving supervisors would leave the North Sea for sunnier places; sunnier fiscally speaking as well as climatically.

And in 2000 the Finance Act contained general powers to treat those trying to reduce tax by working through a partnership or "pocket book company" or by other means trying to avoid being an employee, as caught by Schedule E in any event. We shall return to these new rules and the distinction between "employed" and "self-employed" when we come to deal with Schedule E in the next chapter.

We want to discuss more fully what we called (above) the Case I problem: Is a given sum a trading profit or a capital gain? Another way of putting the same question is, What is trading?

What is Trading? 5–03

There is a kind of definition of "trade" in section 832 of the Taxes Act. We say a "kind of definition" because it is one of those so-called definitions, common in tax legislation, which merely expand a word without defining it. "Trade", we are told, "includes every trade, manufacture, adventure or concern in the nature of trade." Notice that the last few words are "nature of trade", not "nature of *a* trade." Even so, this is little better than defining an elephant as being either an elephant or something which looks and behaves like an elephant.

Judges have also resisted giving an exhaustive definition to "trade", as widened by section 832. There is a useful discussion of the concept, and its problems, in the anti-avoidance case of *Ransom v. Higgs* (1974), HL. This concludes that it is possible for something to be a trade even though no one can actually give the trade a name; see also the consideration of *Ensign Tankers (Leasing) Ltd v. Stokes* in Chapter 2.

One other point to watch is that the same person may be carrying on two or more separate trades at the same time, possibly in the same place. If so, it may be necessary for the trades to be taxed separately.

The question whether a particular person is or is not trading is a question of fact. It was neatly described in one case as "a compound fact made up of a variety of things": *Erichsen v. Last* (1881). We look in a moment at the variety of things that may bear on the decision, but first we draw attention again (as we did in Chapter 3) to the point that an appeal lies from the General or Special Commissioners to the High Court only on a point of law. At first sight, it would seem that a finding by the Commissioners that a person is trading (or is not trading) can never be reversed by the court. This is not so. Following the decision of the House of Lords in the case of *Edwards v. Bairstow and Harrison* (1956), the court can and will reverse the Commissioners' decision if it is of the opinion that (*per* Lord Radcliffe) "the facts found are such that no person acting judicially and properly instructed as to the relevant law could have come to the determination under appeal." His judgment in that case, with that of Viscount Simonds, repays close study.

The badges of trade 5–04

The factors which bear on the question "Trade or No Trade" were graphically described by the 1954 Royal Commission on Taxation as "badges of trade". The Commission listed six badges of trade and though subsequent cases have indicated others those six are still the dominant factors. Quite a useful approach to the problem is to ask oneself, when considering a transaction or series of transactions, if it is not trading, what is it? The rival candidate is usually, though not always, investment. To purchase and then sell an investment is not in itself trading. Another candidate is a hobby, or private and non-commercial activities.

The first point to consider is **what is sold**. Generally, if the subject-matter is such that the purchaser cannot either use it personally or derive an income from it or derive pleasure from it that points towards trading. Thus in *Rutledge v. IRC* (1929) the taxpayer, while in Berlin in connection with a cinema business, bought a million rolls of toilet paper for £1,000. Shortly after his return to England, he sold the whole lot to one purchaser at a profit of over £10,000. It was held that this was an adventure in the nature of trade. Notice that in this case, as in many others, the fact that there was only one transaction (a one-off as the saying is) did not prevent its being held to be trading.[2] Contrast the case of *Salt v. Chamberlain* (1979). Mr Salt was smitten by computers. He thought he had hit the jackpot by inventing a fool-proof method of investing in shares. He didn't and it wasn't. He lost a lot of money and tried to claim it as a trading loss. The court held that the shares were bought as investments. One test was whether the subject-matter itself produces income. Subsequently, however, in *Marson v. Morton* (1986) it was suggested that land could constitute an investment even though it was not income producing.

The second point is **length of ownership**. This is not a compelling consideration, but there is something in it. A quick re-sale points towards trading but see also the fifth point, below.

The third point is **repetition**. Although, as we have seen, a single transaction can amount to trading, there are situations where a single transaction would not be trading but that kind of transaction repeated several times would be trading. In *Pickford v. Quirke* (1927) a director of a spinning company formed a syndicate which bought the shares of a mill-owning company and then sold the assets of that company at a profit. He then took part in three similar transactions, although the members of the syndicate were not always the same people. The Court of Appeal held

---

[2] There was a rumour that this case should really be called the case of the *imaginary* toilet rolls. It is said that the taxpayer invented the story of the toilet rolls to explain an increase in wealth, in the same way as many taxpayers claim that their wealth has arisen from betting-winnings (which are not taxable). It is said that this taxpayer thought that the toilet roll story would not be taxable. It is the tax law equivalent of the alleged non-existent snail in the ginger beer bottle.

that he was carrying on a trade, even though each transaction considered by itself was not an adventure in the nature of trade.

The fourth point is **supplementary work** in connection with the realised property. In *Martin v. Lowry* (1927), HL the taxpayer (who had had nothing to do with the linen trade) purchased from the Government its entire surplus stock of aeroplane linen, about 44 million yards. He found difficulty in selling it, and so he had to advertise extensively, rent offices and engage a manager and staff. He sold the linen to more than a thousand purchasers over a period of about 12 months and made a profit of nearly £2 million. It was held that the operations constituted trading. In *Martin v. Lowry* there was a definite sales organisation, but there are cases where simple supplementary work has been held to make the transaction of buying and selling into trading. Thus in *IRC v. Livingston* (1927) three individuals, a ship-repairer, a blacksmith and a fish salesman's employee, who had not previously been connected with each other in business, bought a cargo steamer, converted it (partly by their own labour) into a steam drifter, and sold it at a profit. The Court of Session overruled a finding of no trade, and held that this was a trade.

The fifth point is **why the sale took place**. There may be some explanation why something is sold which negatives the idea of trading. In *West v. Phillips* (1958) a builder built some houses to hold as an investment and some for resale. Later on he decided to sell the investment houses, and he did so through the same organisation that sold his trading houses. The Special Commissioners held that there was trading, but the Court of Appeal reversed them, holding that the taxpayer decided to sell his investment houses because of rent control and the rising cost of repairs and higher taxation, and that in respect of the investment houses he was not trading.

The sixth point is **motive**. Although a trade may be held to exist even where there is no intention to make a profit, the absence of such an intention points against trading, whereas where there is such an intention that points towards trading. It is an important factor in a borderline case. Just such a case was *Taylor v. Good* (1973) where the taxpayer bought a house at an auction without really intending to, in the hope that he might live there. He later sold it, making a profit, but the Court of Appeal held he did not intend to trade when he bought it, and had not traded with it (see also *Kirkham v. Williams* (1991)).

So much for the case law on trading. Some activities have been declared by statute to be trading. The most important are farming and market gardening. Section 53 of the Taxes Act states that "All farming and market gardening in the United Kingdom shall

73

be treated as the carrying on of a trade ... " There are also "statutory trades" listed in section 54. Finally, other provisions give priority to trading income over other charges where, for example, interest is earned on balances outstanding from customer or on current trading accounts, where a dividend is received as trading income, or where certain property income is received as trading income.

5–05   **What is a Profession?**

We must now turn to Case II, professions and vocations. Neither term is defined by the statutes, so the judges have done the job instead. In *IRC v. Maxse* it was said that the hallmark of a profession is the use of intellectual skill, with or without manual skills. In individual cases it will be a matter of fact whether, on balance, say a photographer running a shop is a professional photographer taxable under Case II, or a trader taxable under Case I, or possibly both at the same time, because the trade is separate from the profession.

"Vocation" is a calling, the way in which someone spends his life. In ordinary speech it carries a rather starry-eyed idea of nurses or others dedicated to their work. This seems to mean that they carry on their work without worrying about mundane things like pay. It is somewhat ironic to find that the leading case on vocations is a case about a bookmaker. The case is *Partridge v. Mallandine* (1886). But, although the work of a bookmaker, a jockey and a racing tipster have all been held to be vocations, a full-time gambler is not! This was decided in *Graham v. Greene* (1925), for the sensible reason (if illogical) that the Revenue would stand to lose far more than it gained from such people, because of loss claims! Anyway, betting and gaming taxes ensure such people contribute their share to the Exchequer.

5–06   **The Computation of Profits**

THE IMPORTANCE OF ACCOUNTS
What we have said so far may suggest that the charge to tax is concerned with individual items of income. This is true of value added tax, and in individual tricky cases for income tax, but not in the vast majority of income tax cases. Remember that there is a charge not on receipts, but on annual profits and gains.

The fundamental point about an assessment on this basis is that taxpayers need to produce accounts to find out for themselves if they have made a profit and for self-assessment purposes.

It is the professional task of accountants to produce accounts of profits and losses, or income and expenditures, over a set period, usually a year. Professional accountants do this in accordance with the accepted practices of their profession, some of which have been formally laid down as statements of standard accounting practice (SSAPs) or as financial reporting standards (FRSs). An example of the former is SSAP 2, which sets out the fundamental accounting concepts that should guide the preparation of accounts.

Companies' accounts are limited by guidelines. Most companies must produce and publish annual accounts which follow the forms and formats laid down in the Companies Acts. Furthermore, the accounts must be independently audited by professional auditors who must certify that the accounts comply with legal requirements, and also reflect a "true and fair view" of the company's profits for the period.

As the prestige of the accounting professions and their role in tax matters grew so the question of relationship between tax law and accounting practices and principles became sharper. The underlying question of the relationship is whether evidence that proper principles of accounting practice requires that an item be dealt with in a certain way should be decisive of its treatment in tax law. For example, if accountancy principles treat an item as revenue expenditure, to be included in the profit and loss accounts, can the item be treated as a capital expense for tax purposes?

Courts will now readily accept more than in the past that accounts prepared in accordance with accepted principles of commercial accountancy are adequate for tax purposes as a true statement of the taxpayer's profits, etc. However, such accounts will not be acceptable for tax purposes to the extent that they or particular items contained within them conflict with any express or implied statutory rule or are contrary to principles established by case law. It is noteworthy in the latter respect that Sir Thomas Bingham M.R. in *Gallagher v. Jones* (1993), CA said:

> "I find it hard to understand how any judge-made rule could override the application of a generally accepted rule of commercial accountancy which (a) applied to the situation in question, (b) was not one of two or more rules applicable to the situation in question and (c) was not shown to be inconsistent with the true facts or otherwise inapt to determine the true profits or losses of the business."

Parliament has increasingly adopted accounting practices in Finance Acts. For example, the loan relationship provisions rely on accepted accounting practices to compute profits, and ignore the previous law-based distinction between income and capital (see paragraph 13–05). Another approach is to adopt professional accounting definitions of forms of income or expenditure (see the definition of "research and development" in section 837A of the Taxes Act). Perhaps most important is section 42 of the Finance Act 1998. This requires that for all accounting years from 1999 trading profits "must be computed on an accounting basis which gives a true and fair view".

If two or more principles of commercial accountancy, either or any of which is generally accepted, are pertinent in a particular case it is for the court, taking into account the professional evidence submitted to it, to determine what is the correct principle of commercial accountancy to apply—see, for example, *Johnston v. Britannia Airways Ltd* (1994) and, for a review of the cases, *Herbert Smith v. Honour* (1999).

For further consideration of these (and related) matters, see the special issue of the *British Tax Review* entitled *Accounting Standards and Taxable Profits* [1995] B.T.R. 433.

In the more workaday world of tax offices, if sensible-looking accounts are produced by respected accountants, they will usually be accepted without much problem, even if they do "try it on" from time to time.

Profit and loss accounts must follow a basic form, whatever precise rules deal with individual items. They must show the totals of relevant forms of income for the period and, against that, the totals of relevant expenditures. They must also show the opening and closing balances of trading stock (or opening and closing values of work in progress). The profit is the excess of income over expenditure, adjusted to reflect any increase or decrease in stock or work in progress between the start and end of the accounts period. But if gross profits are under £15,000, a simple three-line account is usually enough.

We will now examine the income tax rules determining what should be included as a trading receipt, how trading stock is handled and finally, what expenditures are allowable as deductions. Broadly, these rules also apply where a trade is carried on by a company (see paragraph 13–04). In addition, for corporation tax purposes, the profit, losses and expenses relating to loan relationships entered into by companies for the purposes of a trade are treated as receipts or expenses of that trade.

5–07   TRADING RECEIPTS

The first question to be asked about any receipt is, is it a trading receipt or is it a capital receipt? The reader may wish to refer back at this point to Chapter 4 above.

In some circumstances the answer to the question is perfectly plain. Thus, if a manufacturer sells a factory because a more up-to-date one was built it is clear that the proceeds of the sale constitute a capital receipt, which consequently does not enter into the computation of profits for income tax purposes. It is equally plain that if the same manufacturer sells a widget which has been made in the factory the proceeds of that sale constitute an income receipt which becomes an item in the income tax computation.

In other circumstances, the question "trading receipt or capital receipt?" is quite difficult to answer. This is particularly so where compensation is paid to a trader, and in cases of voluntary payments to traders.

Compensation   5–08

There is a mass of decided cases on this matter. We will look at three. In *Van den Berghs Ltd v. Clark* (1935), HL the appellant English company entered into agreements with a competing Dutch company under which each company agreed to conduct its business on certain lines. After a dispute it was settled that the agreements should be terminated on condition that the Dutch company paid £450,000 to the English company. It was held that this was a capital receipt, and thus was not taxable. Lord Macmillan said that " ... the cancelled agreements related to the whole structure of the appellant's profit-making apparatus."

In *Kelsall Parsons & Co. v. IRC* (1938) the appellants were manufacturers' agents; they held contracts with several manufacturers under which they sold their products for a commission. One of these manufacturers wished to terminate its agency contract and it did so about 16 months before it was due to expire, paying Kelsall Parsons & Co. £1,500 as compensation. This sum was held to be an income receipt, and hence taxable. The loss of this one agency clearly did not relate to the whole structure of the appellants' profit-making apparatus. Lord Normand said (in the Court of Session): "The agency agreements, so far from being a fixed framework, are rather to be regarded as temporary and variable elements of the profit-making enterprise."

In *London and Thames Haven Oil Wharves Ltd v. Attwooll* (1967), CA the taxpayer company owned a jetty which was seriously damaged by a tanker when it was coming alongside. The owners of the tanker paid a sum of money to the taxpayer of which part was apportioned to physical damage to the jetty and part to consequential damage, namely loss of use of the jetty during the 380 days taken up in repairing it. The Revenue did not seek to tax that part of the payment which was apportioned to physical damage, but it did seek to tax the part apportioned to consequential damage. The assessment was upheld by the Court of Appeal. Diplock L.J. gave a limpidly clear judgment. He said:

> "Where, pursuant to a legal right, a trader receives from another person compensation for the trader's failure to receive a sum of money which, if it had been received, would have been credited to the amount of profits (if any) arising in any year from the trade carried on by him at the time when the compensation is so received, the compensation is to be treated for income tax purposes in the same way as that sum of money would have been treated if it had been received instead of the compensation."

The Lord Justice went on to say that two questions have to be asked. First, was the compensation paid for the failure of the trader to receive a sum of money? If the answer to that is yes, there arises a second question: If that sum of money had been received by the trader would it have been credited to the amount of profits of the trader? The same question can be put more shortly, namely, would it have been an income receipt of the trade (and not a capital receipt)? If the answer to that question is yes, the compensation is taxable; if the answer is no, the compensation is not assessable to income tax. In the instant case that part of the compensation which had been apportioned to loss of use of the jetty (1) was paid for the failure of the trader to receive a sum of money, and (2) represented the profit (surplus of receipts over expenses) which would have followed from the use of the jetty during 380 days. So the assessment was correct.

5–09 *Voluntary payments*

A problem which has vexed the courts considerably is the status of a payment made to a trader voluntarily, without a contractual requirement that it be paid. When should such receipts be treated as trading receipts?

It was established by the Privy Council in *Comr of Taxation v. Squatting Investment Co. Ltd* (1954), an Australian case, that the mere fact that a payment was voluntary did not prevent it being a trading receipt. Equally the Court of Appeal in *Simpson v. John Reynolds & Co. (Insurances) Ltd* (1975) confirmed that not all voluntary payments were taxable. That case concerned a payment of £5,000 by clients of the insurance brokers following the discontinuance of use by the clients of the broker's services following a change in control of the clients, a company. Important factors in the decision were that the payment was unsolicited and of an amount not tied to possible future sales, and that the trading relationship between broker and client had ceased. The payment could not relate to future performance. A different Court of Appeal working on different facts, reached a similar conclusion in *Murray v. Goodhews* (1978).

The *Simpson* case was, however, distinguished by another Court of Appeal in *Rolfe v. Nagel* (1982), a case concerning voluntary payments to a diamond broker. It was held that here the sums were compensation for otherwise unremunerated work and were not unsolicited, and were trading receipts. Similar thoughts lay behind *McGowan v. Brown and Cousins* (1977).

TRADING STOCK   5–10

It is important to grasp that trading stock (stock-in-trade) is an essential item in a trader's account—for tax purposes no less than for commercial purposes. Let us take a simple trading account as it is usually presented.

	£	£
Sales for the year		37,000
Opening stock	2,000	
Purchases	21,000	
	23,000	
Less Closing stock	2,800	
Cost of goods sold		20,200
Trading profit		16,800

Notice that in the account we have used the phrase "trading profit". This account does not deal with expenses such as wages, rent, rates, heating, lighting, telephone, postage. Those matters would be dealt with in a further account, so reducing the trading profit to a taxable profit.

Trading profit is the amount by which the proceeds of the goods sold (£37,000) exceed the cost of those goods (£20,200).

If one omitted stock—both opening and closing—from the trading account one would get a different result. One would get sales £37,000, less purchases £21,000 = profit £16,000. But that would be unreal. This trader has not only made a profit of £16,000 on sales during the year compared with purchases during the year; he has also improved his position by having increased his stock during the year from £2,000 at the beginning of the year to £2,800 at the end of the year, an increase of £800.

The closing stock figure for one year becomes the opening stock figure for the next year.

As closing stock represents expenditure on goods not yet sold, that expenditure is credited to the current year and carried forward to be charged in the subsequent year—as opening stock—in which the stock is to be sold.

In *IRC v. Cock, Russell & Co. Ltd* (1949) the court gave its approval to the accountancy practice of permitting a trader to value stock at its cost price or its market price, whichever is the lower, and to treat each item of stock separately. So, when any item of stock is expected to fetch less than its cost, its market value (or "net realisable value") (instead of its cost) is included in the total of closing stock. The effect is to charge immediately in the current year that part of its cost which is considered to be irrecoverable.

In some of the reported cases on the matter closing stock has been described as being a receipt of the current year, and in other cases it has been described as a notional sale from one year to the next. And the use of a figure of less than cost has been described as an exception to the general income tax principle that an unrealised loss (or profit) cannot be brought into a tax computation. We venture to think that these views are based on a misapprehension as to the nature of the item of closing stock in a trading account, and that the correct view is that put forward by Russell L.J. in the Court of Appeal in *B.S.C. Footwear Ltd v. Ridgway* (1971). Russell L.J. said:

"In my view the accepted practice of entering stock in hand at cost at the terminal date of the first period and the opening date of the second period arises from the fact that the expenditure has not contributed anything directly to the figures of gross profit in the first period. It is unused expenditure, to be carried forward into the second period, in which it is estimated that it will contribute on sale to the gross profit of that period. But if it is estimated that on sale it will not contribute to the gross profit of the second period—that is, if it is estimated that it will sell below cost—the shortfall is to be regarded in the course of stock valuation as irrecoverable and may properly be treated as a loss incurred in the first period. This I believe to be the basis of the principle that for tax purposes market value if below cost may be taken as the value of stock in hand."

WORK IN PROGRESS. "Work in progress" is the phrase used to cover such things as goods in the process of manufacture. A manufacturer, at the end of a particular accounting period, will have some items in his factory which are partially but not wholly constructed. Such items are brought into account in the same way (broadly) as is closing stock, although this may not be a simple exercise (see *Duple Motor Bodies v. Ostime* (1961), HL). And the same principle applies to many other things besides partially manufactured goods; it applies for example to partially performed contracts of a professional person.

THE RULE IN SHARKEY V. WERNHER. This case established the rule that if you transfer an asset from a taxable activity of yours to a non-taxable activity you must bring in to your accounts the market value of the asset which you have transferred just as though you had sold it. *Sharkey v. Wernher* (1956), HL concerned Lady Zia Wernher. Lady Zia carried on a stud farm, the profits of which were assessable to income tax under Case I. She also owned horses and ran them at race meetings as a recreation, in respect of which activity no liability to tax arose. In one year she transferred five horses from the stud farm to her racing stables. The House of Lords held that the horses must be treated as having been disposed of by way of trade, and the sum which should be regarded as having been received on their disposal must be a sum equivalent to their market value. Lord Simonds neatly observed that the same point arises when "the owner of a stud farm diverts the produce of his farm to his own enjoyment or a diamond merchant, neglecting profitable sales, uses his choicest jewels for the adornment of his wife, or a caterer provides lavish entertainment for a daughter's wedding breakfast. Are the horses, the jewels, the cakes and ale to be treated for the purpose of income tax as disposed of for nothing or for their market value or for the cost of their production?" And the House of Lords (with one dissentient) answered "Market value."

Some years later the Revenue sought to apply the same rule to an author. In *Mason v. Innes* (1967), CA, Hammond Innes (another celebrity) wrote a book called *The Doomed Oasis* and, before its publication, presented the copyright in it to his father as a gift. The Court of Appeal held that the rule in *Sharkey v. Wernher* did not apply. Their decision was apparently based on two points: first, that the taxpayer was carrying on a profession and not a trade, and that a professional person does not have stock-in-trade; secondly, that his accounts were not on an earnings basis but on a cash basis. Neither of these points seems wholly convincing.

SECTION 770 OF THE TAXES ACT. The rule in *Sharkey v. Wernher* is a common law rule, but there is a similar statutory rule in section 770A of the Taxes Act and Schedule 28AA. Where the buyer and the seller are under common control ("associated") the Revenue may substitute in the accounts of either party the notional market price of the thing sold for the price in fact charged, thus counteracting a transaction at an over-value or an under-value. The section does not apply where the under-value or over-value will be reflected anyway in the accounts of the benefitted party, which is the case where he (or it) is taxable as a United Kingdom trader. The section is clearly aimed at "transfer pricing" between the United Kingdom and overseas. Bear in mind that where the section does not apply, the rule in *Sharkey v. Wernher* may apply.

5–11   TRADING EXPENSES
The legislation relating to trading expenses is couched in very negative terms. There is no section stating what expenses are deductible under Cases I and II of Schedule D. This is very different from Schedule E, where there is a section (section 198 of the Taxes Act) which states positively what expenses are deductible by the holder of an office or employment.

For Cases I and II of Schedule D there are two negative enactments. Section 817(1) of the Taxes Act declares that: "In arriving at the amount of profits or gains for tax purposes ... no other deductions shall be made than such as are expressly enumerated in the Tax Acts." And section 74 of the Taxes Act declares: "Subject to the provisions of the Tax Acts, in computing the amount of the profits or gains to be charged under Case I or Case II of Schedule D no sum shall be deducted in respect of"—and this preamble is followed by 15 lettered paragraphs ((a) to (p)) containing non-deductible expenses. If these two enactments (section 817(1) and section 74) had been taken absolutely literally the result would have been that no expenses at all would have been allowable under Cases I and II. A judge once said that the life of the law is not logic but commonsense. And in this case commonsense has triumphed over logic without much difficulty. After all, section 18 (of the Taxes Act) states that tax is to be charged under Cases I and II in respect of the annual profits or gains arising or accruing from any trade, profession or vocation. If you keep a shop and sell goods for £6,000 it would be absurd if you were assessed to tax on £6,000 if you had spent £3,000 on buying the goods in the first place and £1,000 on rent of the shop. Your profit or gain is not £6,000; it is £2,000. It is now settled law that some expenses are deductible under Cases I and II.

Section 74 presents the reader with a seemingly random list of things. In practice, by far the most important is paragraph (a), which follows the fashion by also being drafted in the negative! It provides that:

82

"no sum shall be deducted in respect of ... any disbursements or expenses, not being money wholly or exclusively laid out or expended for the purposes of the trade, profession or vocation ... "

The other items in the list should not be neglected. They separately prevent deduction of expenses amongst other things, for private purposes (para. (b)), deductions for capital (paras (f) and (g)) and losses (paras (e) and (k)).

Specific sections elsewhere in the Act (for example sections 84 and 592(4)–(6) make express provision authorising deductions of particular sums. Other sections (such as section 577) expressly prohibit the deduction of particular sums.

In the absence of other specific provisions, section 74, aided by the judges, has provided the guidance for what is deductible. In general, three tests must be met:

(i)   the expenditure is revenue, not capital, in nature
(ii) the expenditure was incurred wholly and exclusively for the purposes of the trade
(iii) the deduction is not prohibited by section 74.

We say "in general" because there are a few untidy corners. They arise in part from the nature of section 74. It is not clear whether the list of items (a) to (p) is cumulative or disparate, that is, whether a payment which is approved by one paragraph will still be disallowed if it seems to fall foul of another paragraph. Further, interest may be deducted even though it is capital: section 74 (f), and deduction for capital expenditure on the supply of implements appears to be sanctioned by section 74(d): *Hinton v. Maden & Ireland Ltd* (1959), HL. It is for this reason that the whole of section 74 is important. But it is clear that where the other paragraphs are silent, paragraph (a) must be applied.

Revenue, not capital, expenditure 5–12

The same distinction falls to be made in regard to expenditure as in regard to receipts. It is not an easy distinction to make. In one case Lord Greene M.R. remarked, " ... in many cases it is almost true to say that the spin of a coin would decide the matter almost as satisfactorily as an attempt to find reasons." (*British Salmson Aero Engines Ltd v. IRC* (1938), CA). But judges do not toss coins, at least not visibly. So we must look at some reasoning.

The first point to be clear about is that (as we pointed out in Chapter 4 above) a payment which is a revenue receipt in the hands of the payee is not necessarily an item of revenue expenditure by the payer. Equally a payment which in the hands of the recipient is a capital item may be a revenue expenditure on the part of the payer. The two things have to be looked at separately. The principles, however, are the same whether one is considering receipts or expenses.

In some cases of expenditure the matter is perfectly clear. If a manufacturer expends money on a new factory, that is capital expenditure; if he spends money on raw materials, that is revenue expenditure. Adam Smith's distinction between fixed capital and circulating capital is of some help here.

However, in cases where the matter has been less clear–cut reliance has been placed often on the classic statement to be found in the speech of Lord Cave in *British Insulated and Helsby Cables Ltd v. Atherton* (1926), HL: "When an expenditure is made, not only once and for all, but with a view to bringing into existence an asset or an advantage for the enduring benefit of a trade. I think that there is very good reason . . . for treating such an expenditure as properly attributable not to revenue but to capital." There is no doubt that this is a helpful general statement, but some qualification is needed. First, it is clear from later cases that "enduring benefit of a trade" must be taken as meaning "a thing which endures in the same way that fixed capital endures": see *per* Rowlatt J. in *Anglo-Persian Oil Co. Ltd v. Dale* (1931), approved and adopted by Lord Wilberforce in *Tucker v. Granada Motorway Services Ltd* (1979), HL. Secondly, there may be expenditure which has an enduring effect, but which, nevertheless, is not deemed to be capital in nature. Thirdly, the identification of an "asset or advantage for the enduring benefit of a trade" may not be easy. For example, if a taxpayer borrows money for a term, is he to be treated as only receiving cash to be used in his business or is he effectively securing a continuance of his trade [and hence an advantage for his trade] for the duration of the loan?

Probably four main factors emerge from the welter of decided cases on the point: the nature of the benefit acquired in exchange for the payment; the manner in which that benefit is to be used; the means by which it is obtained (periodical payments or lump-sum payment); and, more recently, how the expenditure is treated in standard accounting practice. Different weights are to be attached to these four factors in different circumstances. In *Regent Oil Co. Ltd v. Strick* (1966), HL Lord Reid said:

> "Whether a particular outlay by a trader can be set against income, or must be regarded as a capital outlay, has proved to be a difficult

question. It may be possible to reconcile all the decisions, but it is certainly not possible to reconcile all the reasons given for them . . . The question is ultimately a question of law for the Court, but it is a question which must be answered in light of all the circumstances which it is reasonable to take into account, and the weight which must be given to a particular circumstance in a particular case must depend rather on commonsense than on a strict application of any single legal principle."

There is one particular kind of expenditure which deserves to be mentioned separately. This is the setting aside of a sum of money to cover depreciation. It is well settled that such expenditure is of a capital, not a revenue, nature. However, it must not be thought that income tax law gives no assistance in respect of depreciation; it does give such assistance, but it gives it, in the form of allowances, called Capital Allowances, see Chapter 8, below.

Wholly and exclusively for the purposes of the trade 5–13

The second test that an expense must pass if it is to be an allowable deduction arises from paragraph (a) of section 74. This paragraph differs from the other paragraphs in section 74 in that instead of referring to some special item of expenditure it is a general test applicable to all expenditure.

"WHOLLY"

It seems that the word "wholly" relates to *quantum*. The whole amount of the expenditure must be laid out for the purposes of the trade, or rather the expense is only allowable up to the amount of it which is laid out for the purposes of the trade.

"EXCLUSIVELY"

The word "exclusively" has proved difficult to apply. The classic statement of the law is in the judgment of Romer L.J. in *Bentleys Stokes & Lowless v. Beeson* (1952), CA. This case was concerned with business entertainment expenditure. At the time of the case there was no special rule relating to such expenditure; there is such a rule now (in section 577 of the Taxes Act) disallowing it save in the case of a very limited number of exceptions. Romer L.J. said:

> "It is . . . a question of fact. And it is quite clear that the purpose must be the sole purpose. The paragraph says so in clear terms. If the activity be undertaken with the object both of promoting business and

also with some other purpose, for example, with the object of indulging an independent wish of entertaining a friend or stranger or of supporting a charitable or benevolent object, then the paragraph is not satisfied though in the mind of the actor the business motive may predominate. For the statute so prescribes. *Per contra*, if in truth the sole object is business promotion, the expenditure is not disqualified because the nature of the activity necessarily involves some other result, or the attainment or furtherance of some other objective, since the latter result or objective is necessarily inherent in the act."

And so the Court of Appeal allowed the expenditure which had been incurred in entertaining clients.

Lord Justice Romer made it all sound very easy, but in practice it has not proved easy to separate sole purpose cases from dual purpose cases, and one is sometimes left with the feeling that honesty is not the best policy. In *Bowden v. Russell & Russell* (1965) the sole principal of a firm of solicitors visited America and Canada with his wife to attend the annual meeting of the American Bar Association in Washington and the Commonwealth and Empire Law Conference in Ottawa. It was his intention to have also a holiday with his wife. The court held that the expenses incurred in connection with the conferences were not deductible, because they were incurred for a dual purpose, the advancement of his profession and the enjoyment of a holiday.

Can there be apportionment?

These rules and the doctrine of "dual purpose" have been applied somewhat unhappily for many years. Unhappily because of the point already made and because they do not allow sums incurred for two purposes (such as telephone rentals and car expenses) to be apportioned. But in practice every accountant knows that they can be apportioned, as long as one is not too greedy, whatever the strict provisions of the law. Take, for example, *Lucas v. Cattell* (1972). This was actually a Schedule E case but, as we shall see, these parts of the deductions rules are the same for both Schedules. Lucas was required by his employers to have a telephone at home, but they refused to meet the expense of the telephone rental. For several years the Revenue allowed Lucas to deduct a small part of the rental. One year he demanded more! One is reminded of Lionel Bart's famous song from *Oliver*. The result was predictable. Lucas ended up with nothing. His payment was not wholly and exclusively for his employment; and the rental payment could not be severed so that part could be said to be deductible. (On this underdeveloped aspect of the rule, see Lord Reid in *Ransom v. Higgs* (1974), HL.)

The "object" test

Then Ann (now Lady) Mallalieu, a barrister, gave the courts a chance to make some sense of the rules. They tried, but they found it difficult to resolve the issues and by a four-to-one majority the House of Lords overruled the Court of Appeal and Chancery Division and left the law in as much a muddle as ever: *Mallalieu v. Drummond* (1983), HL.

The facts could not be simpler. Mallalieu claimed £500 for replacement items of court dress, their laundering and cleaning. This was revenue expenditure which she incurred to comply with the official guidance to barristers on dress in court. It was undisputed evidence that, at the time she bought the clothes, her only conscious motive was to comply with these professional requirements.

The judgment of Lord Brightman (for the majority) made clear that there was another source of unease about the rules in his mind. It is often felt that the expenses rules are over-generous to the self-employed as compared with employees. So his Lordship observed, the case was really about "the right of any self-employed person to maintain ... partly at the expense of the general body of taxpayers, a wardrobe of everyday clothes which are reserved for work."

After reciting the dual purpose rule, Lord Brightman reminded himself that the "object" of the expenditure was the decisive factor in applying the dual purpose rule. But, he said, the object of expenditure must be distinguished from its effect. Further, the conscious motive of the taxpayer in making the expenditure was not the deciding factor in establishing the "object". "It is inescapable that one object, though not a conscious motive, was the provision of the clothing that she needed as a human being." He adopted the judgment of Goulding J. in *Hillyer v. Leeke* (1976), which, in effect, rested its conclusion on the "self-evident truth" approach to the question.

Implicitly, this seems to overrule the test laid down in the *Bentleys* case (and cited by Lord Elwyn-Jones in his short, powerful dissent) without mentioning it. So we must now judge the object of an expense objectively, distinguishing its effect. But how do you judge the object of a British medical consultant's flight to the South of France to see a patient (or was it partly to have a holiday?) objectively? Further, for an example of the anomalies to which the application of this test may give rise, see *Watkins v. Ashford Sparkes and Harward* (1985). In *McKnight v. Sheppard* (1999) the House of Lords returned to the subject. The case concerned the deductibility of a fine incurred under a professional disciplinary procedure. Pragmatically, their Lordships decided the issue was one of policy and that taxpayers generally should not be required to help pay the fine.

"FOR THE PURPOSES OF"

Returning to the words of the section, note that it says that the expenditure must be "for the purposes of" the trade. This has been held to mean: "for the purpose of earning the profits": *Strong & Co. Ltd v. Woodfield* (1906), HL, *per* Lord Davey. Damages that were paid by the owners of a licensed house to a guest who was injured when one of the chimneys fell on him were held not to be deductible. Despite criticism, this case and its test were approved by the majority in the *Mallalieu* case.

5–14   **Specific expenses**

We want now to make special mention of certain types of expenditure.

TRAVEL TO WORK AND AT WORK. There are no special rules in the Acts governing the deduction of travel expenses by traders, so the general rules apply. However, there seems to be a lot of misunderstanding about expenditure on travel from home to work and from work to home. Some people think that home to work (and return) travel is not allowable for Schedule E taxpayers but is allowable for Schedule D taxpayers. This is not correct. It is quite true that there is a big difference in the rules relating to expenditure under Schedule E and under Schedule D, and we shall be looking at the difference in the next chapter. But in practice the courts have reached, albeit by different routes, similar conclusions about the allowability or otherwise of travel expenses under both Schedules. This is because the phrase in Schedule E, "travelling in the performance of the duties", more or less balances the phrase in Schedule D, "wholly and exclusively for the purposes of the trade" (as applied to travel).

In *Newsom v. Robertson* (1953), CA a barrister who had chambers in Lincoln's Inn and lived at Whipsnade was held not entitled to deduct the expenses of travelling between the two places. This was so even though he had at his home a library of law books, and worked at home in the evenings and at weekends. On the other hand, in *Horton v. Young* (1972), CA a self-employed bricklayer was held entitled to deduct the expenses of travelling from his home to the various sites on which he worked. At first glance this may seem to be inconsistent with *Newsom*'s case. But this is not so. Mr Horton kept at his home his tools and account books and made his contracts there. It was held that his home was his base, whereas in Mr Newsom's case it was held that his chambers were his base. If your home is your base, travel to work and back home is wholly and exclusively for the purposes of your trade or profession. If your home is not your base then such travel is not wholly and exclusively for the purposes of your trade or profession; it is partly because you choose to live at, *e.g.* Whipsnade.

A later case caused some consternation. This is *Sargent v. Barnes* (1978). A self-employed dental surgeon had a dental laboratory which was on the route between his home and his surgery. He called at the laboratory on his morning and evening journeys for the purpose of collecting dentures and discussing work with his technician. He claimed to deduct the expenses of travel between the laboratory and his surgery. His claim failed, the judge holding that the expenditure was not wholly and exclusively for the purposes of the taxpayer's profession. The journey did not "cease to be a journey for the purpose of getting to or from the place where the taxpayer chose to live". There is another interesting point in this case—because of a mistake. The General Commissioners were muddled when they heard the appeal, and thought the Schedule E rules applied, and that to travel was necessary.

LEGAL AND ACCOUNTANCY CHARGES. The professional costs incurred in a tax appeal are not allowable. This is because the tax is not an expense in earning a profit—it is the way the profits are spent: *Smiths Potato Estates Ltd v. Bolland* (1948), HL. But as a matter of practice the fees paid to an accountant for preparing self-assessment returns are allowed, and so are fees paid for advice on tax liability.

PENSIONS AND PENSION CONTRIBUTIONS. A pension paid by an employer to a former employee will be held to be wholly and exclusively laid out for the purposes of the trade except in so far as it is excessive. Whether annual contributions by a trader to a fund to provide pensions for his employees when they come to retire are deductible depends on the nature of the pension scheme to which the contribution is made. Where such contribution is to an "exempt approved" scheme (see section 592 of the Taxes Act) it is deductible as an expense. Contributions to an "unapproved" scheme are not deductible, unless the employee thereby receives a benefit under the scheme which is chargeable to tax or he is taxable by virtue of section 595 of the Taxes Act on the money paid by the employer (section 76 of the Finance Act 1989).

INTEREST. Interest is quite capable of being wholly and exclusively laid out for the purposes of the trade and, if it is, it is a deductible expense. This is immensely important in practice.

5–15 *Not prohibited*

The third test that an expense must pass if it is to be deductible is that it must not be prohibited by any of the specific paragraphs of section 74. We have now looked at the effect of paragraph (a), and have noted the other paragraphs. We will not deal with them all in detail, but will take a further look at paragraphs (d) and (g).

REPAIRS AND IMPROVEMENTS. Remember that the paragraphs are stating sums which are not deducted. Paragraph (d) says, "any sum expended for repairs of premises occupied ... for the purposes of the trade, profession or vocation, beyond the sum actually expended for those purposes." And paragraph (g) says, "any capital employed in improvements of premises occupied for the purposes of the trade, profession or vocation." So the upshot is that expenditure on repair is allowable, whereas expenditure on improvements is not.[3] In a famous passage Buckley L.J. (in *Lurcott v. Wakely & Wheeler* (1911), CA said:

> "Repair is restoration by renewal or replacement of subsidiary parts of a whole. Renewal, as distinguished from repair, is reconstruction of the entirety, meaning by the entirety not necessarily the whole but substantially the whole subject-matter under discussion."

In subsequent cases the distinction made by Lord Justice Buckley between repair and renewal has been taken to be the same as the statutory distinction between repair and improvements. His idea of "the entirety" seems attractive, but of course it means that everything depends on what the court regards, in any particular case, as the entirety. In *O'Grady v. Bullcroft Main Collieries Ltd* (1932) the expense of replacing a chimney by another on a different site was held to be not deductible. But in *Samuel Jones & Co. (Devondale) Ltd v. IRC* (1951) the expense of replacing a factory chimney was held to be deductible. In the first case the court regarded the chimney itself as the entirety; in the second case the court regarded the chimney as part of a larger entirety, namely the factory.

The distinction between repair and improvements runs into (in some circumstances it is virtually the same as) the distinction

---

[3] See further the useful article by P.F. Smith, "Repair or renewal" [1982] B.T.R. 360.

between revenue and capital expenditure. In *Law Shipping Co. Ltd v. IRC* (1924) a trader bought a ship in a state of disrepair. The periodical survey of the ship was overdue, but she was ready to sail, with freight booked, and she did sail. When that voyage was over, the ship underwent survey, and the owners had to spend some £50,000 on repairs, of which some four-fifths was attributable to the disrepair of the ship at the time of purchase. It was held by the Court of Session that that latter expenditure was in the nature of capital expenditure and was therefore not deductible. In *Odeon Associated Theatres Ltd v. Jones* (1973), CA the appellant company bought a large number of cinemas which had not been kept in repair. Some years later they carried out repairs which had been outstanding at the time of purchase. The cinemas were usable in their unrepaired state, but they were not up to the standard set by the new owners. The Special Commissioners made a finding of fact that on the principles of sound commercial accountancy these deferred repairs would be dealt with as a charge to revenue in the accounts of the company. The Court of Appeal held that the cost of the repairs was deductible as revenue expenditure. The *Law Shipping* case (above) was distinguished on three grounds: (1) in that case, but not in this case, the purchase price was less by reason of the disrepair; (2) in that case but not in this case the asset could not (except temporarily) earn profits until it had been repaired; and (3) in that case there was no evidence of accountancy practice, whereas in this case there was such evidence and it pointed towards deductibility.

The Basis of Assessment   5–16

Thankfully, the complex rules that used to determine which income related to which year have been swept away recently. All trading income is computed on a current year basis. This means that the income taxed in any year is the income earned in that year. For everyone's convenience, the income of the year is taken to be the income of the accounting year of the trade that ends in the current tax year. For example, if Pru Trader keeps accounts on a calendar year basis, then Pru Trader's accounts of the calendar year 2000 are treated as being Pru Trader's taxable trading income for the tax year 2000–01. Special rules apply in the first two years of a business and in the final year, to stop both double counting and avoidance. Other rules deal with cases where the accounts are drawn up for periods that are longer or shorter than 12 months, and adjustments can also be made to deal with pre-trading expenses and post-trading income (known as "post-cessation receipts").

5–17   Post-cessation Receipts

The phrase "post-cessation receipts" means sums which are received after the cessation of a trade, profession or vocation for items sold, or services rendered, before the cessation.

Almost all trades now have accounts computed on an earnings basis. The earnings basis is described in section 110(3) of the Taxes Act:

> "The profits or gains of a trade, profession or vocation in any period shall be treated as computed by reference to earnings where all credits and liabilities accruing during that period as a consequence of its being carried on are brought into account in computing those profits or gains for tax purposes ... "

An earnings-based set of accounts therefore catches sums earned before, but received after a trade ends. Any basis other than the earnings basis is called "a conventional basis" (*e.g.* in section 103(2) of the Taxes Act). This is rather a curious phrase, especially as it is the earnings basis which is the most usual. One meaning of "convention", according to the dictionary, is "practice based on consent". So we take it that here the meaning is that the taxpayer and the Revenue have agreed to depart from the earnings basis. The Revenue rarely do agree, but in some cases, such as authors, earnings are uncertain until received.

The cash basis can, however, result in sums "disappearing" when a trade ends. This is stopped by anti-avoidance provisions. The enactments are now contained in sections 103–110 of the Taxes Act. Section 103 brings into charge to tax (under Case VI) all post-cessation receipts of a taxpayer who had been on the earnings basis and some post-cessation receipts of a taxpayer who had been on a conventional basis. Section 104 brings into charge (under Case VI) such post-cessation receipts of a taxpayer who had been on a conventional basis as are not caught by section 103. (Certain receipts are expressly excepted and are not caught by either section, *e.g.* a lump sum paid to the executors of an author for the assignment of a copyright.)

5–18   Casual Earnings

Case VI of Schedule D is a residuary case or, less politely, a ragbag. Section 18 of the Taxes Act charges under Case VI "tax in respect of any annual profits or gains not falling under any other case of Schedule D and not charged by virtue of Schedule A or E".

Case VI has two aspects, which one might call the "general aspect" and the "particular aspect". By the "particular aspect" we mean that certain kinds of income are specifically directed by other sections to be charged under Case VI. These items include post-cessation receipts, income from settlements which is deemed to be that of the settlor (see Chapter 11), and deemed income from artificial transactions in land (see Chapter 7).

Turning to the "general aspect" of Case VI, the ambit of this aspect is not as wide as it might at first seem to be. "Annual profits or gains" is the same phrase as that which governs Cases I and II. Indeed the phrase covers the whole of Schedule D. It follows that profits, to be taxable under Case VI, must be of the same kind (*ejusdem generis*) as profits which are taxable under Cases I, II, III, IV or V. Let us remind ourselves of three points about the phrase "annual profits or gains". First, "profits" and "gains" mean the same thing. Secondly, since what is taxable is profits, expenses incurred in earning the profits are deductible. Thirdly, "annual" does not mean that the profits must be recurring, but it does mean that the profits must be income profits and not capital profits. It follows that a profit from buying something and then re-selling it is not assessable under Case VI. If the buying and re-selling is done in the course of trading, the profit is assessable under Case I. If the buying and re-selling is not done in the course of trading, the profit is assessable (if at all) to capital gains tax. In *Jones v. Leeming* (1930), HL, Leeming and three other people obtained options to buy two rubber estates in the Malay Peninsula which they subsequently sold at a profit. The Commissioners found that the transaction was not a concern in the nature of trade. The House of Lords held that on that finding the profits could not be assessed under Case VI.

So what *is* caught by the general aspect of Case VI? In *Scott v. Ricketts* (1967), CA, Lord Denning said that what is caught includes "remuneration for work done, services rendered, or facilities provided". A good example of a Case VI profit is in *Leader v. Counsel* (1942). A group of racehorse owners purchased a stallion. If any member of the group did not have a mare which required the services of the stallion he could sell his nomination to anyone else. It was held that there was not a trade, but that these receipts from the user of property were income receipts and were taxable under Case VI.

Similarly, income from activities which do not form part of a profession or vocation, but would do so if repeated, may be charged to tax under Case VI. For example, writing one newspaper article does not make someone into a writer. Case VI also catches income made by selling one's story to the newspapers.

93

The wife of one of the Great Train Robbers sold her story to the *News of the World*. In *Alloway v. Phillips* (1980), CA, the court held that the £39,000 she received derived from her contract with the newspaper, and that her rights under that contract were "property", so that she was liable under Case VI.

Gifts, betting winnings and "winnings" by finding are not assessable under Case VI any more than they are under Case I or Case II.

There are four final points to be made about assessment under Case VI.

First, assessment is on a current year basis, and income tax under Case VI is computed on the full amount of the profits or gains arising in the year of assessment (section 69 of the Taxes Act). Secondly, "arising" has been held to mean "received": *Grey v. Tiley* (1932), CA. So assessment is on the cash basis rather than the earnings basis. Thirdly, losses under Case VI are not so favourably treated as losses under Cases I and II, because a Case VI loss can only be set off against Case VI profits, not against other kinds of income. Fourthly, income falling within the general aspect of Case VI is, except in rare circumstances, investment income and not earned income: see the definition section, section 833(4)(c) of the Taxes Act. Income falling within some particular aspect of Case VI may or may not be earned income depending on the circumstances. For example, post-cessation receipts are earned income if the profits of the trade which has ceased would have been earned income, but, if not, not: Taxes Act, s.107.

5–19   **Pensions and Pension Income**

A self-employed individual does not have an employer to pay him a pension when he retires; he must make his own provision for retirement. Before July 1, 1988, it was fiscally advantageous for such individuals to make provision for their retirement by entering into approved retirement annuity contracts (see sections 619–629 of the Taxes Act). Since that date, as a result of a fundamental reappraisal by the government of pension provision for both the employed and self-employed, it has not been possible to enter into retirement annuity contracts. They have been replaced by personal pensions (see sections 630–655 of the Taxes Act). In 2001, pensions are completely changed again by the Finance Act 2000, to introduce "stakeholder pensions".

Personal pensions, similarly, receive favourable tax treatment. Thus, tax relief takes the form of deducting from the individual's earnings contributions to approved personal pension schemes (see section 639). In other words, there is relief on the amount of the contributions. The relief, however, is limited to a percentage of the individual's net relevant earnings.

In addition, net relevant earnings are subject to an earnings cap (£91,800 in 2000–01). Effectively this means the *maximum* contribution (qualifying for relief) which the individual can make to personal pension schemes is limited to the percentage for his age range of £91,800. If an individual has unused relief this may be carried forward (section 642) but not beyond 2001, or if he has made excess contributions an election may be made for such contributions to be carried back (section 641) but, again, not from 2001.

The relief described above is, of course, directed to the time when the individual is still working, helping him to build up provision for when he retires. Such provision is enormously increased by the fact that the scheme itself into which he pays his contributions is exempt from income tax (section 643(2)) and also from capital gains tax (section 271(1)(h) of the Taxation of Chargeable Gains Act 1992).

NI contributions by traders   5–20

The self-employed are required to pay two kinds of National Insurance contribution. There is a flat-rate contribution called Class 2, payable for each week in which an individual is ordinarily self-employed, and which entitled the payer to a limited range of social security benefits. There is also a Class 4 contribution which earns no benefit entitlement and is, in effect, an additional rate of income tax on some self-employed.

Class 2 is payable by those who are ordinarily self-employed and more than 16. There is no definition of "ordinarily", but it is clear that individuals do not cease to be ordinarily self-employed just because they go on holiday for a week. For contributions purposes someone is self-employed if employed gainfully in employment other than employed earner's employment. The distinction between the employed and the self-employed is as important here as anywhere. This is not just because of the very considerable difference in the contributions paid by the employed compared with the self-employed, but because of the differing benefits the two categories can receive.

Categorisation is the only real problem with Class 2. Note, however, that an employee can also be self-employed at the same time, and pay Class 2 contributions as well as Class 1 contributions, subject to a maximum annual limit (see below). The Class 2 contribution is a flat-rate weekly amount of £2.00 for 2000–01. Those whose earnings from self-employment are lower than that year's exception level £3,825 for 2000–01, need not pay the contributions if they wish. This is a voluntary limit. Someone not paying contributions cannot receive benefits either.

Next, we ought to deal with Class 3. This class is a class of voluntary contributions that may be paid by anyone not paying Class 1 or Class 2 contributions. It is therefore not a tax. It may be a good idea to pay them sometimes, but this is the individual's choice.

Class 4 is payable by many of the people who pay Class 2 contributions. Class 4 is entirely separate in law from Class 2, and is entirely parasitic on Schedule D, Cases I and II. The rate for 2000–01 is 7.0 per cent from £4,385 (lower profits limit) to £27,820 (upper profits limit).

CHAPTER 6

EMPLOYMENT INCOME

INTRODUCTORY 6–01

In the last chapter we considered the taxation, under Cases I and II of of Schedule D, of self-employed individuals. Now we have to consider the taxation of employed individuals. The income tax on employment incomes accounts for some 75 per cent of the whole yield from direct taxes.

The Schedule we are concerned with is Schedule E. It is set out in section 19 of the Taxes Act, and contains three cases, Cases I, II and III. In this chapter we confine the discussion to situations where no foreign element is involved. Cases II and III necessarily involve a foreign element (see paragraphs 26–18, 19), and Case I can involve a foreign element, though it far more commonly does not. In this chapter therefore we shall be dealing solely with Case I, in so far as it does not involve any foreign element.

Section 19(1) declares:

> "The Schedule referred to as Schedule E is as follows: ... Tax under this Schedule shall be charged in respect of any office or employment on emoluments therefrom which fall under ... Case I: ... for any year of assessment in which the person holding the office or employment is resident and ordinarily resident in the United Kingdom ... "

Two important points are contained in that passage, being the two factors which must be present if tax is to be charged under Schedule E: (1) there must be an office or employment; (2) there must be emoluments which are derived from that office or employment. (The beautiful symmetry of this proposition is broken by the fact that some social security benefits are taxable under Schedule E, even although those benefits cannot be said to derive from an office or employment: Taxes Act, section 617. Occupational pensions are also taxable under Schedule E, but that does not militate against the proposition because they *are* derived from an office or employment.)

Office or Employment 6–02

"Employment" is a much wider word than "office", but the word "office" fulfils a useful function in that it catches some

97

situations which might not be regarded as employments. An office was described by Rowlatt J. in *Great Western Railway Co. v. Bater* (1920) as "a subsisting, permanent, substantive position which has an existence independent of the person who fills it, and which is filled in succession by successive holders." A good example would be a judge, and that illustrates the point made above: a judge is taxed under Schedule E; it would be disrespectful (and, we think, inaccurate) to describe him as "employed", but he is undoubtedly the holder of an office. Another example is a company director. If he has a service agreement with his company he is probably employed; if he does not he is probably not employed. But in either case he is an office-holder, and he is taxed under Schedule E. This is so even if the company of which he is a director is what is called a "one man company" and he is the one man.

These examples were easy to determine, but what of the status of part-time officials such as inspectors of government inquiries and part-time Rent Assessment Committee chairmen? The Government takes the view that such people are office-holders in most cases, but the holders frequently disagree, as it would suit them better to regard themselves as self-employed.

This conflict came before the courts in *Edwards v. Clinch* (1982), HL and caused them considerable problems. A bare majority of the House of Lords decided that a civil engineer who sat from time to time as a chairman of government inquiries, being appointed separately to separate inquiries, was taxable under Case II of Schedule D and was not an office-holder. The majority broadly endorsed the approach in the *Bater* case, but emphasised that the performance of the office was less important than its existence independent of the holder of the office. It was, it might be added, agreed that the engineer was not an employee.

"Employment" is a difficult word to define, and the tax legislation does not make the attempt. Nor have the Tax Law Rewrite team. In one case, Rowlatt J. said: "I thought of the expression 'post'." This question of "employed" or "self-employed" was noted in the last chapter (see paragraph 5–02). It is worth noting just how important the distinction is in tax law. Not only is it of vital importance in distinguishing between Schedule E and Schedule D, but it is also crucial to deciding whether someone is carrying on "his" business so as to be liable to register for VAT. Again it is central to the determination of liability to Class 1 (as against Class 2 and Class 4) NI contributions, and the benefits that follow from such contributions. Much of the early case law about the divide arose from NI contribution cases, such as the

Global Plant case (1971) and the *Ready Mixed Concrete* case (1968), both against the Secretary of State for Social Services.

However, case law has also developed in the field of employment law. In those cases the status of the individual for tax and NI contributions is sometimes prayed in aid. Not infrequently the same person has claimed to be self-employed for tax and social security purposes, but an employee so as to claim unfair dismissal or redundancy payments or the benefits of health and safety laws.

In *Young and Woods Ltd v. West* (1980), CA the court drew attention to this and pointed out that corrective action ought to be taken by the tax authorities to reassess individuals who were successful in claiming rights as employees, adding that in such cases, the "employees" themselves might gain little out of belatedly claiming a change of status.

In another employment case, namely *O'Kelly v. Trusthouse Forte* (1983) C.A., the Court concluded that the question whether somebody was working under a contract of service was a question of fact to be decided by the competent body. Interestingly, the conclusion that was so reached was in reliance on an income tax case, *Edwards v. Bairstow* (1956) (see paragraph 3–05). In recent years, the Revenue and the Department of Social Security have worked together to good effect in this area. This led to the transfer in 1999 of responsibility for deciding if individuals were employed or self-employed for all social security purposes from the DSS to the Revenue.

The leading case in this field is *Fall v. Hitchen* (1973). The taxpayer was a professional ballet dancer engaged by Sadler's Wells. Under his contract he was paid £18 a week to rehearse, understudy and dance for a minimum period of rehearsals plus 22 weeks and thereafter until the contract was ended by a fortnight's notice on either side. He was permitted to accept outside work when not required by the Sadler's Wells manager. Pennycuick V.-C. held that he had been correctly assessed under Schedule E. The importance of the case is that it decides that the test of whether a person is an employed person is the same in a tax context as it is in a social security or tort context: is he employed under a contract of service as distinct from a contract for services? The judge said:

> " . . . unless some special limitation is to be put on the word 'employment' in any given expression 'contract of service' appears to be coterminous with the expression 'employment'. I can find no such context in relation to Schedule E. I do not see how it could be said that emoluments arising from a contract of service are not emoluments arising from an employment within the meaning of the charging words in Schedule E."

A person may be a professional person and yet be employed This became clear in the case of doctors. A full-time hospital doctor is clearly employed. And in *Mitchell and Edon v. Ross* (1960), CA it was held by the Court of Appeal that a part-time consultant under the National Health Service was assessable under Schedule E in respect of that appointment and at the same time was assessable under Case II of Schedule D in respect of his private practice. (The case went to the House of Lords but not on the above point. In the House of Lords it was held that expenses incurred (but disallowed) under the Schedule E office could not be allowed under the Schedule D profession.)

6–03 *Personal Service Companies*

Another borderline problem with professionals is the "one man service company" where the taxpayer sets up a company, and the company contracts to supply the individual's services. This was queried in *Cooke v. Blacklaws* (1984), but held by the court to be valid for tax purposes. The Finance Act 2000, Sched. 12, introduces new rules countering so-called artificial self-employment from April 2000. They cover many ways of providing services through an intermediary not already covered by existing arrangements of "the lump" and agency workers (see Chapter 5). All earnings and benefit to workers within the rules are treated as Schedule E payments subject to the PAYE scheme. Parallel regulations apply almost identical rules to NI contributions liability.

The rules are drawn widely, and apply potentially to any worker personally performing services for the purposes of the business of a client, but doing so indirectly through an intermediary. "Intermediary" can include a partnership of which the worker is a partner, or a company in which the worker holds at least 5 per cent of the shares. This catches all one-person "pocket book" companies set up to supply the individual's services to a third party. Such practices have been widespread, particularly to avoid the employer's Class 1 NI contribution. The rules will also end the long-running disputes between the Revenue and many area of business that led to such cases as *Hall v. Lorimer* (1994), CA.

A person cannot hold an office or employment as *part of a* profession for income tax purposes, because the Schedules are mutually exclusive. So if a person is a holder of an office or contract of service, the income must be taxed under Schedule E. This was emphasised in the House of Lords in *IRC v. Brander & Cruickshank* (1971), HL. Although the rule was heavily criticised in that case by Lord Donovan, and is not always strictly observed in practice, it remains the law in income tax cases.

Emoluments Therefrom   6–04

As we have seen, Section 19 of the Taxes Act taxes emoluments from an office or employment. Section 131(1) of the Taxes Act declares: "Tax under Case I ... of Schedule E shall ... be chargeable on the full amount of the emoluments falling under that Case, subject to such deductions only as may be authorised by the Tax Acts, and the expression 'emoluments' shall include all salaries, fees, wages, perquisites and profits whatsoever." Notice that the subsection does not define "emoluments", it merely states what is included in that expression. The Concise Oxford dictionary definition of "emolument" is "profit from office or employment, salary". So the idea of the payment being *derived from* the office or employment is inherent in the word "emolument" itself. As Lord Radcliffe said in *Hochstrasser v. Mayes* (1960), HL:

"... it is not sufficient to render a payment assessable that an employee would not have received it unless he had been an employee ... it is assessable if it had been paid to him in return for acting as or being an employee."

Lord Templeman in *Shilton v. Wilmshurst* (1991), HL, set out the test to be applied in determining whether a payment should be treated as an emolument under section 19. He said:

"Section [18[1]] is not confined to 'emoluments from the employer' but embraces all 'emoluments from employment'; the section must therefore comprehend an emolument provided by a third party, a person who is not the employer. Section 181 is not limited to emoluments provided in the course of the employment; the section must therefore apply first to an emolument which is paid as a reward for past services and as an inducement to continue to perform services and, second, to an emolument which is paid as an inducement to enter into a contract of employment and to perform services in the future. The result is that an emolument 'from employment' means an emolument 'from being or becoming an employee'."

In that case, Peter Shilton, the England goalkeeper, was paid £75,000 by Nottingham Forest on his transfer from Nottingham Forest to Southampton. The question was whether that payment should be treated as derived from his employment with Nottingham Forest (and hence a terminal payment or "golden

---

[1]   Now section 19 of the Taxes Act.

handshake") or as an emolument from his forthcoming employment with Southampton. The tax treatment of the payment was dependent on the answer to this question. The House of Lords decided that it was an emolument of his employment with Southampton as it was an inducement for him to sign for Southampton and subsequently to play for that team. It made no difference that the payment was made by a third party, *i.e.* Nottingham Forest, which had no interest in how Shilton performed for Southampton.

In the course of his judgment in *Shilton v. Wilmshurst* (1991), HL, Lord Templeman indicated that a payment would not be taxable as an emolument under what is now section 19 if attributable to something other than being or becoming an employee, *e.g.* if it was paid to relieve distress. This view was endorsed in *Mairs v. Haughey* (1993), HL, in which it was decided that a payment to employees to relinquish their contingent rights under a non-statutory redundancy scheme was not taxable. This payment took its character from the nature of the payment it replaced, namely, a redundancy payment which might otherwise have been made. Lord Woolf said, "a characteristic of a redundancy payment is that it is to compensate or relieve an employee for what can be the unfortunate consequences of becoming unemployed".[2]

It is central to Lord Templeman's test (and, indeed, to many of the cases in this area) that for an emolument to be taxable it must be a "reward for services". It might be asked, therefore, whether it is conceivable that a payment which is not a "reward for services" can be an emolument taxable under section 19 of the Taxes Act. *Hamblett v. Godfrey* (1987), CA, in which the Court of Appeal decided that a payment of £1,000 made to those employees of GCHQ who agreed to give up their right to belong to a trade union was taxable as an emolument arguably provides (notwithstanding attempts in later cases to suggest otherwise) an example of such an instance. There is a good review of the case law in the Court of Appeal judgment in *EMI Group Electronics v. Caldicott* (1999).

6–05   GIFTS

The most difficult area in which to draw the line between emoluments and non-emoluments is in the field of gifts. There is a mass of decided cases on this matter, and it is not easy to discern in them any clear-cut principle. It is tempting to say that if a payment is made by an employer it must be an emolument and if

---

[2]   However, redundancy payments may be taxed under s.148 of the Taxes Act, see below, para 6–18.

it is made by other persons it is not an emolument. But the cases do not bear that out; the most one can say is that a payment made by an employer is *likely* to be held to be assessable. In *Ball v. Johnson* (1971) a bank clerk who was paid £130 by the bank which employed him for having passed the examinations of the Institute of Bankers was held not to be assessable on that amount. In *Calvert v. Wainwright* (1947) a taxi-driver was assessed on the tips paid to him by his "fares", who could not be considered to be his employers. Again, it is tempting to say that if a payment is made in pursuance of a term of the contract of employment it must be assessable and if it is made without legal obligation it cannot be assessable. But that again is not borne out by the cases.

In *Ball v. Johnson* (above) the £130 was almost paid under a contractual obligation; a term of his employment required him to sit for the examinations, and it was stated in the bank's handbook that it was the usual practice to make such a payment. But perhaps *Ball v. Johnson* is rather an exceptional case. We think one can assert that a payment made in pursuance of the contract of employment is almost, but not quite, bound to be assessable. After all, because it is obligatory it is not a gift, so what is it? But the converse is definitely not true; it is not true to say that if a payment is not in pursuance of a contractual obligation it cannot be assessable. In *Wright v. Boyce* (1958), CA, a huntsman was held to be rightly assessed on Christmas presents of cash received from followers of the hunt even though his contract of service conferred no right to the gifts. The payments were made in pursuance of a custom. Custom seems to be a very important factor in this area of the law.

The world of sport has produced some interesting cases in this field. In *Seymour v. Reed* (1927), HL, where a benefit match was held for a professional cricketer on his retirement, the gate money was held not to be assessable. But in *Moorhouse v. Dooland* (1955), CA, money collected from the crowd for a professional cricketer for outstanding performances was held to be taxable. A cynic might think that the distinction between these cases is the distinction between county cricket and Lancashire League cricket, but the Court of Appeal were able to make more ortho-dox distinctions: in *Dooland's* case there was a contractual right to have a collection made whenever his performance was out-standing; and collections had been made for him not once but several times.

The case of *Moore v. Griffiths* (1972) arose out of England's winning the World Cup in 1966. The Football Association paid £1,000 to each member of the squad. These payments were held

103

not to be taxable. Brightman J. held that the payments had the quality of a testimonial or accolade rather than the quality of remuneration for services rendered, and he set out a number of factors which pointed to that conclusion. One factor was that "the payment had no foreseeable element of recurrence" (on which one might comment "You can say that again"). Another factor was that "each member of the team, regardless of the number of times that he played or whether he was a player or reserve, received precisely the same sum of £1,000. The sum therefore was not in any way linked with the quantum of any services rendered."

That last factor raises an important and constant theme in these cases. A payment may be unconnected with services rendered, either (as in the *Bobby Moore* case above) because it is given to more than one person without measuring their separate merits, or (more commonly) because it is given to one person precisely as an appreciation of his merits, but his merits as a human being rather than as an employee. There is a flavour of this latter idea in *Seymour v. Reed* (above) and in *Calvert v. Wainwright* (above), where Atkinson J. said:

> "Suppose somebody who has the same taxi every day, which comes in the morning as a matter of course to take him to his work, and then takes him home at night. The ordinary tip given in those circumstances would be something which would be assessable, but supposing at Christmas, or when the man is going for a holiday, the hirer says: 'You have been very attentive to me, here is a 10-shilling note,' he would be making a present, and I should say it would not be assessable because it has been given to the man because of his qualities, his faithfulness and the way he has stuck to the passenger."

6–06 ## BENEFITS IN KIND

So far we have been talking about payments made to an employee in actual money. But an emolument may take a form other than money. This is clear from the presence of the word "perquisites" in the definition (section 131(1)).

At this point it is necessary to distinguish between what one might call the common law principle and certain statutory modifications of that principle. Legislation has intervened in two ways: (1) it has declared that for *all* employees (and office-holders) certain things shall be regarded as emoluments which under the common law principle would not be emoluments; and (2) it has introduced a separate code for employees earning £8,500 or more and directors. Once upon a time, the £8,500 level applied only to a few employees. Now it is not much above the minimum wage. So, we will deal with "special" rules first.

The Benefits Code 6–07

We must first study the rules which apply to directors,[3] however little they earn, and to non-director employees who earn £8,500 or more. The rules are statutory and set up a kind of code. In Revenue jargon, those people are often referred to as "P11D" people, by the number of the form used to tell the Revenue about their benefits.

The question whether a person has earnings of £8,500 or more has to be tested on the assumption that the code applies and also that benefits in respect of living accommodation and vouchers are included, and without (at this stage) making any deduction for allowable expenses. So an employee receiving £8,000 and reimbursed expenses of £1,000 is in the code, even though the bulk of the £1,000 is tax deductible. Also, separate employments with the same employer are treated as one employment, and so are employments with employers who are under a common control. But the code does not catch people just because their total earnings (*i.e.* from other employments or professions) exceed that total.

The code is now set out in sections 153–168G of the Taxes Act as amended by subsequent Finance Acts.

THE PRINCIPLES OF THE CODE 6–08

Before going into the details of the code, we need to state the main differences in the taxing of people who are within the code as compared with people outside the code. There are three such differences.

First, *any sums paid to a person within the code in respect of expenses are to be treated as emoluments*: see section 153 of the Taxes Act. For a person outside the code that is not so. A reimbursement of deductible expenses is not an emolument, and in practice a round-sum payment for expenses, if reasonable in amount, is not treated as an emolument. For a person within the code not only a round-sum payment for expenses but even a reimbursement of expenses is an emolument. Mind you, this is not fatal; if he expends, or has expended, the payment in such circumstances that the expenditure is deductible under the ordinary principles, the potential taxability of the allowance is balanced by the deductibility of the expense, so no tax becomes due. But there is an important point here: the onus of proving that

---

[3] A director is not caught as such if he does not have a material interest (= 5 per cent or more) in the company and either he is a full-time working director or the company is non-profit-making (or charitable). But, of course, he may be caught as being an employee who earns £8,500 or more.

a receipt is an emolument lies on the Revenue, whereas the onus of proving that an expenditure is deductible lies on the taxpayer. So for a person within the code the payment in respect of expenses is treated by statute as being an emolument, and the onus is on the taxpayer to prove that the emolument is balanced by deductibility. This point is illustrated by *Owen v. Pook* and *Taylor v. Provan*. In *Owen v. Pook* the taxpayer was not within the code, and it was held that the reimbursement of his travel expenses was not an emolument at all. In *Taylor v. Provan* the taxpayer was within the code, and it was held that the reimbursement was an emolument. It so happened that Mr Taylor was held to be entitled to an equalising deductibility, but it was a near thing; three Law Lords said yes, two said no. There is an element of absurd circuity about an emolument which is reduced to nil by deductibility, and section 166 of Taxes Act recognises this by permitting an inspector to grant a dispensation to an employer (and hence to his employees) when satisfied that the arrangements for paying expenses are such that no tax will be involved. A dispensation carries the great advantage that the dispensed expenses are left out of account in calculating whether a particular employee is within the code.

Secondly, for people outside the code, benefits which are not convertible into money are not taxable emoluments. (There are a few statutory exceptions which we look at below.) For people within the code the principle of convertibility is irrelevant, with the result that (with a few statutory exceptions and a few extra-statutory concessionary exceptions) *all benefits whether convertible into money or not are emoluments*: section 154 of the Taxes Act. But here again all is not lost; the ordinary principles of deductibility are available to off-set the emoluments where the facts warrant such deduction.

Thirdly, for a person outside the code a benefit in kind is valued (with certain statutory exceptions such as non-cash vouchers) at the value which it has to the employee, and not at the expense to the employer of providing the benefit. For a person within the code *a benefit in kind is valued by reference to the expense of the employer in providing it* (called the "cash equivalent"). This point can be clearly seen by comparing *Wilkins v. Rogerson* (1961) and *Rendell v. Went* (1964), HL. In *Wilkins v. Rogerson* the employee (who was outside the code) was taxed on the second-hand value of the suit which his employer bought for him. In *Rendell v. Went* the taxpayer (who was a director and so within the code) was charged with causing death by dangerous driving, for which he would be liable, if convicted, to imprisonment for a term up to five years. The employing company had

106

special need of Mr Rendell's services at that time, and they were most anxious that his services should not be lost to them by reason of his imprisonment. Mr Rendell at first arranged for the Automobile Association (AA) to conduct his defence, but the company arranged for their own solicitors to defend him (with counsel) at the company's expense. The company paid out £641 in costs. If the AA had conducted the defence Mr Rendell would only have had to pay £50 or £60. It was held by the House of Lords that Mr Rendell was taxable on the sum of £641, because that was the cost to his employers of providing the benefit.

In *Pepper v. Hart* (1993), HL, consideration was given to the method by which the cost of providing a benefit could be measured. The taxpayers were nine masters and the bursar employed by an independent boys' school. The school ran a concessionary fees scheme under which members of its staff were entitled to have their sons educated at the school on payment of 20 per cent of the sum charged to the public at large. The concessionary fees more than covered the additional cost to the school of educating the taxpayers' sons, and, as the school was not full to capacity in the tax years when the taxpayers' sons were educated under the scheme, the school did not lose fees which could otherwise have been obtained. It was not disputed that this was an emolument of the taxpayers' employment: at issue, however, was the cost to the school in providing this benefit.

The Revenue argued that the cost to the school in providing this benefit should be calculated by reference to a rateable proportion of the expenses incurred in running the school as a whole for all the boys, *i.e.* the *average* cost. On this basis, the cash equivalent approximated to the level of school fees paid by the public at large. On the other hand, the taxpayers argued that the only expense incurred by the school in connection with the education of their sons was the *additional* or *marginal* cost. This amounted only to those expenses *directly* attributable to the education of the taxpayers' sons, *e.g.* the cost of their food, laundry and stationery, all of which were covered by the concessionary fees paid by the taxpayers. Consequently, the cash equivalent was nil.

The House of Lords by a majority of six to one accepted the taxpayers' argument. However, it was an argument which was accepted only after the House of Lords had departed fundamentally from previous practice by having recourse to parliamentary materials as an aid to the construction of the predecessor of section 156 of the Taxes Act.

In summary, the general approach is that all those within the code are taxed on the cash equivalent of all benefits in kind received, and on all sums received as expenses, subject to exemptions and allowable deductions.

Now let us look at some specific rules of the code.

6–09 ## LIVING ACCOMMODATION EXPENSES

The first point concerns certain expenses connected with living accommodation, and it is dealt with in section 163 of the Taxes Act. This section is a beneficial section because it cuts down (or at least limits) what would otherwise be the tax charge. The section applies where the provided living accommodation comes within the three exceptions stated in section 145(4) of the Taxes Act (necessary for proper performance of duties, customary for better performance of duties or part of special security arrangements) (paragraph 6–16). In those premises, the provision to the employee of the following things, though it is an emolument, is subject to a tax limit; heating, lighting, cleaning, repairs, maintenance, decoration, furniture, and normal appurtenances and effects. The limit is that the taxable amount of the emolument shall not exceed 10 per cent of the employee's emoluments from that employment for the year (less capital allowances and certain pension contributions). So, if a person within the code, with an income of £9,000, enjoyed such benefits to an amount of, say, £1,500 in a particular year, he would only be taxable (in this respect) on an emolument of £900.

6–10 ## CARS AND RELATED BENEFITS

Traditionally the biggest "perk" from a job is the use of a company car. Under general principles the use of a company car cannot be taxed in the hands of an employee. The employee cannot sell the car, nor hire it out, so cannot convert the benefit into cash. Provided the scheme under which the employee acquired the use of the car did not provide a way of converting the benefit, there was nothing to tax.

The legislation, however, taxes those within the code on the private benefit they get from being given the use of a car, *i.e.* the cash equivalent of this benefit as determined by the code. In past years, the cash equivalent was often regarded as far less than the real value of the car. Changes since 1993 mean that the cash equivalent may now be higher than the true value. From 2002 the tax charge will depend on exhaust emissions. The provisions apply where there is no transfer to the employee of the property in the car. (Where there is a transfer of the property in (ownership of) the car its value is taxable on ordinary "common law" principles, and, being convertible into money, it is taxable in the hands of all employees.)

Under section 157 and Schedule 6, as amended, the cash equivalent is 35 per cent of the price of the car. Broadly, the price is the list price (which may be provided by the manufacturer, importer or distributor) together with accessories, delivery charge, VAT and car tax (section 168A). The cash equivalent may, however, be reduced to 15 per cent if the employee was required by his employment and did use the car for at least 18,000 miles of business travel. It is reduced to 25 per cent if the business travel amounted to at least 2,500 miles but less than 18,000 miles. A further reduction of 25 per cent may be made if the car is four years old or more at the end of the year. In the case of a car which is 15 years old or more and worth £15,000 or more (classic cars) the market value is adopted unless it is less than the list price (section 168F). In any event, there is a limit of £80,000 on the value of any car.

If a car is included in a "car pool" no charge to tax arises in respect of the use of that car. The conditions are that the car was used by more than one employee, that it was not normally kept overnight at an employee's house, and that any private use of it was merely incidental to its business use (section 159).

Sections 159AA and AB of, and Schedule 6A to the Taxes Act tax the employee on the private benefit from the use of a van provided by the employer. The cash equivalent is £500 if the van is less than four years old at the end of the year or £350 if it is older. There are special provisions where the use of a van is shared.

Tax is also levied on persons within the code on what might be described as car related benefits. For example, the "perk" of free petrol provided by employers for private as well as business use of company cars may be taxed (see now section 158 of the Taxes Act).

Finally, since 1991, an *employer* pays Class 1A contributions on company cars and fuel provided for the private as well as business use of a company car at 12.2 per cent of the taxable value.

BENEFICIAL LOAN ARRANGEMENTS 6–11

Where a person within the code has the benefit of a loan which is obtained by reason of his employment and the loan is either without interest or at a rate of interest less than the "official rate" (*i.e.* the rate prescribed from time to time by the Treasury) the cash equivalent of the benefit is treated under section 160 of the Taxes Act as an emolument. The cash equivalent is the difference between the amount of interest actually paid in the year and the amount of interest which would have been payable at the official rate. However, the tax charge does not arise if the aggregate amount of all such loans at any time of the year does not exceed

£5,000 (section 161(1)). Further, certain loans are excluded, *e.g.* loans made to employees on terms comparable to loans made to members of the public at large where the employer's business includes the making of loans. Relief may be available in respect of a loan to the extent that it is used for a qualifying purpose (see section 353 of the Taxes Act).

Where in any year there is released or written off the whole or part of a loan which was obtained by reason of a person's employment, an amount equal to that which is released or written off is treated as an emolument.

EMPLOYEE SHAREHOLDINGS
6–12

Section 162 of the Taxes Act applies where a person within the code acquires shares in a company at an under-value in pursuance of a right or opportunity available by reason of the employment. The employee is treated as having an interest-free loan ("the notional loan"), so bringing him within section 160. The loan is treated as outstanding until (a) the whole amount outstanding is made good, or (b) the debt is released, or (c) the shares are disposed of, or (d) the employee dies. In case (a) the tax charge comes to an end; in cases (b) and (c) the employee is taxed as if the notional loan had been written off; in case (d) there is no income tax charge.

Section 162 also imposes a charge to tax where shares are acquired by a person employed or about to be employed as a director or in employment within the code in pursuance of a right or opportunity available by reason of the employment, whether or not they were acquired at an under-value, and the shares are disposed of for a consideration which exceeds their then market value. The amount of the excess is treated as an emolument.

In practice, section 162 is not very important because when shares are held, for example, in an approved employee share ownership plan a participant is not chargeable to tax under section 162 on any free, matching or partnership shares awarded under the plan.

THE CODE AND LOOPHOLES
6–13

Although the code, as the examples we have used show, is wide ranging in its application to benefits provided for directors and employees who earn £8,500 or more, it is not all-embracing. Indeed, some benefits are expressly excluded (see, for example, the provision of certain child care facilities, section 155A). Equally, there are occasions when a taxpayer discovers a loophole in the code, *i.e.* benefits which, perhaps, should be caught by the code but escape it! Of course, it may not take long for such a loophole to be plugged. An intriguing aspect of Finance Acts is to discover what steps have been taken to close a particular loophole (or loopholes). Occasionally, the introduction of such steps is heralded by a Chancellor of the Exchequer with some feeling. Thus in his budget speech in 1991, the Chancellor of the Exchequer, Norman Lamont said:

> "I turn now to one of the great scourges of modern life: the mobile telephone. I propose to bring the benefit of car phones into income tax and simplify the tax treatment of mobile phones by introducing a standard charge on the private use of such phones provided by an employer ... I hope that as a result of this measure, restaurants will be quieter and roads will be safer."

But he failed! The charge was removed in 1999, and replaced instead by a general exemption to tax on mobile phones (s. 155AA).

The Old Rules on Benefits   6–14

Even the common law does not confine "emoluments" to money payments. It recognises that benefits in kind, and hence a number of fringe benefits, are emoluments. But it takes the view that benefits in kind are taxable only if they can be converted (although not necessarily are) into money. In the important case of *Tennant v. Smith* (1892), HL, Lord Halsbury said that the benefits which are taxable are "substantial things of money value ... capable of being turned into money". And in the same case Lord Watson used the expression: "that which can be turned to pecuniary account". The dividing line then is convertibility into money. If a thing can be turned into money it is assessable; if it cannot be turned into money it is not assessable. On this principle the following items (by way of examples) are not taxable; free travel, free board and lodging, free meals, free uniforms, free education. None of these can be turned into money. But if an employer, instead of providing, *e.g* a free meal, gives his employee a cash payment with which to buy a meal, that payment is taxable.

A clear example of a benefit convertible into money occurred in *Weight v. Salmon* (1935), HL. The directors of a company by resolution each year gave Mr Salmon the privilege of subscribing for unissued shares at par value, which was below market value. It was held that the difference between par and market value was assessable to tax.

Another good example of a "perquisite" convertible into money is to be found in the case of *Wilkins v. Rogerson* (1961),

CA. The employer decided to give certain of his employees a suit, overcoat or raincoat as a Christmas present. The employer made an arrangement with a tailor. The employee went to the tailor and got fitted out with a suit. The tailor sent the bill to the employer. It was held that there was an emolument, and that its value was the amount for which the employee could turn the suit into money; that is, the second-hand value of the suit.

If the arrangement had been that the employee contract with a tailor to get a suit made and that the employer should then discharge the employee's obligation to the tailor the value of the emolument would have been the contract price of the (new) suit. This is a general principle; if an employer discharges an obligation of the employee to a third party that constitutes an emolument, the value of which is the sum paid by the employer. For example, if an employer pays the gardener's wages and other expenses of an employee's residence, thus discharging the employee's liabilities in those respects, the employee is taxable on the amounts so paid. This is called "the rule in *Nicoll v. Austin*" (1935).

One particular application of this principle is worth separate mention. Sometimes an employer agrees to pay an employee's income tax or agrees to pay a wage or salary "free of tax". In that case the amount of the tax is an emolument; the employer is discharging an obligation of the employee to a third party (the Revenue). The employer must gross-up the net salary and pay tax on that grossed-up amount.

Before we leave the common law, let us reflect on the state in which the law has been left. The judges have done a thorough job of trying to fill the gaps in the statute, but the end result, for all their efforts, is still confusing.

Take, for example, the provision by an employer of clothes for an employee. He could choose to give the employee a distinctive uniform, or ordinary smart clothing. Alternatively, he could lend the clothing to the employee whilst still technically remaining the owner. Or again, the employer could allow the employee to go out and buy clothes and then pick up the bill, or he could give the employee a sum of money, for the employee to buy clothes himself.

A shrewd employer will, of course, pay staff in the most "tax-efficient" way. In many cases, paying staff partly in kind often meant that employers could give their staff more for less. Even after the introduction of the code and its slow spread to most employees, there were still advantages in reduced NI contributions. As we see later in this chapter, from 2000 most benefits in kind are subject to an employer's Class 1A contribution. This reduces further the advantages of not paying cash.

Vouchers 6–15

One way to provide "tax efficient" benefits was through the use of credit cards, stamp schemes, season tickets and other versions of "plastic" or "paper" money. The Revenue tackled all these approaches under the title of "vouchers". The legislation distinguishes between cash vouchers and non-cash vouchers.

By section 143 of the Taxes Act a cash voucher (which includes a stamp or similar document) is taxable and is subject to the PAYE system. A cash voucher would have been taxable anyway under the common law principle stated above, and the real purpose of this enactment is to bring cash vouchers into the PAYE system, and ensure that tax is deducted by the employer, thus avoiding the necessity of a separate assessment on each recipient employee. This is done by section 203I of the Taxes Act.

A cash voucher is any voucher capable of being exchanged for a sum of money greater than, equal to or not substantially less than, the expense incurred in providing the voucher.

Non-cash vouchers are dealt with by sections 141 and 203G of the Taxes Act. A non-cash voucher is a voucher which is not a cash voucher and which is capable of being exchanged for money goods or services (or any combination of those things). The section has two effects. First, it treats the employee, if he or his spouse or family receives the voucher, as having received an emolument. Consequently certain things that were not previously taxable (because they were not convertible into money) become taxable, *e.g.* free holidays. Secondly, it requires that the emolument be valued at the cost to the employer of providing the voucher and not at the value of the goods or services ultimately received by the employee. So if the employer in *Wilkins v. Rogerson* (above) were now to provide an employee with a voucher exchangeable for a suit, the emolument would be valued (in effect) at the contract price of the (new) suit, and not merely at the suit's second-hand value. But provided no voucher is used in the process of getting the suit, it would seem that the comparatively happy result in *Wilkins v. Rogerson* could still be achieved.

There are equivalent rules to put NI contribution liability on vouchers in the same way as income tax.

Share schemes for employees 6–16

The simple fact that companies are owned by their share-holders has been seen by some as one solution to the friction that occurs between employees and their corporate employers. If employees become shareholders in their employing companies, they will identify more closely with them and be "better" employees. Since the late 1970's, employee share ownership has been politically a Good Thing (and not just under Conservative governments).

One sure way of making other people indulge in a Good Thing is by making it tax-privileged. To this end there has been a welter of legislation aimed at encouraging employee share ownership, starting in 1978. However, as will be seen, one approach which was perceived to be over generous has been abandoned.

The Finance Act 1978 (a Lib-Lab measure resulting from the then alliance between the Labour and Liberal Parties) introduced approved profit sharing schemes. These are schemes whereby companies (usually) appropriate part of their profits for distribution to employees in the form of share capital. The shares are paid not direct to the employees but to a trust. If the trustees are allowed by the employee to hold the shares for a period of years (which has been reduced over the years and presently is three) then the benefit of the shares may be received totally free of income tax.

In 1980, a second tax-privileged means of encouraging employee share ownership was approved. This was the Save As You Earn Scheme, or, as the Tax Acts call it, the Savings-Related Share Option Scheme. Employers offer their employees an option, at a discount on market prices, to purchase shares, valid for a period of years. The employee enters a savings contract (also free of tax) to save the cash to buy the shares by regular monthly instalments, usually over a minimum of five years (three year contracts are now permissible), and at the end of the period to use the savings to buy the shares. In such cases, again if the schemes are Revenue approved, there is no charge to income tax.

In 1984, a further scheme was introduced, the approved share option scheme not tied to a savings contract. This was referred to as the "executive" share option scheme. It could be directed at selected employees to whom, under such a scheme, substantial benefits might accrue. However, in 1995, the Chancellor of the Exchequer (possibly influenced by adverse publicity about "fat cats") decided that these schemes were too much of a Good Thing! Consequently, the income tax privileges associated with these schemes, were withdrawn in 1995.

Then in 1999 a review of all share schemes was announced. As a result, approved profit sharing schemes are being phased out from 2000, and replaced with new *employee share ownership plans* (ESOPs, a name borrowed from the USA). The ESOP rules are in the Finance Act 2000, Sched. 8. ESOPs must be open to all employees. They are wider in scope and potentially more generous than previous schemes, and they do not require trusts to be established. Save As you Earn schemes are not being phased out, and may prove an effective option-based alternative to ESOPs.

The Finance Act 2000, Sched. 14, reintroduced an executive share scheme. But this scheme, known as *enterprise management incentives,* is narrowly targeted only at key employees of small, free-standing entrepreneurial companies.

Further, an employee may acquire shares under unapproved schemes, *e.g.* a share incentive scheme. A share incentive scheme is a scheme whereby an employee can buy shares in his employing company or, indeed, in any other company, immediately and in pursuance of a right conferred or an opportunity offered as an employee (or director) and not in pursuance of an offer to the public. The tax treatment of such schemes is far from simple and we propose only to draw your attention to the following instances when a charge to tax may arise in respect of shares so acquired and in the light of which the attractiveness of such schemes from a tax perspective may be diminished. Thus, for example, in relation to incentive shares held in the employer's company, section 78 of the Finance Act 1988 charges to tax an increase in value of such shares brought about by an alteration to the rights or restrictions attaching to shares in the company. Also, holders of incentive shares may receive special benefits by virtue of their ownership of the shares, *e.g.* benefits not available to at least 90 per cent of the shareholders of the same class as the holders, which are taxed under section 80 of the Finance Act 1988. Nevertheless, share incentive schemes can be attractive for purposes other than tax and, in particular, provide an effective means by which employees involve themselves with their company (and/or its subsidiaries).

Finally, an employee may benefit from the establishment by his employer of an employee share ownership trust—known as an ESOT—which satisfies sections 67–74 of, and Schedule 5, to the Finance Act 1989. Under such a qualifying ESOT an employer sets up and funds a trust. The primary purpose of the trust is the acquisition of shares in the founding employer (using the funds contributed) to be held principally for the benefit of its employees. Particular tax advantages are available to the employer who is entitled to a corporation tax deduction for contributions to the trust (section 67).

Provision of accommodation   6–17

Section 145 of the Taxes Act declares that where living accommodation is provided for a person (or for members of his family or household) by reason of his employment he is to be treated as being in receipt of emoluments of a value equal to the excess of the annual value of the premises over what he actually pays for the premises (if anything). Annual value is defined in section 837 of the Taxes Act, as being (in summary) the market rent on the footing that the tenant pays the rates and the landlord pays for repairs and insurance. That is the general rule, but if the employer (or other person providing the accommodation) is paying rent for the premises (*i.e.* is not the freehold owner) and the rent which the employer pays is greater than the annual value, the employee's emolument is valued at the excess of the rent which the employer pays over the rent which the employee pays. From any amount to be treated as emoluments the employee can deduct such expenses (if any) as would have been deductible if the employee had paid for the accommodation in full himself. The rules for what expenses are deductible are discussed in the next section.

There are three exceptional situations (section 145(4)) in which the provision of accommodation does not count as an emolument, namely: (a) where it is necessary for the proper performance of the employee's duties that he should reside in the provided accommodation; (b) where the accommodation is provided for the better performance of the duties, and his is one of the kinds of employment in the case of which it is customary for employers to provide living accommodation; and (c) where, there being a special threat to his security, special security arrangements are in force and he resides in the accommodation as part of those arrangements. Exceptions (a) and (b) do not apply if the employee is a director of the providing company or an associated company unless he has no material interest in the company and either he is a full-time working director or the company is non-profit making or is established for charitable purposes only. Employees earning £8,500 or more who are not directors have the benefit of the exceptions although they may be taxed on associated living expenses (see paragraph 6–08).

Where the cost of providing living accommodation exceeds £75,000, the employee may be charged to tax on an *additional* emolument. In essence, the employee is taxed on the additional value to him of the accommodation which is measured by applying the official rate of interest to the amount by which the cost of providing the accommodation exceeds £75,000.

6–18   **Deductible Expenses**

Tax is chargeable under Schedule E "on the full amount of the emoluments ... subject to such deductions only as may be authorised by the Tax Acts" (section 131(1)) of the Taxes Act). There are three differences between the expenses which are deductible under Schedule E and those which are deductible under Schedule D, Cases I and II (see paragraph 5–13). The first is a practical difference, namely that whereas profits under Cases I and II do not begin to make sense until one visualises an account with expenses on one side and receipts on the other, expenses play a much smaller part in Schedule E. Many employed people have no expenses (no deductible expenses, that is) at all. The second difference is that whereas the Schedule D legislation merely states what expenses are not deductible, Schedule E states in a positive form what expenses are deductible. And the third difference is that the rules are much more restrictively worded under Schedule E, so that many expenses which would be deductible under Schedule D are not deductible under Schedule E. One justification for the difference between the two Schedules is that it may be expected that, if an employer requires an employee to incur expenditure on its behalf, it will reimburse the employee. This cannot be so for the self-employed person.

The expenses which are deductible under Schedule E are set out in section 198(1) of the Taxes Act:

> "If the holder of an office or employment is obliged to incur and defray out of the emoluments of that office or employment—
> (a)   qualifying travelling expenses; or
> (b)   any amount . . . expended wholly, exclusively and necessarily in the performance of the duties of the office or employment;
> there may be deducted . . . the amount so incurred and defrayed."

The words "wholly" and "exclusively" are not applied to the expenses of travelling, but only to other expenditure. The words "in the performance of the duties" relate to both kinds of expenditure, as also does the word "necessarily." The presence of this word "necessarily" is one feature which makes the Schedule E rules more stringent than the rules of Schedule D, from which it is absent. Another feature which has that effect is the presence of the words "in the performance of the duties" which is a narrower phrase than the Schedule D words "for the purposes of the trade, profession or vocation".

We will look at travelling expenses first. The expense of travel from one's home to one's work is not deductible. This basic rule is established by *Ricketts v. Colquhoun* (1926), HL. Mr Ricketts was a barrister residing and practising in London. He was also the Recorder of Portsmouth (a part-time office). He claimed to deduct from the emoluments of his Recordership the expenses of travelling between London and Portsmouth and also his hotel expenses in Portsmouth. It was held by the House of Lords that neither the travelling expenses nor the hotel expenses were incurred in the performance of his duties, but rather before and after, and moreover, the expenses were attributable to the Recorder's own choice of residence and were not necessary to the office as such. This latter, very objective, point was rather softened by a later decision of the House of Lords, *Taylor v. Provan* (1975) (see below).

The cost of travel from one place of work in an employment to another place of work in the same employment is deductible. In *Owen v. Pook* (1970), HL, Dr Owen was a G.P. at his residence in Fishguard, and he also held a part-time appointment at a hospital in Haverfordwest, 15 miles away. Under his appointment Dr Owen was on stand-by duty to deal with emergency cases and he was required to be available by telephone. His responsibility for a patient began the moment he received a telephone call at home. It was held by a majority of the House of Lords that the duties of Dr Owen's employment were performed in two places (where he received the telephone calls and the hospital) and that he could deduct the expenses of travel between those places. This is akin to the Schedule D cases where a taxpayer is held to have his base at his home. But it is not identical, it is wider; sometimes Dr Owen received telephone calls when he was not at home. It seems to have been regarded as more important when he received the calls than where. But undoubtedly the case does establish that if his home is one of the places at which a taxpayer works (and rightly works) under his contract of employment, then the cost of travel from home to another place of work under the contract is deductible.

These and other leading cases on the vexed questions of travel costs still stand in principle, but are now supplemented by detailed statutory rules in section 198 and Schedule 12A of the Tax Act.

Let us now look at expenses other than travel expenses. These must be incurred wholly, exclusively and necessarily in the performance of the duties.

"Wholly" and "exclusively" are words which do not occur in relation to travelling expenses. For the importance of that point, remember *Sargent v. Barnes* (paragraph 5–13 above). In connection with non-travelling expenses the words proved to be of some importance in *Hillyer v. Leeke* (1976). Mr Hillyer was required by his employer to wear a suit at work. So he bought a suit which he wore at work but on no other occasions. He claimed to deduct the cost of the suit. It was held that the expenditure had not been incurred wholly and exclusively in the performance of his duties. He wore the suit not merely for the purposes of the employment, but also to provide cover, warmth and comfort for himself. This decision was approved by the House of Lords in *Mallalieu v. Drummond* (1983) (see paragraph 5–13).

The word "necessarily" has caused many a claim to founder. Stemming from *Ricketts v. Colquhoun* (above) the test is, as Donovan L.J. put it in *Brown v. Bullock* (1961), CA: " ... not whether the employer imposes the expense ... but whether the duties do." A bank manager was required by his employers (it was "virtually a condition of his employment") to be a member of a London club. It was held that the subscription fee was not a deductible expense. This is a harsh doctrine, and it may in time come to be softened if some of the ideas in *Taylor v. Provan* begin to percolate through. But it will still be the case that the expense must not be necessitated merely by the personal circumstances of the taxpayer as distinct from the necessities of the job. Thus in *Roskams v. Bennett* (1950) Mr Bennett was the district manager of an insurance company. Because of bad eyesight he could not drive a car, and so he found it necessary to maintain an office at home. It was held that the expense occasioned thereby was not deductible. In *Baird v. Williams* (1999) the attempt of a Clerk to General Commissioners to deduct the interest on a loan to buy an office for hearing tax appeals similarly failed.

The phrase "in the performance of the duties" has had similar effects on non-travel expenses as on travel expenses. In *Simpson v. Tate* (1925) a county medical officer of health joined certain medical and scientific societies so as to keep himself up-to-date on matters affecting public health. His claim to deduct these subscriptions was rejected, the court holding that the expense was incurred, not in the performance of the duties, but so that the taxpayer might keep himself fit to perform them. This seems a very restrictive doctrine, and indeed this particular point has been altered by statute. Section 201 of the Taxes Act now permits deduction of (we quote the marginal note to the section) "fees and subscriptions to professional bodies, learned societies, etc." But the doctrine still stands where it has not been changed by statute. In *Fitzpatrick v. IRC (No.2)*; *Smith v. Abbott* (1994) HL, journalists incurred expenditure in purchasing newspapers and journals. They claimed to deduct this expenditure. The House of Lords by a majority (4–1) rejected this claim. Lord Templeman said "a journalist does not purchase and read newspapers in the performance of his duties but for the purpose of ensuring that he will carry out his duties efficiently". The rule surely tends to discourage employees from making themselves better employees.

6–19   Golden Handshakes

One of the pleasures of studying tax law is that it is bedecked with vivid phrases which start as slang and are then taken into the dictionary, if not into the statute book. One such phrase is "Golden Handshakes." These can, more prosaically, be called "terminal payments".

In the first instance, it is, of course, important to establish that a payment is a golden handshake. However, once this is established it is necessary to distinguish three different kinds of payment on the termination of an office or employment.

First, where there is a contractual provision that a certain sum will become payable if the contract is determined early, that sum is treated as remuneration for services and is taxed under Schedule E.

Secondly, if employer and employee agree that the employee will stay on at a reduced salary and the employer makes a payment to an employee in connection with this agreement, that payment is treated as being in anticipation of future services and is taxed under Schedule E.

Thirdly, where a payment is made which is not related to services rendered or to be rendered, but is paid as consideration for the release of the employer's obligation under the contract of employment, *it is not taxable under the ordinary principles of Schedule E*, but is taxable under special statutory provisions which were first enacted in 1960. The provisions are now contained in sections 148 and 188 of the Taxes Act.

Section 148 applies to:

"any payment (not otherwise chargeable to tax) which is made, whether in pursuance of any legal obligation or not, either directly or indirectly in consideration or in consequence of, or otherwise in connection with, the termination of the holding of the office or employment or any change in its functions or emoluments, including any payment in commutation of annual or periodical payments (whether chargeable to tax or not) which would otherwise have been so made."

(The words from "including" onwards catch a payment in commutation of pension rights.) The section is clearly very wide in its scope. One important kind of payment which it catches is a redundancy payment. (This point is confirmed by section 580(3) of the Taxes Act.) Some payments (listed in section 188) are exempted from section 148, such as: (a) any payment made in connection with the termination of an office or employment by the death of the holder, or made on account of injury to or disability of the holder; (b) any sum chargeable to tax under section 313 of the Taxes Act (which charges to tax any sum paid to an employee for a restrictive covenant); (c) payments under approved retirement benefit schemes.

Payments which are caught by section 148 are treated as earned income received on the following date: (a) in the case of a commutation payment, the date of commutation; (b) in the case of any other payment, the date of the termination or change in respect of which the payment is made.

Tax is not charged under section 148 on the first £30,000 of any payment. This figure may be calculated by aggregating two (or more) payments from the same employment or from associated employers. Because of this threshold this is one of the rare circumstances where it is advantageous to be a Schedule E taxpayer rather than a Schedule D taxpayer. A similar sort of payment made to a Schedule D taxpayer would in most situations be taxable, and taxable in full without any exemption for the first £30,000. See *IRC v. Brander & Cruickshank* (1971), HL.

The £30,000 exemption raises a point stemming from what is called "the Gourley principle". That principle was laid down by the House of Lords in *British Transport Commission v. Gourley* (1956). Mr Gourley was injured in a railway accident, and was unable to work again. He sued in tort for damages for (amongst other things) loss of earnings. It was estimated that if the plaintiff had not been injured his earnings over the rest of his working life would have come to £37,000. The defendants argued that since the plaintiff's earnings would have been taxed, the damages should be reduced to take account of that factor. It was estimated that Mr Gourley's earnings *after tax* would have been only £6,000. So the issue was whether his damages should be £37,000 or £6,000. The House of Lords decided for £6,000. *Gourley's* case was brought in tort, but the same principle applies to breach of contract. The reasoning of the principle is that the plaintiff ought not to make a profit out of the tort or breach of contract. The principle only applies where two factors are present: (1) what the award represents is lost receipts which, if they had been received, would have been taxed; and (2) the award itself is not taxable. The principle has been applied to awards of damages for wrongful dismissal which fell within what is now section 148. In *Shove v. Downs Surgical plc* (1984) the judge awarded damages well over the £25,000 limit (the threshold at that time). He reasoned that, if liability to pay taxes was not too remote in assessing loss then, likewise, liability to pay tax on the compensation was not too remote. He therefore ordered net damages of £60,000 to be increased to £83,000 so as to provide for income tax payable on the lump sum compensation.

6–20 ## Pension Income

Many employees, when they come to retire, do not receive any occupational pension. They may get the flat rate state retirement pension ("old age pension") and the state earnings related pension (SERPS). Payments received under this state system are taxable under Schedule E and count as earned income.

An increasing number of employees do enjoy an occupational pension. When such an employee retires, and begins to receive periodical pension payments, he is taxed on those payments under Schedule E and they count as earned income.

During employment such an employee will probably have been subject to some kind of pension scheme, under which he paid contributions and the employer also paid contributions. Two questions arise: are the employee's contributions deductible in computing emoluments? and are the employer's contributions treated as emoluments of the employee?

The answer to the first question is that the employee's contributions are not deductible unless the pension scheme is what is called an "exempt approved scheme" under section 592 of the Taxes Act or it is a "statutory scheme" (section 594). In either instance, the employee's contributions are deductible up to a limit of 15 per cent. of annual remuneration. In practice, any general scheme will try to be "exempt approved" because of the high degree of tax-privilege accorded such schemes by successive governments. A very important further advantage of an "exempt approved scheme" is that the fund of the scheme is itself exempt from income tax and also capital gains tax (section 592 of the Taxes Act and section 271 of the Taxation of Chargeable Gains Act 1992 respectively).

The answer to the second question is that the employer's contributions are treated as emoluments of the employee unless the scheme is an "approved scheme" (not necessarily an "exempt approved scheme") or a statutory scheme (see section 596 of the Taxes Act).

An employee whose employer does not offer an occupational pension scheme or whose employer runs a scheme which the employee opts not to join may take out an approved personal pension scheme. Contributions to such a scheme are treated similarly to those made in respect of the types of occupational pension considered above. Thus, the employee's contributions, within specified limits, are deductible whilst contributions by an employer are not treated as emoluments of the employee (see generally, sections 639–646 of the Taxes Act).

Social Security Income 6–21

The tax treatment of social security benefits is not straightforward, and will form a separate part of the drafts produced by the Tax Law Rewrite Project. Currently, section 617 of the Taxes Act contains two lists. The first is of benefits charged to tax under Schedule E. The second is of payments exempted from any charge to tax. In practice, recipients of some benefits for a long period will not earn enough to pay income tax once the personal reliefs are taken into account. Those receiving most, but not all, benefits are exempted from NI contributions.

The picture is further complicated by the conversion of some social security benefits into tax credits, which are offset directly against tax payable (see paragraph 12–22). The main new benefit is the working families' tax credit (the old family credit). As a result, the pattern of taxation of social security and other personal benefits is confusing, if not confused. Very broadly, payments to the unemployed and retired are taxable, while payments to the seriously disabled and for children are exempt, and payments to lower-paid employees result in a direct reduction of tax bills and sometimes in cash payments from the Revenue.

The Mechanics of Schedule E 6–22

All income taxed under Schedule E counts as earned income. It is collected by means of the Pay As You Earn system (PAYE). That name indicates two things: first, that the tax is on a current year basis, and, secondly, that the tax is collected bit-by-bit as the year goes on. It is collected by the employer by means of deducting the appropriate amount for tax from each weekly or monthly payment that he makes to his employees. The employer is then under a duty to hand over the tax to the Revenue. Every employed person earning over a certain amount (the amount being varied from time to time by statutory instrument in line with variations in the tax threshold) is given a code number by the inspector. This code number tells the employer the amount of allowances and reliefs that any particular employee is entitled to. By applying the code number to the cumulative tax tables with which he is supplied by the Revenue, the employer can know how much tax to deduct from the pay of a particular employee in any particular week (or month) of the tax year. On occasions, a negative code, called a K code, is used. The employer must then, instead of making a deduction from the employee's pay, make an addition to it. This may happen where, for example, an employee receives a benefit in kind which is not within the PAYE system and where it is worth more than his personal allowances.

It is obvious from this (very brief) account that the employer is acting as a collector of tax (unpaid) for the Revenue.

For many years, tax was charged on the emoluments earned by an employee over the tax year (the earnings basis). This often led to problems with regard to emoluments received after the tax year in which they had been earned. Consequently, emoluments are now taxed on a receipts basis, *i.e.* when they are "received" by the employee (for the meaning of "received", see section 202B of the Taxes Act). Special provision is made for an emolument received after an employment has come to an end, *i.e.* it is treated as an emolument of the last year of employment.

Technically, most benefits in kind are outside the PAYE scheme, because they are not payments of income. But some benefits are treated as "notional payments", see sections 203F–203L of the Taxes Act, inserted by the Finance Act 1994 and strengthened by the Finance Act 1998. Further, there is some judicial support for this practice, see, for example, *Beecham Group Ltd v. Fair* (1984).

In theory the PAYE system should produce the result that at the end of the tax year an individual employee has paid (by deduction) exactly the correct amount of tax. In many, cases it does so in practice. If it turns out that too much tax has been deducted, the taxpayer can either get a repayment from the Revenue or have the credit taken into account in determining his code number for a subsequent year.

6–23   National Insurance Contibutions

The authority for levying and collecting contributions is contained in Part I of the Social Security Contributions and Benefits Act 1992 (and the identical sections in the almost identical Northern Ireland Act of that year). Just 19 sections and two Schedules do much of the work of the Income Tax Acts. Well, not quite. Much of the detail of contribution liability is contained in regulations, of which the Social Security (Contributions) Regulations 1979 (S.I. 1979 No. 591) are the most important. Even so, the legislative authority is much less detailed than the equivalent income tax provisions. The reason is that, until recently, the system worked on a much rougher sense of justice. But the rough justice also meant complications for employers forced to calculate two separate monthly tax bills based on inconsistent rules: one for PAYE and one for the modified PAYE scheme applied to NI contributions.

The inconsistencies came partly because PAYE and the modified PAYE were run by different government departments, and appeals were handled by different appeal systems. Since 1998 there have been a series of reforms which, when fully realised, will merge income tax and NI contributions for employees in all but name. Three key reforms bring this about. First, the Social Security Contributions (Transfer of Functions) Act 1999 authorised the transfer of all contributions staff and responsibilities from the DSS to the Revenue. Secondly, contribution liability is being extended, in effect, to cover all forms of income subject to Schedule E and PAYE. Thirdly, all contributions appeals were transferred to the tribunals dealing with income tax appeals, and the courts that supervise them.

We must now examine in turn the various classes of contribution. In summary they are:

Class 1   contributions from employees and their employers

Class 1A   contributions by employers for employees' benefits in kind

Class 1B   contributions by employers for PAYE settlements for employees

Class 2   contributions from the self-employed

Class 3   voluntary contribution from the non-employed

Class 4   contributions from traders and professionals.

Class 1   6–24

This class applies to anyone over 16 who is an earner in employed earner's employment and who in any period receives earnings in excess of a lower limit for that period: section 6. That sentence was full of jargon (all quoted from the Act), and needs translating. What it means in practice is that anyone who has cash earnings that will get taxed under Schedule E will, if those earnings are more than a set minimum limit for any period, be liable for a contribution.

Arriving at that conclusion is not made easy by the exact words of the Social Security Act. That tells us that an "earner" is someone who has earnings. "Earnings" include any remuneration or profit derived from an employment: section 3(1). But it is clear from the Act that the self-employed are engaged in employment as much as employees. The key comes in section 2(1). It tells

125

us that an employed earner is someone gainfully employed either under a contract of service or in an office, with emoluments chargeable to income tax under Schedule E. As the presence of the lower limit prevents a charge to contributions on someone not receiving emoluments from employment, the reference to "gainful" employment seems superfluous.

Ignoring a few loose ends, the charges of Schedule E, as provided by section 19 of the Taxes Act 1988, and Class 1 apply to the same group of people, employees and office holders. We will talk simply of employees.

Where an employee has earnings for a period which exceed a set minimum, called the primary threshold, for any period, called an earnings period, contribution liability arises. The liability is of two kinds:

First, there is the primary contribution. This is paid by the employee personally. Then there is the secondary contribution to be paid by the employer. This must not be passed on to the employee. Both the primary and the secondary contributions are percentages of the earnings of the employee for that earnings period, up to a set maximum called the upper earnings limit.

Two things need to be determined so that the contribution can be levied. One is *earnings* and the other the *earnings period* during which those earnings are earned or treated as earned.

Earnings

Earnings are broadly equivalent to emoluments from Schedule E. But it is only broadly equivalent. The important rule from *Tennant v. Smith* (p.96) about benefits in kind does not operate. Why? In truth, there is no strong reason why, if the terms of the primary legislation are studied, but the case has never been applied to contributions largely because ... it has never been applied. Instead, the matter was left in the Contributions Regulations. Regulation 19 lists a whole series of payments to be disregarded in working out the total of earnings. In particular, this excludes from charge "any payment in kind or by way of the provision of board or lodging or of services or other facilities": reg. 19(1)(d). Also excluded are tips from third parties (such as those received by employed taxi drivers), pensions, benefits under profit-sharing schemes and other matters. Once these are excluded, the charge is to be on the gross earnings from the employment. There are no provisions about deducting expenses or any equivalent of the deductions from total income available for income tax, such as capital allowances or personal allowances. In summary, if payments or earnings are in cash, or are convertible into cash by surrender (rather than sale), then contributions are payable. If the payment is in kind, then until recently no contribution was payable. But see now Class 1A.

Note that the charge is on the earnings from *each* employment. If an earner has two or more employments with the same employer, these are added together. If there are separate employers, the earner must pay a primary contribution separately on the earnings of each job, and each employer must pay a secondary contribution.

Earnings periods

There are complicated rules for defining *earnings periods*. The contribution scheme has no equivalent of PAYE coding, averaging out contribution liability through the year. This is because it is felt to be necessary to have the contributions determined at the time they are paid, so as to enable swift decisions to be taken about entitlements to benefits that may be based on those contributions. To enable this to happen, the liability for each period has to be calculated separately, the basic period being a week or month. Detailed rules are needed to stop avoidance, and the Contributions Regulations provide them.

Rates

The rates of liability are adjusted every year to ensure a correct rate of flow into the National Insurance Fund, bearing in mind the outgoing of that year. For 2000–01, the rates of Class 1 contribution are: employee's contribution rate is 10 per cent of earnings from £76 (primary threshold) to £535 (upper earnings limit). Employer's contribution is 12.2 per cent from £84 (secondary threshold) to £535.

Note that we called the 10 per cent rate the *standard* rate. This is because there is a *reduced* rate, paid by certain married women and widows. They can only pay at this low rate if they opted out of the scheme before 1978. There is also a *contracted-out* rate, again lower than the standard rate. Despite the names used, this is paid by the majority of employees, particularly those in the public sector. The contracted-out rate applies where the employer is providing employees with an occupational pension payable in place of part of the state retirement pension, or where the employee has opted out of both the state pension and any occupational pension, paying a personal pension instead. In exchange for losing the right to part of the state pension, both employer and employee pay reduced amounts. But they will usually be paying for occupational pensions. Finally, a person over pensionable age does not pay a primary contribution, but the employer does.

6–25   **Class 1A**

Eh? This class of contributions is an example of the brilliant art of compromise that is a strength of the British—or, perhaps, an example of why our laws are frequently such a shambolic mess. The Class 1A contribution is in fact a fringe benefits payroll tax. It has nothing to do with social security except that the money is paid into the National Insurance Fund. No entitlement to benefit arises from it. It is a charge on any employer that provides employees with benefits in kind in such circumstances that the employees are liable to income tax on them. If the employee has to pay income tax under that section, then the employer has to pay a Class 1A contribution. If not, not. See section 10 of the Contributions and Benefits Act 1992. Procedure apart, that is the end of the relevant law.

The contribution was brought in as a compromise. In most countries, social contributions are payable on benefits in kind as well as on cash earnings. The fact that this was not so in Britain meant that considerable tax advantages accrued to those who received benefits in kind. Cars formed the most usual benefit in kind and, when first introduced, Class 1A related only to cars. But the British system cannot readily tax benefits in kind to ordinary contributions because of the special rules on earnings periods. Nor can employers be charged income tax on benefits in kind in the way they do in some states (such as Australia). However, if the tax privilege was to be removed from benefits in kind, an employer levy was necessary. So, what was simpler than to use the one employers' payroll tax that was available?

CHAPTER 7

PROPERTY INCOME[1]

"Land", observed Anthony Trollope, "is about the only thing that can't fly away."[2] This is a thought that has occurred to landowners, would-be landowners and the Revenue. The taxation of land has a long and tangled history. Income from land in the United Kingdom is now taxed under Schedule A but by reference to the "profits from a business carried for the exploitation, as a source of rents or other receipts, of any estate, interest or rights in or over land ...." This requires some explanation. Schedule A had its origins in the Finance Act 1963. However, before our attention is directed towards these provisions we should look briefly at some history, with a view to, hopefully, throwing some light upon the present position.

History   7–01

Originally, Schedule A was a tax on the *ownership* of land. From that it followed that it caught not only landowners who let out their land but also owner-occupiers. It was based on annual values. These annual values were supposed to be revised every five years, but in fact the last revision was made in 1935–36, and after that year they became hopelessly out-of-date and absurdly low. The Finance Act 1940 then introduced a system of taxing landlords (under Case VI of Schedule D) on what were called "excess rents", that is on rents received to the extent that they exceeded the annual values fixed under Schedule A.

Then the Finance Act 1963 re-modelled the whole system. Tax on owner-occupiers was abolished. They had, after all, only been subjected to income tax on the basis of a notional income (equal to the annual value) not a real income. And in practice many owner-occupiers had been able to eliminate any tax charge by making a "maintenance claim" in respect of repairs, insurance, etc. So far as non-occupiers were concerned the Finance Act 1963

---

[1] This is the current title being used by the Tax Law Rewrite Project, rather than "Income from Land". "Land" in tax law, as in law generally, includes buildings (except where the context requires otherwise).

[2] See *The Law Chronicle of Barset*, Chap. 58. Further, as Mark Twain once perceptively remarked, they don't make it any more.

combined the Schedule A and excess rents provisions into a new taxing code which was labelled Case VIII of Schedule D.

For the next six years there was no Schedule A; that label was vacant. Then by the Finance Act 1969 Case VIII was re-named "Schedule A". The remodelled Schedule A, which, in essence, taxed the annual profits or gains derived from certain rents[3] and other receipts arising from the ownership of land or an interest in land, then held sway until it was superseded for income tax purposes by the new Schedule A which was introduced by the Finance Act 1995 (at which point it might properly be referred to as the old Schedule A!) on first introduction is applied only to companies, but the charging provisions in Section 15 were rewritten with effect from 1998 for both companies and individuals. Schedules 5 to the Finance Act 1998 is one of the first enacted examples of the "rewrite approach" to amendments.

The income of a Schedule A business is now treated, for computation purposes, in a similar way to the income of a trade under Case I of Schedule D. However, these Schedules remain separate and distinct and income of a Schedule A business is neither trading nor earned income.[4]

Finally, for the sake of completeness, it should be mentioned that there was a Schedule B tax until it was abolished by the Finance Act 1988. Originally, this was a tax on *occupiers* of land which was payable in addition to any Schedule A liability. So an owner-occupier paid both with the important exception that dwelling-houses and trade premises were exempted from Schedule B.[5] However, from 1963 until its abolition, Schedule B was confined to taxing the occupation of woodlands "managed on a commercial basis and with a view to the realisation of profits", and, moreover, an occupier of woodlands might avoid an assessment under Schedule B, which was based on one-third of the annual value of the woodlands, by electing to be assessed under Case I of Schedule D.

7–02

Schedule A

INTRODUCTION

Before we look at some of the essential features of the new Schedule A it is as well to deal with, albeit superficially, a question

---

[3] This included certain capital payments deemed to be rent—see the treatment of premiums (below, paragraph 7–07).

[4] But note the special rules which apply to income from furnished holiday lettings (see below, paragraph 7–06).

[5] Farms used to fall under Schedule B, until farming was transferred by statute to Case I of Schedule D.

which inevitably arise as a consequence of what we have said thus far. Why was the new Schedule A introduced? The answer lies primarily in the quest for simplification to facilitate the introduction of self-assessment. The new Schedule A is undoubtedly simpler in many respects than the old Schedule A and some of the anomalies associated with the latter, *e.g.* the taxation of income from furnished lettings under Case VI of Schedule D rather than Schedule A have been eradicated. It has also been argued that the new Schedule A rules are merely a reflection of Revenue practice preceding the change. This simplification was reinforced by the further changes in 1998.

7–03

THE CHARGE TO TAX
Our starting point for consideration of the parameters of the new Schedule A must be the new basic charging provision enacted in section 38 of the Finance Act 1998 and incorporated into section 15 of the Taxes Act. The charging provision says:

> "Tax is charged under this Schedule on the annual profits arising from a business carried on for the exploitation, as a source of rents or other receipts, of any estate, interest or rights in or over any land in the United Kingdom".

In short, central to the new Schedule A is the notion of a business carried on for the exploitation of land or an interest in land, *i.e.* a Schedule A business. Compare with that the wording in the original version of section 15 enacted in 1988.

7–04

SCOPE
Most commonly, the new Schedule A taxes the profits or gains made by an individual from the business of letting property, *i.e.* the rents received or to which the individual is entitled, less any items of allowable expenditure (see further below). However, it also extends to other sources of profits or gains. First, it catches certain capital payments made by a tenant to a landlord and which are referable to the grant of a lease, *i.e.* premiums which may be taxed as if they are payments of rent. The substantive rules relating to the taxation of premiums under the new Schedule A (which are considered below, paragraph 7–07) are broadly the same as those which apply under the old Schedule A. Secondly, receipts other than rent (actual or deemed) may give rise to profits or gains taxable under the new Schedule A provided, of course, that the receipts are derived from the exploitation of land or an interest in land. Some guidance as to the nature of these "other receipts" is given by *Lowe v. Ashmore* (1971) and *McClure v.*

131

Petre (1988)[6] from which it is apparent that the receipts must be income not capital receipts. In the latter, the taxpayer received a payment in return for the grant of a licence to dump waste on his land. It was held that the payment was a capital receipt and, therefore, not taxable under Schedule A. By granting the licence, the taxpayer deprived himself of a right, namely, the right to dump, which he could otherwise have enjoyed over his land. The payment was the consideration for the disposal of that right. The taxpayer had realised part of the value of his freehold.

Under the new Schedule A, each source of income, *e.g.* each letting where the individual has granted a number of leases is treated as part of a single Schedule A business, and the taxation of the individual in respect of that business is determined by taking into account the income generated and pertinent expenses incurred by such sources as a whole.

7–05
COMPUTATION

Section 21A of the Taxes Act provides for the profits and losses of a Schedule A business to be computed (with some exceptions) in accordance with the rules for computing trading profits under Case I of Schedule D. The Schedule A computation includes all relevant receipts and outgoings of the business for the year of assessment. The charge to tax is calculated on an earnings basis (see above, paragraph 5–17).

The rules for computing profits under Case I of Schedule D are considered in paragraph 5–05, although some aspects of these rules in the context of the new Schedule A are alluded to in the next section.

7–06
PARTICULAR CHARACTERISTICS

The unitary approach to taxation under the new Schedule A means, in principle, that *all* lettings of property by an individual, whether furnished, *i.e.* where part of the rent payable is attributable to the use of furniture, or unfurnished, should be within the parameters of the new Schedule A.[7] Indeed, this is broadly true, although in need of further elaboration in relation to two types of furnished letting, namely furnished holiday lettings and what are known as "rent a room" lettings.

---

[6] Both cases were concerned with the construction to be given to the words "other receipts arising ... from or by virtue of ... ownership of an estate or interest in land or right over ... land or any incorporeal hereditament ... " which appear in the charging provision of old Schedule A.

[7] Previously the profits or gains from furnished lettings by individuals were taxed under Case VI of Schedule D.

The commercial letting of furnished holiday accommodation by individuals or companies is *treated* as a trade. This is set out in section 503 of the Taxes Act which applies to furnished holiday lettings rules which normally only apply to trades, *e.g.* the loss relief rules for trades.[8]

A "rent a room" letting arises where an individual rents out a spare furnished room in his only or main residence (see section 59 and Schedule 10 to the Finance (No.2) Act 1992). This is not a step which an individual would necessarily take without encouragement. That encouragement is provided by a tax incentive. An individual is eligible for relief from income tax if the income from a "rent a room" letting or lettings in a particular year of assessment does not exceed £4,250. If the income exceeds this amount, the individual may choose either to be taxed on the excess over £4,250 or to be taxed on the actual profit made (*i.e.* gross receipts less actual expenses).

Finally, another important facet of the new Schedule A is that in computing the annual profits or gains of a Schedule A business allowable expenses of the business may be set off against any Schedule A income of the business accruing in that year of assessment. An allowable expense is an income expense incurred wholly and exclusively for the purpose of the Schedule A business which does not constitute prohibited expenditure within section 74 of the Taxes Act (see paragraph 5–11).

Premiums   7–07

The next section may be regarded, with hindsight, as perhaps a well-meant mistake. It is common form with commercial lettings in some areas for the consideration payable by the tenant to come in two forms. The first is the annual rent. The second is a lump sum, usually paid at or before the beginning of the lease. In principle, the lump sum is capital. Nowadays it is liable to capital gains tax. But in 1963 when the first fundamental revision of Schedule A occurred there was no capital gains tax, so such sums went tax-free. If premiums were not taxable there would be an obvious and simple tax-avoidance device—don't charge a rent, just take a premium, which, being a capital sum, would not be subject to income tax because it is not an *annual* profit or gain.

The normal meaning of "premium" in relation to land is a lump sum paid for the granting of a lease. But for income tax

---

[8]   Section 504 sets out rigorous conditions which must be satisfied before a letting qualifies as a furnished holiday letting for the purposes of section 503.

purposes "premium" has an extended meaning, as we shall see. Presently, the broad principle is that certain premiums are deemed to be income and are charged to income tax. The substantive rules relating to the treatment of premiums under the new Schedule A, which are considered in the remainder of this section, are broadly the same as those which apply under the old Schedule A. The detailed provisions in section 34 to 39 are concerned to stop up various tax-avoidance devices which would otherwise be open. This is an excellent field in which to observe the battle between tax avoiders and the Revenue.

A premium (or part of a premium) which is not caught for income tax may be caught for capital gains tax. Conversely, that part of a premium which is caught for income tax is not chargeable to capital gains tax.

There are three main heads of charge on premium income: (1) under section 34, premiums and like sums are chargeable; (2) under section 35, where a lease is granted at an undervalue the "amount foregone" may be chargeable on a subsequent assignment of the lease; (3) under section 36, where land is sold with a right to reconveyance the difference between the selling price and the reconveyance price may be chargeable to tax.

Let us look first at section 34. Subsection (1) is the provision which catches a "premium" in its normal meaning. It says:

"where the payment of any premium is required under a lease, or otherwise under the terms subject to which a lease is granted, and the duration of the lease does not exceed 50 years, the landlord shall be treated for the purposes of the Tax Acts as becoming entitled when the lease is granted to an amount by way of rent (in addition to any actual rent) equal to—

$$P - \frac{(P \times Y)}{50}$$

where P is the premium and Y is the number of complete periods of 12 months (other than the first) comprised in the duration of the lease."

Notice that the way the subsection taxes a premium is to treat the landlord as being in receipt of rent which is then part of the profits of the Schedule A business. Notice also that a lease for more than 50 years is not caught by section 34, and that the nearer a lease gets to being for 50 years the less income tax is payable. Thus a premium on a lease for 49 years is reduced by 48/50, or 96 per cent, leaving only 4 per cent taxable. A lease for nine years is reduced by eight-fiftieths (or 16 per cent), leaving 84 per cent taxable. A lease for one year enjoys no reduction at all. But remember also that the part of the premium not caught by income tax *is* liable to tax in so far as a chargeable gain arises. Because of this sliding scale there are detailed rules (in section 38) for ascertaining the duration of leases.

We now come to some extended meanings of the word "premium". Section 34(2) treats as a premium a requirement on the tenant to carry out works on the premises (beyond mere maintenance and repairs). The deemed premium is of an amount equal to the increase that the requirement makes in the value of the landlord's reversionary interest. So the premium provisions cannot be avoided by requiring works rather than a cash payment.

Section 34 also deals with other kinds of disguised premium. Subsection (4) deems a sum to be a premium if it becomes payable by the tenant in lieu of rent or as consideration for the surrender of the lease. Subsection (5) deems a sum to be a premium if it becomes payable by the tenant as consideration for the variation or waiver of any of the terms of the lease.

Where a premium (or a deemed premium, as above) is payable by instalments the tax may be paid in corresponding instalments spread over a maximum of eight years. Before that there was no time-limit, and ingenious leases appeared under which a premium was to be paid over a period of, say 250 years, with the bulk becoming payable in the 250th year.

Section 35 deals with another possible avoidance device. A premium paid on the *grant* of a lease is taxable (as we have seen), but a premium paid on the *assignment* of a lease is not taxable under the provisions we have so far looked at. Therefore, if it were not for this section 35, a simple avoidance would be for A to grant a lease to B (a relative, say, or a friendly company) at a very small premium or without any premium at all and then for B to assign the lease to C (a stranger) at a premium. Section 35 catches this situation. Suppose the market is such that A could have required a premium of £1,000 on the grant of the lease to B, whereas in fact he took a premium of only £200, then £800 is said to be "the amount foregone". If B later assigns the premises for £1,400 he is charged to tax (under the new Schedule A); on the excess of £1,400 over the amount of the original premium (£200), except that the chargeable amount cannot exceed the amount foregone. So on these figures the chargeable amount would have been £1,400 less £200 (= £1,200), but the upper limit is £800, and so the chargeable amount is £800. If B had assigned the premises to C for a premium of £500 the chargeable amount would have been £300. In that circumstance the Revenue would not have collected tax on the whole of the amount foregone, but they would be able to pick up the balance on subsequent assignments by C, D, E, etc.

Section 36 deals with yet another avoidance device, namely selling land subject to a right of reconveyance. If A, a landowner, is minded to take a premium of, say, £7,000, on granting a lease to B, he could, instead, sell the land to B on terms that he, A, could buy back the land from B for the sale price minus £7,000. Section 36 ensures that on such a transaction A is charged to tax (under the new Schedule A) on £7,000. If the sale contains a right for A to take a lease back of the premises from B, the lease back counts as a reconveyance. This lease back procedure is very common in practice, because it is a neat way of solving a liquidity problem or a cash-flow problem, and, as it is not very wicked, section 36 contains a proviso excepting such a transaction from the tax charge if the lease back is granted, and begins to run, within one month after the sale. That seems a very arbitrary way of marking out the exception, but it does enable (as it is intended to do) a genuine lease back arrangement to be free of the tax charge under section 36. But capital gains tax may be chargeable on the transaction; also if the lease back is at more than a commercial rent, only the commercial rent will be an allowable business expense (section 779 of the Taxes Act); also in certain circumstances a proportion of the sale price may be taxed as though it were income (section 780 of the Taxes Act).

7–08   Rent factoring

The ever-ingenious tax professions developed a way round even these wide provisions. They did so by rent factoring, that is, selling or transferring the right to receive rent without transferring the freehold or leasehold giving rise to the right to receive it. Sections 43A to 43G of the Taxes Act were added by the Finance Act 2000 to treat amounts received under such arrangements as rent received as part of a Schedule A business. This happens if the recipient records any form of financial obligation in the accounts related to the receipt. In other words, sums that would otherwise have been converted into financial payments and receipts remain as rent.

7–09   "Artificial Transactions in Land"

These transactions are governed by section 776 of the Taxes Act. Subsection (1) of section 776 states the reason for the section: "This section is enacted to prevent the avoidance of tax by persons concerned with land or the development of land." This is achieved by treating certain capital gains (see below) arising on the disposal of land as income. The rationale of section 776 can be best understood if one looks at its history and antecedents. One must bear in mind that the section dates from before there was a capital gains tax. In those days an owner of land who sold the land could make a tax-free profit, unless he was a dealer in land. If he was a dealer in land he was taxed on the gain as an item in his trading profit (and still is: see, for example, *Pilkington v. Randall* (1966) and compare *Marson v. Morton* (1986)). He could avoid this tax by forming a company to hold the land and then selling the shares, rather than selling the land as such.

Section 776 seeks to block this device by a very wide-ranging provision. At first it was little used, and thought to be of little importance, despite its wording. However, a series of largely successful Revenue contests in the courts in the 1980s indicated that it might be potentially a very wide section indeed: see *Yuill v. Wilson* (1980) in the House of Lords, and *Page v. Lowther* (1983) and *Yuill v. Fletcher* (1984) in the Court of Appeal. But these decisions must now, in turn, be read in the light of two significant developments. First, it may be questioned whether the section is needed in view of the approach adopted by the courts in cases such as *Furniss v. Dawson* (1984), HL, (see above, paragraph 2–11). Secondly, it is inevitable that the importance of the section has been reduced since 1988 by the unification of the rates of tax for capital gains tax and income tax. Notwithstanding these caveats, the section may apply wherever:

(1) land, or property deriving value from land, is acquired solely or mainly to realise a gain on its disposal; *or*
(2) land is held as trading stock; *or*
(3) land is developed solely or mainly to realise a gain on disposal when developed,

and a disposal of the land gives rise to a capital gain. The whole of the gain is treated as income taxable under Case VI of Schedule D for the year in which the gain is realised. For this purpose, "disposal" includes disposal of control over land, so covers the case of land owned through companies, where the companies' shares, rather then the land itself, are transferred.

Even more broadly, the gains can be treated as the income of any person by whom the gain is realised or who provides directly or indirectly an opportunity to realise it. This is wide enough to catch a "mastermind" who has taken no actual part in the process of making a gain, as was illustrated in the two *Yuill* cases mentioned above.

The section is unusual even in tax-avoidance law, and almost unprecedented in general statute law, in containing a statement of its purpose in subsection (1). But it is not clear whether this provision adds anything to the operation of the section.

7–10   Tailpiece

In considering the taxation of receipts from land, one should bear in mind that as well as income tax (in connection with rents and premiums and section 776 gains) a transaction in land may attract capital gains tax. There is also stamp duty of up to four per cent to be paid on sales of land. The four per cent is on the value of the land transferred, so is a capital tax, not an income tax. It can also apply to leases and to sales of shares in property flowing companies. This tax is specific to, and should be studied as part of, conveyancing.

CAPITAL ALLOWANCES[1]

INTRODUCTORY

When we were considering the computation of trading profits, we saw that the cost and depreciation of capital assets are regarded as being of a capital not of a revenue character. But this does not mean that no relief is given for tax purposes in respect of such capital expenditure. It is given by a separate system of "capital allowances". We consider the manner in which such relief is given later in this chapter. Initially, however, we must determine when capital allowances are available.

The law on capital allowance is the first part of tax law to be rewritten fully by the Tax Law Rewrite Project. At the time of writing an informal draft bill has been prepared, and a formal bill is expected to be published in 2000. Further, the Finance Act 2000 has dealt with some necessary tidying and rationalising. The chapter is based on the terms used in the informal bill. This is designed to replace the Capital Allowances Act 1990, a self-contained consolidation measure, and subsequent amendments. It is a comment both on rewrite-style and the growth of the law in this area that the 1990 Act had 165 sections, some of fiendish complexity, and some subject to repeated amendment. The 2000 draft has 622 clauses.

Capital allowances are available as follows:

- plant and machinery allowances;
- industrial and agricultural buildings allowances;
- mineral extraction allowances;
- scientific research allowances;
- know-how allowances;
- patent allowances;
- dredging allowances;
- assured tenancy allowances.

It can be seen from the list that many items of capital expenditure do *not* attract any allowance. Also, the allowances are broadly confined to income taxable as trading income. One exception is the allowances for machinery and plant, which are available to persons carrying on a profession (or vocation) or to persons in employment, as well as to traders: section 27 of the Capital Allowances Act 1990.

The law relating to capital allowances can be traced back to the Income Tax Act 1945. The system of providing relief for capital expenditure through the availability of capital allowances introduced by that Act is the foundation upon which the present law is based. Of course, that is not to say that the system has not been subject to considerable change over the years. The consolidation Act in 1990, the Capital Allowances Act 1990, as amended by subsequent Finance Acts, is the primary source of the present law.

Before looking at aspects of the substantive law two important questions must be addressed—first, what is the rationale for capital allowances and, secondly, the distinct but interrelated question of the rate(s) at which capital allowances should be available?

8–02 **Why capital allowances**

It is implicit in the opening remarks in this chapter that the availability of capital allowances should in some measure be an acknowledgement of the need to take account of the depreciation in value or obsolescence of capital assets acquired by a business. However, for many years, successive governments perceived capital allowances principally as a means of encouraging businesses to invest, and a system of generous allowances developed which enabled a business to write off capital expenditure markedly in advance of any actual depreciation or obsolescence. Thus, by 1984, a business, if it wished, could set the whole of the cost of buying machinery and plant against its taxable profits for the year of purchase, together with most (and sometimes all) of the cost of industrial buildings. This was achieved by claiming the appropriately named first year and initial allowances respectively. In many instances, however, it was not the desire to invest *per se* which prompted expenditure by a business, but the prospect of claiming these allowances with a view to cutting down taxable profits in the year the expenditure was incurred. Such practices, which were intended to exploit the generosity of the system, brought forth the following lament by Chancellor of the Exchequer, Nigel Lawson, in his Budget Speech in 1984. He said:

" . . . Over virtually the whole of the post-war period there have been incentives for investment in both plant and machinery and industrial, although not commercial, buildings. But there is little evidence that these incentives have strengthened the economy or improved the quality of investment. Indeed, quite the contrary ... too much of British investment has been made because the tax allowances make it look profitable rather than because it would be truly productive. We need investment decisions based on future market assessments not future tax assessments."

However, it was a lament which acted as a prelude for a fundamental restructuring of the capital allowances system brought about initially by the Finance Act 1984. The general policy was to phase out the generous first year and initial allowances and to provide, thereafter, for the writing down of such capital expenditure solely on the basis of writing-down allowances applicable over a number of years and at rates which bore some resemblance to actual depreciation. Broadly, this policy has been maintained to the present day, although first year and initial allowances were briefly resurrected in respect of machinery, plant and industrial buildings for one year beginning on November 1, 1992.

We will now look at allowances on plant and machinery, and then (much more briefly) at some other allowances.

Allowances on Plant and Machinery   8–03

Neither machinery nor plant are defined in the tax legislation, and it is often a matter of some difficulty to decide whether a particular item is entitled to an allowance. The meaning to be given to the word plant has been particularly problematic and no attempt was made to codify it in the Rewrite Bill. This is typified by Parliament's enactment in 1994 (see Schedule AA1 to the Capital Allowances Act 1990, inserted by section 117 of the Finance Act 1994) of a rule that buildings and structures *cannot* qualify as plant (subject to the proviso that buildings and structures already so qualifying would continue to do so). The Schedule sets out those individual items or assets which fall with these expressions and which *cannot* qualify as plant. But, interestingly, it also lists items or assets which although within the definition of these words may nevertheless qualify as plant. In respect of an item in the latter category, it is open to the taxpayer to establish in the light of the meaning given to plant by the courts that it does in fact qualify. It is to the approach of the courts that we now look.

It is an interesting fact that the case most often cited as a starting point for judicial statements about the meaning of plant is not a tax case at all, but a tort case. The case is *Yarmouth v. France* (1887), DC. A workman brought a claim under the

Employers' Liability Act 1880 for damages for injuries caused by a defect in his employer's "plant", namely a vicious horse. Lindley L.J. (in holding that the horse was plant) said:

" . . . in its ordinary sense [plant] includes whatever apparatus is used by a business man for carrying on his business—not his stock-in-trade, which he buys or makes for sale; but all goods and chattels, fixed or movable, live or dead, which he keeps for permanent employment in his business."

From that beginning a huge structure of case law has been built up as to what may constitute plant. The item must be a good or chattel; it must have some degree of durability; it must be an item *with* which a trade is carried on as distinct from an item which comprises part of the premises or setting *in* which it is carried on.

It is this latter distinction which has often been difficult to draw, although it is established that an item which becomes part of the premises in which the trade is carried on cannot be plant (except in those cases where the premises are themselves plant for example, *IRC Barclay, Curle & Co. Ltd* (1969), HL), and that this will be so even if the item also has a distinct business purpose, *e.g.* to embellish the premises with a view to pleasing and attracting customers. The determination of whether an item has become part of the premises depends on whether it is more appropriate to describe the item as having become part of the premises as opposed to having retained a separate identity. This is a matter of fact and degree, and a court may take into account whether the item retains visually a separate identity, the degree of permanence with which it is affixed, the incompleteness of the premises without it and the extent to which it was intended to be permanent. In *Wimpey v. Warland* (1989), CA, the court was concerned with whether various improvements including tiling on floors and walls, glass shop fronts, raised and mezzanine floors, staircases and false ceilings which were undertaken at the taxpayer's fast food restaurants were plant. It was conceded that the improvements were designed to attract potential customers and to provide a particular atmosphere which the taxpayer considered conducive to the meals served. Nevertheless, the Court of Appeal decided that the improvements were not plant as they had become part of the premises. In circumstances where items have not become part of the premises, it has been accepted by the courts that they may be plant if the taxpayer's business includes the provision of atmosphere and the items are designed to create that atmosphere (see *IRC v. Scottish and Newcastle*

Breweries (1982), HL); a possibility also countenanced by Schedule AA1 to the Capital Allowances Act 1990.

It is obviously easier to apply the ideas inherent in Lindley L.J.'s statement in *Yarmouth v. France* to a trade than to a profession, and in *Daphne v. Shaw* (1926) it was held that law books bought by a solicitor and used in his practice were not plant. However, 50 years later, in *Munby v. Furlong* (1977), CA, *Daphne v. Shaw* was overruled by the Court of Appeal. Mr Munby, a barrister, won his claim for capital allowances in respect of law reports and textbooks bought in his first year of practice. Lord Denning said:

> "Counsel for the Crown ... would confine a professional man's 'plant' to things used physically like a dentist's chair or an architect's table or, I suppose, the typewriter in a barrister's chambers; but, for myself, I do not think 'plant' should be confined to things which are used physically. It seems to me that on principle it extends to the intellectual storehouse which a barrister or a solicitor or any other professional man has in the course of carrying on his profession."

Lord Denning divided what he called "a lawyer's library" into three parts: first, a set of law reports; secondly, textbooks; thirdly, periodicals, including current issues of law reports.[1] Expenditure on this last group was, said Lord Denning, revenue expenditure; expenditure on the first two groups was capital expenditure, and qualified for capital allowances.

Claiming allowances

8–04

If an item constitutes either machinery or plant, capital allowances may be available to a trader who has incurred capital expenditure on acquiring that item wholly and exclusively for the purposes of his trade[2] and where as a result of that expenditure the item belongs to the trader (see section 24 of the Capital Allowances Act 1990). The meaning of the phrase "wholly and exclusively" has been considered in Chapter 5, although it might be useful to add that where capital expenditure is incurred for the acquisition of plant or machinery to be used partly for trade and partly for other purposes the system of apportionment in section 79 of the Capital Allowances Act 1990 may be applied. The word

---

[1] To which might be added now computer software. Capital expenditure in respect of which may qualify for capital allowances under Capital Allowances Act 1990, s. 67A.

[2] For the availability of capital allowances in respect of capital expenditure by a trader on machinery or plant used otherwise than in the course of his trade, see Capital Allowances Act 1990, s. 61.

"belongs" has an extended meaning for these purposes. Thus, an item of machinery or plant may be deemed to belong to a person even though technically it belongs to another! This is best explained by the following example. Where a lessee of a building incurs capital expenditure on the provision of machinery or plant, which he is required to provide under the terms of his lease, for the purposes of a trade carried on by him (in circumstances where that machinery or plant is not installed or fixed so as to become part of the building or land) then the machinery or plant will be deemed to belong to him and in respect of which he may claim capital allowances (see section 61(4) of the Capital Allowances Act 1990).

8–05   **Using allowances**

Finally, before we look at how allowances for expenditure on machinery or plant work, we must mention the methods of using the allowances. As we saw at the beginning of this chapter, one of the principal attractions of the system of allowances which operated before the changes introduced by the Finance Act 1984, was the opportunity for a trader, who was subject to income tax, to use capital allowances, particularly in the year of purchase, as a *deduction from profits*. Originally, this method of using capital allowances was adopted because it was considered inappropriate to treat the capital allowances of an individual trader as *expenses* in view of the complications arising from the fact that trading profits were taxed on a preceding year basis. However, now these complications are a thing of the past. Consequently, capital allowances are no longer a deduction from profits but treated as a trading expense in the computation of profits. This does not mean, however, that capital allowances are to be equated with revenue expenditure. Substantial differences, which emphasise the continued importance of distinguishing between revenue and capital expenditure, remain. Thus, for example, in the computation of profits, allowable revenue expenditure may be generally set off in full and at once against trading income, whereas this is certainly not true of capital expenditure qualifying for writing-down allowances which must be spread over several years (see below).

8–06   *Allowances*

For many years, there were two kinds of allowances on plant and machinery known as first year and writing-down allowances. However, first year allowances are not always available. When first year allowances are available they operate in tandem with writing-down allowances. But, as we have already seen, the applicability of a writing-down allowance is dependent on the extent to which a business is entitled to or utilises a first year allowance.

A first-year allowance is a percentage (up to 100 per cent in some cases) of the qualifying expenditure incurred by the tax-payer on the plant or machinery in the year in which the capital expenditure is incurred. It is subject both to the same conditions as writing-down allowances and (usually) additional conditions designed to secure a focused economic objective.

Writing-down Allowances   8–07

Where a person carrying on a trade incurs capital expenditure on the provision of an item of machinery or plant wholly and exclusively for the purposes of the trade and in consequence of that expenditure the item belongs to him a writing-down allow-ance may be available on a 25 per cent per annum reducing balance basis. A writing-down allowance may also be claimed by a person who is exercising a profession and by the holder of an office or employment who purchases an item of machinery or plant "necessarily provided for use in the performance of his duties".

A trader may claim a writing-down allowance at the rate of 25 per cent year by year. Suppose X buys a machine in year one for £1,600. X can have an allowance of 25 per cent of £1,600 = £400. This leaves a balance of £1,200. In year two X can have an allowance of 25 per cent of £1,200 = £300. In year three X can have an allowance of 25 per cent of (£1,200–£300) £900 = £225. And so on in accordance with this reducing balance basis. The £675 at the end of year three is commonly called the "written-down value" of the machine. The legislation calls it the "qualifying expenditure". It is equal to the original expenditure *less* the allowances already given, so it is the amount which "qualifies" for further allowances in the future.

Pooling   8–08

All items of machinery and plant belonging to a trader are treated as being in one "pool", except where the item is expressly excluded, *e.g.* certain cars costing more than £12,000 (see sec-tions 34–36 of the Capital Allowances Act 1990), or where at the election of the taxpayer a short-life asset is not pooled in order to allow it to be written down over the period of its prospective useful life (for up to four years): section 37 of the Capital Allowances Act 1990.

Where there is a pool, the 25 per cent is calculated on the qualifying expenditure of the pool as a whole. Each new expenditure increases the qualifying expenditure in the pool. Each disposal of an item of machinery or plant reduces the qualifying expenditure in the pool by an amount equal to the disposal value of the item. If the price obtained for the sale of an item exceeds the amount of qualifying expenditure in the pool, a "balancing charge" is made on the taxpayer. Let us continue our example of X (above) to see how the pooling system works. During the period described above, X only had one machine. Suppose that later on X acquires several more machines, and that at the end of year six X has qualifying expenditure in the pool amounting to £6,000. In year seven X gets a writing-down allowance of 25 per cent of £6,000 = £1,500, leaving £4,500. In year eight X buys a new machine for £3,500. The qualifying expenditure becomes £8,000. In year nine X sells a machine for £8,400. A "balancing charge" is made on X in the sum of £400 because the sum received is larger than the qualifying expenditure. A balancing charge is (notionally) a receipt and therefore falls within the income tax net. If X were to sell the machine, not for £8,400 but for £7,600, there would be no balancing allowance; all that would happen would be that the qualifying expenditure in the pool would go down from £8,000 to £400. When X permanently discontinues the trade there will be a balancing charge or a balancing allowance depending on whether the proceeds of sale of all the machinery and plant in the pool amount to more than or less than the qualifying expenditure.

8–09   Industrial Buildings

Allowances are available for capital expenditure on "an industrial building or structure" to be occupied for the purposes of trade. The kinds of buildings covered are carefully defined (see section 18 of the Capital Allowances Act 1990) and are mainly confined to buildings, e.g. mills and factories employed in what might be described generically as productive industries. This tends to exclude commercial office buildings, residential buildings and retail trade buildings, although amendments over the years have seen the definition extended to cover, for example, hotels, commercial buildings in enterprise zones and workshops. Notwithstanding this detailed definition in section 18, definitional problems still exist as epitomised by *Copol Clothing Ltd v. Hindmarch* (1984) in the House of Lords, where an allowance was denied to a warehouse owner (see also *Carr v. Sayer* (1992)). Where capital expenditure is incurred on a building which is not wholly "industrial" as defined by section 18 allowances may still be claimed in respect of that expenditure provided not more than a quarter of the expenditure on the building is attributable to the "non-industrial" part (section 18(7)).

There are two kinds of allowances on buildings, known as *initial allowances* and *writing-down allowances*. Presently, initial allowances are unavailable (save the 100 per cent initial allowance available in respect of capital expenditure incurred on an industrial building in an enterprise zone) and have been so since 1986 except for a brief renaissance for one year beginning on November 1, 1992. The writing-down allowance is 4 per cent of the *original* expenditure, with no pooling, so that, the allowance will apply evenly over 25 years.

Agricultural Land and Buildings   8–10

The expenditure concerned here is expenditure on the construction of farmhouses, farm buildings, cottages "or other works". In the case of a farmhouse only a maximum of one-third of the expenditure qualifies for the allowance.

The allowance comprises a writing-down allowance of 4 per cent, which, as with the Industrial Buildings allowance, allows a total write-off over a period of 25 years.

Other Capital Expenditure   8–11

The other kinds of capital allowance listed at the beginning of this chapter are merely noted here. But it is, perhaps, apposite to add in passing that, notwithstanding the generally diminished importance of first year or initial allowances since the middle of the 1980s, it is still possible, in some instances, to enjoy capital allowances which write off capital expenditure in one year (see, for example, the 100 per cent capital allowance available for scientific research).

CHAPTER 9

TRADING LOSSES

9–01   *THE TREATMENT OF LOSSES*

This chapter is concerned with losses arising in a trade or profession. This is because, unlike losses arising under Case VI, or under Schedule A, these losses can be set off against taxable income from other sources. The tax position of a trade or profession is calculated by subtracting from the income the relevant expenses. If that calculation leaves a credit balance there is a taxable profit. But if it leaves a minus quantity there is a loss. Thus far, a loss is calculated in just the same way as a profit is calculated. In particular a trader cannot claim for tax purposes to have made a loss merely because a loss is made on one trans-action. For example, if a builder undertakes to build a house for £75,000 and in the event it costs him £80,000 to build the house, he cannot claim to have made a loss of £5,000. What matters is the overall relationship of trading income and expenses through-out a whole year's operation of the trade.

There are four main ways in which relief for losses may be given: set-off against general income and capital gains; carry-forward against subsequent profits; carry-back of terminal losses; and a special mode of relief for losses in the early years of a trade. We will look at these in turn.

9–02   **Set-off Against General Income and Capital Gains**

By section 380 of the Taxes Act a person who sustains a loss in any trade or profession carried on by him either solely or in partnership may make a claim for relief. The relief works by way of setting off the loss in the trade, etc., against profits in some other trade or indeed against any income of the claimant in the same year. If the claimant's income of that same year is not sufficient to absorb the whole of the loss then the balance may be set off against the claimant's income of the preceding year.

The amount of the loss for the purposes of section 380 gen-erally includes capital allowances which are *treated* as trading expenses (see section 140 of the Capital Allowances Act 1990).

By section 384 a loss is not available for relief under section 380 unless it is shown that the trade was being carried on on a commercial basis and with a view to the realisation of profits. And by section 397 an even more stringent rule applies to farming and market gardening, namely that a loss cannot be relieved under section 380 if in each of the prior five years a loss was incurred. The point of these two sections (ss.384 and 397) is to exclude from loss relief against other income "hobby-trading" and particularly "hobby-farming". Hobby-farming is a pretty popular activity. It arises in this way: a person with a substantial income (say a stockbroker) buys a farm and spends a great deal of money on building it up as a capital asset. If he could contrive to have no farming profits because of vast capital expenditure and set the farming losses against his stockbroking profits he could lay a gigantic nest-egg largely at the expense of the Revenue. The Revenue has disobliged.

A claim for relief under section 380 against general income may be extended to the claimant's capital gains of the same year (see section 72 of the Finance Act 1991). However, the loss must be set off against the general income before relief can be given against capital gains. If the claimant's capital gains of that year are not sufficient to absorb the whole of the loss then the balance may be set off against the claimant's capital gains of the preceding year (this also applies to existing businesses during the transitional year).

Carry-Forward Against Subsequent Profits 9–03

Section 385 provides for the carrying forward of a loss in one year against the profits in a subsequent year of the same trade or profession. Notice that it must be the *same* trade, etc. In that respect this relief is totally different from the relief under section 380. A loss can be carried forward under section 385 indefinitely, but it must be set off against the first subsequent assessment and then, so far as it remains not fully relieved, against the next assessment, and so on. If a loss has been partially relieved under some other provision (*e.g.* section 380), the unrelieved amount may be carried forward. Or a trader can ignore section 380 and go straight for section 385 relief.

It may happen that the profits of a particular year are not big enough to absorb a loss which is being carried forward into that year. In that case, interest or dividends (if there are any) arising to the trader will be treated as though they were trading profits. This point needs a bit of explanation. If interest or dividends which have borne tax by deduction are received by a trader they are not included in the computation of his profits under Case I. The present point (in section 385(4)) is that those receipts can nevertheless be *treated as* profits, and a carried-forward loss can be relieved against them by means of a repayment of tax.

Another point which may arise under section 385 relates to payments out by the trader under section 349. (See Chapter 11, below.) Section 349 applies where an annual payment is made otherwise than wholly out of profits brought into charge to income tax. This would be so, for example, where the payer had no profits in the year in which he made the payment. Under section 350 the payer would then have to pay over to the Revenue the tax deducted in making the annual payment. The point here is that section 387 says that in such a case, provided the payment was made wholly and exclusively for the purposes of the trade (or profession) the grossed-up amount of the payment can be treated as a loss and given relief under section 385 (We say "grossed-up" because the section 387 says "the amount on which tax has been paid".)

Another point on section 385 concerns interest, meaning payments of interest outwards. If a trader makes a payment of interest that will, prima facie, be an expense of his trading. But if he has an overall loss the interest will not get relieved. And if he has insufficient other income, the interest will not get relieved under section 353 of the Taxes Act either. The present point is that by section 390 (of the Taxes Act) the amount of the interest payment may be carried forward under section 385 "as if it were a loss."

The general rules for section 385 relief are that not only must the prior loss and the subsequent profit be incurred in the same trade, but also the claimant must be the person who incurred the loss. However, there is an important exception to these general rules in section 386 which provides that where a business carried on by an individual (or individuals) is transferred to a company, the individual may claim to set off under section 385 any losses which he incurred before the transfer against income derived by him from the company after the transfer. The consideration for the transfer of the business must consist solely or mainly of the allotment of shares in the company. The income from the company may take the form of director's remuneration or salary or dividends. Further, a partner does not usually lose the relief available under section 385 when there is a change in the membership of a partnership, *e.g.* when a partner joins or leaves the partnership. This is so because a partner is deemed to be a sole trader/professional in respect of his share of the partnership profit or loss (see further paragraph 12–06). Therefore, his ability to carry forward his share of any such loss against his share of the partnership profits from the same trade or profession in subsequent years is normally unaffected by a change within the partnership (save where the actual trade/profession is subsequently carried on by him alone, see below).

Carry-Back of Terminal Losses   9–04

By section 388 terminal losses (meaning losses outstanding at the termination of a business) may be set off against the profits of a trade or profession in the year of cessation and for the three years of assessment preceding the year in which the cessation or discontinuance occurs.

If the business is carried on by a partnership the position is as follows. A partner may claim relief for terminal losses when his deemed sole and separate trade, etc., is discontinued. Broadly, this occurs when he ceases to be a partner, where the actual trade or profession is subsequently carried on by him alone, or when the actual trade or profession ceases. Also on what one might call a statutory discontinuance caused by a change of partners. In the latter case the retiring partner can have relief but the continuing partners cannot. This is fair, because (as we have just seen) they can, despite the discontinuance, have relief against subsequent profits.

Losses in the Early Years   9–05

The three heads we have so far looked at provide for relief for losses by set-off against any income or capital gains of the same or the preceding year; against profits of the same trade, etc., in any following year; and (for terminal losses) against profits of the same trade in the year of cessation and for three previous years. This relief, which is provided for in section 381, works by way of a set-off of losses in the year of commencement of a trade or profession and/or in the next three years of assessment against any income of the taxpayer for the three years of assessment preceding that in which the loss is sustained. The relief applies to sole individuals and to partners. It does not apply to companies. Of course, a new company would not have any previous income, so the possibility of this relief could not arise. But an existing company sometimes sets up a new trade; it will not qualify for this relief. There is a provision to exclude hobby-trading from the relief. This seems a wise precaution on the part of the Revenue. In genuine cases, however, section 381, in effect, provides a subsidy to a loss-making new business.

SAVINGS AND INVESTMENT INCOME

10–01   **TAXING UNEARNED INCOME**

This chapter deals with the untidiest and most confusing part of the income tax: its treatment of non-earned, non-business income. Taxation of savings and investments is untidy because the ways in which people save and invest have changed out of all recognition since the income tax was introduced, but the income tax rules have not kept pace with the changes. It is confusing because different governments based their approaches on different priorities for encouraging savings and for taxing "unearned" income. Thus, while some forms of unearned income are exempt from tax, other forms are subject to deduction at source even if paid by one private individual to another.

The main forms of savings and investment income of individuals are: pensions or annuities paid after retirement; dividends or other distributions paid in respect of company shares; interest on loans, including government stock and company debentures; annuities (both purchased and unpurchased); royalties (for example, for the use of intellectual property rights or for mineral rights); and annual payments made under trusts, covenants, agreements or court orders (for example, payments following a divorce or for a child, or to or by a charity). In reality, there may be little difference to the investor in receiving income from an investment or a capital gain from it, but the tax rules treat most forms of capital gain entirely separately from income. Here we are concerned only with income.

Pensions paid from savings made through a pension scheme are usually treated as deferred earnings (see paragraph 6–20). Dividends and distributions received by individuals in respect of shares in British companies are taxed under Schedule F. This is noted below. Dividends, interest and other income from foreign sources is taxed under Cases IV and V of Schedule D and we deal with that later. Interest from government stock, such as gilt-edged securities, used to be dealt with under Schedule C, but there are now no special rules for this kind of income. The main income tax rules, covering interest, annuities, royalties and annual payments, are in Case III of Schedule D. Capital gains received from investments or savings are taxed under the capital gains tax.

The rules for non-earned income of companies are different to those for individuals. Companies do not pay tax on dividends or distributions received from other British companies. Most other receipts from investments are taxed under the "loan relationship" rules which apply in broadly the same way to income and capital receipts, to business income from loans and returns on investments, and to both local and foreign source income.

Case III   10–02

At first glance, Case III looks even more of a rag bag than Case VI. According to section 18(3) of the Taxes Act, it covers: interest, annuities, "other annual payments", discounts and income from public revenue securities. Sections 119 and 120 of the Act add mining rents and royalties and the Finance Act 1996 brings certain discounted securities within Case III.[1]

We concentrate on the taxation of interest, annuities and annual payments. These are examples of what has been called by judges "pure profit income". It is pure profit in the sense that there are no expenses to set against it. This can, perhaps, be best appreciated by contrasting pure profit income with other kinds of income.

Trading income is the best contrast. A sum of money received by a trader in the course of the trade is a credit item in calculating his profits but it is not in itself in full a profit. Against it there have to be set various expenses; the cost of buying the thing which he has now sold and the overhead expenses of the selling organisation. In short, the receipt is not pure profit.

For many years, a particular feature of the taxation of annuities and other annual payments has been the operation of special rules (now contained in sections 348 and 349 of the Taxes Act) by virtue of which the payer deducts tax when making the payment, so that the recipient (payee) receives the income net of tax, *i.e.* a withholding tax is applied. However, the importance of these special rules has been considerably diminished, although the special rules still have significance.

In our consideration of the taxation of interest, annuities and other annual payments, the starting point must be to ascertain what these terms mean.

---

[1] For corporation tax purposes, non-trading profits from loan relationships are also taxed under the rules of Case III of Schedule D.

Interest has been defined as "payment by time for the use of money". There was an interesting discussion about what can and what cannot count as interest in the avoidance case of *Cairns v. Macdiarmid* (1983), CA. Interest on a judgment is taxable. At one time there seemed to be a doubt as to whether interest awarded by a judge as an addition to damages was truly income and so taxable. Now it is well settled that such interest is taxable. There is one exception, by statute. Section 329 of the Taxes Act declares that interest on damages for personal injuries or death under the Law Reform (Miscellaneous Provisions) Act 1934 is "not to be regarded as income for any income tax purpose".

An **annuity** is an income which is paid year by year. Many annuities arise under a will or similar instrument of gift. But it is possible to buy an annuity whereby a capital sum is used to pay for a regular income .

An **annual payment** is much more difficult to define. Not the least part of the difficulty is that tradition forces us to define the "income" as "payment". We can reduce the difficulty if we confine ourselves to defining such an annual payment *as falls within Case III of Schedule D.*

10–03   Taxing Annual Payments

In some ways, this has been facilitated by changes incorporated into section 347A of the Taxes Act. The effect of section 347A, subject to the exceptions set out below, is to deny any effect for income tax purposes to many annual payments made by individuals[2]—effectively to ignore such payments for tax purposes and in respect of which, therefore, Case III of Schedule D is redundant. It might be wondered what prompted such a dramatic step. The answer lies in the fact that before this change was made, and notwithstanding the existence of fairly wide ranging anti-avoidance rules which sought to counteract tax advantages which might be gained from the use of covenants and other income settlements,[3] this was a fruitful area for tax saving. Thus, in appropriate circumstances, an individual payer could treat the payment as a charge on his income and deduct it in computing total income, and the payee might not be liable to tax and seek to

---

[2] "Individual" has a limited meaning. For example, a trustee is not an individual for these purposes. Therefore, a beneficiary of a discretionary trust who receives income payments from the trustees will be assessed under Case III of Schedule D.

[3] For the present anti-avoidance rules pertaining to income settlements *not* caught by section 347A, see below, Chapter 11.

recover the tax paid by the payer from the Revenue. The other reason why this kind of device is much less useful now is the reduction in income tax rates. And where section 347A applies these potential tax savings are no longer possible. A payment shall not be a charge on the payer's income (and that his income shall be computed without any deduction being made on account of the payment) and the payment shall not form part of the income of the person to whom it is made if caught by the section.

Section 347A is stated expressly *not* to apply to:

(1) a payment of interest;
(2) a payment made for bona fide commercial reasons in connection with the individual's trade, profession or vocation, *e.g.* a payment under a partnership retirement annuity;
(3) a payment made for a non-taxable consideration (see section 125(1) of the Taxes Act).

Consequently, such payments continue to be taxed under Case III of Schedule D.

The nature of annual payments   10–04

The above discussion gives an insight into some of the annual payments which might, notwithstanding section 347A, still *fall within Case III of Schedule D*; nevertheless it begs the question what *is* an annual payment? The courts have identified the following five characteristics of an annual payment.

First, the **ejusdem generis** rule of interpretation applies. The context is highly important. Section 18 says: "Case III—tax in respect of— ... any interest of money, whether yearly or otherwise, or any annuity or other annual payment ... ". A payment, to be an "other annual payment", must be the same kind of payment as is interest and an annuity. Secondly, the payment must be made under a **binding legal obligation**. A gift, even if it be in money and even if it be one of a series, is not an annual payment. But it is important to appreciate that a payment under a covenant is an annual payment. How can this be, since a covenanted payment is (most commonly) given for no consideration? The answer is that a covenant is a promise under seal, and the seal creates a legal obligation.

Thirdly, the payment must have the quality of **recurrence**. But this requirement is not very exacting. Payments which are variable or contingent are not prevented from being recurrent. Also a

155

payment does not need to be made only once a year; weekly or monthly payments can be annual payments provided they may continue for more than a year.

Fourthly, the payment must be, in the hands of the recipient, **pure profit income** and not a receipt which enters into the computation of profit. In *IRC v. National Book League* (1957), CA, the League (a charity) decided to raise the membership subscription except that those members who entered into seven-year covenants could continue to pay their subscriptions at the existing rate. Over 2,000 members executed deeds of covenant, and deducted tax in making the covenanted payments. The League claimed repayment of the tax from the Revenue, arguing that the payments were annual payments within Case III. The argument was not upheld. The subscriptions were not pure profit income of the League, because the League had to provide benefits, such as the amenities of a club, in return for the subscriptions. *The National Book League* case left a few questions unresolved because the judges propounded alternative tests for deciding what was pure profit income. However, in *Campbell v. IRC* (1970), HL, the House of Lords (although *obiter*) had another look at the question. They adopted the phrase "pure profit income" to describe Case III, but were at pains to emphasise that non-commercial benefits resulting from a payment, such as having one's name printed in an advertisement or receiving a copy of an annual report, did not count.

Fifthly, the payment must be of the nature of **income, and not capital**, in the hands of the recipient. The point arises when A sells property to B in return for instalment payments. Are the instalments income or capital? A payment may be of a revenue nature from the point of view of the payer and yet may be of a capital nature in the hands of the payee. If it is of a capital nature in the hands of the payee it cannot be an "annual payment" even from the point of view of the payer. If it is of an income nature in the hands of the payee it may or may not be of a revenue nature from the point of view of the payer. In *Vestey v. IRC* (1962) Lord Vestey sold a block of shares valued at £2 million for the sum of £5.5 million payable without interest by 125 yearly instalments of £44,000. It was held that the instalments should be dissected into capital and interest, and that the interest element was taxable income of the payee.

In *IRC v. Church Commissioners for England* (1977), HL the Church Commissioners sold to their tenant the reversion on a lease in consideration of rent charges payable annually for 10 years and totalling £96,000 a year. The tenant was not willing to buy for a single lump sum. The House of Lords held that these payments were pure income in the hands of the payee and were not to be dissected into capital and interest elements. The church commissioners, being a charity, were entitled to repayment of the tax which had been deducted by the payer from each payment. (The same rent-charges had previously been held—also by the House of Lords—to be capital payments from the point of view of the payer: *IRC v. Land Securities Investment Trust Ltd* (1969), HL.)

Sections 348 and 349   10–05

As we have seen interest, annuities and certain other annual payments fall within Case III of Schedule D. Broadly, as a result of changes incorporated into section 64 of the Taxes Act, the basis of assessment under Case III of Schedule D is now on a current year basis.

But often such payments are not directly assessed under Case III because they are within the special rules mentioned at the beginning of the chapter and as such are subjected to a withholding tax, namely deduction of tax at source under section 348 or section 349 of the Taxes Act. Sections 348 and 349 apply to annuities and certain other annual payments, *e.g.* to a payment made for bona fide commercial reasons in connection with a trade, profession or vocation annuity and also (with slightly different rules) to patent royalties and certain mining royalties.

The distinction between section 348 and 349 is as follows. Section 348 deals with payments which are made wholly out of profits or gains brought into charge to income tax, whereas section 349 deals with payments which are not made, or not wholly made, out of profits or gains brought into charge to income tax. Notice that the phrase is "income tax", not just "tax": so a payment made by a United Kingdom company cannot fall within section 348 because a United Kingdom company pays corporation tax, not income tax. This point is affirmed by section 7(1) of the Taxes Act.

The basic idea behind section 348 is that the payer has alienated part of his income. If the payer promises to pay the payee £1,000 a year in circumstances where the section applies, the law regards that £1,000 as being the payee's income and not the payer's. So the payee should pay the tax on it and not the payer. The section empowers the payer to deduct tax at the basic rate from the £1,000 and pay the payee the net amount. The amount deducted is treated as tax paid by the payee. As he is paying out of his taxable income, the payer keeps the amount deducted to recoup himself for the tax which he has paid (or will pay) on the

£1,000. This is a classic example, indeed *the* classic example (it has been in the tax system since 1803) of a withholding tax operating. The payer is acting as a collector (unpaid) for the Revenue. The *machinery* of section 348 is that the payer pays the tax on the amount of the payment and recoups himself by deducting tax from the payment. The *effect* is that the payee in reality bears the tax and the payer does not.

If, on the other hand, the payer pays the payee not out of taxable income but out of capital, then a new income springs up in the hands of the payee which has not been taxed. So the payer deducts tax (at basic rate) from his payment to the payee, but this time section 349 applies and the payer *must* deduct tax in making payment to the payee and he *must* hand over the amount deducted to the Revenue, though the Revenue has an alternative power to assess the payee. In the section 348 situation, by contrast the payer *need not* deduct tax from his payment to the payee; but he may, and if he has any sense he will, in order to recoup himself for the tax he has to pay. If the payer does not make a deduction from his payment to the payee and if, for extraneous reasons, the Revenue cannot get the tax out of the payer they can make an assessment on the payee.

Another difference between the sections is that under section 348 (out of taxable income) tax is to be deducted at the basic rate applicable to the year of assessment when the payment is due, whereas under section 349 (not out of taxable income) tax is to be deducted at the basic rate applicable to the year of assessment when the payment is actually made (see *IRC v. Crawley* (1987)).

If the payee is not liable to tax at the basic rate, the whole or part of the amount deducted may be reclaimed from the Revenue. If the payee is liable to the higher rate of tax, as may be so, for example, in the case of a person in receipt of a payment made for a bona fide commercial reason etc., the annual payment counts as part of his total income and for this purpose the net amount received must be grossed up.

If the payer is liable to the higher rate of tax, the cost of the payment can be set against total income for the purposes of the higher rate as well as basic rate.

10–06 ## Why worry about annual payments?

We have spent a considerable time on the complexities of annual payments and collection of tax at source for several reasons. It illustrates some fundamental issues about levying income tax in Britain. First, the system must deal fairly with transfers of income under trusts and covenants but must also seek for that reason to curb avoidance. Secondly, the aim is to collect tax at source where possible, but that is not always easy given the flexibility of British trust laws. Third, there is no general statutory provision to curb abuse of the tax law. The case of *IRC v. Duke of Westminster* (1931) shows that a valid covenant can transfer income effectively from anyone to anyone for income tax purposes in the absence of statutory provisions.

As a result, covenants have been used widely to make tax-efficient transfers of income. It is necessary to understand this in order to understand also the measures used to stop such wide use of covenants. We see in Chapter 11 the general rules now preventing effect being given for income tax purposes to covenants diverting income, for example, to a taxpayer's young children or by way of gift. Before the current rules applied, covenant were used very widely. Parents, funded student children through university most effectively by covenants of income. Divorced spouses paid maintenance to ex-spouses or separated children through covenanted payments, and whole books were devoted to the best ways of doing it. Maintenance covenants ceased to have all effect for tax purposes finally only in 2000. And until 2000, when section 41 of the Finance Act 2000 took effect, covenants were the standard way to make larger gifts to charities. (They were used in 1999 by 1.6 million people, but have since been replaced by a simpler system—see below). In each case the sums covenanted were tax-deductible at the highest rate of tax of the payer, so a tax payer could for example spend £60 on giving someone else £100.

Annuities 10–07

Many annuities arise under a will or similar instrument of gift. These are taxed under sections 348 and 349 or Case III as "pure profit income". But it is perfectly possible to buy an annuity "in the market". These purchased life annuities, or some of them, have a special rule applying to them. The relevant section is section 656 of the Taxes Act. The capital content of each periodic payment to the annuitant is exempt from income tax. The capital is found (putting it broadly) by dividing the purchase price of the annuity by the normal expectation of life of the annuitant, calculated at the date when the annuity begins. Once the calculation has been made the figure remains constant for every year. Income tax is charged each year on the amount by which the annuity payment exceeds this capital content, whether or not the annuitant survives for the period of normal expectation.

10–08 Interest

Here we are concerned with interest from the point of view of the payee. We saw at the beginning of this chapter that interest is taxable under Case III of Schedule D. And later on we saw that interest used to be collected at source under the scheme governed by sections 348 and 349. That was so until 1969, but now interest is not within that scheme. There is, however, a somewhat similar provision in section 349(2) which provides for deduction at source; from 1996–97, tax is deducted at the lower rate. But we want to emphasise that section 349(2) only applies to certain kinds of interest and that most interest does not come within this provision. However, as we shall see, sections 477A and 480A of the Taxes Act require collection at source of tax on interest of many kinds, tax is deducted at the lower rate here also. All interest is in principle chargeable under Case III, but it may be assessed under Case I where interest is an income item in the computation of the profits of a trade, or it may be collected at source under section 349(2) of the Taxes Act.

Section 349(2) applies only to "yearly" interest, not to "short" interest, meaning interest where the obligation to pay it is to continue for less than a year. And section 349(2) only applies to certain kinds of yearly interest, as follows: (a) interest paid by a company or local authority (in each case, otherwise than in a fiduciary or representative capacity; that is, where the payer is a trustee or is paying on behalf of someone else); (b) interest paid by or on behalf of a partnership of which a company is a member; (c) interest paid by any person to another person whose usual place of abode is outside the United Kingdom. The reason for (a) and (b) is that companies are under a special system of taxation, and the reason for (c) is that the government wants to be sure of getting the tax before the money goes outside its grasp. There are important exceptions whereby section 349(2) does not apply even though the interest falls within (a), (b) or (c). These include: interest payable in the United Kingdom on an advance from a bank carrying on a bona fide banking business in the United Kingdom, and interest paid by such a bank in the ordinary course of that business. The Finance Act 2000 added other exceptions to stop deductions applying to the London financial markets.

The limited nature of section 349(2) is made good by sections 477A and 480A of the Taxes Act to the extent that section 477A applies to interest paid by building societies whilst section 480A applies to interest paid by banks, local authorities and the Post Office (National Girobank), on "relevant deposits". These deposits cover money deposited on demand or on such terms as may be agreed subject to an upper limit of £50,000 and other exceptions (as where the depositor is itself a bank).

There are also several forms of interest on which income tax is not deducted at source. These include forms of government savings such as National Saving Certificates, and interest received from ISAs (individual savings accounts, see below). Most of these forms of income are also exempted from tax on the recipient, so are preferred forms of savings.

Further, individuals pay a lower basic rate of income tax on most forms of interest than the rate they pay on earnings. Section 1A of the Taxes Act sets the basic rate on interest chargeable under Case III at 20 per cent (in 2000–01), with the starting rate of 10 per cent also applying. This lower rate does not apply to annuities or other annual payments to which Case III also applies.

Taxation of intellectual property   10–09

As the Revenue itself said in 2000: "our current rules governing the tax treatment of intangible assets are complex, inconsistent and out of date." This quotation is from a Revenues technical paper, *Reform of the Taxation of Intellectual Property* (2000). Consultation was still continuing at the time of writing. It is clear that reform is needed and will occur, but the form it will take is not yet decided. Before reform, royalties from all patents and some other forms of intellectual property were taxable under Case III. Patent royalties, but not royalties for other forms of intellectual property, could also be caught by section 348(2) or section 349(1)(b). Copyright royalties were treated as Case II income if received by the author but as investment income taxable under Case III or Case VI if received, for example, by the author's widow. There was considerable inconsistency in handling lump sum payments for the purchase or use of intellectual property both in the hands of the recipient and as regards capital allowances that the payer might claim. Yet other rules applied to other forms of tangible assets.

Reform is needed especially because of the extent to which a value of a transaction such as the sale of assets can be shifted into the intellectual property licenses necessary to use those assets. For example, much machinery is of little value without the software systems that control the electronics which, in turn, control the machines. This process has been called the "dematerialisation of wealth". In such cases, a buyer buy "bundled rights" to both machinery and software, with much of the value being in the intellectual property rights. New rules are needed to unbundle these rights in a way that could not have been foreseen when the present rules were written. A favoured proposal for reform is adoption of an accounts-based approach that takes all relevant receipts and expenditures into account for tax purposes as they are taken into account under a standard accounting approach.

10–10   Dividends and distributions

An individual receiving a dividend or other distribution from a British company is liable to pay tax on that distribution under Schedule F. Under a former tax system known as ACT (advance corporation tax), companies paid an amount of ACT to the Revenue when paying a dividend. The shareholder was credited with an equivalent amount of income tax. The effect was that the basic rate income tax payer paid no further income tax on dividends. Only higher rate taxpayers were liable. ACT is now being phased out. While this takes place, shareholders are entitled to a limited tax credit (10 per cent of the dividend in 2000).

Individual shareholders are subject to a special lower rate of income tax, the "Schedule F ordinary rate". That rate is 10 per cent in 2000–01. The effect of this special rate, when taken with the residual tax credit, is to cancel out Schedule F liability for a basic rate taxpayer. There is also a special Schedule F higher rate. This is 32.5 per cent in 2000, and has the same effect as if the basic rate were 22 per cent and the higher rate were 40 per cent.

Individuals can avoid all income tax if they hold their shares through a tax preferred scheme (for example, see paragraph 6–16).

10–11   Tax-preferred savings schemes

Governments have for some time sought to encourage savings by individuals by providing tax-preferred savings schemes. A new set of schemes were launched in April 1999. They are known as ISAs—individual savings accounts. A taxpayer may save up to £7,000 a year in an ISA (in 2000–01). This is invested in shares or some forms of loan or life assurance. Any dividends or interest payments are tax-free. Details of schemes are widely available from banks, building societies and other savings institutions. Their practical importance is considerable. Over £17 billion was invested in 6.7 million ISAs in the first nine months of the tax year 1999–2000.

10–12   Charities

It may appear to add to the untidiness by including a note on charity payments and income in this chapter but, until reforms in

2000, many charity payments by individuals took place in the form of covenants (and therefore as annual payments) to which section 348 usually applied. Significant reforms implemented in the Finance Act 2000 abolish the need for covenants, but still give generous tax support of gifts to charities. Under amendments introduced by section 38 to 45 of the Finance Act 2000, any gift of cash or in kind to a charity is treated as made net of tax at the basic rate. The charity receiving the gift can claim the notional deduction of tax back, if the giver is a taxpayer. If the giver gives through a payroll deduction scheme run by the giver's employer, the government adds another 10 per cent to the amount given in addition to the rebated tax. And if the giver is liable to higher rate tax, then the amount of the gift can be deducted for higher rate tax purposes as well. These are considerable incentives to charitable giving.

THE TAXATION OF TRUSTS AND ESTATES

We need to look now at the way in which the income tax system works in relation to trusts and to the estates of deceased individuals.

In the general law—quite apart from tax law—there is a fundamental difference between the position of a person entitled to income of a residuary estate and a person entitled to income arising under a trust. The former is not entitled to anything until it is paid to him or at least appropriated to him: see *Corbett v. IRC* (1938), CA. The latter is entitled to his share of the income of the trust from its inception, or, more strictly, to his share of the income of the investments which constitute the trust fund: see *Baker v. Archer-Shee* (1927), HL.

We will look at the two situations in turn.

11–01   **Trust Income**

The existence of trusts causes great difficulties for tax legislators and for everyone else connected with tax, including students of tax law. Tax law would be very much simpler if there were no trusts. Lest that statement sound naive it may be pointed out that trusts fulfil a prominent role in tax planning. Nevertheless, many civil law countries do not recognise the concept of trusts at all. The subject is additionally complicated in Britain because Scottish trusts law is as developed as, but is markedly different from, English trusts law. Scottish lawyers rightly resent the fact that the (English-drafted) provisions in tax statutes are often passed in ignorance of Scottish law, although the provisions are supposed to work evenly on both sides of the border. But even confining ourselves to English law, the difficulties in squaring our trusts laws and our tax laws are considerable: for inheritance tax they have proved fiendish.

For income tax there is a kind of two-tier system: to some extent income tax is charged on the trustees; to some extent it is charged on the beneficiary.

THE CHARGE ON THE TRUSTEES 11–02

Trustees are not "individuals" for the purposes of income tax, but they are "persons". Consequently they are liable to basic rate tax, for example, on the profits of a trade or Schedule A business carried on by them and, on the other hand, they are not entitled to any personal reliefs. Trustees are not liable to the higher rate of tax, again because they are not individuals and higher rate tax is charged only on individuals.

By section 686 of the Taxes Act a special rate of tax (known as the rate applicable to trusts) is charged on income arising to trustees if it is income which is to be accumulated or which is payable at discretion (whether or not the trustees have power to accumulate income). So, putting it broadly, the rate applicable to trusts is payable by accumulation trusts and discretionary trusts and by trusts which are subject to section 31 of the Trustee Act 1925. (That is the section which gives trustees power to apply income for the maintenance, education or benefit of an infant.) The rate applicable to trusts for 2000–01 is 34 per cent. Not the whole of the income is charged, because expenses of managing the trust are deductible in calculating the liability to tax which arises from the difference between the rate applicable to trusts and the lower rate (if the income is savings income) or basic rate if it is income other than savings income. There is also a special "Schedule F trust rate" of 25 per cent, applying to dividends (and their tax credits).

The trustees of a discretionary trust may be subject to a further charge to tax when they come to make a distribution of income to a beneficiary. Such a charge will arise if the rate of tax is higher in the year of distribution than it was in the year in which the income arose to the trustees. This matter is dealt with by section 687 of the Taxes Act.

THE CHARGE ON THE BENEFICIARY 11–03

A beneficiary's income from a trust forms part of total income for determining reliefs and the rate of tax. It would be nice and neat if one could say that one works out the beneficiary's tax bill and then gives a straight credit for the tax already paid by the trustees. Unfortunately this is not precisely so. There is a case called *Macfarlane v. IRC* (1929) (Ct. Sess.) which held that although trust expenses are not deductible in computing the trustees' income, they are deductible in computing the beneficiary's income. That position now, with the advent of the rate applicable to trusts, is more complicated, because although trust expenses are not deductible in computing the trust's liability to basic rate tax, they are deductible in computing the trust's liability to tax which arises from the difference between the rate applicable to trusts and the lower or basic rate. Indeed, to further compound this complication, such expenses must normally be set off, in the first instance, against savings income. However, one can say this: the tax charge on the beneficiary *takes into account* (to some extent) the tax already charged on the trustees!

Income to which a beneficiary is *entitled* forms part of total income whether or not it is received. This follows from the general principle stated above, namely that a beneficiary who is entitled at all is entitled from the very inception of the trust. Of course this principle does not apply to a discretionary trust; if there is a discretion whether to pay any particular beneficiary, there is no entitlement until the discretion is exercised. When a sum is actually paid to such a beneficiary that sum forms part of his total income and is taxed under Case III of Schedule D. Whether one is talking of a fixed trust or a discretionary trust, payments in kind may, just as much as money payments, constitute income. This would be so, for example of a right to occupy a house rent free.

A payment may perfectly well be income in the hands of a beneficiary, even although it is made out of the capital (and not the income) of the trust. However, a payment out of capital does not become income in the hands of a beneficiary simply because it is to be used for an income purpose by that beneficiary (see *Stevenson v. Wishart* (1987), CA.

An important tax point arises in connection with income which is accumulated by a trust. One has to make a distinction here between a vested interest and a contingent interest. This is a matter of general law rather than tax law and it involves some fairly complicated points But broadly the distinction is that a vested interest is one which (generally) cannot be upset, whereas a contingent interest is one which is dependent on some contingency happening. The clearest example is where a trust provides that X is to have a certain interest under the trust when he attains a certain age. As X may never attain that age the interest is until then contingent. When X has attained that age the interest becomes vested. (A person may attain a vested interest in income before attaining, or without ever attaining, a vested interest in the capital of the fund.) For a person who has a vested interest in the income of a trust, that income (as has been said above) forms part of total income, and that is so even if it is not in fact received. But for a person who has only a contingent interest, until that contingency occurs, the income of the trust is not income. It follows that if the trust's income is accumulated it is not his income and it does not become so even if the contingency occurs (*e.g.* attaining the age of 18) and the accumulations are paid. The payments reach the beneficiary as capital. The leading authority on this point is *Stanley v. IRC* (1944), CA.

Estate Income 11–04

What we are considering here is income arising during the period of administration of the estate of a deceased individual. When an individual dies the estate is administered by executors or administrators. The generic name for these is personal representatives; for tax purposes there is no need to distinguish between the two species.

As with trusts, so with estates, there is a kind of two-tier system of income tax. Personal representatives are like trustees in that they are chargeable to basic rate tax, are not chargeable to the higher rate of tax, and do not qualify for personal reliefs. In another respect, however, personal representatives differ from trustees; they are not chargeable to tax under the rate applicable to trusts (section 686(6)).

How is the beneficiary taxed? That depends on the nature of the benefit. If the will gives an annuity, the annuity payments are part of total income from the date of death. So far as legatees are concerned it is perhaps worth stating the fairly elementary point that a legacy as such is not subject to income tax because it is not income; it is capital. But a legatee may be entitled to interest or (in the case of a specific legacy) to income from the date of death. In those cases the legatee is chargeable to income tax on the interest or income.

Residuary beneficiaries

What we have to look at in more detail is the position of a residuary beneficiary. One has to distinguish between a beneficiary who has a limited interest in the residue of the estate and a beneficiary who has an absolute interest in the residue. A person has an absolute interest if he has an interest in the capital, and a person has a limited interest if he does not have an absolute interest. An example of a person with a limited interest is a person who gets a life tenancy. Everything that is paid to him by the personal representatives must be income for the simple reason that he is not entitled to any capital. Therefore very little complication arises in his case. Each sum that is paid to him during the administration counts (grossed-up) as part of his total income for the year of assessment when it is paid. At the end of the administration period any final payment is regarded as the income of the beneficiary in the year of assessment in which the administration ends.

A beneficiary who has an absolute interest has, by definition, an entitlement to capital. Therefore it is by no means certain that everything paid to him during the administration of the estate is income. To get at his tax liability the income element must be sorted out from the capital element. The first step is to calculate the "residuary income" of the estate for each year of assessment during the administration period. To arrive at residuary income the personal representatives are permitted to deduct certain management expenses. The residuary income of the estate is divided into a residuary income for each beneficiary according to his share. For example, if there are three absolute beneficiaries each with an equal share the residuary income of each is one-third of the residuary income of the estate. Then any sums which are paid to a beneficiary are treated as income for the year of assessment in which they are actually paid in so far as (grossed-up) they do not exceed his residuary income. In so far as they do exceed it they are treated as capital. Finally, if at the end of the administration the beneficiary has not received all the residuary income which is his due, the outstanding amount is regarded as having been paid immediately before the end of the administration period.

11–05   Anti-avoidance Rules

We must now consider the detailed rules relating to settlements in Part XV of the Taxes Act, which are intended to curb the use of settlements for tax avoidance. Section 660 G (1) of the Taxes Act provides that for the purposes of Part XV a settlement includes "any disposition, trust, covenant, agreement, arrangement or transfer of assets". Broadly speaking, this encompasses two types of settlement, namely, income settlements and capital settlements. An income settlement is a settlement which involves the transfer of income only, *e.g.* a covenant. A capital settlement is a settlement which involves the transfer of income-producing property, *e.g.* a trust. An income settlement is the handing-over of fruits; a capital settlement is the handing-over of a fruit tree. An income settlement may provide for payment to trustees or for payment direct to the beneficiary; a capital settlement necessarily involves trustees. In neither instance, however, can a transaction constitute a settlement unless there is an element of bounty; a bona fide commercial transaction is not a settlement for the purposes of Part XV (see *IRC v. Plummer* (1979), HL and *Chinn v. Collins* (1981), HL).

The background to Part XV is that settlements, historically, have been a favourite means of tax avoidance, particularly when individuals faced high marginal rates of tax. Indeed, in the absence of statutory intervention, the potential for tax-saving through settlements is self-evident—any settlement would enable an individual with a high rate of tax to unload income on to a comparatively poor member of the family to the advantage of the family viewed as a whole, because the poor member has a lower rate of tax or may not be liable to tax at all. Not surprisingly, therefore, governments have over the years sought to counteract the fiscal efficacy of settlements. The rules in Part XV of the Taxes Act are the most recent attempt. Where applicable, the rules in Part XV deem income arising under a settlement during the life of the settlor to be the income of the settlor for *all* income tax purposes. In such instances, the income is treated as arising first in the settlement and then as being transferred to or reverting to the settlor. The important phrase, however, is "where applicable" for many income settlements (annual payments) made by individuals are denied any effect for income tax purposes as a result of section 347A of the Taxes Act. Therefore, in respect of such settlements, the rules in Part XV are redundant.

The rules in Part XV of the Taxes Act fall into three categories:

(1) rules which apply where the settlor (or spouse) retains an interest in the settled property (section 660A);
(2) rules which apply where a benefit is received by unmarried minor children from a parental settlement (section 660B);
(3) rules which apply where the settlor (or his spouse) has received a capital sum from the settlement (sections 677–678).

These rules are now considered first in relation to capital settlements and then, in so far as they may be applicable, with regard to income settlements.

Capital Settlements   11–06

SETTLEMENTS WHERE THE SETTLOR RETAINS AN INTEREST

Broadly, section 660A(1) of the Taxes Act deems all income arising under a settlement during the life of the settlor to be the *income of the settlor* for all income tax purposes unless the income arises from property in which the settlor has no interest.

The settlor is treated as having an interest where that property or any derived property (see section 660A(10)) is, or will or may become, payable to or for the benefit of the settlor or spouse in any circumstances whatsoever (section 660A(2)). Section 660A(3) provides that a spouse of the settlor does *not* include a prospective or separated spouse or a widow or widower. Thus, it is the existence of the interest which attracts the charge to tax under section 660A and, perhaps, the most compelling example of where such an interest exists is where a settlement can be revoked and, on revocation, property reverts to the settlor or spouse (but note *IRC v. Wolfson* (1949), HL).

The operation of section 660A(1) is limited by section 660A(4) and (5) by virtue of which the settlor is not to be regarded as having an interest if his interest can only take effect on the occurrence of certain specified events, *e.g.* the bankruptcy of a person who is or may become entitled to the property or any derived property or on the death at any age of a child of the settlor who had become beneficially entitled to the property or any derived property at an age not exceeding 25. In addition, section 660A(1) does not apply to the income arising under a settlement by one party to a marriage to provide for the other after divorce, annulment or separation to the extent that the income is payable for the benefit of that other (section 660A(8)). Further, an outright gift by one spouse to the other, of property from which income arises, is not usually treated as a settlement for the purposes of section 660A(1) (see section 660A(6)).

If section 660A(1) applies, the settlor is charged to tax under Case VI of Schedule D, and the income is treated as the highest part of his income. However, the settlor may recover any tax so paid from the trustees or any other person to whom the income is payable under the settlement (section 660D(1)).

11–07 BENEFITS RECEIVED BY UNMARRIED MINOR CHILDREN FROM PARENTAL SETTLEMENTS

Generally, any income arising under a settlement which is paid during the life of the settlor to or for the benefit of an unmarried minor (including a stepchild or illegitimate child) of the settlor is treated by section 660B(1) of the Taxes Act for all income tax purposes as the income of the settlor. However, section 660B(1) will not apply where the income is treated as the income of the settlor under section 660A, nor will it apply where the income paid to a child under such a parental settlement does not exceed, in total, £100 in any tax year.

In addition, if income arising under a capital settlement in favour of the settlor's unmarried minor children is retained or accumulated by the trustees such income is not treated under section 660B as income of the settlor. In certain circumstances, such a capital accumulation settlement can be used to secure tax savings for the family when it is viewed as a whole. For example, if the accumulated income belongs to the beneficiary because he has a vested interest, *e.g.* when capital is settled for a minor absolutely, there may be liability to basic rate tax, but this will, broadly speaking, have been borne by the trustees. Section 686 of the Taxes Act does not apply because the income belongs to the beneficiary (see section 686(2)(b)). Moreover, depending on his other income and allowances, the beneficiary may be able to recover tax paid by the trustees so that the income as long as it remains within the settlement (or is distributed after the beneficiary has reached 18 or married under 18) will in some instances be free of income tax. However, if the beneficiary's interest is contingent, the accumulated income does *not* belong to him. Here the only tax-saving lies in the difference between the tax charged on the income at the rate applicable to trusts, namely 34 per cent, (none of which is recoverable because the income is neither that of the settlor nor the beneficiary) and the tax which would have been payable if the income had been received by the settlor whose marginal rate of tax is 40 per cent. A 6 per cent saving, in itself, may not warrant setting up such a settlement.

Income which is not accumulated but distributed is caught by section 660B. This will be so, for example, where income is applied for the child's maintenance, education or benefit under section 31 of the Trustee Act 1925. And it is no good the trustees thinking that they can avoid section 660B by accumulating income and using capital for maintenance, etc., of the unmarried minor beneficiary. This device is stopped by section 660B(2) which provides that any sum whatsoever paid out for the benefit of an unmarried minor child of the settlor shall be deemed to be income (and not capital) to the extent that there is "available retained or accumulated income". "Available retained or accumulated income" is the aggregate amount of income which has arisen under the settlement since its inception *less* income already treated as income of the settlor or a beneficiary, income paid to or for the benefit of a beneficiary other than an unmarried minor child of the settlor and income properly spent on trust expenses (section 660B(3).

If section 660B applies, the settlor is charged to tax under Case VI of Schedule D, and the income is treated as the highest part of his income. However, as with section 660A(1), the settlor may recover any tax so paid from the trustees or any other person to whom the income is payable under the settlement (section 660D(1)).

11–08   CAPITAL SUMS PAID TO THE SETTLOR

Section 677 of the Taxes Act (as amended by the Finance Act 1995) attacks capital sums paid *to* the settlor (or his spouse) out of the settlement. "Capital sum" is defined to include "any sum paid by way of loan or repayment of a loan" (section 677(9)). This is the key to the understanding of what the section is primarily aimed at. It is designed to stop a settlor (who is a higher-rate taxpayer) making a settlement, causing the trustees to accumulate rather than distribute the income, and causing them to let him (or his spouse) have the income in the form of a loan. For "other" capital sums which fall within section 677, see sections 677(9) and (10).

Where a capital sum is paid by the trustees to the settlor (or his spouse) such sum (grossed up at the rate applicable to trusts) is to be treated for all income tax purposes as the income of the settlor (and charged to tax under Case VI of Schedule D) to the extent that such sum falls within the amount of "income available". "Income available" means, broadly speaking, the aggregate of all income arising to the settlement since its inception which has not been distributed and is not deemed to be income of the settlor under some other provision (section 677(2)). The point of this is that what the section is attacking is the payment out as capital of money which came into the settlement as income.

If in the year in which the capital sum is paid such sum exceeds the income available, the excess is carried forward and charged to the settlor in the following year (in so far as there is income available up to the end of that year) and thereafter, if necessary, subject to a maximum of 11 years. However, if the capital sum is paid by way of loan no charge can be raised in any year after that in which the loan is wholly repaid (section 677(4)).

Section 678 of the Taxes Act stops the dodge of ensuring that the payment of a capital sum was made not by the trustees to the settlor but by an associated company which was in some way put in funds by the trustees. The section deems such sums to be paid by the trustees to the settlor and thus to be within the scope of section 677.

The settlor receives a tax credit for tax paid by the trustees, but cannot recover from the trustees any tax for which he may be responsible as a result of the operation of section 677 (*cf.* the position under sections 660A and 660B).

Income Settlements 11–09

Section 347A stops most forms of income settlements (chiefly covenants) being effective to avoid income tax. The income of the payer being computed for income tax purposes without any deduction for the payments. Where section 347A does not apply to an annual payment, the income will be treated as the income of the settlor (payer) under section 660A, unless he can show that the income arises from property in which he has no interest or that the income is expressly excluded from the operation of section 660A(1). In the latter respect, section 660A(1) does not apply to income paid under a settlement by one party to a marriage to provide for the other after divorce, annulment or separation to the extent that the income is payable for the benefit of that other (section 660A(8)). In addition, section 660A(9) provides that income which consists of annual payments made by an individual for bona fide commercial reasons in connection with his trade, profession or vocation or qualifying charitable donations falls outside section 660A(1).

173

CHAPTER 12

THE TAXATION OF INDIVIDUALS

12–01 We have entitled this chapter "The Taxation of Individuals" because "individual" excludes companies (which, in tax law as in law generally, are "persons" but are not "individuals") and also excludes trustees and personal representatives, to whom special tax rules apply, as we saw in the last chapter. Since 1990 husbands and wives are taxed separately as individuals.

Even when we have been through the process of identifying an individual's taxable income under each charging section in the Taxes Act, the process of working out an individual's tax bill is quite complicated. We state the process here in a series of steps. It is not easy to reduce it to simplicity, because one has to accommodate "income", "total income", and "taxable income" (which are not the same) and various kinds of deductions (and reductions) which operate at different stages of the process. But here goes:

1. "Income" is income under any particular Schedule. It is either (see, for example, interest, annuities and annual payments in Schedule D, Case III) pure income or (as, for example, in Schedule D, Case I) the balance of income over expenditure.

2. "Total income" is the sum of the incomes under the Schedules minus what are called "charges on income", that is, such things as annuities and some annual payments which the taxpayer pays out (see section 835 of the Taxes Act) and certain specified interest payments.

3. Total income is not the same as "taxable income". To arrive at taxable income one deducts from total income certain income tax reductions.

4. To work out the tax bill of an individual one applies to taxable income the various tax rates. One then deducts the reliefs which are given by reducing that bill. One has now arrived at the "tax payable", being an actual sum in hard cash. One can call this the "tax bill".

Now let us look in more detail at the steps in the process.

174

Income 12–02

The amounts of income which an individual has under each Schedule are added together to make up the schedular or statutory income. Each Schedule has its own rules for computing that kind of income which falls within it. What requires to be stated here is that some items of receipt are not subject to tax. Important examples are students' grants and scholarships, some social security benefits such as child benefit, and the first £70 of National Savings Bank interest. Brief mention should also be made of ISAs (individual savings accounts)—see Chapter 10.

Kinds of Income 12–03

An individual's income may include items of the following kinds:

(a) Income not taxed by deduction before receipt 12–04

An important example of this kind of income is income from a trade under Case I of Schedule D. Another example is income from rents under Schedule A.

(b) Income taxed by deduction before receipt 12–05

This is where we take account, as we must, of all receipts which were subject to withholding taxes. The point we want to make here is that income taxed by deduction of tax before receipt has to be grossed-up, that is, converted into a gross sum, for the purpose of computing total income. We will explain grossing-up in a moment. The most important example of income taxed by deduction before receipt is salary or wage income. Tax is charged under Schedule E and is deducted by the employer under the PAYE system. The gross amount, which includes the tax calculated according to the various tax bands, is included in total income, but of course the employee is credited with the tax deducted by his employer.

Interest received from a building society or a bank is also subject to deduction of tax before receipt.

GROSSING-UP. An employee usually knows what his or her gross pay is (because the pay slip must state what it is) and so grossing-up does not present any problem. Moreover, it is, perhaps, simpler (and we are very much in favour of simplicity when it is a matter of arithmetic) to consider the mechanics of grossing-up in the case of taxable interest. The payer will deduct tax at the basic rate. If the lender receives £78 (net), the gross amount is £100. The gross amount is made up of the net payment (£78) plus tax deducted at the basic rate (at present 22 per cent), £22. With less obvious figures, you gross-up by multiplying the net amount by 100 over 78. The explanation (for simple lawyers, not accountants) is that if basic rate is 22 per cent, net income is gross (which is 100 per cent) less 22 per cent of gross, so net income is 78 per cent of gross. Dividends must also be included with the tax credit. But a special tax rate applies—see paragraph 10–10.

12–06   *Trust income*

A beneficiary under a trust has to include in the total income an amount equal to his share of the trust income, grossed-up. He will have received the share after deduction of tax. He will be credited (depending on the circumstances) with all or some of the tax paid by the trustees. The taxation of trust income is dealt with in paragraph 11–03.

12–07   *Partnership income*

A partnership is defined in the Partnership Act 1890 as the relation which subsists between persons carrying on business in common with a view of profit. There is no definition of partnership in the tax legislation, but the existence of partnerships is, as might be expected, acknowledged.

Three non-tax points we wish to make are extremely elementary, but we have found that they come as a surprise to some students. First, a partnership is quite different from a company registered under the Companies Acts, of which the main species is a limited company, *e.g.* Imperial Chemical Industries plc. Thus a partnership, unlike a registered company, is not, in English law, a legal entity separate from its members (although, as we shall see, under the old regime it is for purposes of assessment and collection treated as though it were a separate legal entity). Nevertheless, the name of a partnership may contain the word "Company", or "Co.", *e.g.* Price & Co. This does not make it a company in law; it is a partnership. The word "firm" is equivalent to the word "partnership", and should not be used in reference to a company. Secondly, there is no requirement of law or practice that the shares of each partner in the profits (or losses) of the partnership should be equal. Thirdly, a company can be a partner in a partnership.

Section 111 of the Taxes Act provides:

"Where a trade or profession is carried on in partnership, the partnership shall *not*, unless the contrary intention appears, be treated for the purposes of the Tax Acts as an entity which is separate and distinct from those persons." [*Emphasis added*.]

Broadly speaking, the responsibility for the tax payable on the profits of a trade or profession carried on in partnership lies not with the partnership but with the individual partners. Assessments are made on the individual partners, not on the partnership. Each partner is treated as if his share of the partnership profits is derived from a separate trade or profession carried on by him alone, *i.e.* as a sole trader or professional. This notional sole trade or profession is deemed to begin when he becomes a partner. It comes to an end when he ceases to be a partner or where the actual trade or profession is subsequently carried on by him alone or when it is actually discontinued. The partners are individually liable for tax in accordance with their respective shares in the partnership profits during the period in which the profits accrued.

Classification of Income   12–08

Earned, Investment and Savings Income

For nearly 90 years (since 1907) the law of income tax made a distinction between two kinds of income, earned income and unearned income, and until 1984 taxed the latter more heavily than the former. At one time the system was to have a "standard rate" of tax applicable to all income, but to have also a relief on earned income. In this respect, the system between 1973 and 1984 was to have a "basic rate" of tax applicable to all income, and also to have a further rate imposed (as well) on unearned income. This further rate was called in the legislation "additional rate", but it has now been repealed. Since 1992, the situation has become more complicated, with different rates applying to different kinds of income.

The legislation does not use the phrase "unearned income", but rather "investment income". And it does not define investment income except to say that investment income is any income other than earned income. Earned income is defined in section 833 of the Taxes Act. Broadly, it includes all income derived from an office or employment which is chargeable under Schedule E and any income which is charged under Schedule D and is immediately derived by an individual from the carrying on of his trade, profession or vocation either as an individual or partner.

This definition is consonant with commonsense, but there are some difficult borderline cases.

Income which is charged under Schedule A (see Chapter 7), notwithstanding its computation according to the principles of Case I of Schedule D, is investment income.

The Finance Act 1996 revives, in part, the notion that earned and investment income may be taxed at different rates. However, its approach is to identify a species of "investment income", which it refers to as "savings income". Savings income includes, for example interest from banks and building societies, interest from authorised unit trusts, interest from gilts and other securities and purchased life annuities. Dividends and similar payments from United Kingdom companies are also treated to a special rate.

12–09   Total Income

It is necessary to find a taxpayer's total income for two purposes: first, to determine whether it is enough to entitle him to personal reliefs; secondly, to determine liability (if any) to the higher rate of tax.

To arrive at total income one deducts what are called "charges on income" and certain payments (outward) of interest.

12–10   *Charges on Income*

A charge on income arises when a taxpayer binds himself by a legally enforceable arrangement to make payments to another person or body on a regular basis. The basic theory is that if a person alienates part of his income it ceases to be his income, and so does not form part of his total income. Instead, it becomes the income of the payee, and he [it] pays the tax instead. The theory of alienation has been drastically cut down by tax legislation, but it still stands in a few circumstances. For example, a covenant of income by partners of a partnership to a retired partner is a charge on the income of the payers (see paragraph 10–03).

12–11   *Deductible Interest Payments*

We are not speaking here of interest paid out as one of the expenses of a business; that is deductible *in computing* the income of that business. We are speaking of payments of interest in respect of which an individual can secure relief from income tax by deducting them *from* income. Relief of this sort was at one time widely available. It has been progressively restricted over recent years. In particular, what used to be called "mortgage interest relief", a deduction for interest paid when buying a home was abolished in 2000.

Perhaps not surprisingly, these exceptional cases do not include many of the payments of interest with which most people are conversant, *e.g.* on a bank overdraft or under a credit card arrangement or hire purchase contract. Rather they relate to instances where the loan for which the interest is being paid is for one of a number of specified purposes which are discussed below. However, even if the loan is for one of these purposes there are two general restrictions which come into play: first, relief is only given up to the amount of reasonable commercial rate of interest, see section 353(3) of the Taxes Act; and secondly, no relief at all is given if the sole or main benefit that might be expected to accrue to the claimant from the transaction under which the interest is paid was the obtaining of a reduction in tax liability by means of such relief: section 787 of the Taxes Act.

In outline, the rules for the specified purposes are as follows:

1. Loan applied in acquiring an interest in a close company, co-operative, employee-controlled company or partnership

The relief given in each of these instances is intended to encourage the development of small businesses. Broadly, this objective is pursued by granting relief to a claimant where the loan is used to invest in or to provide finance for any of the above enterprises and where the claimant is closely associated with that enterprise as an employee, shareholder, or partner as appropriate. 12–12

2. Loan to purchase machinery or plant 12–13

This relief helps partners and employees. If a partner borrows money to acquire machinery or plant for use by the partnership he can get relief on the interest, and so can an employee who borrows money to acquire machinery or plant which he uses for the purposes of his employment. This relief (both for partners and employees) is limited to three years' interest.

3. Loan to pay inheritance tax 12–14

This relief is available to the personal representatives and is some help to the estate in what is often the difficult task of getting together enough ready cash to pay the tax. It may be claimed where the loan in respect of which the interest is paid is used by the personal representatives to pay inheritance tax due on personalty to which the deceased was beneficially entitled. Only one year's interest is deductible.

12–15   **Taxable Income**

Having arrived at an individual's total income, the next step is to convert it into taxable income. This is achieved by the deduction of certain personal reliefs from his total income.

12–16   *Personal Reliefs*

There are a small number of personal reliefs set out in chapter I of Part VII (see sections 257 to 278) of the Taxes Act. As we shall see, all individuals are entitled to at least one allowance or reduction of tax. But the number of allowances and reductions has been radically reduced in recent years. Before we look at what is left, we must note some general points.

First, if an individual's total income in any year is less than the reliefs they are to that extent lost. There is no provision for carrying the balance forward into future years or back into past years. Secondly, until recently, a feature of the "unified system" of income tax which was introduced in 1973 has been that all personal reliefs operated by way of *deductions* from total income. For most reliefs this system still applies. So if a relief is say £100, it does not mean £100 off the tax bill, but only £100 off the taxable income. In other words, the relief is whatever tax on £100 comes to, according to the tax rate of a particular individual which means, of course, that the relief is worth more to the higher rate taxpayer. However, some reliefs no longer operate in this way. Rather they are effected not as *deductions* from total income but as *reductions* in the individual's tax bill. Broadly, the individual's tax bill is reduced by an amount equal to a percentage of the value of the relief. When we consider the specific reliefs we will make it clear which of these alternative means of granting "relief" apply. Thirdly, the value of personal reliefs is adjusted or reviewed each year to take account both of the needs of the Exchequer and the rate of inflation (and, of course, on occasions more political considerations). In theory, the room for manoeuvre is restricted by the requirement that the value of the main reliefs be linked to changes in the retail prices index, *i.e.* to be raised each year by the amount necessary to maintain their true values. In practice, Parliament may determine otherwise (section 257C of the Taxes Act). Finally, there is a matter of terminology. All reliefs are called collectively "personal reliefs", whereas usually, but not exclusively, a specific relief is called an allowance (although it would now be more accurate to refer to a reduction in some instances).

Let us now look at the personal reliefs in more detail.

THE PERSONAL ALLOWANCE 12–17

The personal allowance may be claimed by all taxpayers resident in the United Kingdom. It allows a claimant (for 2000–01) a deduction of £4,385 from total income. Any such claimant, *however young*, is entitled to the personal allowance and there is every incentive to use it for, as we have seen, if it is not used it is wasted—it cannot be carried forward or back nor can it be transferred to anyone else.

Where a claimant is during the tax year aged 65 or over the personal allowance is increased. For a claimant who is between 65 and 74 years of age during the tax year, the allowance increases from £4,385 to £5,790; for a claimant who is aged 75 or over it is increased to £6,050. This extra relief (sometimes called "the age allowance") is reduced where the claimant's total income exceeds £17,000 (section 257(5) of the Taxes Act).

THE MARRIED COUPLE'S ALLOWANCE 12–18
(REDUCTION)

This has been abolished for tax years starting with 2000–01 unless one or both of the couple are over 65. It is a reduction of the tax bill, equal to 15 per cent of the yearly allowance, giving a tax reduction of up to £300.

ADDITIONAL RELIEF IN RESPECT OF CHILDREN 12–19

This is also abolished from 2000-01 to be replaced in 2001–02 by a children's tax credit: see the new section 257AA and Schedule 13 to the Taxes Act 1988. The tax credit will be 10 per cent of £4,420 in 2001, reducing for those paying higher rate tax. It can be claimed by taxpayers looking after one or more children aged under 16. It is intended to operate with working families tax credit (see below).

OTHER ALLOWANCES 12–20

There is relief for blind people (but not for those suffering any other disability). The blind person's allowance for 2000–01 is £1,400 and is available as a *deduction* from the claimant's total income.

Finally, for the sake of completeness, we should mention an entitlement which is neither a relief nor an allowance, namely, child benefit. This is a tax-free payment (usually made on a weekly or monthly basis) to a mother (in most cases) in respect of each of her children who is aged under 16, or under 19 and in full-time education. And we must return to rather different forms of tax credit (below) that may *increase* income.

12–21   The Tax Bill

Having deducted from total income certain of a taxpayer's personal reliefs, we have arrived at taxable income. We must now proceed to establish what amount of tax is payable. This is primarily determined by the rate or rates of tax applicable to an individual's taxable income.

12–22   *The Rates of Tax*

If one searches for any consistency of application or purpose in the rates of tax which are applied to taxable income one searches in vain as the following brief excursus through recent history shows.

From 1973–74 a new method of charging income tax came into force and surtax was abolished. Income tax is all one tax, though levied at various rates. Until 1977–78 there were the basic rate, higher rates and additional rates. For 1978–79 there was a lower rate. The introduction of a lower rate complicated the system, mainly because of the many cases in which at that time income tax was "deducted at source" at the basic rate. It also greatly complicated the PAYE codes. On the other hand it was thought that the introduction of a lower rate had achieved one social good by reducing the number of people caught in the "poverty trap". The poverty trap is the situation in which a family can actually be worse off if the bread-winner gets a rise than they were before. This absurdity arises from the interaction (at a certain low level of income) of income tax, national insurance contributions and means-tested social benefits. It was found, however, when detailed research was undertaken that the main beneficiaries were married women. So it was abolished. From 1984–85 there was another change in the rate structure. The additional rate, levied on investment income over a certain threshold at the rate of 15 per cent, was abolished. Again, research suggested that in practice it operated in a different way to that which theory suggested. It was mainly paid by retired people. This left a basic rate and a series of progressive higher rates of tax. From 1988–89 a single higher rate of tax of 40 per cent was introduced.

Since then there has been the resurrection from 1992–93 of a lower rate (levied at 20 per cent) as a first step towards the government's proclaimed goal of achieving a basic rate of 20 per cent; a goal further enhanced from 1996–97, by the taxation of savings income of many taxpayers at the lower rate. A special 10 per cent rate was applied to dividends (with a special higher rate) in 1999 to offset the effect of other reforms of corporation tax. And in 1999 a new "starting rate" of income tax of 10 per cent was imposed on the first slice of taxable income. This was aimed specifically at poverty trap victims. It is hoped that it works better than in 1979.

For the tax year 2000–01, income tax is charged on an individual's taxable income at the following rates.

Starting rate

The starting rate is 10 per cent, and applies to the first £1,520 of an individuals taxable income.

Savings rate

The savings rate is 20 per cent and it applies to savings income in place of the basic rate.

Basic rate

The basic rate is 22 per cent and it applies to the taxable income of an individual between £1,521 and £28,400.

Higher rate

The higher rate is 40 per cent and it applies to the taxable income of an individual in excess of £28,400.

Where an individual's taxable income includes savings income the rate of tax charged on the savings income is the lower rate, save where the individual is liable to tax at the higher rate when more tax is payable. Savings income is treated as the top slice of an individual's income, and an individual with other income will be entitled to set against that other income the totality of the lower rate band.

Example

Ali has taxable income (after allowances and reliefs) of £40,000 of which £5,000 is savings income taxed at source, and £1,000 is a dividend on British shares (including tax credit). Tax liability is:

10% of	£1,520	= £152 and	
22% of	£26,880 (£28,400 – £1,520)	= £5,913 and	
32.5% of	£1,000 (gross dividend)	= £325 and	
40% of	£10,600 (£39,000 – £28,400)	= £4,240	

Total Tax = **£10,630.60**

The 20 per cent rate is not used because savings income is "top sliced", that is, taxed after earned income as the top slice of income. The overall effective average rate of tax on taxable income in this example is 26.5 per cent or, on total income adding back the personal allowance for someone under 65 in 2000, 23.9 per cent.

If we assume that all Ali's earnings are subject to Schedule E and NI contributions, the figures should also include employee's NI contributions at 10 per cent of £535 less £76 weekly, an annual total of £2386.80. This brings the overall average effective rate of tax on Ali's total income to 29.3 per cent.

At this point, one might be forgiven for thinking that the computation process is complete and that the individual's tax bill has been ascertained. In some cases this will be so, but in others account must also be taken of reliefs which take effect by reducing the individual's tax bill. Broadly, there are three types. First, such relief may be available to an individual as a "reward" for supporting a government-backed initiative—for example, the respective reliefs available to an individual, who furthers the government's aim to foster investment in small businesses by acquiring shares in a venture capital trust or in a qualifying company under the enterprise investment scheme. Secondly, as we have already seen (paragraph 12–17), some personal reliefs, *e.g.* the married couple's allowance are effected not as deductions from total income but as reductions in the individual's tax bill. In addition, an individual may be entitled to double taxation relief (see below, paragraph 26–08). Finally, we must note a new kind of relief that can turn some people's tax bills into *increases in income*: tax credits!

12–23   **Tax Credits**

Just ahead of the new millennium, Parliament enacted the Tax Credits Act 1999. It was the most dramatic change to individual income tax since Adam Smith invented the idea ahead of the

Napoleonic War (or was it Colbert who did so more than a century earlier?). Unlike personal allowances or reliefs, a tax credit is cashable. As a result, some of those entitled to a tax credit will get more from the Revenue than they pay in income tax and contributions. This is truly revolutionary stuff. It means a "taxpayer" may not pay any tax. On the contrary, he or she may be a "taxgainer". As with those who "pay" zero-rated VAT, there will be the strongest incentive to get the tax forms filled in—money back. Here's how.

There are two forms of tax credit: working families' tax credit (WFTC) and disabled person's tax credit (DPTC). WFTC has taken over from the former social security benefit called family credit. But it is now run by the Inland Revenue and, from April 2000, is paid to qualifying employees through their pay packets with their earnings. WFTC can be claimed by any employee (or self employed individual) who is both working at least 16 hours a week and looking after one or more children. Broadly, if someone is getting child benefit for looking after a child, then he or she can also claim WFTC.

Working families tax credit   12–24

WFTC is income-related and takes into account any savings above a limit, currently £8,000. A claimant is credited with a set weekly amount—a personal credit—along with a credit for each child, depending on the age of the child. The personal credit is at a set level for each claimant or couple, with a higher figure if someone is working more than 30 hours a week. The claimant can also claim a weekly childcare credit if paying for one or more children to be looked after by a registered childminder. This gives a maximum weekly tax credit. This is then reduced as the income and capital of the claimant (and partner, where there is one) rises. Remember that the claimant (or partner) must be working at least 16 hours a week to claim. Earnings are assumed to be at not less than the national hourly minimum wage. So there will always be some earnings.

The amount of tax credit is reassessed every six months. Taken together with the income tax personal allowances and credits and the removal of NI contributions from the lowest paid, its effect is to provide a minimum level of "earnings" after all adjustments for a working family looking after children. In 2000 this was said to be about £10,000 for the year for a small family. There are two central features of the scheme. First, the government gives resources to, rather than takes them from, the family under the combined effect of income tax and contributions. This includes every family—unlike income tax on its own, or benefits that need claiming, no one is left out. Secondly, the cash is paid to the employee as part of the pay packet by the employer. It is specifically intended to be a work-related credit. Those who do not work will get less.

For example, A and B are a young couple with two young children. A stays at home looking after them whilst B works 25 hours a week at the minimum wage. B will (in 2000) earn about £90 a week. A and B claim WFTC, which is paid to B with the weekly pay packet. Each week B earns £90. The personal allowance (and child tax credit from 2001) will stop B having to pay much income tax. This will be at the starting rate of 10 per cent. And there will be a small deduction for NI contributions each week. This qualifies B for state benefits, including statutory sick pay. B will then receive the cash value each week of the personal credit, plus the allowance for the two children. This will be worth about £100 a week. As a rough example, let us say that B loses deductions of £5 a week, but gets a credit of £100 a week. B's weekly pay will then be £90-£5 +£110, a total take home payment of £195. If B were a single parent having to employ a childminder, then, in addition, the first £140 of those costs would be met each week (in 2000). The message is intended to be clear—it is better to be a working taxpayer than "on benefit".

The self-employed cannot receive tax credit through a pay packet. They get it instead paid weekly directly to them by the Revenue. But again the message is the same—if you are not a "taxpayer" you cannot benefit.

12–25 Disabled person's tax credit

DPTC is a similar benefit for the working disabled (with or without children). It is aimed at providing a state subsidy to earnings to recognise that may disabled people are less competitive in the job market, and also have extra expenses in keeping themselves at work.

WFTC and DPTC are still experiments. But they are part of a shift of the welfare payments system from social security to tax. Separate legislation in 1999 also moved responsibility for statutory sick pay and statutory maternity pay to the Revenue along with, as we have seen, NI contributions. Employers have also been given the job of collecting the repayment of student grants (another sort of income tax, in the widest sense). In 2000, the Government announced further reforms for 2003, abolishing WFTC by splitting the employment credit payable to the parent from the child credit payable for each child. Watch this space!

CHAPTER 13

THE TAXATION OF COMPANIES

CORPORATION TAX

A company does not pay income tax or capital gains tax; the tax which it pays is corporation tax. Corporation tax is charged on the "profits" of the company, and "profits" means income and chargeable gains: Taxes Act, s.6. The amount of any income shall be computed in accordance with income tax principles (Taxes Act, s.9(1)), and the total amount of chargeable gains shall be computed in accordance with the principles of capital gains tax (Taxation of Chargeable Gains Act 1992, s.8).

So we have already covered a lot of ground but remember that the 1996 Finance Act applies different rules for companies with regard to all forms of debt, known as "loan relationships". In addition, there are many matters peculiar to companies which we have yet to look at.

What is a "company"? It is defined in the Taxes Act, s.831[1] as meaning (except in certain contexts) "any body corporate or unincorporated association, but does not include a partnership, a local authority or a local authority association."[2] (An authorised unit trust is deemed to be a company, but some special rules apply to it; see Taxes Act, s.48.)

A non-resident company, *i.e.* one not incorporated in the United Kingdom and whose central management and control are located elsewhere, is not within the charge to corporation tax unless it carries on a trade in the United Kingdom through a branch or agency. If so it is chargeable to corporation tax on trading income from the branch on income from property held by the branch and on chargeable gains accruing from the disposal of assets within the United Kingdom in the same circumstances as

---

[1] ss.831–842A is a group of sections headed "Interpretation" and it is well worth looking at.

[2] Nor does it include the Conservative Party's Central Office—that is not an unincorporated association. But members' clubs are included: *Conservative and Unionist Central Office v. Burrell* (1982); *Blackpool Marton Rotary Club v. Martin* (1990) (C.A.). In a member's club there is no liability on the members to share profits or losses as there is in a partnership.

would make an individual chargeable. In so far as it is not liable to corporation tax, a non-resident company is liable to income tax on the same footing as a non-resident individual.

13–02   Why tax companies?

It may be asked, why have a tax on company profits at all? Why not simply tax, in the hands of the shareholders, what emerges from the company in the form of distributions? The answer originally was because of the different rates of tax between income tax and capital gains tax. Taxing only distributions would have meant that that would enable a company to be used as a kind of receptacle in which profits could be stored up tax-free; distribution (and hence income taxation) could be avoided by storing up the profits for years on end and then eventually selling the shares (causing only liability to capital gains tax at a flat rate). This "receptacle problem" (a problem for the Revenue) is particularly acute in the case of narrowly-owned companies, such as one-member companies and family companies. Special rules were devised to deal with such companies, called "close" companies and, although the harmonisation of income tax and capital gains tax rates has solved *most* of the "receptacle" problems, other possible tax advantages remain. These include the use of investment companies to avoid higher rate tax on "hidden" distributions.

13–03   To incorporate or not?

The question whether a particular individual or partnership would gain (tax-wise) by forming a company is not easy to answer except in very general terms, or alternatively in minutely particular terms with a full knowledge of all the circumstances of a particular case. In general, a major pointer is the comparison between the individual's marginal rate of income tax and the relevant rate of corporation tax. This has changed very sharply recently. For example, back in 1979 when the first edition of this book was written the top rate of income tax had just fallen from 98 per cent to 75 per cent. The main rate of corporation tax was then 52 per cent. By 2000 that had dropped to 30 per cent. The "small companies" rate is 20 per cent, the basic rate of income tax on savings. If he does form a company, the individual trader will become a director and be taxable under Schedule E (and PAYE) (instead of Case I or II of Schedule D) and will be subject to the rules about benefits from higher-paid employment but will, be better off as regards pension arrangements.

The change from Case I or Case II income tax to corporation tax is done by a discontinuance of the trade (see Taxes Act, s.63); loss relief (income tax) can be carried forward (Taxes Act, s.35); and hold-over relief (capital gains tax) is available.

The decision whether to trade individually or by means of a company is not wholly, perhaps not even primarily, a tax decision. There is one great advantage of incorporation, namely limited liability even for a single member company, although for small companies that may be largely illusory in practice. Also, it is easier for a company to arrange finance (either from inside or outside the business) for expansion, particularly by the use of a floating charge. The disadvantage from more (and expensive) paperwork arising from the requirements of the Companies Acts has to some extent been reduced for small companies in recent years. And, of course, it must be borne in mind that some *professions* do not permit their practitioners to become incorporated. A final point is that, until 2000, individuals could impose a "pocket book" company between themselves and their clients or customers to save some income tax and NI contributions. The Finance Act 2000 contains anti-avoidance provisions to stop this (see paragraph 6–04).

The corporation tax, along with income tax and capital gains tax, is under the care and management of the Commissioners of Inland Revenue, and the detailed provisions for administration set out in the Taxes Management Act 1970 apply to corporation tax. It is important to appreciate, at the outset, that corporation tax *is* the income tax and capital gains tax on companies. Its administration is closely tied in with that of income tax and CGT.

The substantive law of corporation tax is to be found, for the most part, in sections 6–13A, Part VIII (sections 337–344), Part X (sections 392A–413), and a few sections of the Taxation of Chargeable Gains Act 1992, and Chapter II of Part IV of the Finance Act 1996 and section 117 and Schedule 18 to the Finance Act 1998.

Taxable Periods 13–04

Corporation tax is levied by reference, not to "years of assessment", but to "financial years". A financial year begins on April 1 and ends on March 31. And each financial year is named by reference to only one calendar year and that is the year in which it begins, not the year in which it ends. So the financial year 2000 is the year from April 1, 2000, to March 31, 2001. Assessment is on a current year basis; the tax assessment for 2000 being based on the profits of 2000. But where a company's accounting period does not correspond to the financial year, the profits of the accounting period are apportioned into the appropriate financial years. This is important in that the rate of tax may differ in the two financial years.

Companies became subject to self-assessment in 1999. Large companies pay the tax due in quarterly instalments during the year, with rather more generous treatment for smaller companies—but then the many small companies pay hardly any serious amounts of tax.

For many years, tax was paid in advanced when dividends were made. But this system (ACT or advance corporation tax) is now being phased out and, for simplicity we ignore it save for the brief summary of the effect on shareholders at paragraph 10–10.

13–05   Rates

In 1982, before reforms started, the main rate of corporation tax was 52 percent. It was then steadily reduced and is now 30 percent. Nonetheless, the effective rate of corporation tax paid by most companies increased significantly. Why? Because many of the exemptions and deductions were withdrawn or reduced in value. As Newton did not quite say, what comes down must go up—in the upside down world of tax.

To help out the small guys, there is also a "small companies rate". This is a bit of a misnomer, because it is nothing to do with the sizes of the company or its assets. It is a "small profits tax" with a rate of 20 per cent. It is levied on profits up to £300,000, and there are tapering provisions on profits over that amount up to a total of £1.5 million. At that level the full 30 per cent is payable. And to help out the really small guys, there is since 1999 a starting rate of 10 per cent on profits up to £10,000. This tapers up to 20 per cent when profits reach £50,000. For example, a company with profits of £50,000 pays tax at 20 per cent, of £10,000. A company with profits of £40,000 pays 10 per cent on the first £10,000 (£1,000 payable), plus 22.5 per cent on the next £30,000 (a total amount payable of £7,750).

13–06   Computation of Profits

A company is charged to corporation tax on its total profits; that is, its income plus its chargeable gains. (Profits = income + chargeable gains). It is declared in the Taxes Act, s.9 that in general a company's income is to be computed on income tax principles, excluding income tax enactments which make special provision for individuals. This, however, does not mean that there are no differences at all. One difference is that the rules for computing a company's income and gains from either borrowing or lending are different from those for individuals (see below). But the differences are minor compared with the broad principle which (we say again) is that a company's income is computed on income tax principles. If the law of income tax changes during the accounting period of a company, the law which applies for the computation is the law applying to the year of assessment in which the accounting period *ends*.

Similarly, section 8 of the Taxation of Chargeable Gains Act 1992 declares that the chargeable gains of a company are to be computed on the principles of capital gains tax. That is subject to what we say about "loan relationships" below.

The income of a company is allotted to Schedules and cases as is the income of an individual. So, for example, a company's trading income is assessed under Case I of Schedule D and its income from rents under Schedule A. The rules for determining what expenses are deductible are as for income tax.[3] Under Case I, directors' emoluments are on the same footing as salaries and wages of the company's employees; they are deductible to the extent that they are reasonable.

The several classes of income of a company together with the total of its chargeable gains constitute the total profits of the company.

Loan Relationships 13–07

Chapter II of Part IV of the Finance Act 1996 introduced a new regime for companies in respect of all profits and losses made by companies on loans. In general the idea is to treat all such profits and losses as income, whether or not for individuals they would be treated as capital gains or losses. (The original idea was to apply these rules to individuals as well but that did not find favour during the consultation process). The new rules apply whether the company is the borrower or lender. The most

---

[3] Occasionally the problems posed under income tax rules arise from the fact that it is a company which is involved. For example payments made by a holding company to assist a subsidiary company were deductible under Schedule D, Case I from the holding company's profits since they would have been so deductible by the subsidiary and were made purely for the benefit of the holding company: *Robinson v. Scott Bader Co. Ltd* (1981). On the other hand, money spent by a holding company which was for the purpose of a trade carried on by its subsidiaries was not deductible—it was not spent wholly and exclusively for the purposes of the holding company's trade: *Vodafone Cellular Ltd v. Shaw* (1995).

obvious category is the treatment of interest paid by a company on its debentures from the company's point of view.

The 1996 rules apply to what are termed "loan relationships". These are defined as any relationship in which a company is either a creditor or debtor for a money debt, whether in sterling or another currency, which under the general law is a loan. Thus all forms of bond and corporate debt are covered. In calculating the profits and losses from such relationships companies may use one of two accounting methods: an accruals basis, under which payments and receipts are allocated when they accrue to the accounting periods to which they relate; or a mark-to-market basis, which means that a loan relationship must be accounted for in each accounting period at a fair value. In general companies may use whichever method they use in their statutory accounts prepared for Companies Act purposes.

The central concepts of the new regime (in sections 82 and 83 of the 1996 Act) are: (i) that where companies enter into loan relationships for the purposes of a trade, the profits, losses and expenses relating to those relationships (known in the legislation as debits and credits) will be treated as receipts of expenses of that trade; ie they will form part of the Schedule D, Case I computation; and (ii) in the case of profits and losses arising from other, *i.e.* non-trading, loan relationships any net profit (taking into account the company's other income subject to those rules) will be taxable under the rules of Case III of Schedule D.

Any net loss on a non-trading loan relationship, calculated in the same way, may be used to give relief in one of four ways. First, it may be used against any profits for corporation tax of the year in which the loss occurred; secondly by way of group relief (see below); thirdly by way of carry back against similar non-trading profits of the preceding three years; and fourthly by carry forward against non-trading profits generally of the company for succeeding accounting periods.

These new rules apply to all interest payments made by companies but do not apply to payments which are distributions for corporation tax purposes so that the basic distinction remains between dividends payable on shares and interest payable on debentures. The former cannot be deducted from taxable profits. The latter are now part of the tax computation as outlined above. Perhaps the most significant feature of the new rules is the general shift from capital gains tax rules to income tax rules for the many forms of corporate and government debt.

Deductions from Total Profits 13–08

Having arrived at the total profits of the company the next thing to do is to consider what items are permitted to be deducted in order to determine the amount on which corporation tax is to be charged. There are four kinds of permitted deductions: (1) charges on income; (2) management expenses of an investment company; (3) minor capital allowances; (4) losses. We will deal with these in turn.

CHARGES ON INCOME 13–09

It will be remembered from Chapter 12 ("The Taxation of Individuals") that, for income tax, certain payments out are called "charges on income" and are deductible in computing "total income". Those deductions are separate from the deductions which are expenses in earning the income under any particular Schedule or Case. The position is similar for corporation tax. Payments out which are expenses in earning the income under a particular Schedule or Case are deductible in computing the income of a company under that Schedule or Case. That still leaves some payments out which, although not deductible *in computing* income, are deductible *from* (or "against") the total profits of the company. Many payments are not deductible in either way. Those which are deductible against total profits are called "charges on income": see section 338 of the Taxes Act. Of course deductibility is only completely effective if the charges on income are less than the total profits. If the charges exceed the total profits in a particular accounting period, and the charges include payments made wholly and exclusively for the purposes of a trade carried on by the company, then up to the amount of that excess (or of those payments, if less) the charges are deductible as if they were trading expenses of the trade for the purpose of computing a trading loss: Taxes Act, s.393(9). Or, where a company is a member of a group of companies, it may in certain circumstances "surrender" its excess of charges on income to another company in the group: Taxes Act, s.403(7).

There are various conditions with which a payment must comply if it is to count as a charge on income. The conditions are set out in section 338. In summary, a payment is not to be treated as a charge on income in any of the following circumstances: if the payment is charged to capital; if the payment is not ultimately borne by the company; if the payment is not made under a liability incurred for a valuable and sufficient consideration (subject to the rules for charitable donation, below)[4]; if (in the case of a non-resident company) the payment is incurred for the purposes of its overseas operations, if it would be deductible in computing the company's taxable profits.

Certain further stringent rules apply to payments made by companies to non-residents: see Taxes Act, ss.338(4) and 340.

A company that makes a gift of a sum of money to a charity is treated as if it made an annual payment of the sum: Finance Act 2000, s. 40.

13-10 MANAGEMENT EXPENSES OF AN INVESTMENT COMPANY

Another possible deduction from total profits applies to an investment company. Such a company, if resident in the United Kingdom, is permitted to deduct its management expenses: Taxes Act, s. 75. The point of this provision is to make up for the fact that an investment company, unlike a trading company, has no opportunity of deducting expenses of management in the actual computation of profits. "Management expenses" are given a wide meaning by the courts, but they must relate to some act of management and not be part of the cost of acquiring an asset; *e.g.* a commission paid by one investment company to another company in return for that company's guarantee of a loan raised by the first, was held by the Court of Appeal to be an acquisition and not a management expense. It was part of the price of raising the loan.[5] A similar, but more restricted, provision applies to insurance companies: section 76.

13-11 MINOR CAPITAL ALLOWANCES

Another possible deduction relates to what one might call the "minor" capital allowances. An example is the agricultural buildings allowance for non-traders. The rules are complicated, but in

---

[4] It must be made in *return for* consideration and not just in the hope of receiving consideration. Thus in *Ball v. National & Grindlay's Bank* (1973), money paid under a covenant for the education of overseas employees' children in order to retain their services was held not to be a charge on income. It was a hope of a business advantage only. It is an open question whether payment by the company for the benefit of A with consideration supplied by B will be a charge on income.

[5] *Hoechst Finance Ltd v. Gumbrell* (1983), CA.

certain circumstances such an allowance can be implemented by way of a deduction from total profits.

LOSSES 13–12

Losses of companies under corporation tax are dealt with in ways similar to losses of individuals under income tax. Let us first make the general point that a loss in a trade is computed in the same way as trading income is computed. In other words, the computation process may lead to a plus answer or a minus answer.

There are two main ways in which a trading loss of a company may be relieved: see the Taxes Act, ss. 393, 393A.

Carry-forward 13–13

The company may claim, to set off a trading loss of one accounting period against trading income from the same trade in succeeding accounting periods. Relief is given against the first available year and then each successive year as appropriate. For the purposes of this carry-forward relief, if a company in a particular accounting period has an excess of "charges on income" over profits and the charges on income include payments made wholly and exclusively for the purposes of a trade carried on by the company, then, up to the amount of that excess or of those payments, whichever is the less, the charges on income so paid shall in computing a loss be deductible as if they were trading expenses of the trade: Taxes Act, s. 393(9).

Set-off against current and previous profits 13–14

The company may claim to set off a trading loss in any particular accounting period against profits of whatever description (including chargeable gains) of that accounting period. If the loss is not in this way completely absorbed, it can be set against the profits of preceding accounting periods, subject to the limitation that the loss can only be carried back for accounting periods falling within the previous three years. Such a claim must be made within two years and relief is given against a later accounting period before an earlier period. The company must have been carrying on the same trade in the carry-back period. Set-off against general profits, but not carry forward relief, is not allowed unless either (a) the trade is being carried on in the exercise of functions conferred by an Act of Parliament or (b) the trade is being carried on on a commercial basis. It will be noticed that (b) above is parallel to a requirement for income tax (section 384) designed to exclude hobby-trading from the relief. And the special rules for hobby-farming (section 397) apply to corporation tax as well as to income tax.

13–15 *Case VI*

Apart from the above modes of loss relief there is also a limited relief for Case VI losses. The company may claim to set off the loss against any other Case VI income for the same or any subsequent accounting period.

13–16 *Company reconstructions*

Where a company ceases to carry on a trade and another company begins to carry it on, the change of company is ignored if the fundamental ownership (*e.g.* by shareholding) is (to the extent of three-quarters or more) the same before and after the change of companies. So if Company A has accumulated losses, and its trade is transferred to Company B (and the common ownership test is satisfied) Company B can use the carry-forward provisions and set off the accumulated losses against profits of the transferred trade[6] (but not against other profits): Taxes Act ss. 343, 344. There are restrictions if Company A is insolvent at the time of transfer.

13–17 *Change of ownership*

Sometimes the converse case arises; that is, the company carrying on the trade remains the same but the underlying ownership changes. There used to be a brisk business in the sale of companies which were bulging with unrelieved tax losses. This commerce was largely struck down by a section which is now the Taxes Act, s. 768. If in any period of three years there is both a substantial change in the ownership of a company and a "major change in the nature or conduct of a trade carried on by the company" past trading losses will not be available for carry-forward relief. A substantial change in ownership is basically a change in the ownership of more than 50 per cent of the voting share capital. Nor is the relief available if "at any time after the scale of the activities in a trade carried on by a company has become small or negligible, and before any considerable revival of the trade, there is a change in the ownership of the company."

---

[6] Company B can merge the trade with another carried on by it, but the relief will only apply to profits of the transferred trade: *Falmer Jeans Ltd v. Rodin* (1990).

The point of this latter provision is to strike at what was once a common practice keeping a company in existence simply because it was big with losses. Similar rules apply to prevent losses incurred *after* the change of ownership from being carried back against profits incurred *before* the change under the three year carry-back reliefs: Taxes Act, s. 768A.

Group relief 13–18

A company which is a member of a group or of companies may "surrender" a loss to another company which is a member of the same group. This enables the transferee company to claim loss relief: Taxes Act, ss. 402 and 403(1). The claimant company must use the relief in the year it was surrendered. A group for this purpose is where 75 per cent of the ordinary shares of one company is owned by the other. The availability of this relief has, however, led to the creation of strange "groups" of companies the object of which is to allow a profitable company to take the benefit of a loss of a company with insufficient profits. This has led in turn to complex anti-avoidance legislation and many complex cases as to what constitutes a group for this purpose.

A similar relief is available within a consortium of companies which together own trading companies.

Distributions 13–19

Some payments out made by a company are "distributions" and some are not. A dividend is a distribution; interest on loan stock is not. A distribution which is made by a company resident in the United Kingdom is chargeable to income tax on an individual recipient under Schedule F. A payment which is not a distribution is not subject to Schedule F, though it may be chargeable to tax under some other Schedule. For example, interest on loan stock is chargeable on an individual under Case III of Schedule D.

What is a distribution? 13–20

The concept of "distribution" is defined in the Taxes Act, ss. 212 and 218, as amended. The definition is widened where the paying company is a "close company": see Chapter 21, below. A distribution is never deductible from the total profits of the paying company, be it close or non-close.

The definition of "distribution" is involved, but putting the matter broadly it covers (amongst other things) dividends (including capital dividends) and anything else (other than a repayment of share capital) distributed in respect of shares in cash or otherwise out of the assets of the company (meaning that the cost falls on the company) and where the company does not receive any new consideration for that which it distributes. It follows that a bonus issue is not a distribution, because there is no cost falling on the company; and a rights issue is not a distribution, because there is new consideration.

13–21 *What is not a distribution?*

The Companies Act 1985 gives companies power to repurchase their own shares and to issue redeemable ordinary shares without requiring a court order. The avowed intention of these provisions was to provide small companies with shares which would be attractive to an outside investor in that he could resell to the company and not be "locked-in" with no opportunity to sell the shares. (Private companies in general have no open market for their shares.) But such a repurchase or redemption will be a distribution for tax purposes in so far as it amounts to more than the original investment. The Government therefore introduced an exemption from the distribution rules for certain repurchases and redemptions. We may say, however, that the exemption is extremely limited and in some cases will frustrate the intentions of the companies legislation.

There is one other exemption from the distribution rules allowed for by sections 213 to 218 of the Taxes Act. This will be on a "demerger"—*i.e.* splitting up one company into two or more. In certain circumstances an issue of shares by the original company to the members of the new companies will not invoke the distribution rules. As with purchases and redemptions this relief only applies to trading companies when the de-merger is wholly or mainly for the benefit of the trade. Advance clearance is again possible and desirable.

13–22   Close companies

Lurking in sections 414 to 422 of the 1988 Act are the remaining legislative "ruins" of a once-great Revenue weapon for use in tax collection: the provisions aimed at breaking-open close companies. What are left are complicated definitions which have limited practical effect. So instead of the full treatment in previous editions of this book, we will attempt only a brief summary.

The aim of the provisions was to break down the fiscal "walls" of companies to ensure that they were not used to hide money from the national coffers. (The more polite euphemism of "lifting the corporate veil" suggests making love, but these were wartime measures). The sections contain complicated language but the key issue was to define the targets so that they could not move out of range, and then provide high-calibre ammunition is much lower. Close companies were at their most important when the top rate of income tax was 98 per cent and anything was, in most people's view, better than incurring that rate. Further, there could be double tax when dividends were paid out, as both the company and the shareholder were taxed. The obvious answer was to keep the money in the company and not to pay it out as a dividend—or to pay it out in disguised ways such as loans. The "ammunition" consisted of provisions that deemed dividends to occur, deemed loans to be dividends, and so on.

The targets were all companies that were, in effect, closely controlled. There were elaborate definitions that caught any combination of arrangements where private companies were controlled by five or fewer groups of people or by their directors.

In practice, the sections are of limited importance for two very different reasons. The first is that in the modern "global" economy, companies move out of range by the simple process of decamping to an offshore jurisdiction. The second is that the tax burden is now much lower. Now that the top rate of 40 per cent the pressure to avoid it not so intense. Put it this way; you can now keep at least 60 per cent of your income at the top end, while when these provisions were introduced you could keep about 2 per cent.

PART THREE

Taxation of Capital Gains

CAPITAL GAINS TAX

INTRODUCTION 14–01

Capital gains tax is, not surprisingly, a tax on capital gains. It is not a tax on income and is generally free from any overlap with income tax. Nor is it a tax on capital as such (as a wealth tax would be) but only on gains. It is in this latter point (gains) that it differs from inheritance tax. Both inheritance tax and capital gains tax are concerned, broadly speaking, with the movement of capital from one person to another, but whereas on such a movement inheritance tax charges tax on the whole amount of capital which moves, capital gains tax charges tax only on the gain as between the value it has at the time of this movement (*e.g.* sale by A) compared with the value it had on the occasion of its last previous movement (*e.g.* purchase by A). There are a few occasions when there will be a charge to both taxes where some limited relief is available, but on the whole they are complementary. In general, inheritance tax was designed to tax voluntary transfers whereas capital gains tax was designed to tax commercial transfers. But changes made to both taxes have led to the paradoxical position that lifetime gifts are now subject to capital gains tax and only rarely to inheritance tax.

The social idea behind capital gains tax is that it is too arbitrary, and therefore unfair, to tax a person on his income (*e.g.* dividends) and not to tax a person on his capital gains (*e.g.* buying shares on the stock exchange and selling them at a higher price). The latter is thought of as being as much a taxable resource as the former.[1]

But the theory was initially spoiled by high rates of inflation. If you bought something in 1978 for £400 and sold it in 1982 the probability is that you would have got around £600 for it. On paper you have made a gain of £200; in real terms you have not made any gain at all. Until 1982 the legislation made no allowance for such a paper gain. In fact the point was tested in court, and in *Secretan v. Hart* (1969) it was held that no adjustment for

---

[1] But see "The Meade Report and the Taxation of Capital" [1979] B.T.R. 25.

inflation (or to put it in another way, for the fall in the value of money) was allowable.

The tax was originally introduced in 1965 and taxed all gains accruing after March 1965. Conservative governments between 1979 and 1997 sought to reduce the impact of the tax (by introducing extensive reliefs) and to remedy the perceived injustice of taxing inflated gains. In 1982 a form of index-linking was introduced, which was refined in 1985 so that relief was available for the effects of inflation from March 1982. Thus if a person bought an asset in 1972 for £1,000 and sold it in 1992 for £11,000 he would be able to discount from the total gain of £10,000 a sum for inflation from 1982 to 1992. But he or she was still liable in full for all gains incurred before 1982. In 1988, therefore, it was decided to take out of the charge all gains, paper or real, incurred before 1982. Thus in our example the gain would be calculated by taking the market value of the asset at March 1982, say £7,000, and deducting that from the sale price of £11,000. That gain of £4,000 would then also attract relief for inflation between 1982 and 1992.

In 1998 the relatively new Labour Government decided that, for individuals, there should be no more relief for the effects of inflation but that instead relief should in future be given according to the length of time that the asset has been held by the taxpayer. The avowed intention was to discourage short-term gains. This taper relief, as it is known, reduces the chargeable gain by a percentage which increases the longer the asset has been held, but only to a maximum achieved after four years for a business asset and 10 years for other assets. The old relief is still available, however, for inflation between 1982 and 1998 and there is still no charge for any gains accruing before 1982. The result is that if a taxpayer sells an asset in 2001 for say £50,000, having bought it for £10,000, the apparent gain of £40,000 will be reduced in three different ways, depending upon when he acquired the asset. If he acquired it in May 1998 he will only be able to claim taper relief based on the length of his ownership from that date. If he acquired it in May 1988, he will first be entitled to claim a deduction for inflation between May 1988 and April 1998 and then taper relief on that reduced amount calculated as if he had begun to own the asset in April 1998. If he acquired it in May 1978 his gain will be calculated from the market value of the asset in March 1982, with a reduction for inflation from that time to April 1998 and taper relief from then on. We will go into more details of all this in the next chaper.

For administrative and assessment purposes capital gains tax, which applies only to individuals and not companies, is similar to income tax and is thus subsumed into the system of self-assessment and payment already explained. It is assessed and charged annually and payment is due by January 31 of the year following the year of assessment. For companies, chargeable gains, although computed in general in the same way as for individuals, are then liable to corporation tax and not capital gains tax. Unlike individuals, however, companies are still entitled to relief for the effects of inflation. Taper relief does not apply to them.

The law relating to capital gains tax was consolidated in the Taxation of Chargeable Gains Act 1992. **Unless otherwise stated all references in this part of the book are to that Act.** Most amendments made since then have been incorporated into that Act. It is, as we shall see, quite a technical tax and there have been many cases for the courts to decide. Those which relate to the principles of the tax are included below.

Rates of Tax   14–02

Since 1988 the rates of capital gains tax and income tax have been harmonised: section 4. Until then capital gains tax was charged at a flat rate of 30 per cent. A taxpayer's chargeable gains are now treated as if they were the top slice of that person's taxable income and thus the appropriate income tax band—starting, basic (applicable to savings income) or higher—will apply. Where the gain straddles two bands it will be taxed proportionately at the two rates. But the two taxes remain separate so that, for example, personal allowances cannot be set off against capital gains tax and capital losses cannot be set off against income tax.

Instead, an individual subject to capital gains tax can take advantage of the "exempt amount" for each year. This is specified by a statutory instrument issued in advance by the Treasury for each tax year and is index-linked unless Parliament decides otherwise: section 3. The amount for 2000–01 is £7,200. Tax is therefore only payable in so far as an individual has taxable gains (chargeable gains less allowable losses) in excess of that amount in the year. The exempt amount is in effect the tax threshold for the year in question and so fulfils the same role for capital gains tax as the personal allowances do for income tax. Because capital gains tax is charged by reference to a transaction it is therefore possible to limit such transactions between years so as to maximise the use of this exemption.

Spouses are taxable as separate individuals for capital gains tax as for income tax. Thus they both have an exempt amount.

However, there are two consequences for the tax if the spouses are living together. For this purpose a married woman is deemed to be living with her husband unless they are legally separated or the circumstances are such that the separation is likely to be permanent: section 288(3). The first consequence is that a transfer of assets between the spouses is treated as if neither a gain nor a loss has occurred (so that the transferee is deemed to have acquired the asset at the price paid by the transferor) (see below) and the second is that they can only have one main residence to qualify for exemption from the tax (see paragraph 16–05). Thus a cohabiting couple can each have a house which they can sell free of the tax, but not so married couples.

Trustees, who may be liable to pay the tax in relation to changes in the beneficial ownership of the trust property, are only entitled to half the annual exempt amount (Schedule 1, para. 2). Personal representatives, however, are entitled to the full amount for the year of the death and the two following years. After that they cease to have any exempt amount (section 3(7)). Both trustees and personal representatives are taxed at a fixed rate of 34 per cent.

14–03 The Charge to Tax

Section 1(1) declares: "Tax shall be charged in accordance with this Act in respect of capital gains, that is to say chargeable gains computed in accordance with this Act and accruing to a person on the disposal of assets."

This subsection contains in summary form the whole of the law relating to capital gains tax. We shall know that law when we know what a chargeable gain is, how the Act requires computation to be made, what a person is, what an asset is, and what a disposal is. This chapter tells us what a chargeable gain is and what amounts to a person, an asset and a disposal; *i.e.* the basic charge. The next chapter concerns itself with the computation of the gain and the final chapter with the various exemptions and reliefs from the tax.

14–04 CHARGEABLE GAINS

All gains other than exempted gains are chargeable gains (section 15(2)). The chargeable gain is, broadly speaking, the difference between the cost of the asset and the consideration received on its disposal. The cost is usually referred to as the "base cost". It is important to realise that the consideration received by A on a disposal to B will be B's base cost on a subsequent disposal to C. Capital gains tax operates thus by charging the gains on an asset by reference to specific events, known as disposals. In general, as we have seen, where an asset was acquired before March 31, 1982, the base cost will be its market value at that date.

Although each asset disposed of in a year of assessment has to be considered separately, the tax is charged on the total amount of chargeable gains in the year after deducting allowable losses (section 2(2)).

The key requirements for a charge are the disposal of an asset by a chargeable person. Let us now examine each of these in turn (in reverse order).

PERSONS   14–05

"Person" has the same meaning as in income tax law. So not only individuals are persons but so also are companies and trustees and personal representatives which have been covered above. As we have seen, however, companies are liable to corporation tax and not capital gains tax on their gains. A partnership (or firm) is not a "person" in the law of England. In Scottish law a partnership is a "person". For capital gains tax purposes in all parts of the United Kingdom partners are treated separately as individuals for their share of the gains or losses arising from the disposal of partnership assets or other partnership dealings: section 59. The same principle will also apply to members of a limited liability partnership.

Residence, etc.   14–06

A person is chargeable to capital gains tax in respect of chargeable gains accruing to him in a year of assessment during any part of which he is resident in the United Kingdom, or during which he is ordinarily resident in the United Kingdom (section 2(1)). The meaning of "resident" and "ordinarily resident" are the same as for income tax (section 9).

On the other hand, the disposal of an asset which is situated in the United Kingdom only imposes tax on a person who is not resident and not ordinarily resident here if he is carrying on a trade through a branch or agency in the United Kingdom and the asset is connected with the trade (section 10(1)). To prevent an individual from acquiring a temporary residence outside the United Kingdom and then disposing of a U.K. asset free of tax, section 10A provides a charge on such gains realised during the period of non-residence which is triggered by the individual's return to the United Kingdom. The section applies if the individual was resident or ordinarily resident in the United Kingdom for some part of four of the seven tax years prior to departure from the United Kingdom, and the period of non-residence is less than five full tax years. In general, the gains will be computed as if the individual had been resident in the year in question but will be charged at the rate applicable in the year of return.

An individual who is resident or ordinarily resident but not domiciled in the United Kingdom is taxed only if the proceeds are remitted to the United Kingdom on gains from the disposal of assets outside the United Kingdom (section 12(1)), and losses on the disposal of such assets are not allowable losses (section 10(4)). In *Young v. Phillips* (1984), the disposal of letters of allotment to shares in a United Kingdom company, although taking place in Sark, was held not to fall within section 12(1). The letters carried rights enforceable in the United Kingdom and so were not assets situated outside the United Kingdom.

14–07 ASSETS

All forms of property are assets, and this is so whether they are situated in the United Kingdom or not. Thus a United Kingdom resident is liable for disposal of non-U.K. assets. (Section 275 contains rules for determining where certain kinds of assets are situated.) Section 21(1) declares that the following items are included amongst assets: (a) options, debts and incorporeal property generally; (b) any currency other than sterling; and (c) any form of property created by the person disposing of it, or otherwise coming to be owned without being acquired. Notice that head (c) brings into charge things which were never acquired but were on the contrary created by the taxpayer, such as a building, the copyright of a book, and (very importantly) the goodwill of a business[2] which of course may have been built up from nothing. Some items, as we shall see later, are expressly stated not to be chargeable assets.

Since assets are defined by reference to all forms of property it is important to note that this will include all interests in property; for example a lease of land is itself an asset as well as the land. The major item in practice for capital gains tax is company securities. There was originally some doubt as to whether purely personal rights could be assets for this purpose; these would include assets such as the right of a protected tenant under the Rent Acts or a right to damages for an action in tort. Such rights cannot be

---

[2] See, *e.g. Butler v. Evans* (1980). In *Kirby v. Thorn EMI plc* (1987), the Court of Appeal held that where a company, having sold three subsidiaries, agreed not to compete with their businesses it had disposed of its goodwill in those businesses. That was an asset. They overruled the judge's opinion that the company was merely fettering its freedom of commercial activity.

assigned or sold. Damages, but not the right to sue for damages (see below), are in fact exempt by virtue of section 19(5), which suggests perhaps that otherwise they would be assets. The point was resolved in *O'Brien v. Benson's Hosiery Ltd* (1980), HL, where B was appointed a director of the company in 1968 on a seven-year contract. In 1970 the company released him from this contract in return for a payment of £50,000. The Revenue sought to assess the company on this receipt on the basis that it had disposed of an asset, *viz.* its rights against B under the contract. The House of Lords, reversing the Court of Appeal, held that these rights were assets. The fact that the company could not assign their rights did not matter. The important point was that they could be turned to account, as in fact they had been in this case. As we shall see even the fact that an asset has no obvious market value does not prevent it being an asset—one can always calculate a hypothetical market value.

Non-assignable rights under a contract are therefore assets. Can the same be said of a disputed or moral claim? In *Scott v. Ricketts* (1967), £39,000 was paid by a developer to an estate agent "in consideration for the withdrawal of any claim he may have". It was clear that he only had a moral claim and it was held that Case VI of Schedule D could not apply since it was not "analogous to the sale of an asset". Some assistance may be derived from the decision in *Zim Properties Ltd v. Procter* (1985) that a right to sue for damages in the tort of negligence was an asset on the basis that it could be turned to account (*e.g.* by a compromise settlement). The judge, applying the *O'Brien* test, thought that all such actions would be assets unless clearly frivolous or vexatious. "Assets" is a wider concept than "property". Since in practice the question will only arise if the "assets" are turned into account (*e.g.* there is a disposal), the *O'Brien* test suggests that all such rights and claims will be assets if the point arises. Put another way, we can almost say that if you can dispose of something in any of the ways possible under the Act, it is an asset.

Disposals   14–08

The basic event on which capital gains tax depends is the disposal of an asset. Whenever a disposal takes place a calculation must be made to see whether there has been a gain or a loss or neither.

The word "disposal" has first of all to be given its ordinary meaning before going on to consider the extended meaning given to it by the Act. In its ordinary meaning a disposal occurs whenever the owner of an asset (which, remember, may be an abstract entity such as a right) divests himself of his entitlement to the asset. Thus the ordinary meaning includes sale, exchange and gift.

It is very important to grasp that the making of a gift is a chargeable event. At first sight this may seem very odd. Clearly the giver of a gift has made a disposal, but how on earth can he be said to have made a gain? The point was challenged in court in *Turner v. Follett* (1973), CA. It was inevitably held that a gift is a chargeable event. In section 17 it is now enacted that where a person acquires an asset by way of gift the disposal of it to him (as well as the acquisition of it by him) shall be deemed to be for a consideration equal to its market value. So if a father gives to his son an asset which he bought for £10,000 and at the time of the gift its market value is £14,000, father has made a chargeable (albeit notional) gain of £4,000. But notice that if the gift is a gift of British money there is no charge to *this* tax (though there may be to inheritance tax) because sterling is not an asset; section 21(1)(b). Otherwise, there would be no yardstick to measure gains.

When capital gains tax was introduced there was no other charge on gifts (except those within seven years of a death). Capital transfer tax, introduced in 1975 originally applied to all gifts and there was therefore a potential double charge to tax on a gift. When capital transfer tax mutated to inheritance tax most gifts (except those made within seven years of a death) were again excluded from the charge. Thus the relief from capital gains tax introduced in 1980 to avoid the double charge was substantially repealed.

The market value rule for gifts stated in section 17 applies not only to a disposal by way of gift but also to a disposal "otherwise than by way of a bargain made at arm's length". The idea is that if two people are closer than arm's length away from each other their dealings may be not wholly governed by commercial considerations, with the result that a deal may be done at less than market value. This might be so, for example, where a young man sells his sailing dinghy to his friend. In such a case the disposal is deemed for the purpose of capital gains tax to be at market value. So if Fred bought a boat for £5,000 and later sold it to Greg for £7,000 when its value was really £10,000, Fred has a chargeable gain of £5,000 and Greg gets a base cost of £10,000. In *Zim Properties Ltd v. Procter* (1985) a potential negligence action was held not to have been acquired at arms length or by way of bargain and was thus acquired at market value at the date the right of action accrued.

Where the parties to a transaction are "connected persons" the transaction is automatically treated as a transaction otherwise than by way of a bargain at arm's length; section 18(2). "Connected person" is defined in section 286(2) as follows: "A person is connected with an individual if that person is the individual's husband or wife, or is a relative, or the husband or wife of a relative, of the individual or of the individual's husband or wife." And by section 286(8) "relative" means "brother, sister, ancestor or lineal descendant". There are also definitions in section 286 of "connected person" in relation to trusts, partnerships and companies.

Where the parties are not connected persons the question as to whether they are at arm's length or not is a question of fact, which amounts in effect to deciding whether there was an element of gift involved. In *Bullivant Holdings Ltd v. Ellam* (1998), it was held that where X purchased a 25 per cent shareholding in a company from Y for £12,500, they were at arm's length and so that was X's base cost, even though X had acquired a 50 per cent holding in the same company on the same day from Z, which had had its market value of £350,000 attributed to it as X's base cost since X and Z were connected persons.

Where there is a gift or a sale at an undervalue the donor or vendor is primarily liable for the tax, subject to the relief mentioned above, but if he does not pay it the donee or purchaser can in certain circumstances be required to pay it.

Section 17 also applies the market value rule to cases where the consideration cannot be valued, or is connected with the loss of employment, reduction of emoluments or is in respect of the provision or services. In *Whitehouse v. Ellam* (1995) it was said that there must be a direct link at the time of the disposal between the disposal and the loss of emoluments.

Now we come on to the extended meanings of "disposal" for the purposes of the tax.

Part disposals 14–09

First, "disposal" includes a part disposal (section 21(2)). Thus where a person disposes of less than the whole of an asset (or disposes of less than his whole interest in an asset) that counts as a part disposal of the whole asset and not a disposal of part of the asset (see *Watton v. Tippett* (1996)). Generally speaking, the gain accruing on the disposal is calculated by reference to a proportion of the cost of the entire asset. A part disposal also includes the disposal of an interest in an asset, which interest is created by the disposal and did not exist before the disposal. If the owner of freehold land grants a lease (for a premium) over the land the granting of the lease is a part disposal, notwithstanding that the lease only comes into existence at the moment when the part disposal takes place. The freeholder has disposed of part of his interest in the land. While we are talking of leases let us point out that a premium for a lease is only chargeable to capital gains tax in so far as it is not chargeable to income tax (Schedule 8, para. 5(1)). This is part of a wider principle, namely that any sum charged to income tax is not to count as part of the consideration for a disposal for the purposes of capital gains tax (see section 37(1)).

14–10 *Deriving capital sums from assets*

The second extended meaning of "disposal" is this: if a capital sum is derived from assets by their owner there is assumed to be a disposal of those assets, notwithstanding that no asset is acquired by the person paying the capital sum (section 22(1)). The clearest example of this is where a shareholder receives a capital distribution in respect of his shares. This section also applies to fix the charge on those rights and claims, discussed above, which are only assets if they can be turned into account. The "turning to account" is the derivation of a capital sum from the asset, hence the disposal and the charge: *O' Brien v. Benson Hosiery (Holdings) Ltd* (1979), HL; *Zim Properties Ltd v. Procter* (1985). In the latter case it was stated to be a matter for the exercise of common sense as to the asset from which the sum is derived. It might be the right to payment itself or the property giving rise to that demand (*e.g.*, by a vendor of a house). The section was also applied in *Kirby v. Thorn EMI plc* (1987) to a company entering into a restrictive covenant not to compete with the business it had just sold. It had derived a capital sum from an asset (its goodwill).

Section 22(1) then goes on to say that the principle applies in particular to four defined circumstances: (a) capital sums received by way of compensation for any kind of damage or injury to assets or for the loss, destruction or dissipation of assets or for any depreciation or risk of depreciation of an asset. An example would be compensation for infringement of copyright; another example would be damages paid by a tortfeasor for physical damage done to an asset; (b) capital sums received under a policy of insurance covering the risk of any kind of damage, etc., to assets. This hardly needs examples; (c) capital sums received in return for forfeiture or surrender of rights, or for refraining from exercising rights. An example would be a payment received by A

212

for releasing B from his obligation under a contract;[3] (d) capital sums received as consideration for use or exploitation of assets. This seems to point towards such transactions as the grant of a right to use a copyright. In *Chaloner v. Pellipar Investments Ltd* (1996) it was said that this head could not apply where the owner granted a lease over his property. That would be a part disposal under section 21(2). The head might apply where the owner retained full title to the property, *e.g.* on the grant of a licence. The question might be asked as to why a taxpayer should argue for a disposal under head (d) rather than for a part disposal. The answer is that a disposal under heads (a)–(d) takes place when the capital sum is received (section 22(2)), whereas a part disposal takes place on the grant and, as in the case itself, that can affect the computation of the gain.

Section 22 has produced other problems of interpretation for the courts. In *Marren v. Ingles* (1980) the House of Lords held, demonstrating admirable common sense, that the meaning of "notwithstanding that no asset is acquired by the person paying the capital sum" was "whether or not" he acquired such an asset, *e.g.* absolute title to an asset on payment of a contingent sum. In *Davenport v. Chilver* (1983) the judge decided that if a capital sum was received within one of the specific headings (a–d) the section could apply even if the capital sum did not strictly derive from an asset as required by the general wording of the section (*e.g.* access to an independent compensation fund).

In *Davis v. Powell* (1977) money paid to a tenant farmer as compensation for disturbance on the ending of his lease as required by the Agricultural Holdings Act 1948 was held not to be *derived* from the lease but from the statutory right to compensation. Nor was it money received under (c) as money received for the surrender of rights under the lease—there was no element of bargain but simply a statutory computation. A similar result has been applied to business tenancies: *Drummond v. Austin-Brown* (1983), but not where the right to compensation is an independent property right, *e.g.* to a compensation fund for loss of foreign appropriated property, see *Davenport v. Chilver* (1983).

Loss, destruction and negligible value   14–11

The third extended meaning of "disposal" is set out in section 24(1):

---

[3]   *e.g.* the disposal of the company's rights in *O'Brien v. Bensons' Hosiery (Holdings) Ltd* (1979), see para. 14–07, above.

" ... the occasion of the entire loss, destruction, dissipation or extinction of an asset shall ... constitute a disposal of the asset whether or not any capital sum by way of compensation or otherwise is received in respect of the destruction, dissipation or extinction of the asset."

The *entire* loss, destruction, etc., of an asset would normally mean that it had become valueless, so the deemed disposal is a disposal for a nil consideration. The next subsection—section 24(2)—deals with a situation where there has not been entire loss, destruction, etc., but where the value of an asset has become "negligible". The effect here is that the owner is deemed to have sold and immediately re-acquired the asset at its then market value. The deemed disposal, being at a negligible value, may well give the owner a loss (compared with the price for which he had acquired the asset); the point of the deemed re-acquisition is that if the value of the asset picks up so that there is a gain on its subsequent disposal, that gain is calculated by reference to this new, low, acquisition value. This subsection only applies if the taxpayer makes a claim to the Revenue to that effect.[4]

In deciding whether an asset becomes entirely lost, destroyed, etc., or whether it merely becomes of negligible value, if the asset in question is a building it is treated as an asset separate from the land on which it stands. But the owner is deemed to have disposed of the land (as well as of the building) and also to have immediately re-acquired the land at its then market value. The effect of this is that any loss relief that the owner gets in respect of the building will be reduced by the amount of any appreciation in the value of the land itself since he acquired it.

Let us look now at the inter-relation between the destruction, etc., of an asset and the receipt of a capital sum. If an asset is totally destroyed that will produce a loss, because the deemed disposal is for a nil consideration. If the destroyer pays a sum in damages or an insurer pays insurance money that may reduce or wipe out the loss. Suppose A bought an asset for £6,000. Subsequently it was totally destroyed. A is deemed to have disposed of the asset for nothing. That produces a loss of £6,000. A few weeks later an insurance company pays A £6,000. That produces a gain of £6,000. The one balances the other, so all in all there is no loss or gain. Of course, the insurance company may pay A less than £6,000, say £5,500, in which case there is an overall loss of

---

[4] The disposal (loss) is deemed either to have taken place at the date of the claim or at any earlier time within two years prior to the tax year at the claim, if specified in the claim. It cannot be deemed to take effect any earlier: *Williams v. Bullivant* (1983).

£500. Or the insurance company may pay A more than £6,000, say £7,000, in which case there is an overall gain of £1,000. There are provisions in section 23 whereby in some situations tax on such a gain may be deferred until there is a disposal in the future. This is a kind of "hold-over" relief. ("Hold-over" relief is another splendid piece of tax jargon, to be found nowhere in the dictionary, but everywhere in the Acts. There are several kinds of hold-over relief in CGT, all amounting only to postponements of tax, rather than complete exemptions.) For example, if our friend A spends the insurance money within one year of receipt on buying a replacement asset for £7,000 the £1,000 gain is dealt with by deducting £1,000 from the acquisition cost of the replacement asset. This will have the effect of increasing by £1,000 the gain to A when he comes to dispose of the replacement asset in the future. So A will be in exactly the same position as he would have been in if the asset had never been destroyed. Suppose A sells the asset (the replacement asset) eventually for £9,000. When he sells the asset, he deducts £1,000 from the replacement cost (which was £7,000) so his gain is £9,000 minus £6,000 = £3,000. If the original asset (which cost £6,000) had never been destroyed his gain would equally have been £3,000. These provisions apply not only to insurance money received but also to damages received. A somewhat similar system operates where an asset is not destroyed but only damaged.

We have now dealt with the extended meanings of "disposal," except for some which occur in connection with settled property (on which see below at paras 14–22 *et seq.*).

What we must do now is to look at some particular disposal situations.

DISPOSALS FOR A DEFERRED OR CONTINGENT CONSIDERATION

14–12

Suppose that A sells an asset to B for £500 payable immediately and £100 per month payable for the next 10 months. The consideration received by A for that asset for capital gains tax purposes is £1,500 (£500 + 10 × £100) and he is deemed to have received this amount at the date of sale (date of the contract, unless it is a conditional contract in which case it is the date on which the condition is fulfilled[5], section 28). Section 48 makes it clear that no allowance is to be made for the fact that A will not

[5] See *e.g. Hatt v. Newmann* (2000). A conditional contract is one where all the liabilities under the contract are conditional and not where, *e.g.* property is to pass only on payment of all instalments under a contract of sale: *Lyon v. Pettigrew* (1985).

receive the full amount at that time. This is an example of a disposal for a deferred consideration (*i.e.* a future payment which will become payable).

The position is more complex in relation to disposals for a contingent consideration (*i.e.* a future payment, which may or may not become payable, usually of an uncertain amount). This has caused problems which had to be resolved by the House of Lords in *Marren v. Ingles* (1980). In that case the taxpayer agreed to sell 60 shares in an unquoted company for £700 each, payable immediately, and a stated percentage of the sale price quoted for those shares if the company was floated on the stock exchange. When the company was floated the purchaser became liable to pay the taxpayer £2,825 for each share. Clearly there was a disposal of assets for at least £700 each but how to deal with the additional amount?

The Revenue did not seek to charge the tax by reference to a single disposal on the original agreement but by reference to two disposals—one of the shares on the agreement and one of the right to the contingent payments under section 22(1) as the receipt of a capital sum derived from that right on payment of the extra amount. After much technical argument by the judge and the Court of Appeal on the merits of applying section 22(1), the House of Lords held that the section could apply whether the purchaser was thereby acquiring full title to the shares or simply extinguishing a liability to pay an additional sum. The judge, Slade J, also discussed whether section 17 could have applied (*i.e.* a disposal where the consideration cannot be valued is to be charged at market value) or whether it could be regarded as two part-disposals, but expressed no opinion on the matter. Section 48, which provides that deferred or contingent consideration be added back onto the proceeds of the disposal as if paid at the time, relates only to the first disposal, and in a *Marren v. Ingles* situation any such contingent consideration can only be valued then on an actuarial (*i.e.* reduced) basis. The second disposal catches the full amount actually paid. Thus the argument of the taypayer in *Marson v. Marriage* (1980) that since the original disposal was prior to 1965 (at that time the starting date for the tax) and the contingent payments (in that case for land subsequently developed) after 1965, section 48 required all the considerations to be regarded as pre–1965 and so out of the charge, failed, and the principle of *Marren v. Ingles* was applied.

APPROPRIATIONS TO AND FROM STOCK IN TRADE

It will be remembered that under the principle of *Sharkey v. Wernher* (1956), HL where a trader disposes of part of his stock in trade not by sale but for his own use he must, for the purposes of income tax, bring into his accounts as a receipt the market value of the asset at that time. And of course the converse applies—where a trader transfers an item from his own recreational enjoyment into his trade he can show in his accounts the market value of that item as an expense of the trade.

Now, how does capital gains tax bear on these events? Where a person who is a trader transfers a personal asset to his trade that appropriation is treated as a disposal, thus involving a gain or a loss compared with its earlier acquisition cost: section 161(1). But he can, if he wishes, avoid payment of capital gains tax by electing to bring the asset into trading stock not at its then market value simply, but at its then market value reduced by the amount of the chargeable gain or increased by the amount of the allowable loss (section 161(3)). (A partner can only make this election if the other partners concur.) Take the case of a gain: the effect is that the item appears in his trading account amongst "purchases" at a figure below its true value by the amount of the gain, thus swelling his trading profits for that year by that amount.

In the converse case, where a trader transfers an item of trading stock to his personal enjoyment he is treated as having acquired it for a consideration equal to the amount then brought into the accounts of the trade in respect of that item for income tax purposes. Thus the closing figure for the item for income tax purposes is taken as the base cost for capital gains tax purposes: section 161(2). For income tax purposes no doubt the trader would like to put a low figure on the item, thus reducing his trade receipts and so his profits. But a low figure for income tax means a low base cost, which will in the end involve him in more capital gains tax.

The practical importance of the provisions we have been discussing is reduced by the presence of an exemption from capital gains tax in the case of a disposal of an asset which is tangible movable property and which is a wasting asset: see below at paragraph 16–07. But of course not all stock in trade is tangible movable property. It may be tangible without being movable (*e.g.* land) or movable without being tangible (*e.g.* stocks and shares).

14–14 CAPITAL DISTRIBUTIONS BY COMPANIES

Where a person receives a capital distribution (other than a new holding, on which see the next heading) in respect of shares in a company, he is treated as if in consideration of that distribution he had disposed of an interest in the shares (section 122). This applies for example when a company makes a "rights" issue of shares[6] and a shareholder sells his rights. Another example of its application is when a liquidator makes a repayment of capital to shareholders in the course of a winding-up. If, however, the amount of any capital distribution is "small"[7] as compared with the value of the shares the occurrence is not treated as a disposal, but instead the amount of the distribution is deducted from the expenditure allowable as a deduction in computing a gain when the shareholder comes to dispose of the shares in the future. This of course has the effect of increasing the gain and hence the tax. It is a kind of hold-over relief.

14–15 COMPANY ADJUSTMENTS

There are detailed provisions (in sections 126–140) as to the bearing of capital gains tax on the re-organisation of a company's share capital, the conversion of securities and the amalgamation of companies. We will not go into all the details here. One example is this: where a company makes a "bonus" issue or a "rights" issue of shares and a shareholder takes up the shares (a "new holding") the new shares are treated as acquired when the original shares were acquired, and the acquisition cost of the total holding is the cost of the original shares plus the sum (if any) which the shareholder pays for the new holding. In the case of a company amalgamation (or take-over) then, subject to certain conditions, the exchange of shares in one company for shares in another company does not count as a disposal. This rule led to a great deal of tax avoidance and the relief has been subjected to two conditions, namely that the change must be effected for bona fide commercial reasons and it must not form part of a scheme or arrangements of which the main purpose or one of the main purposes is avoidance of tax liability: see section 137.

14–16 TRANSFER OF BUSINESS TO A COMPANY

Where a person (other than a company) transfers a business as a going concern (and with its assets) to a company wholly or partly in exchange for shares, the gain on the transferred assets is

---

[6] This is an issue of shares which are offered first to existing shareholders.
[7] The Revenue takes the view that "small" means less than £3,000 or 5 per cent of the value of the shares, if greater.

computed but not charged to tax. The gain is apportioned between the shares received and any other consideration received. That part of the gain attributed to the shares is not assessed but is deducted from the allowable cost of the shares when the transferor of the business comes to dispose of them in the future. So it is a form of roll-over relief. The part of the gain attributed to the consideration other than shares (*e.g* cash) is assessed at once in the normal way. This matter is dealt with a section 162.

DEBTS 14–17

The "satisfaction" of a debt is a disposal by the creditor. "Satisfaction" of a debt includes payment-off of the debt, and it also includes assignment of the debt. It may be worth discussing what the creditor whose debtor pays him a debt is disposing of. The answer is that he is disposing of the debt itself, which is a chose in action—a species of right. There are many circumstances in the law of capital gains tax where it is more obvious that a person is acquiring something (*e.g* money in satisfaction of a debt) than that he is disposing of something. If one looks closely one sees that he is disposing of the right to obtain that which he acquires. Where does the capital gain come in in connection with a debt? The answer to that is that the capital gain is the difference between what the creditor lent and what he gets back as a capital sum.

Although, in general, satisfaction of a debt is a disposal (section 251), so far as concerns the original creditor no chargeable gain accrues on the disposal. And the same is true of the original creditor's personal representative or legatee. At first sight this seems very good of the Revenue, but the point is really directed against losses. It is a general principle of capital gains tax law that a loss cannot be claimed from a transaction upon which, if there had been a gain, it would not have been a chargeable gain. This principle is modified for debts which prove to be bad debts by section 253, introduced in 1978. That section was enacted because huge losses had been incurred during the slump of the mid–1970s. The section provides that where a loan or part of a loan *to a trader* becomes irrecoverable the original creditor or a guarantor can claim the loss as an allowable loss.

The rule that no chargeable gain (and hence—subject to section 253—no allowable loss) can arise to the original creditor (or his personal representative or legatee) does not apply to a "debt on a security." The courts have struggled to decide what exactly amounts to a debt on a security. The most recent decision is that of the Court of Appeal in *Taylor Clark International Ltd v. Lewis* (1998). It does not mean the same as a secured debt, *e.g.* a debt secured by a mortgage or charge. Instead it is said to encompass debts which are really held as investments, and so can lead to a gain or loss, whether protected by a security or not. One important factor seems to be whether the debt is held in a marketable form. The obvious example is loan stock of a company or local authority (see section 132(3)(b)). However, gains on what are known as "qualifying corporate bonds" (company debentures) are exempt from the charge to capital gains tax for individuals and so cannot give rise to any allowable losses (section 117).[8]

The assignee of a debt (as distinct from the original creditor) does make a chargeable gain (or an allowable loss) when the debt is satisfied, whether it be a debt on a security or not. This rule (if it stood alone) would open the way to a great deal of tax avoidance, because it is very easy to contrive a loss on a debt. So there are provisions to stop up these possibilities. A loss made by a person on the disposal of a debt is disallowed if he acquired the debt from a "connected person": section 251(4). So if A sells a debt to B for £1,200 and later X (the debtor) pays up £1,000 to B, B cannot claim a loss of £200 if A and B are connected persons. If this were not so, and B *could* claim a loss, it would be a way of B making a gift of £200 to A, to which gift the Revenue would be contributing.

Sometimes a creditor takes property instead of money in satisfaction of a debt. In that case the base cost of the property is its then market value and no more. This looks as though it is going to prejudice the creditor when he comes to sell the property. And so it does in the case of a creditor who is not the original creditor, but is a person who has acquired the debt by assignment. So if A assigns to B a debt of £5,000 for £5,000 and then X (the debtor) hands over to B in satisfaction of the debt property worth £4,500, the base cost of the property is £4,500. So if, later, B sells the property for £5,200 he has made a gain of £700. But if the *original* creditor (A) (not having assigned the debt) accepts from the debtor in satisfaction of the debt property worth £4,500 the chargeable gain to A, when he comes to sell the property, is not to exceed the chargeable gain which would have accrued to him if he had acquired the property for a consideration equal to the amount of the debt. So if the debt was £5,000, the property was worth £4,500 and A later sells it for £5,200, A's chargeable gain is £200 (not £700). These matters are dealt with in section 251(3).

14–18   OPTIONS

An option is an asset. The grant of an option is treated as a disposal. Where the option is exercised the grant and the exercise

---

[8] Companies may still get relief on such losses under corporation tax rules.

are treated as all one transaction. So if A grants to B an option to buy certain property and B subsequently exercises the option and buys the property, the sum paid for the option and the sum paid for the property are added together to ascertain the disposal cost (for A) and the acquisition cost (for B). Supposing, on the other hand, that an option is granted and then abandoned (*i.e.* not exercised): A is left with the gain on the grant of the option; for B the abandonment of the option does not count as a disposal for the purposes of section 24 (total loss, asset becoming of negligible value, etc.)—with the result that, although he has lost money, he does not get any loss relief. On the other hand if the option is abandoned by agreement for a consideration, *i.e.* A pays B to release the option, that will be a disposal by B under section 22(1) (derivation of a capital sum from an asset). Thus if the option is released for a nominal amount loss relief will be available. These and other rules are set out in sections 144–147, as interpreted by Vinelott J. in *Golding v. Kaufman* (1985).

VALUE SHIFTING   14–19
This is the dramatic and cryptic heading given to sections 29 to 34. Section 29 begins with a general introduction, and it then proceeds to deal with four specific situations.

First, if a person having control of a company exercises his control so that value passes out of his shares (or other rights) or out of the shares (or rights) of a person with whom he is connected into other shares (or rights) that is a disposal of the shares (or rights). An example would be if A, who holds the only shares which carry voting rights in a company, were to pass a resolution to transfer the voting rights to the shares held by other shareholders. It is, after all, a kind of gift. For a more sophisticated example, see *Floor v. Davis* (1980) (H.L).

Secondly, if there has been a shift of value as above, and subsequently the transferor disposes at a loss of some other asset which has depreciated in value by reason of the shift, that loss is not an allowable loss.

Thirdly, if there is a sale and lease back of land or other property and then subsequently there is an adjustment of the rights and liabilities under the lease which is favourable to the lessor, that counts as a disposal by the lessee of an interest in the property. The idea behind this rule is that the seller has really sold the property for less than its true value. Suppose A, the owner of a factory, sells the freehold of it to B for £100,000 and B immediately leases it back to A at a rent of £5,000 a year. Later an adjustment is made in the terms of the lease in favour of B, so that in effect B is to get £6,000 a year from the property. On this footing the price that A received for the freehold turns out be less than what he could have got for it, with the result that A paid less capital gains tax on the disposal of the freehold than he "should" have done. This present provision, by treating the adjustment in the lease as a disposal by A, enables the Revenue to pick up the lost tax.

Fourthly, if an asset is subject to some right or restriction and then the person entitled to enforce the right or restriction abrogates it, that abrogation counts as a disposal by that person of the right or restriction. An example of this would be if A, who had chartered a ship from B, were to release B from his obligations under the charterparty. That would be a disposal by A of his rights under the charterparty.

Section 30 was enacted (originally in 1977) to strike at some tax avoidance schemes which were based on transferring some of the value of a chargeable asset into a non-chargeable asset. The section is in very wide terms and has the potential to become a general anti-avoidance weapon. It will not apply if the taxpayer can show that tax avoidance was not the main purpose of the scheme.

Sections 31 to 34 (enacted in 1989 and amended in 1999) are aimed at preventing a group of companies from selling a subsidiary company with a reduced value, having shifted that value into other companies within the group prior to the sale.

14–20   HUSBAND AND WIFE

As we have seen, disposals *between* spouses who are living together are treated (by section 58) "as if the asset was acquired from the one making the disposal for a consideration of such amount as would secure that on the disposal neither a gain nor a loss would accrue to the one making the disposal."[9] Broadly the effect of this is that the transferee takes the asset at the base cost which it had in the hands of the transferor. But it is a little better than that, because the words of the section seem to imply that if there are some incidental costs of the inter-spousal transfer the base cost for the transferee is to include those costs. Thus if H bought an item for £100 and subsequently transferred it to W and the costs of the transfer were £5, the base cost for W (looking to a future disposal by her) would be £105. W's base cost will also include an amount to cover inflation since H bought the asset, or from March 1982 if later up to 1998. On a subsequent disposal

---

[9] This rule does not apply if (a) the asset is trading stock of the transferor or is acquired as trading stock of the transferee, or (b) the disposal is by way of *donatio mortis causa*.

by W taper relief will be calculated by reference to the date when the asset was acquired by H.

Death

Until 1971 death was in itself a chargeable event for capital gains tax thus providing a double charge with estate duty (the predecessor of inheritance tax). The Finance Act 1971 abolished the charge. But a person's death still has important consequences—for his or her survivors. The subject of death is now dealt with in section 62 of the 1992 Act. Section 62(1) provides:

" ... the assets of which a deceased person was competent to dispose—
(a) shall be deemed to be acquired on his death by the personal representatives or other person on whom they devolve for a consideration equal to their market value at the date of death; but
(b) shall not be deemed to be disposed of by him on his death ..."

The main point of the phrase "assets of which a deceased person was competent to dispose" is to exclude settled property in which the deceased had an interest. Settled property is governed by different rules which are discussed under the next heading. To take an example, if, when A dies, he is the life tenant under a settlement, he is not "competent to dispose" of the settled property. One can speak of property of which a deceased person was competent to dispose as being his "free estate".

The effect of section 62(1) is that so far as concerns the deceased's free estate, the death does not give rise to a charge to capital gains tax, but it does give rise to an "uplift" in the base cost of his assets. This, of course, is advantageous for the future. If A bought an asset for £50,000 and later died when its market value was £60,000, the base cost becomes £60,000. On a future disposal of the asset for £65,000, the gain is £5,000 and not £15,000 so that £10,000 gains have been written off. It must be borne in mind, however, that inheritance tax will (or may) be payable on the death of A on the full value of £60,000. Indeed the idea behind the exemption from capital gains tax on death is that death should not be an occasion of charge to both taxes. But it goes a bit further than that, because there is no charge to capital gains tax on death even if there is no charge to inheritance tax either, as for instance where assets are left to a surviving spouse. (See para. 19–01 below).

The next question which arises is this: when the personal representatives come to dispose of the assets in the course of the administration of the deceased's estate, is that disposal a chargeable event? The answer is that if the disposal is to a legatee that is not a chargeable event, but if the disposal is to anyone else it is a chargeable event.

A legatee gets as his base cost the market value of the asset at the time of the deceased's death; section 62(4). "Legatee" is given by section 64(2) and (3) an extended meaning. It includes any person taking under a testamentary disposition (a will) or under an intestacy or partial intestacy, whether he takes beneficially or as trustee. And where the personal representatives appropriate assets to satisfy a legacy, the person taking under the appropriation is deemed to be a legatee. Also, by section 62, subsections (6) to (9), if the deceased's dispositions are varied by an instrument in writing made by the persons entitled within two years of the death, the variations do not count as disposals, except such variations as are made for a consideration (other than a consideration consisting of some other variation).

A disposal by personal representatives otherwise than to a legatee *does* involve a chargeable gain or allowable loss. This is so, for example, if they sell an asset in order to pay inheritance tax, or if they simply re-arrange the investment portfolio. There is no provision for personal representatives to offset their losses against gains of the deceased. If the deceased had, in the year of assessment in which he died, an excess of losses over gains these may be "rolled backwards" for the preceding three years before taper relief is applied: section 62(2).

14–22 Settled Property

"Settled property" is defined in section 68 as "any property held in trust[10] other than property to which section 60 ... applies." So the first thing to do is to find out what section 60 is all about. It deals with the situation where one person is nominee for another person or is a bare trustee for another person. Neither a nominee nor a bare trustee counts as a trustee, and the property they hold is not settled property. The property is treated as though it were vested in the person for whom the nominee or bare trustee is holding it, *i.e.* the beneficiary. Unfortunately (from the point of view of clarity) section 60 itself does not use the phrase

---

[10] A unit trust scheme does not count as a trust (nor does an investment trust company). Both count as companies, though with some special rules of their own.

"bare trustee," but there is an illuminating translation of the phrase used in the section, namely "trustee for another person absolutely entitled as against the trustee, or for any person who would be so entitled but for being an infant or other person under disability (or for two or more persons who are or would be jointly so entitled) ... ". The phrase "bare trustee" does occur in the marginal note to section 60. Section 60(2) says this:

> "It is hereby declared that references in this Act to any asset held by a person as trustee for another person absolutely entitled as against the trustee are references to a case where that other person has the exclusive right, subject only to satisfying any outstanding charge, lien or other right of the trustee[11] to resort to the asset for payment of duty, taxes, costs or other outgoings, to direct how that asset shall be dealt with."

The words "jointly so entitled" in section 60 do not refer only to persons who are technically joint tenants; they cover also persons who are tenants in common. So *concurrent interests* can exist (whether in the form of a joint tenancy or a tenancy in common) without the property in which the interests subsist being settled property, provided the "tenants" can direct the trustee how the asset shall be dealt with: see *Kidson v. MacDonald* (1974). This point is not confined to real property; the word "jointly" refers to "persons who are, as it were, in the same interest", whatever the subject matter of the trust (*per* Walton J. in *Stephenson v. Barclays Bank Trust Co. Ltd.* (1975)). On the other hand it was held in both those cases that where there are *interests in succession* (*e.g.* where there is a trust for A for life with remainder to B) the trustees can never be bare trustees and the property must be settled property. This is because, although A and B are *together* entitled absolutely as against the trustee, they are not entitled "jointly" and so section 60 can never be satisfied.[12]

If the beneficiaries' interests are contingent they are clearly not absolutely entitled as against the trustees, even if the only contingency is on their obtaining the age of majority. They are not absolutely entitled "but for their infancy" but because they only have contingent interests: see *Tomlinson v. Glyns Executor Co.* (1970).

---

[11] This does not include payment of an annuity under the trust. Thus the presence of an annuity prevents the beneficiaries being absolutely entitled: *Stephenson v Barclays Bank Trust Co. Ltd* (1975).

[12] In *Booth v. Ellard* (1980) it was accepted that the interests of the beneficiaries must be concurrent and all must be the same. See also *Harthan v. Mason* (1980).

The essential criteria for a bare trust is that the beneficiary (or beneficiaries) must be able to direct the trustees as to how to deal with the trust property and to give a valid receipt for it. Actual transfer is not required, just the right to do so: *Stephenson v. Barclays Bank Trust Co. Ltd* (1975). This has been applied to what are known as "putting arrangements." Thus where all the members of a private company transferred their shares to trustees and subjected themselves to restrictions on transfer they were held to be absolutely entitled since they could collectively end the trust and so destroy or override any discretions or powers vested in the trustees.[13] Similarly where a family entitled to farming property set up a trust in which each member's interest was equivalent to their previous entitlements there was held to be no settlement for capital gains tax purposes.[14] The importance of this is that there is no exit charge if one member takes his interest out of the trust (see para 14–25, below). On the other hand, in the case of class gifts, *e.g.* "to such of my grandchildren born within 21 years of my death", the beneficiaries cannot be absolutely entitled until the class has closed, *i.e.* there can be no more potential beneficiaries. Until then the size of each grandchild's share is unknown.[15] Different considerations apply where each potential beneficiary has a defined share, *e.g.* "one quarter to each of my grandchildren on attaining 21". In this case when each beneficiary attains a vested interest (*i.e.* attains 21) the question of whether he becomes absolutely entitled to that part of the settled property depends upon whether he can require the trustee to appropriate that part of it to him. In the case of land held on trust, for example, the trustees have a power to postpone sale by law, and this can only be overridden by the court or by all the beneficiaries acting together. Thus in *Crowe v. Appleby* (1975) such beneficiaries were held not to be absolutely entitled against the trustees. The position would usually be different if the trust property consisted of money or quoted securities which are easily divisible.

If the trustees are not bare trustees then "any property held in trust" is settled property.

We must now consider the events connected with settled property which count as disposals.

14–23 ## PUTTING PROPERTY INTO SETTLEMENT

A transfer of property into a settlement is a disposal of the *entire property* thereby becoming settled property: section 70.

---

[13] *Booth v. Ellard* (1980).
[14] *Jenkins v. Brown* (1989).
[15] For this purpose any individual is deemed to be capable of having children until he or she dies: *Figg v. Clarke* (1997).

This is so even if the donor takes some interest as a beneficiary under the settlement or is a trustee or the sole trustee of the settlement. This is a pretty harsh rule. Suppose Mr Smith wishes to give his house to his nephew, but to retain for himself the right to occupy the house for the rest of his life, so that the nephew will only come into occupation when S dies (S for Smith and also for "settlor"). S can only carry out this transaction by putting the house into settlement. It is a transfer of property into a settlement and so it is treated as a disposal of the entire property. That means that the deemed consideration for the disposal is the whole capital value of the house. This does not accord with the reality, because in reality all that S has given away is the remainder interest. The same point can occur the other way round: S may want to allow his aged aunt to live in the house for her life. He makes a settlement under which the aunt gets a life interest and he retains the remainder interest. There is a charge to tax based on the value of "the entire property" when this transfer is made. In reality all that S has given away is a tiny fraction of the value of the entire property.

DISPOSALS BY TRUSTEES
14–24

Trustees, though they are not "individuals," are "persons", and they are chargeable to capital gains tax at 34 per cent. They are chargeable, for example, on gains made in the course of switching investments in the trust's portfolio. But where the settler or the settler's spouse has an interest in the settlement the gains are taxable as if they had been realised by the settler and not the trustees, *i.e.* at the possible higher rate of 40 per cent.

There is also one general situation (special to trustees) where they are *deemed* to dispose of assets comprised in the settled property. This is where a person becomes absolutely entitled to settled property and is known as the "exit charge" (section 71(1)). In addition, although there is no deemed disposal, there is a deemed re-acquisition by them where an interest in possession terminates by reason of the death of the person entitled to it (section 72(1)). In general, as we shall see, the fact that the trustees are so liable means that the disposal by a beneficiary of an interest in the settlement is not a chargeable disposal, otherwise there would be a double taxation. There is an exception to this, however, where the interest disposed of is one in which the settler or the settler's spouse has an interest. We will look at these situations in turn.

(1) A person becoming absolutely entitled
14–25

Suppose assets are held in trust for A contingently on his attaining the age of 25. When A becomes 25 that is an occasion of charge under section 71(1). The assets are deemed to have been disposed of by the trustee and immediately re-acquired by him in his capacity as a bare trustee within section 60(1), for a consideration equal to their market value. After that it makes no difference whether the trustee hands over the property to A at once or keeps it as bare trustee for him. The actual handing over of the property to A is not a chargeable event because it is deemed to be A's already by virtue of section 60(1). The upshot is that the trustees pay tax on the gain represented by the increase in value of the assets between the time when they were put into trust and the time when A became 25, and A takes as his base cost the market value on the day when he attained 25.

If an asset has fallen in value so as to create a loss on the deemed disposal by the trustees, that loss is transferred to A only if the trustees cannot set it off against gains arising at the same time or earlier in the same tax year. But A can only use that loss to offset a subsequent gain by him on the disposal of that asset, or if the asset is land, any asset which is derived from it. In no circumstances can a loss incurred by the trustees on the actual disposal of an asset be transferred to A (section 71(2)).

Where the event which causes a person to become absolutely entitled is caused by the *death of* the person entitled to an interest in possession (including an annuity), no chargeable gain accrues on that disposal (section 73(1)(a)). All that happens is that the trustee is deemed to dispose of the settled property and immediately re-acquire it as a bare trustee. The effect is that there is an uplift of the base cost to the market value at the time of the death. The person who becomes absolutely entitled acquires the property at the up-to-date value. This, of course, is advantageous to him when he comes to dispose of the property in the future. Suppose property is settled on A for life, with remainder to B absolutely. On A's death B becomes absolutely entitled. There is no charge to capital gains tax (even if there is no charge to inheritance tax either) but there is an uplift in line with the general rule on deaths.

There is a special exception to this advantageous rule where there arises what is called "reverter to the disponer". The background to this point is that no inheritance tax is payable on the death of X where X has been given a life interest by S (settlor) in such terms that the property reverts, on X's death, to S. If in this situation S could also get, on the death of X, an uplift in the base cost for purposes of capital gains tax that would be too favourable to S. So he cannot; see section 73(1)(b). If, on the life tenant's death, property reverts to the disponer (settlor), the disposal and re-acquisition shall be deemed to be for such consideration as to secure that neither a gain nor a loss accrues to the trustee. Thus, suppose S grants a life interest to X in property which at the time of the grant is worth £10,000. X dies at a time when the market value of the property is £14,000. The property reverts to S. The trustee is treated as re-acquiring the asset for £10,000 (not £14,000) and that figure (£10,000) becomes S's base cost.

(2) Termination of an interest in possession by death
14–26

This situation is dealt with by section 72(1). Naturally, the termination of an interest in possession by the death of the person entitled to it and the absolute entitlement of some person often happen on the same event. If property is held in trust for A for life with remainder to B, the event of A's death brings about the termination of a life interest (A's) *and* the absolute entitlement of some person (B). In this situation it is section 71(1) which applies. Section 72(1) applies only where there is a termination of an interest in possession by the death of the person entitled to it but still no one becomes absolutely entitled. This would be so, for example, where property is settled on A for life, remainder to B for life, remainder to C absolutely, and A dies. On A's death there is the termination of his interest by his death but no one becomes absolutely entitled; B becomes entitled for life and section 72(1) applies. On B's death (or surrender) section 71(1) applies, because C does become absolutely entitled. If B died before A, however, section 72(1) would not apply since B's interest is not in possession. Nor would section 71(1) apply because no one would become absolutely entitled.

Section 72(1) applies only on the death of the person entitled to the interest in possession (including an annuity) and provides that there is no charge to tax, but there is an uplift in the base cost in the same way as section 73 operates in relation to a section 71 charge.[16] There is still an uplift (and no charge to tax) even if the property is exempt from inheritance tax (*e.g.* because the property passes from a deceased husband to his widow). There is no uplift under section 72 where an interest terminates otherwise then on a death, *e.g.* by a surrender. Only section 71 can apply in that case if someone becomes absolutely entitled.

It is important to note that the exemption from charge and base uplift given by section 73(1)(a) and the base uplift given by section 72 (which we have just been speaking about) only apply where the event causing a person to become absolutely entitled or causing the termination of an interest in possession is the death of

---

[16] Section 72 applies to a life interest in part of the settled property. This includes any form of joint interest: *Pexton v. Bell* (1975), CA.

the person *entitled* to the interest. If A is life tenant (with remainder to B) and A dies still holding the life tenancy, there is no charge to capital gains tax, only an uplift. But if A (life tenant) assigns his interest to X, there is a charge when A dies, even though X's interest comes to an end on A's death. B becomes absolutely entitled, and section 71(1) imposes a charge to tax. The charge is not relieved by section 73(1)(a) for the reason that B's becoming absolutely entitled is not caused by the death of the person *entitled* to the interest because A was not (at death) *entitled* to it. Similarly, if A is life tenant under a settlement for A for life, then for B for life, then for C absolutely. If A is still holding the life tenancy when he dies there is the termination of a life interest and an uplift of the base price, because the termination arises on the death of the person entitled. But if A had assigned his interest to X there is a charge on A's death; section 72(1) does not apply and there is no uplift of the base price.

The charge to tax under section 71(1) which arises on the death of a former life tenant who has assigned his interest will be in addition to a charge to inheritance tax.

14–27   **TRANSFERS BETWEEN TRUSTS**

Trustees are liable for capital gains tax in respect of their own settlement. By virtue of section 69 the trustees for the time being are regarded as one body for this purpose, so that there is no charge on a change of trustees. The position is more complex, however, where under a power in the settlement the trustees transfer assets to another trust, of which they may or may not be the trustees. The crucial question is whether the second settlement can be regarded as a separate settlement or as merely a subsidiary part of the first. If they are separate settlements then it appears that the trustees of the second trust will become absolutely entitled as against the trustees of the first, and an exit charge can be made under section 71(1), discussed above. In *Hoare Trustees v. Gardner* (1978) the judge decided that the second trustees need not be beneficially entitled as against the original trustees, nor did the section require them to be absolutely entitled as against the whole world (clearly they were not so as against the second beneficiaries). This was so even though the trustees of both trusts were identical.

If the second settlement is, however, merely a subsidiary of the first trust then the trustees of either trust will be liable for the gains of both but there will be no exit charge. This has been a particularly useful device for the Revenue where one set of trustees is non-resident and so not chargeable to the tax. In *Roome v. Edwards* (1982) Lord Wilberforce laid down the test to determine whether there are one or two settlements as follows: "The question whether a particular set of facts amounts to a settlement should be approached by asking what a person, with knowledge of the legal content of the word under established doctrine and applying this knowledge in a practical and common-sense manner to the facts under examination would conclude." In that case, since the original settlement was still in existence and the second settlement was treated as being held on the trusts of the first as added to and varied by the first, the two settlements could be treated as one.

Each case depends upon its facts and there are no golden rules. Separate administration and separate trust accounts may be relevant.[17] In *Bond v. Pickford* (1983) the Court of Appeal drew a distinction between trustees transferring property under a power which altered the operative trusts of a settlement, thus allowing removal of the assets from the original settlement altogether (*i.e.* powers in the wider form) where there would be a charge under section 71, and powers in a narrower form which do not confer such authority. In that case a power to allocate funds for discretionary beneficiaries which were subject to the rules of the trust was held to be a narrower form power. The trustees of the original settlement continued to be responsible in that capacity for the allocated funds. The Revenue have indicated in a Statement of Practice (SP 7/84) that there will be no charge under section 71(1) (and so no separate settlement) if there is an exercise of a power in the wider form if either it is revocable or where the trusts declared are not exhaustive so that they may at some time come back into the trusts or reference still has to be made to the trustees' original powers of administration or disposition. There will equally be no deemed disposal if the duties of the trustees of the second settlement fall to the trustees as trustees of the first. Separate identity of the trustees is irrelevant, as is the location of the mechanical powers of the trustees. However, in *Swires v. Renton* (1991), Hoffmann J. suggested that even if the funds were transferred under a wider form power the question remained as to whether there was a new settlement or whether it was being "grafted onto" the existing settlement. If any reference back to the original settlement was required then this would indicate that no new settlement had been created.

---

[17] Vinelott J. in *Ewart v. Taylor* (1983) regarded this as an important factor together with the fact that the transfer to the second settlement was part of a scheme to wind up the first, in finding that the two settlements were separate.

14–28 TAX POSITION OF THE BENEFICIARIES

The legislation is not notably generous to trustees or beneficiaries, but beneficiaries do have one crumb of comfort. It is to be found in section 76(1). If a person, other than the settlor or settlor's spouse, is holding an interest under a settlement and that interest was created for his benefit, then, unless the trustees are non-resident, no chargeable gain arises if he disposes of his interest. Thus, suppose property is held in trust for A for life with remainder to B absolutely. If A assigns (*e.g.* sells) his life interest that is not a chargeable event. The same is true if B sells his remainder interest. And if it happens that B dies while A is still alive, B's personal representatives can sell B's remainder interest without tax arising. But a person who acquired an interest for consideration in money or money's worth (other than consideration consisting of another interest under the settlement) and then sells the interest is liable to tax on any gain involved. So if X bought A's life interest (or B's remainder interest) and then sold it at a gain he would be liable to tax. And if X, having bought B's remainder interest and still holding it when A died, would be treated as disposing of the remainder interest in consideration of obtaining the settled property itself and so a charge to tax would arise: section 76(2).

There is an exception to the general rule that the disposal of a non-purchased interest is not a chargeable event where the relevant interest is held in a settlement in which the settlor or his spouse has an interest. Where such an interest, whether owned by the settlor or not, is disposed of for actual consideration (other than another interest in the settlement) the trustees will be deemed to have made a disposal of the assets to which that interest relates to themselves at market value: section 76A and Schedule 4A. Unless the interest is in a specific fund or in a specific fraction of the income or capital, this means a deemed disposal of all the trust assets. This is intended to prevent, *e.g.* a settlor transferring an asset into a settlement (using one of the roll over reliefs) and then selling his interest in the settlement, thus effectively transferring the asset tax free. Liability for the tax falls on the trustees, but they have a right of recovery from the person disposing of the interest.

The legislation also permits adjustments of the interest of several beneficiaries amongst themselves without a charge to tax arising. "Partition" of settled property is quite a common occurrence. A, a life tenant, may surrender his life interest in part of the trust property in return for an interest in the capital. A is not treated as acquiring his interest in capital for money or money's worth because he has acquired it in exchange for "another interest" (*i.e.* his life interest) "under the settlement" and that does not count as money or money's worth. Consequently if A were to carry out the above transaction and then sell his interest in capital (a remainder interest) at a gain, he would not be liable to tax.

PAYMENT OF THE TAX

14–29

A beneficiary may become liable to pay tax which has been assessed on the trustees. This will be so where the tax is not paid within six months of its due date and the asset concerned or a part of it or the proceeds of it are transferred by the trustees to the beneficiary. He can be assessed at any time within two years from the due date on the chargeable gain or, in the case of a transfer of a part, on a proportionate part of the chargeable gain; section 69(4).

Chapter 15

GAINS AND LOSSES

Putting it very broadly the amount of a chargeable gain or of an allowable loss is arrived at by comparing the consideration received on the disposal of an asset with the cost of its acquisition. What we must now do is to look in more detail at the way in which the computation is done. If the asset is a foreign asset the consideration received and the costs of acquisition must be converted into sterling at the rate of exchange applicable at each event so that the gain or loss may be affected by fluctuations in exchange rates.[1] And by section 16(1) a loss is to be computed in the same way as a gain.

We will look first at the general rules of computation laid down in Part II, Chapter I (sections 15 to 20) and Chapter III (sections 37 to 52) of the Act. Applying those rules will produce what may be referred to as the **gross gain**. But, as we have seen, we then have to look at the rules providing for relief from the effects of inflation (limited to periods up to April 1998 for individuals) and taper relief for individuals for periods after that date. Applying those rules to the **gross gain** produces the **chargeable gain,** *i.e.* the amount upon which tax is actually payable at the rates set out in the previous chapter once the total of chargeable gains exceeds an individual's exempt amount for that year.[2] Next we shall look at the special rules where the asset disposed of was owned by the taxpayer on March 31, 1982. These are necessary because it should be remembered that no gains accruing before then are taxable. There are further special rules where the asset was owned on April 6, 1965, *i.e.* when the tax was first introduced (a somewhat diminishing band). Finally we look at the position where the computation produces a loss rather than a gain.

---

[1] *Bentley v. Pike* (1981); *Capcount Trading v. Evans* (1993), CA. This is not the position with regard to income taxation.

[2] Companies pay corporation tax on their chargeable gains and have no exempt amount.

General Rules—Computing the Gross Gain   15–01

Income receipts and expenditure

First, there is to be excluded from the consideration for a disposal any sum which is taken into account for income tax (section 3). An example would be the whole of the consideration for the sale of an asset by a dealer in such assets. Another example would be that part of a lease premium which was chargeable to income tax. Special rules apply to assets which have enjoyed capital allowances.

Similarly expenditure which would be allowable in an income tax computation is not allowable for capital gains tax (section 39). In making this decision the section requires that the asset is presumed to be a fixed asset of a trade and the question asked whether the expenditure would have been allowable in an income tax computation of that, hypothetical, trade (the statutory hypothesis).[3] Since under income tax law extensive repairs may be carried out to an asset and still be allowable for that tax, (*Odeon Cinemas Ltd v. Jones* (1972)), this, in practice, restricts many claims.

Consideration   15–02

This is basically the gross money price paid. If the consideration is in money's worth it can be valued (exchange of assets is a disposal). Remember also that where the consideration cannot be valued it will be taken to be the market value of the asset. That rule, in section 17, also applies to gifts and sales at an under-value.

Sometimes the relevant consideration may depend upon the terms and form of the transaction adopted by the parties. The courts will apply the agreed terms of the parties unless they are a sham or a fraud. It is not open to the taxpayer to argue that some other construction should be put upon the agreement simply because it would have achieved the same economic effect and be more advantageous for tax purposes.[4] Further, as we have seen, section 48 provides that where the right to receive payment is postponed (*e.g.* on a payment by instalments) or contingent, the whole amount is treated as the consideration at the time of the

---

[3] See, *e.g. Emmerson v. Computer Time International* (1977), CA.
[4] *per* Lightman J. in *Spectros International plc v. Madden* (1997). See also *Fielder v. Vedlynn Ltd* (1992).

disposal without any discount for delay in payment or the possibility that it might not be paid at all, although if either of the latter can be subsequently shown to have happened an adjustment can be made.[5]

An example of these rules of interpretation by the courts and the operation of section 48 is the case of *Garner v. Pounds Shipowners and Shipbrokers Ltd* (2000), HL. The taxpayers sold an option to purchase land to M for £299,750. That money was paid to independent stakeholders who were to pay over the money only when the taxpayers obtained the release of some restrictive covenants over the land or as directed by M. If the taxpayers failed to obtain those releases then the money was to be repaid to M unless M decided in any event to exercise the option. The releases were achieved by the taxpayers at a price of £90,000. The stakeholders then paid £309,750 to the taxpayers and £90,000 to the holders of the restrictive covenants. In the event the option was never exercised. The question arose as to what was the consideration for the grant of the option (and not the land).

The House of Lords held that the consideration for the grant of the option was the full £399,750. In doing so they distinguished the earlier case of *Randall v. Plumb* (1975). In that case consideration for an option to purchase land was paid directly to the taxpayers on terms that they would have to repay part of it if planning permission was not subsequently obtained. Walton J. allowed a discount from the consideration paid for the option by taking into account the contingent possibility of repayment. This is allowed as an adjustment under section 48. The House of Lords expressly approved that decision but said that it had no application to the present case since the whole amount was paid to the taxpayers and no part of it was ever repaid to M. A payment to a third party did not alter the consideration received by the taxpayers for the grant of the option since it was clear that the parties had agreed that the payment of £399,750 was for the grant of the option only and not for both the option and the taxpayer to obtain the release of the covenants. The parties were bound by their clear agreement. If the contingency was directly related to the value of the consideration (as in *Randall v. Plumb*) it could be taken into account in computing its value but if it was related to

---

[5] The actual consideration must be irrecoverable and not just its sterling equivalent (*i.e.* where because of the need to convert foreign currency transactions into sterling at the rate in force at the time when the contract was made, the amount ultimately received when the instalments are paid, calculated at the rates then in force, is less in sterling terms than that originally charged): *Goodbrand v. Loffland Bros North Sea Inc* (1998).

matters which did not directly bear upon that value it did not follow that it should be taken into account. As we shall see in a moment they were also unable to deduct that £90,000 as allowable expenditure.

Allowable expenditure   15–03

The gain (or loss) is computed by deducting the allowable expenditure from the consideration. As we shall see the expenditure may in some cases be increased to take account of inflation. Section 38(1) provides the following heads:

(a) expenditure wholly and exclusively incurred in the acquisition of the asset (together with the incidental costs) or, if the asset was not acquired, the expenditure incurred wholly and exclusively in producing it (*e.g.* the expenditure incurred in writing a book and thereby creating a copyright). Where the taxpayer acquired the asset on a market value disposal to him, *e.g.* a gift, that will form his acquisition cost;

(b) the expenditure incurred wholly and exclusively for the purpose of enhancing the value of the asset being expenditure reflected in the value of the asset at the date of disposal (*e.g.* extensions to a building) and expenditure incurred wholly and exclusively in establishing, preserving or defending one's title to, or right over, the asset (*e.g.*, the costs involved in taking out probate);

(c) the incidental costs of making the disposal.[6]

The expenditure under (a) and (b) must be "wholly and exclusively" for the acquisition of the asset or for establishing, preserving or defending title to the asset. This has enabled the court to disallow an acquisition cost where acquiring the asset was part of an avoidance scheme,[7] but in *IRC v. Richard's Executors* (1971) the House of Lords, by a narrow majority, held that those words must be given a reasonable interpretation in allowing the costs of obtaining a valuation for estate duty purposes as an expense establishing title since such a valuation was a necessary prerequisite for obtaining their title to the estate.

In *Garner, v. Pounds Shipowners and Shipbreakers Ltd* (2000)[8] the taxpayers also failed to have the £90,000 paid to the

---

[6] Inheritance tax payable on a gift may also be allowable if a claim is made for roll-over relief on a gift of business assets; see paragraph 16–12.

[7] *Eilbeck v. Rawling* (1982).

[8] See para. 15–02, above.

owners of the restrictive covenants deducted from the consideration for the grant of the option under either paragraphs (a) or (b). Since the option could have been exercised by M whether or not the restrictive covenants were removed, the obligation to do so could not be said to be wholly and exclusively incurred by the taxpayers in providing the option for the purposes of paragraph (a). Further, for paragraph (b) neither the obligation nor the payment of £90,000 was reflected in the value of the option (as opposed to the land itself) at the date of the agreement. The option was to purchase specified land at a specified price. In effect the expenditure was extraneous to the option and it was even arguable that the obligation to remove the covenants was part of the asset (option) being disposed of so that it could not also be expenditure relating to it. As the House of Lords pointed out, the position might have been different if M had exercised the option since the £90,000 may then have been deductible from the purchase price for the land itself as distinct from the option.

Expenditure or consideration received on two or more assets may be apportioned between those assets if it is just and reasonable, so that where a company sold the shares of a subsidiary company and agreed to waive a debt owed to it by that subsidiary, the consideration received for the sale of the shares was held to be divisible between the two disposals—the sale of the shares and the waiver of the debt: *Aberdeen Construction Group Ltd v. IRC* (1978). If, however, the consideration for the shares and the waiver are expressed as separate sums no further adjustment can be made: *Booth (E.V.) (Holdings) Ltd v. Buckwell* (1980).

In the absence of fraud or collusion the acquisition cost (base price) is the value placed on the amount provided by the parties in the contract at the date of the acquisition. Thus if an asset is acquired by a company issuing new shares, credited as fully paid up, to the vendor, it is the value placed on those shares by the parties which forms the acquisition cost of the company for any subsequent disposal: *Stanton v. Drayton Commercial Investment Co. Ltd* (1982). The Revenue's argument that market value should apply was rejected. Expenditure, to be allowable, however, must be in money or money's worth. In *Oram v. Johnson* (1980) personal work by the taxpayer on renovating an old cottage was not allowed as an expense as enhancing the value of the asset; nothing had passed out from the taxpayer. If he had used a builder the expenditure would have been allowable.

In *Administrators of the Estate of Caton v. Couch* (1997), it was held that whilst the cost of employing a valuer to value shares in a private company was allowable as an incidental cost of their disposal, subsequent costs in negotiating that value with the Revenue and in (successfully) appealing against an assessment were not so allowable.

It will be recalled that there are many instances where there is deemed to be a disposal (and re-acquisition). Can there be incidental costs of such a notional disposal? Section 38(4) says (rather laconically):

> "Any provision ... introducing the assumption that assets are sold and immediately re-acquired shall not imply that any expenditure is incurred as incidental to the sale or re-acquisition."

It has been held in the courts that real expenditure on a notional disposal is allowable (*e.g.* legal costs), but that notional expenditure is not. Real lawyers' fees could arise, for example, in respect of a deemed disposal and re-acquisition by trustees on the death of a life tenant. Such real fees are deductible. But where the deemed disposal and re-acquisition arises because the asset in question was held by the taxpayer on March 31, 1982 (see para. 15.09 below) the taxpayer cannot say: "If I had really sold and re-bought the shares on the stock exchange on that day I would have incurred brokers' fees and stamp duty, and I claim to deduct those notional expenses."

Certain kinds of expenditure are not deductible, notably expenditure on insuring an asset in respect of damage, injury, loss or depreciation. Another notable non-allowable expenditure is the payment of interest (except as provided by section 40 in relation to loans for construction work taken out by companies where the resulting building, etc. is being disposed of).

A word must be said about Value Added Tax. If VAT has been suffered on the purchase of an asset but that VAT is available as input tax for set-off in the purchaser's VAT account, the cost of the asset for the purposes of capital gains tax will be the cost exclusive of VAT. Where no VAT set-off is available, the cost will be inclusive of the VAT which has been borne. Where an asset is disposed of any VAT chargeable as output tax will be disregarded in computing the capital gain (because the disponer will have to pay over the VAT to Customs and Excise). If the disponer is not selling in the course of a business VAT is not chargeable. VAT which is payable for services (such as stockbrokers' services) is deductible as part of the incidental costs. (See the Revenue's Statement of Practice 8/73.)

15–04 *Part disposals*

Where there is a part disposal the amounts of acquisition or production expenditure (see (a) above) and subsequent expenditure (see (b) above) have to be apportioned between the part disposed of and the part retained (section 42). The apportionment is done by applying to the total of expenditure the fraction

$$\frac{A}{A + B}$$

where A is the consideration for the part disposal and B is the market value of the property retained. To take an example, suppose Mr Smith owns an asset which has a base cost of £10,000 and he sells part of that asset for £7,000 and the market value of the part he retains is £21,000. The "attributable" expenditure is:

$$£10,000 \times \frac{£7,000}{£7,000 + £21,000} = £2,500$$

So the gain on this part disposal is £4,500 (*i.e.* the difference between the sale consideration (£7,000) and the attributable expenditure (£2,500)). The balance of expenditure (£7,500) which was not allowed on this part disposal is carried forward for use on any future disposal of the part of the asset which was retained.

15–05 *Wasting assets*

There is a restriction on the amount of expenditure that may be deducted in respect of what are called "wasting assets". A wasting asset means (*per* section 44(1)) an asset which has a predictable life not exceeding 50 years. Plant and machinery are expressly regarded as having a life not exceeding 50 years. The residual or scrap value of the asset is deducted from the acquisition cost and the resulting sum is written-off on a straight line basis over the life of the asset. Let us take an example. Suppose Mr Jones bought an asset which had a predictable life of 30 years. He paid £10,000 for it. Ten years later Mr Jones sold the asset for £8,000. It has a scrap value of £1,000. The computation for calculating the gross gain on the occasion of the sale goes like this:

Proceeds of sale		£8,000
Less: cost	£10,000	
Deduct scrap		
value	£1,000	
	£9,000	
Deduct amount		
written-off		
$\frac{10}{30} \times £9,000$	£3,000	
	£6,000	£6,000
	Gross chargeable gain	£2,000

Notice that this procedure, on the above facts, converts what at first sight looked like a loss (cost price £10,000; sale price £8,000) into a gain. The idea behind this is that if you buy a wasting asset and use it for a number of years and then sell it you have had the enjoyment of part of its useful life and you have sold it when its prospective useful life is diminished. So the Act deals with this situation by providing that the buying price must be notionally reduced to take account of the enjoyment of the asset which you have used up.

Amongst other things, a life interest in settled property is a wasting asset when the predictable expectation of life of the life tenant is 50 years or less. The legislation is somewhat inconsistent in that it counteracts by these artificial means the inherent depreciation of a wasting asset, such as a life interest, but it charges in full as an ordinary chargeable gain the inherent appreciation in a naturally appreciating asset such as, for example, a remainder interest.

A lease is a wasting asset when its future duration is 50 years or less.[9] But for leases the straight line basis of writing-off is not used. What is used is a fixed Table set out in Schedule 8. On this Table the line of wastage is curved and it accelerates as the lease approaches its end since leases depreciate more rapidly towards the end of their life.

Computing the chargeable gain   15–06

Having calculated the gross gain (*i.e.* the consideration for the disposal less the allowable expenditure) the actual chargeable gain is calculated for individuals by the application of a relief for

---

[9] Where a lease for less than 50 years could be extended for 50 years under the Leasehold Reform Act 1967 that does not affect the position of the lease which remains as a wasting asset: *Lewis v. Walters* (1992).

241

the effects of inflation (known as indexation relief) for periods when the asset was owned between April 1982 and April 1998 and by taper relief thereafter up to the date of disposal. Companies continue to receive indexation relief until the date of disposal and do not fall within the taper relief regime. Remember that an individual is entitled to an annual exempt amount of chargeable gains before tax is actually payable, that losses may be set off against chargeable gains (see below) and that there are a number of exemptions and reliefs which may further reduce the gain in specific situations (see the next chapter).

For individuals, therefore, how the chargeable gain is calculated depends upon when the asset was acquired. There are four relevant categories which we must take in turn. The first is where the asset was acquired after April 5, 1998 where only taper relief is available (post-1998 assets); the second is where the asset was acquired before that date but after March 31, 1982 where indexation and taper reliefs are available (post-1982 assets); the third is where the asset was acquired before April 1, 1982 where, as we have seen the asset is rebased to wipe out gains accruing before then (pre-1982 assets); and the fourth is where the asset was acquired before April 6, 1965 when the tax was first introduced (pre-1965 assets).

15–07   *Assets acquired by individuals after April 5, 1998*

Under section 2A and Schedule A1 the gross gain is to be reduced by taper relief which reduces that gain for tax purposes according both to the length of time the asset has been held and whether or not it is classed as a business asset. The intention is to discriminate against short term gains. The relief works by reducing the amount of the gain to a percentage according to a table set out in section 2A(5). Losses, which are not tapered, are to be deducted first before any taper relief is applied but they can be used in the way most favourable to the taxpayer, *i.e.* against those gains with the least taper relief available.

To qualify for taper relief the asset must have been owned for the requisite number of whole years (taken from the date of the acquisition). There is no relief for a part year of ownership. The table (as amended in 2000) is set out below:

Gains on disposals of business assets		Gains on disposals of non-business assets	
Number of whole years in qualifying period	Percentage of gain chargeable	Number of whole years in qualifying period	Percentage of gain chargeable
1	87.5	–	–
2	75	–	–
3	50	3	95
4 or more	25	4	90
		5	85
		6	80
		7	75
		8	70
		9	65
		10 or more	60

The table makes it clear that there will be no reduction for a non-business asset until it has been held for three whole years and that the maximum relief will be obtained after 10 years when a plateau is reached. After that 60 per cent of the gross gain will still be chargeable. For a business asset the minimum period of ownership is one year (with a higher reduction) with only a four-year maximum relief so that only 25 per cent of the gain will be chargeable thereafter. This relief has been introduced as a replacement for two reliefs, indexation relief and retirement relief. The latter, which is set out in paragraph 16–11, applies broadly to the disposal of a business by an individual aged 50 or over, and provided in its 1998 version a substantial reduction in the charge for gains up to £1 million if the business had been owned for 10 years or more. That relief is being phased out as taper relief takes effect which is the avowed reason why business assets are treated much more favourably for taper relief purposes. But retirement relief applied to gains which had already been reduced by indexation. Exactly how beneficial taper relief will be in practice depends perhaps upon future inflation rates since they are no longer relevant to the figures in the table.

An example as to how taper relief will work is where Alfred acquires an asset in June 2000 for £10,000 and sells it in July 2004 for £25,000. His gross gain is therefore £15,000. If the asset is a non-business asset, since he has four whole years of ownership, that gain will be reduced to 90 per cent of the gross gain so that his chargeable gain will be £13,500 irrespective of any inflation over that time. If the asset were a business asset the

243

chargeable gain would be only 25 per cent of the gross gain, *i.e.* £3,875.

It is clearly important therefore to decide what amounts to a business asset. The answer in Schedule A1 (as amended in 2000) is that there are four categories (which are in general much wider than those eligible for retirement relief): (1) Shares in a qualifying company. This is defined as a trading company[10] which is either: (a) an unlisted company; or (b) any listed or unlisted company of which the taxpayer is an officer or employee[11] or (c) any listed or unlisted company in which the taxpayer owns 5 per cent or more of the voting rights. An unlisted company for this purpose is one which is not listed on the Stock Exchange and is not a 51 per cent subsidiary of a listed company; (2) Other assets used by the taxpayer for the purposes of a trade carried on by him as a sole trader or partner; (3) Assets owned by the taxpayer and used for a trade carried on by a qualifying company; and (4) Assets used by the taxpayer for the purposes of an office or employment of a trading employer.

Where an asset has been partly a business asset and partly a non-business asset during the relevant period, the gross gain is to be apportioned according to the time the asset has been a business and non-business asset and taper relief is to be applied to the respective parts of the gain as if they had been separate assets during the whole period of ownership. Thus if Brian acquires shares in June 2000 for £10,000 and sells them in July 2004 for £20,000 he has a gross gain of £10,000. If the shares were in a qualifying company only for the last two years of ownership, and thus were business assets for two years and non-business assets for the other two, the gross gain is to be apportioned accordingly at 50:50. Half the gain (£5,000) is reduced to the business asset percentage for four years (25 per cent, i.e. £1,250) and the other half to the non-business percentage for that period (90 per cent, *i.e.* £4,500).

One final point to note on taper relief is that the period of ownership is calculated from the date of acquisition of the asset and there is no reduction in taper relief if the value of the asset is enhanced by subsequent expenditure on that asset in the meantime. Thus if Clarence buys an asset for £10,000 in 1999, spends £100,000 enhancing it in 2006 and sells it in 2007 for £200,000,

---

[10] The relief also applies to shares in the holding company of a trading group and certain joint venture companies. Provided the company exists for the purpose of trading commercially and for profit there is no restriction on non-business assets held by the company, *cf.* retirement relief.

[11] There is no requirement that the office or employment be full-time, *cf.* retirement relief.

taper relief applies on the gross gain (£90,000) for the full eight years.

Assets acquired after March 31, 1982 and, for individuals, before April 6, 1998

Until the 1998 changes, the gross gain was reduced by indexation relief to produce the chargeable gain. This was done by calculating the indexation allowance which was then deducted from the gross gain but only so as to reduce the chargeable gain to nil—it could not be used to create a loss. Under the 1998 changes this relief still applies for individuals to assets acquired between April 1, 1982 (when indexation relief was first introduced) and April 5, 1998 (after which it has been replaced by taper relief). For companies it still applies in full, even to an asset acquired after April 5, 1998. It is necessary therefore to set out how that relief works and then to consider how it fits in with taper relief for individuals.

Indexation relief is set out in sections 53 to 57. In essence the relief works by calculating the indexation allowance for each item of allowable expenditure, *e.g.* acquisition costs and enhancement costs and then deducting that amount from the gross gain, but not so as to create a loss. Losses are not index-linked.

Section 54 provides the basic rules for calculating the indexation allowance available against the gain. It is the *indexed rise* in each item of allowable expenditure, calculated separately.

The indexed rise is $\dfrac{RD - RI}{RI}$

where RD = Retail Prices Index for the month of disposal and RI = Retail Prices Index for the month of the expenditure. Each item of expenditure must therefore be calculated separately. Because of this, RI will vary according to the expenditure in question. For expenditure incurred after the asset was acquired, RI is the month in which that was first reflected in the nature of state of the asset. To prevent too much mathematical labour the indexed rise need only be calculated to the third decimal place and it is then easier to express it as a percentage. If there should ever be a time of negative inflation RD will be taken to be the same as RI so that the allowable expenditure will not be reduced by this calculation! An example may help to show how the relief works in full for companies:

245

X Ltd disposes of an asset in June 2003 having acquired it in June 1996.

RD = Retail price index in June 2003 which is, let us say, 654.0.

RI = Retail price index in June 1996 which is, let us say, 512.0.

The indexed rise is $\dfrac{RD(654.0)-RI(512.0)}{RI(512.0)}$

which is equal to 0.2578125 or 0.258 to the third decimal place.

Expressing that as a percentage the indexed rise is therefore 25.8 per cent. We can now apply the indexed rise to the disposal. If X Ltd disposed of the asset for £50,000 having paid £20,000 to acquire it then its gross gain, *i.e* without the indexation allowance, will be £30,000. The indexation allowance is £20,000 × 25.8 per cent = £5,160. This will reduce the chargeable gain from £30,000 to £24,840.

For individuals, section 53(1A) prevents any indexation allowance being claimed for any item of expenditure on or after April 6, 1998 and section 54(1A) provides that for allowable expenditure incurred before that date RD is to be taken as April 1998. The net effect is that indexation relief is available up to April 5, 1998 and taper relief thereafter. But there are two twists in the application of taper relief. First, section 2A(9) provides that where a non-business asset was held before March 17, 1998 (Budget Day), then for taper relief purposes an extra year is added onto the qualifying period. Secondly, in calculating whole years of ownership for pre-1998 assets, the relevant period is a tax year and not years running from the date of acquisition. An example may make this clearer:

X acquires a non-business asset in June 1996 for £20,000 and sells it in July 2003 for £40,000. His gross gain is therefore £20,000. He is entitled to indexation relief from June 1996 (RI) until April 1998 (the fixed RD) on his acquisition cost. Suppose the indexed rise, calculated as above, is 0.052, which translates to 5.2 per cent. X's indexation allowance is therefore 5.2% of £20,000, *i.e.* £1,040. That is deducted from the gross gain to produce the indexed gain of £18,600. That indexed gain is then reduced by taper relief for the period from April 1998 to the date of disposal, July 2003. This amounts to five whole years for the purposes of taper relief but, because the asset was owned before

March 17, 1998, X is entitled to an extra year. Thus the relief is applied on the basis of six years' worth of non-business taper *i.e.* to 80 per cent of the indexed gain. The tapered and so chargeable gain is therefore £14,880.

To summarise the procedure: (1) calculate the gross gain; (2) apply indexation relief to April 1998 to obtain the indexed gain; and (3) apply taper relief to the indexed gain, remembering, if it is a non-business asset, to add on an extra year.

Assets acquired before 1 April 1982 but after 5 April 1965   15–09

Subject to one important difference the calculation of the chargeable gain for pre-1982 assets is the same as for pre-1998 assets set out above. The difference is that pre-1982 assets are subject to rebasing in the calculation of the gross gain as if they had been acquired at market value at March 31, 1982. That date is also RI for the purposes of indexation relief. For such assets therefore both RI and RD are fixed for individuals, RD being April 1998. Subject to that the three steps set out above should be used to calculate the chargeable gain for individuals. We need, however, to go into the process of rebasing since, as ever, it is not always straightforward. There are also different rebasing rules for assets held before April 6, 1965 which are dealt with next.

It is section 35 which takes all gains accrued before March 31, 1982 out of the charge to tax. That date was chosen because indexation relief starts at that point. Section 35 (2) accordingly provides that where a taxpayer disposes of an asset which he held on March 31,1982 then "in computing ... the gain or the loss accruing on the disposal it shall be assumed that the asset was on March 31, 1982 sold by the person making the disposal, and immediately reacquired by him, at its market value". Thus the base price of that asset is uplifted to its market value at that date. Thus it can be said to have been "rebased" to March 1982. Where the taxpayer has acquired the asset after March 31, 1982 on a no gain/no loss transfer, *e.g.* as between spouses, from a transferor who owned the asset on March 31, 1982, the transferee is also deemed to have owned it then and rebasing will apply.

Given the constant presence of inflation in the period before 1982, rebasing to March 31, 1982 will almost certainly reduce the gross gain from what it would have been without such rebasing, *i.e.* by taking the original cost as the base price. But certain assets fluctuate in value irrespective of underlying inflation and it is possible, for example, that an asset was actually worth less in March 1982 than when it was originally purchased.

In such a case rebasing would actually increase the gain. There are therefore two exceptions to this rebasing rule.

First, where a computation without rebasing would have produced a loss and a computation with rebasing would produce a gain, or vice versa, then the disposal is treated as one which has made neither a gain nor a loss. Secondly, where a computation without rebasing would have produced a smaller gain or a smaller loss than one using rebasing, then that smaller gain or loss is to be chargeable or allowable as the case may be. In working out the computation without rebasing, indexation relief must be taken into account from 31 March 1982 calculated on the higher of the market value of the asset at that time or the original base cost (section 55 (2)).

To take some simple examples of all this (ignoring indexation and taper reliefs):

1. A buys a painting for £10,000 in 1976. Its market value in March 1982 is £15,000 and he sells it in 2001 for £20,000. Rebasing will apply so that the gross gain is £5,000 and not £10,000.

2. B buys a painting for £10,000 in 1976. Its market value in March 1982 is £30,000 and he sells it in 2001 for £20,000. Rebasing would then produce a loss of £10,000 whereas without rebasing there would be a gain of £10,000. Accordingly there is neither a gain nor a loss.

3. C buys a painting for £10,000 in 1976. Its market value in March 1982 is £5,000 and he sells it in 2001 for £20,000. Rebasing would then produce a gain of £15,000 whereas without rebasing there would be a gain of £10,000. Since without rebasing there would be a smaller gross gain than on rebasing, that smaller gain will be chargeable.

Note that under these rules if rebasing produces a smaller loss than non-rebasing that smaller loss is the only one which is allowable—the non-rebasing alternative is only available if that produces a smaller loss.

All this is very complex and requires taxpayers to keep records relating to events prior to March 1982. Accordingly any taxpayer may elect that rebasing will apply to all disposals made by him of all assets held by him at March 31, 1982. Once made this election cannot be revoked and it must be a blanket election. It is a matter of mathematics to work out whether any particular taxpayer should make such an election, which must be made within two years of the first such disposal: section 35 (5).

Assets owned before April 6 1965   15–10

Capital gains tax has never applied to gains accruing before April 6, 1965, the date when the tax first came into effect. There have always therefore been special rules where a taxpayer is disposing of an asset which he held on that date and these can now be found in Schedule 2. Obviously, however, since, as we have seen, all pre-March 31, 1982 assets can be rebased to that date, those rules have been largely superseded by the 1982 rebasing provisions. Those provisions do, however, require a computation to be made without such rebasing for comparison purposes so that if the asset is a pre-April 6, 1965 asset the rules in Schedule 2 will be used for that purpose. That is the only distinction between pre-1982 assets and pre-1965 assets.

The basic rule for computing the comparative gross gain or loss of a pre-April 6, 1965 asset is known as the straight line apportionment rule. This involves taking the original cost of the asset as the base cost, calculating the gain over the whole period and then apportioning the gain between the period of ownership prior to April 6, 1965 and that after April 5, 1965 on a straight line basis. That gain will then be used as the comparison with the 1982 rebased gain in applying the 1982 rebasing rules. For example:

D buys a painting for £1,000 in April 1955 and sells it for £51,000 in April 2005. The total gain (ignoring indexation and taper reliefs) is £50,000. This was accrued over a 50-year period, 10 of which were prior to April 1965 and 40 after that date. Thus 40/50ths of the gain is deemed to have accrued after April 1965 and so £40,000 is the chargeable gain. If the painting had a market-value of £60,000 in March 1982 (it was in fashion then) rebasing to that date would produce a loss of £9,000. Accordingly under the 1982 rebasing rules since one method produces a gain and the other a loss there would be neither a loss nor a gain.

One complication in making the straight line apportionment computation is the impact of indexation relief. This must be calculated on the asset's market value at March 31, 1982. But is it to be applied after the gain has been time-apportioned or before? To see the difference, in the example above suppose the indexation relief (calculated to April 1998) is £4,000. If that is taken off after the time apportionment it will reduce the gain from £40,000 to £36,000. If it is taken off before then the total gain of £50,000 will be reduced to £46,000 and three-quarters of that will be chargeable, *i.e.* £34,500. In *Smith v. Schofield* (1993) the House of Lords reluctantly held that on the wording of Schedule 2 the latter was the correct procedure despite the fact that it attributed post-1982 inflation relief to gains made before the tax was even introduced.

15–11 *Special rules for shares—pooling arrangements*

Until indexation relief was introduced in 1982, shares of the same class in the same company held by a taxpayer were treated as a single asset, *i.e.* a pool of shares. Every time some were bought they were added to the pool (and the acquisition cost added to the acquisition costs of the pool) and when some were sold they were deducted from the pool and charged as a part disposal of the single pooled asset. Thus, if half the shares were sold, half the allowable expenditure of the pool was available. Between 1982 and 1985 such pooling was abolished but in 1985 new rules reinstated the pooling arrangements and accommodated indexation relief.

The 1985 system is set out in sections 104 to 114. It still applies for shares held by companies, but under section 110A it no longer applies to shares held by individuals because of the demands of taper relief whereby the length of ownership of each share has to be identified. It is necessary therefore to look at the 1985 system and then to see how it relates to the 1998 system for individuals.

The 1985 rules require all holdings of shares in the same company to be separated out into those acquired after April 5, 1982 (new holdings) and those held before that date (old holdings). New holdings are treated as a single asset so that when some are sold an appropriate part of the allowable expenditure (cost of the pool to date minus expenditure already allowed) is available. Indexation relief is worked into this structure as follows. On every acquisition of shares, after the first, the existing pool of expenditure is indexed up to that date and then the additional expenditure is added on. Similarly on every disposal, the pool of expenditure is indexed up from the last time it was indexed up (on an acquisition or previous disposal) and an appropriate proportion of that indexed pool is used up, with the remainder being carried forward. Thus there is a rolling programme of indexation. That actual indexation is done in the same way as for other assets by reference to the retail prices index or RPI of the month the pool was last indexed and the RPI for the month of acquisition or disposal.

250

Old holdings are by definition finite in that no more can be acquired. Thus there can only be disposals and under the 1985 system indexation relief can be applied in the normal way on each disposal by applying indexation relief to the appropriate part of the pool of allowable expenditure from April 1982 to the date of disposal.

Although the 1985 rules require that the two pools be kept entirely separate, section 107 provides three identification rules on the disposal of shares within either of the two pools. When such shares are disposed of they are to be identified as follows: (1) with any such shares acquired on the same day; (2) then with any such shares acquired within the previous 10 days; and (3) then with any such shares on a last-in first-out basis. The effects of (1) and (2) are that no indexation relief at all is allowable and the practical effect of (3), which means that the most recently acquired shares are deemed to have been disposed of first, is that the new holding will be presumed to have been sold before the old holding.

The 1985 rules still apply to companies but for individuals pooling has been abolished for any shares acquired after April 5, 1998. Accordingly, both pre-existing pools of old and new holdings are frozen with their allowable expenditure indexed up to that date. Subsequent acquisitions are treated as any other asset. Section 106A also replaces section 107 for identifying shares disposed of by an individual. Thus when an individual disposes of shares they are to be regarded as being shares which were acquired in the following order: (1) shares acquired after April 5, 1998 on a last-in first-out basis; (2) with shares in the frozen new holding pool; and (3) with shares in the frozen old holding pool. Taper relief will then be applied as with any other asset.

That order is subject to special rules designed to prevent what was known as "bed and breakfasting". That was a simple tax planning device whereby the taxpayer sold a number of shares on the market at the close of business on one day and bought them back again at the start of trading on the next day. Thus there would have been a disposal which if it gave rise to a gain would have been calculated not to exceed the exempt amount for the year. Consequently there would be no actual charge but the taxpayer's base cost was increased to the repurchase cost. Without this the taxpayer may not have been able to take advantage of the exempt amount. Section 105 has always provided that any shares sold must be identified first with any shares acquired on the same day, but that does not prevent the scheme working since they are sold on day 1 and re-acquired on day 2. Section 106A(5) therefore provides that any shares sold must (before any other identification rules are applied) be identified with shares acquired in the 30 days following the disposal. That will prevent simple bed and breakfasting but it will not of course prevent a taxpayer selling the shares, giving the proceeds to his or her spouse, who then buys back the shares the following day.

15–12 **Losses**

We want to collect together under this heading certain leading points about losses. Some of the points have been mentioned before; some are new.

Losses are, in general,[12] computed in the same way as gains are computed; section 16(1).[13] If a transaction is such that a gain (if there had been one) would not be a chargeable gain, then if a loss occurs (instead of a gain) that loss is not an allowable loss; section 16(2). This provision has some very important consequences. A good example arises in connection with the disposal of gilt-edged securities or qualifying corporate bonds (see para. 16.03 below).

Capital gains tax is charged on the total amount of chargeable gains in a year of assessment after deducting any allowable losses. Losses are not subject to taper relief so that the full amount of a loss is available, however long the asset has been held. But losses must be deducted from gains in the same year of assessment before taper relief is applied to them. These points are to be found in sections 2(2) and 2A(2). The effect is that part of the relief for losses may be lost if it is used to cancel part of a gain which would not have been taxable anyway because of taper relief. However, section 2A(6) provides that losses may be set off against gains in a way which is most advantageous to the taxpayer, *i.e.* to cancel out gains which have the least taper relief. Where there are more losses than gains in the same year of assessment, the surplus losses may be carried forward to future years again to cancel out untapered gains.

If in any year a person has a taxable amount (chargeable gains minus allowable losses) not exceeding the exempt amount for that year the accumulated losses of earlier years are not required to be used in eliminating that taxable amount. For example if at the end of year 1 a person has accumulated losses of £5,000, and in year 2 his taxable amount is £4,000, no part of the £5,000 needs to be used in knocking down the £4,000 to nil. He goes

---

[12] But see the application of taper relief below.
[13] In general, losses must be realised but remember the deemed disposal provisions where an asset has been destroyed, extinguished or become of negligible value, where an allowable loss may be claimed.

252

forward into year 3 with his accumulation of losses (£5,000)
intact: section 3(5)(a). Similarly, if his taxable amount in year 2
had been £8,000, he need only use so much of his accumulated
losses as is needed to reduce that taxable amount to the exempt
amount and the remaining losses could be carried forward into
year 3: section 3(5)(b). The same principle applies to losses
carried *back* from the year in which an individual dies. Note that
in no other circumstances can losses be carried back.

Losses incurred in a disposal to a "connected person" are only
allowable against gains made on subsequent disposals to the
same connected person: section 18(3).

CHAPTER 16

EXEMPTIONS AND RELIEFS

An exemption arises where either some asset is expressed not to be a chargeable asset or some gain is expressed not to be a chargeable gain. A relief arises where although there is a chargeable asset and a chargeable gain the full amount of tax is not exacted or the chargeable gain is postponed. Remember that there is an annual exemption for all gains accruing to an individual up to the exempt amount for the year in question. This chapter deals with the more important exemptions and reliefs.

16–01   ## Hold-over Relief for Gifts Immediately Chargeable to Inheritance Tax

Between 1980 and 1989 all gifts between individuals were eligible for what is known as hold-over relief from capital gains tax. This was because gifts were also subject to inheritance tax and it was thought inequitable to apply both taxes. This general relief was, however, abolished in 1989 on the (slightly flawed) basis that inheritance tax now rarely applies to lifetime gifts. Hold-over relief still applies to gifts of business assets (see paragraph 16–12 below) and under section 260 gifts which attract an immediate charge to inheritance tax. Section 260 also applies to some specific types of gift which are exempt from inheritance tax. Before we look at this current relief it is important to understand the concept of a hold-over relief since it applies in other areas we shall come to (gifts of business assets, replacement of business assets, transfer of business to a company).

Hold-over relief works by allowing the amount of the chargeable gain which would otherwise be payable on a disposal from A to B to be deducted from the acquisition cost of B rather than chargeable on A. Suppose A buys an asset for £10,000. He disposes of it to B for £15,000. Ignoring indexation and taper relief A would therefore make a gain of £5,000. If hold-over relief is available then instead of charging that gain on the disposal, B will be deemed to have acquired the asset for £10,000 (*i.e.* £15,000–£5,000). If B subsequently disposes of the asset to C for £20,000 he will therefore be treated as having made a gain (once more ignoring indexation and taper relief) of £10,000 (£20,000–£10,000). Thus A's original gain of £5,000 and B's actual gain of £5,000 are both chargeable on B's disposal to C. In other words hold-over relief postpones or holds over A's gain, it does not exclude it. A further consideration is that taper relief will apply only to the length of ownership of B, there is no provision for rolling over accrued taper relief, nor is taper relief applied to the held-over gain to be deducted from B's acquisition cost.

If B's disposal to C had also been eligible for hold-over relief then B's gain of £10,000 would not be chargeable but C's acquisition cost would be reduced by that amount, and so on. Thus whilst the general relief for gifts applied it was possible by simply making a series of gifts of an asset to postpone all the gains. If the final donee died so that the asset passed under his will or intestacy those held-over gains would disappear because of the provisions (already dealt with para. 14.21) whereby his executors would be deemed to acquire the asset at its then market value but make no chargeable gain on transferring the asset to the beneficiary.

Hold-over relief for all types of gift is now only available where the gift would attract an immediate charge to inheritance tax: section 260. This means that the gift must be a chargeable transfer for inheritance tax purposes. It does not apply, however, to gifts which are potentially exempt transfers, because they will only be chargeable to inheritance tax if the donor dies within seven years of making the gift so that there is no immediate charge to the tax. Even if they do then become chargeable no hold-over relief is available. These concepts are discussed at para. 18–02, below, but the effect broadly is that the relief only applies to the creation or termination of a discretionary trust. Provided there is a charge to inheritance tax, however, it does not matter that the amount of tax actually payable is negligible–see *Melville v. IRC* (2000), paragraph 18–02 below. The relief is not available to companies or where the donee is neither resident nor ordinarily resident in the United Kingdom. Where it applies the relief for gifts of business assets does not apply. A claim for hold-over relief must be made jointly by the donor and donee and if made entitles the parties to postpone the gain in the way set out above.

The relief also applies to bad bargains taxable on full market value under section 17. In that case the amount which can be held-over is the difference between the price paid and the market value, *i.e.* the gift element. Finally we should note that the relief is available to certain gifts which are exempt from inheritance tax altogether thus taking them outside the tax net. These include gifts to political parties and to maintenance funds for historic houses.

16–02   Some Miscellaneous Exemptions

Private motor cars are not chargeable assets. It was just not worth the effort of trying to tax them. Nor are savings certificates or premium bonds chargeable, nor betting winnings.

There is no chargeable gain when a person disposes of foreign currency which he had acquired for personal expenditure abroad.

Sums obtained by way of compensation or damages for any wrong or injury suffered by an individual in his person or in his profession are not chargeable gains. Were it not for this provision, the law might otherwise produce the slightly macabre result that someone who received compensation, for example, for an injury at work, would be regarded as part-disposing of himself for CGT purposes.

There are also exemptions for gains arising from individual savings accounts and a relief for transfers of shares into an approved employee share-ownership plan.

16–03   Gilt-edged Securities and Qualifying Corporate Bonds

A gain is not a chargeable gain if it accrues on the disposal of certain specified gilt-edged securities and qualifying corporate bonds: see sections 115, 117 and Schedule 9. The list of specified gilt-edged securities has been added to from time to time by statutory instrument and now comprises virtually all government stocks. At first sight this seems a generous gesture on the part of the Revenue, but losses occur in dealings on the gilt-edged market, and the rule that where no chargeable gain (if there had been a gain) would have arisen there can be no allowable loss has meant that this exemption has frequently operated to prohibit losses rather than to exempt gains. Qualifying corporate bonds, which similarly cannot give rise to a loss, are defined to include normal non-convertible corporate debentures, but for companies most qualifying corporate bonds have been subsumed into their trading profits for corporation tax purposes and taken out of the chargeable gain regime.

16–04   Life Assurance and Deferred Annuities

In principle the receipt of policy monies under a policy of life assurance, or the receipt of the first instalment of a deferred annuity, is a disposal (a disposal of the right in return for the money). But no chargeable gain arises where the money is paid to the original holder of the policy or his personal representatives or trustees. Nor is there a chargeable gain if he surrenders (or they surrender) the policy. But if the policy is assigned for money or money's worth (*e.g.* sold) and then the policy money is paid to the assignee (or the policy is surrendered) that is a chargeable event. This matter is dealt with by section 210.

Private Residences   16–05

This point is dealt with in sections 222–226. A gain on the disposal by an individual of a dwelling-house or part of a dwelling house is not a chargeable gain if the house was the individual's only or main residence. This exemption in practice takes most people's main asset out of the charge to capital gains tax and is extremely important in practice in a country where most families now own their own homes. But the benevolence does not extend (as we shall see) to inheritance tax; for that tax a private residence is no different from other property. The capital gains tax exemption does not apply if the house was acquired wholly or partly for the purpose of realising a gain from its disposal: section 224(3).

To get the full capital gains tax exemption the house must have been the individual's only or main residence throughout his period of ownership, ignoring any period of ownership prior to March 31, 1982, except that it does not matter if it has not been such for all or any part of the last 36 months of his ownership. The point of this exception is (we take it) to meet the case where an individual has moved to a new house before he has been able to sell his old one. If the house has not been the taxpayer's only or main residence throughout his period of ownership a fraction of the gain is exempted corresponding to the period of occupation. In certain circumstances a period of absence can be disregarded. These include periods, where the taxpayer was employed abroad and any period not exceeding three years. Where the taxpayer has to live in job-related accommodation the exemption will apply to a house bought as a future main residence even if he never lives in it.

The relief applies to a dwelling-house which is the taxpayer's sole or main residence. In *Goodwin v. Curtis* (1998), the Court of Appeal upheld a decision of the General Commissioners that mere temporary occupation of premises by a taxpayer is not sufficient to make it his residence for the purposes of the relief. Thus there is a distinction between temporary accommodation and a permanent residence. In that case the taxpayer had already

257

advertised a farmhouse as being for sale before he moved into it. He lived in it for just over a month until the sale was completed. In the view of the Court of Appeal the facts indicated that there was an insufficient degree of permanence for it to be his residence. Each case will depend on its facts, but the important criterion will be the intention of the taxpayer when he occupies the house and not the length of occupation. A clear intention to occupy the house permanently will be sufficient, even if he has to move out after a short time, *e.g.* because he has changed jobs, whereas a longer period of occupation which is always temporary may not be so.

What amounts to a dwelling-house or part of a dwelling-house for this relief has been the subject of several cases. It has been held to include a caravan (admittedly connected to mains services),[1] but this is always a question of fact.[2]

More difficulties have arisen as to what amounts to part of a dwelling-house. This has for example been held to include the disposal of a bungalow built in the grounds of a house for the gardener and housekeeper[3] so that a dwelling-house can clearly consist of more than one building. The criteria applied to decide whether the building being disposed of is part of the dwelling house or a separate entity have varied. Initially the question asked was whether the two buildings together formed an entity so that taken together they could form a dwelling-house. Thus in *Williams v. Merrylees* (1987) Vinelott J. held that a lodge built some 200 yards from the main house could form part of a single dwelling-house with the main house, the dwelling-house being split up into different buildings fulfilling different functions. The scale and layout of the buildings was important. But in the same year, Walton J. applied a much more precise (and restrictive) test in *Markey v. Saunders* (1987). To succeed in a claim for relief the taxpayer would have to show that the second building (1) increased the taxpayer's enjoyment of the first dwelling; and (2) was very closely adjacent to it. Since the employee's bungalow in that case was a long way from the main house and was screened from it, the judge was able to decide that it did not form part of the taxpayer's dwelling-house.

The Court of Appeal in *Lewis v. Lady Rook* (1992) seem to have adopted this narrower geographical (or proximity)

---

[1] *Makins v. Elson* (1977).
[2] *Moore v. Thompson* (1986), where the caravan was not connected to main services and only occupied sporadically it was held not to come within the exemption.
[3] *Batey v. Wakefield* (1981).

approach as opposed to the entity approach. The test set out in that case was to ask whether the building being sold was within the curtilage of, and appurtenant to, the main building so as to constitute an entity which could be described as a dwelling-house. The Court of Appeal were cheerfully of the opinion that everyone would know what the curtilage of a house was, but it is nowhere defined in the tax legislation.[4] Because of this uncertainty more litigation on this issue may follow. In *Honour v. Norris* (1992) the above test was said to be applicable to the "country house" situation but not to the facts of that case. The taxpayer had acquired four separate flats in a block of flats and the fourth, acquired to accommodate their grown up children and their guests, was sold separately. The judge refused to lay down any general test for such urban cases. On the facts the fourth flat had never formed part of a single entity—it had been acquired as a separate unit conveniently close to the others. It was like a country house owner acquiring a bungalow in the nearby village.

The exemption also applies to land occupied and enjoyed with the dwelling house, up to half a hectare in area. If this land is disposed of separately from the house it must be disposed of first, otherwise it will no longer be occupied and enjoyed with the house at the time of its disposal.[5] A larger area may be allowed if it is required for the reasonable enjoyment of the house, given the size and character of the house: section 222. There is no requirement that the land is actually physically attached to the house, *e.g.* if it is the natural garden of the house. On the other hand land owned apart from the house will not count just because it is used as a garden.[6]

If the gain accrues from a disposal of a dwelling-house part of which is used exclusively for the purposes of a trade, business, profession or vocation the exemption applies only to that part of the gain which falls to be apportioned to the "private" part of the house. (This is a point to be weighed against the income tax advantage of claiming that a part of one's house is being used

---

[4]   There are many cases in other areas as to what amounts to the curtilage of a building. One example, for the purposes of the Housing Act 1980, is the definition laid down in *Dyer v. Dorset County Council* (1988) that the curtilage is a small area of land which is part and parcel of the building it contains or is attached to it. But in *Skerrits of Nottingham Ltd v. Secretary of State* (2000), the Court of Appeal said that it was wrong to include smallness as a criterion. It was a question of fact and degree, so that a manor house might well include stables and other outbuildings. The Court also said that "curtilage" was an expression which not even lawyers could define precisely!

[5]   *Varty v. Lynes* (1976).

[6]   *Wakeling v. Pearce* (1995).

exclusively for business, etc., purposes.) Similar provisions apply to any reconstruction, conversion or change of use of the property, but it seems that such events will only justify an apportionment if they amount to a change in the taxpayer's occupation[7]: section 224.

If the owner lets his house during his period of ownership the part of the gain attributable to that period is chargeable on a straight line basis (*e.g.* owned 10 years during which it was let for two, one-fifth of the total gain is chargeable). Further relief is available under section 223(4) where the house is let as residential accommodation.[8] The chargeable gain is then reduced by the lower of the exempt gain (*i.e.* four-fifths of the gain in the example above) or £40,000. In practice lodgers are not treated as affecting the relief.

The exemption also applies to occupation of a dwelling-house held under a settlement by a person entitled to occupy it under the settlement: section 225. Usually this will be the life tenant but it can include a beneficiary under a discretionary trust where the trustees have a power to allow this.[9]

A married couple can only have one residence or main residence. If they are not separated it is no good claiming that Mon Repos is the man's main residence and Dunromin is the wife's main residence: section 222(6). Where a taxpayer, or a husband and wife, have two or more residences, they must choose which is to be the "main" residence. This choice must be made within two years of the acquisition of a second or subsequent residence in which case it will be backdated for that period. In *Griffin v. Craig-Harvey* (1993) the court held that the taxpayer had no right to make an election after two years from the second acquisition, a decision which leaves many taxpayers out of time to make an election. If there is no election the inspector of taxes can decide which is the taxpayer's main residence.

16–06   Chattels Disposed of for £6,000 or Less

Section 262 provides that "a gain accruing on a disposal of an asset which is tangible moveable property [*i.e.* a chattel] shall not be a chargeable gain if the amount or value of the consideration for the disposal does not exceed £6,000." Section 262 does not apply to a disposal of currency of any description, nor to a disposal of commodities by a person dealing on a terminal

---

[7]   *IRC v. Green* (1982).
[8]   This includes taking in hotel guests: *Owen v. Elliott* (1990).
[9]   *Sansom v. Peay* (1976).

market. A terminal market is not defined but it means a market in which you can buy or sell, *e.g.* cocoa, for a price fixed now but for delivery at some future date (*e.g.* three months hence). It is sometimes called a futures market. Notice that the figure of £6,000 refers to the amount of the consideration, not to the amount of the gain.

Where the amount of the consideration exceeds £6,000 there shall be excluded from any chargeable gain so much of it as exceeds five-thirds of the difference between the consideration and £6,000.

But the section is far from generous as regards losses. If there is a disposal at a loss, and the consideration for the disposal is less than £6,000, the consideration is deemed to be £6,000. Thus if a chattel was bought for £6,200 and sold for £5,800 the actual loss (£400) is not allowable; the loss relief is limited to £200.

If two or more assets forming part of a set of articles (say a set of Chippendale chairs) are disposed of by the same seller to the same buyer (or to different buyers who are acting in concert or who are connected persons) whether on the same or different occasions, the two or more transactions are treated as a single transaction.

The disposals of two (or more) quite separate articles qualify separately for the relief. It is no bar to getting the relief that you have (in the same year) sold a table for £6,000 and a stamp for £6,000, or even for that matter two unconnected stamps for £6,000 each.

Tangible Moveables which are Wasting Assets   16–07

No chargeable gain (or, more likely, an allowable loss) shall accrue on the disposal of an asset which is tangible moveable property (*i.e.* a chattel) and which is a wasting asset: section 45. It will be recalled that a wasting asset is an asset which has a predictable life not exceeding 50 years. This exemption applies (unlike the exemption mentioned above) irrespective of the amount of the disposal consideration.

Replacement of Business Assets   16–08

Sections 152 to 159 are the operative sections here. They provide not a complete exemption from tax but a relief in the hold-over form. The relief arises when a trader disposes of business assets (of certain types) at a gain, and uses the disposal consideration to acquire replacement assets. The relief is given by allowing the trader to defer payment of tax on the disposal gain and (instead) to deduct the untapered gain which he makes on the disposal of the old assets from the acquisition cost of the new assets. This will have the effect of increasing the tax payable when he comes (if he does) to dispose of the new assets in the future. Remember also that taper relief will only apply to the length of time that the trader has held the new asset. Accrued taper relief on the old asset cannot be carried forward; nor is it applied to reduce the gain to be deducted from the acquisition cost of the new asset.

To get the relief the trader must acquire the new assets within three years after the disposal[10] (or within 12 months before the disposal). Once the replacement asset is acquired it must be used in the taxpayer's trade "on the acquisition." A gap will prevent the relief applying.[11]

It is possible to acquire the "new" asset one year before the disposal of the old asset, provided of course that the old asset was part of the trader's assets when the new asset was acquired. But in *Watton v. Tippett* (1997) no relief was allowed where a trader, having bought a single asset, disposed of part of it within a year and claimed to deduct the gain from the cost of the part retained. The original cost for the whole asset could not be severed since the part retained had never been acquired as such.

The relief only applies to assets set out in classes in section 155 (which can be added to by a Treasury Order). These are currently: (i) land and buildings; (ii) fixed plant and machinery[12]; (iii) ships; (iv) aircraft; (v) hovercraft; (vi) goodwill; (vii) satellites, space stations and spacecraft (!); (viii) certain farming quotas; (ix) fish quotas; and (x) rights of members of a Lloyd's syndicate. The old and new assets need not be of the same type, however.

There is no relief for a non-resident where the replacement asset is outside the charge to tax because it is outside the United Kingdom: section 159. In addition there is no relief if the new assets were acquired wholly or partly for the purpose of realising a gain from their disposal. There are further restrictions if the replacement asset is a wasting asset.

Where the whole of the proceeds of sale are not reinvested in acquiring a new asset, the amount not reinvested will be treated as a chargeable gain and only the balance will be held over.

---

[10] This period can be extended by the Revenue, but there is no appeal against their refusal to do so: *Steibelt v. Paling* (1999).

[11] See *Campbell Connelly & Co. Ltd v. Barnett* (1993). There are special rules for groups of companies in this respect. In practice, if an asset requires capital expenditure on it before it can be used in the taxpayer's trade, the relief will apply if the work is completed within a reasonable time and it is then used in the trade. See *Steibelt v. Paling* (1999).

[12] Thus excluding moveable machinery: *Williams v. Evans* (1992).

Similarly where the new asset is only partially used for the purposes of the business the relief will be restricted to the proportion used in the business.[13]

Transfer of Business to a Company   16–09

Hold over relief is also available where an unincorporated business (and not just its assets) are transferred to a company in return for shares in the company; ie where the business is incorporated: section 162. The untapered gains on the disposal can be deducted from the acquisition cost of the shares and time for taper relief will begin to run only on their acquisition. The company is deemed to acquire the assets at market value (section 17 will apply).[14] Retirement relief (below) may, if available, be deducted first before this relief is applied.

Concessions applicable to hold-over business reliefs   16–10

The operation of the two reliefs discussed above are amplified by a number of published extra-statutory concessions which in effect allow a gain to be deferred in the same way as hold-over relief even though the statutory provisions might not strictly be applicable. As we have seen, the basic principle of hold-over relief is that there is no charge on the first gain but that that amount is then deducted from the acquisition cost of the replacement asset thus increasing the gain on any disposal of that asset. It appears that under the wording of these concessions there is no undertaking required from the taxpayer at the time when the first gain is deferred that it will be so deducted from the acquisition cost on the second disposal. Further it appears that the Revenue have conceded that they have no powers to compel any such deduction. Consequently for events occurring only after March 9, 1999, sections 248A and 248B now give them the power to assess the held-over gain under a concession as it would have been under the sections. This was not made retrospective, however, so some taxpayers appear to have been able to both have their cake and eat it.

Retirement Relief   16–11

Under sections 163 and 164 and Schedule 6 so-called retirement relief is available to an individual who is disposing of his business interests. The relief is always known as retirement relief

---

[13] For an unfortunate example of this restriction see *Todd v. Mudd* (1987).
[14] See, *e.g. Gordon v. IRC* (1991).

although it is not limited to retirement situations. There are a mass of detailed rules relating to this relief which has been immensely important in practice since it lowers the impact of capital gains tax on the transfer of family businesses between the generations. The relief takes the form of excluding what would otherwise be chargeable gains up to a specified cash amount. Following the introduction of taper relief, however, retirement relief is being progressively phased out by the simple expedient of reducing the amount of excluded gains year by year. The relief will cease to apply altogether for disposals in the year 2003–04 and subsequent years. The rules for the relief remain unchanged until then. The following is an outline of how the relief works.

To qualify for the relief the following three elements must be present:

   (i) the taxpayer must be either over the age of 50 at the time of the disposal or retiring on the grounds of ill health and must have owned the property for at least one year;

  (ii) the disposal must be either a material disposal or another qualifying disposal; and

 (iii) the disposal must be of chargeable business assets.

Thus, provided the taxpayer is over the age of 50 he need not be retiring. There are detailed rules on what amounts to a retirement under that age on the grounds of ill-health and the Revenue's decision on that point cannot be appealed. Provided criteria (ii) and (iii) are met such an individual is entitled to claim the relief provided he has owned the property being disposed of for a minimum of one year. But to claim the full amount of the relief he must have owned it for 10 years. (There are provisions which allow successive businesses and ownership of a business between spouses in succession to be included in this total).

If the taxpayer is entitled to the full relief then, in the tax year 2000–01, the chargeable gain will be totally exempt up to an amount of £150,000 and will be exempt as to half of the gain between £150,000 and £600,000. If the taxpayer does not have ten years of ownership then the relief is scaled down proportionately, losing 10 per cent for each year below 10. Thus if the taxpayer has owned the business for five years (*i.e.* half of the 10 required for full relief), he will have total relief on gains up to £75,000 and the half relief on additional gains up to £300,000 (*i.e.* half the full amounts). The relief is also available if the assets have been "owned" by the holder of an interest in possession under a trust and the disposal is by the trustees. The relevant amounts for the tax year 2001–02 are relief for full gains up to

£100,000 and half gains above that up to £400,000, and for the tax year 2002–03, relief for full gains up to £50,000 and half gains above that up to £200,000. After that year the relief will cease to apply.

What then amounts to a material disposal so as to attract this relief? There are three types of material disposal. The first is a disposal of a business or part of a business, *e.g.* by a sole trader or a partner. The second is a disposal of assets owned by the taxpayer which at the time when the business ceased were in use in that business,[15] provided the business was owned by the taxpayer either on his own or in partnership with others or by his personal company (see below for what that means).

The courts have often been faced with difficulties arising when a trader has disposed of business assets which prima facie fall within the second head. But to fall within that head the taxpayer must show that the business has ceased prior to the disposal[16] and that the asset was used by the business which has ceased.[17] It follows that unless the business has ceased, a trader disposing of business assets cannot fall within the second head. The question which then arises is whether such a disposal can fall within the first head as the disposal of part of a business. In *McGregor v. Atkinson* (1977) the taxpayer carried on a mixed farming business on 35 acres. He sold about five acres to a developer and carried on his business on the remaining land. His claim to retirement relief failed because it could not be said that the five acres sold were a separate part of his business. His business was continuing substantially as before. Thus he could not be said to be disposing of part of a business within the first head.

But in subsequent cases it was accepted that it was possible for the first head to apply where the taxpayer disposed of assets which had the effect of bringing to an end part of a business. The first head was not limited to the disposal of part of a business as a going concern.[18] In deciding whether there has been a disposal of the whole or part of a business the courts will look at the position before and after the disposal of the assets and ask

---

[15] In *Clarke v. Mayo* (1994) the court accepted the argument that this need not be construed literally to mean the instant before the business ceased and preferred the test as to whether the assets were being disposed of as part of the taxpayer's withdrawal from the business.

[16] See *Marriott v. Lane* (1996) as to the problems of a temporary cessation.

[17] In *Plumbly v. Spencer* (1999) the Court of Appeal held that where the assets belonged to the taxpayer it was sufficient if either he or his personal company owned the business in which the assets were used.

[18] In *Pepper v. Daffurn* (1993) and *Wase v. Bourke* (1996) the claim failed only because the cessation of part of the business predated the disposal of the assets and so could not have been caused by it.

whether the changes caused by the disposal amount to a cesser of the whole or part of a business. Thus in *Jarmin v. Rawlings* (1994) the taxpayer, who was a dairy farmer, decided to change to stored cattle and sold some land and buildings used for milking, together with his milk quota. Relief was allowed on the basis that by disposing of those assets he had disposed of the dairy farming business which was a business in its own right. Applying the test is a question of fact. Thus in *Barrett v. Powell* (1998) the taxpayer farmed land as a tenant farmer. He surrendered his tenancy but was allowed by the landlord to continue farming on the land for two years. He was refused relief on the disposal of the tenancy because at that time his business had not ceased and, although precarious, was still continuing.

The third type of material disposal is a disposal of shares in a personal company by a full time working officer or employee of that company. A personal company is one in which the taxpayer owns 5 per cent or more of the voting rights. In *Palmer v. Maloney* (1999) the Court of Appeal said that to be regarded as a full-time working officer or employee at the company, a tax payer must spend all the normal working hours working for the company, i.e by reference to other full-time workers. If that is the case then the fact that the taxpayer has an additional job elsewhere will not affect the position. He does not have to show that all his working hours are devoted to the company.

The relief is also available for "other qualifying disposals". These are disposals of assets held by the taxpayer for the purposes of his office or employment and of business assets held by an individual partner or by a shareholder of a personal company on his withdrawal from that business.

Finally the relief only applies in so far as the disposal relates to chargeable business assets. Thus, for example, if the material disposal is of shares in a personal company there will be no relief for gains attributable to shares held by that company as investments. This is a business and not an investment relief.

The ultimate replacement of retirement relief by taper relief is both more and less generous. For example, whilst retirement relief operates to exclude all gains up to a certain amount, taper relief applies without any age limits and to unlimited gains. Further there is a much more generous definition as to what can amount to a business asset for taper relief (all holdings in unlisted trading companies; 5 per cent holdings in listed companies; and any holdings by employees or officers in listed trading companies whether or not they are full-time). On the other hand taper relief can never exclude more than 75 per cent of the gain which may still penalise small businesses.

Whilst the two reliefs co-exist the procedure is that retirement relief is to be applied to the chargeable gain (indexed up to 1998 where appropriate) and taper relief is then applied to the gain as reduced by retirement relief.

Gifts of Business Assets   16–12

There is a relief for gifts of business assets which is now enacted in section 165. The relief arises where an individual makes a disposal otherwise than under a bargain at arm's length to a person resident or ordinarily resident in the United Kingdom of an asset used for the purposes of a trade, profession or vocation carried on by the transferor or by his personal company or by a trading company which is a subsidiary of his personal company but only if the transferee is not a company. The relief also applies to a similar transfer of shares of an unquoted company or of the transferor's personal company. The relief is additional to retirement relief (above), but it only applies to the extent that the transfer was not relieved by that relief.

Unlike retirement relief this relief is a hold-over relief so that the amount of the untapered gain can be deducted from the deemed acquisition cost of the donee (market value under section 17). Because the donee will therefore become liable to a potentially higher capital gains tax bill on a subsequent disposal any claim for this relief must be made by both the donor and donee. Remember also that taper relief will not apply to reduce the gain held-over and will apply only to the donee's period of ownership when he disposes of it.

Where the relief is available on sales at an undervalue only the amount of that undervalue is available for the relief. If the gift was the subject of a charge to inheritance tax the donee can add that tax paid to his acquisition cost.

Charities   16–13

A gain which accrues to a charity and is applicable and applied for charitable purposes is not a chargeable gain: section 256(1). But if property is held on charitable trusts and then ceases to be so held there is a deemed disposal at market value and any gain so accruing is chargeable: section 256(2). Where a charity has an interest under a trust, money paid to it by the trustees on the disposal of surplus assets are not gains accruing to the charity but to the trustees, unless it is a bare trust.[19]

---

[19] *Prest v. Bettinson* (1980).

Turning now to a disposal *to* a charity, such a disposal if by way of gift is exempt from capital gains tax under section 257 in the sense that neither a gain nor a loss is treated as accruing on the disposal. If the charity subsequently disposes of the property which was given to it, and disposes of it at a gain, the gain will not be a chargeable gain if the gain is applicable and applied for charitable purposes.[20]

---

[20] An outright transfer by a charitable company to another charity is deemed to be applied for charitable purposes: *IRC v. Helen Slater Charitable Trust* (1980).

PART FOUR

Inheritance Tax

THE EVOLUTION OF INHERITANCE TAX

Ever since 1894 there has been a tax aimed at non-commercial transfers of capital, charging tax on the whole of the value so transferred. The current version of this tax is known as inheritance tax, although as we shall see it is neither calculated by reference to what a person inherits nor limited to inheritance on a death. It differs from capital gains tax which taxes only the gain on a transfer, does not apply on a death and applies in the main to commercial transfers of capital. The relationship between the two taxes is usually complementary, although there are overlaps in the area of lifetime gifts, where paradoxically capital gains tax is more likely to apply than inheritance tax.

17–01

The evolution of inheritance tax can be traced back to estate duty introduced in 1894. That tax charged all the property of an individual which passed on his death, unless specifically exempted. In its final form this included not only property which the deceased owned at his death and which passed under his will or intestacy but also property which was deemed to pass on his death. Such property included the full value of any settled property in which the deceased had an interest (including certain discretionary trusts) and the value of any gift made by the deceased either within seven years prior to his death or at any time if the deceased had retained any interest in the property given. The whole amount of the property so passing on the death was then aggregated and tax charged on that amount. Thus estate duty was a mutation duty (*i.e.* one charged on the property passing from the deceased) and not an acquisition duty (*i.e.* one charged according to the amount each person acquired on the death). But only a death triggered a charge.

In 1974 the incoming Labour Government announced its intention to repeal estate duty, which it finally did in 1975. The replacement was known as capital transfer tax. The central idea of this tax (introduced as the precursor of a wealth tax which never materialised) was to charge all non-commercial transfers of capital (known as chargeable transfers) made by an individual throughout his lifetime, with death being regarded as the final

271

transfer. The important concept was that all such transfers were taxed on a cumulative basis. Thus the rate of tax for each successive transfer was calculated on the basis of the transferor's cumulative total at that time. Thus if X, having already made transfers of £100,000, made another transfer of £50,000, the rate of tax for that transfer would be calculated at that applicable for transfers between £100,000 and £150,000, and so on, until on X's death the rates payable would depend upon his whole cumulative total of lifetime transfers. The value of each transfer was calculated not on the value of the transfer as such but on the loss to the transferor. There were special rules for settlements. The law on capital transfer tax was consolidated in 1984 into the Capital Transfer Tax Act.

But by then this principle of taxing all transfers made by an individual throughout his lifetime had been reduced by the rule that the cumulative principle should only apply to gifts made within the previous ten years. Thus in our example above, if X had made the £100,000 transfers more than 10 years before the transfer of £50,000, the latter would be taxed only on the rates between £0 and £50,000. If only £60,000 of the earlier transfers had been made within the past 10 years, the rate of tax on the £50,000 transfer would be calculated according to the rates between £60,000 and £110,000. More importantly, on a death the deceased's cumulative total would only be those transfers made within 10 years of the death and not those throughout his lifetime. In 1986 even more fundamental changes were made to the structure of capital transfer tax and the resulting product was renamed as the inheritance tax we have today. **Even the 1984 consolidation, as amended, was renamed the Inheritance Tax Act 1984[1] and references to sections in the following chapters are to that Act unless otherwise stated.**

What then were these changes? Apart from a simplification of the rates of the tax, the major change was to take most lifetime transfers out of the charge to the tax altogether.[2] With one or two exceptions[3] lifetime transfers will only be chargeable if either they were made within seven years prior to the death of the transferor or the transferor has retained a benefit in the property transferred. Virtually all lifetime transfers are now regarded as

---

[1] Technically the law provides that the 1984 Act *may* be referred to as the Inheritance Tax Act 1984 rather than the Capital Transfer Tax Act, but, in practice, everybody does so.

[2] Thus triggering the reintroduction of the charge on lifetime gifts under capital gains tax.

[3] Notably those relating to discretionary trusts which are immediately chargeable.

potentially exempt transfers which will only become retrospectively chargeable in their own right if the transferor dies within seven years of making them. Since the cumulative principle for those transfers which are chargeable was reduced from 10 to seven years, on a death the deceased's cumulative total relates to those transfers charged (at the time or retrospectively) within the past seven years.

Inheritance tax has therefore resurrected the old estate duty concepts that a death rather than a lifetime transfer is the trigger for a charge to the tax and that gifts made within seven years and those with a reservation of benefit (gifts with reservation) become chargeable on that death. But many aspects of capital transfer tax also remain. Charges on a death and on settlements remain much as before, the way in which the value of the transfer is calculated is still the loss to the transferor, there is still a limited form of cumulation and in certain cases there is a charge even though no death has occurred. Thus inheritance tax is a hybrid between estate duty and capital transfer tax, which charges more than just an inheritance on a death and which does so by reference to the total of the transfers made by the transferor and not by reference to the amount inherited; *i.e.* it is still a mutation and not an acquisitions tax. One curious consequence of the changes to this tax is that most lifetime gifts will not be chargeable to inheritance tax (the non-commercial tax) on the full value transferred but to capital gains tax (the commercial tax) on the notional gain made by the donor. Where both taxes are chargeable there is, as we have seen in paragraph 16–01, a relief from capital gains tax.

In the following chapters we shall examine the scope and effects of this hybrid known as inheritance tax. The first question which needs an answer is what amounts to a chargeable lifetime transfer so as to give rise either to an immediate lifetime charge or to a retrospective charge if the transferor dies within seven years, explaining as we go the way in which gifts with reservation fit into this. Then we need to examine the charge which arises on the death of the transferor. Having established what is chargeable or potentially chargeable we need to look at the various exemptions and reliefs which are available against this charge. Having thus established the net charge so to speak we then examine how the charge is actually calculated and who ultimately has to account for and pay the tax. Because settlements are the subject of many special rules these are dealt with in a separate chapter.

CHAPTER 18

CHARGEABLE TRANSFERS

Inheritance tax is only chargeable if there is a *chargeable transfer*. These may be made either during the transferor's lifetime or on his death, although, as we have seen, most of the former do not attract an immediate charge to the tax. Instead they may become retrospectively chargeable if the transferor dies within seven years of making them. Until then they are known as *potentially exempt transfers*. There are special rules for lifetime transfers in which the transferor retains some interest in the property transferred, known as *gifts with reservation*. This chapter deals with what is meant by a chargeable lifetime transfer, what is a potentially exempt transfer, the rules for gifts with reservation, transfers on death, and one or two special charges, *e.g.* involving close companies as defined for corporation tax purposes). Settled property, being inevitably the most complex area, is dealt with separately in Chapter 21. Remember that there are many exemptions and reliefs which apply to these various charges—these are set out in the following chapter.

18–01   ## Lifetime Transfers

Section 1 declares: "Inheritance tax shall be charged on the value transferred by a chargeable transfer." What, then, is a "chargeable transfer"? The answer is in section 2(1): "A chargeable transfer is a transfer of value which is made by an individual but is not an exempt transfer."

So we need to know what is a transfer of value, what is the value transferred, what is an individual and what is an exempt transfer.

A *"transfer of value"* is defined by section 3(1) as: " ... a disposition made by a person (the transferor) as a result of which the value of his estate immediately after the disposition is less than it would be but for the disposition: and the amount by which it is less is the *value transferred* by the transfer." The two essential criteria for a charge are therefore a disposition and a loss to the transferor's estate.

The word *"individual"* is not defined by the Act, but of course it is a word well-known in tax law; it does not include companies, nor trustees nor personal representatives. However, as we shall see later, certain dispositions made by trustees of settled property give rise to charges to tax as if they were chargeable transfers, and transfers of value made by companies which are close companies may also give rise to tax liability.

Transfers which are *"exempt transfers"*, and therefore not changeable transfers, are dealt with in Chapter 19.

It is also as well to say here (and we shall see some examples of this later on) that some kinds of property are designated as *"excluded property"*, though these are mainly overseas assets. Transfers of such property are not taken into account; section 3(2).

Loss to the transferor's estate   18–02

It is very important to appreciate that the *value transferred* by a transfer is measured under section 3(1) by the diminution in value of the transferor's estate, and not by the increase in value of the transferee's estate, which in this legislation is not limited to the property of a dead person. Of course, in many circumstances the result would be the same whichever measure one took. If Albert gives a motor car to his son Ben, Albert's estate is diminished and Ben's estate is increased by the same amount, namely the value of the car. But there are circumstances in which this is not so, and some of them are very important. For example, if Albert owns 51 per cent of the shares in a company and Ben owns none, and then Albert transfers 2 per cent of the shares to Ben, the diminution in Albert's estate is much greater than is the increase in Ben's estate, because Albert has given up control of the company and Ben has not obtained control.

The word *"estate"* is defined in section 5(1) as "the aggregate of all the property to which [a person] is beneficially entitled, except that the estate of a person immediately before his death does not include excluded property". We shall deal with excluded property later.

The word *"property"* is stated in section 272 to include "rights and interests of any description." It thus includes (and the importance of this will be seen later) an interest under a settlement such as a life tenancy. In particular, section 5(2) includes any general power of appointment as being part of a person's estate. The definition of a general power for this purpose seems to continue the estate duty concept[1] of any power which a person can appoint

---

[1]   See *e.g. Re Parsons* (1943).

in his own favour, *e.g.* "to such person as X shall appoint", or "to such of X, Y, and Z as X shall appoint". It follows that the exercise of such a power will be a transfer of value (disposition plus loss to the estate) and also in some cases the omission to exercise it (loss to estate and gain to the estate of the person entitled in default of appointment—section 3(3)).

The meaning of property in the context of a loss to the transferor's estate was considered by Lightman J in *Melville v. IRC* (2000). The taxpayer had settled property on discretionary trusts (an immediately chargeable transfer) but had included a provision in the trust deed whereby he had the right to require the trustees to transfer the whole of the trust fund back to him at his request at any time 90 days after the date of the settlement and also had a veto on any exercise by the trustees of their powers of appointment under the trust. The judge held that those rights were property under section 272 and therefore formed part of the taxpayer's estate for the purposes of section 3(1). There was no reason to apply any other meaning to the word property, as defined, than as including anything which was capable of producing value being realised and turned into money. It followed that the loss to his estate consequent on the transfer into the settlement was negligible. It did of course remain a chargeable transfer, since there was some loss, for the purposes of relief from capital gains tax (see para. 16-01) which was the object of the exercise.

One very important aspect of this diminution principle is that if the transferor pays the inheritance tax the tax is itself taxable, because his estate is diminished not only by what he transfers to the transferee but also by what he has to pay to the Revenue. The payment of the tax forms part of the loss to the transferor's estate. So there is a grossing-up process. We will deal with this concept more fully later on.

18–03 *Disposition*

It will be noticed that the definition of transfer of value includes the word "disposition". There is no general definition of this but it probably includes not only obvious transfers such as sales and gifts but also disclaimers[2] and waivers of possible future rights.[3] There have been two attempts since 1975 to charge interest-free

---

[2] Some disclaimers are expressly excluded from the charge, (*e.g.* of a legacy within two years of death: s.142). So it presumably follows that other disclaimers are included.

[3] Again some waivers, (*e.g.* of future dividends not declared for at least one year afterwards: s.15) are expressly excluded from the charge.

loans but both have been repealed and the position remains obscure. It is, however, provided by section 3(3) that a disposition can be merely the omission to exercise a right. This provision prevents many possible avoidance devices. For example, but for this provision Albert could make a tax-free transfer to Ben (his son) by engaging him, for a lump sum paid in advance, to work for a specified time in his (Albert's) business and then standing by and omitting to sue for damages when Ben does not turn up. Section 3(3) only applies, however, if, as the result of an omission by you, your estate is diminished and another's is increased, and it can be avoided if you can show that the omission was not deliberate.[4]

Associated operations   18–04

It is stated in section 272 (the definitions section, well worth looking at) that a "disposition" includes "a disposition effected by *associated operations*" and "associated operations" are defined by section 268. They are

"(a) operations which affect the same property ... or
 (b) any two operations of which one is effected with reference to the other, or with a view to enabling the other to be effected or facilitating its being effected, and any further operation having a like relation to any of those two, and so on: whether those operations are effected by the same person or different persons, and whether or not they are simultaneous; and 'operation' includes an omission."

A simple example of how this provision might work arises from an attempt to manipulate the exempt transfer provisions. As we shall see transfers between spouses are, in general, exempt and each individual may make exempt transfers up to £3,000 in each tax year. Suppose Albert is a wealthy taxpayer who has already given £3,000 to his son, Ben in the current year. Albert could give £3,000 to his wife Zoë, who could then give that money to Ben, using her exempt amount. None of the transfers is a chargeable transfer. Under the associated operations provisions the transfer of the second £3,000 to Ben could be treated as if it had been made by Albert and so chargeable if Albert were to die within seven years, even if Zoë is still alive.

The definition of associated operations is very wide and it is interesting to compare it with the *Ramsay* principle devised by

---

[4] Does this include for example failure to exercise a beneficial option owing to lack of funds?

the courts. The section has been before the courts on two occasions, both involving settlements. In *Macpherson v. IRC* (1988) the trustees entered into two transactions which together had the effect of lowering the charge to tax on the second. The House of Lords had no difficulty in deciding that these were associated operations but the case is worth noting because their Lordships imposed a restriction on the width of the section by insisting that each operation must be relevant to the scheme which created the benefit for the transferee. In *Hatton v. IRC* (1992) where two settlements were created within 24 hours of each other and the first was set up with a view to the second being created, Chadwick J. also applied the associated operations rules. The consequence was that each settlor was treated as being a settlor of both settlements, which had the effect of negating the sought for exemptions from the tax. It is possible that this approach will also apply to joint and reciprocal settlements.

If the associated operations provision applies then the consequence is that the chargeable transfer is deemed to take place at the time of the last of them: section 268(3). There is one statutory exception in section 268(2). The grant of a lease for full consideration is not to be associated with any operation effected more than three years earlier, *e.g.* a gift of the landlord's reversion.

18–05   *Non-commercial transfers*

It has been said above that inheritance tax is (in part) a tax on non-commercial transfers, *i.e.* "gifts tax". That phrase is not used in the legislation, but it is made clear by the use of other words *"gratuitous benefit"* in section 10(1) that the tax only bites on transfers which contain an element of gift. Sales at market value are not taxable because they do not involve any diminution in the value of the seller's estate. If Albert owns a car which is worth £800 and he sells it to Charles for £800 Albert's estate has the same value after the sale as it had before the sale; he has merely exchanged one asset (the car) for an equivalent asset (cash). But suppose Albert sells the car, not for £800, but for £500. That may occur either (1) because Albert wished to confer a benefit on Charles or (2) because he made a bad bargain. A gift (as in (1)), is taxable: a bad bargain (as in (2)), is not taxable. This point is dealt with in section 10(1) which declares:

"A disposition is not a transfer of value if it is shown that it was not intended, and was not made in a transaction intended, to confer any gratuitous benefit on any person and either—

278

(a) that it was made in a transaction at arm's length between persons not connected with each other, or

(b) that it was such as might be expected to be made in a transaction at arm's length between persons not connected with each other ..."

The subsection requires two conditions to be met; a subjective non-donative intent *and* the objective fact stated in (a) or the apparently objective fact stated in (b).[5] Where the parties are connected (*i.e.* they are relatives, linked in a trust, partners or involved with a close company) the criterion imposed by (b) of what would be expected to amount to an arm's length sale was discussed in *IRC v. Spencer-Nairn* (1991).

This was an unusual case in that the vendor was unaware that he was selling to a connected person (a company) and had negotiated on the basis that they were unconnected. He sold the property for £94,000 below the market value because he mistakenly thought that he was liable for repairs to the property. The Revenue agreed that he had no gratuitous intention but argued that the discrepancy between the market value and the actual value of the land meant that it was not one which could have been expected on an arm's length sale. The Scottish Court of Session dismissed the argument that any such discrepancy would automatically invoke the section, stating that it was merely one factor which had to be taken into account. They decided that a hypothetical arm's length vendor should be taken to have had the actual vendor's (reasonable) belief that he was liable for repairs and so, since the price was not unreasonable given that belief, they found for the taxpayer. They were impressed by the fact that the price had been negotiated between persons who thought they were acting at arms length. One consequence of this decision is therefore that in assessing what can be expected on an arm's length sale certain subjective factors, such as the reasonable belief in this case, are to be taken into account.

Notice that section 10(1) has the very desirable result that payment for services is not a transfer of value. If you pay a fee to a solicitor (for example) your estate has been diminished by the

---

[5] On a sale of shares in an unquoted company it is also necessary to show that the price was either freely negotiated or one that could have been so negotiated. Thus transfers by close companies are outside the definition.

amount of the fee but you are saved from tax by section 10(1). You need only pay the solicitor, not the Revenue as well.

18–06   *Potentially exempt transfers*

Lifetime transfers do not necessarily attract an immediate charge to tax. Only those which are not potentially exempt transfers as defined in section 3A become immediately liable to a charge. A potentially exempt transfer (PET) is defined as (i) one made by an individual, (ii) which would otherwise be a chargeable transfer, (iii) which is made to another individual or is made to, or is connected with, a settlement in which an individual has an interest in possession or which is an accumulation and maintenance settlement or is a disabled trust.[6] Thus transfers to companies and the various charges involving discretionary trusts (other than accumulation and disabled trusts) are not potentially exempt transfers. They are therefore immediately chargeable transfers.

In the case of a transfer to an individual the transfer will only be a PET if the property becomes part of that individual's estate or his estate is increased. Thus if David decides to pay his grandson's school fees and does so by paying the school direct he has not made a PET—the grandson's estate has not been increased. It would be a PET if David gave the money to his son who then used the money to pay the school fees as the son's estate will have been increased. Gifts with a reservation, *i.e.* where the donor retains some interest in the property, are the subject of special rules, set out in the following part of this chapter.

We will explain the somewhat tortuous rules for calculating the charges to inheritance tax in Chapter 20. For the moment it is sufficient to note that a lifetime transfer which is not a PET attracts an immediate charge based on the cumulative total of such transfers within the previous seven years. The current rate for immediately chargeable lifetime transfers is 20 per cent on cumulative transfers above £234,000. Thus if Edward, having made no previous transfers, creates two discretionary trusts in 2000 and 2001, each with a value of £234,000—the first will be tax free but the second will be chargeable at 20 per cent.

If the transfer is a PET then there is no immediate charge to tax and if the transferor lives for more than seven years there will be no charge at all. If, however, the transferor dies within that period the PET becomes chargeable at the appropriate rate for deaths (which is currently double the rate for lifetime transfers, subject

---

[6]   These terms are discussed in Chapter 21, below.

to some relief if he has survived at least three years) as laid down at the date of death rather than at the rate in force when the transfer was made unless the former is higher. The effect of a PET ceasing to be exempt because of the death is that it retrospectively becomes a chargeable transfer. Thus it will have to be taken into account in working out the transferor's cumulative total for subsequent lifetime transfers. This can retrospectively affect the liability for those other transfers. Thus if in our example above, Edward had made a PET of £234,000 in 1999, which subsequently becomes chargeable on Edward's death in 2001, not only is that transfer itself charged to tax but the relevant cumulative total of previous transfers for the discretionary trust transfer in 2000 will change from zero to £234,000 and the latter will become chargeable at 20 per cent.[7]

Gifts with reservation of benefit

18–07

With the introduction of the potentially exempt transfer regime in 1986 it was inevitable that measures would be taken to prevent a transferor making a gift, *e.g.* of his house to his son or daughter, whilst retaining a benefit in that property, *e.g.* by continuing to live in the house. If the transferor lived for more than seven years after making the gift he would avoid any inheritance tax and would have passed on his house to his son or daughter tax free, whilst in practice having made no material change in his circumstances. To prevent taxpayers having their cake and eating it in this way the concept of a gift with reservation was introduced by section 102 of and Schedule 20 to the Finance Act 1986. In fact this concept was really reintroduced because it had been necessary for such a provision under estate duty law to prevent exactly the same abuse. The basic legislation is similar to that for estate duty and some of the cases decided under those rules are relevant here. One issue which also arose under the old rules was decided in such a way by the House of Lords under the new rules that additional legislation, sections 102A, 102B and 102C was introduced in 1999.

One problem with using the former estate duty concept of a gift is that it does not always square with the inheritance tax concept of a transfer of value. Thus, whilst a bad bargain may be a

---

[7] In fact, as we shall see, because Edward has died within seven years of setting up the discretionary trusts, additional tax above the 20 per cent becomes payable, up to the full death-rate, depending on the length of time Edward survived.

transfer of value if it is between connected persons because there will be a loss to the transferor's estate and it will not fall within the gratuitous benefit exemption, it is hard to see that there is any element of bounty so as to classify it as a gift.[8]

Section 102 of the Finance Act 1986 applies when an individual disposes of any property by way of gift and either:

(a) possession and enjoyment is not bona fide assumed by the donee at, or before the beginning of the relevant period; or

(b) at any time in the relevant period the property is not enjoyed to the entire exclusion, or virtually the entire exclusion,[9] of the donor and of any benefit to him by contract or otherwise.

The *relevant period* in which both possession and enjoyment must be assumed and the entire exclusion of the donor is assessed, is seven years prior to the death of the donor. Thus if at any time in the seven years prior to his death the donor was not so excluded or possession was not taken up by the donee, the gift will be regarded as one subject to a reservation. It follows that if any such benefit is given up and possession has been assumed more than seven years before the death then there is no gift with a reservation and in fact no charge to inheritance tax.

There are two possible consequences of a gift being regarded as one subject to a reservation. First, whenever it was made, if the gift is still subject to a reservation at the date of the donor's death, the property given is deemed to be part of the donor's estate at death and so chargeable as if he had never given it away. Secondly, if the gift ceases to be subject to a reservation within seven years before the donor's death, the donor is treated as if he had made a PET at that date. Thus the property will be retrospectively charged under the PET rules as if the donor had made a chargeable transfer of the property at the date when the reservation ceased.

Using, in part, the old estate duty cases it is possible to shed some light on how the courts will interpret the various parts of section 102 of the Finance Act 1986. With regard to the concept of the donee assuming bona fide possession in paragraph (a) it is

---

[8] It is also arguable that a disposition which is deemed by the 1984 Act not to be a transfer of value, *e.g.* one for the maintenance of the family (see paragraph 19–19), will still be a gift for this purpose.

[9] This was not present in the original estate duty provisions and is intended to allow *e.g.* the donor of a house to return to it on visits or a short holiday.

clear that to do so the gift must be a perfect transfer in equity.[10] This was the decision in *Letts v. IRC* (1954). Looking at paragraph (b), it has been held that the donor will not be entirely excluded from possession of the property unless that is the position in fact as well as in law. Thus in *Oakes v. Commissioner of Stamp Duties* (1954), a settlor who settled property in which he had no interest was caught when he was appointed as a trustee with a right to remuneration, and in *Stamp Duties Commissioner of New South Wales v. Permanent Trustee Co.* (1956), where the settlor borrowed the interest arising from the settlement on his daughter, with no legal entitlement to do so, a similar result applied.

The inclusion of a benefit "by contract or otherwise" is intended to catch collateral benefits to the donor. In *Att.-Gen. v. Seccombe* (1911) it was held that such benefits had to be the subject of a legal entitlement. It is doubted whether that would now be the law. Schedule 20 expressly excludes two factual situations from being a reservation of a benefit. Paragraph 6 provides that actual occupation of land by the donor in return for full consideration in money or where the donor comes back into actual occupation of land owing to his incapacity and it is for reasonable provision for his care and maintenance by the donee who is a relative of the donor, are not to be regarded as a reservation of a benefit by the donor.

The most complex of the old cases were those which drew a distinction between a benefit reserved out of the property given away and a benefit retained by the donor which was never given away in the first place. The importance of this is that in the second case the property actually given away has never been the subject of a reservation. This is easier to state than to apply in practice, however. The trick is to separate the part retained by the donor from the part given away. This is sometimes explained by reference to *vertical and horizontal separation*.

For example if Fred owns two adjoining houses and gives one to Gillian whilst retaining the other this is said to be vertical separation. The fact that Fred has retained one house does not mean that he has retained any benefit in the other which thus becomes a PET.

Suppose instead Fred creates an interest in his property and then gives away the rest, he has horizontally separated the two and so has no benefit in the part given away. It would be different

---

[10] Remember that in general equity will not perfect an imperfect gift so that if any formalities required to effect a gift have not been undertaken by the donor, there is no perfect gift.

if he gave away the whole property and was then given back the interest in it—he would have reserved a benefit in the property.

With regard to such horizontal separation the timing of the separation is crucial. The original authority for its effectiveness is *Munro v. Commissioner of Stamp Duties* (1934), where the donor gave away land subject to his interest as a partner in its use which had been created prior to the gift. He was held to have given away only the land subject to the partnership interest. He had not reserved his interest as a partner, he had simply never given it away at all. This decision was distinguished in *Nicholls v. IRC* (1975) where the donor gave his land away subject to a condition that it was leased back to him by the donee. He was held to have given away the whole property and reserved the benefit of the lease. The lease had not been created by a prior transaction unlike the partnership interest in *Munro*.

The only case on the new provisions was also directly on this point of horizontal severance. In *Ingram v. IRC* (1999), HL, the donor transferred property to trustees and, in an attempt to avoid the decision in *Nicholls*, *at the same time* created the right to a lease of the property to herself. The Court of Appeal agreed with the general principle as to the timing of the separation in *Nicholls* but it was rejected by the House of Lords. In their opinion a gift of the freehold of land with a condition that a lease back to the donor be granted was not a gift with reservation. All that the donor had given away was the reversion in which she had no benefit. *Nicholls* was distinguished on the basis that in that case there was an additional reservation under a different head because the donee had covenanted to repair the land and so the donor, in occupation of it under the lease, was not entirely excluded from benefit by contract. This allowed the House of Lords to decide that the general reservation point in *Nicholls* was *obiter*.

The success of what was known as the "lease carve out scheme" in *Ingram* "disappointed" the Revenue, who then, in time-honoured fashion, took the first opportunity to introduce legislation to reverse the decision. The main section is section 102A inserted into the Finance Act 1986. It applies only where the gift is of an interest in land and where it would not otherwise be a gift with reservation under the general rules.[11] In practice it is of course in relation to land that such schemes will mainly apply because of the possibilities of creating horizontal interests in land. The section provides that where X makes a gift of an interest in

---

[11] Such as a reservation of benefit by a contract (the covenant to repair) as in *Nicholls*.

land there will be a gift with a reservation if within the relevant period[12] either: (1) X (the donor) or his spouse has a *significant right or interest* in relation to the land; or (2) X or his spouse is a party to a *significant arrangement* in relation to the land (section 102A(2)).

An interest, right or arrangement is significant for this purpose if it *entitles* or *enables* X to occupy all or part of the land or to enjoy some right in relation to all or part of the land[13] otherwise than for full consideration in money or money's worth (section 102A(3)). This means that for the section to apply it must be X who occupies the land or enjoys the right, even if it is his spouse who has the interest. Thus if X gives some land to Y on condition that it is leased back to X's spouse, but X occupies the land with his spouse's consent, it will be caught because X's spouse has an interest which is a significant one since it has enabled X to occupy the land. The use of the word *enables* may cause problems since it is far less precise than *entitles*. For example, suppose that X gives land to Y on condition that it is leased back to Z who is not X's spouse. Z then allows X to occupy the land. Is X a party to a significant arrangement, *i.e.* one which enables him to occupy the land?

An important limit on the scope of section 102A is that subsection (5) exempts interests or rights which X or his spouse were granted more than seven years before the gift of land.[14] Thus, at first sight, if X grants his spouse a lease in year one and gives the reversion to Y in year nine, there will be no reservation even if X continues to occupy the land. But this seven-year period does not apply to arrangements, so that any arrangement made at any time before the gift will count if it is significant. Therefore, if the above example can be regarded as an arrangement, it will still be a gift with reservation since X's occupation will make it significant. Thus it can be seen that these provisions apply to interests, etc., created well before the gift and not just to lease carve out schemes of the *Ingram* type. Under the old rules the Revenue used to ignore events prior to the gift if they were "prior independent transactions".[15]

Section 102A does not apply in certain circumstances where the general rule in section 102 would not apply, *e.g.* occupation by X due to unforeseen circumstances. Nor does it apply where X

---

[12] Remember that this is the seven years before X's subsequent death.

[13] This will include rights such as shooting rights, etc.

[14] Be careful not to confuse this with the period of seven years before X's death in which the significant right, interest or arrangement must still exist before there can be a charge, whenever the gift was made.

[15] Which of course they seldom were in practice.

gives Y a lease and retains the reversion (section 102A(4)(b)) which is the converse to a lease carve out.

More fundamentally section 102A does not apply to gifts of an undivided share (*i.e.* in England the creation of a tenancy in common) in land. In fact in such a case even the general provisions in section 102 are not to apply (section 102C(6)). Instead section 102B applies. Under that section, where X gives Y an undivided share in his land so that X and Y become tenants in common, he will have made a gift with reservation unless: (1) X does not occupy the land;[16] (2) X occupies the land to the entire exclusion of Y for full consideration in money or money's worth[17]; or (3) X and Y occupy the land and X does not receive any benefit, other than a negligible one, provided by Y or at his expense for some reason connected with the gift. This last situation will therefore protect X if Y pays only his fair share of the outgoings of the land. There will also be no charge where X occupies the land due to unforeseen circumstances.

The final question involving gifts subject to a reservation is that if they do become chargeable what property is actually subject to the charge? The answers to this are to be found in Schedule 20 to the Finance Act 1986. If the property originally given is still held by the donee unchanged in form then of course it will be that property, valued now, which is chargeable. But if the donee has parted with the original gift an alternative is required. In outline, if the donee sells or exchanges the asset for full consideration then that sum or replacement asset becomes the subject of any charge. In other cases the property with which he parted (including any replacement asset taken in full exchange) becomes the subject of the charge. The same rules apply broadly to gifts into a settlement.

18–08   Transfers on Death

Section 4(1) declares that: "On the death of any person tax shall be charged as if, immediately before his death he had made a transfer of value and the value transferred by it had been equal to the value of his estate immediately before his death." It is this enactment which brought in inheritance tax as a replacement of estate duty.

The effect of section 4 is that the deceased is deemed to have made a disposition of all his assets the moment before death. The

---

[16] Since section 102 does not apply X can receive rent, etc., from the land provided he is not in occupation of it.

[17] This is similar to the position under sections 102 and 102A.

total of those assets must then be added to the cumulative total of his chargeable lifetime transfers made in the past seven years and charged at the appropriate rate (currently 40 per cent on transfers above £234,000). The rate of tax on a death is twice that on a lifetime transfer, although the former may also be liable to capital gains tax. We have already seen that the death of the transferor will make all PETS made within the past seven years retrospectively chargeable (and part of the cumulative total for subsequent previous transfers) and that a gift still subject to a reservation at the death will also become chargeable at the rates for a death. The death will also increase the rate of tax already paid on an immediately chargeable lifetime transfer made within seven years prior to the death. One minor blessing is that since the deceased has transferred all his assets on his death there can be no question of grossing up the transfer to include the tax payable— that must come out of the assets transferred. Questions as to who pays the tax and who ultimately bears the cost (*e.g.* as between the beneficiaries) are the subject of Chapter 22.

What is the point of deeming the transfer of value to have been made "immediately before" the death, not "on" the death? Presumably it is to knock out any argument that at the moment of death certain interests of the person dying cease to exist and therefore do not form part of his estate. This argument could have been put forward, for example, in relation to the interest of a joint tenant which is extinguished "on" the death: section 171(2).

Similarly exercising a power of appointment by will does not affect the fact that such a power formed part of the estate immediately before the death. Estate has the same meaning as for lifetime transfers. Moving the deemed transfer from the moment of death to "immediately before" the death also makes it easier for the legislation to lay down its own code of rules, untrammelled by the general law, as to which assets are to be treated as forming part of the estate and which are not. Such a code is laid down in sections 171 to 177. For example, there is an allowance for reasonable funeral expenses under section 172.

It is important to know what is the tax position if two (or more) persons die (for example in a car accident) virtually at the same instant. The law of succession to property in such a case is stated in section 184 of the Law of Property Act 1925, namely that the younger person is deemed to have survived the elder person. For tax purposes, however, section 4(2) provides that "where it cannot be known which of two or more persons who have died survived the other or others they shall be assumed to have died at the same instant." Suppose that the two persons are Albert and his son Ben. The effect is that the estate left by Albert to Ben is charged to tax on Albert's death but not also on Ben's death. Similarly, if Ben has left anything to Albert, that estate is charged on Ben's death but not also on Albert's death. Where the order of death *is* known (*e.g.* Albert dies five minutes before Ben) section 4(2) does not apply, but there may be "Quick Succession Relief": see paragraph 19–13. An alternative is to provide in a will that property will only pass to a beneficiary if he survives the testator by a specified period. Such survivorship clauses if limited to six months will avoid a double charge in such cases: section 92.

18–09   **Other Charges**

This rather curious chapter title is taken from the Finance Act 1975 where "Other Charges" was used as a cross-heading to describe four sections, 39–42, grouped together in that Act as being, broadly speaking, anti-avoidance measures. It is a fair comment on the haste with which the 1975 Bill was prepared that these problems had not been thought through very thoroughly. Indeed, when the Bill was first published the problem of close companies (obvious with hindsight) had not been dealt with at all. When the 1984 consolidation took place some attempts at rationalisation over the 10 years was evident. Section 39 (beefed up in 1976) become sections 94 to 98 *and* section 102 *and* section 202. Section 41 was repealed before it came into effect. But sections 40 and 42 (now sections 262 and 263) still defy classification and were assigned to the "Miscellaneous and Supplementary" part of the 1984 Act.

18–10   *Close companies*

In general, inheritance tax is not charged on companies because they are not "individuals". But, by section 94, where a company which is a close company makes a transfer of value a tax charge may arise. Such transfers cannot be PETs and so attract an immediate charge to the tax. The intention is to prevent such companies from being used to avoid the tax. Tax is charged as if each participator, domiciled here, had made a transfer of value proportionate to his interest in the company.[18] But against this can be set the amount (if any) by which the value of his estate

---

[18] We have come across these terms for corporation tax purposes. But see section 96 which excludes the ownership of preference shares for this purpose.

is increased. So (for example) a reduction of capital would be a gratuitous transfer by the company, but no tax would be payable because each member's estate would be increased by the amount received. His estate (for this purpose) does not include any rights or interests in the company.

Section 98 provides that where there is an alteration of such a company's shares or debentures or rights attaching to them so that there is a loss to a transferor's estate there will be a chargeable transfer by the participators. This is to prevent value being passed in ways that it might be impossible to establish that the transferor shareholder has made a disposition, *e.g.* on a reduction of capital or a purchase by a company of its own shares. The sections are aimed at various avoidance devices, and consequently section 102 provides that a "close company" includes not only a company which is a close company for purposes of corporation tax but also a company which would be such a close company if it were resident in the United Kingdom.

Future payments   18–11

This matter is dealt with (in rather obscure language) by section 262. Where a transfer of value takes the form of a disposition for which payments are made (or assets are transferred) more than a year after the disposition, each payment is taxed separately when it is made, the tax being based on a proportionate part of the value transferred. For example, if A buys a property for more than its market value, that is, on the general principles of the tax, a transfer of value by A of the amount by which the price exceeds the market value—the gratuitous element. The effect of this present section is that if A agrees to pay by instalments, each instalment counts as a separate transfer of value. (The rule does not apply to a disposition for no consideration at all, such as an ordinary seven-year covenant.) The point of the section is (presumably) to spread the amount of value transferred. Thus some of the instalments may fall within seven years before A's death, thus attracting a charge, whereas the earlier ones may escape such a charge under the PET rules.

Interest-free loans   18–12

This matter was originally intended to be dealt with by section 41 (of Finance Act 1975) but that was replaced by Finance Act 1976, s.115 before it came into effect. That section was itself repealed and there are no specific provisions now to deal with interest-free loans. The position is therefore covered only by the general provisions of the Act. It follows that a fixed-term loan of money or assets may be a transfer of value. For example, if A lends B £1,000 interest-free for five years, gratuitously, A is making a transfer to B of the then value of using the money for that period. But if the loan was repayable on demand, there would be no value transferred, and no inheritance tax charge.

18–13 *Annuity purchased in conjunction with life policy*

Section 263 imposes a charge to tax where the purchase of an annuity is an associated operation with the issue of a life policy on the life of the annuitant and the policy is vested in someone other than the purchaser of the annuity. The purchaser is treated as making a transfer of value at the time the life policy becomes vested in that other person. The amount of the transfer of value is whichever is the less of the following: (a) the sum paid for the annuity plus premiums paid under the policy up to the time of the transfer; (b) the greatest benefit capable of being conferred at any time by the policy. Such transfers are PETs.

It seems that this special charge to tax is additional to the charge which may arise (if no exemption applies) from the transferor's keeping the policy on foot by paying the premiums, each premium payment being a transfer of value.

The reason why the Revenue are so concerned about back-to-back policies is that a linked contract for life assurance and an annuity with the same company can be obtained on very favourable terms, because if the company loses on the assurance policy it will gain on the annuity contract. Because of this background, it seems that the Revenue will be prepared to treat the arrangements as not being associated operations (and hence not taxable) if the life policy has been issued on no different terms from those which would have been obtainable without the annuity link.

18–14 *Settled property*

The application of inheritance tax to settled property is the subject of Chapter 21, below.

EXEMPTIONS AND RELIEFS

The legislation gives relief from tax in various ways. Some kinds of property are declared to be excluded property. Some transactions are declared not to be transfers of value. Some transfers of value are declared to be exempt transfers, thus attracting no tax. Some transfers of value, though they are taxable, attract a reduced amount of tax. Some apply to lifetime transfers only, some to transfers on a death and others to all types of transfer.

No great benefit would accrue from expounding the exemptions and reliefs under separate heads corresponding to the various modes of relief mentioned above. Until the 1984 Act they were somewhat randomly placed through the legislation, and even the 1984 consolidation has to resort to calling two of its nine parts "Miscellaneous". In order to continue to show how the history of this tax lacks coherence the order in which the exemptions and reliefs are expounded in what follows is based largely (but not wholly) on the order in which they stood in the Finance Act 1975 and then on the order in which further reliefs have been added since. References in this chapter are, however, to the 1984 Act.

We list first those transfers defined as exempt transfers.

Transfers between spouses: section 18   19–01

Transfers between spouses are exempt transfers. This is true both of lifetime transfers and of transfers on death. This exemption is obviously of immense importance in family planning, by which *we* mean tax planning from the point of view of the family as a whole.

The exemption is stated in section 18:

> "A transfer of value is an exempt transfer to the extent that the value transferred is attributable to property which becomes comprised in the estate of the transferor's spouse, or, so far as the value transferred is not so attributable, to the extent that that estate is increased."

This is a rather curious phrase. The first part of it gives exemption to the straightforward case where one spouse transfers some item of cash or property to the other spouse. The second part of the phrase deals with less clear-cut cases. An example would be a case where one spouse forgives a debt owed to him (or her) by the other spouse. The forgiveness is a transfer of value, but it is an exempt transfer because, although no property becomes comprised in the estate of the forgiven spouse, that estate is increased by the amount of the debt.

The exemption does not apply if the disposition takes effect on the termination *after the transfer of value* of any interest or period. So if H (husband) leaves property to X (any third party) for life and then to W (H's wife) the exemption does not apply. Similarly if H leaves property to X for 10 years and then to W. Also, the exemption does not apply if the disposition depends on a condition which is not satisfied within 12 months. An example would be if H left property to W provided she survived him by 18 months. But the exemption is not excluded by reason only that the gift is conditional on one spouse surviving the other for a specified period. So a survivorship clause in a will does not knock out the exemption provided the survivorship period is not more than 12 months. In practice wills are commonly drawn with a survivorship period of 30 or 60 days.

As an anti-avoidance measure, the exemption does not apply if the spouse has purchased the reversionary interest in the property: see section 56(2).

There is no requirement that the spouses must be living together. But if the transferor spouse is domiciled in the United Kingdom and the transferee spouse is domiciled abroad, the exemption has a limit of £55,000 (calculated as a value on which no tax is payable. *i.e.* without grossing-up).

19–02   **Values not exceeding £3,000: section 19**

Transfers of value made by a transferor in any one year are exempt to the extent that the values transferred by him do not exceed £3,000. The values are to be calculated for this purpose as values on which no tax is payable; in other words, without grossing up. The year ends on April 5. Unused relief may be carried forward into the next year to be used after the amount for that year. The shortfall cannot be carried forward any further. Thus if in year 1 X gives away £2,500 he can carry forward £500 to year 2. If in that year he gives away £3,200 he uses the £3,000 for that year and £200 from year 1. The remaining £300 is lost.

As husband and wife are separate chargeable individuals for the purposes of inheritance tax, each can make gifts to (for example) their children up to £3,000 per year without either of them incurring any inheritance tax. Compare this to the capital gains tax rules.

Where the transferor makes more than one transfer of value in a tax year the relief is given against earlier rather than later transfers. Where, as in most cases, a transfer is a PET then the relief is first given against any transfers which are not PETs in that year. If the PET subsequently becomes chargeable it will be treated as having been made at the end of the year in which it was made and in so far as the exemption for that year is still available it can be claimed retrospectively against the retrospective charge.

This exemption only applies to lifetime transfers, not to transfers on death.

Small gifts to same person: section 20   19–03

Transfers of value made by a transferor in any one tax year to any one person are exempt to the extent that the values transferred by them (calculated as values on which no tax is chargeable) do not exceed £250. This exemption does not apply to transfers on death, and it only applies to lifetime transfers which are "outright gifts", as distinct from gifts in settlement. It does not apply to part of gifts in excess of £250.

Learned articles have been published arguing that the wording of the legislation is such that this "small gifts exemption" and the £3,000 exemption" (and some other exemptions) are not wholly independent and that in some circumstances they are not cumulative.[1] The position is unclear, however, and there is a good argument that the two exemptions are cumulative. So we think one can say that a taxpayer (Albert perhaps) can give up to £250 to any number of different persons in a year and can also make £3,000 worth of gifts, all exempt from tax: e.g. £3,250 to B plus £250 to C plus £250 to D and so on through the alphabet (if his generosity runs so far).

Normal expenditure out of income: section 21   19–04

A transfer of value is an exempt transfer if, or to the extent that, it is shown (a) that it was made as part of normal expenditure of the transferor: and (b) that (taking one year with another) it was made out of his income; and (c) that, after allowing for all transfers of value forming part of his normal expenditure, the

---

[1] See particularly David Feldman in [1977] B.T.R. 164.

transferor was left with sufficient income to maintain his usual standard of living.

Some guidance as to what is meant by "normal expenditure" for this purpose was provided by Lightman J. in *Bennett v. IRC* (1995). Mrs Bennett had been given a life interest under her husband's will with her sons taking the whole amount after her death. Initially the income produced by the trust fund was sufficient to meet her needs, which were described by the judge as "modest". Subsequently the income produced by the fund increased substantially and she instructed the trustees that since she did not require any additional income, the surplus income should be paid out to the sons. Her needs did indeed continue to be modest. The trustees did as instructed, although on a conservative basis. Mrs Bennett died unexpectedly two years after giving this instruction and the Revenue sought to charge the payments to the sons as PETs by her, which were activated by her death. The sons argued that the normal expenditure out of income exception applied.

Lightman J. said that for expenditure to be normal, each payment had to be shown to conform to an established pattern of expenditure by the payer. Such a pattern could be established by proof of the existence of a prior commitment or resolve (*e.g.* a regular payment) or by reference to a sequence of payments, *e.g.* by paying the instalments on a life assurance policy.[2] Thus a death bed commitment would not satisfy either requirement. There was no need, however, either for a legal obligation or a minimum period. The amount need not be fixed and the recipient need not be the same, so that, *e.g.* paying the costs of elderly relatives' nursing home expenses would suffice. The fact that the income was unreasonable or idiosyncratic did not mean that it was not normal for the particular individual. Applying all this to the facts, the judge held that the exception applied in this case. There was a pattern in respect of the surplus income, which she genuinely did not need, and the payments to the sons had been made in accordance with that pattern.

This exemption applies only to lifetime transfers, not to transfers on death.

19–05   **Gifts in consideration of marriage: section 22**

A gift in consideration of marriage is not defined in the legislation. It has been established by case law that a gift is a gift in

---

[2] For an example of a case where there was no pattern of expenditure, see *Nadin v. IRC* (1997).

consideration of marriage if it fulfils three requisites: it is made on the occasion of a marriage; it is conditional on the marriage taking place; and it is made for the purpose of, or with a view to encouraging or facilitating, the particular marriage: see the estate duty case of *IRC v. Lord Rennell* (1964), HL.[3]

Transfers of value made by gifts in consideration of marriage are exempt under section 22 (if they are lifetime transfers or certain transfers under a settlement, as distinct from transfers on death) to the extent that the values transferred by such transfers made by any one transferor in respect of any one marriage (calculated net) do not exceed:

(a) in the case of gifts satisfying the conditions set out below by a parent of a party to the marriage, £5,000;
(b) in the case of other gifts satisfying those conditions, £2,500; and
(c) in any other case, £1,000.

The conditions which have to be met to obtain the £5,000 or £2,500 exemption are:

(i)   it is an outright gift to a child or remoter descendant of the transferor (thus each parent can give £5,000, and each grandparent £2,500, to the couple); or
(ii) the transferor is a parent or remoter ancestor of either party to the marriage, and either the gift is an outright gift to the other party to the marriage or the property comprised in the gift is settled by the gift; or
(iii) the transferor is a party to the marriage, and either the gift is an outright gift to the other party to the marriage or the property comprised in the gift is settled by the gift.

There are limits on who can benefit. To qualify for exemption an outright gift must be to a party to the marriage; and a settled gift can only include certain persons (notably the parties to the marriage and their issue) as beneficiaries or potential beneficiaries.

Gifts to charities: section 23   19–06

Transfers of value to charities are exempt transfers. There is no limit as to the amount and the exemption applies to both lifetime and death transfers. There are provisions which prevent the relief

---

[3]   Provided these conditions are fulfilled the motive of the donor is irrelevant. See *Re Park Dec'd.* (*No.2*) (1972).

applying if the transfer is not an immediate and outright transfer, or if it could be used for other purposes.

19–07   **Gifts to political parties: section 24**

There is a similar unlimited exemption for gifts to political parties defined as one with either two members of Parliament or one member and at least 150,000 votes at the last general election.

19–08   **Gifts to housing associations: section 24A**

There is also a similar unlimited exemption for gifts to housing associations.[4]

19–09   **Gifts for national purposes, etc.: section 25**

A transfer of value is an exempt transfer if it is made to certain bodies (sometimes referred to as "heritage bodies") being certain galleries, museums, libraries, national collections and preservation bodies, universities, university colleges, local authorities, or any government department. The bodies given this benefit are listed in Schedule 3. The exemption applies to lifetime and death transfers, and there is no limit in amount. The reference to "any government department" makes it doubly sure that such museums as the Victoria and Albert Museum are within the exemption.

19–10   **Cash options under approved annuity schemes: section 152**

All the provisions listed above are exempt transfers. The reliefs that follow take several different forms for no particular reasons, so each should be looked at as self-contained.

Where, under an approved annuity scheme, an annuity becomes payable on a person's death to the deceased's widow, widower or dependant and the scheme gave an option for the deceased to require that, instead, a sum of money should be paid to his personal representatives, that option will not involve that the deceased be treated as being beneficially entitled (under section 5) to that sum. In other words, that sum does not form part of his estate.

---

[4] These are defined by reference to the Housing Associations Act 1985.

Death on active service, etc.: section 154   19-11

This exemption applies to death on active service against an enemy (or on other service of a warlike nature) and to death arising out of such service.[5] The exemption operates by means of excluding section 4, the section which charges to tax a transfer on death.

Visiting forces and staff of allied headquarters: section 155   19-12

This paragraph gives certain exemptions to pay and tangible movables of members of visiting forces of designated countries (not being citizens of the United Kingdom and colonies) and personnel attached to a designated allied headquarters.

Relief for successive charges: section 141   19-13

This is generally called "quick succession" relief. Prior to 1981 two somewhat confusingly different forms were in operation, one relating to deaths and the other to settlements. Under the new "unified" relief the tax charge on a death or a fixed interest settlement is reduced if the death or settlement charge occurs within five years after some previous chargeable event relating to the same property. For a death the previous charge may be of any type, but for a settlement it must have been a previous charge on that settlement, or the creation of the settlement itself.

The relief operates by way of a "tax credit" against tax payable on the second charge by reference to a percentage of the tax paid on the first. This will be 100 per cent if the gap between the two transfers is one year or less, reduced by 20 per cent for each subsequent year between the transfers, so that if the gap is more than four years it will only be 20 per cent.

Conditional relief for works of art, historic buildings, etc.:   19-14
sections 30-35A (as amended)

The things to which this conditional relief relates are chattels of pre-eminent interest, works of art, scientific collections, land and buildings which are of outstanding scenic, architectural, historic or scientific interest and chattels historically associated with them. The sections apply to all transfers including discretionary trusts, but the relief can only be sought in relation to a PET if it subsequently becomes chargeable. It is provided (no doubt as an

---

[5] This includes service in Northern Ireland.

anti-avoidance measure) that for relief to apply to a lifetime transfer the property must have either been owned for six years or the transferor must have acquired the property on a death which was itself a "conditionally exempt transfer" (see below). The relief must be claimed within two years.

To gain the relief the property has to be "designated" by the Revenue, and "undertakings" have to be given concerning preservation, access, etc. The rules relating to these undertakings were tightened in 1998, so that, for example, it is no longer sufficient to allow public access only by prior appointment. A transfer is then called a "conditionally exempt transfer" so that any tax payable will be postponed. It is conditional because if an undertaking is not observed tax becomes payable on the current value of the asset by reference to the transferor's cumulative total, but at the lifetime rate if the conditionally exempt transfer was not made on a death. Also, tax becomes payable on a subsequent sale or disposal of the property (including disposal on death). There are two cases where a subsequent disposal is not a chargeable event: (a) if the subsequent death or gift is itself a conditionally exempt transfer or the undertaking previously given is replaced by an undertaking given by such person as the Revenue think appropriate; (b) if within three years of the death the deceased's personal representatives (or, in the case of settled property, the trustees or the person next entitled) give the property or sell it by private treaty to one of the "heritage bodies" listed in Schedule 3 (see para. 19–09, above) or transfer the property to the Revenue in satisfaction of tax. Where the conditionally exempt transfer loses its exemption on a subsequent gift which is a PET, any inheritance tax triggered will be available as a tax credit against the tax payable if the PET becomes chargeable.

The point of the exemption which has been discussed under this head,[6] as distinct from the heritage bodies exemption discussed above is that an ancestral home (for example), or a Rembrandt in an ancestral home, can be kept in the family.

A maintenance fund can be set up under section 27. It is possible for property to be settled on trusts to finance the maintenance, repair or preservation of, or public access to, historic buildings or adjoining land without liability to inheritance tax. This relief, again, takes the form of a conditional exemption which becomes chargeable on the fund failing to meet the criteria.

---

[6] It is sometimes called the "national heritage exemption". So we have the "national heritage exemption" as well as "heritage bodies" and "heritage property".

Voidable transfers: section 150   19–15

This relief refers to transfers set aside by law. An example would be a gift made within five years before bankruptcy, because such a gift could be set aside (under the Insolvency Act 1986, s. 339) by the transferor's trustee in bankruptcy. If a transfer is so set aside, tax is repaid (with tax-free interest) and also the transfer is wiped out from the transferor's cumulative total of values transferred.

Relief for business property: sections 103–114   19–16

This relief was brought in in 1976 in response to claims that without some such relief many small businesses would face closure because of the tax on transfers, *e.g.* from parent to child. The relief has been liberalised by subsequent amendments and, in many cases, stands at 100 per cent. Transfers of value in this context include not only lifetime transfers but also transfers on death and chargeable events in relation to settled property.

Where the whole or part of the value transferred by a transfer of value is attributable to the value of any relevant business property, the whole of that part of the value transferred shall be treated as reduced by either 100 or 50 per cent. The value transferred is to be calculated as a value on which no tax is chargeable, *i.e.* without grossing up. Relevant business property means:

  (i) a business or an interest in a business. This includes sole traders and partners disposing of all or part of their interests in a business[7]; a business for this purpose does not include the making or holding of investments;

  (ii) a holding of shares in or securities of a listed company which, together with others held by the transfer, gave him control of the company on all questions affecting the company[8];

  (iii) a holding of securities in an unquoted company which together with other such securities and unquoted shares

---

[7] In *Fetherstonhaugh v. IRC* (1984) a sole trader who used land owned by a settlement of which he was the life tenant in his business was allowed the relief on that land under this head. In *Russell v. IRC* (1988) the relief was allowed where a legatee was entitled to a cash sum payable only out of the proceeds of sale of a business.

[8] Control is to be assessed at the time of the transfer. In assessing whether the transferor has voting control of a company no account is to be taken of the fact that other shares are held by an individual who cannot in practice exercise his votes, *e.g.* a five- year-old child: *Walding v. IRC* (1996).

> held by the transferor, gave him control of the company (as defined above);
>
> (iv) a holding, of any size, of shares in an unquoted company;
>
> (v) any land or building, machinery or plant which was used wholly or mainly for the purpose of a business carried on by a company of which the transferor had control (as defined above) or of which he was a partner.

Certain items are excluded from the definition of relevant business property, *e.g.* shares or securities of a company which is in the process of liquidation, or surplus cash not required for the future use of the business.[9]

And, putting it broadly, property is not relevant business property unless it has been owned by the transferor throughout the two years immediately preceding the transfer. But there are provisions adjusting this rule where there have been replacements of property, the incorporation of a business, and acquisitions of property on the death of a spouse.

The relief is given by reducing the value of the net business assets that have been transferred. The relief is given automatically. For transfers within categories (i), (iii) and (iv) this relief is 100 per cent, so that most family businesses will be outside the tax. For categories (ii) and (v) the relief is 50 per cent. It is generally better therefore for a taxpayer's company to own the plant and machinery etc., used in its business, rather than the taxpayer.

Where the transferor makes a PET of relevant business property and then dies within seven years so that it becomes a chargeable transfer, the relief will only be available if the transferee still owns the property (or what is known as replacement property) and it would have qualified for the relief immediately before the transferor's death. Similar rules apply where additional tax is payable on a lifetime transfer on the death of the transferor within seven years (see Chapter 20). There is no such clawback, however, where a beneficiary sells the business after inheriting it on a death.

In deciding whether the relief applies to a gift subject to a reservation (either one which is still in existence at the transferor's death or which ceased only within the last seven years and so is a deemed PET), the criteria in the various categories are applied to the donee and not the donor, although the ownership of the donor can be added to that of the donee to establish the two year

---

[9] *Barclays Bank Trust Co Ltd v. IRC* (1998).

minimum ownership requirement. Paradoxically, however, in assessing whether the shares give control of the company, the shares will be regarded as being owned by the donor.

Business property relief may be available where agricultural relief is also available. In such cases agricultural relief takes priority, through business property relief is also important to farmers and farm owners.

Relief for agricultural property: sections 115–124C   19–17
(as amended)

This relief applies to lifetime transfers and transfers on death, and it applies to transfers involving settlement as well as to "outright" transfers. It was included in the 1975 Act, but drastically remodelled and extended in 1981.

Short-term purchasers of farms are excluded from the relief; for the relief to apply, both the transferor and the land must fulfil certain conditions. The transferor must have either occupied the land for agricultural purposes throughout the last two years or have owned the land for the last seven years, it having been occupied by someone for agricultural purposes during that time. A person who inherits a farm from his or her spouse, provided the spouse fulfilled the above condition, can transfer the farm with benefit of the relief. For the land to qualify it must be agricultural property in the United Kingdom. If one farm has been replaced by another, it is sufficient if occupation of the farms viewed together lasted for at least two out of five years immediately preceding the transfer.

The relief, where it is available, takes the form of reducing the "agricultural value of the agricultural property". "Agricultural property"[10] means:

> "agricultural land or pasture and includes woodland and any building used in connection with the intensive rearing of livestock and fish if occupied with agricultural land or pasture and the occupation is ancillary to that of the agricultural land or pasture; and also includes such cottages, farm buildings and farm-houses, together with the land occupied with them, as are of a character appropriate to the property".[11]

---

[10] This includes land used for "short rotation coppicing" by virtue of section 154 of the Finance Act 1995. In essence this is the planting and harvesting of permanent trees within 10 years. It also includes "habitat land" and genuine farm cottages.

[11] Section 115(2). If the buildings do not fall within that test, *e.g.* because they are very valuable compared to the farmland involved, they cannot be included as agricultural land: *Starke v. IRC* (1995).

"The agricultural value" is "the value which would be the value of the property if the property were subject to a perpetual covenant prohibiting its use otherwise than as agricultural property": section 115(3). Thus there is no relief for any development value, although business relief may be available for that.

The reduction is either of 100 or 50 per cent. In broad terms owner occupiers are entitled to a 100 per cent reduction, whilst agricultural landlords are entitled to a 50 per cent reduction unless the tenancy began or a tenant succeeds to the tenancy after August 1995 when 100 per cent relief is now available, although of course on the value of the reversion and not the whole farm. The reduction in value because of the agricultural tenancy will, of course, reduce the inheritance tax payable on the land. There are no limits as to size of the farm or as to amount of the relief. As with business relief, this relief is given automatically. It is given in priority to business relief but both may be available. The availability of the relief for PETs and gifts with reservation is governed by the same rules as those for business relief.

Transfers of shares or debentures in a farming company controlled by the transferor can qualify for agricultural property relief.

19–18   **Relief for woodlands: sections 125–130**

Relief is available where any part of the value of a person's estate immediately before his death is attributable to the value of land in the United Kingdom on which trees or underwood are growing but which is not agricultural property. Deathbed purchases of woodland as a tax avoidance ploy will not work. For the relief to apply the deceased must either have been beneficially entitled to the land throughout the five years immediately before his death or have become beneficially entitled to it otherwise than for a consideration in money or money's worth, *i.e.* by a gift or inheritance.

The relief takes the form of leaving out of account, in determining the value transferred on death, the value of the trees or underwood. Notice that the relief does not apply to a lifetime transfer and also that it is only the value of the timber which is relieved, not the value of the land on which it is growing.

The relief is not absolute; a subsequent lifetime transfer of the timber can give rise to a retrospective charge to tax at the full rate at the date of the transfer. Tax will be charged on the sale proceeds of the timber if the transfer is for full consideration; otherwise on the then net value of the timber. If the transfer following the death is itself a chargeable transfer, *e.g.* a gift, there may be a tax charge on that disposal as well as the retrospective tax charge relating to the death, but the value transferred by the subsequent disposal will be calculated as if the value of the trees or underwood had been reduced by the amount of tax charged in respect of the death. Business relief (at 50 per cent) will be available if the growing timber formed a business asset of the deceased at the date of death.

If another death occurs, and there has been no disposal between the first death and the second death, the second death wipes out any possibility of a tax charge arising in respect of the first death.

Dispositions for maintenance of family: section 11   19–19

The official Revenue view is that section 11 only applies to lifetime transfers, and not to transfers on death. The point has never been tested in the courts, but the Revenue view is probably correct, for one or other (or both) of two reasons: (1) The section uses the word "disposition". It is noticeable that the section relating to death (section 4) nowhere uses the word "disposition". It would seem to be a fair inference that wherever in the inheritance tax legislation the word "disposition" occurs the enactment is referring only to lifetime transfers; (2) the section uses the phrase "not a transfer of value", and it may well be (as some commentators assume) that wherever the legislation gives an exemption by saying that such-and-such shall "not be a transfer of value" that exemption is confined to lifetime transfers and does not cover transfers on death.

Section 11(1) declares that a disposition is not a transfer of value if it is made by one party to a marriage in favour of the other party or of a child of either party and is:

(a) for the maintenance of the other party; or
(b) for the maintenance, education or training of the child for a period ending not later than the year in which he attains the age of 18 or, after attaining that age, ceases to undergo full-time education or training.

"Child" includes a step-child and an adopted child. A similar disposition in favour of an illegitimate child is exempt, but in this case only if the child is the child of the disponer (not of the other party to the marriage). A similar disposition in favour of a child who is someone else's child is exempt if the child is not in the care of a parent of his. But in this case, if the disposition is made after the child attains 18 years of age, it is only exempt if the child has for substantial periods before attaining that age been in the care of the disponer.

Also, a disposition is not a transfer of value if it is made in favour of a dependent relative of the disponer and is a reasonable provision for his or her care or maintenance. Here there is an explicit reference to reasonableness (of amount), whereas in the case of a disposition to a spouse or child there is no explicit mention of reasonableness. However, such a limit seems to be implicit, because it is stated that, where a disposition satisfies the conditions to a limited extent only, so much of it as satisfies them and so much of it as does not satisfy them shall be treated as separate dispositions.

The section gives exemption to a disposition made on the occasion of a decree of divorce or nullity. But it equally applies to a disposition made during an on-going marriage. It is true that so far as a disposition to a spouse is concerned section 11 is not needed because a transfer to a spouse is exempt anyway, but so far as a child is concerned section 11 is very useful as it exempts a payment made by a parent to assist (for example) a child who is a student if the payment is outside the "normal expenditure out of income" exemption (see para. 19–04 above).[12]

The section is made to apply to a disposition on the occasion of the dissolution or annulment of a marriage (and to a disposition varying a disposition so made) by subsection (6) which provides that in relation to those events "marriage" (see subsection (1)) includes a former marriage. In *G v. G* (1975) a High Court judge held that the court has power to defer a decree absolute in order to prevent inheritance tax arising.[13]

19–20 **Alteration of dispositions taking effect on death, etc.: sections 17, 29A, 93, 142–145**

The scheme of the sections is this: certain re-arrangements of the deceased's estate shall not be treated as transfers of value and tax shall be charged on the death as if the deceased had left his property in accordance with the re-arrangements. The main provisions can be stated in six numbered points.

(1) By section 142(1), where within two years after a person's death any beneficiary makes an instrument in writing which

---

[12] The section may not apply if the child leaves school, goes out to work and re-enters full-time education after the age of 18. Has he already ceased to undertake full-time education?

[13] Such orders will usually be exempt under s.10 (no gratuitous benefit).

effects a variation or disclaimer of any of the dispositions (whether effected by will or under the law relating to intestacy or otherwise) of the property comprised in the deceased's estate immediately before his death, the variation or disclaimer shall not be a transfer of value and tax shall be charged as if the variation had been effected by the deceased or (as the case may be) the disclaimed benefit had never been conferred. In the case of a variation, written notice of election must be given to the Revenue within six months after the date of the instrument by the parties thereto and also, where the variation results in additional tax being payable, by the deceased's personal representatives. But the personal representatives can only decline to join in an election if insufficient assets are held by them for discharging the additional tax. Additional tax could become payable, for example, if some item of property which had been left by the deceased to his widow is now, by family agreement, to go to his daughter.

The section does not apply to a variation or disclaimer which is made for any consideration in money or money's worth other than consideration consisting of the making of another variation or disclaimer relating to the same estate. For the purpose of this section the deceased's estate includes excluded property but not settled property in which he had an interest in possession. It does not matter whether or not the administration of the estate is complete, and it does not matter that a benefit has been received under the original dispositions, and there is no objection to the variations extending beyond the deceased's family or beyond the original beneficiaries. Where a variation results in property being held in trust for a person for a period which ends not more than two years after the death the disposition at the end of the period is treated as though it had had effect from the beginning of the period.

In *Russell v. IRC* (1988), Knox J. upheld the Revenue's argument that section 142 could not apply where the beneficiaries, having already executed one deed of variation, executed a variation of that deed. The section only allows the first one to count as being read back into the will. On the other hand in *Lake v. Lake* (1989), Mervyn Davies J. held that a deed of disclaimer could be rectified by the court if the wording had failed to give effect to the joint intention of the parties, even though the amended wording would substantially improve the parties' tax position.

(2) By section 144, where by his will a settlor creates a settlement in which there is no interest in possession, but within two years of death the settled capital is paid to a beneficiary, or a person acquires a beneficial interest in possession, or the settlement becomes an accumulation and maintenance settlement then

the event in question will not be chargeable as a capital distribution (see Chapter 21) and tax will be charged on the death as though the event in question had been provided for by the will.

In *Frankland v. IRC* (1997) the section was held by the Court of Appeal not to apply to a variation within the first quarter after the death of the settlor because within that time no capital distribution charge is levied and the section requires that, without its application, a capital distribution charge would otherwise apply. The section was not ambiguous and the absurdity not too great!

(3) Section 143 deals with the case where assets are left to a legatee with a request (which is not legally binding) that the legatee should distribute them in accordance with the testator's wishes. If within two years after the death the legatee does so distribute the assets, the transfers by the legatee are not transfers of value and tax shall be charged in relation to the death as if the property had been bequeathed by the will to the transferees. (Such a provision in a will is called a precatory trust; it is quite common, particularly in respect of household effects, etc.)

(4) Section 145 deals with the case where a surviving spouse elects, under section 47A of the Administration of Estates Act 1925, to redeem for a capital sum his or her life interest which arises under the intestacy rules. Where such an election is made, the election does not count as a transfer of value and tax is charged in relation to the death on the footing that the surviving spouse had from the outset been entitled to the capital sum.

(5) By section 93, where a person becomes entitled (on death or otherwise) to an interest in settled property but disclaims the interest, then, if the disclaimer is not made for a consideration in money or money's worth, the inheritance tax provisions shall apply as if he had not become entitled to the interest.

(6) Section 29A is rather different in that it is in reality an anti-avoidance provision. It applies whenever there is an exempt transfer on a death, *e.g.* to a charity,[14] and the exempt beneficiary subsequently makes a disposition of property, which does not derive from that transferred on the death, in settlement of a claim against the deceased's estate. In that case the exemption on the death is reduced by the amount transferred by the exempt beneficiary. Thus if Paul agrees with a charity to leave them £100,000 in his will if the charity will then pay £50,000 to his mistress (who may have a claim against his estate), the effect of section 29A will be that only £50,000 of the gift to the charity will be exempt.

---

[14] Other exempt transfers covered are those to spouses, political parties, housing associations, maintenance funds and employee trusts.

Family provision orders: section 146   19–21

A court has power, under the Inheritance (Provision for Family
and Dependants) Act 1975 to order that provision be made for
the family and dependants of a deceased person out of his estate,
and for this purpose to change the destination of property. When
a court makes an order of this kind the property shall be treated
for the purposes of inheritance tax as if it had on the deceased's
death devolved in accordance with the order.

Dispositions allowable for income tax or conferring retirement   19–22
benefits: section 12

A disposition made by any person is not a transfer of value if it
is allowable in computing that person's profits or gains for the
purposes of income tax or corporation tax. It is difficult to think
of a disposition which is allowable for income tax (or corporation
tax) and yet which would need this section to protect it from
inheritance tax; most commonly such a disposition would be a
disposition for value and would consequently be excluded from
inheritance tax by section 10 (no gratuitous intent). Perhaps
certain kinds of business gifts would "fit the bill".

Contributions to approved retirement benefit schemes and
approved personal pension schemes for employees and also dispositions to provide in some other way comparable benefits on or
after retirement for an employee not connected with the disponer,
or, after the death of the employee, for his widow or dependants,
are not transfers of value.

Dispositions by close company on trust for benefit of   19–23
employees: section 13

A disposition of property made to trustees by a close company
whereby the property is to be held on trust for the employees is
not a transfer of value. The conditions of exemption are very
strict and in practice not much use is made of this provision.

Waiver of remuneration: section 14   19–24

Sometimes an employee or, more commonly a director, waives
(or repays) his remuneration for a period to his employer (company). If nothing were done about it, such waiver or repayment
would be a chargeable transfer by the employee or director.
Section 14 declares that the waiver or repayment shall not be a
transfer of value provided that it is brought into charge in

computing the profits or gains of the employer for income tax or corporation tax.

19–25   Waiver of dividends: section 15

A person who waives any dividend on shares of a company within 12 months *before* any right to the dividend has accrued does not by reason of the waiver make a transfer of value.

19–26   Grant of an agricultural tenancy: section 16

A grant of an agricultural tenancy is not a transfer of value if it is made for full consideration in money or money's worth. Otherwise the almost inevitable reduction in the value of the property (such leases have controlled rents) would lead to a charge.

19–27   Tailpiece

After such a long chapter on exemptions and reliefs, the reader may be thinking that there is not much left of the tax, particularly since most lifetime transfers are exempt unless the transferor dies within seven years. But the reality is that, though the exemptions and reliefs are a major factor and the charge to tax is therefore to quite an important extent avoidable, there is still much for the tax to bite on particularly on a death, since, unlike CGT, there is no private residence exemption.

In the next chapter we shall look to see the strength of the bite.

CHAPTER 20

COMPUTATION

Inheritance tax is charged on any lifetime transfer of value which is a chargeable transfer, and also on the deemed transfer of value made by a deceased person immediately before his death. Remember that a PET becomes a chargeable transfer on the death of the transferor within seven years and that a gift subject to a reservation still in existence at death is part of the deceased's estate. If the reservation has ceased before then the gift becomes a PET at that time. As we shall see, the existence of PETs complicates the computation rules.

In the case of a lifetime transfer the charge is on the value transferred. In the case of a deemed transfer on death the charge is on the value of the deceased's estate. Section 3 declares that: " ... a transfer of value is a disposition made by a person (the transferor) as a result of which the value of his estate is less than it would be but for the disposition; and the amount by which it is less is the value transferred by the transfer." So for a lifetime transfer, one has to compare the value of the transferor's estate (remember that "estate" can refer to a living person's wealth, as well as to a dead person's) before the transfer with its value after the transfer. For a discussion as to how that comparison is to be made see paragraph 18–02 above. For a death transfer this comparison does not arise. (The tax charges relating to settled property are discussed in Chapter 21.)

Rates of Tax 20–01

As we have already seen the rates of inheritance tax are applied on a cumulative basis so that in essence each chargeable lifetime transfer is charged at the appropriate rate taking into account previous chargeable transfers within the last seven years. This principle is applied equally on a death so that the rate takes into account the chargeable transfers made seven years prior to the death. Only if the transferor lives for more than seven years after making a transfer will it be taken out of the calculation. The effect of the transferor dying within seven years of making a chargeable transfer or a PET is discussed below.

The current rates for inheritance tax are very much simplified from those originally introduced. Schedule 1 currently provides that for a charge on a death the rate for the first £234,000 of cumulative transfers is nil. For all cumulative transfers above that amount the rate is 40 per cent. Section 7 provides that for a lifetime transfer the rates are half those on a death, *i.e.* nil and 20 per cent. For peace of mind it is better to regard the band up to £234,000 as being charged at a nil rate rather than as being exempt.

Thus if Fred, having made chargeable transfers of £234,000 in the previous seven years makes another one of £100,000, that transfer will be charged at 20 per cent, since he will have exceeded the nil rate band. If his cumulative total had been £184,000, the £100,000 transfer would then have been chargeable at £50,000 × nil per cent and £50,000 × 20 per cent. In effect, therefore, Fred can make up to £234,000 of chargeable transfers in each seven year period without actually having to pay any tax. The position would have been the same if Fred, with a cumulative total of £234,000, had died and left an estate of £100,000, except that that estate would then have been taxed at 40 per cent. The fact that lifetime rates are half those on death is counterbalanced by the fact that capital gains tax may well be payable on a lifetime transfer whereas it does not apply on a death.

20–02 **The effect of a death on chargeable transfers and PETs made within the previous seven years**

To avoid taxpayers making immediately chargeable transfers shortly before death so as to attract the lower rate of tax, section 7(4) provides that where the transferor dies within seven years of making a chargeable transfer the rates applicable on a death will be retrospectively imposed on that transfer. Since the transfer will have already borne tax at the lifetime rate there is in effect an additional charge to tax (on the transferee) based on the original value of the transfer. That additional charge is computed by working out what the amount of tax would be if the current death rate had applied and deducting from that the tax already paid on the original transfer. However, in making this calculation, if the transferor has survived more than three years after making the transfer, only a percentage of the death rate will be used. This is known as taper relief. Thus if the transferor survives for six years only 20 per cent of the death rate will be used; for five years, 40 per cent; for four years, 60 per cent; and for three years, 80 per cent.

To take an example:

Suppose that George having already made chargeable transfers of £234,000 in the previous seven years makes a gift of £20,000 (gross) to a company. Tax at 20 per cent will be payable, *i.e.* £4,000. If George dies two years later the Revenue will claim extra tax from the company. The full death rate will be applied to give a figure of £8,000 tax (at 40 per cent) and the company will have to pay the extra £4,000. If George had survived for four years only 60 per cent of the death rate tax would be used to give a figure of £4,800 tax so that the company would only be liable to find an extra £800 tax.

Sometimes the application of taper relief means that no extra tax is payable on the death (*e.g.* if George had lived for more than five years in the above example, the recalculation at 40 per cent of the death rate would give a total of £3,200, which is less than the £4,000 already paid). There is no refund of any of the original tax, however. Section 131 provides that if the gift has fallen in value between the gift and the subsequent death, the additional tax is calculated on that reduced value,[1] but the original value remains as part of the transferor's cumulative total for the purposes of calculating the rate applicable to the transfer of his death estate.

The position is slightly more complicated where the transferor dies within seven years of making a PET (including a gift with reservation where that reservation has ceased within seven years of the death). As we have seen the PET will then become chargeable (on the transferee) in accordance with the transferor's cumulative total at the time when the PET was made, on the value then transferred (unless it has since fallen in value, when that lower value can be used). The rate of tax will, however, be the death rate applicable at the date of death (unless the rates have increased in which case the rates at the time of the transfer are used). Once again taper relief, calculated as above, will be available to lower the amount payable but of course there is no deduction for tax already paid since none was payable at the time. Thus, in the example above, if the gift had been made to Harry instead of a company, no tax would have been payable at the time. On George's death, Harry would have become liable to tax at £8,000 in the first scenario and £4,800 in the second.

But this activating of the charge has another effect. Since the transfer is no longer a PET it will be treated as if the transferor had always made a chargeable transfer at that time. Thus

---

[1] This does not apply to wasting assets, *i.e.* those which are inevitably going to decrease in value.

although it was not originally included in the transferor's cumulative total it will have to be so included retrospectively. Accordingly the tax payable on previous chargeable transfers may have to be recalculated on that basis.

To take a simple example:

Ian, having made no previous chargeable transfers, makes a PET of £200,000 to John. The next year he makes an immediately chargeable transfer to trustees of £100,000. Ian's cumulative total prior to that (at that time) is nil so that the chargeable transfer is within the nil band. If Ian dies within seven years the PET becomes chargeable so that Ian's cumulative total at the time of the transfer to the trustees is recalculated at £200,000 and that transfer will now fall as to £34,000 into the nil band and £66,000 into the 40 per cent band (death rate applies as it was within seven years of the death).

Where the transferor has made a combination of PETs and chargeable transfers within seven years of his death the recalculations are almost endless.

20–03   *Transfers of more than one property*

It is provided by section 265 that where the value transferred by a chargeable transfer is determined by reference to the values of more than one property the tax chargeable on the value transferred shall be attributed to the respective values in the proportions which they bear to their aggregate, but subject to any provision reducing the amount of tax attributable to the value of any particular property. The "but subject" part of the subsection means that if, for example, on death X leaves a farm to Y and shares in Unilever plc to Z, Z does not enjoy any part of the agricultural property relief. The main part of the subsection means that, for example, if A leaves property worth £60,000 to B and property worth £40,000 to C, the tax is spread evenly over the whole value transferred. The gift to B bears 60 per cent of the tax bill and the gift to C bears 40 per cent.

20–04   *Transfers on the same day*

Transfers on the same day by the same transferor present some difficulty. The basic principle is stated in section 266(1): where the value transferred by more than one chargeable transfer made by the same person on the same day depends on the order in which the transfers are made, they shall be treated as made in the order which results in the lowest value chargeable. For example, if on the same day A makes a chargeable transfer to B (A paying the tax) and a separate chargeable transfer to C (C paying the tax), the gift to B will have to be grossed up, (see para. 20–08 below), whereas the gift to C will not. So it is "cheaper" in tax terms to count the gift to B before the gift to C, because the grossing up will come at a point lower down the scale. The legislation permits that. Then, the order of the gifts having been established, section 266(2) declares that there shall be an "effective rate," namely the tax which would have been charged if the transfers had been a single transfer. So A pays tax on the gift to B and C pays tax on the gift to himself, both at the same rate.

Transfers reported late   20–05

This is dealt with by section 264. Where an earlier transfer is not notified to the Revenue (see Chapter 23, below) until after the tax has been paid on a later transfer the position depends upon the gap between the transfers. If the gap is seven years or more there is no problem since they would not be cumulated together anyway and so tax plus interest is payable on the earlier transfer at the rates then applying. If the gap is less than seven years the earlier (unreported) transfer is charged at the rate then applying and the extra tax which should have been collected on the second transfer (because of cumulation) is now charged on the first one (plus interest).

Liabilities   20–06

In considering this topic it is necessary to distinguish between liabilities resulting from a chargeable transfer and other liabilities.

Liabilities resulting from a chargeable transfer   20–07

One has to remember that the value transferred is the amount by which the transferor's estate immediately after the disposition is less than it would be if the disposition had not been made.

A chargeable transfer may give rise to inheritance tax and at the same time to two other taxes—capital gains tax and sometimes stamp duty. Also there may be incidental costs of the transfer, such as conveyancing fees. All these items, if paid by the transferor, will diminish the value of his estate immediately after the transfer. So, in the absence of any provision to the contrary, they would all increase the amount of the "value transferred" and so increase the amount of tax payable. The Act does make provisions to the contrary, to some extent. Section 5 provides that in determining the value of the transferor's estate immediately after the transfer, his liability to inheritance tax on the value transferred shall be taken into account, but not his liability for any other tax or duty. And by section 164 the incidental expenses (if borne by the transferor) shall be left out of account.

The great point to grasp is that when one is considering liabilities immediately *after* the transfer, the effect of taking a liability into account is to increase the diminution in value of the transferor's estate and so increase the value transferred and so increase the inheritance tax. Conversely, the effect of leaving a liability out of account is that that liability (*e.g.* liability to capital gains tax or liability to pay conveyancing fees to one's solicitor) does not increase the inheritance tax.

And if the capital gains tax is borne by the transferee, that is treated (for inheritance tax) as actually reducing the value transferred: section 165. And the same is true of the incidental expenses of making a transfer, if these are borne by the transferee: section 164.

There are special rules about debts due to foreign residents (section 162(5)).

20–08 *Grossing up*

The principle of grossing up a lifetime transfer is embedded in section 5. If the transferor is to pay the inheritance tax, his liability to the tax is to be taken into account in calculating the diminution in his estate caused by the transfer. If A makes a chargeable transfer to B of £x in cash or of property worth £x (tax free), A's estate is diminished by £x plus the relevant inheritance tax. So £x must be grossed up to find what sum must be paid by A to the Revenue to put £x into the hands of B free from any liability to the tax. If one calls that sum £y, A must pay £x to B and £y to the Revenue.

If A makes a transfer to B, stipulating that B must pay the inheritance tax on it, no grossing up arises. This is because A's estate is not diminished by inheritance tax, since he is not going to pay any of it. Since most lifetime transfers are now PETs, any tax which becomes chargeable will only be due after the transferor's death on the transferee so that no grossing up occurs.

In a general sense there is no grossing up either in the case of a transfer on death. This is because grossing up is, in effect, built into the situation since it is only the sums net of tax which will reach the beneficiaries. However, where a specific gift is left by will "tax-free" a kind of grossing up has to take place to determine the entitlements of other beneficiaries: see Chapter 22 below, under the heading "Incidence".

With regard to the actual process of grossing up, in principle it is just like grossing up for income tax. If A wants to put into the hands of B £40,000, one has to work out what sum, after deduction of tax, will leave £40,000 clear. But in practice it is often very much more complicated than is the income tax process. This is because (a) the tax on any particular transfer has to take account of the transferor's previous tax history under the principle of cumulation and (b) the particular gift itself may cross the rate bands.

The principle of grossing up is perhaps best explained as follows:

If A makes a net chargeable transfer (*i.e.* after tax) of £100,000 to B Ltd the tax is calculated in the following way: tax payable on £100,000 = £x. The loss to A's estate is therefore £100,000 + £x. The tax actually payable is therefore the tax on (£100,000 + £x) = £y. A's cumulative total carried forward for the next transfer is thus £100,000 + £y. £y in effect represents an element of tax on tax (£x).

If, however, A makes a gross chargeable transfer of £100,000 to B Ltd, he will actually pay to B Ltd £100,000 less £x (the tax on £100,000). The loss to A's estate will thus only be £100,000 and that will be his cumulative total for future transfers.

The effects of grossing up are therefore to increase both the tax payable on the individual transfer and the cumulative total of the transferor. On the other hand the transferee will receive a set amount, in our example £100,000 and not an amount variable according to the tax payable. As we have seen, however, this concept has been much reduced in importance by the introduction of PETs. It is limited to those lifetime transfers which are not PETs.

Other liabilities   20–09

What we are talking about here is liabilities other than those which result from a chargeable transfer. The importance of the topic is that it is clearly relevant to the comparison which has to be made in the case of lifetime transfers between the value of a person's estate before and after the transfer (its relevance is to the "before" part) and it is clearly relevant to the valuation of a person's estate on death.

A liability is not taken into account unless it is a liability imposed by law or it was incurred by the transferor for a consideration in money or money's worth: section 5(5). Thus an outstanding mortgage on a house would be deductible but not a voluntary covenant.

In establishing the value of an estate on death section 5(5) is supplemented by section 103 of the Finance Act 1986. This section disallows what are known as "artificial debts". These are defined as debts for which the consideration was either directly derived from the deceased or provided by another person to whose resources the deceased contributed. In the latter case there must be a causal link between the contribution of the deceased and the debt transaction. A simple example of this section applying is where Jane gives away a valuable asset to Kate and three years later she buys it back for full market value but leaves the debt outstanding until the date of her death five years later. The gift to Kate will not be taxable since it was a PET made more than seven years before her death and the debt owed to Kate, having been made for full consideration, would be deductible under section 5(5). But since the consideration for the debt, the asset, derived from Jane's estate it would not be allowable under section 103 of the 1986 Act.

Where an artificial debt is paid off during the deceased's lifetime, the repayment is treated as a PET: section 103(5) of the 1986 Act. Thus if Jane repaid Kate a year before her death it would become a chargeable transfer on her death. This will probably not apply, however, if Jane pays Kate the full amount immediately on buying the asset back—no debt has been incurred.

Before we leave liabilities, notice this general point about them: if it is a question of valuing an estate *before* a transfer (or immediately before death) it is advantageous to the taxpayer if a liability can be taken into account: if it is a question of valuing an estate *after* a transfer it is disadvantageous if a liability is to be taken into account.

20–10 Relief Against Double Charges

Section 104 of the Finance Act 1986 allows regulations to be made to prevent double charges to inheritance tax applying in certain situations. The Inheritance Tax (Double Charges Relief) Regulations 1987 apply such a relief in four situations:

(1) Where A makes a PET of some property to B, B transfers the property back to A (*e.g.* in his will), and A then dies within seven years of the PET. The double charge arises because the property

would be chargeable on the gift to B (the PET has become chargeable) and also on A's death (it forms part of his estate). The solution is to either charge the property as part of A's estate at his death and ignore the PET or to tax the PET and ignore the value of the property on A's death, whichever produces the lower amount of tax.

(2) Where A makes a gift subject to a reservation which is also a chargeable transfer, *e.g.* a gift of his house to a company but he continues to live in it, and he dies still enjoying that reservation (or did so within seven years of his death). Since tax will have been paid on the chargeable transfer and the house will form part of his estate on his death (or will be a chargeable PET) there is again the potential for a double charge. The solution again is to take the lower of charging the house as part of A's estate at death and to ignore the gift or to tax the gift and ignore the house as part of A's estate (or as a chargeable PET).

(3) Where A makes a chargeable transfer (or chargeable PET) of money to B and B lends an equivalent sum back to A. A then dies with the loan to B outstanding. The double charge here arises because the debt would not be allowed under section 103 of the Finance Act 1986 as an artificial debt (see above). Thus the money given is chargeable on the transfer and as part of A's estate on death. The regulations provide that the tax payable is to be the lower of taxing the transfer and allowing the debt against the estate or ignoring the transfer and disallowing the debt.

(4) Where A makes a chargeable transfer (but not a PET) and the transferee returns the property to A, which is beneficially owned by A on his death within seven years of the original transfer. The double charge in this case is the additional tax which will be payable on the original transfer because of A's death within seven years and the tax payable on the property as part of A's estate at his death. Again either the original transfer or the value of the property on A's death is to be ignored, although there is no relief for the tax already paid on the transfer.

Valuation 20–11

Open market value

The basic principle of valuation is stated in section 160. Except as otherwise provided the value at any time of any property shall be the price which the property might reasonably be expected to fetch if sold in the open market at that time. This is generally called "open market value" and takes us into the realms of a hypothetical sale.

The subsection then goes on to say (perhaps rather inconsistently) that the price shall not be assumed to be reduced on the ground that the whole property is to be, hypothetically, placed on the market at one and the same time. So if A owns 100,000 shares in XYZ Ltd the shares are valued (in the absence of an actual sale) without any reduction for the fact that if such a parcel of shares were put on the market at one time the price would be depressed.

The definition of open market value continues the valuation rule which existed for estate duty purposes. The general judicial definition is that it is the best price available from a hypothetical purchaser in the market and not necessarily the highest price.[2] If there are a range of prices which competent valuers would consider as open market values then the highest is no more likely than the lower. It seems that some account may be taken of the existence of a special purchaser, e.g. the owner of adjoining land, who might pay "over the odds" to acquire the property.[3] If there is no open market, e.g. there are restrictions on sale, the property is to be valued under what is known as the *Crossman* principle on the assumption that a hypothetical purchaser buys freely in a hypothetical market but, having bought it, becomes subject to the restrictions.[4] This is particularly the case with private company shares which usually[5] have some form of restriction attached to them. Section 168 provides that in such a case the hypothetical purchaser buying in the hypothetical market must be assumed to know all the information which a prudent prospective purchaser might reasonably require to know if he were buying from a willing vendor at arms length.[6] This is in itself an exception to the basic rule that it is the market value of the property and not its intrinsic value which counts, e.g. a painting will be valued at its then market value even if it later turns out to be a forgery.

The *Crossman* principle has also been applied where the property is subject to some form of liability other than a restriction on sale. This was the decision of the Court of Appeal in *Alexander v. IRC* (1991). The property was a flat in which the deceased had acquired a leasehold interest at a discount under a statutory scheme. Under the lease the tenant had to repay that discount to the landlord if the lease was sold within five years. The tenant died within the first year. What was the value of the lease? The

---

[2] *Re Hayes W.T.* (1971); cf. *Ellesmere v. IRC* (1918).
[3] *IRC v. Clay* (1914); c.f. *IRC v. Crossman* (1937).
[4] *IRC v. Crossman* (1937); *Re Lynall* (1972).
[5] See Charlesworth and Morse, *Company Law* (16th ed.), pp. 194–200.
[6] e.g. whether the company's profits are increasing. The whole concept has a touch of Lewis Carroll about it.

Court of Appeal held first that the obligation to repay was an incumbrance on the property incurred for a consideration and so fell to be taken into account in valuing the property. They then held that the value of the flat for inheritance tax purposes was what a hypothetical purchaser would pay to acquire the lease subject to the obligation to repay the discount if there was a sale within five years but disregarding the fact that his own (hypothetical) purchase would have given rise to such a liability.

In *Walton v. IRC* (1996) the deceased owned an interest in a tenancy (as a partnership asset). The other interest was held by one of his sons and the landlords were the deceased and his two sons. The court upheld a valuation of that interest on the basis that since it could not be assigned without the landlord's consent and that might be withheld, it could not take into account the value of the land if the lease and reversion were merged. The intentions of the actual landlords could be taken into account; there was no requirement to use a hypothetical landlord.

Restriction on freedom to dispose: section 163   20–12

The rule referred to above on restrictions on sale could lead to abuse. To avoid this there is a complex provision which is best understood if we take one particular kind of restriction on freedom to dispose, namely an option. Suppose A grants to B an option to purchase a house. If the option price is the same as the then market price, say £50,000, there is no transfer of value. If the option price, say £35,000, is less than the then market price there is a transfer of value unless B pays for the option a sum (£15,000) equal to the difference between the prices. If, later, B exercises his option and buys the house for £35,000 when it is worth £60,000, the amount of the "value transferred" depends on how much consideration B gave for the option. If B gave no consideration, the "value transferred" by the sale is £25,000 (the gratuitous element). If B gave £15,000 for the option, the "value transferred" by the sale (assuming B pays the tax) is £45,000 (£60,000–£15,000) less £35,000 = £10,000.

Valuation of related property: section 161   20–13

The concept of "related property" is an important one. Property is related to the property comprised in a person's estate if (a) it is in the estate of his spouse, or (b) it is (or has been within the preceding five years) the property of a charity, political party, etc., and became so on an exempt transfer made by him or his spouse.

Where the value of any property *would be* less than the appropriate portion of the value of the aggregate of that and any related property, it *shall be* the appropriate portion of the value of that aggregate. That is the rather obscure wording of section 161(1). We have italicised "would be" and "shall be" in the hope of making it a bit clearer. But it needs an example. The background is that the enactment is intended to stop up a tax-avoidance device. Suppose A owns 70 of the 100 issued shares in XYZ Ltd. Mrs A owns none. A transfers 30 shares to his wife. Controlling shares are worth say £10 each; non-controlling shares are worth say £6 each. The transfer to Mrs A is exempt. The legislation ensures that after the transfer A's holding is valued (*e.g.* on his subsequent death) as being worth not merely $40 \times £6$ (*i.e.* £240), but $\frac{40}{70}$ of the value of the combined (controlling) holding. The combined value is £700, so A's holding is valued at £400, and Mrs A's holding is valued at £300.

A relief is provided (by section 176) where property was valued on death on the related property basis and is subsequently (within three years of the death) sold for a lesser amount to those who inherited the property on the death on an arm's length sale.

20–14   *Value of lessor's interest: section 170*

In a settlement the life tenant is treated as owning the whole settled property and the holder of the reversionary interest is treated as owning nothing, because his interest is "excluded property" (see Chapter 21). In addition a lease for life, if the lease was not granted for full consideration, is treated (see section 43) as a settlement, but with the modification that the lessor's interest is not excluded property. This present section (section 170) provides that the value of the lessor's interest in the property shall be taken to be such part of the value of the property as bears to it the same proportion as the value of the consideration, at the time the lease was granted, bore to what would then have been the value of a full consideration. So, if L grants a lease for life to T at 75 per cent of full consideration, L's interest in the property is taken to be 75 per cent of the value of the property. (And T's interest is taken by section 50(6) to be 25 per cent of that value.)

20–15   *Value of life policies, etc.: section 167*

This section provides that the value of certain life policies and contracts for deferred annuities shall be treated as not less than the total of premiums paid (minus any surrender value paid, *e.g.*

on a partial surrender) where that would be higher that its market value at the time of a lifetime transfer. This does not apply on a death.

Value transferred on death   20–16

Inheritance tax is charged on the death of a person as if, immediately before his death, he had made a transfer of value and the value transferred by it had been equal to the value of his estate immediately before his death: section 4. His estate does not include "excluded property": section 5(1). It does include property over which he had a general power to appoint or dispose, settled property in which he had a life interest (except, in certain circumstances, where the property reverts on the death to the settlor or the settlor's spouse) and his share in a joint tenancy.[7]

On a death, therefore, the whole of the deceased's estate must be valued on the open market basis on the assumption of a hypothetical sale of all the estate immediately before the death. The methods of ascertaining such a value are the same as for lifetime transfers (see para. 20–11 above). One rule which is peculiar to ascertaining the market value on a death, however, is that where by taking a number of items together a higher price could be obtained that must be done, *e.g.* by valuing a set of Hepplewhite dining chairs as a single unit rather than by reference to each chair. (The related property rules, above, prevent this being avoided by transfers of part of such a set to a spouse and part to another). This is known as the process of "lotting"[8]. In *Gray v. IRC* (1994), this approach was applied by the Court of Appeal to aggregate the deceased's partnership interest in a farming business, including a lease of the land farmed, with the deceased's freehold reversionary interest in that land. The fact that taking the two together did not form a natural unit of property was irrelevant. The only question was whether a prudent hypothetical vendor would have adopted this course of action in order to obtain the most favourable price without undue expenditure of time and effort.

The Act also lays down some detailed rules, as follows.

(i) An allowance shall be made for reasonable funeral expenses (section 172).

(ii) Certain changes (whether increases or decreases) in the value of the estate which occur *by reason of* the death are treated

---

[7] Which is still in existence the moment before death.
[8] That phrase had been used in the House of Lords case which established this principle: *Buccleuch v. IRC* (1967).

as having occurred before the death. An example of an increase would be the proceeds of a life insurance policy; these proceeds count as part of the estate. An example of a decrease would occur if a restaurant business lost value through the death of its successful proprietor; this fact is to be taken into account in valuing the business as part of the deceased's estate (section 171). An allowance is also made for the extra expense of administering or realising foreign property (section 173).

(iii) Sections 178 to 189 provide some relief where "qualifying investments" (notably quoted shares and holdings in an authorised unit trust) are sold within the 12 months following the death for less than the value at the date of death. In that case the sale proceeds can be substituted for that value.

(iv) Sections 190 to 198 provide a similar relief where land (which may include buildings) is sold within three years of the death for less than the value at death. To claim this relief legal title to the land must have been conveyed. A mere exchange of contracts, although a sale in equity, is not sufficient.[9]

---

[9] *Jones v. IRC* (1997).

CHAPTER 21

SETTLED PROPERTY

What is Settled Property?   21–01

Part III of the 1984 Act now presents the inheritance tax rules for
settled property in a deceptively tidy manner. The original aim of
these rules was said to be to ensure that property within settlements bore the same levels of taxation in the longer term as did
unsettled property. The general approach adopted has, from the
beginning, been to seek to tax the beneficial entitlement or
possession of trust property, ignoring the legal title and the status
of the trustees. (Compare this with the capital gains tax
approach, which concentrates instead on legal title.) However,
converting the general aim and approach into workable yet fair
legislation has proved a difficult task, not least because views of
what is "fair" taxation of wealth vary widely. In consequence, the
1975 proposals were heavily amended in 1976. They were subject to a substantial review in 1980, and recast in 1982. The
impact of the introduction of PETs in 1986 caused additional
changes to be made.

"Settled property" is not separately defined; it is simply property comprised in a settlement.[1] What, then, is a settlement, for
the purposes of the Act? Section 43 states that it is a disposition
whereby property is for the time being:

(1) held in trust for persons in succession; or
(2) held in trust for any person subject to a contingency; or
(3) held on discretionary trusts; or
(4) held on trust to accumulate the income; or

---

[1] Whether there is one or more settlements has proved to be a problem for
capital gains tax (see para. 14–27 above). Similar problems will arise with
inheritance tax. In *Minden Trust (Cayman) Ltd v. IRC* (1985) the exercise of
a power under a trust which transferred the entire trust property was held to be
a settlement.

(5) charged (otherwise than for full consideration)[2] to pay an annuity; or

(6) subject to a lease for life if the lease was not granted for full consideration.[3]

Property subject to provisions equivalent to heads (1) to (5) above under the law of a foreign country can constitute a "settlement." Foreign settled property is, however, excluded property unless the settlor was domiciled in the United Kingdom at the time the settlement was made.[4]

Neither a tenancy in common nor a joint tenancy is as such a settlement, but either of them will be a settlement if it also falls under any of the heads enumerated above.

21–02   **Putting property into a settlement**

Putting property into a settlement is basically the same as any other lifetime or death transfer for inheritance tax purposes. In the case of a lifetime transfer into a settlement it will be a PET if the trust created is either one in which there is an interest in possession (a fixed interest trust) or it is an accumulation or maintenance trust or a disabled trust. If the trust is a discretionary trust then the transfer is immediately chargeable. Where the settlor retains an interest in the settled property, remember to apply the rules on gifts with reservation (see paragraph 18–07, above).

21–03   **Classification of settlements for charging purposes**

The remainder of this chapter is concerned with the impact of inheritance tax after the property has been put into a settlement. For this purpose the Act makes a sharp distinction between (1) settled property which is held on fixed interest trusts, that is to say, where some person is beneficially entitled to an interest in possession (*e.g.* where there is a life tenant) and (2) settled

---

[2] An annuity not charged on property (*e.g.* an annuity purchased from an insurance company) is not a settlement. Even an annuity which is charged on property is not a settlement if it is granted for full consideration. Hence (probably) an annuity granted by continuing partners for a former partner or his dependants is not a settlement.

[3] Presumably the point of this is to prevent a person from seeking to avoid the rules relating to settled property by granting a lease for life instead of a life tenancy.

[4] But not reversionary interests—see the end of this chapter. Domicile here has its extended meaning for inheritance tax purposes.

property in which no one has a beneficial interest in possession (*e.g.* where the property is held on discretionary trusts).[5]

There are also (3) some special kinds of settlement such as accumulation and maintenance settlements which are subject to special rules. We will deal with these three categories in turn, but the reader should bear in mind that some of the property in a settlement may fall within one of these categories and some within another, and that even the same property may change its category from time to time.

The important question therefore is whether there is a beneficial interest in possession in the settled property. The Revenue published a statement on February 12, 1976[6] setting out their understanding of the term "interest in possession." In particular they dealt with the position where a person is entitled to the income of the property subject to a power of revocation or appointment or a power of accumulation. It is accepted that, in general, it is entitlement to the income as it arises which indicates a beneficial interest in possession (*e.g.* section 50 defines the size of the interest by reference to the proportion of income received). The Revenue's point was that it must be immediate entitlement to the income, so that if there is a power to accumulate income there is no interest in possession, the trustees can withhold current income as it arises, whereas in the case of a power of revocation or appointment over, the trustees can only deprive the beneficiary of future income, thus leaving him with a beneficial interest in possession in the meantime.

This view was tested all the way up to the House of Lords in *Pearson v. IRC* (1980). In that case the settlor's daughter was entitled to the income under the settlement subject both to a power of appointment exercisable by the trustees and a power to accumulate the income until appointment. Both sides agreed that the power of appointment did not prevent the daughter from having a beneficial interest in possession until it was exercised. The judge, Fox J., and the Court of Appeal also found that the power to accumulate did not prevent this either. The daughter still had a present right to present possession, the classic meaning of an interest in possession. By a majority of three to two, however, the House of Lords upheld the Revenue's argument that a power to accumulate does prevent the person taking in default of accumulation from having a beneficial interest in possession. Lord Keith, in the majority, concluded that the daughter only had

[5] See "Discretionary and Fixed Interest Settlements" by G.F.R. Whitehead [1983] B.T.R. 303.
[6] See, *e.g.* [1976] B.T.R. 418.

the right to a later payment if the trustees either by inaction or decision did not accumulate the income—she had no absolute right to the income as it accrued.

Several points may be made on this decision. First of all it is a classic example of the working of the English judicial system. In all, six judges found for the taxpayer and only three for the Revenue, yet the Revenue view is the law. Further, the majority of the House of Lords contained not one specialist property lawyer (unlike most of the other judges involved). Secondly, the decision, as Lord Russell (in the minority) implied, is based on two basic misconceptions: (1) as to the nature of a vested interest subject to defeasance; and (2) as to the difference between trusts and powers. What the daughter had was an interest vested subject to defeasance, a perfectly acceptable form of beneficial interest in English law which gives the owner the right to the income until it is taken away. The obsession with it being an "absolute" interest is irrelevant. Powers of accumulation, like powers of revocation or appointment, are only powers, *i.e.* they must be exercised unanimously to take effect. If one trustee disagrees then the power will not apply and the income be paid under the underlying trust, in this case to the daughter. The reader is referred to the speech of Lord Russell for a perfect example of what the law ought to be.

It may be noted, however, that the decision is not all bad for taxpayers. It may be desirable to provide that X receives all the income of a trust but does not have a beneficial interest in possession. That should be possible by giving X a right to the income subject to a power of accumulation which is not intended to be exercised.

Whatever the merits of its application in *Pearson*, the test is still quite clear: does the beneficiary have a present right to present possession, *i.e.* in general to the income as it arises? This test was applied in *Moore & Osborne v. IRC* (1985)[7] where it was held that the sole member of a class of discretionary beneficiaries could not claim an immediate entitlement to the income unless the class was closed, *i.e.* so that there was no possibility of another member of the class coming into existence. So long as that remained a possibility he was not so entitled and so had no interest in possession for inheritance tax purposes. The potential beneficiaries in this case were himself, any wife he might marry, and any children he might have. In fact he died unmarried and childless, but he did not have an interest in possession immediately before his death.

---

[7] See also *Stenhouse's Trustees v. Lord Advocate* (1984).

The entitlement to income being the usual test, it follows that even if the beneficiary has no right to the capital (*e.g.* he has a contingent interest), a statutory (or agreed) right to the income will suffice. The most common example is a contingent beneficiary's right to the income, once he has attained the age of majority, by virtue of section 31 of the Trustee Act 1925. It is clear that such a right is sufficient to create an interest in possession for this purpose. Thus in *Swales v. IRC* (1984) an appointment to D if and when her eldest child attained 21, operated to give D a right to the income under section 31(i)(ii) of the 1925 Act and so an interest in possession.

An interest in possession can exist where the settled property does not produce an income provided that the beneficiary has a present right to present possession of the settled property. Obviously this cannot be measured in terms of the income arising, but rather in terms of actual possession. In *IRC v. Lloyds Private Banking Ltd* (1998), H and W were tenants in common of their house. On W's death, her undivided share was left to her daughter but on terms that if H chose to continue to live in the house, paying all the bills, he was to be allowed to have exclusive possession of the house until his death. The judge held that this effectively gave H a determinable life interest in half of the house since it enabled him to live in the house undisturbed for the remainder of his life (his right to occupy the other undivided half of the house came from his own interest as a tenant in common—but on its own it would not have been enough for sole occupancy) and that was a present right to present possession.

The effect of powers generally in relation to the use of income or the right to possession arising under the trust depends upon whether they are classified as administrative (thus not affecting the beneficiary's right to the income (or possession) as it arises) or dispositive (with the opposite effect). In the *Lloyds Private Banking* case the judge held that W's trust was a dispositive provision. In *Miller v. IRC* (1987) the Court of Session held that a power to use income to maintain the capital value of the fund was an administrative power so that the there was an interest in possession. The criterion was said to be that administrative powers are those relating to the prudent management in discharge of the trustees' duty to maintain the trust estate. A dispositive power is one which diverts income away from one beneficiary for the benefit of others. It is understood, however, that the Revenue are not entirely happy with this distinction and they stand by their subsidiary argument in *Pearson* that a power to use income to pay taxes, etc., which would otherwise be payable out of capital prevents an interest in possession from arising.

21–04   Where There is a Beneficial Interest in Possession

The basic point to grasp here is that the person holding the beneficial interest in possession is treated "as beneficially entitled to the property in which the interest subsists": section 49(1). So if A is entitled to a life interest in Blackacre he is treated for the purposes of the tax as though he were the owner of Blackacre itself. And if B is entitled to a life interest in a settled fund worth £500,000 he is treated as though he were the owner of £500,000. But if a life tenant is entitled to part only of the income of settled property his interest is taken to subsist in only a proportionate part of the capital. So, if B were entitled to, say, half the income of the settled fund he would be treated as the owner of £250,000.

It follows that a reversionary interest is not an interest in possession. A reversionary interest is defined in section 47 as "a future interest under a settlement, whether it is vested or contingent . . . " A future interest cannot be an interest in possession because it is not "*in possession*". An interest in possession means an immediate entitlement: a present right of present enjoyment. There is a distinction in the general law between a reversionary interest and a remainder interest, but the definition quoted above makes no distinction of this kind—both are reversionary interests. So, if property is held on trust for A for life with remainder to B absolutely, A has an interest in possession and B has a reversionary interest.

It was pointed out above that in this situation A is treated as though he were the owner of the settled property itself. If B is also to be treated as owning something there will be some degree of double taxation. So the legislation treats B as owning nothing. This is achieved by declaring a reversionary interest to be "excluded property": section 48. The effect of this is most clearly seen in relation to a death. Section 5 provides that "the estate of a person immediately before his death does not include excluded property". So, if property is settled on trust for A for life with remainder to B, and B dies while A is still alive. B's reversionary interest is not taxed on B's death.

There are three (perfectly reasonable) exceptions to this principle. A reversionary interest is not excluded property if (1) it has at any time been acquired for consideration, or (2) it is one to which either the settlor or his spouse is beneficially entitled (see para. 21–10 below), or (3) it is the interest expectant on the determination of a lease for life which is treated as a settlement. The problem of purchased reversions is dealt with at the end of this chapter.

Another kind of interest which is not an interest in possession is a contingent interest. This again is because a contingent interest does not carry an immediate entitlement and so is not "in possession". If property is held on trust for A if he attains the age of 25 years, A's interest in the capital of the trust is contingent upon his attaining that age. Until he is 25, he does not have an interest in possession in the capital. But a very important point arises here. He may well, as we have just seen, become entitled (by statute[8] or otherwise) to the *income* of the trust on attaining his majority, namely 18 years of age. Where that is so, his interest in income vests in possession at 18. And his interest in income is sufficient to make him a person "beneficially entitled to an interest in possession". In other words, a contingent gift of capital which carries what is generally called "the intermediate income" confers an interest in possession as in *Swales v. IRC* (1984).

During the time that the estate of a deceased person is being administered a person who will be entitled to an interest in possession when the administration is completed is treated as having the interest from immediately after the death: section 91. Of course this only matters if the beneficiary dies or disposes of his interest during the administration period.

There is one interest which is an interest in possession under the Act, though under the general law it would not be an interest in settled property at all. This is the interest of the lessee where the lease is treated as a settlement because it was granted for life and for less than full consideration. That the lessee's interest is an interest in possession emerges, by implication, from section 50(6).

THE CHARGING PROVISIONS 21–05

We must now look at the circumstances in which a charge to tax arises in respect of settled property where there is a beneficial interest in possession, or (to put it in more popular terms) where there is a "fixed interest settlement," as distinct from a "discretionary settlement". In most cases where these charges arise otherwise than on the death of the person entitled to the interest in possession they are PETs and so only chargeable if the life tenant dies within seven years. They will only be immediately chargeable to tax if either a company becomes entitled to the property or a discretionary trust is thereby created. In the discussion below these lifetime charges will be assumed to be PETs.

Death of the beneficial owner 21–06

Let us again take the simple case of a settlement by which property is settled on A for life with remainder to B. A, the life

---

[8] See the Trustee Act 1925, s.31, as amended.

tenant, dies. A's life interest is part of his estate immediately before his death (section 5) and so is taxed under section 4, just as is his unsettled property. The only special point that arises (and it is one that has already been made) is that (under section 49) A is treated as owning the settled property itself. So, if the subject-matter of the trust is Blackacre, what falls to be valued on A's death is Blackacre itself, and not merely A's life interest in Blackacre. Apart from this (very important) valuation point, there is no difference on the occasion of death between a life interest and any other kind of property (except that the tax is normally payable by the trustees out of the settled property).

We now turn to look at the two circumstances in which a PET may be made during the lifetime of the life tenant.

21–07   *Termination of an interest in possession*

This circumstance is dealt with in section 52(1) as follows:

"Where at any time during the life of a person beneficially entitled to an interest in possession in settled property his interest comes to an end, tax shall be charged . . . as if at that time he had made a transfer of value and the value transferred had been equal to the value of the property in which his interest subsisted."

Notice the valuation point cropping up again in the last few words: what has to be valued is the property itself, not the value of the interest merely. There is no grossing up. The deemed transfer of value will be a PET. An example of an interest coming to an end during the lifetime of the life tenant would be where property is held on trust for X until she shall remarry and she does remarry. Another example would be where property is held on trust for Y for life with remainder to Z, and Y surrenders his life interest to Z.

21–08   *Disposal of an interest in possession*

This depends on section 51. Where a person beneficially entitled to an interest in possession in any property comprised in a settlement disposes of his interest, the disposal is not a transfer of value but is treated as the coming to an end of his interest. So if a section 51 situation arises, it is equated with a section 52 situation: that is to say, disposing of the interest is treated as a coming to an end of the interest. So, if A gives away to X his life interest in Blackacre, a tax charge arises just as if his interest had come to an end. Consequently there is a PET by A (without grossing up) on the whole value of Blackacre.

It is interesting to follow up what happens if A does give away (or, for that matter, sell) his life interest in, say, Blackacre to X. There then arises what is called an "interest *pur autre vie*". This describes the interest which X acquires. He has an interest in Blackacre "for another's life"; that is, his interest lasts only as long as A lives. When A dies, X's interest comes to an end, and a PET arises (under section 52). If X were to die while A was still alive, X's interest (the interest *pur autre vie*) would pass by his will or on intestacy to say, Y. The interest would be part of X's estate and tax would be charged (under section 4) on X's death. Y would then hold the interest and, if A were then to die, Y's interest would end, and a PET would arise under section 52. There might be quick succesion relief: see para. 21–11, below.

Note that although section 3(4) treats such deemed disposi- tions in the same way as actual dispositions, that subsection is expressly excluded from the operation of sections 19 to 22, so preventing the annual exemption and exemptions for small gifts, expenditure out of income and wedding gifts operating here.

Extension of the termination and disposal rules 21–09

If the point were not dealt with in the legislation it would be very easy to minimise the tax by depreciating the value of settled property by various transactions between the trustees and per- sons connected with the settlement.[9] The point is dealt with by section 52(3). If such a transaction takes place there is a deemed partial termination of the interest and so a PET arises. Thus, for example, if the trustees let a house rent-free to a beneficiary on a lease a tax charge will arise. A depreciatory transaction by an individual is taxable on the ordinary principle that it diminishes his estate. But trustees do not have an estate. That is why it is necessary to have this express rule.

Qualifications to the termination and disposal rules 21–10

We now have to look at a number of qualifications to the disposal and termination rules.

NEW ENTITLEMENT. If A's life interest terminates but he becomes on the same occasion entitled to the property or to

---

[9] See, *e.g. Macpherson v. IRC* (1988).

another interest in possession in the property, there is no PET unless the later interest is of less value than the former, in which case there is a deemed transfer of value equal to the difference: section 53(2) and section 52(4). This exception is a logical consequence of the principle that the holder of an interest in possession is treated as the owner of the property. If property is settled on trust to pay the income thereof to A for eight years and thereafter to A absolutely, there is no tax charge when the eight years are up and A takes the property absolutely; he was already treated for tax purposes as the absolute owner of the property. Thus there has been no loss to his estate. But if the trust was to pay the income to A for eight years and then to divide the property three-quarters to A and one-quarter to B, there would be a PET on that division. There is a notional loss to A of one-quarter of the settled property. Mind you, it may not be a real loss, because what A has after the eight-year period may well be (and probably will be) more valuable than what he had before. But it is a notional loss (and so taxable) because during the eight-year period he was treated as though he were the owner of the whole trust property, whereas after the division he is the owner of only three-quarters of it. The same point applies to an agreed "partition" between a life tenant and a remainderman, which is quite a common occurrence in practice. The proportion of the property which is partitioned to the remainderman is caught for tax as being property in which the interest of the life tenant comes to an end.

DISPOSAL FOR A CONSIDERATION. If the life tenant disposes of his interest for a consideration (that is, sells it as distinct from giving it away) the value transferred is reduced by the amount of the consideration: section 52(2). So if A, the life tenant of settled property worth £700,000, sells his life tenancy for £200,000, a PET arises not on the whole £700,000 but on £500,000. One might think that this provision would mean that no PET at all would arise if a life tenant were to sell his interest for its full market value. This is not really so because in practice a life interest (except in very rare circumstances) is always worth less than the property itself in which the interest subsists. The full market price of a life interest in Blackacre is almost certain to be less than the value of Blackacre itself. So if the life tenant sells his interest in Blackacre even for the full market price of the interest there may still be a PET on the disposal.

A reversionary interest in the property does not count in this connection as consideration. So in a partition (discussed under the previous heading) the fact that the life tenant gets in return for his life tenancy part of the remainderman's reversionary interest does not reduce the amount of tax chargeable on the partition.

REVERTER TO SETTLOR. The word "reverter" is lawyers' old-fashioned jargon for reversion. So what we are talking about here is the situation where S settles property on X with a provision that on a certain event the property is to revert to S. It is provided by section 53(3) that if the interest comes to an end during the settlor's life and on the same occasion the property reverts to the settlor, tax shall not be chargeable. The reason for this exception from charge is that it is considered desirable that a person should be able to provide a life interest (or other interest) for his dependants without a charge to tax when the property reverts to him. An example might occur on a divorce; one spouse might want to transfer the matrimonial home to the former spouse until the children of the marriage reach (say) school leaving age, with a provision that the house should then revert to the first spouse. Section 53(3) ensures that when the reversion takes place no tax charge arises. It is dealing with the situation where the interest comes to an end during the life of the beneficiary—in our example during the life of the former wife. Parallel provision is made by section 54 for the case where the "reverter to settlor" occurs on the occasion of the death of the beneficiary. An example would be where a man gives a life interest in a house to his widowed mother.

The operation of this relief requires the identification of who is the settlor. In *Fitzwilliam v. IRC* (1993) the House of Lords decided that it could include anyone who consciously provided the funds for the settlement but not someone who gave the funds unconditionally to another who then created the settlement.

The relief does not apply if the settlor or his spouse had acquired the reversionary interest for consideration. The point of this rule is to stop an avoidance device. Suppose a settlor (S) were to settle £50,000 on X for life, remainder to Y. If it were not for this rule, S could, when X was old and about to die, buy Y's reversionary interest for £50,000. In this way he could pass the £50,000 to Y without any tax arising.

REVERTER TO SETTLOR'S SPOUSE. A similar exception applies where the property reverts not to the settlor but to the settlor's spouse, provided the spouse is domiciled in the United Kingdom at the time the reversion occurs: section 53(4).

TRUSTEE'S REMUNERATION. Sometimes a trustee is remunerated for his services as a trustee by being given an interest in possession in the settled property (or in some part of it). Section 90 declares that provided the interest does not represent more than reasonable remuneration, no tax charge shall arise on the termination of the interest.

21–11   *Relief for successive charges*

There is "quick succession" relief for successive charges on interests in possession under section 141 in the same way as on a death transfer. Thus if there is a charge on a fixed interest settlement, by the activating of a PET, within five years of a previous chargeable transfer of the settled property (including the creation of the settlement), the value chargeable is reduced by a percentage. If the period since the last chargeable transfer is one year or less the reduction is 100 per cent; if the period is not more than two years the reduction is 80 per cent; if the period is not more than three years the reduction is 60 per cent; if the period is not more than four years the reduction is 40 per cent; if the period is not more than five years the reduction is 20 per cent.

21–12   *Close companies*

We have seen (see para. 18–10 above) that by sections 94 to 98 a transfer of value of unsettled property by a close company can be apportioned to the participators. A close company may also be involved in settled property in various ways.

Where a participator in a close company is a trustee of settled property in which the company has an interest in possession a transfer of value by the company can be apportioned to the interest holder. This is effected by deeming there to be a partial termination of his interest: section 99. Such a charge will not be a PET.

Where a close company is itself entitled to an interest in settled property the participators are treated as being the persons beneficially entitled to that interest according to their respective rights and interests in the company: section 101. Again these transfers will not be PETS.

21–13   *Fixed interest trusts and PETS*

As we have seen, gifts into fixed settlements and the lifetime charges on such settlements will usually be PETs and so only chargeable if the settlor or the life tenant dies within seven years. However, there will still be an immediate charge where the settlor creates a discretionary trust (other than those specifically protected such as accumulation and maintenance trusts), or where such a trust arises as the result of the termination of the life tenant's interest. A combination of PETs and chargeable transfers may, however, enable a discretionary trust to be set up effectively free of tax. To prevent this sections 54A and 54B were introduced in 1986.

The scheme would work like this:

> Mary, a wealthy settlor with a cumulative total of chargeable transfers of £234,000, settles a further £200,000 on Naomi, who has made no previous chargeable transfers, for one month and then for discretionary beneficiaries. The gift into the settlement by Mary will be a PET. Further, when Naomi's interest terminates, the chargeable transfer will be deemed to have been made by her and so fall entirely within the nil band of tax. Provided that Mary lives for seven years there will therefore be no charge to tax without sections 54A and 54B.

Those sections provide, however, that in this situation tax will be charged on the termination of Naomi's interest as if the deemed transfer of value under section 52 had been made by a hypothetical transferor having the cumulative total of the settlor at the date of the creation of the settlement. Thus such a transferor would inherit Mary's cumulative total and the transfer would then attract tax at the lifetime rate. The sections only apply if the life interest was created immediately, is not created by an exempt transfer (*e.g.* a life interest given to the settlor's spouse), and terminates within seven years of the creation of the settlement and during the lifetime of the settlor.

Where There is No Beneficial Interest in Possession   21–14

We now turn to look at the totally different regime of tax charges which applies to settled property in which, or part of which, for the time being there is no beneficial interest in possession. The charging provisions are contained in Chapter III of Part III of the 1984 Act, sections 58 to 85. These charges are immediately chargeable and do not fall within the PET regime.

The sections apply to what the legislation refers to as "relevant property". By section 58(1) relevant property means settled property (which we have already defined) in which no qualifying interest in possession exists. Section 59 defines such a qualifying interest as one to which an individual (or a company whose business it is to buy such interests) is beneficially entitled. It follows that with settled property there is either a beneficial interest and Chapter II of the Act applies, or there isn't and

Chapter III applies. Section 58(1), however, also excludes from the definition of relevant property certain types of settlement in which there is no interest in possession—these settlements are specially favoured for tax purposes and have special rules of their own. They are dealt with in the next part of this chapter. For the moment it is sufficient to note that these include charitable trusts and accumulation and maintenance settlements for persons under 25. It is also important to remember that a settlement may comprise both relevant and non-relevant property, *e.g.* part may be a discretionary trust and part be subject to a beneficial interest in possession or be a charitable trust.

There are three questions to be answered in relation to relevant property, which we may loosely describe as discretionary trusts. First, when will there be a charge to inheritance tax? Secondly what property will actually be charged? Thirdly at what rate is the tax to be charged? The problem with discretionary trusts is that, unlike fixed interest trusts, there is, by definition, no person entitled to an interest in possession regarded as owning the whole settled property for inheritance tax purposes, and so there will be no automatic charges on the death of such a person (or on an assignment of his interest, etc.). Fixed interest trusts are, in the nature of things, subject to a charge on the whole settled property at least once every generation (*i.e.* every 30 years or so). Similarly, the rates charged on fixed interest settlements are those applicable to the holder of the beneficial interest in possession—by treating the whole settled property as being in his ownership no special problems arise. Neither of these connecting factors are available for discretionary trusts.

The answer provided is, roughly, to charge a discretionary trust to tax every 10 years in such a way as to provide a charge on the whole settled property every 30 years or so, and to charge any property leaving the settlement in the meantime. The 10-year charge is known as the *principal charge*, the exit charges as *interim charges*. In relation to both types of charge the three questions above must be answered, but it is important to keep them separate in your mind. The rules, particularly as to the calculation of rates involved, are complex, and further difficulties arise because of the more generous treatment of discretionary trusts in existence before March 27, 1974, *i.e.* the date when the tax was introduced. This is because the tax regime for discretionary trusts was altered dramatically from that under estate duty law and it was thought unfair to apply the full rigour to such trusts. In general the basic difference is that a post March 26, 1974 settlement carries with it the cumulative total of the settlor at the date of the settlement whereas an earlier one does not.

It is now time to examine the charges.

THE PRINCIPAL OR 10-YEAR CHARGE 21–15

When will there be a charge?

Section 64 provides that on the tenth anniversary of the date on which the settlement commenced and on every subsequent 10-year anniversary, a principal charge to inheritance tax is to be levied. However, section 61 provides that no date prior to April 1, 1983 could be such an anniversary. It follows that settlements created prior to April 1, 1973 could not have a chargeable 10-year anniversary until after April 1, 1983. It therefore became something of a lottery as to how soon such a settlement (created before this tax was thought up) would be taxed. For example, a settlement created on April 1, 1973 will have been taxed on April 1, 1983 but a settlement created on March 31, 1973 will not have been taxed until March 31, 1993! What price tax planning?

It is obviously important therefore to decide when a settlement was created. Section 60 provides that this is when the property first becomes comprised in it, whether it was at this stage a discretionary trust or not, but for post March 26, 1974 settlements where a settlor, or his spouse, has an interest in possession when the settlement is first created, the property is only treated as having become comprised in the settlement when neither he nor his spouse have such an interest (section 80).

What is subject to the charge? 21–16

A 10-year charge is levied on the value of the relevant property comprised in the settlement, valued at the date of the charge. Since the whole amount is being charged no question of grossing up can arise. It is important to remember that this is all that is being charged when grappling with the rules as to the calculation of the applicable rates.

What rate is to be charged? 21–17

Here one has to distinguish between pre-March 27, 1974 settlements and others.

SETTLEMENTS CREATED AFTER MARCH 26, 1974. The rate of tax is calculated according to section 66. It is three-tenths of the effective rate of tax payable on a *notional chargeable transfer* made by a *notional transferor* with a *notional cumulative total* charged at the lifetime rates.

The *notional chargeable transfer* consists of:

(i) the relevant property which is actually being charged, valued now;
(ii) other property comprised in the settlement which is not relevant property (*e.g.* in which there is a beneficial interest in possession or which is a charitable trust), valued at the time it entered the settlement; and
(iii) property comprised in any related settlement (section 106 defines that as one made by the settlor on the same day as the settlement except a charitable trust). These should be avoided.

The *"transferor's" notional cumulative* total is:

(i) the settlor's seven-year cumulative total of chargeable transfers at the date of the creation of the settlement; and
(ii) the full amount charged to interim charges (see below) in the 10 years prior to the anniversary.

There is an additional sting in the tail. If the settlor has added property during the 10-year period his cumulative total at that time will be used if it is higher than his total at the time of the creation of the settlement. Conversely, however, if property is comprised in the settlement but has ceased during the 10-year period to be relevant property the amount upon which an exit charge has been made can be deducted from the cumulative ladder (section 67).

In an attempt to display these rules in a different way it may be helpful to give an example.

X, with a cumulative total of previous chargeable transfers of £234,000, created a settlement on December 1, 1990, of £100,000. Half is on discretionary trusts and half with an interest in possession. On the same day he made an accumulation and maintenance settlement (not relevant property) worth £50,000. At that time X had a seven-year cumulative total of £234,000.

The 10-year charge will arise on December 1, 2000. Let us suppose that the discretionary half of the settlement is then worth £150,000.

The notional transfer will be

£150,000 (chargeable relevant property)

£50,000 (value of fixed interest part of settlement at date of settlement)

£50,000 (related accumulative and maintenance settlement)

£250,000

The notional cumulative total, since there have been no exit charges, is that of the settlor at the date of creation of the settlement, *viz.* £234,000

therefore calculate the notional tax at lifetime rates on such a transfer of £250,000

i.e. tax on £484,000

less tax on £234,000

= £X

Next, express £X as a percentage of £250,000 to give the effective rate of tax, *i.e.* Y per cent. (Under the current simplified rates this is relatively easy.)

The rate chargeable is then $\frac{3}{10}$ Y per cent.

Remember that rate is then charged on £150,000 only, *i.e.* the value of the relevant property at the anniversary.

Under section 66(2) in applying this rate to the relevant property, if part of that property has not been subject to the discretionary trusts for the whole 10-year period (*e.g.* additions to the property) the tax payable on that part of the relevant property is to be reduced by one-fortieth for each completed quarter of a year prior to its becoming comprised in the settlement.

Thus if a settlement of £500,000 is subject to a 10-year charge of £30,000 under the rules above, but £100,000 was only added two years prior to that charge, the tax payable on that £100,000 is reduced as follows:

the tax payable on that part is $\dfrac{£100,000}{£500,000} \times £30,000 =$ £6,000; and

that figure (£6,000) is reduced by $\dfrac{32}{40}$, *i.e.* reduced to £1,200.

Settlements created prior to March 27, 1974. Section 66(6) amends the above rules for settlements in existence at the introduction of what is now inheritance tax. The basic concept is, however, the same. *i.e.* three-tenths of the effective rate on a notional chargeable transfer made by a "transferor" with a notional cumulative total.

In this case, however, the notional transfer consists only of the chargeable relevant property and no account is taken of either other property in the settlement or related settlements.

The notional cumulative total consists only of the amount subject to exit charges during the 10-year period. The settlor's prior total is ignored unless he has made an addition to the property after the March 1982 in which case his cumulative total then will be included.

In the first example given above therefore the notional transfer would be £150,000 and the notional cumulative total nil. The nil band would therefore apply.

21–18   THE INTERIM OR EXIT CHARGES

When will there be a charge?

Section 65(1) provides that there will be a charge to inheritance tax if either (a) any part of the property ceases to be relevant property (*e.g.* on an advance of capital to a discretionary beneficiary) or (b) the trustees carry out a depreciatory value-shifting transaction which has the effect of reducing the value of the settled property, *e.g.* a loan to a beneficiary at a low rate of interest, etc. (This is similar to the charge on fixed interest settlements under section 52(3).)

The donative intent exception in section 10 applies to the second of these charges, as in effect does section 3(3), omission to exercise a right being regarded as equivalent to a transaction.[10]

There is no charge in the first quarter after the creation of the settlement or 10-year charge[11] for trustees' costs and expenses, or for income distributions (*i.e.* income in the hands of the recipient). Nor is there a charge if the property ceases to be relevant property because it becomes comprised in a charitable trust (section 76).

---

[10] The associated operations provisions also apply. See *MacPherson v. IRC* (1988).
[11] For an unexpected consequence of this see *Frankland v. IRC* (1997), CA.

What is subject to the charge?   21–19

Section 65(2) provides that the interim charges are to be levied on the amount by which the relevant property after the event is less than it would be but for the event. This is the standard measure for inheritance tax, in effect the loss to the settlement's estate. It follows that unless the tax is paid by the beneficiary (*i.e.* it is a gross transfer) the transfer will have to be grossed up for tax purposes.

What rate is charged?   21–20

In this case it is necessary to distinguish between whether there has been a 10-year principal charge or not. With regard to exit charges prior to the first 10-year charge there was a distinction between pre-March 27, 1974 settlements and others. The former have by now all had such a charge and so those provisions are redundant.

All settlements prior to the first 10-year charge. Section 68 requires us to apply the *appropriate fraction* of the effective rate of tax on a *notional chargeable transfer* made by a "transferor" with a *notional cumulative total*.

The appropriate fraction is:

$$\frac{\text{number of quarters since the settlement commenced}}{40}$$

except for property which has not been in the settlement for the whole of that time, in which case for that property one uses only the number of quarters since it became relevant property.

The *notional transfer* consists of:

(i)   the value of the settled property at the commencement of the settlement;
(ii) the value of any related settlement;
(iii) the value of any addition to the property, valued at the date of entry.

The *notional cumulative total* is the settlor's cumulative total at the date of the settlement, ignoring any transfers made on that day.

To take an example:
A set up a £200,000 discretionary trust on January 4, 1994. He had previously made chargeable transfers of £50,000. Also

341

on January 4, 1994 he set up a £70,000 trust for charity. On February 10, 2000 the trustees advanced £30,000 to F absolutely.

There is an interim charge on £30,000 (ceases to be relevant property). There has been no previous 10-year charge.

To find the rate:

notional transfer

= £200,000 (value of settled property in 1990)
+ £70,000 (related settlement)
£270,000

notional cumulative total = £50,000 (settlor's total in 1990)
therefore calculate tax on   £320,000
less tax on   £50,000
=   £x

express £x as a percentage of £270,000 to give effective rate = y per cent.

The appropriate fraction is

$\frac{3}{10} \times \frac{24}{40}$ (no. of quarters since 1990 = $\frac{9}{50}$
so the rate chargeable on £30,000 is $\frac{9}{50}$ of y per cent.

ALL SETTLEMENTS AFTER THE FIRST 10-YEAR CHARGES. In such cases section 69 provides a simpler way of calculating the rates on an interim charge. It is simply the appropriate fraction of the rate charged on the last 10-year charge (ignoring any deduction for added property). We can for once dispense with notional transfer and the like.

The appropriate fraction is:

$$\frac{\text{number of quarters completed since the last 10-year charge}}{40}$$

The only complication is if at the time of the interim charge the settlement includes relevant property which was not there at the 10-year charge. In that case the 10-year charge has to be recalculated to include the added property, valued at the time it becomes relevant property.

21–21   Special Kinds of Settlement

As we have said before, some special types of settlement are not relevant property and as such are not liable to the interim and

342

principal charges even though there is no beneficial interest in possession. Similarly, the creation of such a trust is a PET. However, if the property ceases to be held on the specified trusts there is a flat rate charge which increases according to the length of time the property has been exempt and so avoided the 10-year charge. This is subject to a maximum of 30 per cent and no period prior to March 13, 1975 will be counted.

The list of these trusts can be found in section 58(1). These include trusts for the benefit of employees, superannuation schemes, charitable trusts, and protective trusts. One of the most important is an accumulative and maintenance settlement and this may be used as an illustration of how these settlements are treated for inheritance tax purposes. In general it should also be remembered that if a discretionary trust is changed to become a specially favoured trust the property will cease to be relevant property and an interim charge will accrue. That does not apply on a change to a charitable trust, however.

ACCUMULATION AND MAINTENANCE SETTLEMENTS

21–22

One can think of these settlements as being settlements for the benefit of young people.

Where a discretionary trust comes within the definition of an accumulation and maintenance settlement it is relieved from the normal tax charges relating to discretionary settlements since it is not relevant property. Its creation will also be a PET.

The matter is dealt with in section 71, which applies to any settlement where:

(1) one or more persons ("beneficiaries") will become entitled to the settled property or to an interest in possession in it at some specified age not exceeding 25;

(2) there is no interest in possession in the settled property;

(3) any application of the income must be for the maintenance, education or benefit of a beneficiary;

(4) to the extent that it is not so applied, the income must be accumulated; and

(5) not more than 25 years have elapsed since the latest time when conditions (1) to (4) above became satisfied, except that this rule does not apply if all the persons who are or have been beneficiaries are or were (putting it broadly) grandchildren of a common grandparent.

There has been some dispute as to the meaning of the word "will" in condition (1). In *Baron Inglewood v. IRC* (1983) the

Revenue argued that this requires that the beneficiary will *inevitably* become entitled to an interest if he attains the specified age. The taxpayer argued that it was sufficient if *at the present time* someone will and that such things as powers of revocation do not prevent the section applying. The Court of Appeal decided for the Revenue. The settlement has to ensure that one or more of the beneficiaries will attain a vested interest under 25 to come within the section. If his interest is capable of being taken away by the settlement (such as by a power of revocation) that cannot be the case. This involved the Court of Appeal in distinguishing such powers from, *e.g.* the power of advancement under section 32 of the Trustee Act 1925—the latter being classed as administrative powers or auxiliary powers.

There are several tax advantages applying to settlements which fulfil the above requirements. There is no 10-year anniversary charge, no interim charge, *e.g.* on the advancement to a beneficiary, no charge on the death of a potential beneficiary under the specified age or on a beneficiary obtaining an interest in possession by reaching the specified age.

There will be a charge if either (i) the property ceases to comply with the conditions or (ii) the trustees involve themselves in a depreciatory value-shifting transaction (*cf.* similar charges on fixed interest and discretionary trusts). The charge is a tapering charge based on the number of quarters of a year from the time when the conditions were first fulfilled to the date of charge. It is a flat rate charge on the scale set out in section 70:

0.25 per cent for each of the first 40 quarters (10 years—10 per cent).

0.20 per cent for each of the next 40 quarters (11–20 years—further 8 per cent).

0.15 per cent for each of the next 40 quarters (21–30 years—further 6 per cent).

0.10 per cent for each of the next 40 quarters (31–40 years—further 4 per cent).

0.05 per cent for each of the next 40 quarters (41–50 years—further 2 per cent).

Thus if the time lapse is 15 years the rate is 14 per cent. The maximum rate is 30 per cent after 50 years, which cannot occur before March 13, 2015, given the earliest allowed starting date.

It is important to note the effect of section 31 of the Trustee Act 1925 on these rules. That section gives trustees a statutory power to pay maintenance to a potential beneficiary up to the age of 18. It also, unless excluded, gives that beneficiary a right to receive the income between the ages of 18 and the required age. It follows that a gift to X "when he is 30" will give X the right to the income at 18—he will therefore have an interest in possession at that age and so have the right to such an interest at an age under 25. The Revenue have agreed that this will satisfy the conditions for section 71 to apply. Unless section 31 of the Trustee Act is excluded, such as by a direction to accumulate the income until the beneficiary reaches 30, it does not therefore matter what age is specified as entitling the beneficiary to the capital, he will receive the income, and so get an interest in possession, at 18.[12]

By a further concession the conditions will be fulfilled even if no age is specified in the deed if it is clear that the beneficiary will become entitled to the property, if at all, by age 25, *e.g.* to X in 21 years' time, X being three years old.

The Purchase of a Reversionary Interest   21–33

We have seen (notably at para. 21–04 above) that except in certain circumstances a reversionary interest in settled property in the United Kingdom is excluded property, thus giving effect to the principle that for inheritance tax purposes the life tenant owns the whole settled fund and the reversioner owns nothing.

There are a number of special provisions in the legislation, however, some of which are designed to prevent over-charging in respect of reversionary interests and some of which are designed to prevent tax avoidance.

The most important provision is that a purchased reversion is not excluded property: section 48(1)(a). This is to prevent an obvious form of avoidance. Suppose that £200,000 is settled on A for life, remainder to B. C purchases B's remainder for £60,000, which is its market value. This is not a chargeable transfer since there will be no loss to C's estate and in any event no donative intent by B (protected by section 10). C has depleted his free estate by £60,000 and gained the reversion. If he could thus give the reversion to D as excluded property he would in effect have given D £60,000 free of inheritance tax. Thus there is a charge on the gift to D, a reversion, once purchased is not excluded property.

The position is more complex if the reversion is purchased by the owner of a prior interest in the settlement.

Suppose that property having a value of £200,000 is settled on A for life with remainder to B. And suppose further that A has

---

[12] This is equally true if the contingency is otherwise than attaining a specific age. See *Swales v. IRC* (1984).

free estate (*i.e.* unsettled property) worth £100,000. If A were to die his estate would have a value of £300,000. If A (before dying) were to buy from B the reversionary interest for its full actuarial value (say £80,000) he could do so without any tax charge, because although A's life interest terminates he becomes on the same occasion absolutely entitled to the property: see section 53(2). The reversion merges with the life interest and the property ceases to be settled property. If A were now to die, his estate would have a value of only £220,000, made up of £200,000 (the former settled property) plus £20,000 (his free estate, previously £100,000 but diminished by the £80,000 which he has paid to B). In this way tax would be saved. The "trick" lies in having brought into his estate something which in reality increases his wealth, but which (for the purposes of the tax) he already owned, and in having depleted, by that transaction, his taxable estate.

The legislation meets this avoidance device by treating A as having made a gift to B of £80,000, and so as having made a PET of that amount. This is done by means of section 55 which says:

" ... where a person entitled to an interest (whether in possession or not) in any settled property acquires a reversionary interest expectant (whether immediately or not) on the interest, the reversionary interest is not part of his estate ... "

Thus, although A gives full value to B for the reversionary interest, and although there is no donative intent, he is treated as having paid £80,000 for nothing, and so as having made a transfer of value amounting to £80,000. The usual exemption for lack of donative intent in section 10 is expressly excluded from applying to a section 55 transaction.

LIABILITY AND INCIDENCE

In this chapter we deal with two matters which are separate but related, namely liability and incidence.

Liability is concerned with who is to pay the tax to the Revenue. The previous legislation, dealing with Estate Duty, described this duty to pay the tax as "accountability". That was somewhat confusing, because there is also a separate duty to deliver to the Revenue an account. The inheritance tax legislation describes the duty to pay the tax as "liability" which is much clearer.

Incidence is concerned with who is ultimately to bear the burden of the tax. So, for example, an executor may be under a duty to pay the tax to the Revenue. He then looks to the rules of incidence to see against what beneficial interests under the will he is to charge it.

Liability   22–01

The following persons may, in various circumstances, be liable to pay the tax: transferor, transferee, trustee, beneficiary, settlor, personal representative. Does anyone feel left out?

The details are set out Part VII, sections 199 to 214, of the 1984 Act.

For *chargeable*[1] *lifetime transfers of unsettled property* the persons liable are: (a) primarily the transferor and then the transferee; and (b) so far as the tax is attributable to the value of any particular property, any person in whom the property is vested (whether beneficially or otherwise) at any time after the transfer or who at any such time is beneficially entitled to an interest in possession in the property; and (c) where by the chargeable transfer any property becomes comprised in a settlement, any person for whose benefit any of the property or income from it is applied.

---

[1] There rules are modified for PETs which become chargeable transfers on the transferor's death within seven years and for any additional "death rate" payable on such a death. See below.

347

For *chargeable transfers of settled property* the persons liable are: (a) primarily the trustees of the settlement; and (b) any person entitled (whether beneficially or not) to an interest in possession in the settled property; and (c) any person for whose benefit any of the settled property or income from it is applied; and (d) where the chargeable transfer is made during the life of the settlor and the trustees are not for the time being resident in the United Kingdom, the settlor.

For *transfers on death* the persons liable are: (a) in respect of unsettled property and in respect of settled property being land in the United Kingdom which devolves upon them, the deceased's personal representatives[2]; (b) in respect of settled property, the trustees; (c) so far as the tax is attributable to the value of any particular property, any person in whom the property is vested (whether beneficially or otherwise) at any time after the death or who at any such time is beneficially entitled to an interest in possession in the property; and (d) so far as the tax is attributable to the value of any property which, immediately before the death, was comprised in a settlement, any person for whose benefit any of the property or income from it is applied after the death.[3]

Where the transferor dies within seven years of making a chargeable transfer the additional tax which becomes payable (*i.e.* the difference between the lifetime rates and the death rates) is principally the liability of the transferee. Similar rules apply where the transferor dies within seven years of making a PET and the transfer becomes chargeable. But if, for example, the transferee does not pay within 12 months the personal representatives are liable. All concerned are advised to take out insurance against such a contingent liability.

In any circumstances where two or more persons are liable for the same tax, each is liable to the Revenue for the whole of it. But, of course, the Revenue cannot get more tax than is due.

References in the above contexts to any property include references to any property directly or indirectly representing it. So one does not escape the tax charge merely by selling the original property and investing the proceeds in some other property. (For the tax position of the purchaser, see paragraph 22–03 below.)

---

[2] This liability is a personal liability of the personal representatives and not a liability of the deceased which they assume. See *IRC v. Stannard* (1984).

[3] Liability also extends to anyone who interferes or "intermeddles" in the estate to become an *executor de son tort*. See *IRC v. Stype Investments (Jersey) Ltd* (1982).

Transfers between spouses   22–02

Where a transferor is liable for any tax and by another transfer of value made by him any property becomes the property of a person who at the time of both transfers was his spouse, that spouse is liable for so much of the tax as does not exceed the value of the property at the time of the transfer to that spouse. See section 203, which is designed to stop up a rather crude avoidance device—namely, make a transfer of value to someone overseas and make also an exempt transfer of the rest of one's estate to one's spouse, and leave the Revenue to whistle for their money.

Exception of purchaser from liability   22–03

A purchaser of property is not liable for tax attributable to the value of the property purchased, unless the property is subject to an Inland Revenue charge (on which see para. 23–06, below): section 199(3).

Limitations of liability   22–04

There are limitations on the extent to which a person is liable for the tax. For instance, a personal representative is liable only to the extent of the assets he has received or might have received but for his own neglect or default. Somewhat similar limitations apply to trustees, beneficiaries and transferees: see section 204.

Incidence   22–05

We now come to the question of who is to bear the ultimate burden of the tax, bearing in mind that the person who pays the tax may not be the person on whom the burden should ultimately fall.

Problems of incidence are most acute in relation to tax arising on death. In the case of lifetime transfers it is a matter between the parties as to who bears the tax. The main effect, as we have seen, will be as to whether "grossing up" is necessary.

Whilst prima facie each item of property comprised in a person's estate at death carries its own burden of tax this general principle is largely reversed by section 211. Tax attributable to the value of property in the United Kingdom which vests in the deceased's personal representatives and which was not, immediately before the death, comprised in a settlement, is to be treated as part of the general testamentary and administration expenses of the deceased, unless the will provides to the contrary. This of course means that, apart from any jointly owned property passing by survivorship which will not vest in the personal representatives, the tax attributed to the bulk of the average testator's estate will be treated as part of the general testamentary and administration expenses of the deceased for it is only in exceptional circumstances that the average estate includes overseas property. The incidence of tax for the average testator is therefore to be determined by the Administration of Estates Act 1925, s.34 and Part II of the First Schedule thereto under which where the deceased has left a will effectively disposing of the residue of his estate the burden will be thrown on that residue.

This process is reinforced by the tendency of testators to include in their wills directions that particular gifts should be paid free of inheritance tax. As we shall see in a moment, such a direction does, however, have another potential effect on the incidence rules on death. There is one exception to this power of testators to make tax free gifts. Suppose a testator gives his residue equally to his wife and his mother, with a direction that the mother's share is to be free of inheritance tax. The gift to the spouse is exempt, whilst that to the mother is chargeable. Section 41 provides that such a chargeable residuary gift must bear its own tax so that the direction that such tax shall be borne by the exempt gift of residue to the spouse is void. This means that the net share actually received by the mother will be less than that received by the spouse since the former will be reduced by the tax payable on it. If the testator actually wishes the spouse and mother to receive equal net shares (*i.e.* after tax has been paid) this can be achieved if the will makes it clear that the mother's share of the residue, before tax, is to be enlarged by an amount which will ensure that when the tax is deducted from it her net share is equal to that of the spouse.[4] But this must be very clearly expressed and the courts will not infer it simply because the more likely explanation that the executors were intended to pay the tax due as a testamentary expense out of the gross residue before the shares were divided is prohibited by section 41.[5]

It is important on a death to calculate the estate rate, *i.e.* the rate of tax which applies to the whole estate, taking into account the nil band. Thus if A dies, having made no previous chargeable transfers, leaving a chargeable estate (ignoring exempt transfers) of £334,000, tax will currently be chargeable at nil on £234,000 and at 40 per cent on £100,000. Thus the tax bill will be £40,000.

---

[4] *Re Benham's Will Trusts* (1995).
[5] *Re Ratcliffe* (1999).

Applied across all the assets this gives an average rate of 13.33 per cent. That rate will then be deducted from any legacies which have to bear their own tax before the money is paid over to the legatee. Tax-free legacies will be paid in full with the tax coming out of residue. This apparently simple calculation is, however, as in many areas of tax law, not always quite so simple.

Partially exempt transfers on death   22–06

In many cases the rule that inheritance tax is a testamentary expense to be paid out of residue causes no problems. Thus where all the legacies are both chargeable and tax free and the residue is also chargeable, the whole tax bill (at the estate rate) is charged on the residue. Similarly, if the legacies are either all exempt, or are to bear their own tax under the terms of the will, the residue and the tax-bearing legacies will simply bear their own tax at the estate rate. But problems arise in three not uncommon cases. These problems are the subject of sections 36 to 42. The following is an outline of the effect of these sections, which in practice involve many complex calculations:

(i)   Where the testator leaves a legacy free of tax[6] and an exempt gift of residue; *e.g.* £200,000 to my daughter, free of tax, residue to my wife. In this case, in order to work out how much tax should be charged on the legacy (*i.e.* the estate rate since the residue is exempt) it must be grossed up (in the same way as a net lifetime transfer). The tax then payable on that grossed up legacy is deducted from the residuary gift and the daughter will receive the net £200,000.

(ii) Where the testator makes both tax-free legacies and those which must bear their own tax, together with an exempt gift of residue. Grossing up only the tax-free legacies would not be enough (since there are other legacies involved in assessing the tax liability) but grossing up all the legacies would be too much (since those bearing their own tax are not required to be grossed up, just as with a gross lifetime transfer). The solution is to gross up the tax-free legacies at a rate of tax applicable to a hypothetical transfer of the total of the grossed up tax-free legacies and those bearing their own tax. This is known as "double grossing up".

---

[6]   Remember this will be the case unless the will provides to the contrary.

In essence, the tax-free legacies are first grossed-up in the normal way, then the rate for grossing up a second time is calculated on a transfer of the total of that grossed up figure plus the tax-bearing legacies (say 20 per cent). The tax-free legacies are then grossed up again at that rate. The estate rate of tax is then calculated on the total of those doubly grossed up legacies and the tax bearing legacies (say 25 per cent). That rate will then be deducted from the residue in respect of the tax-free legacies and from the tax-bearing legacies in respect of their own tax.

(iii) Where the testator leaves both tax-free and tax-bearing legacies, as above, but the residue is partly chargeable and partly exempt. In this case, the tax-free gifts are again subject to a double grossing up, but the second grossing up must be at a rate calculated on a hypothetical transfer of the total of the grossed up tax-free legacies, the tax-bearing legacies and the chargeable part of the residue (divided after deducting the single grossed up tax-free legacies and the tax-bearing legacies). After the tax-free legacies have been so doubly grossed up, the estate rate is calculated on the total of the doubly grossed up legacies, the tax-bearing legacies and the chargeable part of the residue (now divided after deducting the doubly grossed up legacies and the tax-bearing legacies). That rate is then charged on the residue as a whole in respect of the tax-free legacies. Only after that will the residue be divided and the estate rate applied to the chargeable part. That rate will also be deducted from those legacies bearing their own tax.

CHAPTER 23

ADMINISTRATION AND COLLECTION

Section 215 of the 1984 Act announces that inheritance tax "shall be under the care and management of the Board" (*i.e.* the Commissioners of Inland Revenue). Part VIII of the 1984 Act (sections 215 to 261) provides detailed rules concerning the administration and collection of the tax.

Delivery of an account: section 216

23–01

The personal representatives of a deceased person are under a duty to deliver an account to the Revenue specifying to the best of their knowledge and belief all appropriate property[1] and its value. And a similar duty rests on a transferor and a trustee[2] of a settlement concerning a lifetime transfer which is not a PET. The transferee must deliver an account in respect of a PET if the transferor dies within seven years and the personal representatives must also deliver an account of any PETs made by the deceased in the seven years prior to the death, again to the best of their knowledge and belief. If there are no personal representatives appointed within 12 months of the death the duty to account falls on those beneficially entitled to the property or an interest in the property (including certain discretionary beneficiaries). There is no duty to account on a death if the estate does not exceed £200,000 and certain other conditions are fulfilled.[3] The phrase "best of their knowledge and belief" means the personal knowledge of the individual. This includes documents in his possessions or custody but he is not required to be an information gatherer.[4]

---

[1] Including any interests in possession or general powers of appointment held by the deceased.

[2] This includes a foreign trustee of a foreign trust made by a U.K. settlor: *Re Clore (dec'd) (No. 3)* (1985).

[3] These are: there is no settled property; not more than £50,000 is outside the U.K.; the estate does not include any gifts subject to a reservation; and the deceased died domiciled in the U.K. having made no chargeable *inter vivos* transfers within seven years of the death other than transfers of money or quoted securities of less than £75,000: S.I. 1981 Nos. 880 and 881, as amended by S.I. 1998 No. 1431; made under s.256.

[4] *Re Clore (dec'd) (No 3)* (1985).

353

Personal representatives must deliver their account within 12 months from the end of the month in which the death occurs or within three months of the time when they first acted (if this period expires later).

Any other person must deliver his account within 12 months from the end of the month in which the transfer took place, or (if it expires later) the period of three months from the date on which he first became liable for tax. (There are special rules about conditionally exempt works of art, etc., and about timber.) There are penalties in default unless there is a reasonable excuse (section 245).

Personal representatives cannot get probate until they have paid the tax, and they cannot sell any of the estate assets (so as to get cash with which to pay the tax) until they have got probate. That looks like a vicious circle. But the problem can be overcome. The personal representatives can submit a provisional account and pay tax on that, then get probate, then sell off some of the estate assets, then submit a corrective or supplementary account and pay tax on that.

23–02   **Returns by certain persons acting for settlors: section 218**

There is a special provision concerning overseas settlements. Where any person, in the course of a trade or profession (other than the profession of a barrister) has been concerned with the making of a settlement and knows or has reason to believe that the settlor was domiciled in the United Kingdom and that the trustees of the settlement are not or will not be resident in the United Kingdom, he must within three months of the making of the settlement make a return to the Board stating the names and addresses of the settlor and of the trustees of the settlement. This requirement does not apply to a settlement made by will nor to any other settlement if such a return has already been made by another person or if an account has been delivered in relation to it. The provision applies to (amongst others) solicitors and accountants and there are penalties in default (section 245A).

23–03   **Power to require information and inspect property: sections 219, 219A, 219B, 220 and 220A**

The Board, with the consent of a Special Commissioner, may by notice in writing require any person to furnish them within such time, not being less than 30 days, as may be specified in the notice with such information as the Board may require for the purposes of inheritance tax. The notice may be combined with a notice relating to income tax. Legal professional privilege is protected except that a solicitor (not a barrister) can be required to disclose the name and address of his client and (in certain circumstances relating to an overseas client) the names and addresses of his client's clients in the United Kingdom.

In addition, an officer of the Revenue may call by written notice for any documents, accounts or particulars from anyone liable to deliver an account. There is no requirement for the consent of a Special Commissioner but there is an appeal to such a person by the recipient of the notice. There is no further right of appeal by either side. The power is limited to the purpose of determining whether an account is incorrect or incomplete.

If the Board authorises any person to inspect any property for the purpose of ascertaining its value for the purposes of inheritance tax the person having the custody or possession of that property shall permit him to inspect it at such reasonable times as the Board may consider necessary.

There is also provision for bilateral exchange of information with foreign governments relating to inheritance tax and its foreign equivalent. Where such an agreement with a foreign government is in force, the power to require information for inheritance tax purposes applies to information relating to the foreign tax charge.

Determination and appeals: sections 221 to 225   23–04

Instead of the word "assessment" which is the technical term applying to income tax, capital gains tax and corporation tax, the term used in relation to inheritance tax is "determination". The Board make a determination and then serve a notice of determination.

Appeals (which must be made within 30 days of service of notice of determination) go to the Special Commissioners except in two cases as follows: (1) where it is so agreed between the appellant and the Board, or where the High Court (on an application made by the appellant) is satisfied that the matters to be decided are likely to be substantially confined to questions of law and gives leave, the appeal goes to the High Court direct, thus cutting out the Special Commissioner stage; (2) any question as to the value of land in the United Kingdom must be determined by the appropriate Lands Tribunal.

The procedure before the Special Commissioners is similar to that in relation to other taxes.

Appeal lies from the Special Commissioners to the High Court on a point of law only.

23–05 ### Payment of tax: sections 226 to 236

In general, inheritance tax becomes due six months after the end of the month in which the chargeable transfer was made or, in the case of a transfer made after April 5 and before October 1 in any year otherwise than on death, at the end of April in the next year. So in many instances tax is due before the account is due. Tax on PETs is due six months after the death which activates the charge. So is the additional tax payable on the death of the transfers of a chargeable transfer within seven years.

Tax which is due and unpaid attracts interest at prescribed rates and there is no income tax relief for the interest payments. Where there has been an overpayment of tax the repayment by the Revenue carries interest (at the same rates as above) from the date on which the overpayment was made, and this interest is not subject to income tax.

In certain circumstances the tax can be paid by instalments. This facility applies only where the tax is attributable to certain kinds of property: land, controlling shares or securities; other shares or securities which are unquoted and in respect of which certain detailed conditions are satisfied; and a business or an interest in a business to the extent of its net value (as defined).[5]

The instalment provisions apply to transfers on death. They also apply, with certain modifications, to lifetime transfers but only if either (a) the tax is borne by the person benefiting from the transfer or (b) the property is settled property and remains in the settlement after the transfer.

Interest on land is payable in instalments from the date on which the first instalment fell due, but in other cases interest only runs if an instalment is in arrears so that there can be interest-free instalments.

23–06 ### Inland Revenue charge for unpaid tax: sections 237 and 238

The word "charge" in this context is being used in the same sense in which a mortgage is a charge. Section 237 automatically imposes an Inland Revenue charge on all property included in a chargeable transfer[6] and, in the case of settled property, on any property included in the settlement. The holder of the property can thus be liable for the tax. On a transfer on death, however,

---

[5]   Rather special instalment provisions apply to timber in certain circumstances.

[6]   It also applies to the various chargeable events connected with conditionally exempt heritage property.

the charge does not apply to personal[7] or movable property in the United Kingdom comprised in the free estate of the deceased. A purchaser of land where the charge is not registered and a bona fide purchaser of personal property without notice is not subject to the charge; where this is the case the charge attaches to the proceeds of sale.

[7] Until 1999 leaseholds counted as personal property for this purpose.

PART FIVE

Value Added Tax

THE CHARGE TO VALUE ADDED TAX

Value added tax is almost always known as VAT. Even the VAT Act calls it that. So shall we. Not only does it save time, it also avoids awkward questions about whether we have the name right! We call it "value added tax", but the Irish call it "value-added tax", and are probably correct. Why? Because the name is a direct translation from the French *taxe sur la valeur ajoutée*—tax on added value. Somewhere we turned the noun "value" into an adjective.

VAT has turned from a foreign idea into Britain's second biggest tax in one generation. Why? There are two main reasons: a legal reason and a practical reason. The legal reason is that VAT is the only permissible general sales tax in the European Union. When we joined the E.C. in 1973, we were obliged to adopt the tax. As we see below, many of the basic legal concepts of the tax are increasingly a matter of the construction of European law.

The practical reason is that the E.U. is, in fiscal terms, a customs union. For many centuries much English, then British, government revenue was earned from customs duties. Now the UK government gets precisely nothing from customs duties—they are a European tax, and cannot be imposed between the Member States of the E.U. We can only tax goods from other European countries to the same extent as we tax domestic production. So we tax both equally—and that is the heart of VAT.

Introduction   24–01

VAT is a charge on:

- domestic supplies of goods and services;
- cross-border acquisitions from other states in the E.U.; and
- imports from states outside the E.U.

Each of these three charges is a distinct but related part of the tax. However, in this and the following chapter, we shall deal with the tax on the assumption that all relevant aspects of taxable transactions take place in the United Kingdom. International aspects are dealt with in Part Six of the book.

24–02   *VAT as an E.U. tax*

The United Kingdom adopted VAT as part of its Treaty obligations on joining the E.C. Article 93 of the E.C. Treaty provides for the harmonisation of "turnover" taxes in the E.C. This has been effected by the introduction of a number of E.C. Directives on VAT.

The principles of the E.C. VAT were laid down in 1967 in the First VAT Directive (Directive 27/227). Detail was added by a Second Directive, but this was revoked in 1977 and replaced by the Sixth VAT Directive (Directive 77/388). The Sixth Directive has been amended and extended considerably since 1977. In its embellished version, it forms the main text of the E.C. VAT law and its importance cannot be over emphasised since the European Court of Justice (ECJ) has long held that where the provisions of the Directive appear to be unconditional and sufficiently precise and clear, those provisions can be relied upon as a matter of Community law by taxpayers as against any national provision (*i.e.* United Kingdom legislation) which does not properly transpose those terms into domestic law. This doctrine of direct effect has been applied many times to various provisions of the Sixth Directive.[1] In practical terms it is therefore very common now for a dispute before a United Kingdom court as to the effect of a provision in a United Kingdom statute on VAT to be argued in terms of whether it complies with the relevant article of the Directive and we shall come across many such examples as we look at the tax. It follows that the basic framework of VAT is also derived from the Directive, *e.g.* as to what exemptions are permitted[2] or in what circumstances illegal transactions are taxable.[3] Where, however, the national provision could be construed as being consistent with the Directive, but was in fact misconstrued by the parties, there is no remedy under Community law since the matter could have been resolved by the national court on the wording of the domestic provision.[4]

---

[1]   There are many such cases but see *e.g. Finanzamt München III v. Mosche* (1997).
[2]   See *e.g. Norbury Developments Ltd v. CEC* (1999).
[3]   *Fischer v. Finazamt Donaueschingen* (1998).
[4]   *Marks and Spencer plc v. CEC* (2000)

It is not just in the wording of the Directive itself, however, that the influence of Community law is felt. In applying the terms of the Directive the United Kingdom courts are obliged to apply broader Community law principles of construction. This was recognised very early by Nolan J. in *Yoga for Health Foundation v. CEC* (1984). Thus many decisions are based upon E.C. principles such as legitimate expectations, legal certainty, proportionality, non-discrimination, equivalence and effectiveness. There is a particular stress on the principle of fiscal neutrality, *i.e.* that economic operators carrying on the same business should be taxed the same. Thus the ECJ was able to find that the Directive made no distinction between a nursing home run by a company and one run by a partnership.[5] Occasionally, Member States are permitted to opt out of part of the Directive. Such "derogations" as they are called are, however, very strictly construed by the ECJ, again applying Community law principles.[6]

But the Directive is not exhaustive especially with regard to procedural matters. The question then arises as to whether in deciding as to the propriety of a national VAT provision which is not covered by the Directive, the above principles of Community law should be applied or whether it is a matter only for national law. In other words is the whole operation of VAT now a matter for Community Law principles of construction to be applied? In two decisions, Moses J. held that, in the absence of any reference to the matter in the Directive, or of any breach of the Directive, a challenge to the activities of the Customs and Excise in relation to repayment claims for overpayment of tax, which were not caused by any breach of the Directive, must be decided on national principles only.[7] The Court of Appeal[8] has upheld this approach in general, distinguishing between a repayment claim arising from a refusal to allow the deduction of input tax, which is covered by the Directive, and one, as in the case, based on the overpayment of output tax which was not so covered. General principles of Community law could not be relied on where there was no pre-existing Community right.

The Court of Appeal did, however, refer to the ECJ the question as to whether Community law would prevent the national court enforcing a provision of domestic legislation which removed with retrospective effect the right under domestic

---

[5]   *Gregg v. CEC* (1999).
[6]   *Finazamt Bergisch Galdbach v. Skripalle* (1997). But see *Belgocodex SA v. Belgium* (2000) on the rights of Member States to revoke such derogations.
[7]   *Marks and Spencer plc v. CEC* (1999); *R v. CEC, ex parte Building Societies Ombudsman Co Ltd* (1999).
[8]   *Marks and Spencer plc v. CEC* (2000).

law to reclaim overpayment of VAT where that claim had not been exercised within three years. Although, the right to repayment in question in that case had arisen as a result of the operation of direct effect, *i.e.* as a matter of Community law, the question as referred to the ECJ is not so limited and could apply to a claim based purely on national law. As such it potentially raises again the question as to the operation of Community law in areas not specifically within the ambit of the Directive.

Since that reference was made, however, the ECJ itself has ruled that since the Directive does not lay down any procedural rules relating to the operation of VAT it is for the Member States to provide safeguards for those rights (*e.g.* as to payment and repayment of the tax) conferred by Community law[9]. The only restrictions are that they must not treat Community rights less favourably than domestic rights or make it virtually impossible to enforce such rights. But the Court also assumed that the basic principle of Community law of fairness must also apply so that similar situations must be treated similarly unless the difference can be objectively justified, whether or not a Community right as such is in issue. They considered that the whole of VAT falls within the province of Community law principles.

24–03   **VAT in the United Kingdom**

In the United Kingdom, VAT is imposed by the Value Added Tax Act 1994, a consolidation measure, together with significant provisions in delegated legislation. Partly as a result of a series of cases brought against the United Kingdom Government by taxpayers and by the European Commission, many of the differences that used to exist between the E.C. VAT and its United Kingdom version have been removed or at least reduced.

VAT law is a curious mix of broad principles and considerable amounts of detail. This is because of the nature of the tax. In principle it is a very broad-based tax, much broader than income tax or corporation tax. Potentially it applies to any economic transaction under which anyone adds value to any business activity; that is, under which anyone recovers not only the cost of materials used in a transaction, but also the cost of his or her own labour (or that of employees) or a profit. Of course, both are usually the aim. VAT therefore can apply to any economic activity. Further, it applies directly to those activities, not at one remove in the way corporation tax or income tax do. We must in

---

[9]   *Société Financière d'Investissements SPRL v. Belgium* (2000).

every case establish not who makes the money, but who makes the supply, to whom, and of what. Easy? No, because checking on those questions can involve almost any aspect of commercial law and intellectual property law and much of real property law as well. If a problem exists in any of these areas of law, it can exist in VAT also.

At the same time, therefore, United Kingdom VAT law has to follow a European paradigm and deal with considerable detail. Both make the traditional pattern of imposition by means only of primary legislation inappropriate. In practice, there are four tiers of operative legislation. The top tier is formed by the European directives. The next tier is the VAT Act and amending Finance Acts. Below that are orders in Council and other delegated legislation. Then comes the fourth layer: official Notices. These Notices are issued by the Customs and Excise Commissioners and, unusually, have, at least in part, legislative status. Taxpayers to whom the Notices are issued are obliged to follow their contents. By this multiple means, the law is imposed. Supported both by considerable use of the appeals process, and also by agreements with trade organisations, extra-statutory concessions, parliamentary questions, press releases, and more than 80 leaflets of guidance, those who need to do so can find out at least what the local VAT offices think they should be doing. Of this wealth of material, you may find it useful to obtain one Notice in particular. Notice No. 700, *The VAT Guide*, is an excellent summary, with worked examples, of the tax for those who have to operate it. It is available free from your local VAT office.

Administration and appeals   24–04

VAT administration is the task of the oldest British government department, Her Majesty's Customs and Excise. Perhaps this may seem odd. First, the main job of this department is now running VAT, although that tax is neither an excise tax nor a customs duty. Secondly, the customs duties are not Her Majesty's—they "belong" to the European Union and British customs officers act as agents of the E.U. in collecting duties. A third reason for this seeming odd is that VAT is, in practical terms, accounted for by the same taxpayers as pay corporation tax and Schedule D income tax. Why is it not then collected by the Inland Revenue?

The answer is that when we adopted VAT it replaced, among other taxes, a sales tax called purchase tax. This left excise officers underemployed, and VAT solved that problem. This had the unfortunate practical effect of emphasising differences between VAT and income tax rather than common areas, particularly in procedural terms. Not all the differences between income tax and VAT are necessary differences. Naturally, the new VAT was fitted into an existing approach. But even now a taxpayer must deal with two lots of officials and sets of powers while in several other European states one team of tax officials deals with both kinds of tax.

The differences between the taxes also extend to the assessment and appeals systems. We will explain the system of the administering of VAT later, but we need to note that the system does not rely on formal assessments in the same way as income tax. Instead, liability to pay arises whenever a taxable supply of goods or services takes place. If the person making the supply cannot agree with the local VAT office about the application of VAT to that supply, then there is a right to refer the matter to a special tribunal. The tribunal has the right to hear appeals on a long list of things: see section 83 of the VAT Act 1994. Apart from disputes about liability, a major subject of appeals is the imposition of penalties.

Appeals are heard by the VAT and duties appeal tribunal (VADT). Originally set up only to hear VAT appeals, this tribunal now deals with all aspects of the indirect taxes or, in effect, appeals from decisions of the customs and excise authorities. The VADT has the power to deal with any question of law, procedure or fact in an appeal. Appeals from the VADT can only be made on a point of law. This right of appeal is part of the general right to appeal to the High Court from a tribunal granted by section 11 of the Tribunals and Inquiries Act 1992.

VAT in Scotland is exactly the same as in England, save that appeals from the VADT lie to the Scottish courts rather than the English courts. There are, however, not one but two common lines of appeal on Scottish cases and English cases. The first is to the House of Lords. The second, as we have seen, is to the European Court of Justice in Luxembourg.

Because, as we have seen, many of the key issues in imposing VAT depend on the VAT directives, the interpretation of those directives is at the heart of many appeals. Any court or VADT which considers that a question of interpretation of European Community law is necessary to a decision may refer the matter to the European Court before reaching a conclusion in a case. It is the right of the judge or tribunal to decide on a reference, not that of the parties to the case. In the case of a court of final appeal, this right becomes an obligation. An example of this, in addition to those mentioned in paragraph 24–02, is the case of *Apple and*

Pear Development Council v. CEC (1988). The case involved a definition of the term *consideration*. While this caused little problem in the lower courts, the House of Lords found that a decision could not be reached without ensuring that the term was interpreted accurately at the European level. The case was therefore referred to the European Court of Justice from the House of Lords. In other cases, the matter has been referred directly from the VADT.[10] All decisions on such references, whether made from British courts or tribunals or from other E.U. states, bind all British courts and tribunals.

How VAT Works   24–05

As we shall see, VAT is charged on a supply of goods and services by the supplier. It is an indirect tax in the sense that it is charged as part of the purchase price for those goods and services and accounted for by the recipient of that consideration. The tax operates as a *value-added* tax. This requires an examination of the way VAT works from the viewpoint of a trader rather than on a transaction-by-transaction basis. Consider this example:

Alan owns a forest. He sells planks of wood cut from the trees. Beech buys the planks and turns them into chair frames. Caitlin buys the chair frames from Beech, upholsters them, and turns them into chairs. Den buys the chairs from Caitlin, and sells them to customers in his shop. Six of the chairs are bought by Eka for £200 each. How does VAT apply to this series of transactions? Let us assume that A, B, C, and D are all registered for VAT.

A sells the planks from which the parts are made for £10 to B. To this must be added VAT at 17.5 per cent (the appropriate rate). B therefore pays A £11.75. A keeps the £10, but pays the £1.75 to the local VAT office. B sells the chair frames to C for £30, again plus VAT. B therefore charges C £30 plus the VAT, a total of £35.25. Of the £5.25 VAT he receives, B reclaims the £1.75 paid out to A, and hands £3.50 to the VAT office. B's profit is therefore £20. Similarly D pays C £100 plus VAT for

---

[10] There will be no reference if the matter has already been resolved or is clear. But in other cases a reference will usually be made: see *e.g. Town and County Factors Ltd v. CEC* (1998).

the chairs, a total of £117.50. C recoups the £5.25 from the £17.50, handing over £12.25, and keeping a profit of £70.

E pays D £200. VAT is not added to this price, so must be included in it. E is therefore treated as paying D £170.21 plus £29.79 VAT. D keeps £17.50 of the £29.79 VAT, handing the balance of £12.29 over to the VAT office. D's profit is £70.21.

E has therefore paid VAT at the standard rate of 17.5 per cent on the full purchase price paid, the £29.79. VAT has been paid at this rate at each of the four stages of manufacture and sale of the chairs and their components. But at each stage, the seller has kept back the VAT incurred by her or him. The local VAT office has therefore collected only £29.79. A paid in £1.75, B adding £3.50, C adding a further £12.25 and D the final £12.29. This reflects the profits of A (£10), B (£20), C (£70), and D (£70.21). In other words, each has paid VAT on the value-added at that stage of production.

As this example shows, the tax is turned into a value-added tax by allowing each taxable person to collect VAT on the full sale price, but deduct from it any VAT paid out in making the sales. In VAT terms, the VAT collected by a trader is known as the *output tax* (or tax on outputs). The VAT incurred by the trader is *input tax* (or tax on inputs to the business). The VAT payable to the VAT office is the balance of output tax less input tax.

This position is complicated by the fact that there are exempt and zero-rated supplies. We shall deal with those in the next chapter. The detailed rules as to the collection and computation of the tax are also dealt with in that chapter. We must now turn to when the tax will be charged.

24–06   **When VAT Applies**

The three key questions to be answered in determining the structure of VAT are: who are the taxpayers? on what are they taxed? when, and how much, tax is paid?

In a practical sense, the taxpayers of VAT are the final consumers who buy the goods and services subject to the tax. The legal obligation to account for the tax, however, is not placed on them, but on those that supply them. These are called not taxpayers but *taxable persons* in the VAT legislation. This helps us keep in mind that the tax is imposed on transactions rather than persons, although the taxable persons are those required to collect the tax. Who are taxable persons? Section 3 (1) of the VAT Act tells us that "a person is a taxable person for the purposes of this Act while he is, or is required to be, registered under this Act." We will explore below who is in these two categories.

What is subject to VAT? Section 4(1) of the Act says that "VAT shall be charged on any supply of goods or services made in the United Kingdom, where it is a taxable supply made by a taxable person in the course or furtherance of any business carried on by him" while section 4(2) adds that a "taxable supply is a supply of goods or services made in the United Kingdom other than an exempt supply." We must add to this helpful definition the further guidance that *supply* includes all forms of supply, but not anything done otherwise than for a consideration, and that anything which is not a supply of goods but is done for a consideration (including, if so done, the granting, assignment or surrender of any right) is a supply of services (section 5(2)).

But wait a minute. VAT is a European tax. Has the British legislation carried out the requirements of European law? The key provision is Article 2 of the Sixth VAT directive. This provides that "The following shall be subject to value added tax: 1. the supply of goods or services effected for consideration within the territory of the country by a taxable person acting as such ... "

To this we must add Article 4.1 of the directive: "Taxable person" shall mean any person who independently carries out in any place any economic activity specified in paragraph 2, whatever the purpose or results of that activity.

Despite the differences in wording, the structure of the British VAT is that required in E.C. law. We should therefore read the British charging provisions in the light of the European provisions—with two cautions. The same words may appear in the two texts, but with different meanings. For example, we shall see that *taxable person* in the European text does not have the same meaning as *taxable person* in the British text. The second warning is that words in the European text may appear to be ordinary English words when they are not. *Consideration* is an example of this, as again we see below. One reason for this is that the European text exists in several equally authoritative language versions. In practice, the French version is the one that is more equal than the others.

Subject to those warnings that—as in any tax law—we must always remember precisely what each word means, we can use the two sets of provisions to state the key structure of the VAT as it applies to supplies internal to the United Kingdom.

24–07   **The Charge to VAT**

VAT applies to:

- supplies

- of goods and services

- for consideration

- other than exempt supplies

- in the United Kingdom

- by a taxable person

- as part of the economic activities of that person.

Each of these elements must be present, or be deemed to be present, before the tax operates on a supply. A supply made when one or more of the elements of the tax are missing is said to be outside the scope of the tax. It is a criminal offence deliberately to charge VAT on a supply that is outside the scope of the tax. These seven elements are therefore the necessary criteria for the operation of the tax. They are not sufficient to determine tax liability in full, but we shall examine these key issues first, then deal with the other provisions.

24–08   *Supplies*

The phrase *supplies of goods and services for consideration* should seem familiar to a student of commercial law, and who should therefore have heard of the Supply of Goods and Services Act 1982. Unfortunately, the analogy is not valid. None of the words in that phrase bear the same meaning as in English contract and commercial law, although there is a large area of overlap between the two sets of rules in practice. This is both because VAT is a European tax, and cannot be confined by the commercial rules of any one country, and also because the aim of VAT is different. It is to ensure that the tax is collected regardless of the legal niceties of a particular transaction. See, for example, the early case of *CEC v. Oliver* (1980). The High Court had to decide whether a sale through a car auction that was later established to be a void contract was a "supply". Under commercial law principles it was not, but the judge rejected the analogy and found it was a supply. More recently the ECJ has held that an illegal sale was a taxable supply where the trade could have been carried on legally. Only trades which are illegal *per se* are excluded from this application of the E.C. principle of fiscal neutrality.[11]

VAT is a tax on trading transactions, and the main base of the tax is commercial sales. More broadly, the tax operates when someone does something that realises value to that person from some other person. The word used for this is *supply*. I supply you with, say, buttered toast or a musical performance, and you pay me. But I cannot, in the ordinary sense, supply myself with the buttered toast. Nor do I supply myself with the butter or the loaf that I use to make the meal. In other words, self-supply is not a supply. Where, for example, a manufacturer makes bolts that are then used by that manufacturer in making windows to sell to others, the manufacturer supplies windows, not bolts. There must be a customer for there to be a supply.

Exceptions to this general rule exist to avoid distortion of competition in certain market sectors. The exceptions are limited, and in the United Kingdom they are confined to: self-supplies of motor vehicles by vehicle manufacturers, self-supplies of commercial buildings by building developers in certain circumstances, and self-supplies of printed stationery.

Neither British nor E.C. VAT laws define *supply*, beyond the vague guidance in the VAT Act that "supply . . . includes all forms of supply". Nor is a general definition possible. This is because the English term *supply*, useful and concise though it is, is a term untranslatable into many western European languages. There is therefore no equivalent of it in the French original E.C. text, or the German, Spanish or other official texts. Any attempt at defining supply must therefore be made in the context of the kind of supply, of goods or of services.

Despite the warning set out above, lawyers looking at the concept of a supply of goods will be tempted to turn to the commercial law of their own systems to establish when the goods transfer from supplier to customer. Under commercial law rules, that usually occurs when ownership, title, or risk transfers. Of course, if there is title reservation, then ownership does not transfer, although risk may. Is there a supply when goods are handed over, but the ownership is not, and is it relevant that risk passes? For VAT purposes, there are two issues here. First, a supply of the use of goods (for example, equipment leasing) is not a supply of goods at all—it is a supply of services. Secondly, a

---

[11] *Staatssecretaris van Financiën v. Coffeeshop Siberië vof* (1999).

supply of goods does not always take place if and when the local commercial laws determine that title has transferred. This is because supply is a European concept. The Sixth Directive, having refrained from defining supply, defines instead *supply of goods* as *the transfer of the right to dispose of tangible property as owner* (Article 5.1). Following this, the E.C.J. has ruled that in the case of a supply of goods, it is not relevant whether title to the goods has passed under the national law: *Staatssecretaris van Financiën v. SAFE BV* (1991).

VAT is therefore a tax on consumption. In *Parker Hale Ltd v. CEC* (2000) this was held to include the voluntary handing-in of handguns in return for compensation from the Government. A supply of goods would give rise to consumption wherever a right was acquired to dispose of those goods as owner. In that context the fact that the Government intended to destroy the handguns was irrelevant.

The definition of *supply* in the context of a supply of services is even more difficult to establish. It is intertwined with two other definitions, that of services, and that of consideration. This is clear from the British law itself: "anything which is not a supply of goods but is done for a consideration (including, if so done, the granting, assignment or surrender of any right) is a supply of services" (section 5(2)). In *Mirror Group Newspapers Ltd. v. C.E.C* (2000), it was accepted by the court that there were six characteristics of a supply of services. In addition to it not being a supply of goods (see the next paragraph) and being done for consideration, the characteristics are: that it must have constituted a transaction; that something must have been done by the supplier; that which was done must have been capable of being used by and for the benefit of an identified recipient; and that benefit must be regarded as a cost component of the activity of another person in the commercial chain.

24–09   *Goods and services*

There is no general definition in the United Kingdom VAT legislation of *goods*. Instead, we must turn to Schedule 4 to the VAT Act. There we are told (in paragraph 1) that a transfer of the whole property in goods is a supply of goods, but anything less is a supply of services. Likewise, the transfer of possession as part of an agreement for sale is a supply of goods, as is transfer of possession where a sale expressly contemplated. A credit sale or hire-purchase is therefore a supply of goods. Equipment leasing, where a sale might occur, is not.

The main point to grasp is that "goods and services" for VAT purposes can mean whatever the Treasury want them to mean. They can by order treat any transaction as a supply of goods, or of services, or as neither (section 5).

Land is an example of this. Land cannot be moved, so it cannot be goods. But neither is it a service. What, then, do we make of the provision that the supply of a major interest in land is a supply of goods (paragraph 3). For VAT purposes, land has to be deemed to be goods or services. This is because, as we have seen, anything which is not goods is a service. In the binary world of VAT, a sale of land, or of a lease of more than 21 years (a major interest: section 96) is a supply of goods. All else to do with land is a supply of services.

The same is true of other forms of property that do not naturally fit into the deliberately simplified framework of VAT. Supplies of intellectual property, and of the right to use that property are alike treated as supplies of services, even when title is transferred. (This is implied by paragraph 1 of Schedule 5.) Supplies of electricity and similar intangibles are supplies of goods (Schedule 4, paragraph 3).

Tricky problems also occur where a supply is both goods and services. For example, the supply of buttered toast is a supply of the butter, the bread, and the effort of toasting and buttering the bread. Is that goods or services or both? The practical answer may be that it does not matter. The difference between goods and services is only of importance if it changes the amount of tax due, or when the tax is due. The only general difference between goods and service lies in the timing rules about when supplies occur. Otherwise, the problem is the more detailed one of whether a particular supply is charged at one rate of VAT or another. In our example, the tax rate on buttered toast is different to the tax rate on a loaf of bread, so the detail is important. We return to it when we deal with tax rates.

Consideration 24–10

A supply is only subject to VAT if it is made *for consideration*, or is deemed to be made for consideration. The idea behind this requirement is an economic one. To be taxable, a transaction must be one that adds value. Consequently, unless in some way value is realised from a supply, there is nothing to tax. In practice, value is realised if the supplier gets paid for the supply. If nobody pays, there is no added value. It is in this way that the rule has been interpreted by the European Court, in a case which nicely illustrates the clash between traditional English thinking and the more general approach required for VAT.

In *Apple and Pear Development Council v. CEC* (1988), the Council carried out two groups of activities. The first group was of ordinary trading activities. The second group comprised activities financed by a statutory levy, and required by the law establishing the Council. The Council claimed that all its activities were for consideration. Much of the argument about this was framed in terms of the English law of contract. Was the statutory levy consideration for the supplies made to those who paid the levy of the statutory services? The case was argued in this way until it came to the House of Lords. The House noted that the point was one of European law, not English law, and found a reference to the ECJ was necessary.

The European Court noted that the question was a general one. Based on a linguistic analysis of the multilingual forms of the texts of the directives, the court laid down the test that there must be a payment for a supply, and that the payment and supply must be directly linked. In accordance with practice, the European Court left it for the national court to determine whether there was a direct link on the facts of the particular case.

The direct link test means that not all supplies for which payments are made are supplies for consideration (or against payment). There must be a legal relationship between the parties, reciprocal performance and the remuneration received must constitute the value actually given by the provider. The European Court itself has ruled in several cases that there was no such direct link; *e.g.* donations to a street musician,[12] payments to a farmer in return for not using land,[13] and the provision of free transport by an employer for its employees.[14]

In the United Kingdom the issue has arisen mainly in connection with supplies by clothing and other companies through "hostesses" holding parties in their own homes. Thus in *Rosgill Group Ltd v. CEC* (1997) at such a party sufficient goods were sold to entitle the hostess either to take a cash commission of £2.89 or to obtain a discount on a blouse of £7.23. She chose the latter, thus paying some £20 for a blouse priced at £28. The Court of Appeal held that the consideration for the supply of the blouse by the company to the hostess was not only the cash she paid but also the holding of the party. There was a direct link between the latter and the supply of the blouse, both con-

---

[12] *Tolsma v. Inspecteur der Omzetbelasting Leenwarden* (1994).
[13] *Landboden-Agrardienste GmbH & Co KG v. Finanzamt Calau* (1998).
[14] *Julius Fillibeck Söhne GmbH & Co KG v. Finanzamt Neustadt* (1998).

tractually (she was entitled to the discount) and causatively (without the party there would have been no supply of the blouse at the reduced price).

A similar direct link was found in *CEC v. Littlewoods Organisation plc* (2000) in relation to the enhancement of commission (up from 10 to 12.5 per cent) credited to an agent selling catalogue goods to others, where the agent used the commission earned to purchase goods for herself rather than taking cash. The only reason for the increased commission was the option to do so under the agency agreement. Thus there was both a contractual and causative link between the services supplied by the agent and the additional amount credited to her.

In a different type of case, *CEC v. Church Schools Foundation Ltd* (2000), the necessary requirements of a legal relationship and reciprocal performance between the money paid and the services performed, were found to exist where the company running the church schools made grants to the foundation (which owned them) with the joint intention that those grants should be used by the foundation in upgrading school premises. Thus there was a supply of services by the foundation to the company in return for a consideration (the grants).

Specific problems concerning supplies   24–11

The basic requirement of a supply of goods or services for a consideration has led to a number of specific problems for the courts to deal with. Three of these are sufficiently fundamental to VAT as to require some consideration at this point.

IDENTIFYING WHAT IS SUPPLIED AND TO WHOM. VAT depends upon a supply to fix upon for there to be a charge. Sometimes identifying exactly who is supplying what and to whom is far from straightforward, but by doing so the VAT position is thereby clarified. To take just three examples. In *CEC v. Diners Club Ltd* (1989) an everyday cash card transaction whereby the card holder used his card to buy goods from a retailer so that there was an assignment of the debt by the retailer to the card company and the payment of that debt by the company less commission, was held to constitute a supply of financial services by the card company to the retailer, in addition to the supply by the retailer to the card company. In *Trustees of Nell Gwyn House Maintenance Fund v. CEC* (1999) the trustees of a maintenance fund for a block of flats were required and did employ staff to provide maintenance, etc., of the building. The House of Lords held that they were supplying the whole services of the staff to the tenants (*i.e.* the total cost of the operation) and not just the act of arranging for the staff to work (*i.e.* the organisation costs only). There is a clear distinction between A paying B for services to be provided by B, and A putting B in funds so that B could arrange for C to provide the services. This was clearly the former.

In *CEC v. Plantiflor Ltd* (2000) the company supplied plants to customers partly by mail order. Delivery, if requested, was by Parcelforce and £2.50 was charged for postage and packing of which £1.63 related to the charge by Parcelforce. The Court of Appeal held that there were three supplies. The first was of the goods by Plantiflor to the customer; the second was of the service of arranging delivery of the goods and packaging the goods, also by Plantiflor to the customer; and the third was of the actual delivery which was supplied by Parcelforce to the customer. There was no fourth supply of services by Parcelforce to Plantiflor. On that analysis the consideration for the supply by Plantiflor to the customer could not include the £1.63 since it was the consideration for the supply by Parcelforce to the customer and to hold otherwise would be to impose VAT twice on the same consideration (although in that case the supply by Parcelforce was in fact an exempt supply).

SINGLE TRANSACTION—MULTIPLE OR SEPARATE SUPPLIES. What is the position when in return for a single consideration a person receives several benefits? Are these separate supplies as in the *Plantiflor* case just discussed, (so that some might be exempt or taxed at different rates) or can they be taken together to form a single supply? If the answer is the latter then a second question is whether that multiple supply is exempt, etc.

This problem has arisen several times. In *British Airways plc v. CEC* (1990)[15] the Court of Appeal held that a supply of in-flight catering on a domestic flight was integral to the flight itself and so was not a separate supply. In *CEC v. United Biscuits (UK) Ltd* (1992) the Court of Session in deciding that a supply of biscuits in a decorative tin was a supply of biscuits which happened to be in such a container and not a separate supply of the biscuits and container, said that the test was whether one supply was either an integral part of the other or incidental to it. In *CEC v. Wellington Hospital* (1997) the Court of Appeal said that in applying this test it was not appropriate to look at the whole transaction and see whether one part of it was ancillary to the whole, but rather to

---

[15] See also *Virgin Atlantic Airways Ltd v. CEC* (1995).

ask whether one element was so dominated by another that it lost its separate identity for tax purposes.

The situation was clarified by the ECJ in *Card Protection Plan Ltd v. CEC* (1999). It is essential to identify the essential features of the transaction. There will be a single supply if one or more elements can be regarded as the principal supply and others can be regarded as ancillary. "Ancillary" in this context means that it does not constitute an aim in itself but only a means for customers of enjoying the principal service supplied. Itemising the different services in price terms might be significant, but is not conclusive This approach has since been followed by the House of Lords in *CEC v. BT plc* (1999) in relation to a delivery charge imposed on the purchase of a new car, and the Court of Appeal in *Pilgrims Language Courses Ltd v. CEC* (1999) to the provision of accommodation, etc., on residential educational courses. In both cases there was found to be a single supply of the car and the teaching respectively. The House of Lords stressed that the commercial reality of the situation should be looked at.

In *Co-operative Wholesale Society Ltd v. CEC* (1999), however, Keene J. held that where there were two distinct elements to the supply, which were alternatives for the customer, it could not be said that one was ancillary or incidental to the other. In *Sea Containers Services Ltd v. CEC* (2000), the same judge held that where part of the supply constituted a separate aim in itself it could not be regarded as incidental or ancillary to the other part and the fact that it only accounted for 17 per cent of the consideration did not alter that fact.

In *CEC v. FDR* (2000), the Court of Appeal adopted the following approach, without intending to lay down any rules, to this question of multiple supplies. The first thing is to identify, if possible, what the "core" activities of the supplier are and then to consider whether there are other supplies which are ancillary to the core. This may produce one of three results. One is that there is a single core activity (referred to as the "apex"); the second is that the core involves a number of supplies which are integral to each other (referred to as the "table-top"), in addition, in either case, to the ancillary supplies; and the third is that there are no core as distinct from ancillary supplies—they are all equal for VAT purposes. In the apex model the VAT treatment of the core and ancillary supplies will be determined by the status of the single core supply. In the table-top model it will be necessary to look again at the elements of the core supplies to determine the taxable status of the core on the facts (*e.g.* by a numerical process) and then apply that to both the integral core and ancillary supplies. If it is not possible to separate out core supplies from ancillary supplies, then there can be no such single application of VAT status and each supply must be dealt with separately[16].

WHERE THERE ARE TWO SUPPLIES TO DIFFERENT CUSTOMERS BUT ONLY ONE PAYMENT OF CONSIDERATION BY ONE CUSTOMER. This problem arises because just as in income tax, and for similar reasons, VAT has a rule that where a business makes a supply of business assets otherwise than for a consideration then there is a deemed supply at the cost to the supplier (Schedule 4 paragraph 5).[17] In *CEC v. Telemed Ltd* (1992), Telemed produced medical videos which it distributed free to doctors. The videos contained advertisements for drug companies for which it charged a fee. It was argued that the company was therefore making two supplies, one of the services to the drug companies for a fee and one of the videos to the doctors which were caught by paragraph 5. This was rejected by the judge on the basis that the company only supplied the videos as part of its contractual obligation to the advertisers. This approach was followed by the House of Lords in *CEC v. Professional Footballers Association* (1993) in deciding that trophies presented at an annual dinner and met out of the cost of tickets for the dinner were not separate supplies under paragraph 5. There was a direct link between the consideration paid for the tickets and the awards.

24–12 *Taxable supplies and exempt supplies*

All supplies within the scope of the tax are taxable supplies unless they are exempt supplies (VAT Act, s.4 (2)). A supply is exempt if, and only if, it is one of the kinds of supply listed in Schedule 9 to the 1994 Act. This copies into the United Kingdom law directly operative provisions of E.C. law. Exemption covers some major kinds of economic activity such as financial supplies and many kinds of health, education and welfare activity. We examine some of these at paragraph 25–03 when discussing liability to VAT.

24–13 *Taxable persons*

The structure of European VAT is such that anyone making a taxable supply for consideration can be regarded as a taxable person. United Kingdom VAT does not work this way. Instead, it

---

[16] See *e.g. Bothupswana National Corporation Ltd v. CEC* (1993).

[17] Such as gifts given by petrol companies to customers who have collected vouchers: *Kuwait Petroleum GB Ltd v. CEC* (1999).

sets a threshold of activity before the imposition is necessary. Anyone whose level of activities is at or above the level of the threshold is required to register with the VAT office for the locality, and to impose VAT on all taxable supplies made. If there is a failure to register, VAT will be deemed to have been charged by the taxpayer. Those not required to register may, however do so on a voluntary basis.

For VAT purposes, a *person* is any individual or any body of persons with separate legal personality that is engaged in economic activities. This includes non-profit organisations that do not pay income tax or corporation tax such as charities and clubs as well as companies. It also includes any national or local government body. For this reason, a government department may charge VAT on its supplies. This is to prevent distortions in competition between commercial organisations and other bodies. As a result, many organisations not required to make returns for direct tax purposes have to comply with the VAT rules. In addition, a partnership is also treated as a separate person (unlike the income tax approach). A partnership is therefore separate from the individual partners.

Companies and other large organisations can register divisions or separate parts of the organisation separately. For example, if only part of an organisation is making supplies to which VAT applies, that part can register separately from any other part. This excludes those other parts from the requirements of VAT, but it also means that any supplies made by that part of the organisation to the other parts are subject to VAT.

By contrast, a group of companies can make a common registration for VAT in the name of one of the companies. Where this happens, supplies between companies within the group are outside the scope of the tax. It is only supplies by the group to others that are caught. For this purpose, two companies are in a group if both are based in the United Kingdom and one controls the other or both are controlled by the same third person (VAT Act, s.43A). Each of the companies must be involved in an economic activity, so that a company that is purely a holding company has to be left out (*Polsar Investments* (1993)). This sensible idea of grouping has been abused widely. The result is that strict anti-avoidance provisions were introduced by the Finance Acts 1996 and 1999, allowing spurious use of grouping to be counteracted.

A person (in the sense just described) is required to register for VAT if the total turnover from taxable supplies in any period of 12 months is £52,000 or more or if there are reasonable grounds to believe that the rates of taxable supplies in the next 30 days will exceed £52,000. (These are the 2000 figures—they are adjusted

379

every year.) Any exempt supplies or supplies outside the scope of VAT are excluded from the total. The total is calculated on the assumption that no VAT is charged on the supplies. Note that the amount is for turnover, not profit. It is irrelevant that the person is making a loss, or is not in business to make a profit. It also applies to persons, not to businesses. If I run two businesses, one as a farmer, and one as a sports journalist, I must account for total turnover from both my activities even though they may be treated separately for income tax purposes. The test is applied each month on a rolling basis. However, if the person can show that supplies for the current year are below £50,000 (in 2000), then the requirement to register does not apply. There is some scope for abuse of this provision by dividing turnover between different legal persons to ensure each is below the limit. Where that happens, the VAT office has the right to impose a group registration to bring all the associated avoiders into the tax net.

A person not required to register under any of these provisions has the right to register on a voluntary basis. Why should anyone want to become a taxpayer voluntarily? In the case of a tax like income tax, there are few, if any, good reasons. VAT is not a tax like income tax. As we shall see later, a VAT payer may actually receive money from the government, rather than pay it. Few businesses can resist a government handout!

A further reason is that those who are registered for VAT usually prefer to buy from others who are registered—it is cheaper. Someone who expects to have to register a business in any event may find it advantageous to register before being compelled to do so. Not all traders that could ask for voluntary registration do so. Some refrain from registering in order to avoid VAT. The joke is that they end up paying more VAT by doing so! We see why in the next chapters.

Economic activities

The final element in the structure of VAT is that activities are only relevant if they are economic activities of the taxable person (in European law) or, in the United Kingdom text, *in the course or furtherance of a business carried on by him*. In this phrase, business is defined as including any trade profession or vocation (section 94). In practice, although the United Kingdom legislation has continued to use the reference to business, it is more helpful to think of the more general, and broader, European phrase. In part, this is because it is clear that VAT is wider than the implicit reference in section 94 to Schedule D, Cases I and II of the Taxes

Act might imply. Most things within Schedule A are also within the scope of the tax, as are many things within Cases V and VI of Schedule D. So also are many situations where the charge to capital gains tax or its corporate equivalent will apply.

The early cases concentrated on the meaning of a "business". Thus in *CEC. v. Royal Exchange Theatre Trust* (1999) the raising of money by a charitable trust to convert the Manchester Corn Exchange into a theatre and the subsequent gift of the theatre was held not to be a business. Similarly a charity that supplied goods to beneficiaries without payment, or for a token fee, was not acting as a business: *Whitechapel Art Gallery v. CEC* (1986), where the running of an art gallery to which free admission was granted was accepted as outside the scope of VAT. An interesting example of a marginal case is the decision in *Lord Fisher v. CEC* (1981), which established that shooting (and equally hunting and fishing) one's own land with one's own friends contributing to one's costs is not always a business.

More recent cases have, however, been argued on the basis of the "economic activities" test in the Directive. The House of Lords in *ICAEW v. CEC* (1999) had to decide whether the regulatory services provide by the Institute of Chartered Accountants on behalf of the Government in respect of insolvency practitioners, licensed auditors, etc., fell within VAT. After reviewing the decisions of the ECJ, they held that the Institute was not carrying on an economic activity. It was not enough that it was making supplies for a consideration, there was no element of commercial activity. What was needed were activities of an economic nature. Their Lordships also thought that the United Kingdom test of a business also required an economic content, so that the Institute were not carrying on a business.

The tax applies to economic activities of taxable persons *acting as such*. An individual buying a house to live in, or buying a car for private use, is not engaging in an economic activity but a private activity. This is true also when the house or car is sold. There is a complication here to which we must return. If a private person sells a car, there is no VAT on the sale. If a car dealer sells it, there is VAT. The same thing applies to antiques, and to horses and ponies. Whether VAT applies therefore partly depends on the identity of the seller, not the kind of goods. This can cause problems, and special rules apply to these occasional or second-hand goods.

24–14   *Agents and employees*

VAT only applies to the person carrying on the economic activity or business. The most important group of people excluded from VAT by this rule are employees. An employee is carrying on the employer's business as agent, and is not in business by himself or herself. VAT therefore does not apply to the payment of earnings by employer to employee. If the employee's services are supplied to some third party, any VAT is applied to the charge made by the employer to the third party for those services. The effect of this important exclusion is that the added value on which someone is charged includes the total of all payments to employees.

The rule applies to office holders such as company directors as well, unless the office holder is holding that office as part of a separate business. For example, a partner in a firm of solicitors may act as a director of a client's business in order to advise the client. Fees paid to the director, or the partnership, should be subject to VAT (section 94(4)). This may be contrasted with the purist view under which such fees can only be subject to Schedule E income tax, not Schedule D (*IRC v. Brander and Cruickshank* (1969)). This also means that a one-person company that pays out its profits to its owner as an employee is in the same position for VAT purposes as a company that pays out the profits to its owner as a dividend (dividends also being outside the scope of the tax).

Behind this rule is a distinction also of fundamental importance for income tax. Is an individual working as an employee or as a self-employed person? The borderline between the two is the borderline between Schedule D and Schedule E for income tax purposes. Nor is there any different definition for VAT purposes than that for income tax purposes—whether taxpayers are in business on their own. Or, as the E.C. Directive has it, a taxable person *acting as such*.

The position is more complex for other agents. By definition, an agent is someone making supplies on behalf of someone else. If the person is an agent rather than an independent contractor, the supply is not made by the agent but by the agent's principal. Take the case of an auctioneer. The auctioned goods are not owned by the auctioneer, but the buyer usually does not know the identity of the seller. The buyer of, say, antique furniture has therefore no way of knowing if the seller is a registered person for VAT purposes, or whether the sale is an economic activity within the scope of VAT. At the same time, the only activity on which an auctioneer is liable for VAT as an agent is the service as an agent. To avoid complications, auctioneers and other agents where the agency is not disclosed are treated as making the supplies themselves. If the agency is disclosed, the VAT is imposed by the principal.

COMPUTATION AND PAYMENTS

If the British VAT were a simple form of value-added tax with a single rate, the previous chapter would have covered many of the problems. It is not, and it does not. In this chapter therefore we must discuss the rate structure of the tax, the extensive way in which exemptions apply to the tax, how the value of a taxable supply is found and the rules as to the payment of the tax, including how input tax is deducted.

25–01 ## The VAT Rate Structure

The simplest form of VAT would have one rate of VAT applying equally to all goods and services. But the United Kingdom structure is far more complex.

Article 12 of the E.C. Sixth VAT Directive imposes a two-rate structure on the VAT of the Member States: a main rate of not less than 15 per cent, and a lower rate of between 4 per cent and 9 per cent . . . or so it says. In fact, it allows for several other rates as well.

The United Kingdom rate structure has the following rates:

- a standard rate of 17.5 per cent;
- a reduced rate, of 5 per cent, on domestic fuel supplies, the installation of energy-saving materials in residential accomodation, the installation of central heating systems and home security goods under government-funded schemes for certain pensioners, and the installation of heating system measures under government-funded schemes for the less well-off (see Schedule A1 for details);
- special rates for special regimes, such as the 4 per cent flat rate scheme for farmers;
- 0 per cent (the zero-rate) both for international supplies and a wide range of UK supplies (see para. 25–02, below).

In addition, there are supplies outside the scope of the tax, exempt supplies, and supplies deemed not to be supplies or either goods or services.

As a result, the United Kingdom has one of the most complex rate structures for VAT in the developed world. The structure gives scope for many disputes and distortions to competition. The United Kingdom also has the only major system to use its VAT as a subsidy for certain kinds of domestic activity. Why? The zero-rates reflect the exemptions that used to apply to taxes before VAT. However, the zero-rate in VAT is not the same thing as a zero sales tax. It is in reality a subsidy resulting in regular repayments of tax to those who sell zero-rated goods because since they are still making taxable supplies, they will have no output tax (zero-rated) but will be able to reclaim their input tax. Add to the predictable consumers' resistance at a rate increase, the pressure to retain the monthly tax rebate paid to those who are zero-rated, and we see why the lobby for the status quo is a strong one. This is so although it makes the British VAT one of the most inefficient around. We see a similar situation in the lower rate of VAT on fuel supplies. The debate over the attempt to increase the VAT on domestic fuel to the standard rate from a zero-rate resulted in a government defeat in the Commons and the original compromise of 8 per cent has since been reduced to 5 per cent. It is precisely because of this that we must spend some time looking at the rate structure.

There is a strict order for determining at what rate, if any, VAT applies to a supply:

1. Exclude any supply that is outside the scope of the tax, or deemed not to be a supply of goods or services. If it is not excluded:
2. See if the supply is one of those listed as zero-rated. If it is not listed:
3. See if the supply is exempt. If it is not exempt:
4. See if any special tax regime or reduced rate applies. If it does not:
5. Apply the standard rate.

The order is important because it means that anything to which a special category does not apply is to be taxed at the standard rate, without exception. We noted the scope of the tax in the last chapter and the categories of reduced rate supplies at the beginning of this chapter, but we must now explore zero-rating, exemption, and the special regimes.

25–02   *Zero-rated supplies*

A supply is zero-rated if it is listed in Schedule 8 to the 1994 Act. The Schedule is divided into (currently) 16 groups, several of which are of considerable complexity.

Several themes run through the Schedule. The first is of international supplies: see Group 7 (international services), Group 8 (transport), Group 10 (gold), Group 13 (imports, exports, etc.) and Group 14 (tax-free shops) for the main relevant groups. The policy here is to ensure that no British VAT gets hidden in the cost of any goods or services offered on the international market. Any VAT imposed on a supply or its inputs in the United Kingdom before export is therefore rebated in full, and no VAT is applied on export. The purpose is to keep British goods and services as competitive as possible.

A second theme is that of supplies of a social or community nature. These include: Group 1 (food), Group 2 (domestic sewerage and water supplies), Group 3 (books), Group 4 (talking books for the blind), Group 5 (construction of homes and some other buildings), Group 6 (listed buildings), Group 8 (transport), Group 9 (houseboats and caravans used as homes), Group 12 (medicines), Group 15 (charities), and Group 16 (children's clothes and protective clothing).

The reason for zero-rating these supplies is linked in part to the underlying E.C. law. That lays down those forms of supply that should be exempted, leaving others to be taxed. Most states taxed them at a reduced level, but this has been deemed politically inappropriate in the United Kingdom, so they have been zero-rated. This practice was sanctioned by the ECJ as being compatible with the Directive in *EC Commission v. UK* (1988). It follows that, unlike exempt supplies, the categories of zero-rated supplies are a matter for United Kingdom legislation. The Sixth Directive does not specify a particular rate of tax for any taxable supply and so the Court of Appeal in *Marks and Spencer plc v. CEC* (2000) refused a challenge to zero-rating based on direct effect.

Zero-rating is, however, expensive to the Treasury. It involves actually paying out money. Governments have been quietly reducing the scope for this since they introduced the tax.

One result of this and the benefits of zero-rating is that the Schedule is now of considerable complexity. Each group contains a detailed list of what exactly amounts to a zero-rated supply. By way of illustration let us look at Group 1 which is headed "Food". This is defined as any supply within four categories of which the most important is food of a kind used for human consumption. But that general class is subject to no less than seven lists of excepted items, which are therefore standard rated, unless they fall within a further seven further lists of items overriding those excepted items, in which case they become zero-rated again. The intention is, we assume, to charge non-basic foodstuffs but to zero-rate the essentials of life. Thus zero-rating does not apply for example to confectionery but it does apply to cakes and biscuits "other than biscuits wholly or partly covered with chocolate or some product similar in taste and appearance". This means that, for reasons which are not entirely clear, chocolate cakes are zero-rated but chocolate biscuits are standard-rated. That in turn leads to disputes as to whether a particular product is a cake or a biscuit or neither.[1]

There is also a general exception to zero-rating for a supply "in the course of catering". That in turn is defined as including a supply of food for consumption on the premises on which it is supplied (*i.e.* food eaten in a restaurant or café) and any supply of *hot* food for consumption off the premises.[2] What is meant by hot food in this context is further defined as food which has been heated "for the purposes of enabling it to be consumed at a temperature above the ambient air temperature" and at the time of the supply is above that temperature. Such detailed statutory wording has inevitably led to disputes as to how it is to be applied in practice. In *John Pimblett and Sons Ltd v. CEC* (1988), the Court of Appeal, no less, were faced with the situation of a retail baker who sold fresh pies for consumption off the premises. Fresh pies are of necessity hot. The Court of Appeal held that the predominant purpose of the baker was to supply fresh and not hot pies so that they did not fall within the definition.[3]

Other groups have also led to litigation. Thus in Group 3 (Books, etc.), we have legal definitions as to what amounts to books[4] and newspapers[5] and in Group 8 (Transport) detailed

---

[1] See *e.g.* *CEC v. Ferrero UK Ltd* (1997) as to the position of wafer products.
[2] Because that definition is inclusive only it means that even cold food supplied in the course of catering may be standard-rated. In such a case it has been held that what amounts to a supply in the course of catering is to be decided by giving those words their ordinary meaning, so that where customers bought a "party tray" from the delicatessen counter of a supermarket, which had been pre-ordered, that was not a supply in the course of catering since most people would regard the hostess and not the supermarket as doing the catering: *CEC v. Safeway Stores plc* (1997).
[3] See also *Malik v. CEC* (1998) on the position of food which was cooked and then kept hot before delivery.
[4] *Odhams Leisure Group Ltd v. CEC* (1992); *CEC v. Colour Offset Ltd* (1995).
[5] *Geoffrey E Snushall Ltd v. CEC* (1982).

reasons as to why a roller coaster could not be included as being the transport of passengers.[6]

25–03   *Exempt supplies*

A supply is exempt if it is within the terms of Schedule 9. The Schedule presents a similar exercise to Schedule 8, and again contains several themes. The chief difference is that behind Schedule 9 are detailed provisions in Article 13 (A, B, and C) of the Sixth Directive. The details of this Schedule are therefore decided by reference to the Directive, as interpreted by the ECJ. The exemptions are construed strictly but not so as to go against the express wording. Where the United Kingdom provision is wider than the Directive it is not open to the Customs and Excise to rely on the Directive although, of course, the UK wording will have to be changed.[7]

For that reason, of strict construction, the meaning of education (one of the groups of exempt supplies) was construed as meaning a course, or a class or lesson of instruction rather than in the broader sense of widening the mind, by Carnwath J. in the *North of England Zoological Society v. CEC* (1999). The context of the Directive pointed that way.

One group of exemptions deals with supplies where it has proved extremely difficult to apply VAT. The main group of this kind is Group 5 (financial services), and linked with it is Group 2 (insurance). The chief problem is isolating the value-added in a financial supply such as a loan, or under insurance against a risk. There are also complexities in some kinds of supplies of land (Group 1), and in betting (Group 4). In practice, it can prove easier to put excise taxes on these kinds of supply, and leave them excluded from VAT. This happens in most European countries (including the United Kingdom) with insurance and betting and with many land transactions. The question of VAT on financial supplies also causes a direct overlap with income tax.

A second group of supplies are those made to individuals rather than for commercial purposes, and left out for social reasons. These include education (Group 6), health and welfare (Group 7), burials (Group 8), and community activities including associations (Group 9), sports events (Group 10) and charity fund-raising (Group 12). The oddments include postal services (Group 3). Why add VAT to stamps when the state runs the

---

[6]   *CEC v. Blackpool Pleasure Beach Co* (1974).
[7]   See *CEC v. Civil Service Motoring Association Ltd* (1998), *per* Mummery L.J.

postal service? Another is works of art (if there is an IHT or CGT exemption applying).

Zero-rating and exemption compared   25–04

The reason for zero-rating is the need to impose tax on supplies that cannot be exempted under E.C. law. Ironically, however, zero-rating is more advantageous than exemption, so the effect in the United Kingdom of the European rule is the reverse of that intended. For this reason the E.C. Commission objected for many years to British zero-rating. As a result, it forced several previously zero-rated supplies to be either exempted or taxed at the standard rate.

Zero-rating is known in E.C. circles as exemption with credit. They intend this to emphasise the fact that those making zero-rated supplies can claim refunds for input tax incurred for the purpose of those supplies. This is because they are technically taxable supplies, although no new tax will be paid. By contrast, an exempt supply is one for which no input tax credit is possible. The comparative effect of these categories depends on the identities both of suppliers and those being supplied.

It is largely a matter of indifference to taxable persons receiving inputs to make taxable supplies whether the inputs are taxed at the standard rate or at a zero-rate. The only difference is one of cash-flow. They must pay the input tax on the standard-rated supply before reclaiming it. By contrast, an exempt supply to a taxable person is more expensive. This is because the supplier will probably pass on any input tax as part of the non-taxable price for the supply. The recipient therefore pays for that VAT, but cannot reclaim it. In other words, a taxable person would rather buy supplies taxed at the standard rate than exempt supplies. This also explains why taxable persons may prefer to deal with a registered supplier rather than a supplier that chooses to remain unregistered when under the compulsory limit for registration.

An ordinary consumer cannot claim back any VAT. Nor can a claim be made by someone who makes only exempt supplies, or who is not registered for VAT. In each case, they have to bear the cost of VAT whether it is express or hidden. For them, therefore, zero-rated supplies are better than exempt supplies, because there is less total VAT. For them exempt supplies *are* taxed supplies, while zero-rate taxable supplies are not.

25–05 *Partial exemption*

A problem arises for those who make both taxable supplies and exempt supplies, whether or not they are mixed. The supplier, if registered, is entitled to an input tax credit for input tax incurred for the purpose of taxable supplies. It is not entitled to a tax credit in respect of input tax for exempt supplies. Anyone in this position must therefore take steps to identify which inputs relate to the taxable supplies, and which relate to the exempt supplies. The ECJ has rules in *Midland Bank plc v. CEC* (2000) that there must be an immediate and direct link between a particular input transaction and a taxable rather than an exempt output transaction for the input tax to be deductible. Some of the complexities of this are discussed in paragraph 25–12 below. In practice many input supplies are linked to both exempt and taxable output supplies, *e.g.* electricity used by a shop which sells both taxable and exempt goods. Many such traders agree a percentage with their local VAT offices so that, for example, they can claim 60 per cent of the input tax as a fair share of total inputs.

25–06 *Special regimes*

VAT also lends itself to the development of a multiplicity of special schemes. As with the schedules on zero-rating and exemption, we derive little benefit from a detailed study of these schemes, but they do solve some tricky practical problems.

One series of special schemes (provided for in official Notices in the 727 series) is that for retailers. These are designed to deal with the problems of those selling a mixture of goods that are taxed at different rates, or are exempt. Examples are the supermarket, high-street retailers and even the corner shop. They can agree with the local VAT office to avoid having to make separate calculations of VAT on every sale, or having to separate zero-rated goods from standard-rated goods.

Another set of special schemes are those dealing with goods sold by dealers but bought by them from private customers. For example, if I sell my private car to a dealer, I add no VAT to it. But I bought my car from a garage and paid VAT when I did so. If the dealer charges VAT on the whole price of the car when selling it to another customer, it is being double taxed. To avoid this, a *margin scheme* operates. In effect, the dealer has to account for VAT only on the difference between the price paid to me and the price for which the car is sold. Similar regimes apply to antiques.

A further group who get special attention are farmers. The problem here is the assumed aversion of farmers from keeping accounts. Yet someone buying from a farmer wants an input tax credit for any supply, on which the farmer would charge VAT. The compromise, made at European level, is a deemed input tax equal to 4 per cent of the output.

Having established that there is a charge to VAT and what the appropriate rate is, the final questions for domestic supplies are: what is the value of the supply so that the amount can be calculated? When is that tax charged? And how is it actually accounted for to the Customs and Excise?

Valuation   25–07

On how much do we impose the VAT? Section 19 of the 1994 Act provides that where the consideration for a supply is in monetary form, the value is the amount that, when the VAT is added, equals the consideration. For example, if the price I pay for a supply is £117.50, the VAT rate being 17.5 per cent, then the value of the supply for VAT purposes is £100. Similarly, if the price I pay is £100, then the value of the supply is £85.10, with VAT of £14.90 *i.e.* 17.5 per cent of £85.50 payable. This suggests that if we offer you a price for a product, the price is VAT-inclusive, rather than VAT-exclusive.

Section 19 is the United Kingdom's implementation of Article 11A of the Directive, which has direct effect. As originally enacted it was found to be inconsistent with some of the provisions of Article 11A and was amended in 1992 to provide only the general rules set out above. Article 11A is in fact far more detailed and so all the recent disputes as to valuation of a supply have in fact been decided by reference to that Article rather than the section.

Article 11A(1) provides that the taxable amount of a supply is "everything which constitutes the consideration which has been or is to be obtained by the purchaser, the customer or a third party for the supply, including subsidies directly linked to the price of such supplies". Article 11A(2) provides that this is to include any incidental expenses and taxes other than VAT itself. What is an incidental expense depends upon first deciding exactly what the supply amounts to. If the supply, properly ascertained, consists of two elements, X and Y, it is not then permissible to use Article 11A(2) to argue that X is an incidental expense of Y for the purpose of whether there is a single supply in which X is subsumed into Y. Article 11A applies only therefore to determine the value of the consideration so ascertained (*i.e.* X and Y). Thus in *CEC v. BT plc* (1999) where the House of Lords held that the supply was a composite supply both of a new car and its delivery direct to the customer, it could not be said that the delivery costs were incidental expenses of the supply of the car under Article 11A(2).

This distinction between the consideration for a supply and the value of that supply for VAT purposes arose in relation to the question as to whether a subsidy is part of the value of a supply under Article 11A(1). In *Keeping Newcastle Warm v. CEC* (2000), there was no dispute that a flat rate £10 subsidy, paid under a Government scheme for assisting energy savings, formed part of the consideration for the supply of energy saving advice by the suppliers. But they argued that since this subsidy was not linked to the price of the supplies it did not fall to be included in the value of the supply within the wording of Article 11A(1). The judge accepted that there could be a difference between the consideration for, and the value of, a supply. He then referred to the ECJ the issue as to whether subsidies which are not linked to the price of a supply (and so not expressly included in the wording of Article 11A(1)) could still form part of the value of that supply.

The value of a supply is therefore inextricably linked to the consideration for the supply, which as we have seen in the previous chapter means what is received as a direct link for the supply. It is important to stress again that it is necessary first to decide precisely what the supply is, and what the consideration for it is, before applying any part of Article 11A. Article 11A (including the permitted deductions set out below) cannot be used in that process; it is concerned only with the value of the consideration of that supply once ascertained. Thus in the *Trustees of Nell Gwyn House Maintenance Fund v. CEC* (1999) where, as we have seen, it was held that the trustees were supplying to the tenants of a block of flats not only the maintenance staff but also the whole costs of the maintenance of the block, it was not permissible to then argue that the payments for the staff were received from the tenants as repayment for expenses paid out on their behalf under Article 11A(3)(c), discussed below.

25–08   *Non-cash consideration*

Where there is an element of non-cash consideration involved in the supply, the question is of course what monetary value to give it. There have been many European and United Kingdom cases on which formula is to be used. The situation seems to have clarified itself, however, into deciding in each case what is the "subjective value" of the consideration to the supplier. Sometimes this is an approximate value which the parties can be said, either expressly or impliedly, to have attributed to the consideration which, particularly in the case of services is otherwise difficult to value. This is the case in the "hostess" cases such as *Rosgill Group v. CEC* (1997). In that case, the consideration and therefore the value of the supply was not just the cash paid by the hostess for the blouse (remember she paid about £20 for a blouse worth £28 retail) but also the fact that she had held a party. The latter was non-cash consideration which had therefore to be given a monetary value. In that case that the value to the supplier of the services of providing the party was found on the attribution principle to be the cash discount on the blouse (£8) which she had received as a result of holding the party. In such cases the fact that the goods supplied in return for services have a catalogue price makes the attribution of the monetary value straightforward. A similar result obtained in *CEC v. Littlewoods Organisation plc* (2000) in relation to the reduction in price of catalogue goods in return for the services of agents in selling such goods to others. If no such attribution by the parties can be discovered, however, the monetary value of the supply is the cost to the supplier.

It follows that the key question is whether the parties have attributed a value to the non-cash consideration.

In *CEC v. Westmorland Motorway Services Ltd* (1998) a coach driver was provided by the motorway service station with a free meal if he took a coach party of 20 or more people there and remained there for at least half an hour. Clearly there was a supply of a meal to the driver for a consideration but what was its monetary value? There were two possible cash valuations: what it cost the service station to provide the meal (cost price) or some other (higher) value attributed to it by the parties (*i.e.* in this case what it would have cost the driver to buy the meal—the retail price). The Court of Appeal held that on the facts the parties had impliedly attributed the latter value. That result is less likely where there is no retail price for the goods because they are not available for general purchase[8] in which case the value will be the cost to the supplier.

---

[8] See e.g. *Empire Stores Ltd v. CEC* (1994)

393

A different approach was taken by Carnwath J in *CEC v. Bugeja* (2000) where the judge said that the attribution of a value by the parties approach, adopted in *Rosgill* and *Westmorland*, need not apply where the subject of the supply was goods not services and where the consideration received was not therefore intangible or incapable of being valued by any normal method. In that case the taxpayer sold videos. A customer paid £20 for the first video, but if the customer returned the video (they had security tags on them) the next video would only cost £10. It was clear that the consideration for the supply of the second video was £10 plus the return of the first video. The CEC argued that the value of the returned video was therefore also £10 because without it the customer would have had to pay £20 (by analogy with the hostess cases). Carnwath J. held that on the evidence that most of the returned videos were destroyed by the supplier and that he could buy replacements for about £3, that figure would best express the subjective value of the returned video to him. That approach was, however, doubted by Lightman J in the *Littlewoods* case.

25–09   *Allowable deductions*

Article 11A(i) is subject to Article 11A(3) which allows certain items to be deducted from the consideration. These are (a) price reductions for early payment; (b) price discounts and rebates allowed at the time of the supply; and (c) amounts received by the supplier from a customer as repayment for expenses paid out on behalf of the customer to a third party. With regard to such expenses under paragraph (c), there is a clear distinction between expenses paid to a third party C which have been incurred by A in the course of making his own supply of services to B and as part of the whole of the services rendered to him by B, which would not be deductible under paragraph (c); and where specific services have been supplied by C to B (not A) and A has merely acted as B's known and authorised representative in paying C, which would be so deductible. In *CEC v. Plantiflor Ltd* (2000) the company (A) sent plants by mail order to customers (B) and charged B the costs required by Parcelforce (C) to deliver the plants. The Court of Appeal, having found that the delivery was a specific supply by C to B and not part of any supply by A to B, duly allowed that amount as an expense with regard to the consideration for the supply by A to B.

Price rebates and discounts at the point of sale are allowed under Article 11A(3)(b). These include a coupon received on the purchase of a full-price film which entitles the purchaser to a discount on a second purchase of a film,[9] but not "free gifts" obtainable after accumulating a number of coupons on the purchase of petrol. There cannot be a rebate or discount of 100 per cent.[10]

Allied to the test that in valuing non-cash consideration it is the amount received by the supplier which matters, is the principle that it would be unjust to tax a supplier on a figure which is in excess either of what he actually receives or the customer actually pays. An example may make this clearer. In *Argos Distributors Ltd v. CEC* (1996), Argos sold vouchers redeemable at its shops, only for goods to the value shown on the vouchers, to employers, who then gave them to their employees as incentives. Argos sold the vouchers to the employers at 95 per cent of their face value. Thus, for example, suppose Argos sold a voucher with a face value of £100 to Fred for £95. Fred gave that voucher to his employee Sid, who bought goods worth £100 from Argos with it. What was the value of the supply by Argos to Sid? The ECJ held that it was the amount actually received by Argos for those goods, *i.e.* £95. That was the amount which Argos actually received for the goods and fiscal neutrality required that VAT be charged on no higher figure.[11] For those interested there are more complex examples of this principle in action.[12]

Accounting for VAT   25–10

As we have seen the VAT payable to the VAT office is the balance (if positive) of output tax less input tax. If the balance is negative then a claim for repayment can be made. This balance requires accounting rules to determine when VAT is to be collected and returned to the VAT office, and what input tax can be deducted from the output tax. VAT laws have a special language for this as well:

- *Tax periods* are the periods for which taxable person must make returns to the VAT office.

---

[9] *Boots Co plc v. CEC* (1990). The coupon was held to have no monetary value but was instead a document obliging Boots to sell the second film at a discount. Such an argument could not apply where the returned goods have an actual value such as the videos returned by the customers in *CEC v. Bugeja* (above). In that case there can be no argument based on there being a discount.

[10] *Kuwait Petroleum (GB) Ltd v. CEC* (1999).

[11] The Advocate General in that case thought that the 5% could not be a discount under Article 11A(3)(b) since it was not given to the customer (Sid) at the point of sale. The Court did not express any views on that point.

[12] See *e.g. Elida Gibbs Ltd v. CEC* (1996) and *North Anderson Cars Ltd v. CEC* (1999).

- *A tax invoice* is the formal document required when a supply is made.
- *The tax point* is the time when VAT has to be charged on a supply, and therefore determines the tax period in which output tax on a supply must be returned.
- The *tax credit* is the amount of input tax that can be set against output tax for each tax period.

25–11 *Tax periods*

All registered persons must make regular returns to the VAT office and there are provisions for assessments in default. In the case of larger traders, this is done on a quarterly basis so that it is received by the VAT office within a month of the end of the quarter. For smaller traders, annual accounting is possible. Under this scheme returns are only made once a year and arrangements are made for instalments payments of VAT, monthly or quarterly, depending on the size of turnover, throughout the year on an estimated basis. Some traders are allowed to make monthly returns. These include exporters because, as we shall see, their returns amount to requests for refunds of tax, and so involve a payment by the VAT office to them.

Each return requires that the trader total up the output tax on all outputs made in the period covered by the return. A tax credit can then be claimed for all input tax incurred during the period, provided that the input tax is claimable as part of the credit. Tax payable must be sent with each return; excess input tax will be repaid within 10 days.

In each case, the trader must have documentary evidence to substantiate the amounts returned. These are open to inspection by the VAT office who may make retrospective assessments. In the case of most transactions, the required evidence is a *tax invoice*. The actual amount payable is based on these invoices, although small traders may pay on a cash basis, *i.e.* the difference between output tax collected and input tax paid.

25–12 *Tax invoices*

Each taxable supply must be documented in the required way. In most cases, this is by the issue of a special invoice recording the transaction, called a tax invoice. A taxable person supplying goods or services to another taxable person must issue the latter with an invoice recording the key details of the supply. These include the VAT registration details of the supplier (including the VAT number that all registered persons are given on registration), names and addresses, the amount payable for the supply, and the amount of VAT on the supply. In this way, documentary evidence is recorded of the precise details of the transaction, including both the person who should be paying the VAT to the local VAT office, and the person who will be reclaiming that amount as input tax. This is one of the secret efficiencies of VAT: if the purchaser does not have a tax invoice, no input tax can be claimed. If the purchaser produces the tax invoice, the VAT office has the information to check that the supplier has paid in the VAT.

Tax points 25–13

Tax point is VATese for the time of supply. When does a supply occur? The answer cannot be defined in terms of passing of title. Instead, the rule must be completely practical—it has to be applied by the sales assistant or bookkeeper recording the transaction. In addition, revenue protection requires that the tax point is something that cannot be postponed or avoided.

The solution adopted by section 6 is a two-tier one. The formal time of supply of goods is either when the goods are delivered (or made available) to the customer, or when payment is made for the supply, whichever is earlier. In the case of services the alternative to earlier payment is when the supplies are rendered. In practice, the tax point is the time when the tax invoice is issued. To tie the two together, the law requires that the tax invoice be issued not later than 14 days after the formal time of supply, in which case the date of the invoice will become the tax point. Normal practice with sales of goods is to issue the tax invoice at the same time as the sale and payment, but the rules give a little flexibility.

All taxable persons must include in their tax returns all supplies where the tax point is within the period covered by the tax return, whether or not the payment has actually been made. They will also want to claim a tax credit for all input tax where the tax point is in that period.

Tax credits 25–14

A registered person can claim a tax credit for all input tax incurred in a tax period in making taxable outputs. The United Kingdom system is contained in sections 24 to 26 which mirror, but which have largely been ignored in legal disputes in favour of the wording of the Sixth Directive. The two key conditions are that the claimant holds tax invoices for the sum of input tax claimed (Sixth Directive, Article 18(1)),[13] and that there was an immediate and direct link between the input tax transaction and a particular taxable output transaction the input tax was incurred *for the purposes of* taxable outputs (Sixth Directive, Article 17(2)). The Treasury has power to disallow some kinds of input tax regardless of the reason for it is incurred (section 26). This power is allowed by European law under Article 17(6). The British rules disallow expenditure on a number of inputs, in particular on private cars (with exceptions such as the purchase of cars for resale),[14] most forms of business entertainment,[15] and expenditure on accommodation provided for staff.

There is an inherent policy conflict in these rules. The tax authorities are concerned to maximise tax revenues. From their viewpoint, input tax is lost tax, and is therefore to be discouraged. But VAT is a tax on value-added, that is, a tax on the differences between inputs and outputs. Any attempt to reduce the entitlement to input tax so as to tax more than the value added is wrong in principle. The dilemma is heightened by the natural temptation of taxpayers to claim as much input tax as possible. I may say that the new power boat I purchased was bought directly for the purpose of my (taxable) business. The tax authorities, watching me cruising down the river on a Sunday afternoon, may not be entirely convinced that I am doing it to impress my customers. They see an age-old variant of the battle over deductible expenses turning up in a new guise.

There is inevitably a lot of case law building up about this issue, just as there has been in income tax over the wholly and exclusively rule. The ECJ itself has said in *Midland Bank plc v. CEC* (2000), that the diversity of commercial and professional transactions makes it impossible to set out a single method of determining the necessary relationship between input and output transactions in order for input tax to become deductible. It is for the national courts to decide how to apply the direct and immediate link test of the facts of each case, taking into account all the surrounding circumstances.

---

[13] This includes any document regarded by a Member State as an invoice and allows Member States to require additional evidence under national rules for the prevention of fraud: *Reisdorf v. Finanzampt Köln-West* (1997).

[14] This exclusion is valid even though cars are essential tools in the business concerned or could not be used for private purposes: *Royscot Leasing Ltd v. CEC* (1999).

[15] As to what this amounts to see *e.g. BMW (GB) Ltd v. CEC* (1997) and *CEC v. Kilroy Television Co Ltd* (1997).

In the earlier UK cases where the UK's legislative equivalent of article 17(2), *i.e.* whether the input tax was incurred for the purposes of the taxable supplies, was applied, it was decided that the test was essentially a subjective one. In *Ian Flockton Developments Ltd v. CEC* (1987) the taxpayer engineering company successfully claimed input credit arising from the costs of maintaining and running a racehorse. Where there was no obvious connection between the expenditure and the business it was for the trader to show a link but its subjective intention was paramount. In that case it had been found as a fact that the company's intentions were to use the racehorse for the purposes of the business.

This issue has since been discussed by, on the wording of the Directive the ECJ on many occasions. That court has established certain ground rules which distinguish the question from the narrower one in income tax. In particular the court has repeatedly emphasised the distinction between the acquisition of goods or services by a taxable person and the taxable use to which they are to be put. It is the former that gives rise to the input tax credit. The use to which they are to be put simply determines the extent of that deduction[16]—there is no concept of "wholly and exclusively" as in income tax. With regard to the general issue as to whether the goods or services for which input tax credit is sought has an immediate and direct link to the business carried on by the trader, the relevant European cases were analysed by the House of Lords in *CEC v. Redrow Group plc* (1999). The company built and sold new houses. As part of a marketing scheme they paid prospective purchasers' estate agents' fees on selling their own houses. The company instructed the estate agents and monitored their activities. These expenses were not payable if the sale of the new house fell through. The House of Lords held that the input tax attributable to those fees was deductible. It was not necessary to show that there was a direct link between the payment of the input tax and the specific supply by the taxpayers to the purchasers (output tax).[17] The test was whether the input supply was received in connection with the business for the purpose of being incorporated within its economic activities. The fact that a third party benefited was irrelevant. On the facts the supply of services by the estate agents to Redrow fell within those criteria.

---

[16] *Lennartz v. Finanzamt Munchen III* (1995); *Belgium v. Ghent Coal Terminal NV* (1998).

[17] It is not clear how this approach is reconcilable with the approach of th ECJ in *Midland Bank plc v. CEC* (2000) which seems to require such a link. It could, however, be an application of the direct link test, which was allowed by the ECJ.

There is, however, a clear need to make such direct links if the trader is making both taxable and exempt supplies since there is no input tax credit in relation to supplies to the trader which are used for the purposes of exempt supplies (Article 17(2) applies only to taxable transactions). The solution in the VAT (General) Regulations 1995 is to identify input supplies which are used exclusively for the business of making taxable or exempt supplies as appropriate[18] and then to apportion those supplies which are not exclusively used for one such set of supplies (*e.g.* the cost of office equipment) according to the ratio of taxable to exempt supplies. Further if an input is initially related to a taxable supply but is actually used in relation to an exempt supply, no deduction is allowed.[19]

The question of identifying a link between an input and output transaction for the purposes of a business which consisted of the making of both exempt and taxable supplies, came before the ECJ in *Midland Bank plc v. CEC* (2000). The bank had acted in relation to a take-over for a client (a taxable supply of services), although its general banking business involved both exempt and taxable supplies. After the take-over was completed, the bank was sued for negligence in relation to the advice given to the client and so hired expensive UK lawyers to act for it. The bank now sought to deduct the input tax on the lawyers' bill from the output tax it charged its client for the take-over advice. The ECJ held that for there to be an immediate and direct link between the two, the former must be part of the cost components of the latter. In this case the legal action was a consequence of the advice and not a cost component of it. Accordingly the only direct link was with the bank's business as a whole and so the input tax was deductible only in part.

25–13 *Bad debt relief*

Since liability to account for VAT arises at the tax point there would be a problem for a trader who has issued a tax invoice in one quarter, and so accounted for the output tax on that invoice, if the customer subsequently defaults on payment so that the trader never actually receives that tax. From 1990 onwards therefore there has been an allowance for such bad debts. Section 36 currently provides that any debt (whether in cash or in kind)

---

[18] See *e.g. CEC v. Harpcombe Ltd* (1996).
[19] *Tremerton Ltd v. CEC* (1999). This may not be so if the reason for the change is beyond the trader's control or the taxable supplies never materialised: *Midland Bank v. CEC* (2000).

which is more than six months old and which has been written off in the trader's books is eligible for such relief (*i.e.* the output tax paid can be reclaimed). The original supply must have been at open market value. There is no relief where the right to repayment of the debt has been assigned to a third party and the third party has been paid. Repayment of the relief is also required if the debt is subsequently repaid.

International Tax

CHAPTER 26

INCOME TAX

We must now turn our attention to an aspect of tax law left on one side in our earlier discussions. This is the question of the effect on our taxes of a foreign element. Arguably this is the most fascinating area of our tax laws. It is certainly one of the most complicated. It is also one to which much attention is now devoted in the United Kingdom. This is because of the ease with which money and other assets can be moved in to and out of the United Kingdom. Since the creation of the single internal market in the European Union, funds may be moved as freely as goods and people around the member states.

26–01

What makes the international side of tax so fascinating? It is in part because it involves a complex study of comparative law. Everywhere else (bar the Cayman Islands) has tax laws of some kind. Just as our domestic history and politics have shaped our own tax laws into particular forms, so the tax laws of all other states tend to differ for individual reasons. The chances are also that when there is a foreign element to a British tax problem, there will also be foreign tax to pay. This gives rise to the problem of *double taxation*, where the same income or property gets caught within the tax jurisdictions of more than one country at the same time. The effect is that, unless special rules apply, punitive rates of taxation are applied to international trade. The consequent distortion of trade benefits no one in an open economy. To avoid problems, rules to prevent double taxation have been developed, and they are another aspect of the fascination of the subject. The problems are, in practice, most severe in the area of income and corporation taxes, and we deal with these first.

Behind double taxation and the treatment of any foreign elements in tax liability is an elementary rule of housekeeping. It suits the Exchequer to regard income or property as covered by United Kingdom taxes wherever possible for financial reasons. What we look at in this part of the book is the way in which our tax laws tackle those foreign elements, and how they deal with the problems of double taxation.

We tackle these issues in reverse order, dealing first with the occurrence of double taxation. There is a reason for this. The rules dealing with double taxation may override and replace the

United Kingdom's usual rules for dealing with a foreign element. Further, the special rules apply more often than the underlying national legislation. So the prior question must be: what double taxation rules apply here? Only then should we look at the United Kingdom's own rules. They deal with two broad issues: whether a person is regarded as covered by the tax laws, and whether those laws reach to the form of income or property, or to the transaction or arrangement, which it is sought to tax here. But before we deal with either of these rules, we must answer another question: Whom does the United Kingdom try to tax?

26–02 Who Is Caught By United Kingdom Tax?

The first factor in deciding whether United Kingdom tax is payable by a potential taxpayer under either a DTA or general United Kingdom law is the legislation which is regarded as applying to the person. (DTAs are explained at paragraph 26–07).

In deciding whether a person is subject to the tax laws of the United Kingdom or some other country, or both, the United Kingdom follows general world practice in ignoring the nationality of a taxpayer and concentrating instead on where the person is based or lives. For this purpose the law deals with individuals separately from businesses. For individuals it uses three concepts: residence, ordinary residence and domicile. In summary, residence may be regarded as where the taxpayer is living now, ordinary residence as where the taxpayer is normally living, and domicile is where the taxpayer has his permanent home. But these are misleadingly brief summaries, and we must expand them further.

In looking at these terms, we should bear in mind a warning given by the House of Lords in *Shah v. Barnet London Borough Council* (1983), HL, a case about the entitlement of overseas students to British education grants. The case involved the House of Lords in interpreting the concept of "ordinary residence". The Lords made it clear that, unless special rules were laid down by Parliament in particular cases, this and similar concepts had the same meaning throughout the law and not separate meanings for each different kind of law. They are also largely a question of looking at the facts. There are few special rules in United Kingdom tax law.

26–03 *Residence*

Residence is of pervasive importance in every income tax situation in which there is a foreign element. This is because the general rules are that:

(a) someone who is resident in the United Kingdom is liable to income tax on worldwide income, and

(b) anyone not resident here is taxable in the United Kingdom on income arising here.

Despite the importance of the concept of residence, the legislation on the meaning of residence is a mixture of a few statutory pronouncements to which have been added a considerable body of case law. Apart from law, the *practice* of the Revenue is important in this field. The general idea is that someone is resident where they are living for a time in *that* tax year. The problem of applying the concept of residence to the facts of individual cases engaged the courts in some of the earliest tax appeals, such as in *Re Young* (1875) (Court of Session). Since then, elaborate rules have evolved in a mixture of law, concession, and practice.

Section 336 of the Taxes Act declares that a person who is in the United Kingdom for some temporary purpose only and not with a view or intent of establishing his residence here, and who has not actually resided in the United Kingdom at one time or several times for a period equal in aggregate to six months in any year of assessment is not chargeable as a United Kingdom resident, but that a person who has so actually resided shall be so chargeable for that year. This is the United Kingdom version of a general international rule known as the "183 day rule"—that someone comes within the local tax jurisdiction after having been there for 183 days. It is implicit in the section that a person may be held to be resident here even though he has been present for less than six months, provided his presence has what is called a "residential quality". There are three main aspects of this.

First, a person who has a home here (a residence, but use of that word confuses things!) may be treated as resident in a tax year of assessment if present here only for a short period—or possibly even if not present at all. There is a statutory qualification to this rule. It is declared by section 335 of the Taxes Act that if a person works full time abroad the question of residence in the United Kingdom must be determined without regard to any place of abode (residence?) maintained here. Also, (with regard to Schedule E) where the employment is in substance one of which the duties fall to be performed outside the United Kingdom, merely incidental duties performed here are treated as performed abroad.

Secondly, a person who does not maintain any home here, but pays regular visits to the United Kingdom, is regarded as resident if these visits form part of the individual's habit of life. This vague test, based on the case law, is interpreted by the Revenue in its code on residence (published as IR 20) as meaning more than 91 days in each of four years.

Thirdly, section 334 of the Taxes Act states that when a Commonwealth citizen or citizen of the Republic of Ireland, whose ordinary residence has been in the United Kingdom, leaves the country for the purpose only of occasional residence abroad, actual residence in the United Kingdom is treated as continuing.

In applying these tests, it is important to remember that an individual may be resident in the United Kingdom and another state—possibly more than one other state—at the same time.

Residence of companies is as important to decide for tax purposes as residence of individuals. For many years this was decided by a judicial test, offered by Lord Loreburn in *de Beers Consolidated Mines v. Howe* (1906), HL: "A company resides . . . where its real business is carried on . . . and the real business is carried on where the central management and control actually abides." This was a common sense application of the idea of residence to something which is purely a creation of the law. But it has a distinct disadvantage for tax purposes in the days of email and executive jets. The central management and control of a company can be wherever the directors chose to meet to take their decisions. So, if the directors of a British-registered company, all of whom are resident in Britain, decide to take the corporate jet together for a trip to Bermuda once a month for their monthly board meeting at a small office they maintain there, where is the company resident? Bermuda may be British, but it is also an offshore jurisdiction outside the British tax jurisdiction.

The common law rule was therefore supplemented in 1988 (by Finance Act 1988, s. 66) by a second rule, adopting a prevalent international rule into the United Kingdom. This is that any company incorporated under the laws of the United Kingdom is resident here for tax purposes. This rule applies alongside the old rule. Any foreign incorporated company with central management in the United Kingdom is also resident here.

Because many states operate double tests like those now applying in the United Kingdom, it is common for a company to have more than one residence, although this can be inconvenient for some companies and also for the tax authorities. To avoid both these sets of problems, both tests are overridden by a rule relating to our double taxation rules. If under those rules, which we note below, the company is to be regarded as resident outside the United Kingdom, then it is not a United Kingdom resident for any tax purposes (Finance Act 1994, s. 249).

Ordinary residence   26–04

In 1928 in *Levene v. IRC*, HL Viscount Cave said " . . . I think
that [ordinary residence] connotes residence in a place with some
degree of continuity and apart from accidental or temporary
absences". In 1983 in *Shah v. Barnet London Borough Council*,
HL, Lord Scarman, giving judgment on behalf of all their Lordships, noted that the words bore the same meaning in 1983 as
they did in 1928, and that that was their ordinary meaning, He
added his own description, that the words refer to "a man's
abode in a particular place or country which he has adopted
voluntarily and for settled purposes as part of the regular order of
his life for the time being, whether of short or long duration".
We have noted that the Revenue has based its "four year rule"
on its own view of this case. Following these tests, it is possible for
a person to be ordinarily resident in two places, and therefore two
countries, at once. It is also possible for a person to be resident
here without being ordinarily resident here, and the reverse.

Domicile   26–05

Domicile also has no special meaning in tax law. Internationally, it is a confusing term because it is the French equivalent of
"residence", but the French and English meanings of domicile are
far removed from each other. The nearest equivalent is permanent residence, but the individual's permanent home would be a
better way of putting it. An individual can only have one domicile, and at birth that is where the person is born. The domicile of
origin, as this is called, can be replaced by a domicile of choice,
but not easily, and only if both the intent of the individual and the
factual pattern of the individual's life, dictate this. The result is
that a person may spend many years away from home but still be
domiciled there.

Double Taxation Relief   26–06

United Kingdom tax laws provide for a relief called double
taxation relief to apply to any case where a person has to pay
income tax, capital gains tax, corporation tax or inheritance tax
at the same time as paying a similar foreign tax. This is subject to
exceptions based mainly on the grounds that a foreign tax is not
of the same kind as these taxes. Relief is provided by two means.
By far the more important means is through application of
bilateral treaties with other states known in the United Kingdom
as double taxation agreements (DTAs). Where there is no

agreement, the tax authorities here provide a foreign tax credit against United Kingdom taxation, known as unilateral relief.

26–07   *Double Taxation Agreements*

The best practical answer to double taxation problems between the United Kingdom and any other state is for the authorities of both states to sit down and work out what to do about the various problems of overlaps and gaps individually. They are greatly assisted in doing this by the existence of standard forms of agreement which most states follow closely. The most important model is the OECD Model Tax Convention. This is used for British agreements. (OECD is the Organisation for Economic Cooperation and Development, based in Paris, and of which the United Kingdom is a very active member.) Another model is the United Nations Model Double Tax Convention.

Once the treaty negotiators have worked through problems thrown up by both sets of tax laws, and sorted out the answers, they draw up an agreement which binds the two states to follow the answers whenever the problems arise. The United Kingdom authorities do not need legislative powers to do this, because agreeing treaties can be done on the authority of the royal prerogative. It would be possible to deal with individual foreign problems by individual provisions in Finance Acts but, with only rare exceptions, this does not happen. The necessary legal authority to require the authorities—and taxpayers—in this country to comply with the answers is given under a general provision. You will find it in section 788 of the Taxes Act 1988, with equivalent provisions in the TCGA 1992, and the IHTA 1984.

Section 788 provides that if Her Majesty by Order in Council should declare that arrangements have been made with the government of any overseas territory with a view to double taxation relief, "then, subject to the provisions of this Part of this Act, the arrangements shall, *notwithstanding anything in any enactment*, have effect ... ". The words in (our) italics mean what they say. Anything in an Order in Council can override anything in any of the taxing Acts—or, indeed, any other Act except the European Communities Act 1972 (which contains the same words referring to E.C. law). Orders in Council are quite common, and the United Kingdom has concluded more than 100 DTAs with other governments. Most follow the standard patterns of the Model Tax Conventions.

Individual DTAs are negotiated in the form of Conventions binding in international law on the two states. In practice parts of each Convention need renegotiating from time to time as the tax systems of the two states are amended. Parts of DTAs are revised by Protocols.

The United Kingdom has concluded DTAs with many states, including all our European Union partners and main trading partners. Most of these agreements are aimed to be comprehensive, dealing with most—usually all—the problems likely to arise. We note the individual answers given in the standard forms of DTA below.

Until recently, it was an aim of many states to reach agreements with all their neighbours. But this has given rise to a practice known as "treaty shopping" and has also encouraged "tax havens". If a country has a DTA with the United Kingdom, overlap of taxes is usually avoided. If at the same time the other state has very low, or nil, tax rates applying to income protected from United Kingdom taxes, it will become fiscally very attractive. A place with a favourable (to the taxpayer) tax regime is often called a "tax haven"—though "no tax haven" or the French term "paradis fiscal" might be more accurate. Recently the OECP has been coordinating action to stop "harmful tax practices" of these states, many of which were put in an OECD list in 2000.

They have also been adopting special provisions in their treaties or national laws to stop "treaty shopping". This is the use by a taxpayer of a treaty between states of which the taxpayer is not a resident. This can be done, at least in theory, by the taxpayer setting up a company in one of the states and using it as a "conduit" company to pass income through the state under the treaty provisions. Treaties concluded by some states, particularly the United States (and to a lesser extent the United Kingdom) therefore contain provisions designed to ensure that the treaty provisions can only be used by those who are genuine residents of the two states for income that genuinely relates to the states.

The forms of relief from double taxation   26–08

The first form of relief offered by a DTA that follows the usual form of the Model Conventions is a series of "tiebreaker" provisions designed to ensure that an individual or company that is treated as a resident for national tax purposes by both states has resident status in just one of the states. In the case of companies, this is done by replacing the national rules by a single rule: the company is resident in the state (of the two) where its centre of effective management is to be found. Note that this is different to either of the British rules, but overrides both of them. The centre of effective management is where the day-to-day management decisions are taken—usually the same place as its head office.

The tiebreaker rules for individuals consist of a series of rules that give preference in turn to the centre of economic interests of the individual, the individual's real home, and the individual's nationality.

The effect of these rules is to ensure that only one of the two states has a worldwide claim to tax over any taxpayer. But it also creates a problem. Companies and individuals may have genuine strong economic links with both states. By removing the residence link between the taxpayer and one of the states, that state's claim to tax may be removed or reduced excessively compared with the income being earned by the taxpayer in that state. To deal with this, DTAs have special rules about "permanent establishments" (or PEs as they are usually termed). A PE is a branch or agency of the taxpayer established on a continuing basis in the other state. If a PE exists, the state where the PE is has extended rights to tax income of the taxpayer effectively connected with the PE. At the same time, the tax paid with respect to the income of a PE in one state is available for foreign tax credits in the other state, to limit the maximum level of taxation that can be imposed.

The second form of relief given by a DTA is a series of provisions that attribute the rights to tax different forms of income between the two states to reduce the scope for double taxation. The rights to tax some forms of income are attributed primarily to the state where the income arises (the source state). This applies to taxation of income and capital gains from land. The rights to tax cross-border transfers of income are often shared between the two states, with the source state having a limited right to tax. For example, many DTAs provide that both states can tax interest paid by a lender in one state to a borrower in the other state, but they limit the source state to a maximum of perhaps 10 per cent tax. Yet other forms of income can be taxed in the state where the taxpayer is resident (the state of residence)—remembering that the taxpayer is for these purposes only resident in one state. This is true of trading income (see below).

The third form of relief given by a DTA is by requiring states to limit any double taxation that does occur. This can be done in two ways. Where the source state taxes a form of income, the state of residence may either exempt the income from further tax, or give a foreign tax credit for the tax paid in the source state against any tax payable in the state of residence. The United Kingdom rarely gives relief by way of exemption, relying instead on the granting of foreign tax credits. For example, where a source state is entitled to levy a 10 per cent tax on interest paid to a taxpayer resident in the United Kingdom, the United Kingdom tax authorities allow the taxpayer to set the tax paid in the source state directly against tax due here. The United Kingdom therefore only collects the difference between the total tax payable in the United Kingdom and the tax already paid in the source state. It grants this foreign tax credit in accordance with the provisions of United Kingdom law. These are the same whether or not a DTA exists.

Unilateral relief

26–09

Where we have no DTA with another territory, or where the agreement does not apply to a particular foreign tax (for example a local income tax), unilateral relief is available under United Kingdom law, by section 790 of the Taxes Act 1988 and equivalent provisions in the TCGA 1992 and IHTA 1984. These sections empower the authorities to grant relief unilaterally as if there were a DTA in effect.

As already noted, the actual relief is given in the form of a foreign tax credit, whether the entitlement to the relief arises under a DTA that has been incorporated into our law by an Order in Council, or where it is being granted under the more general authority of section 790. The taxpayer has to show that the tax has actually been paid to the foreign tax authority, that the tax is either a tax expressly covered by a DTA or a similar tax to the United Kingdom income tax, corporation tax or capital gains tax, and that the tax relates to the same income as the United Kingdom charge to tax. Where a credit is allowed, the tax due in the United Kingdom will be reduced by the amount of foreign tax paid. This relief prevents the tax paid being more than the higher of the rates of tax of the two territories. If the United Kingdom rate is higher than the foreign rate, only the difference between the two is payable here.

The rules allowing a foreign tax credit prevent the taxpayer claiming back excessive foreign tax credit. In particular, if the United Kingdom tax on a form of income is lower than the foreign tax, so that the tax credit is potentially greater than the United Kingdom tax bill, the credit is limited to the amount of the United Kingdom tax bill. Also, the taxpayer cannot add two or more claims for foreign tax credit from different countries or different sources together to achieve a cross-subsidy from lower foreign tax bills to higher foreign tax bills. The credit rules have to be applied separately to each form of income and each foreign state.

Finally, if neither of the above forms of relief operate, section 811 may come to the aid of those subject to a double charge to income or corporation tax. This section allows relief by way of deduction. It treats the amount of income taxable in the United Kingdom as equal to the gross income less the amount of overseas tax paid.

26–10   **Foreign Incomes and Gains**

We now look in turn at how each of the schedules and main charging sections deal with foreign elements, remembering of course that in any individual case a double taxation agreement of the kind discussed above may override the general rules. For this reason, we shall also examine how the OECD Model Tax convention (MTC) and, where it differs, a typical British double tax agreement (DTA) deal with the issues.

26–11   *Schedule A*

Schedule A is charged expressly on land in the United Kingdom, so the only foreign element that could arise is the identity of the taxpayer. However, any foreign association of the recipient of a rent is irrelevant under the rules of the Schedule. Article 6 of the MTC (which is followed in most DTAs) provides that tax may be collected by the state where the land is, authorising taxation under Schedule A of foreign landowners. Income from foreign land is taxed under Schedule D.

26–12   *Schedule D, Case I and II*

At first sight it would seem that trades or professions carried on abroad are within Case I or Case II. Section 18(1)(a)(ii) of the Taxes Act relates to "any trade, profession or vocation whether carried on in the United Kingdom or elsewhere." Despite these words it is clear from case law that if a trade is carried on *wholly* outside the United Kingdom it is not within Case I. Instead it will be caught in Case V. This is equally true of a profession or vocation. See *Colquhoun v. Brooks* (1889), HL But if the trade or profession is carried on *partly* here, then Case I or Case II applies to the full profits. Case I and Case II apply even if the taxpayer is not resident in the United Kingdom, and whether or not the taxpayer is a British national. Note that all corporate profits of a resident company are regarded as being under Case I, and that Case V does not apply to corporate trading profits. If the company is not a United Kingdom resident, then it is taxed in the

United Kingdom to corporation tax on any profits of a branch or agency here, but to income tax on any other United Kingdom source profits.

The Schedule D rules are normally overridden by rules in our DTAs. Article 7 of the MTC provides that a trade is to be taxed in the state where the trader is resident, unless the trader maintains a permanent establishment (PE) in the other state. (On PEs, see above.) If so, then the state where the PE is may tax trading income effectively connected with the PE. If it does so, the state of residence of the trader must give double tax relief for that tax against any tax it levies on the same income. British DTAs broadly follow this approach. On this basis, the Inland Revenue is authorised to impose tax on the worldwide trading profits or British residents, and on the British trading profits of foreign residents.

In practice, the most significant problem in taxing international trade is dealing with international transactions between associated traders, such as companies in an international group. The principles of international tax are based on cross-border transactions taking place at arm's length prices. They assume that the parties are unrelated commercially. The reality is that much international trade is between associated parties and is not at arm's length. This gives rise to what is called transfer pricing, that is, pricing that does or may transfer profits or costs from one state to another on a non-arm's length basis. The OECD has adopted a detailed code to deal with this. That code was effectively adopted into British law by the Finance Act 1998 and Schedule 8AA to the 1988 Act.

Schedule D, Case III   26–13

The Case applies to interest, annuities or annual payments "payable within or out of the United Kingdom": section 18(2). In practice much of the income falling within this part of the charge of Case III is dealt with by withholding taxes, most of which apply whether or not the recipient is linked to the United Kingdom. For example, interest paid to a foreign recipient is often subject to a withholding. The level of withholding is normally set by the DTA. The MTC recommends a withholding tax of 10 per cent, but an increasing number of British DTAs provide for exemption at source, leaving the interest be to taxed in the county of the recipient only. It is British Government policy to avoid withholding of tax on interest payments, but to seek enforcement of the tax obligations through the exchange of information.

26–14   *Schedule D, Cases IV and V*

These are the only main charging sections aimed specifically at overseas income. Case IV taxes "income arising from securities out of the United Kingdom", and Case V deals with income from "possessions" out of the United Kingdom, except where the income is emoluments caught under Schedule E. "Securities" and "possessions" are not defined. It may be noted that the words go back to the start of income tax, when a possession probably consisted of a sugar plantation, no doubt manned by slave labour. The terms certainly predate that revolutionary new concept called the joint stock company. In practice these terms cause little difficulty. There is no difference of importance between Case IV and Case V. The alternatives to the two cases will be charged under other Schedules or Cases. These may well end up with the same tax "take", because in most cases the charge under either case is on the whole of the income for the relevant year, whether or not it has been received in the United Kingdom. The application of either case to companies is limited. Case IV does not apply to companies since 1996. Either Case I or Case III applies. Case V, as we have already noted, does not apply to profits of resident companies, and foreign profits of non-resident companies are outside the scope of the tax.

If a Commonwealth or Irish citizen is not ordinarily resident in the United Kingdom, or if any other national is not domiciled in the United Kingdom, then he or she will only be charged under these Cases on what is termed a "remittance basis". That means United Kingdom tax will only be charged if the income is received (in any form) in the United Kingdom. Such a person can avoid a United Kingdom tax charge by keeping the income out of this country. This is widely used by wealthier foreign residents in Britain to reduce their exposure to British tax.

Again, these Cases may be overridden by the rules of DTAs. Several rules are relevant. Article 10 of the MTC covers dividends, and provides for a limited withholding tax on the dividend for the state where the dividend is sourced. The rule for foreign rents and trades have already been noted. "Other income" not specifically mentioned elsewhere in a DTA is usually taxable in the state of the resident only.

26–15   *Schedule D, Case VI*

This is the "rag-bag" provision, but, as we have already seen that Cases IV and V are a sort of "overseas rag-bag" there is in practice no point under Case VI of importance here. Nonetheless, we shall see that Case VI is used to cover specific overseas anti-avoidance provisions. If these catch income already taxed in another state, then double tax relief is usually required either by a DTA or by our own rules.

Schedule E   26–16

Schedule E is divided into three Cases which are set out in section 19 of the Taxes Act. That section used the phrase "foreign emoluments" and that phrase is relevant to all three cases. "Foreign emoluments" are "emoluments of a person not domiciled in the United Kingdom from an office or employment under or with any person, body of persons or partnership resident outside and not resident in, the United Kingdom." Notice that there are two factors here, one turning on the domicile of the employee and one on the residence of the employer.

CASE I   26–17
Case I applies where the person holding the office or employment is resident and ordinarily resident in the United Kingdom. The charge to tax is on the *whole* of the emoluments. That is the basic position but there are two possible exceptions. First, there is a deduction in respect of earning from work done abroad during an absence from the United Kingdom of 365 days or more. The deduction is the whole of the amount of the emoluments attributable to that period. Secondly, where the duties of an office or employment are performed wholly outside the United Kingdom and the emoluments are foreign emoluments the emoluments are excepted from Case I.

CASE II   26–18
Case II applies where the person holding the office or employment is not resident, or if resident, is not ordinarily resident, in the United Kingdom. Tax is charged only on emoluments for the year of assessment in respect of duties performed in the United Kingdom. This case can only apply to a person who performs duties here but does not become resident or alternatively does not become ordinarily resident here. Case II is not strictly in line with the principle that a non-resident can only be taxed on a United Kingdom source of income, unless we regard the United Kingdom duties as a "source".

CASE III   26–19
Case III applies to a person who is resident in the United Kingdom (where ordinarily resident here or not) in either of two

situations. The first is where the emoluments are from an employment whose duties are performed wholly outside the United Kingdom and the emoluments are foreign emoluments. Because the duties are performed wholly outside the United Kingdom, this situation is not caught by Case II, and because of this—and also that the emoluments are foreign emoluments—the situation is not caught by Case I. The second situation is where the emoluments are for duties performed outside the United Kingdom and the employee is resident but not ordinarily resident in the United Kingdom. Because the duties are performed outside the United Kingdom Case II does not apply, and because the taxpayer is not ordinarily resident here Case I does not apply. Case III is designed to apply, and does apply, only where Cases I and II do not apply. The charge to tax under Case III is only on emoluments received in the United Kingdom (the remittance basis).

In most cases, this complex set of rules is overridden by the DTA rules. Article 15 of the MTC sets out the rules for taxing foreign employees. The main rule is known as the "183 day rule". Tax on employment income is levied in any year only by the state of residence of an employee working temporarily in another state, unless the employee is in the other state for 183 days or more in the year (or that year and a previous year), and the pay for the work comes from an employer in the state where the work takes place. For example, if I work in another state for two three-month periods, it must be calculated whether or not those periods total 183 days. If they do, I can be taxed in the other state. If the Inland Revenue can also tax me under any of the cases of Schedule E, I will be given double tax relief for the foreign tax.

26–20   *Schedule F*

This applies expressly only to payments by companies resident in the United Kingdom. The extent to which British tax is applied to a dividend being paid overseas depends on the terms of the DTA made with the other state. In the absence of a DTA, a foreign shareholder may lose the 10 per cent credit (see paragraph 10–10). Dividends from foreign countries received in the United Kingdom by individuals are taxable under Case V of Schedule D.

26–21   *Capital gains tax*

The general charge to capital gains tax applies to all assets whether situation in the United Kingdom or not. However, a person is only liable to the tax on a gain if during part of the relevant tax year he is either resident here or ordinarily resident here: TCGA 1992, s.2. Where a person is resident or ordinarily resident here, but is not domiciled in the United Kingdom, then gains from foreign assets will only be charged to tax when received (if ever) in the United Kingdom. Conveniently, section 275 provides a list of rules to identify the location of assets such as debts or shares (why is there not a similar list in the income tax legislation?).

The MTC, Article 13, (followed by many DTAs) provides a series of rules for deciding which state may tax capital gains. Gains on land may be taxed in the state where the land is. Most other forms of capital gain may be taxed in the state of residence of the taxpayer. However, many states still do not charge capital gains tax, or restrict it to gains made in the state. Consequently, the British rules create something of a tax haven for foreign investors here if they realise their profits in the form of capital gains rather than income, and they do not get taxed in their own states.

Anti-Avoidance Provisions   26–22

The full story of this chapter has not been told until we look at special anti-avoidance provisions aimed at catching transaction and arrangements designed to avoid United Kingdom tax. We will note four of these measures, where a determined attempt was made to tackle the "leakage" of taxable income overseas.

Transfer of assets abroad

Section 739 of the Taxes Act was enacted (to quote the near-unique statement of legislative purpose in the section):

> "for the purpose of preventing the avoiding by individuals ordinarily resident in the United Kingdom of liability to income tax by means of transfers of assets by virtue ... whereof ... income becomes payable to persons resident or domiciled out of the United Kingdom ..."

Originally enacted in 1936, these provisions were given an extremely wide interpretation in 1948 in *Congreve v. IRC*, HL. They proved to be oppressively effective until the House of Lords reinterpreted the sections in *Vestey* in 1981, which gave the sections their present shape.

The sections give the Revenue wide powers to deem an individual to be receiving income (chargeable under Schedule D, Case VI) where that individual has power to enjoy overseas income

419

which would be taxable if it were received here. The individual can escape the charge if he can show "to the satisfaction of the Board" that either avoidance of tax was not one of the purposes behind the transactions or that the transactions were bona fide commercial transactions not designed for tax avoidance reasons. But even these provisions have limits: see *IRC v. Willoughby* (1997).

Migration of companies

Section 765 used to contain power for the Treasury to stop a company resident in the United Kingdom becoming non-resident and thus slipping round the tax net. The section was much modified in 1988 to meet E.C. legal requirements. It still contains limits, enforceable by the criminal law, against capital movements outside the E.U.

Controlled foreign companies

Sections 747 to 756 of the Taxes Act contains proposals originally entitled "Tax Havens", and this summarises their purpose. Their methods are better summarised by the present title: controlled foreign companies.

These provisions apply potentially to any company resident outside the United Kingdom in a low tax area but which is controlled by persons resident in the United Kingdom. But they do not apply if the company was quoted, if it followed an acceptable distribution policy, if it engaged only in exempt activities (broadly, that it is trading or operating locally and not mainly with the United Kingdom), or if its profits did not exceed £20,000.

If a company is to be treated as a controlled foreign company, then the profits of the company will be apportioned among those who have an interest in the company in broadly the same way as with a close company, so that income will be deemed to be received in the United Kingdom by those with interests in the controlled foreign company, and will be taxed accordingly. A crucial question here is the residence of a company, but in general the ordinary rules apply.

Originally this legislation was operated, in effect, by Revenue discretion and negotiation. But the introduction of self-assessment ended this approach. The provisions were rewritten by the Finance Act 1998 and strengthened by the Finance Act 2000.

Offshore funds 26–23

This is the rather vague title given to sections 757 and following of the Taxes Act. An offshore fund includes any overseas company, any overseas unit trust or any other overseas method for co-owning property. Introduced in 1984, these measures attack certain material interests in non-qualifying offshore funds. A material interest means any interest which allows the owner to get the market value of his investment back in some way within seven years of investment. A fund is non-qualifying unless the Board of Inland Revenue certifies that the fund is following a full distribution policy, and that the fund does not have a significant investment in other offshore funds or other companies.

Where someone is regarded as having a material interest and the "fund" is non-qualifying, then the provisions treat any gain made by an investor resident or ordinarily resident in the United Kingdom (and calculated along the same lines as gains for capital gains tax) as an income gain chargeable under Schedule D, Case VI.

VALUE ADDED TAX

27–01   Unlike the income taxes, value added tax was invented expressly with international aspects in mind. The introduction and subsequent growth in importance of the tax in Britain—and in most other countries—is a reflection of the successfully way in which the tax can be accommodated to most aspects of the growth of world trade. It is because its essential features make it a *neutral* tax, that is one that does not discriminate between different kinds of supply.

The approach is fundamentally different to the approach to income tax discussed in the previous chapter. As we saw, the UK and most other states seek to impose income tax both on locally-sourced income and on taxpayers who are resident in the jurisdiction. Double tax agreements are then used to avoid or reduced double taxation. That approach does not work for indirect taxes. They are imposed without reference to the identify of taxpayers and must therefore be imposed by reference to each separate supply. Traditionally, this was done by customers duties imposed on all imports of goods (and sometimes also on xpors) and excise taxes on internal supplies of specific kinds of goods. But customs duties have little place in an international trading economy based on free, non-discriminatory trade. They have no place at all in the Single Market of the European Union.

The E.C. adopted VAT partly because it deals better than most forms of taxation with three aspects of taxing international trade. The first is the *principle of equal treatment*. A state must treat all other states on equal terms. In other words, if a Member State removes customs duties from goods imported from another state, it must also remove them from similar goods imported from any other state. This is the primary commitment of all Member States of the World Trade Organisation under GATT 1994 (the 1994 adoption of the General Agreement of Tariffs and Trade) and is set out in Article I of that treaty. It is also in the GATS (General Agreement on Trade in Services). The result is that a state must have one set of tariff rates for all imports.

The second aspect is the *removal of customs duties*. The WTO, and the GATT before, it have been instrumental in removing or reducing customers duties on most goods in most states. This has resulted in the effective abolition of customs duties on exports in all member states of the WTO, and significant reductions on imports. In reality, this means that other forms of tax have had to take the place of customs duties in providing revenue for national governments The obvious way of doing this is to impose internal indirect taxes so as to collect the customs duties in another way. But this could reintroduce the discrimination both against imported or exported goods generally, and also against imports from specific states.

To counter internal discrimination, the GATT also imposes the *principle of national treatment*. This is in Article III of the GATT. It requires that states do not impose, directly or indirectly, taxes or charges on imported goods that are more burdensome than the taxes and charges imposed on "like" products made locally. In other words, a state cannot impose a higher level of tax on imported products than on locally made products. There is, again a similar rule in the GATS. In theory, a state is free to impose higher taxes on its own goods than on imported goods, but such taxes rarely last long in an open market as they make imports cheaper than equivalent local goods. That reality, along with the principle, prevents states replacing customs duties by equivalent internal taxes. It means that any form of internal indirect taxation must be both non-discriminatory as regards the state of origins of imported goods, and neutral as between imported goods and locally made goods.

Indirect taxes in the European Union 27–02

The E.U. has taken the abolition of discriminatory taxes as far as it can. Article 25 of the Consolidated E.C. Treaty abolishes all internal customs duties within the European Customs Area (ECA). This consists of the fifteen Member States of the E.U., plus the other members of the European Economic Area (EEA), Turkey and a few small states or territories such as the Isle of Man. Article of the Consolidated E.C. Treaty imposes Article III of the GATT in a strong and directive effective way within all Member States. There are equivalent provisions elsewhere in the EEA and ECA.

This effect is confirmed by the E.C. VAT Directives. These impose a single form of VAT on all Member States in a way entirely consistent both with Article 90 and the abolition of customs duties, and with a further provision preventing Member States introducing any other general indirect tax in addition to the E.C. form of VAT. Finally, the introduction of the single market meant further measures to ensure that VAT was not collected at the frontiers but internally only. These measures have also been adopted elsewhere in the EEA.

We will examine how this works in Britain and where problems remain, by looking first at VAT on goods, and then at VAT on services.

27–03 ### VAT on cross border supplies of goods

VAT can be imposed on imports and exports in two ways. They can be taxed at either end of a cross border supply. Either VAT can be imposed on a destination basis—on imported goods, or it can be imposed on an origin basis—on exported goods. The form of VAT adopted by the E.U. for goods is the destination based form. Remember that the basic income tax rule for traders is that they pay tax where they are resident, so the income tax will be charged on the exporter, while the VAT is being charged on the importer.

All exported goods are zero-rated. Consequently, the exporter, if registered, can claim back any input tax paid in buying or making any goods for export. In this way, there is no UK VAT on goods exported from the United Kingdom. The goods are therefore imported into the other state free of all United Kingdom tax. This prevents British exports being prejudiced in the other state by a British tax burden.

Within the E.U. the working of this rule is strengthened by allowing the overseas trader to register in the UK so as to claim the tax back here when the goods are exported by the trader. An overseas trader who carried out business in this way with several European states is free to register in each of those states. Otherwise, it may be appropriate for the trader to bring the goods into a country where it is registered before exporting them.

VAT is imposed on all goods imported into the United Kingdom. Since the United Kingdom became part of the E.U.'s single market goods brought into the UK from other Member States are no longer regarded as imports. They are referred to instead as *cross border acquisitions*. Goods are only regarded as imports if they enter the UK directly from a non-Member State, for example outside Europe. In the case of imports, VAT is imposed at the appropriate British rate on the value of the goods at the customs frontier. Remember that the rate of tax on imported goods must be the same rate as that charged on those goods if supplied internally. Any E.C. customs duties are imposed at the same time. VAT is due on the value of the goods including any customs duty and import costs.

This applies on all imports, whether brought in by a registered person or by others. Registration is not necessary for the levy of VAT on imports. The only important exceptions to this for most people are the travellers' personal allowances, or so called "duty-free" goods—in practice this means free of VAT and excise duty as well as customs duty. This depends on specific E.C. regulations that exempt goods brought in by travellers such as tobacco and alcoholic drinks.

Different rules apply where goods are brought into the UK from other Member States. Anyone who brings in cross border acquisitions amounting to more than the internal limit for registration in a year must register for VAT if not already registered. The key difference is that registration is by reference to the total value of acquisitions, rather than supplies (see Schedule 3). VAT is imposed on cross border acquisitions by registered persons on the value of the goods on delivery to the first destination in the UK and not at the frontier. That is why goods are not stopped for customs and VAT purposes as they come through the Channel Tunnel. Registered taxpayers are required to declare the inward supply of all goods subject to VAT to them in their VAT returns. The assumption of the system is that the goods will have been supplied by another trader who is registered in the other country. A procedural requirement that all VAT registration numbers be disclosed allows this process to be checked. All VAT numbers issued to traders in any state in the E.U. are unique to avoid any confusion.

There are additional rules to prevent avoidance or evasion. Anyone who receives cross border acquisitions of more than £70,000 in a year, and who is not otherwise registered is also required to register (the rules are in Schedule 2) and to make the necessary returns to the VAT office.

Other problems are dealt with by specific rules or by abrogating the destination basis of the tax. Cars taken across a frontier as a private transaction are liable to VAT in the state where they are first registered. So a car bought in, say, France, and then registered in Britain will be subject to VAT at the British rate, provided of course that the formalities are met. Goods bought by mail order impose a significant problem, as there is no easy way on checking on them in the states to which they are sent. Instead they are taxable supplies in the state from which they are supplied. A British customer ordering goods from France will therefore pay the French rate of VAT on those goods. In an ideal world that would perhaps make no real difference to the purchaser. In practice, it can result in significant savings even after postage is paid! The growth of Internet sales make this ever more significant. This is the same as a British customer buying goods in France and bringing them in personally. In both cases, the British private customer cannot claim a rebate of French tax, and offer instead to pay the British tax.

The travellers' personal allowances, or "duty free", no longer applies to VAT in the E.U. A British traveller buying goods, in say, Belgium, therefore pays the Belgian tax and pays no further tax in Britain. But because the rates of tax in some other Member States are significantly lower than in Britain, it can still save money to buy taxed goods in other countries and import them into Britain.

Despite these added complications, the imposition of VAT on cross border supplies of goods is relatively straightforward. This is because customs officials are used to handling such matters and, if enforcement resources are adequate, most goods can be intercepted or traced.

27–04   **VAT on cross border supplies of services**

By contrast with goods, cross border supplies of services are far more difficult to handle. In part this is because the "customs approach" to collecting VAT cannot work on services. By definition, nothing tangible crosses the frontier, even where services are exported to, or imported from outside Europe. Indeed to talk of the "export" of services is somewhat artificial in many cases. For example, a British firm of lawyers is asked to give advice on an ongoing basis to a Canadian business. How is that advice given? The Canadians could second someone to Britain to receive the advice, or a British legal team could go to Canada (perhaps setting up an office there) or they could both meet on a regular basis, in say Ireland or the advice could be given by conference telephone calls, or by email, or by courier, or by fax, or by post, or most probably by a combination of all those means. Where is the advice supplied? Would it make any difference if the legal advice is applied to a business in Denmark rather than Canada?

Nonetheless, the problems of cross-border supplies of services are essentially the same as those of cross-border supplies of goods. Discrimination should be avoided and excessive taxation of "exported" services will hurt the exporting state. At the same time, steps needs to be taken to control avoidance.

VAT avoidance is all too easy in the electronic age. Take the supply of telephone services. The general rule in the E.U. used be that telephone services (that is, the supply of the service of allowing you to make a telephone call) were regarded as supplied where the telephone service supplier was based. So, if you make a call via British Telecom to say, Sweden, then you pay British VAT. If you use the Swedish telephone services then you pay Swedish VAT. It did not take too long for people to discover that the best services to use were those based in countries with no VAT. The rule had to be changed and was. Currently, Britain along with other developed states is working out how to collect tax on services supplied via the Internet. There is no easy answer. The estimates of tax already being lost are enormous and, as they say in the best (downloaded, foreign) films, "you ain't seen nutt'n yet".

The E.U. so far, has come up with a series of expedient answers rather than a single overall approach. This has been supplemented as we shall see by national action.

The main E.U. approach is to abandon the destination basis of tax as the general rule. Indeed it has abandoned the rule of basing the tax on where the supply occurs. Instead, the general rule is that VAT is to be imposed on a supply of services where the supplier is in a separate state to the person supplied, by reference to the *residence of the supplier*. This is in effect the same basic rule as that for income tax, save that the supplier of services of VAT purposes is the recipient of the income for income tax purposes. But what rate of tax should be applied? If the rate is a zero-rate, then the net result is that tax is imposed in theory, but in practice the "taxation" of suppliers means that the supplier can claim back the input tax and cross-border services are made tax free.

To deal with this, there are a series of specific rules. They are found in the "place of taxable transactions" rules in the E.C. Sixth VAT Directive. Supplies of services are dealt with in Article 9. Supplies related to land are subject to VAT where the land is. Supplies of transport services take place where the transport services are provided. For international journeys over state territory, this can result in the journey being divided up and being chargeable in more than one state. However, if international transport is zero rated, the only significance of this is in claiming input tax.

Services relating to cultural, artistic, sporting, scientific, educational, entertainment or similar activities (including organising such activities and providing ancillary services to them) occur where the services are supplied. This rule also applies to services related to movable tangible property and to ancillary transport services (such as port services).

A wide range of commercial services are regarded as taking place where the customer is located. This is of course the main rule for the supply of goods. These rules apply if either the supply is to a customer established outside the E.U., or if the supply is to a registered taxpayer established in a different E.U. state to the supplier. In other words, these are businesses to business supplies for VAT purposes. The significance of this is that they can be audited within the E.U. by the tax authorities of the receiving state. The rule applies if supplies going out of the E.U. are business supplies, not consumer supplies. These rules apply to : intellectual property rights; advertising services; professional services such as legal advice, accountancy, engineering consultants, data processing of information supplies banking, financial and insurance services supplies of staff, supplies of services, by agents for principals and leasing of goods, apart from transport. For example, a law firm supplying services to a business elsewhere in the E.U. or for example to a Canadian business will be regarded as supplying the services where the customer is based. There will therefore be no VAT imposed on the bills for the services by the state where the law firm is based. The means of supplying is therefore irrelevant.

INDEX

Accommodation, 6–17
Accounts
  accounting profession, 5–06
  charges, 5–13
  corporation tax, 13–04
  expenditure, 5–13
  guidelines, 5–06
  inheritance tax, 23–01
  profit and loss, 5–06
  standards, 5–06
  stock, 5–10
  VAT, 25–08–25–09
Accumulation or maintenance
  settlements, 21–03, 21–22
Acts. *See* Legislation
Adjudicator, 1–13
Administration
  inheritance tax, 23–01–23–06
  VAT, 24–04
Administrative law, 1–11
Advance corporation tax
  dividends, 10–10
  phasing out of, 13–04
Advisers, 1–14
Age allowance, 12–17
Agency workers, 5–01
Agents, 24–14
Agricultural land and buildings,
  8–07, 19–17, 19–26
'Annual', meaning, 4–01
Annual payments
  annuities, 10–02, 10–04
  collection, 10–06
  covenants, 10–02, 10–06
  definition, 10–02, 10–04
  income tax, 10–02, 10–06
  interest, 10–02, 10–04
  international aspects of
    taxation, 26–13
  profits, 10–02, 10–04

Annual payments—*contd*
  savings and investment income,
    10–01–10–06
  settlements, 11–10
  trusts and estates, 10–06
Annuities
  annual payments, 10–02,
    10–04
  capital, 10–07
  capital gains tax, 16–04
  deferred, 16–04
  definition, 10–02, 10–04
  disposals, 16–04
  income tax, 10–07
  inheritance tax, 18–13, 19–10
  international aspects of
    taxation, 26–13
  life assurance, 18–13
  options, 19–10
  purchased life, 10–07
  savings and investment income,
    10–01–10–05, 10–07
Anti-avoidance. *See* Tax
  avoidance
Appeals, 1–12
  agreements, 3–02
  Court of Appeal, 1–12
  courts, to, 1–12
  Ensign Tankers case, 2–16
  European Union, 1–12
  General Commissioners, 1–12
  handling, 2–16
  House of Lords, 1–12
  income tax, 3–02
  inheritance tax, 23–04
  judgments online, 2–19
  law and fact, 3–06
  Northern Ireland, 2–06
  reform, 1–12
  reports, 1–12

INDEX

Appeals—*contd*
  self-assessment, 3–06
  Scotland, 2–06
  Special Commissioners, 1–12
  tribunals, 1–12
  VAT, 1–12, 24–04
  withdrawal, 3–02
Armed forces, 19–11–19–12
Artificial transactions in land,
  7–09
Assessment
  casual earnings, 5–19
  corporation tax, 13–04
  expenditure, 5–16
  income tax, 3–02
  inheritance tax, 23–04
  partnerships, 12–07
  VAT, 24–04
Assets
  abroad, transfer of, 26–22
  acquisition after 31 March 82
    and before 6 April 1998,
    15–08
  business, 15–06, 16–12
  capital gains tax, 14–07,
    15–05, 16–08
  gifts, 16–12
  international aspects of
    taxation, 26–22
  leases, 15–05
  meaning, 14–07, 15–06
  replacement, 16–08
  options, 14–18
  tapering relief, 15–06
  tax avoidance, 26–22
  wasting, 15–05, 16–07
Authorities. *See* Tax authorities
Avoidance. *See* Tax avoidance
Avoision, 1–05

Bad debt relief, 25–13
Banks, 10–06
Base, 1–04, 1–09
Beneficial interests in possession,
  21–03–21–04
Beneficial loans, 6–11
Beneficial owners, death of,
  21–06

Beneficiaries, 11–03–11–04,
  14–28
Benefits in kind
  Code, 6–06, 6–08
  directors, 6–06
  emoluments, 6–06, 6–08,
    6–14, 6–22
  employment income, 6–06,
    6–08, 6–14, 6–22
  national insurance
    contributions, 6–25
Betting, 5–19
Bill, 12–21–12–22
Booklets, 2–12
Budget website, 2–19
Business leases, 7–07
Business transfers, 9–03, 14–16

Capital
  annuities, 10–07
  beneficiaries, 11–04
  capital gains tax, 14–14
  circulating, 4–02
  companies, 14–14
  disposal, 14–10–14–11
  distributions, 14–14
  expenditure, 4–02, 5–10
  fixed, 4–02
  income and, 4–01–4–02
  receipts, 4–02, 5–05
  savings and investment income,
    10–05
  settlements, 11–05, 11–06
  trusts and expenses, 11–04
Capital allowances, 8–01–8–11
  allowances,
    initial, 8–07
    types of, 8–06, 8–09
    writing down, 8–06–8–07,
      8–09
  agricultural land and buildings,
    8–10
  corporation tax, 13–09
  deductions, 8–02
  depreciation, 8–01
  draft Bill, 8–01
  expenditure, 8–01, 8–02–8–10
  industrial buildings, 8–09

Capital allowances—*contd*
  investments, 8–01
  losses, 9–02
  minor, 13–11
  plant and machinery,
    8–02–8–08
  pooling, 8–08
  profits, 8–02
  rates, 8–01
  Tax Law Rewrite Project,
    2–17, 8–01
  writing down allowances,
    8–06–8–07, 8–09, 8–10
Capital gains
  gains, meaning of, 4–01
  losses, 9–02, 9–05
  savings and investment income,
    10–01
  set-off, 9–02
  trading income, 5–01
Capital gains tax, 14–01–14–29
  adjustments, 14–15
  annuities, 16–04
  appropriations to and from
    stock in trade, 14–13
  assets,
    gifts of business, 16–12
    meaning of, 14–07
    replacement of business,
      16–08
    wasting, 15–05, 16–07
  capital distributions, 14–14
  charge to tax, 14–03–14–07
  chargeable gains,
    14–03–14–04, 14–06
  charities, 16–13
  chattels for or under £6, 000,
    16–06
  companies, 14–01,
    14–14–14–16, 16–09
  compensation, 16–02
  computation of gains and
    losses, 15–01–15–12
  concessions, 16–10
  connected persons, 14–08
  consideration, 15–02
  contingent consideration,
    14–12
  corporation tax, 13–06

Capital gains tax—*contd*
  damages, 14–07, 16–02
  death, 14–21–14–23
  debts, 14–17
  deferred consideration, 14–2
  disposals, 7–09, 14–04,
    14–06–14–13,
    14–25–14–29
    chattels for or under £6,
      000, 16–06
    meaning of, 14–08–14–11
    part, 15–04
    trustees, by, 14–25–14–29
  distributions, 14–14
  double taxation, 26–21
  employee share ownership
    plans, 16–02
  exemptions, 14–02, 14–13,
    16–01–16–13
  expenditure, 15–01, 15–03
  foreign currency, 16–02
  gains, computation of,
    15–01–15–02
  gifts, 14–08, 16–12
  gilts, 16–03
  history, 2–02
  holdover relief, 14–11, 16–01,
    16–10
  income tax, 2–08, 5–01,
    14–02, 14–13
  indexation, 15–05, 15–07,
    15–09–15–11
  individual savings accounts,
    15–02
  individuals, 14–01
  inflation, 14–01
  inheritance tax, 16–01, 20–07
  international aspects of
    taxation, 26–21
  life assurance, 16–04
  losses, computation of,
    15–01–15–12
  market value rule, 14–08
  motor cars, 16–02
  options, 14–18
  partnerships, 14–05
  personal rights, 14–07
  'persons', 14–05
  premiums, 7–07

Capital gains tax—*contd*
  private residences, 16–05
  purpose, 1–07, 2–01
  qualifying corporate bonds,
    16–03
  ranking, 2–08
  rates, 14–02
  reliefs, 15–01, 16–01–16–13
  reorganisation, 14–15
  replacement of business assets,
    16–08
  residence, 14–06
  retirement relief, 16–11
  securities, 16–03
  self-assessment, 14–01
  settled property, 14–21–14–29
  shares, 14–14–14–15, 15–11
  spouses, 14–02, 14–20
  stock in trade, appropriations
    from and to, 14–13
  tangible movables, 16–07
  tapering relief, 14–01, 15–07,
    15–09, 15–12, 16–11
  transfer of business to
    company, 14–16, 16–09
  trustees, 14–02, 14–25–14–29
  wasting assets, 15–05, 16–07
Capital transfer tax, 17–01
Carry-back of terminal losses,
    9–04
Carry-forward, 9–03, 13–11
Cars and related benefits, 6–09,
    16–02, 25–06
Case law
websites, 2–19
Case stated, 3–05
Casual earnings, 4–02, 5–19,
    6–04
Centralisation, 2–06
Certainty, 1–04
CGT. *See* Capital gains tax
Chargeable gains
  capital gains tax, 14–02–14–04
  charities, 16–13
  computation, 15–06–15–08
  corporation tax, 13–04
  debts, 14–17
  gilts, 16–03
  inflation, 15–06

Chargeable gains—*contd*
  inheritance tax, 16–01
  reliefs, 15–06, 16–11
  retirement relief, 16–11
  wasting assets, 16–07
Chargeable transfers,
    18–01–18–14,
    20–01–20–09, 22–01
Charges
  accountancy, 5–13
  corporation tax, 13–07
  double, 20–10
  expenditure, 5–13
  exit, 21–18–21–21
  income, 12–09, 13–09
  inheritance tax, 18–09–18–13,
    19–13, 20–10, 21–11,
    21–15–21–21, 23–06
  interim, 21–18–21–21
  legal, 5–13
  potentially exempt transfers,
    18–06
  principal, 21–15–21–21
  relief, 19–13, 21–11
  settlements, 21–03,
    21–05–21–21
  successive, 19–13, 21–11
Charging provisions
  capital gains tax, 14–03–14–07
  inheritance tax, 21–05–21–14
  legislation, 2–07, 2–08
  property income, 7–03
  taxes and, relationship
    between, 2–08
  VAT, 24–07–24–10
Charities
  capital gains tax, 16–12
  chargeable gains, 16–13
  corporation tax, 13–07
  covenants, 10–01
  disposals, 16–13
  incentives, 10–12
  inheritance tax, 19–06
  reforms, 10–01
  savings and investment income,
    10–12
Chartered Institute of Taxation,
    1–14, 2–14

Chattels for or under £6, 000,
    16–06
Children
  child benefit, 12–20
  children's tax credit, 12–19
  inheritance tax, 19–19, 19–21,
    21–22
  maintenance, 19–19, 19–21,
    21–22
  meaning, 19–19
  personal relief, 12–18
  settlements, 11–07
Close companies
  collection, 13–22
  corporation tax, 13–22
  definition, 13–22
  distributions, 13–20
  employee trusts, 19–23
  income, 12–12
  inheritance tax, 18–04–18–05,
    19–23, 21–12
  lifting the corporate veil,
    13–22
  loans, 12–12
  settlements, 21–12
  tax avoidance, 18–04
Code, The
  benefits in kind, 6–06, 6–08
  cars and related benefits, 6–10
  emoluments, 6–06, 6–08,
    6–10, 6–22
  employee shareholdings, 6–12
  employment income, 6–06,
    6–08, 6–10, 6–12–6–13
  expenditure, 6–08
  loopholes, 6–13
  PAYE, 6–22
  principles of, 6–08
Collection, 1–08. See also PAYE
  annual payments, 10–06
  close companies, 13–22
  costs, 1–05
  customs duties, 1–05
  interest, 10–06
  Internet, 27–04
  national insurance
    contributions, 6–23
  VAT, 27–04
Commercial leases, 7–07

Commissioners
  appeals, 1–12
  Genera, 1–12
  Inland Revenue, 1–10
  role, 1–10
  self-assessment, 3–04
  Special, 1–12
Companies. See also Close
    companies, Corporation tax,
    Shares
  adjustments, 14–15
  business transfers, 14–16
  capital, 14–14
  capital gains tax,
    14–14–14–17, 16–09
  consortiums, 13–18
  controlled foreign companies,
    26–22
  definition, 13–01
  distributions, 14–14
  employee-controlled, 12–11
  groups of, 13–18, 24–13
  incorporation, advantages of,
    13–03
  interest, 10–08
  international aspects of
    taxation, 26–03, 26–20,
    26–22
  investment, 13–10
  loans, 12–11
    relationships, 10–01
  migration of, 26–22
  non-resident, 13–01
  offshore, 26–23
  partnerships, distinguishing
    between, 12–06
  pocket book, 13–01
  purchase of own shares, 13–19
  reorganisation, 14–15
  residence, 26–03
  savings and investment income,
    10–01
  service, 6–03
  small, 12–11, 13–01, 13–05
  tax avoidance, 26–22
  transfer of business to a
    company, 14–16, 16–09
  VAT, 24–13

INDEX

Compensation, 14–10. *See also* Damages
Competition, 24–08, 24–13, 25–01
Complaints, 1–13
Compliance, 2–11
Connected persons
  arm's length transactions, 14–08
  capital gains tax, 14–08
  definition, 14–08
  international aspects of taxation, 26–12
Consolidation, 2–09
  finding the law, 2–10
  income tax, 2–03
  interpretation, 2–13
  national insurance contributions, 2–04
Consortiums, 13–16
Constitutional law, 1–11
Construction. *See* Interpretation
Construction industry, 5–01
Contributions Agency, 1–10
Controlled foreign companies, 26–22
Co-operatives, 12–12
Corporate veil, lifting the, 13–22
Corporation tax, 1–07, 13–01–13–20. *See also* Advance corporation tax
  accounting period, 13–04
  assessment, 13–04
  capital allowances, minor, 13–11
  capital gains tax, 13–06
  carry-forward, 13–13
  Case IV losses, 13–15
  chargeable gains, 13–06
  charges on income, 13–09
  charging provisions, 2–07
  charities, 13–09
  computation, 13–06
  consortiums, 13–18
  deductions, 13–08–13–11
  distributions, 13–01, 13–19–13–21
  dividends, 12–22

Corporation tax—*contd*
  expenditure, 13–09, 13–10
  financial years, 13–04
  group relief, 13–18
  history, 2–02
  income, 13–06
    charges on, 13–09
  income tax, 13–01, 13–06
  interest, 13–07
  investment companies, 13–10
  loan relationships, 13–06, 13–07
  losses, 13–12–13–18
  management expenses, 13–10
  non-residents, payments to, 13–09
  ownership, change of, 13–17
  payments, 13–09
    non-residents, to, 13–09
  periods, 13–04
  profits, 13–01
    computation of, 13–06
    deductions from total, 13–08–13–11
    set-off against current and previous, 13–14
  rates, 12–22, 13–01, 13–05
  reconstructions, 13–16
  self-assessment, 13–02
  set-off, 13–14
  small companies rate, 13–05
Costs, 3–04
Covenants, 10–02, 10–06, 10–12
Credits. *See* Tax credits
Criminal proceedings, 3–07, 3–09
Cross-border transactions, 27–03, 27–04
Customs, 1–02, 1–10
  collections costs, 1–05
  duties, removal of, 27–01
  European Union, 1–06
  guidance, 2–12
  powers, 1–10
  professions, 1–14
  VAT, 1–10, 24–04, 27–01
  views of, 2–12
  website, 2–19

Damages, 6–18, 14–07. *See also*
  Compensation
Death
  active service, on, 19–11
  alterations of dispositions
    taking effect on, 19–20
  beneficial owners, 21–06
  capital gains tax, 14–21–14–23
  inheritance tax, 18–03, 19–11,
    19–20, 20–02, 20–16,
    21–06, 22–01
  legatees, meaning of, 14–21
  partially exempt transfers,
    22–06
  personal representatives, 14–21
  same time, occurring at, 18–08
  settled property, 14–21–14–29
  termination of interest in
    possession by death,
    14–22
  transfers on, 18–08, 19–20,
    20–02, 22–01
  value transferred on, 20–16
Debts
  artificial, 20–09
  assignment, 14–17
  bad debt relief, 25–13
  capital gains tax, 14–17
  chargeable gains, 14–17
  disposals, 14–17
  inheritance tax, 20–09
  reliefs, 25–13
  satisfaction of, 14–17
  security, on, 14–17
Deductions
  capital allowances, 8–02
  corporation tax, 13–08–13–10
  expenditure, 5–10, 5–15,
    15–03
  income, 12–04–12–05, 12–11
  interest, 10–08, 12–11
  profits, 8–02
  savings and investment income,
    10–03
Definition of taxes, 1–01
Delegated legislation, 2–09
Demergers, 13–22
Depreciation, 5–12, 8–01
Destruction, 14–11

Devolution, 2–06
Directors
  benefits in kind, 6–06
  emoluments, 6–06
  remuneration, waiver of,
    19–24
  VAT, 24–14
Disabled persons' tax credit,
  12–22
Discounts, 25–07
Disposals
  annuities, 16–09
  capital, 14–10–14–11
  capital gains tax, 7–09, 14–04,
    14–06–14–13,
    14–25–14–29, 15–04
  charities, 16–13
  chattels for or under £6,000,
    16–06
  compensation, 14–10
  consideration, 21–10
  contingent consideration,
    14–12
  debts, 14–17
  deferred consideration, 14–12
  destruction, 14–11
  extension of rules on, 21–09
  gains, 15–04
  gilts, 16–03
  inheritance tax, 21–08–21–10,
    20–12
  interests in possession,
    21–08–21–10
  interests, 14–09
  leases, 14–09
  life assurance, 16–04
  loss, 14–11, 15–04
  meaning, 14–08–14–11
  negligible value, 14–11
  options, 14–18
  part, 14–09, 15–04
  personal representatives, 14–21
  private residences, 16–05
  property income, 7–09, 7–10
  qualifications, 21–10
  retirement relief, 16–11
  sale of land, 7–10
  settlements, 14–23,
    21–08,–21–10

Disposals—*contd*
shares, 15–11
spouses, 14–20
stamp duties, 7–10
trustees, 14–24–14–29
Distress, 3–02
Distributions
capital, 14–14
capital gains tax, 14–14
close companies, 13–20
corporation tax, 13–01,
13–19–13–22
demergers, 13–22
income tax, 13–19
meaning, 13–19–13–22
purchase of own shares, 13–22
savings and investment income,
10–01, 10–10
schedules, 13–19
settlements, 11–08
Divers, 5–01
Dividends
advance corporation tax,
10–08
corporation tax, 12–21
income tax, 10–10
inheritance tax, 19–25
losses, 9–03
meaning, 4–01
rates, 12–21
savings and investment income,
10–01, 10–10
Schedule F, 10–10
waiver of, 19–25
Domicile, 26–02, 26–05
Double taxation, 2–09, 26–01,
26–06–26–10,
26–13–26–15, 26–19–26–21
agreements, 26–07
capital gains tax, 26–21
foreign tax credits, 26–09
income, 26–08
interest, 26–08
limits on, 26–08
OECD Model Tax Convention,
26–07, 26–10,
26–13–26–14, 26–19,
26–21
reliefs, 26–06, 26–08–26–09

Double taxation—*contd*
tax credits, 26–09
tiebreaker provisions, 26–08
treaty shopping, 26–07
unilateral relief, 26–09
withholding tax, 26–13,
26–14
Dual purpose rule, 5–13
Dumping, 7–04
Duty free, 27–03

Earned income, 12–08
Earnings. *See* Casual earnings
Economy control, 1–02
Education, 25–06
Efficiency of taxation, 1–05
Electronic tax, 2–19
Emoluments
appointments, 6–17
benefits in kind, 6–06, 6–08,
6–14, 6–22
cars, 6–10
Code, 6–06, 6–08, 6–10, 6–22
directors, 6–06
employment income,
6–04–6–06
expenditure, 6–08
gifts, 6–05
golden handshakes, 6–04, 6–19
international aspects of
taxation, 26–16–26–19
living accommodation
expenses, 6–09
loans, 6–11
meaning, 4–01, 6–04
perks, 6–06, 6–10
sport, 6–05
termination payments, 6–03
Employees
close companies, 19–23
companies controlled by,
12–12
inheritance tax, 19–23
remuneration, waiver of,
19–23
self-employed, difference
between, 5–18
shareholdings, 6–12, 6–16

Employees—*contd*
  trusts for, 19–23
  VAT, 24–14
Employment income, 6–01–6–23
  accommodation, provision of,
    6–17
  beneficial loan arrangements,
    6–11
  benefits in kind, 6–06, 6–08,
    6–14, 6–22
  cars and related benefits, 6–10
  cases, 6–01
  code, 6–06, 6–08, 6–10,
    6–12–6–13
    loopholes and, 6–13
  contracts of service, 6–03
  emoluments, 6–04–6–06
  employee shareholdings, 6–12,
    6–16
  expenses, deductible, 6–18
  foreign element, 6–01
  gifts, 6–05
  golden handshakes, 6–19
  living accommodation
    expenses, 6–09
  national insurance
    contributions, 6–23–6–25
  'office or employment', 6–03
  one man service companies,
    6–02
  part-time officials, 6–02
  pensions, 6–01, 6–20
  professions, 6–02
  Schedule D, 6–02
  Schedule E, 6–01
    mechanics of, 6–22
  self-employed, 6–02
  service companies, 6–02
  social security, 6–21
  VAT, 6–02
  vouchers, 6–15
Ensign Tankers case, 2–16
Enterprise management incentive
  plans, 6–16
Equity, horizontal and vertical,
  1–04
Errors, 3–04
ESCs, 2–09, 2–12

ESOPs (employee share
  ownership plans), 6–16
ESOTs (employee share
  ownership trusts), 6–16
Estate duty, 17–01
E-tax, 2–19
Estates. *See* Trusts and estates
European Convention on Human
  Rights, 2–06
European Union
  appeals, 1–12
  customs duties, 1–06
  direct effect, 24–02
  interpretation, 2–09, 24–02
  judgments online, 2–14
  legislation, 2–09
  nationality discrimination,
    1–06
  preliminary rulings, 2–14
  single market, 2–06
  VAT, 1–06, 2–04, 2–06,
    24–01–24–08,
    24–12–24–13,
    25–01–25–07,
    27–01–27–04
Evasion. *See* Tax evasion
Executive share schemes, 6–16
Exemptions
  capital gains tax, 14–02, 14–13
  inheritance tax, 18–01–18–07,
    19–01–19–27, 20–02,
    20–10, 21–13
  spouses, 19–01
  VAT, 24–12, 25–01,
    25–03–25–05, 25–12,
    27–03
Expenditure
  agricultural land and buildings,
    8–07
  assessment basis, 5–16
  capital, 4–02, 5–12
  capital allowances, 8–01,
    8–02–8–10
  capital gains tax, 15–01, 15–03
  Code, The, 6–08
  corporation tax, 13–07, 13–08
  deductions, 5–11, 5–15, 6–18,
    15–03
  depreciation, 5–10

INDEX

Expenditure—*contd*
dual purpose doctrine, 5–13
emoluments, 6–08
employment income, 6–18
gains, 15–01, 15–03
improvements, 5–15
indexation allowance, 15–09
industrial buildings, 8–09
inheritance tax, 19–04
interest, 5–13
investment companies, 13–10
legal and accountancy charges, 5–13
living accommodation expenses, 6–09
losses, 15–01, 15–03
management, 13–10
normal, 19–04
pensions,
  contributions, 5–13
  income, 5–18
pooling, 8–08
prohibited, not, 5–15
property income, 7–06
receipts, post-cessation, 5–14
repairs, 5–15
quantum, 5–13
revenue, 5–12
Schedule D, 5–11, 5–13
Schedule E, 5–11, 5–13
self-employed, 5–13, 5–18
tax, 1–09
trading income, 5–11–5–18
travel to work and at work, 5–13, 6–18
trusts and expenses, 11–03
wasting assets, 15–05
wholly and exclusively for the purposes of trade, 5–13, 5–20, 7–06, 8–02, 15–03
Expenses. *See* Expenditure
Exports, 27–03, 27–04
Extra-statutory concessions, 2–09, 2–12

Factoring, 7–08
Fairness of taxation, 1–04
Family provision orders, 19–21c

Farming
farm land and buildings, 8–07
inheritance tax, 19–17, 19–26
losses, 9–02
Film industry, 2–16
Finding tax law, 2–10
Food, 25–02
Foreign currency, 16–02
Foreign taxes. *See also* Double taxation, International aspects of taxation
credits, 25–09
enforcement of, 2–06
Furnished property, 7–06
Furniss v *Dawson*, 2–14

GAAR, 2–11
Gains.*See also* Chargeable gains
apportionment, 15–06, 15–10
computation, 15–01–15–12
consideration, 15–02
disposals, part, 15–04
expenditure, 15–01, 15–03
foreign, 26–10–26–21
indexation, 15–05, 15–07, 15–09–15–11
meaning, 4–01
receipts, 15–01
GATS, 27–01
GATT, 27–01, 27–02
General anti-avoidance provisions, 2–15
General Commissioners, 1–12
Ghosts, 1–05
Gifts, 5–19, 6–05, 14–08, 16–01, 16–12
capital gains tax, 14–08, 16–12
casual earnings, 5–19
charities, 19–06
emoluments, 6–05
employment income, 6–05
holdover relief, 16–01
housing associations, 19–08
inheritance tax, 16–01, 18–01–18–07, 19–03, 19–05–19–09
marriage, in consideration of, 19–05
national purposes, for, 19–09

Gifts—*contd*
political parties, 19–07
reservation of benefit, with,
18–07
reliefs, 16–01
small, to same person, 19–03
Gilts, 16–03
Golden handshakes, 6–04, 6–19
Government stock, 10–01
Grossing up, 12–04, 20–08
Group of companies, 13–18,
24–13
Guidance, 2–12

Hearings, 3–04
History of taxation, 2–02
HM Treasury website, 2–19
Historic buildings, 19–14
Holdover relief, 14–11, 16–01,
16–08, 16–10
Holiday accommodation, 7–06
Housing associations, 19–08
Husband and wife. *See* Spouses

Identity of the taxpayer, 1–09
Imports, 27–01, 27–03
Improvements, 5–15
Incentives, 1–05, 7–06, 10–12
Income, 12–01–12–19. *See also*
Casual earnings,
Employment income, Income
tax, Property income,
Savings and investment
income, Trading income
beneficiaries, 11–03
capital and, 4–01–4–02
charges, 12–10, 13–06
child benefit, 12–20
children's tax credit, 12–19
classification, 12–08
close companies, 12–12
computation, 12–11
co-operatives, 12–12
corporation tax, 13–07, 13–08
deductions, 12–04–12–05,
12–11
double taxation, 26–08
earned, 12–08

Income—*contd*
employee-controlled
companies, 12–12
estate, 11–04
foreign, 26–10–26–21
gross, 12–05
grossing up, 12–05
inheritance tax, 12–14
interest, 12–05, 12–11
investment, 12–08
loans, 12–12–12–14, 13–07
losses, 9–02, 9–05
married couple's allowance,
12–18
mortgage interest relief, 12–11
partnership, 12–07, 12–12
pensions, 5–18
personal allowances,
12–17–12–18
personal reliefs, 12–16
plants and machinery, 12–13
receipts, 4–02
reliefs, 12–16–12–18
savings, 12–08
schedules, 12–01, 12–08
set-off, 9–02
settlements, 11–05,
11–06–11–07, 11–09
small businesses, 12–12
tax bill, 12–21–12–22
tax credits, 12–23
taxable income, conversion
into, 12–15–12–20
total, 12–09–12–14
trusts and estates, 11–01,
11–03–11–04, 12–05
types of, 12–03
unearned, 12–08
widow's bereavement
allowance, 12–20
Income tax, 3–01–3–10. *See also*
Employment income, PAYE,
Property income, Savings
and investment income, Self-
assessment, Trading income
agreements, 3–02
annual, 2–03
payments, 10–02, 10–04
annuities, 10–07

INDEX

Income tax—*contd*
appeals, 3–02
assessments, 3–02
capital gains tax, 2–04, 5–01,
14–02, 14–13
charging provisions, 2–07
consolidation, 2–03
corporation tax, 13–01, 13–06
devolution, 2–06
distress, 3–02
distributions, 13–19
dividends, 10–10
fairness, 1–04
handling case on, 3–01–3–10
harmonisation, 14–02
history, 2–02
'income', 4–01
inheritance tax, 19–22
interest, 10–08
international aspects of
taxation, 26–03
legislation, 2–02
meaning, 1–07
premiums, 7–07
progressive, 1–04
purpose, 1–07
ranking, 2–08
rates, 13–01
re-enactment of legislation,
2–03
reform, 2–03
residence, 26–03
returns, 3–02
rich persons, 1–04
Royal Commissions, 2–03
savings and investment income,
10–05
Schedules, 2–07, 2–08
settlements, 11–09
source doctrine, 2–03
starting rate, 12–22
Tax Law Rewrite Project, 2–17
trusts and estates, 11–02,
11–04
VAT, 2–08
Indexation, 15–05, 15–06,
15–09–15–11
Individual savings accounts,
10–11

Information
inheritance tax, 23–03
legal professional privilege,
23–03
tax authorities, 1–11
Inheritance tax, 17–01
accounts, delivery of, 23–01
accumulation and maintenance
settlements, 21–22
administration, 23–01–23–06
agricultural property, 19–17,
19–26
annuities, 18–13, 19–10
appeals, 23–04
appointment powers, 18–01,
18–08
armed forces, 19–11–19–12
assessment, 23–04
beneficial interests in
possession, 21–04
beneficial owners, death of,
21–06
business property, 19–16
capital gains tax, 16–01, 20–07

capital transfer tax, 17–01
change of name, 2–03
chargeable transfers,
18–01–18–14,
20–01–20–09, 22–01
charges, 18–04–18–08, 19–13,
20–10, 21–11,
21–15–21–21, 23–06
charging provisions,
21–05–21–14
charities, 19–06
close companies,
18–09–18–10, 19–23,
21–12
collection, 23–01–23–06
computation, 20–01–20–16
death,
active service, on, 19–11
alterations of
dispositions taking
effect on, 19–20
beneficial owners, of, 21–06
same time, occurring at,
18–08

Inheritance tax—*contd*
death—*contd*
transfers on, 18–08, 19–20,
20–02, 22–01
value transferred on, 20–16
debts, artificial, 20–09
determinations, 23–04
diminution principle, 18–01
disposals,
consideration, for, 21–10
extension of rules on, 21–09
interests in possession,
21–08
qualifications, 21–10
restrictions on freedom of,
20–12
disposition, meaning of, 18–01
dividends, waiver of, 19–25
double charges, 20–10
employees, trusts for, 19–23
estate duty, 17–01
excluded property, 18–01
exemptions, 18–01–18–07,
19–01–19–27, 20–02,
20–10, 21–13
exit charge, 21–18–21–21
expenditure, normal out of
income, 19–04
family maintenance, 19–19,
19–21, 21–22
fixed interest trusts, 21–13
general anti-avoidance
provisions, 2–15
gifts, 16–01, 18–01
charities, 19–06
housing associations, 19–08
marriage, in consideration
of, 19–05
national purposes, for,
19–09
political parties, 19–07
reservation of benefit, with,
18–07
small, to same person, 19–03
grossing up, 20–08
historic buildings, 19–14
history, 2–02, 17–01
holdover relief, 16–01
housing associations, 19–08

Inheritance tax—*contd*
incidence, 22–05–22–06
income, 12–14
income tax, 19–22
information, power to require,
23–03
inspections, 23–03
instalments, 23–05
interest, 23–05
interests in possession,
disposals of, 21–08
termination of, 21–07,
21–09–21–10
interim charges, 21–18–21–21
late reported transfers, 20–04
leases, 18–02, 20–14
land, interest on, 23–05
liabilities, 20–06–20–10,
22–01–22–04
limitations of liability, 22–04
life assurance, 18–13, 20–15
loans, 12–12, 12–14, 18–07
maintenance , 19–14, 19–19,
21–22
marriage, 19–05
meaning, 1–07
national purposes, gifts for,
19–09
open market value, 20–11,
20–16
options, 19–10, 20–12
partially exempt transfers,
22–06
payments, 18–01, 23–05
future, 18–11
personal representatives, 23–01
potentially exempt transfers,
18–02, 20–02, 20–10,
21–13, 23–01
principal charge, 21–15–21–17
property,
exception from liability,
22–03
inspections, 23–03
transfers of more than one,
20–03
valuation of related, 20–13
rates, 20–01–20–05, 21–17,
21–20, 22–05, 23–05

Inheritance tax—*contd*
related property, 20–13
reliefs, 16–01, 19–01–19–27,
 20–02, 20–13, 21–11
remuneration, 19–24
retirement benefits, 19–22
returns and persons acting for
 settlors, 23–02
reversionary interests, purchase
 of, 21–23
same day, transfers on, 20–04
services, payment for, 18–01
settled property, 21–01–21–23,
 22–01, 23–02
settlor, reversion to, 21–10
spouses,
 marriage, in consideration
  of, 19–05
 reversion to, 21–10
 transfers between, 19–01,
  22–02, 22–05
stamp duties, 20–07
successive charges, 19–13
taper relief, 20–02
tax avoidance, 18–01, 18–10
tax free legacies, 22–06
ten year charge, 21–15–21–17
time limits, 23–05
transfer of value, 18–02, 18–11
 meaning of, 18–01
trustees' remuneration, 21–10
trusts, 19–23, 21–13
unpaid tax, charges for, 23–06
valuation, 20–09,
 20–11–20–16
values not exceeding £3, 000,
 19–02
voidable transfers, 19–15
wills, 22–05
woodlands, 19–18
works of art, 19–14
Inland Revenue
Ajudicator, 1–13
agreements, 2–12
commissioners, 1–10
Contributions Agency, 1–10
guidance, 2–12
inspectors, 1–10
offices, 1–10

Inland Revenue—*contd*
professions, 1–14
role, 1–10
views of, 2–12
website, 2–14
Inquiries, 3–08
Inspections, 23–03
Inspectors, 1–10
Instalments
inheritance tax, 23–05
interest, 23–05
premiums, 7–07
Institute for Fiscal Studies
website, 2–19
Institute of Indirect Tax
Practitioners, 1–14
Instruction manuals, 2–12
Intellectual property, 10–09
Interest
annual payments, 10–02–10–05
banks, 10–08
collection, 10–08
companies, 10–08
corporation tax, 13–05
deductions, 10–08, 12–10
definition, 10–02
deposits, 10–08
double taxation, 26–08
expenditure, 5–11
income, 12–05, 12–11
income tax, 10–06
inheritance tax, 23–05
instalments, 23–05
judgments, 10–02
loans, 13–07
losses, 9–03
mortgage interest relief, 12–12
savings and investment income,
 10–01–10–04, 10–08
settlements, 11–06
short, 10–08
yearly, 10–08
Interests in possession,
 21–03–21–04, 21–08–21–10
International aspects of taxation,
 1–06, 26–01–26–22. *See also*
 European Union, Foreign
 taxes, Non-residents

International aspects of
  taxation—*contd*
annual payments, 26–13
annuities, 26–13
anti-avoidance provisions,
  26–22–26–23
assets, transfer abroad, 26–22
associated traders, 26–12
capital gains tax, 26–21
companies, 26–20
  controlled foreign, 26–22
  migration of, 26–22
  residence of, 26–03
cross-border transactions,
  26–12
dividends, 26–14, 26–20
domicile, 26–02, 26–05
double taxation, 2–09, 26–01,
  26–06–26–10,
  26–13–26–15,
  26–19–26–21
emoluments, 26–16–26–19
foreign income and gains,
  26–10–26–21
four year rule, 26–04
gains, 26–10–26–21
income, 26–10–26–21
income tax, 26–03
land, 26–11
183 day rule, 26–03, 26–19
OECD Model Tax Convention,
  26–07, 26–10,
  26–13–26–14, 26–19,
  26–21
offshore funds, 26–23
ordinary residence, 26–02,
  26–05
possessions, 26–14
professions, 26–12
remittance basis, 26–14
residence, 26–02–26–05,
  26–18–26–19
Schedule A, 26–11
Schedule D, 26–12–26–15
Schedule E, 26–16–26–19
Schedule F, 26–20
securities, 26–14
tax havens, 1–06
temporary visits, 26–03

International aspects of
  taxation—*contd*
trade, 26–12
UK, persons caught by,
  26–02–26–05
VAT, 27–01–27–04
vocations, 26–12
Internet, 2–19, 27–03, 27–04
Interpretation, 2–13
ambiguity, 2–13
complexity, 2–13
consolidation, 2–13
European Union, 2–13, 24–02
general anti-avoidance
  provisions, 2–15
legislation, 2–09, 2–13
ordinary meaning, 2–13
rules, 15–02
statutory, 2–13
tax avoidance, 2–13
technical meaning, 2–13
VAT, 24–02
wide, 2–13
Investments. *See also* Savings and
  investment income
companies, 13–10
income, 12–08
management expenses, 13–10
Invoices, 25–10
ISAs (individual savings
  accounts), 10–11

Joint tenancies, 14–22
Judgments
interest, 10–02
websites, 2–19
Judicial review, 3–08
Land. *See* Property income
Law. *See* Tax law
Leaflets, 2–12
Leases
assignment, 7–07
carve-out schemes, 18–06
commercial, 7–07
disposal, 14–09
furnished, 7–06
inheritance tax, 18–06, 20–14
lease-backs, 7–07
premiums, 7–07

INDEX

Leases—*contd*
property income, 7–04,
7–06–7–07, 7–10
reservation of benefits, 18–06
stamp duties, 7–10
wasting assets, 15–05
Legal charges, 5–14
Legal professional privilege,
23–03
Legatees, meaning of, 14–21
Legislation
charging provisions, 2–07,
2–08
consolidation, 2–03, 2–09,
2–10, 2–13
Constitution, lack of, 2–09
debates, 2–09
delegated, 2–09
double taxation agreements,
2–09
European Union, 2–09
extra-statutory concessions,
2–09
income tax, 2–03
interpretation, 2–09, 2–13
Schedules, 2–07, 2–05
Tax Law Rewrite Project,
2–08, 2–07
websites, 2–19
Licences, 7–04
Life assurance, 16–04, 18–13,
20–15
Living accommodation expenses,
6–08
Loans
beneficial, 6–14
cash equivalent, 6–11
companies, 10–01
close, 12–11
co-operatives, 12–11
corporation tax, 13–04
emoluments, 6–11
employee-controlled
companies, 12–12
employment income, 6–11
income, 12–11–12–14, 13–07
inheritance tax, 12–12, 12–14,
18–07
interest, 13–07

Loans—*contd*
loans, 13–07
partnerships, 12–12
plant and machinery, 12–13
profits, 13–07
relationships, 10–01, 13–06
definition, 13–07
relief, 6–11
writing off, 6–11
Losses, 9–01–9–05
apportionment, 15–10
calculation, 9–01
capital allowances, 9–02
capital gains, set-off against,
9–02, 9–05
carry-back of terminal, 9–04
carry-forward, 13–13
subsequent profits, against,
9–03
Case IV, 13–15
computation, 13–12,
15–01–15–02
consideration, 15–02
corporation tax, 13–12–13–18
disposals, 14–11, 15–12
part, 15–04
early year, 9–05
expenditure, 15–01, 15–03
farming, 9–02
group relief, 13–16
income, set-off against, 9–02,
9–05
interest, 9–03
loans, 13–05
market gardening, 9–02
ownership, change of, 13–17
partnerships, 9–03, 9–04
payments, 9–03
professions, 9–01–9–05
profits,
carry-forward against, 9–03,
13–11
set-off, 13–14
qualifying corporate bonds,
15–12
receipts, 15–01
reconstructions, 13–16
relief, 9–02–9–03, 9–05
securities, 15–12

Losses—*contd*
set-off, 9–02, 9–04, 9–05,
13–13
taper relief, 15–12
terminal, 9–04
trades, 9–01–9–05
transfer of businesses, 9–03
Lump, 5–01

Machinery and plant,
8–02–8–08, 12–12
Mail order, 27–03
Maintenance
covenants, 10–06
historic buildings, 19–14
inheritance tax, 19–14, 19–19,
19–21, 21–22
settlements, 21–22
works of art, 19–14
Maladministration, 3–10
Management expenses, 13–08
Manuals, 2–12
Market gardening, 9–02
Marriage, 19–05, 19–19
Married couple's allowance,
abolition of, 12–18
Mistakes, 3–04
Moonlighting, 1–05
Mortgage interest relief, 12–10
Motor vehicles, 6–10, 16–02,
25–06

National insurance contributions,
1–07
benefits in kind, 6–24
Class 1, 6–24
Class 1A, 6–25
collection, 6–23
consolidation, 2–03
Contributions Agency, 1–10
earnings, 6–24
periods, 6–24
employment income,
6–23–6–25
guidance, 2–12
history, 2–02
PAYE, 6–23
primary, 6–24

National insurance
contributions—*contd*
rates, 6–24
Schedule E, 6–23–6–24
secondary, 6–24
self-employed, 5–17–5–18
trading income, 5–17–5–18
National purposes, gifts for,
19–09
Negligence, 1–14
Non-residents. *See also*
Intenrational aspects of
taxation
companies, 13–01
corporation tax, 13–01, 13–07
payments, to, 13–07
Northern Ireland, 2–03

OECD Model Tax Convention,
26–07, 26–10,
26–13–26–14, 26–19, 26–21
Office-holders, 6–02, 24–14
Offshore funds, 26–23
Ombudsman, 1–13
One man service companies,
6–02
Options, 14–18, 15–02–15–03,
19–10, 20–12

Parliamentary Ombudsman, 1–13
Parliamentary proceedings, 2–12
Partnerships
assessments, 12–07
capital gains tax, 14–05
companies, differences
between, 12–07
income, 12–07, 12–12
loans, 12–12
losses, 9–03, 9–04
self-assessment, 3–03
PAYE (Pay-As-You-Earn)
Code, 6–22
national insurance
contributions, 6–23
repayments, 6–22
Schedule E, 6–22
vouchers, 6–15
Payments. *See also* Annual
payments, Distributions

INDEX

Payments—*contd*
corporation tax, 13–07
future, 18–06
inheritance tax, 18–01, 18–11,
23–05
losses, 9–03
non-residents, to, 13–07
services, for, 18–01
settled property, 14–29
termination, 6–04, 6–19
trading income, 5–08
voluntary, 5–08
Penalties
automatic, 3–07
criminal proceedings, 3–07
mitigation, 3–07
personal representatives, 3–09
self-assessment, 3–07–3–09
settlements, 3–09
tax evasion, 3–09
Pensions
contributions, 5–14, 6–20
deferred earnings, as, 10–01
employment income, 6–01,
6–20
expenditure, 5–14, 5–18
income, 5–18
occupational, 6–20
savings and investment income,
10–01
self-employed, 5–18
SERPS, 6–20
Perks, 6–06
Personal reliefs
age allowance, 12–17
children's tax credit, 12–19
income, 12–16–12–20
married couple's allowance,
abolition of, 12–18
personal allowance, 12–17
reductions, 12–16, 12–18
traveller's, 27–03
VAT, 27–03
widow's bereavement
allowance, 12–20
Personal representatives
disposals, 14–21
inheritance tax, 23–01
penalties, 3–09

Personal representatives—*contd*
potentially exempt transfers,
23–01
trusts and estates, 11–04
PETs (potentially exempt
transfers), 18–06, 20–02,
20–10, 21–13, 23–01
Planning. *See* Tax planning
Plant and machinery, 8–02–8–08,
12–13
Political parties, gifts to, 19–07
Pollution tax, 1–02
Pooling, 8–08
Potentially exempt transfers,
18–06, 20–02, 20–10,
21–13, 23–01
Poverty trap, 12–22
Preliminary rulings, 2–14
Premiums
assignment, 7–07
capital gains tax, 7–07
commercial leases, 7–07
disguised, 7–07
income tax, 7–07
instalments, 7–07
lease backs, 7–07
meaning, 7–07
property income, 7–04, 7–07
Schedule A, 7–07
tax avoidance, 7–07
Press releases, 2–12
Principles of taxation, 1–03–1–06
Privilege, 23–03
Professions
customs, 1–14
employment income, 6–02
Inland Revenue, 1–14
international aspects of
taxation, 26–12
losses, 9–01–9–05
trading income, 5–03
Profits
accounts, 5–06
annual payments, 10–02
capital allowances, 8–02
carry-forward, 9–03
computation of, 5–06, 13–04
corporation tax, 13–01, 13–06,
13–08–13–11

Profits—*contd*
  deductions, 8–02
  loans, 13–05
  losses, 9–03, 13–14
  meaning, 4–01
  profit-sharing schemes, 6–15
  set-off, 13–14
  stock, 5–10
  trading income, 5–06
Property. *See also* Property
  income, Settlements
  exception from liability, 22–03
  inheritance tax, 20–03, 20–13,
    22–03, 23–03
  inspections, 23–03
  related, 20–13
  transfers of more than one,
    20–03
  valuation of related, 20–13
Property income, 7–01–7–10
  artificial transactions, 7–09
  capital gains tax, 7–09
  charge to tax, 7–03
  charging provisions, 7–03
  commercial lettings, 7–07
  computation, 7–05
  disposals, 7–09, 7–10
  dumping, 7–04
  expenditure, 7–06
  factoring, 7–08
  furnished accommodation, 7–06
  holiday accommodation, 7–06
  international aspects of
    taxation, 26–11
  leases, 7–04, 7–06–7–07, 7–10
  licences, 7–04
  history, 7–01
  incentives, 7–06
  owner-occupiers, 7–01
  premiums, 7–04, 7–07
  receipts, 7–04
  rent, 7–04
    factoring, 7–08
  rent-a-room letting, 7–06
  Schedule A, 7–01–7–10
    scope of, 7–04
  Schedule B, 7–01
  stamp duty, 7–10
  tax avoidance, 7–09

Purchase of own shares, 13–19

Qualifying corporate bonds,
  15–12, 16–03

Ramsay principle, 2–14
Rates, 1–09
  basic rate, 12–22
  capital allowances, 8–01
  capital gains tax, 14–02
  corporation tax, 12–22, 13–01,
    13–05
  dividends, 12–22
  example of workings, 12–22
  harmonisation, 14–02
  higher rate, 12–22
  income, 12–22
  income tax, 13–01, 14–02
  inheritance tax, 20–01–20–05,
    21–17, 21–20, 22–05,
    23–05
  lower rate, 12–22
  national insurance
    contributions, 6–23
  poverty trap, 12–21
  settlements, 21–14, 21–17,
    21–20
  small companies, 13–01,
    13–05
  starting rate, 12–22
  tax bill, 12–22
  trusts and estates, 11–02
  VAT, 25–01–25–06
Rebates, 25–07
Receipts
  capital, 4–02, 5–07
  capital gains tax, 15–01
  expenditure, 5–17
  gains, 15–01
  income, 4–02
    property, 7–04
    trading, 5–07
  losses, 15–01
  post-cessation, 5–17
  voluntary payments, 5–07
Reconstructions, 13–16
Records, 3–04
Redistribution of wealth, 1–02

Reliefs. *See also* Personal reliefs
  agricultural property, 19–17
  bad debt, 25–13
  capital gains tax, 14–01
  chargeable gains, 15–06
  charges, successive, 19–13,
    21–11
  chattels at or under £6,000,
  corporation tax, 13–16
  double taxation, 26–06,
    26–08–26–09
  gifts, 16–01
  group, 13–18
  historic buildings, 19–14
  holdover, 16–01, 16–08,
    16–10
  indexation, 15–06,
    15–09–15–11
  inheritance tax, 16–01,
    19–01–19–27, 20–02,
    20–13, 21–11
  loans, 6–11
  losses, 9–02–9–03, 9–05,
    13–18
  mortgage interest, 12–12
  private residences, 16–05
  replacement of business assets,
    16–08
  retirement, 16–11
  settlements, 19–13, 21–11
  tapering, 14–01, 15–07,
    15–09, 15–12, 16–11,
    20–02
  tax bill, 12–22
  VAT, 25–13
  woodlands, 19–18
  works of art, 19–14
Remuneration, 19–24
Rent, 7–04, 7–08
Repairs, 5–15
Repayments, 6–21
Replacement of business assts,
  16–08
Reservation of benefit, 18–02
Residence
  capital gains tax, 14–06,
    16–05
  companies, 26–03
  income tax, 26–03

Residence—*contd*
  international aspects of
    taxation, 26–02–26–05,
    26–18–26–19
  ordinary, 26–02, 26–05
  private, 16–05
  temporary, 14–06, 26–03
Retail prices index, 15–05
Retailers, 25–06
Retirement benefits, 19–22
Retirement relief, 16–11
Returns
  income tax, 3–02
  inheritance tax, 23–02
  self-assessment, 3–03
  settlements, 23–02
  VAT 25–09–25–11
Revenue. *See* Inland Revenue
Reviews, 1–13
  judicial review, 3–10
  maladministration, 3–10
  reviewers, of, 3–10
  self-assessment, 3–10
Rewrite Project, 2–08, 2–18,
  6–20, 8–01
Royalties, 1–08, 10–01, 10–07

Sale of land, 7–10
Sanctions, 3–03
Savings and investment income,
  10–01–10–12, 12–07
  annual payments,
    10–01–10–06
  annuities, 10–01–10–05,
    10–07
  capital, 10–05
  capital gains, 10–01
  Case III, 10–05
    scope of, 10–02
  charities, 10–12
  companies, 10–01
  deductions, 10–05
  distributions, 10–01, 10–10
  dividends, 10–01, 10–10
  forms of, 10–01
  government stock, 10–01
  income tax, 10–05
  intellectual property, 10–09
  interest, 10–01–10–05, 10–08

Savings and investment income—
  contd
  pensions, 10–01
  royalties, 10–01
  tax-preferred savings schemes,
    10–11
  trading income, comparison
    with, 10–02
  trusts, 10–01
Schedules
  casual earnings, 5–19
  distributions, 13–17
  exclusivity, 2–08, 6–02
  history of, 2–02
  income, 12–01, 12–07
  income tax, 2–07, 2–08
  international aspects of
    taxation, 26–10–26–20
  losses, 13–15
  national insurance
    contributions, 6–23
  PAYE, 6–22
  premiums, 7–07
  Schedule A, 2–07, 5–19,
    7–01–7–10, 26–10
  Schedule B, 2–07, 7–01
  Schedule C, 2–07
  Schedule D, 2–07, 5–01, 5–11,
    5–19 , 6–01–6–02, 10–01
    Cases I-VI, 2–07, 5–01,
      5–11, 5–19, 5–20, 6–01,
      26–10–26–15
    international aspects of
      taxation, 26–10–26–15
    savings and investment
      income, 10–02–10–05
  Schedule E, 2–03, 5–01, 5–19,
    6–01
    international aspects of
      taxation, 26–16–26–19
    mechanics of, 6–22
  Schedule F, 2–07, 10–01,
    10–10, 26–20
  self-employed, 5–20
School fees, 6–07
Scotland, 2–06, 24–04
Securities. *See also* Shares
  capital gains tax, 16–03
  disposals, 15–12

Securities—*contd*
  gilts, 16–03
  international aspects of
    taxation, 26–14
Self-assessment, 3–03–3–10
  appeals, 3–05–3–06
  case stated, 3–05
  Commissioners, 3–04
  corporation tax, 13–02
  costs, 3–04
  criminal proceedings, 3–07
  errors, correction of, 3–04
  hearings, 3–04
  inquiries, 3–03
  late filing, 3–03
  law and fact, 3–06
  partnerships, 3–03
  penalties, 3–07, 3–09
  prosecutions, 3–09
  purpose of, 2–11
  records, 3–04
  returns, 3–03
  reviewers, reviewing the, 3–10
  sanctions, 3–03
  settlements, 3–09
  tax evasion, 3–08
  time limits, 3–03, 3–04, 3–09
Self-employed
  artificial, 6–02
  employees and, distinction
    between, 5–20
  employment income, 6–02
  expenditure, 5–13, 5–18
  intermediaries, acting through,
    6–02
  national insurance
    contributions, 5–20
  ordinarily, 5–18
  pensions, 5–15
  Schedule E, 5–01
  Schedules, 5–20
  tax credits, 12–22
  trading income, 5–01
  travel to work and at work,
    5–14
  VAT, 6–02, 24–14
SERPs, 6–20
Service companies, 6–02
Services, payments for, 18–01

INDEX

Set-off
  capital gains, 9–02
  income, 9–02
  losses, 9–02, 9–04, 9–05,
    13–12
  profits, 13–14
  VAT, 15–03
Settlements
  accumulation and maintenance
    trusts, 21–03, 21–22
  annual payments, 11–09
  beneficial interests in
    possession, 21–03–21–04
  beneficial owners, death of,
    21–06
  capital, 11–05, 11–06–11–08
    settlor, paid to, 11–08
  capital gains tax, 14–21–14–29
  cash, 3–07
  chargeable transfers, 22–01
  charging, 21–05
    classification for, 21–03
    interim or exit charges,
      21–18–21–21
    principal charge,
      21–15–21–21
    reliefs for successive, 21–11
  children, 11–07
  classification, 21–03
  close companies, 21–12
  concurrent interests, 14–22
  consideration, disposals for,
    21–10
  contingent interests, 21–04
  death of beneficial owners,
    21–06
  discretionary trusts, 21–02,
    21–14
  disposals, 14–23,
    21–08–21–10
  distributions, 11–08
  fixed interest settlements,
    21–05
  fixed interest trusts, 21–13
  foreign law, 21–01
  income, 11–05, 11–06–11–07,
    11–09
  income tax, 11–08

Settlements—contd
  inheritance tax, 21–01–21–23,
    22–01, 23–02
  interest, 11–07
  interests in possession,
    21–03–21–04
    disposal of, 21–08–21–10
    reverter to settlor, 21–10
    reverter to spouse, 21–10
    termination of, 21–07,
      21–09–21–10
  interim or exit charges,
    21–19–21–21
  joint tenants, 14–22
  maintenance and
    accumulation, 21–22
  meaning, 14–22, 21–01
  new entitlements, 21–10
  payments, 14–29
  penalties, 3–09
  potentially exempt transfers,
    21–13
  principal charge, 21–15–21–21
  property, putting into
    settlement, 14–23
  rates, 21–14, 21–17, 21–20
  relief for successive charges,
    21–11
  relevant property, 21–14,
    21–16
  returns, 23–02
  reversionary interests, 21–04,
    21–10, 21–23
  reverter to settlor, 21–10
    spouse of, 21–10
  settlor retains an interest,
    where, 11–06
  spouses, 21–10
  tax avoidance, 11–05
  tax evasion, 3–07
  ten year charge, 21–15–21–21
  tenants in common, 14–22
  trustees, 14–22–14–23
    remuneration, 21–10
  trusts and estates,
    11–05–11–09
    bare, 14–22
  unmarried minor children,
    11–07

Settlements—*contd*
vesting, 14–22
Share option schemes, 6–16
Shares
agricultural land, 19–17
bed and breakfasting, 15–11
bonus issues, 14–15
capital gains tax,
14–14–14–15, 15–11
disposals, 15–11
distributions, 13–19
indexation relief, 15–11
pooling arrangements, 15–11
purchase of own, 13–22
reorganisations, 14–15
Single market, 2–06
Sharkey v *Wernher* rule, 5–10
Small businesses, 12–11, 13–01,
13–03
Social control, 1–02
Social costs, 1–05
Social security, 6–20
Social security contributions. *See*
National insurance
contributions
Source doctrine, 2–03
Special Commissioners, 1–12
Sps (Statements of Practice),
2–12, 2–16
Sport, 6–04
Spouses
capital gains tax, 14–02, 14–20
disposals, 14–20
dissolution of marriage, 19–19
exemptions, 19–01
gifts in consideration of
marriage, 19–05
inheritance tax, 19–01, 19–05,
19–19, 19–21, 21–10,
21–22, 22–02, 22–05
maintenance, 19–19, 19–21,
21–22
private residences, 16–05
settlements, 21–10
Staff of allied headquarters,
19–12
Stamp duties
history, 2–02
inheritance tax, 20–07

Stamp duties—*contd*
leases, 7–10
property income, 7–10
sale of land, 7–10
Standards, 5–06
State earning related pensions,
6–20
Statements of practice (SPs),
2–12, 2–16
Statutes. *See* Legislation
Statutory interpretation, 2–13
Stock
accounts, 5–10
appropriations to and from,
14–13
capital gains tax, 14–13
profits, 5–08
Sharkey v *Wernher* rule, 5–10
trading income, 5–10
work in progress, 5–10
Sub-contractors, 5–01
Sweet & Maxwell website, 2–19

Tangible movables, 16–07
Taper relief, 14–01, 15–07,
15–09, 15–12, 16–11, 20–02
Tax authorities, 1–10–1–13. *See*
also Contributions Agency,
Customs, Inland Revenue
administrative law, 1–11
appeals, 1–12
constitutional law, 1–11
control of, 1–11
enforcement, 1–11
information needs, 1–11
powers of, 1–11
reviews, 1–13
views of, 2–12
Tax avoidance
assets, transfer abroad, of,
26–22
avoision, 1–05
close companies, 18–10
company migration, 26–22
controlled foreign companies,
26–22
Ensign Tankers case, 2–16
general anti-avoidance
provisions, 2–15

INDEX

Tax avoidance—*contd*
  inheritance tax, 18–01, 18–10
  international aspects of
    taxation, 26–22–26–23
  Internet, 27–03 27–04
  interpretation, 2–13
  meaning, 1–05
  offshore funds, 26–23
  premiums, 7–07
  property income, 7–09
  settlements, 11–05
  tax evasion, comparison with,
    1–05
  VAT, 1–05, 27–03, 27–04
Tax bill, 12–20–12–21
Tax bulletin, 2–12
Tax credits
  amount of, 12–22
  children's tax credit, 12–18
  disabled person's tax credit,
    12–22
  double taxation, 26–09
  foreign, 26–09
  income, 12–22
  self-employed, 12–22
  social security, 6–21
  VAT, 25–12
  working families' tax credit,
    12–22
Tax evasion
  avoision, 1–05
  meaning, 1–05
  penalties, 3–09
  prosecutions, 3–09
  settlement, 3–09
  tax avoidance, comparison
    with, 1–05
  VAT, 27–03
Tax havens, 1–06
Tax law, 2–01–2–19. *See also*
    Legislation
  application, 2–14
  E-tax, 2–19
  general anti-avoidance
    provisions, 2–15
  geography, 2–06
  history, 2–02
  finding the law, 2–10
  interpretation, 2–13

Tax law—*contd*
  tax authorities' view, 2–12
  Tax Law Rewrite Project,
    2–07, 2–17
  using tax laws, 2–11
Tax Law Rewrite Project, 2–08,
    2–17, 6–21, 8–01
Tax planning, meaning, 2–11. *See
    also* Tax avoidance
Taxation
  efficiency, 1–05
  fairness of, 1–04
  international, 1–06
  policy, 1–02, 2–06
  principles, 1–03–1–06
Taxes
  anatomy of a tax, 1–09
  base, 1–04, 1–09
  collection, 1–08
  definition, 1–01
  reasons for, 1–02
  social control, 1–02
Taxpayers
  European Convention on
    Human Rights, 2–06
  identity of, 1–09
  protection, 2–06
Tax-preferred savings schemes,
    10–09
Tenancies. *See* Leases
Tenancies in common, 14–22
Termination payments, 6–04,
    6–19
Time limits
  errors, correction of, 3–04
  inheritance tax, 23–05
  self-assessment, 3–03
Tips, 4–02, 6–05
Trading income, 5–01–5–18
  agency workers, 5–01
  capital gains, 5–01
  Case I, 5–01
  Case II, 5–01, 5–05
  casual earnings, 5–19
  construction industry, 5–01
  divers, 5–01
  expenses, 5–09–5–18
  losses, 9–01–9–05
  Lump, 5–01

Trading income—*contd*
national insurance
contributions, 5–20
'professions', 5–05
profits, computation of, 5–06
savings and investment income,
10–02
Schedule D, 5–01
Schedule E, 5–01
self-employed, 5–01
stock, 5–10
sub-contractors, 5–01
receipts, 5–07
'trade', 5–01, 5–03
'trading', 5–03
'vocations', 5–05
Training, 1–14
Transaction taxes, meaning, 1–08
Transfer of businesses, 9–03,
14–16, 16–09
Travel expenses, 5–11, 6–18
Traveller's personal allowances,
27–03
Treasury website, 2–19
Tribunals, 1–12, 24–04
Trusts and estates, 11–01–11–04.
See also Settlements
annual payments, 10–04
beneficiaries, 11–03–11–04,
14–28
capital, 11–04
capital gains tax, 14–02,
14–24–14–29
close companies, 19–23
contingent interests, 11–03
discretionary, 11–02, 21–02,
21–14
disposals, 14–24–14–29
employees, 19–23
expenditure, 11–03
fixed interest, 21–13
income, 11–01, 11–03–11–04,
12–06
income tax, 11–02, 11–04
inheritance tax, 19–23, 21–10,
21–13
personal representatives, 11–04
rates, 11–02

Trusts and estates—*contd*
savings and investment income,
10–01
settled property, 14–22–14–29
termination of interest in
possession by death,
14–26
transfers between, 14–27
trustees, 11–02, 14–02
bare, 14–22
remuneration, 21–10
vested interests, 11–03, 14–22

Unincorporated businesses,
16–09
United Kingdom, composition for
tax purposes, 2–06

VAT, 1–07, 24–01–24–14
accounting for, 25–08–25–09
administration, 24–04
agents, 24–14
appeals, 1–12, 24–04
application, 24–06
assessment, 24–04
bad debt relief, 25–13
car dealers, 15–06
charge to VAT, 24–07–24–10
collection, 27–04
companies, 24–13
competition, distortion of,
24–08, 24–13, 25–01
computation,
consideration, 24–04, 24–06,
24–10–24–11, 25–07
cross-border transactions,
27–03–27–04
Customs and Excise, 1–10,
24–04
customs duties, 27–01
dealers, 25–06
delegated legislation, 2–09
direct effect, 24–02, 25–07
directives, 24–02, 24–04,
25–01, 25–06–25–07,
27–02
directors, 24–14
discounts, 25–07

INDEX

VAT—*contd*
discrimination, 27–04
duty free, 27–03
economic activities,
    24–13–24–14
education, 25–06
employees, 24–14
employment income, 6–02
European Union, 1–06, 2–04,
    2–06, 24–01–24–08,
    24–12–24–13,
    25–01–25–07,
    27–01–27–04
exemptions, 24–12, 25–01,
    25–03–25–05, 25–12,
    27–03
exports, 27–03, 27–04
farmers, 25–06
food, 25–02
GATS, 27–01
GATT, 27–01–27–02
goods, 24–09, 24–11
groups of companies, 24–13
history, 2–02
income tax, 2–08
imports, 27–01, 27–03
input tax, 15–03, 24–04,
    25–05, 25–08, 25–12
international aspects of
    taxation, 27–01–27–04
Internet, 27–03, 27–04
interpretation, 24–02
invoices, 25–10
mail order, 27–03
mixed supplies, 25–04
multiple supplies, 24–11,
    25–04
non-cash consideration, 25–07
notices, 24–03
office holders, 24–14
output tax, 24–05,
    25–08–25–09, 25–12
partial exemptions, 25–05
personal allowances, 27–03
place of taxable transactions,
    27–04
procedural rules, 24–02
    Scotland, 24–04
rate, 25–01–25–06

VAT—*contd*
rebates, 25–07
registration, 24–12, 25–10,
    27–03
reliefs, 25–13
retailers, 25–06
returns, 25–09–25–11
self-employed, 6–02, 24–14
separate supplies, 24–11
services, 24–08–24–09, 24–11,
    27–04
set-off, 15–03
single transactions, 24–11
Sixth VAT Directive, 24–02,
    25–01, 25–06–25–07,
    27–02
special regimes, 25–06
supplies, 24–07–24–12
    cross-border, 27–04
    exempt, 25–03–25–05
    mixed and multiple, 25–05
    taxable and exempt, 24–12,
        25–07, 25–12
    time for, 25–11
    zero-rated, 25–02, 25–04
tax avoidance, 1–05, 27–03,
    27–04
tax credits, 25–12
tax evasion, 27–03
tax periods, 25–09
tax point, 25–11
taxable persons, 24–06, 24–13
traveller's personal allowances,
    27–03
valuation, 25–07–25–13
VAT and Duties Tribunal,
    1–12, 24–04
voluntary registration, 24–12
World Trade Organization,
    27–01
zero-rating, 25–01–25–02,
    25–04, 27–03
Vehicles, 6–10
Visiting forces, 19–12
Vocations, 5–05, 26–12
Voluntary payments, 5–08
Vouchers, 6–15

Wasting assets, 15–05, 16–07

Wealth redistribution, 1–02
Web pages, 2–19
Widow's bereavement allowance,
   12–20
Wills, 22–05
Withholding tax
   double taxation, 26–13, 26–14
   meaning, 1–08
   royalties, 1–08
Woodlands, 19–18
Work in progress, 5–10
Working families' tax credit, 12–23

Works of art, 19–14
World Trade Organization,
   27–01
Writing down allowances,
   8–06–8–07, 8–09, 8–10
Writing off, 6–11
WTO (World Trade
   Organization), 27–01

Zero-rating, 25–01–25–02,
   25–04, 27–03

